DEATH VALLEY
& THE AMARGOSA

A Land of Illusion

DEATH VALLEY
& THE AMARGOSA

A Land of Illusion

RICHARD E. LINGENFELTER

UNIVERSITY OF CALIFORNIA PRESS
Berkeley   Los Angeles   London

To Naomi and Ondi

University of California Press
Berkeley and Los Angeles, California

University of California Press, Ltd.
London, England

Copyright © 1986 by The Regents of the University of California

Library of Congress Cataloging in Publication Data

Lingenfelter, Richard E.
  Death Valley & the Amargosa.

  Bibliography p.
  Includes index.
  1. Death Valley (Calif. and Nev.)—History. 2. Amargosa River Valley (Nev.
and Calif.)—History. 3. Gold mines and mining—Death Valley (Calif. and
Nev.)—History. 4. Gold mines and mining—Amargosa River Valley (Nev.
and Calif.)—History. I. Title. II. Title: Death Valley and the Amargosa.
F868.D2L56 1986   979.4'87   85-20121
ISBN 0-520-06356-2 (alk. paper)

Printed in the United States of America

  4 5 6 7 8 9

Contents

Preface

This is the history of Death Valley, where that bitter stream the Amargosa dies. It embraces the whole basin of the Amargosa from the Panamints to the Spring Mountains, from the Palmettos to the Avawatz. And it spans a century from the earliest recollections and the oldest records to that day in 1933 when much of the valley was finally set aside as a National Monument.

This is the story of an illusory land, of the people it attracted and of the dreams and delusions they pursued—the story of the metals in its mountains and the salts in its sinks, of its desiccating heat and its revitalizing springs, and of all the riches of its scenery and lore—the story of Indians and horse thieves, lost argonauts and lost mine hunters, prospectors and promoters, miners and millionaires, stockholders and stock sharps, homesteaders and hermits, writers and tourists.

But mostly this is the story of the illusions—the illusions of a shortcut to the gold diggings that lured the forty-niners, of inescapable deadliness that hung in the name they left behind, of lost bonanzas that grew out of the few nuggets they found, of immeasurable riches spread by hopeful prospectors and calculating con men, and of impenetrable mysteries concocted by the likes of Scotty. These and many lesser illusions are the heart of its history.

Much has already been written about the history of the valley, but much more has been left untold. A full history of the valley has been attempted only once before—in 1940 by Carl Burgess Glasscock, in *Here's Death Valley*. But Glasscock mixed fact and fantasy and missed many fascinating chapters. Thus the whole story is told here for the first time.

The uncovering of Death Valley's history, like the recovery of its elusive mineral wealth, has been the work of many hands, mining and refining it. The final metal owes much to the ground-breaking labors of Willie Chalfant, Julian Steward, Carl Wheat, Ann and LeRoy Hafen, Ruth Woodman, Eddie Edwards, Harold and Lucile Weight, David Myrick, Russell Elliott, Hank Johnston, George Hildebrand, Linda Greene, and John Latschar, all of whom helped to open its rich lodes of history.

I am indebted to them and to many others for their generous aid in this work. I owe special thanks to Horace Albright, Ruth Anthony, Joan Barton, Teresa Bodine, Nancy Bowers, Dennis Casebier, Hazel Cleghorn, Dan Cronkhite, Hilary Cummings, Mary DeDecker, Shirley Harding, Alan Hensher, Jack Herron, LeRoy Johnson, Joe Kern, George Koenig,

Jim Kubeck, Bill Michael, Germaine Moon, Irene Moran, Lee Mortensen, Jean Muller, Tom Murray, Virgil Olson, George Pipkin, Ken Prag, Virginia Rhode, Gary Roberts, Guy Rocha, Fran Rudman, Joe Samora, Marcia Samelson, Peter Sanchez, Gil Schmidtmann, Victoria Scott, Donnalee Simmons, Debbi Tippett, Richard Terry, Hugh Tolford, Shirley Warren, Walt Wheelock, Sally Zanjani, and Sibylle Zemitis—and most especially to my old friend, Richard Dwyer, and my wife and daughter.

Before you read on, our times require a cautionary note: in the pages that follow, all the prices, wages, assays, and bullion yields are given in values reported at the time, not in today's dollars. If the values sometimes seem trifling for the excitement they generated, remember that those were the days when $4 a day was a good wage and gold was $20 an ounce—and that a large factor is needed to convert to present-day dollars.

Del Mar, California   Richard E. Lingenfelter
July 1985

A LAND OF ILLUSION

The valley we call Death isn't really that different from much of the rest of the desert West. It's just a little deeper, a little hotter, and a little drier. What sets it apart more than anything else is the mind's eye. For it is a land of illusion, a place in the mind, a shimmering mirage of riches and mystery and death.

These illusions have distorted its landscape and contorted its history. One of the simplest lessons of history is that we respond not so much to what is happening around us as to what we believe is happening—not to what we see but to what we believe we see. Rarely has this gulf been wider or more persistent than in Death Valley and the Amargosa.

It is a land of the deluded and the self-deluding, of dreamers and con men. Even its hardest facts are tinged with aberrations.

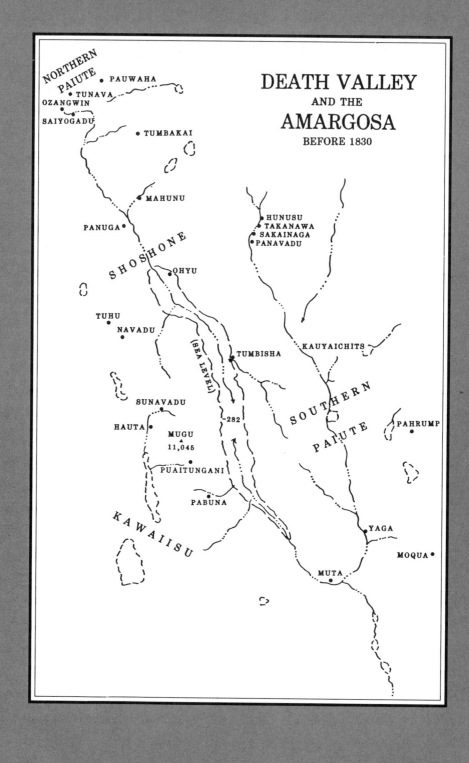

DEATH VALLEY
AND THE
AMARGOSA
BEFORE 1830

NORTHERN
PAIUTE
PAUWAHA
TUNAVA
OZANGWIN
SAIYOGADU

TUMBAKAI

MAHUNU

PANUGA

SHOSHONE

OHYU

HUNUSU
TAKANAWA
SAKAINAGA
PANAVADU

TUHU
NAVADU

(SEA LEVEL)

TUMBISHA

KAUYAICHITS

SUNAVADU

HAUTA

MUGU
▲
11,045

-282

SOUTHERN

PAIUTE

PAHRUMP

PUAITUNGANI

PABUNA

K A W A I I S U

YAGA

MOQUA

MUTA

A Land of Extremes

The sharpest realities of Death Valley are its extremes of depth and heat and aridity. It is, in fact, the lowest, hottest, driest spot in America.

Joel Brooks was the first to guess, in February 1861, that the floor of Death Valley might actually be below sea level. He was better acquainted with the valley than almost anyone else at the time, having helped surveyor Henry Washington run the township lines through the valley four years before, and having just returned the previous spring as a guide for the army. But Brooks was also a braggart and border ruffian, said to have been run out of every town in the southern San Joaquin Valley. He boasted that he had killed more Indians both in battle and in captivity than any man in California, and he didn't stop there; he had most recently killed a man on the Mojave River. A government officer, branding him "a vagrant and outlaw," had concluded, "It is hardly necessary for me to add that his statements are totally unworthy of credit." Still, Brooks was hired as guide for the California boundary reconnaissance party heading for the Death Valley country early in 1861—but then they also brought along camels![1]

Considering his reputation, it is not surprising that when Brooks suggested to his companions that the valley they were about to enter was below sea level, he was answered with unbelieving, if cautious, scoffs and challenges to bet. Sides were quickly drawn and each new barometer reading was anxiously awaited as they moved into the valley. To the chagrin of the doubters, Brooks was right: they paid up on March 11, when the barometer set up on the salt flat below Furnace Creek indicated they were 377 feet below sea level. Later, more conservative analysis of the barometer readings, considering uncertainties in atmospheric conditions, showed that the lowest point reached by the survey was somewhere between 100 and 250 feet below the sea. But the startling fact remained that Death Valley, hundreds of miles from the sea, was well below sea level.[2]

California State Geologist Josiah Whitney eagerly spread the word of the valley's great depth. Perhaps from some notion of the symmetry of nature, he also called attention to the fact that this lowest point in the country was only 60 miles from the highest point, which his colleagues had thoughtfully named for him. But the news was received with as much skepticism as Brook's original suggestion. One of Whitney's own associates, a brash young paleontologist, William Gabb, challenged the

claim, maintaining that his own measurements showed that the valley was
several thousand feet above sea level. Nevada papers championed Gabb,
chiding Whitney for wanting both the highest and lowest spot for California. Whitney's enthusiasm doubtless rubbed salt in a festering wound,
since both these prized points lay within an area that was still the subject
of a smoldering boundary dispute between the two states. Whitney
nevertheless argued that Gabbs had simply mistaken the upper sink of
the Amargosa at Ash Meadows for its lower sink in Death Valley, and
subsequent measurements by the Wheeler survey confirmed this.[3]

The Wheeler survey in the early 1870s, however, triggered a whole
new controversy over whether Death Valley or the Salton Sink was in
fact the lowest spot in the country. This issue wasn't resolved until after
the turn of the century. Wheeler's surveyors reported that Death Valley
wasn't as deep as had been thought, being at most only 110 feet below
sea level. At the same time, surveyors for the Southern Pacific Railroad
route found that the Salton Sink was at least 215 feet below sea level—not
only much deeper than previously supposed but apparently deeper than
Death Valley as well. Thus the Salton Sink was heralded as the nation's
lowest spot. It held that title until 1891, when a government botanical
expedition to Death Valley reported a depth in excess of -351 feet and
won back the honor for Death Valley. A decade later, measurements by
the California state mineralogist and the U.S. Geological Survey pushed
the valley's depth down to -427 feet, and then to -480 feet.[4]

Needless to say, these Death Valley surveys were not all that reliable,
for they were based on barometric measurements, subject to large
meteorological uncertainties. A much more accurate measurement was
finally made in 1907, when the first spirit-leveled line was run into the
valley by L. F. Biggs of the Geological Survey. The lowest point that
Biggs found was only -276 feet, so he announced that Death Valley was
not deeper than the Salton Sink after all, for the Survey reported the sink
to be -287 feet. The controversy could have raged on, because the
California state mineralogist maintained that the deepest part of the Salton
Sink was only -275 feet—one foot less than Death Valley—and then the
Geological Survey revised its Death Valley depth to -274! But by then
it was a moot point, for in the spring of 1905 the rampaging waters of
the Colorado River had turned the Salton Sink into the Salton Sea. Thus
at last, and perhaps only by default, Death Valley regained the title.[5]

The most recent surveys suggest that at its lowest point, some 4 miles
west of Badwater, Death Valley is 282 feet below sea level, making it
without doubt the lowest dry spot on the American continents. But the
figure seems less impressive when we consider that the lowest spot on
earth, the surface of the Dead Sea, is more than a thousand feet lower.

Death Valley has other similarities with the Dead Sea, not only in name but in origin. Death Valley and the Salton Sink owe their depth to the tearing of the western edge of the continent in the global process of seafloor spreading. Death Valley is thus the deepest landward extension of that great spreading rift that has become the Gulf of California and the Salton Sink, much as the Dead Sea basin is the landward extension of the spreading rift that is the Red Sea.[6]

Death Valley is not only the lowest spot in the Western Hemisphere but also the hottest—for a time, in fact, it was the hottest known spot on earth. Yet its early reputation for torrid temperatures was based more on imagination than on fact, and even claims that Death Valley was the hottest spot in California did not go unchallenged.

The first actual measurements of summer temperatures in Death Valley, made by the Wheeler survey in the early 1870s, showed a maximum of 121° F, which the Army Signal Corps proclaimed the highest temperature ever recorded in the United States. But Death Valley lost this distinction in 1884, when a new record of 126° F was set at Mammoth Tank station on the Southern Pacific Railroad in Salton Sink; a year later, the temperature at the same station reached 130° F. Hotter unofficial temperatures were claimed at Furnace Creek Ranch in Death Valley, but when the U.S. Weather Bureau set up a temporary station there in the summer of 1891, the hottest it got was only 122° F.[7]

Death Valley thus remained the second hottest spot until a permanent weather station was established at Furnace Creek in 1911. Then on July 10, 1913, during a heat wave when the temperature reached or surpassed the Mammoth Tank record on three separate days, Death Valley not only regained its title of the hottest spot in the United States but became the hottest known spot on earth, as the temperatures soared to a searing 134° F. It may have been even hotter. The thermometer was only calibrated to 135° F and may not have given accurate readings at that extreme. Only a few people experienced that awful heat wave in Death Valley, and one of them died of it. Peter A. Busch, the thirty-nine-year-old founder of Rhyolite and a veteran of the desert, was returning from Los Angeles in a new Dodge, which he foolishly decided to drive across Death Valley. When the car bogged down on the sandy road west of Stovepipe Wells, Busch and his chauffeur tried to walk out. Only the chauffeur was rescued alive.[8]

Such heat was extraordinary, even for Death Valley. There was a strong wind blowing in the valley that day carrying hot air from the Nevada desert over the Amargosa Range, where it was superheated by compression as it fell over a mile and a half into the valley below. It was a record-breaking but fatal combination. The record of 134° F set that day remains the hottest ever officially measured in the Western Hemisphere; as a world record, it was edged out by two degrees in 1922 at a station in the Sahara.[9]

Death Valley publicists have claimed still hotter unofficial temperatures and have also argued that Furnace Creek Ranch is not the hottest spot in Death Valley. But the official extremes are intolerable enough. Every year since records have been kept, the summer maximum has reached 120° F or more, and half the time it has climbed to at least 125° F![10]

It is not surprising that only a few have chosen to spend the summer there and that those who have had to go to extraordinary means just trying to make life bearable. Before the days of air-conditioning, workmen at the Furnace Creek Ranch slept in the irrigation ditches and the foreman poured water on the floor and slept under a wet blanket in front of a fan. What made even such marginal relief possible was Death Valley's extremely low humidity.[11]

Death Valley is in fact the driest spot in the country. The average rainfall since 1912, when the first records were kept, is only 1.66 inches per year—the lowest recorded anywhere in the Western Hemisphere. There have been years, such as 1929 and 1953, when not a drop of rain was seen in the valley. The most rain that was ever reported in one year was 4.6 inches in 1941. The relative humidity averages less than 20 percent—just a fraction of that to which we have become accustomed in air-conditioned cars, homes, and offices—and on a hot summer day the humidity can drop to a desiccating 3 percent. In air that dry, furniture curls and splits and falls apart.[12]

The rain that does fall in Death Valley generally comes in just a few cloudbursts. The dry baked hills cannot absorb such downpours, so the water bursts down the canyons in scouring flash floods that sweep away everything in their path. It is usually only after such storms that you can get a glimpse of the Amargosa River, Fremont's "bitter water of the desert." The rest of the year the Amargosa is dry over most of its course; the only flow is underground. Enthusiasts have claimed that the Amargosa is, in fact, the "longest underground river in the world." As a local paper noted, since it can't be seen, no one knows just how long it is, so the claim cannot be disputed.[13]

A Name on the Land

Nothing about Death Valley is more compelling or more intriguing than its name and all that it grimly suggests. The name inexorably transforms the land in the minds of those who hear it; no one can wholly ignore it. Because of its stigma the valley cannot be just a place of subtle beauty or even the deepest, hottest, driest spot on the continent. Its beauty is tinged with foreboding and its depth and heat are tainted with apprehension.

The name alone has conjured up seemingly endless horrors in the minds of Sunday supplement writers. Death Valley, one wrote in 1894, is

> the most deadly and dangerous spot in the United States. It is a pit of horrors—the haunt of all that is grim and ghoulish. Such animal and reptile life as infests this pest-hole is of ghastly shape, rancorous nature and diabolically ugly. It breeds only noxious and venomous things. Its dead do not decompose, but are baked, blistered and embalmed by the scorching heat through countless ages. It is surely the nearest to a little hell upon earth that the whole wicked world can produce.[1]

Like a cancer, the name bred other maledictions in its image—on Coffin Peak and the Funeral Mountains, in Deadman Pass and Dry Bone Canyon, and from Dante's View and Hell's Gate to the Devil's Golf Course. The culmination of such morbid mimicry was a widely circulated report that a man named Coffin was working the graveyard shift on the Cemetery Mine in Skull Gulch in the Funeral Range on the rim of Death Valley![2]

But who named Death Valley? Was it one of the forty-niners—the Jayhawkers, or Manly, or Bennett, or Juliet Brier? Or was it some later explorer in the boundary survey or the Blasdel party? There are ample contenders for the honor, both volunteer and nominee. And why was it named? Was it for the only argonaut known to have died there, for the imagined death of a whole wagon train, or just for the threat of death that some forty-niners felt there?[3]

One certainty is that it was not named for an all-but-forgotten gold seeker named Sheldon Death, as his sister once hoped. Nor was it named, as one turn-of-the-century hack writer fancied, for the tragicomic slaughter of a whole "borax stampede during which prospectors went mad from the heat and ran shrieking up ravines where later their bones were found bleaching!"[4]

Juliet Brier, sometimes hailed as "the heroine of Death Valley" for bringing her husband and children through alive, was credited by a latter-day writer with naming the valley, but this seems to be a gratuitous suggestion, for not one of the forty-niners including her husband, ever said she named it. On the contrary, her husband and a few of the Jay-hawkers insisted that Death Valley wasn't named until Governor Blasdel's party supposedly found the "bleaching bones of nine men" in the valley many years later. One reminiscing Jayhawker called Searles Lake, where two of their party died, "Death Valley," but none of the Jayhawkers gave Death Valley that name—they had no reason to do so.[5]

The only argonauts who lingered and actually knew death in the valley were the Bennett-Arcan party. They camped there for nearly four weeks on the verge of starvation while Manly and Rogers trekked out to the settlements and back to rescue them. It was one of their number who died there. And it was when they were finally leaving the valley, camped atop the Panamints, that Death Valley was named. Early on the morning of February 15, 1850, Asabel Bennett and John Arcan climbed with William Lewis Manly to a point just above their camp to scout the route ahead. Then, Manly recalled, "just as we were ready to leave and return to camp we took off our hats, and then overlooking the scene of so much trial, suffering and death spoke the thought uppermost saying:—'*Good bye Death Valley!*'"[6]

But which one of them spoke these words? Manly never says. Perhaps he couldn't recall, or perhaps either modesty or animosity kept him from saying. In an 1877 interview Manly apparently claimed the honor for himself, but thereafter he was noncommittal. Tradition in the Bennett family gives Bennett the honor. If it was Bennett, Manly's failure to credit him may have stemmed from a falling out they had during a trip back to Death Valley in 1861.[7]

It was as a result of that later trip that the name Death Valley first came into popular use. Several exploring and prospecting parties entered the valley between 1850 and 1860, including two led by Bennett, but none ever mentioned the valley by name. Not until Manly and Bennett and a friend, Caesar Twitchell, went to the valley in the winter of 1860–61 was the name resurrected. It was then Twitchell returned home to tell a *Los Angeles Star* reporter in March of 1861 about "a place called 'Death Valley,' so named in 1849," that the name first appeared in print. The name spread quickly as Manly and Bennett camped with others at the newly discovered Coso mines just west of the valley. By April the California boundary party had adopted the name, and later that year it appeared on Farley's map to the new mines. The name was clearly in common use by 1866, when Nevada Governor Blasdel entered the valley.[8]

Death Valley was first put on the map by Minard Farley in 1861. (*Courtesy of Bancroft Library*)

While camped in Death Valley, the Bennetts and Arcans had lived for weeks in the shadow of death, but it was apparently the very real and tragic death of Richard Culverwell, whom Bennett and Rogers had buried just two days before, that was uppermost in their minds when they named the valley. For, as Manly remarked, discussing the naming, "in this lonely place Capt. Culverwell died . . . entirely alone, so our name of the place was a proper one." Richard I. A. Culverwell, an ailing forty-eight-year-old former government clerk from Washington, D.C., was weak from sickness and exhaustion and without food or water when he died about February 9, 1850, several miles south of Bennetts Well. He was the valley's first recorded victim, and his death apparently inspired its name.[9]

But once the name Death Valley was fastened upon the land, that name demanded much more than the solitary death of an ailing argonaut to give it meaning. It required mythical horrors of monumental proportions to justify it, and the valley exacted a very real, seasonal toll of death to sustain it.

The mythical horror that arose to give legitimacy to the name Death Valley—the annihilation of a whole wagon train—grew like a cancer from the ordeal of the Death Valley argonauts themselves. The myth fed on their fading and uncertain memories, on the ubiquitous rumors of their suffering, and on the illusory evidence of their burned and abandoned wagons. And the myth grew with every telling, until it reached such grotesque proportions that it defied all reality.

One of the earliest versions of the myth was that published in 1869 by George Q. Cannon, a member of the Hunt wagon train from which the Death Valley argonauts had separated. He recounted the imagined deaths of eighty-seven emigrants in that

> fearful place . . . lured into its treacherous bosom by the hope of
> finding water. They reached the centre; but the glaring desert and
> the dry barren peaks met their gaze on every hand. Around the valley
> they wandered, and the children, crying for water, perished at their
> mothers' breasts. The mothers soon followed, and the men, with
> swollen tongues, tottered and raved and died.[10]

As others embellished the story, the year of the tragedy drifted about between 1849 and 1856; the emigrants picked up a name, the "Lost Montgomery Train"; they varied from argonauts tricked by a Mormon guide to dissident Mormons fleeing polygamy; and their numbers grew until ultimately there were nearly four hundred whose bones were "scattered for miles by the coyotes and buzzards."[11]

The myth was so well entrenched by the turn of the century that the publication of authentic accounts of the Death Valley argonauts by Manly and others could have little immediate effect upon it. The reality only confused George Wharton James, who in his *Heroes of California* devoted one chapter to the Death Valley argonauts of 1849 and another to "The Unknown Heroes of Death Valley"—a mythical wagon train lost in the summer of 1850. As late as the 1920s, the *Los Angeles Times* still printed melodramatic fantasies about the "terrible slaughter" of Mormon emigrants caught in Death Valley's "murderous maw." Desert scholar Eddie Edwards finally gave the mythical wagon train a full airing and a proper burial in 1964, but who can be sure that it may not still rise again?[12]

Other enthusiasts meanwhile have promoted a whole new myth to push the beginnings of the valley's damnation back into prehistory, claiming that even before the coming of the white men, the Paiute had cursed the valley with the awful name *Tomesha*, meaning "ground afire." This story seems to have been started in 1907 as a one-liner by a young geologist, Sydney Ball, and it was such a good story that it has been eagerly spread ever since. But it was too good to be true, for Tomesha is only a vagrant spelling of Tumbisha, the largest Indian village in the valley, at the mouth of Furnace Creek; only through confusion does it ever seem to have been applied to the valley itself. It is a Shoshone name, probably best translated as "Coyote Rock," from *tumbi*, "rock," and *ishavaip*, "coyote." It certainly has no relation to the Paiute word for fire, *coso*, which has found its proper place in the burnt volcanic country west of the Panamints. But as the history of Death Valley shows again and again, myth and illusion can take on a life of their own that no amount of fact can quiet, so "ground afire" too is surely here to stay.[13]

Death in the Valley

Death Valley has been called "the most advertised graveyard in the world" and it has been claimed that there is "no other spot so forbidding, so desolate, so deadly." Its name alone seems to demand a seasonal toll of death. Indeed, as if the name were a self-fulfilling prophesy, seven men died in the valley that first summer that its name was made known in 1861.[1]

But just how deadly is Death Valley? Discounting the mythical multitude of emigrants, there are little over a hundred known deaths in the valley, due to anything other than old age, in its entire recorded history—an average of less than one death per year. This number pales to insignificance when compared to the tens of thousands that die each year in such lively places as Los Angeles, Chicago, or New York. But in an area as sparsely populated as Death Valley, it is stark evidence that for the uninformed and the overconfident, the valley can be a dangerous and even deadly place in the summer.[2]

What makes Death Valley seasonally dangerous is not so much that it's extremely hot, but that it's extremely dry. Dehydration, not heat stroke, is the principal cause of death in Death Valley. Heat stroke is a problem in hot, humid air where your body cannot keep cool enough by the evaporation of perspiration. In the hot, dry air of Death Valley, the situation is just the opposite: your body is cooled very effectively by evaporation, but at a dangerous rate of dehydration. On an average summer day in Death Valley, you can lose over 2 gallons of water just sitting in the shade; hiking in the sun, you can lose twice as much! Without enough to drink to replace it, the loss of 4 gallons of water is almost certainly fatal, and even the loss of 2 gallons could have fatal results.[3]

The first sensations of thirst begin with the loss of a little over a quart of water. By the time you have lost a gallon you begin to feel tired and apathetic. Most of the water lost comes from your blood, and as it thickens, your circulation becomes poor, your heart strains, your muscles fatigue, and your head aches. With further loss of water you become dizzy and begin to stumble; your breathing is labored and your speech is indistinct. By the time you have lost 2 gallons of water your tongue is swollen, you can hardly keep your balance, your muscles spasm, and you are becoming delirious. You are likely to discard your hat, clothes, and shoes, which only hastens your dehydration and suffering. With a loss of more than 3 gallons of water you will collapse, your tongue and skin shriveled and numb, your eyes sunken, your vision dim, and your hearing almost gone. Bloody cracks will appear in your skin and you'll soon be dead.[4]

Such was the fate of fully two-thirds of those who have died in Death Valley. The remainder were the victims of such diverse fates as homicide, tainted food, climbing accidents, and plane crashes. The summer of 1905, at the height of the Bullfrog rush, was probably Death Valley's deadliest. Thirteen men are known to have died of thirst and heat in the valley that summer, and there were undoubtedly other unknown dead. One newspaper at the time claimed as many as thirty-five died that season.[5]

There is no typical victim: those who have succumbed to the desiccating summer heat in Death Valley range from tenderfeet like Earle Weller and Morris Titus to veteran desert men like Judge Bethune and Jim Dayton. Earle C. Weller was a robust 180-pound twenty-five-year-old with a full red beard; his brother-in-law Edgar Morris Titus, four years his senior, was a much smaller man with a neatly trimmed dark goatee. Caught up in the excitement of the Bullfrog rush they came to Rhyolite from Telluride, Colorado in June 1905. There they joined up with another tenderfoot, John Mullan, and set out with two horses and nineteen burros packed with provisions to prospect in the Panamints. They never got across Death Valley. Taking the wrong fork in the trail down a canyon in the Grapevines, they missed the springs and found only a small seep several miles above the mouth of the canyon. This could scarcely provide water enough for one man, but they made camp there the evening of June 26, while Titus went on down the canyon with some of the burros in search of more water. When Titus failed to return by the following morning Weller took the remaining burros and went looking for him, leaving Mullan in camp with the horses and provisions. Neither Titus nor Weller ever returned. A few days later, on July 1, three men were found in the north end of Death Valley. Two were dead; the third, barely alive and unable to speak, was given water but died an hour and a half later. They had thrown off most of their clothing in their delirium, so there was nothing left to identify them, and they were buried on the spot. Two weeks later Mullan was found in a stupor still waiting at the camp with the provisions; both horses were dead. Mullan was taken to Rhyolite and eventually recovered. Some of the burros wandered into Grapevine Ranch along with one belonging to Judge Lawrence Bethune of Tonopah. It appears that Bethune, an experienced but aging prospector, happened upon Titus and Weller, lost and suffering from thirst, and became exhausted trying to help them. They were the three men buried in the north end of the valley that July. But their graves were never found by Weller's grieving father, who came to Death Valley three years in a row searching in vain for the bodies of his lost son and son-in-law. All that he ever found were seven of their burros and a hastily made sign that his son-in-law had left in the canyon that now bears his name:[6]

HURRY ON! I'M GOING DOWN TO INVESTIGATE THE SPRING.

TITUS

James W. Dayton, summer caretaker of the Furnace Creek Ranch and a former swamper on the twenty-mule-team borax wagons, had made the trip from the ranch to Daggett for supplies many times before. But when he started on July 24, 1899, he complained of not feeling too well. Nonetheless he set out alone on the 150-mile journey with a wagon, six mules, and his dog. Sixteen days later, when word of his departure reached Daggett, Frank Tilton and Adolph Nevares headed for Death Valley to find out why he hadn't arrived. They got to within 20 miles of Furnace Creek Ranch before they found his body. Dayton had curled up in the scant shade of a mesquite bush by the side of the road just half a mile north of the abandoned Eagle Borax Works—not far from where Culverwell had died half a century earlier. Fifty feet beyond was Dayton's wagon with two full canteens and three barrels of water. The wagon brakes were set and all six mules had died in their tangled traces, after a frantic but futile struggle to free themselves. Only his dog had survived, half starved, apparently getting water at the old borax works to sustain him in his lonely vigil. Dayton doubtless died the day he left Furnace Creek, illness making him an easy prey to the desiccating heat. He was buried on the spot. Frank Tilton spoke the last rites: "Well, Jimmie, you lived in the heat and you died in the heat, and after what you been through I guess you ought to be comfortable in hell."[7]

Little was known about most of those who died in Death Valley, and even less is remembered. Their remains were most often buried in unmarked graves; more than a third of the bodies found in the valley were never identified. The few grave markers that were put up were of more use as mile posts to the living than they were to the memory of the dead, as one tenderfoot learned when he got directions to the next spring: "Six miles farther you'd come to 'Tim Ryan, August 9th '05,' and two and a half miles southeast of him you'll find plenty of good water." Ryan could have used those directions himself, for his death was blamed on his having drunk poisonous water at another spring. A neatly carved grave marker for "William Dooley" that once stood on a mound in Wingate Pass served a different purpose. It was said to have been put up by the cagey renegade himself in 1897 to throw an Arizona lawman off his trail. Val "Shorty" Nolan's weathering headboard is still a conspicuous landmark on the road east of Stove Pipe Wells Hotel. Nolan was last seen alive at Beatty on the

Fourth of July 1931, and was found and buried by a movie company in Death Valley that November. But Death Valley's most prominently marked graves are those of two men who didn't die there—Shorty Harris and Death Valley Scotty. They did, however, figure prominently in the valley's history. Shorty, who died in Big Pine in 1934, had asked to be buried beside Jim Dayton, his friend of bygone days, and Scotty, dying enroute to a Las Vegas hospital in 1954, was brought back to his castle for burial.[8]

Death Valley's most widely publicized death, however—one that was reported almost halfway around the world—simply never happened! Dan De Quille, local editor of the Virginia City *Territorial Enterprise,* spun the yarn as filler on a dull day in the summer of 1874 under the headline, "Sad Fate of an Inventor":

> A gentleman who has just arrived from the borax fields of the desert regions surrounding the town of Columbus, in the eastern part of this State, gives us the following account of the sad fate of Mr. Jonathan Newhouse, a man of considerable inventive genius. Mr. Newhouse had constructed what he called a "solar armor," an apparatus intended to protect the wearer from the fierce heat of the sun in crossing deserts and burning alkali plains. The armor consisted of a long, close-fitting jacket made of common sponge and a cap or hood of the same material; both jacket and hood being about an inch in thickness. Before starting across a desert this armor was to be saturated with water. Under the right arm was suspended an India rubber sack filled with water and having a small gutta percha tube leading to the top of the hood. In order to keep the armor moist, all that was necessary to be done by the traveler, as he progressed over the burning sands, was to press the sack occasionally, when a small quantity of water would be forced up and thoroughly saturate the hood and the jacket below it. Thus, by the evaporation of the moisture in the armor, it was calculated might be produced almost any degree of cold. Mr. Newhouse went down to Death Valley, determined to try the experiment of crossing that terrible place in his armor. He started out into the valley one morning from the camp nearest its borders, telling the men at the camp, as they laced his armor on his back, that he would return in two days. The next day an Indian who could speak but a few words of English came to the camp in a great state of excitement. He made the men understand that he wanted them to follow him. At the distance of about twenty miles out into the desert the Indian pointed to a human figure seated against a rock. Approaching they found it to be Newhouse still in his armor. He was dead and frozen stiff. His beard was covered with frost and—though the noonday sun poured down its fiercest rays—an icicle over a foot in length hung from his nose. There he had perished miserably, because his armor had worked but too well, and because it was laced up behind where he could not reach the fastenings.[9]

The People

Despite the severity of the summers, ancient campsites reveal that people have lived in Death Valley for at least ten thousand years, since the end of the last Ice Age, and perhaps even longer. Summer relief has always been close at hand in the cool heights of the Panamints and neighboring ranges, while the weather in the valley the rest of the year is delightfully mild. At the close of the Ice Age and during a wetter interlude some two to five thousand years ago, a deep lake covered the valley floor and even the summers were pleasant. Then the lake shore was dotted with scores of camp sites. In drier, more recent times, settlement in the valley has been pretty much confined to the perennial springs and the mild seasons.[1]

In the nineteenth century and for at least a few centuries before that, the Indians living in Death Valley belonged to three separate tribes—the Shoshone, the Southern Paiute, and the Kawaiisu. The Shoshone occupied the largest part of the valley and surrounding country, settling in the northern half of Death Valley and in the bordering Panamints and Grapevines, as well as in the upper Amargosa River basin from Ash Meadows north. That quarter of the valley and the adjacent country south and east of Furnace Creek, including the southern reaches of the Amargosa River, was settled by the Southern Paiute, while the extreme southern end of the valley and of the Panamint Range was held by the Kawaiisu. Fish Lake and Deep Spring valleys bordering Death Valley on the northwest were settled by the Northern Paiute, who also occupied Owens Valley. Actual boundaries in this barren land were ill-defined at best; all that mattered was who held the springs and pinyon lands, and even these distinctions were blurred by intertribal marriages.[2]

These current tribal names were, of course, unknown to the people themselves. The Death Valley Shoshone simply referred to themselves as *nuwu,* "the people," but their neighbors had many names for them. The Saline Valley Shoshone called them Tsagwaduka, or chuckwalla eaters; the Owens Valley Paiute further west named them the Sivinangwatu, or easterners; the Fish Lake Valley Paiute called them Tavainuwu, or sun people; and the Ash Meadows Paiute referred to them as Koets. Both the Shoshone and the Kawaiisu living in the southern half of the valley were known to those in the north as Mugunuwu from the name Mugu, "pointed," given to Telescope Peak; to the Southern Paiute, they were known as Panumunt, which made its way into English as Panamint, and is now applied both to the Indians and the mountain range. The Ash

Meadows Paiute likewise called themselves *nu,* or people, but were called Sivindu, or easterners, by the Shoshone.[3]

Pine nuts and mesquite beans were the staple foods of the Indians in and around Death Valley. Mesquite, called *ovi* by the Shoshone, grows around the borders of salt flats and in the dunes wherever there is water close to the surface. Mesquite beans were gathered throughout the springtime. The young beans were eaten whole, while the mature beans were either dried and stored or ground into a flour. Pine nuts, called *tuba,* were gathered in the fall from pinyon trees, which grow above the 7,000-foot level in the Panamints, the Grapevines, and adjacent ranges. The nuts fall from the pine cones for a period of two to three weeks after the cones begin to open in the autumn. During this time a single Indian might gather as much as 200 pounds of nuts. These had to serve as the staple and sometimes the only food through the winter. Because each pine bears nuts only once every three to four years, the harvest was unpredictable, and in a bad year a family might face starvation before winter's end.[4]

These staples were supplemented by seeds of sand bunchgrass, wild rye, sunflower, and devil's pin cushion, as well as by wild grapes, *hupi* berries, mariposa lily bulbs, Joshua tree buds, and squaw cabbage greens. Small game such as rabbits, squirrels, pack rats, quail, ducks, and chuckwallas rounded out the diet. Killing a bighorn sheep provided a rare treat. Rabbit drives were the most important communal effort, involving families from several villages and, if successful, ending in a great feast. Rabbit skins were also essential for making blankets and robes. In preparation for a drive, nets of yucca fiber or wild hemp a couple feet high and hundreds of feet long were strung out in a great arc; then men, women, and children completed the circle and began beating the brush to drive the frightened animals into the net, where they were clubbed to death.[5]

Because of the abundance of most essentials, only limited trade was carried on among the Death Valley people through barter and with shell bead money. A string of beads, measured once around the hand, was the common unit of exchange. One string bought about 2 quarts of pine nuts, but a sinew-backed bow cost twenty-four, moccasins as much as forty, and a wife cost a hundred strings of beads. When the white men or *hiko* came, the exchange rate was set at about 8¢ per string, but it fell to about half that as a glut of glass beads led to inflation. The Indians soon switched to the white men's currency.[6]

The mild weather both in the mountains during the summer and in the valley during the rest of the year required little shelter except from occasional wind and rain. The migratory life of the people and the tradition of abandoning a house on the death of an occupant also discouraged elaborate permanent dwellings. The *kahni* or house was thus a simple affair. The winter homes in the valley were roughly dome-shaped, about

10 feet across, built of either mesquite or willow branches, and covered with wattled grass and brush. The summer homes in the mountains were more cone-shaped, built around a tripod of pinyon branches, and covered with boughs and bark. A tule mat usually covered the doorway and a small hole in the roof let out the smoke from a fire pit in the center of the room. Sweat houses—simple saunas—were built on a similar plan but packed with an outer layer of mud to hold in the steam. Among the Paiute and those Shoshone on the upper Amargosa, the sweat house doubled as the village community center.[7]

The villages in Death Valley and along the Amargosa consisted of only a few families, or sometimes just one extended family. Since they were generally a day's travel from one another, social life centered almost exclusively on the family and neighbors in the village. Aside from occasional rabbit drives, the only large communal social gathering was the yearly fall festival. This festival, held after the pine-nut gathering, was celebrated for several days with a circle dance, feasting, gambling, and a mourning ceremony at which all the belongings of anyone who had died that year were burned. Organizing the rabbit drives and the fall festival were the only official functions of the regional chief or *pakwinavi,* "big talker."[8]

The largest and probably the most prosperous Shoshone village in Death Valley was Mahunu, located at the springs in Grapevine Canyon near where Scotty's Castle now stands. Wild grapes, which grew in abundance there, made this one of the most attractive oases in the valley and gave the springs, the canyon, and the mountains their present names. In the mid-nineteenth century, about thirty people lived at Mahunu. They belonged to four families; the best remembered was that of Dock, a shaman and the *pakwinavi* of most of the Death Valley Shoshone. Dock was so fond of sweat baths that he built five sweat houses—one at each camp he frequented.[9]

These families spent the winter and part of the fall and spring at Mahunu, living off its wild grapes, berries, seeds, and a store of pine nuts from the fall. In the spring and fall they hunted migrating duck at nearby Grapevine Springs, where they made artificial ponds to lure the birds and built brush blinds from which to shoot them. When the mesquite beans matured in the late spring the Mahunutsi went to Panuga, now Mesquite Spring, for the harvest. Then they moved up into the Grapevine Mountains for the summer, probably camping at one of the springs just east of the crest. In October before the pine nuts fell, Dock organized rabbit drives on Sarcobatus Flat. Families from Ohyu, now Surveyor's Well, and from villages in Oasis Valley on the Amargosa joined in these drives, which lasted about a month. Then they returned to the Grapevine Range for the pine-nut harvest. After the harvest Dock sent out the word for all to convene at Ohyu for the fall festival. The festival was attended by

Shoshone from the villages of Tuhu at Goldbelt Spring and Navadu in Cottonwood Canyon on the west wide of Death Valley, and occasionally by others from Oasis, Panamint, and Saline valleys. After the festival everyone returned to the winter camps to begin the seasonal round again.[10]

Limited farming began at Mahunu about the time the first white men arrived, but the Mahunutsi probably picked up the idea from the Ash Meadows Paiute, not the whites. Each family cultivated a dozen or more acres. Corn, beans, pumpkins, and squash were the main crops. Later, Dock and Gold Mountain Jack, another Mahunutsi, each started second farms out on the floor of Death Valley at Panuga, where Gold Mountain Jack's family spent about half of their time.[11]

Less is known of the Shoshone, Kawaiisu, and Paiute in the southern half of Death Valley prior to the coming of the white man, but they played a more prominent part in the later history of the valley. After gathering pine nuts high in the Kaiguta, now the Panamint Range, they wintered in at least five main villages: Tumbisha, at the mouth of Furnace Creek; Puaitungani, in Johnson Canyon; Sunavadu, in Wildrose Canyon; Hauta, at Warm Spring in Panamint Valley; Pabuna, in Warm Spring Canyon at the south end of the Panamints; and probably a Kawaiisu village in Butte Valley. Tumbisha was the largest and most cosmopolitan village, its families made up through intermarriage among Shoshone, Kawaiisu, and Southern Paiute. The other villages were mostly Shoshone. The great oasis at the south end of Death Valley, Saratoga Springs, known as Muta to the Shoshone, may have been a temporary camp of the Southern Paiute from Tecopa Hot Springs.[12]

The Panamint Shoshone were the first Death Valley Indians to resist the invasion of white prospectors during the Coso mining rush. When the Owens Valley Paiute rose up against the intruders, the Panamint Shoshone joined in. Early in 1863 they attacked a prospecting camp near Wildrose Canyon, killing four men and driving others out. But the prospectors retaliated, killing nine Panamint Indians, including their chief, whom the whites dubbed Thieving Charley. Other Death Valley and Ash Meadows Shoshone were drawn into skirmishes with the whites before an informal peace was reached about 1867.[13]

Panamint Tom, the last *pakwinavi* of the Panamint Shoshone, pursued a more circumspect course thereafter, living in peace with local white settlers, although he and his brother, Hungry Bill, did make periodic raids far to the south to steal horses from ranches near Los Angeles. Horsemeat was a welcome treat in the Panamint villages when the pine-nut stores ran low in late winter, and the brothers were generous with their spoils. Still, Panamint Tom had a bad reputation among many local whites. For a time they accused him of murdering just about every man reported lost in the south end of Death Valley, when in fact he was one of the few who would brave the summer heat to try to rescue them. He admitted to having killed three whites at one time or another during his life, but many more owed their lives to him.[14]

In the 1880s and 1890s, Tom had a ranch with an orchard of 150 fruit trees at Pabuna, down in the wash of Warm Spring Canyon. But when a cloudburst and flash flood swept away the crops and trees in July of 1897, he moved back to Hungry Bill's ranch at their old village of Puaitungani—which means "mouse cave"—much higher into the Panamints. During the mining boom of the mid-1870s a man named William Johnson had briefly crowded in on them, starting a truck garden there to supply Panamint just over the crest. But Johnson moved on after the boom, leaving only his name in the canyon. Hungry Bill and his family took over the 4 or 5 acres of terraced gardens, planting grapevines and peach trees as well as squash, melons, beans, corn, wheat, and alfalfa.[15]

Two other Panamint Shoshone were prominent in the later history of Death Valley—Indian George and Shoshone Johnny. As a child George was startled one day in the 1850s, when he suddenly came upon a white man at Emigrant Spring; thereafter his father called him Bah-vanda-sava-nu-kee, or Boy-who-runs-away. Much later he came to be known to the whites as Indian George, after Dr. Samuel George hired him as his guide to prospect the Panamints. Sometime after the turn of the century the Bureau of Indian Affairs, figuring he needed a last name, called him George Hansen. Born at Ohyu in Death Valley, George married Panamint Tom's sister, moved briefly to Sunavadu, and then started a ranch in Panamint Valley at the mouth of Hall Canyon. His ranch was a welcome oasis for travelers and is now the Indian Ranch Reservation.[16]

George's cousin Shoshone Johnny, one of Grapevine Dock's sons and first known as Hungry Johnny, made history in 1904 when he showed Bob Montgomery the richest gold mine in all the Death Valley country—the Montgomery Shoshone, the mine that made the Bullfrog boom. Bob sold the mine for over $2,000,000, but for his part Johnny got little more than a grubstake and intermittent remembrances from Bob over the years. Johnny capitalized on his fame for a time and then returned to his home at Sunavadu. He ended his days posing for tourists at Furnace Creek, where he died in October 1953.[17]

Over on the Amargosa River the Shoshone wintered at the two best-watered spots, Oasis Valley and Ash Meadows, at opposite ends of the Amargosa Desert. In the mid-nineteenth century there were several families, totaling about thirty people, at each of these spots. Most of those in Oasis Valley lived at Sakainaga on the Amargosa bottomlands at the mouth of Beatty Wash, about 3 miles from the present town of Beatty. The others were scattered in the nearby camps of Panavadu, Takanawa, and Hunusu—all within just a few miles of one another. Although they occasionally gathered pine nuts in the Grapevine Mountains, the Oasis Valley Shoshone usually went east to the Belted Range and the Shoshone Mountains, where the harvest was more dependable. In addition to gathering wild foods they had also learned from the Southern Paiute to cultivate some staple crops.[18]

When white ranchers began settling in Oasis Valley in the late nineteenth century, most married Shoshone women. This eased somewhat the transition of the Shoshone into the new ways. But Panamint Joe Stuart, the last *pakwinavi* of the Oasis Valley people, still held to some earlier superstitions, so that when lightning killed a woman at his ranch in the summer of 1906, he took it as a bad omen and sold out. Moving up into the Grapevines, he and his family turned to selling firewood to miners at the new camps of Rhyolite and Bullfrog. Panamint Joe died of food poisoning from uncooked ham in June 1909, while he and his wife Maggie were guiding two would-be mining investors and their wives across Death Valley. Maggie led the party on to safety, and for her heroism, mine owner Bob Montgomery gave her a pension of $25 a month.[19]

The people at Ash Meadows, known to their neighbors as Kauyaichits, were mixed Shoshone and Southern Paiute. They went to the Spring Mountains for the pinyon harvest with Southern Paiute from villages to the south. No one recalls how many villages there once were at Ash Meadows, but after white ranchers began moving in, most of the Kauyaichits seem to have gathered onto a single ranch of their own at a spring about a mile east of Longstreet Spring. Although they took up many of the white man's ways, the Kauyaichits frequently found his justice beyond their reach. When their *pakwinavi,* Ash Meadows Charlie, was killed by a drunken white ranch hand in 1907, three of the Kauyaichits trailed the killer into the Funeral range and captured him. Refraining from meting out justice on the spot, they turned him over to the sheriff, only to have a jury set him loose.[20]

The main settlement of the Southern Paiute on the Amargosa was at Yaga, now Tecopa Hot Springs. With about seventy inhabitants, this was the largest Indian village in the Death Valley–Amargosa country. It was also the first village there to be visited by white men, when New Mexican horse traders opened a trail to California in 1830.[21]

Unlike the Shoshone, the Southern Paiute relied more heavily on cultivated crops such as beans, corn, melons, squash, sunflowers, and grapes, although they still gathered pinyon and other wild foods. Horsemeat also became a regular part of their diet once the New Mexican caravans began their annual trek to California, returning each spring with thousands of horses. Resting Spring, just 4 miles east of Yaga, was a favorite stopping place on the trail. Returning caravans paused there for a few days to rejuvenate their herds after the long barren journey from the Mojave River. The herds devoured almost everything edible around Resting Spring, taxing the larder of the Yagats and their neighbors. But enough stray horses turned up dead to help make up for the loss.[22]

The Yagats were loosely associated with the Southern Paiute in three smaller villages to the east: Pahrump, at the springs of that name; Moqua, in the Kingston Range at Horse Thief Springs; and Nogwa, at Potosi Spring. All gathered pinyon in the Spring Mountains and joined together to celebrate the fall festival at Pahrump. Tecopa from Pahrump was *pakwinavi* of all four villages during the latter half of the nineteenth century. Tecopa means "wildcat," but it was an inadequate description for so shrewd and skillful a negotiator as he. The whites imagined that his influence extended all the way from Death Valley to the Colorado River, and he did nothing to discourage the notion. They plied him with gifts, including a favored stovepipe hat, and named a mining camp after him, all to win his aid and blessings in prospecting the surrounding country. In a sort of a self-fulfilling prophesy, his influence in surrounding villages seemed to grow in proportion to the respect that the whites paid him. When he died in 1905, his mourning ceremony drew Paiute from as far as the Colorado River as well as Shoshone such as Panamint Tom from across Death Valley. His son, Tecopa John, who had discovered the famous Johnnie mine north of Pahrump, was named the new *pakwinavi,* but he never matched his father in influence.[23]

At the extreme north end of Death Valley the pinyon groves on the Palmetto and Sylvania mountains were shared by Shoshone and Northern Paiute. Most of the Shoshone lived at Pauwaha, now Lida Spring, although a couple of families chose to winter at Saiyogadu at the head of Tule Canyon and at Tumbakai on the Gold Mountain side of Oriental Wash, both of which open into Death Valley. All but one of the Northern Paiute families in the area settled at Tunava, now Pigeon Spring. The loners lived at Ozangwin near Cucomungo Spring, a few miles to the south. Palmetto Dick, a Northern Paiute, was *pakwinavi* of all the people in that area in the mid-nineteenth century. He organized the rabbit drives near Ozangwin and the fall festival at Tunava. After his death they joined in activities with the Fish Lake Valley Paiute at Sohoduhatu, now Oasis, directed by Big Mouth Tom. The Deep Spring Valley Paiute also took part in these affairs after their own "big talker," Joe Bowers, signed up as a scout for the U.S. Army and moved to an outpost near the mining camp of Palmetto.[24]

Although the coming of white horse traders, prospectors, miners, ranchers, and eventually tourists disrupted the traditional ways of life in Death Valley and the Amargosa country, some of the *nuwu* remain to this day. They may have intermarried with the whites and adopted some of their technology, but they, like the land, have endured.

MORE LOST THAN FOUND

To the early whites who came into it, the Death Valley and Amargosa country was a land where more was lost than found—a stingy land that took much and gave little.

The horse traders and horse raiders who came first found a hard, meager trail across the southern edge of the country, but they lost many horses and occasionally their lives just trying to cross it. Westering gold seekers lost their way into the country and found their way out only after losing their oxen, their wagons, and a few even their lives. Yet on their way out they found gold and silver ledges that dazzled their imagination, but they lost track of all but one of these bonanzas. And those who tried to mine that one gold ledge lost more money in getting out the ore they found than they ever got from it. Others lost their lives just looking for the ledges that were lost, and a couple of lost-ledge hunters found even richer ledges, only to lose them, too.

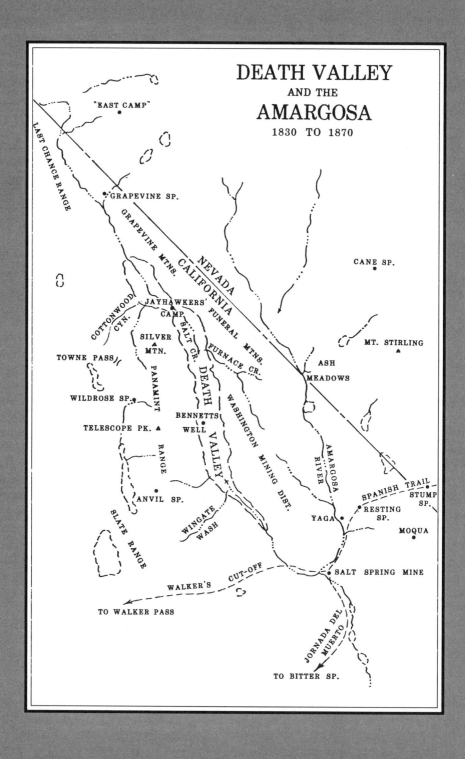

DEATH VALLEY
AND THE
AMARGOSA
1830 TO 1870

LAST CHANCE RANGE

"EAST CAMP"

GRAPEVINE SP.

GRAPEVINE MTNS.

NEVADA
CALIFORNIA

CANE SP.

COTTONWOOD CYN.

JAYHAWKERS' CAMP

SALT CR.

FUNERAL MTNS.

SILVER MTN.

FURNACE CR.

MT. STIRLING

TOWNE PASS

PANAMINT

DEATH VALLEY

ASH
MEADOWS

WILDROSE SP.

TELESCOPE PK.

RANGE

BENNETTS WELL

WASHINGTON MINING DIST.

AMARGOSA RIVER

ANVIL SP.

SPANISH TRAIL
STUMP SP.

SLATE RANGE

WINGATE WASH

YAGA

RESTING SP.

MOQUA

WALKER'S CUT-OFF

SALT SPRING MINE

TO WALKER PASS

JORNADA DEL MUERTO

TO BITTER SP.

Los Chaguanosos

The first white intruders into Death Valley and the Amargosa were horse traders, opening a trail between New Mexico and California in 1830. Over this route, now known as the Spanish Trail, came caravans of traders, then bands of raiders—Los Chaguanosos—who soon dominated the trade, running out hundreds to thousands of horses each year from the ranches and missions of California for eager settlers in the Mississippi Valley. They lost many animals on the deadly jornada across the south end of Death Valley, but it was such lucrative business that they came back year after year, until the gold rush essentially ended the trade. Then tantalizing tales of the Chaguanosos' secret shortcut to California drew an ill-fated band of gold seekers right into the heart of Death Valley.[1]

Antonio Armijo, an enterprising trader in his late thirties, headed the first caravan from New Mexico to California in the fall and winter of 1829–30. Starting from Abiquiu he traveled northwest through Monument Valley, forded the Colorado River in Glen Canyon, trekked across southern Utah, down the Virgin River, and around the south end of the Spring Mountains, and reached the Amargosa River near the Paiute village of Yaga on January 14, 1830. From there the caravan followed the Amargosa, which Armijo named Rio de los Payuches, south into Death Valley until they reached Rio Salitroso, now Salt Creek. They followed Salt Creek out of the valley, trekked around the Avawatz Mountains to Bitter Spring, then traveled up the Mojave River, over Cajon Pass, and on to the San Gabriel Mission, where they arrived on January 31. At the mission and in the neighboring settlements they swapped serapes for horses at roughly two for one, getting animals for barely a fifth of what they would sell for in Santa Fe or farther east. A month later they headed back over the trail to New Mexico with the first herd of horses from California. The success of the trade was assured.[2]

The Spanish Trail has been called the "longest, crookedest, most arduous" trail in the West, and the trek into the south end of Death Valley—the *jornada del muerto* or "journey of death"—was the worst part. There were 45 waterless miles between the drearily named Bitter and Salt springs, whose meager, tainted waters did little to relieve man or beast, and it was fully 80 miles from the Mojave River to Resting Spring, where the first good, sufficient water could be had for stock. The jornada del muerto was soon strewn with the bleaching bones of spent horses, in grim testimony to its name. The Paiute and other Indians along the trail also levied a toll

25

in horseflesh. But even with such losses, the horse trade was an exceedingly profitable business—so much so, in fact, that it quickly attracted those whose only capital was the bravado to take what they wanted. Stolen horses soon made up a large, if not the largest, part of the trade along the Spanish Trail. The thieves were a mixed lot of New Mexican traders, American and Canadian trappers, and Indian raiders, collectively branded Los Chaguanosos by the Californians.[3]

The first of these was a band led by Juan Jesus Villapando, a member of an old New Mexican family. Villapando's band came to California in the winter of 1832–33, posing as traders. Authorities became suspicious when at every ranch they visited, horses and mules turned up missing. Villapando was apprehended at a rendezvous on the Mojave River with nearly two hundred stolen horses, but he escaped to a new rendezvous with his cohorts at the south end of San Joaquin Valley, where they gathered a much larger herd. Despite a government raid that caught three of the thieves and four hundred horses there, Villapando and most of his gang escaped to New Mexico in the spring of 1833, with roughly a thousand horses. To avoid detection their escape route from the San Joaquin Valley to the Spanish Trail must have stayed clear of the Mojave River. Most likely they crossed over Tehachapi Pass, or possibly the pass farther north that Joseph Walker would find the following year, and then traveled along the rift of the Garlock fault from the foot of the Sierra to the south end of Death Valley, striking the Spanish Trail at Salt Spring. This route was much used by later horse thieves and came to be known as "Walker's cutoff," either because it ran to Walker Pass or because it was frequented by the Ute raider Walkara, called Walker by the whites. This was the highly touted shortcut that the argonauts were seeking when they blundered into Death Valley in 1849.[4]

Closer surveillance by the Californians briefly curtailed the horse thieves for a few years, until the province was thrown into turmoil by the revolution and counterrevolution of 1836–37. Among the mercenaries who took part in the revolts was Jean-Baptiste Chalifoux, a Canadian trapper who led a band of Chaguanosos, hired first by one side and then the other. Dissatisfied with their pay after the revolt ended, Chalifoux's band raided the missions of Santa Inez and San Luis Obispo in the fall of 1837, stealing nearly fifteen hundred animals, which they drove from the San Joaquin Valley across the end of Death Valley to the Spanish Trail and on to New Mexico. This was so much more profitable than trapping that Chalifoux returned for another raid in the fall of 1839, but this time he was captured by Mexican troops in the San Joaquin Valley. While the troops were patrolling the central valley, however, a new band of Chaguanosos pulled off the biggest raid of all against the missions and ranches to the south. Outraged Californians chased the thieves all the way into Death Valley.[5]

The great raid of 1840 had its inception at Fort Davy Crockett, a trading post run by Philip F. Thompson and two partners in Brown's Hole on the Green River, in the northwest corner of present-day Colorado. The declining fur trade was forcing many trappers to look for new pursuits, and the stories of Chalifoux's successful raid on the Mexican missions and ranches in California attracted Thompson, an impetuous twenty-nine-year-old Tennessean; Dick Owens, for whom Owens Valley was named; and about a dozen other trappers. With Phil Thompson as their leader, they set out for California in January of 1840. Others of like mind joined en route, so that by the time they reached the missions their number had nearly doubled. Lore has it that among the final raiding party were such familiar names as old Bill Williams, Pegleg Smith, Jim Beckwourth, and the Ute chief Walkara—indeed, there was hardly a mountain man of note who wasn't later linked to the gang.[6]

After a careful reconnaissance of their quarry, the gang launched a series of raids in quick succession. Starting at the Mission San Luis Obispo in late April, they swept through the ranches and missions of southern California, reaching their rendezvous in Cajon Pass by mid-May, with about three thousand horses and mules.[7]

Three posses of irate Californians set out in pursuit of the Chaguanosos. The first posse—two dozen *vaqueros* led by Cucamonga rancher Don Ygnacio Palomares—was barely a day behind the fleeing thieves. But these overeager pursuers rode into an ambush some 50 miles out into the Mojave Desert. Two of Palomares's men were killed and one was wounded. In parting insult, some of the Chaguanosos went after the retreating posse and ran off all their horses, leaving them to struggle on afoot in the desert. In the meantime Juan Leandre, a Los Angeles justice of the peace, joined the pursuit with a small party of reinforcements. When he learned of Palomares's fate he halted at Cajon Pass to await the main posse, under Los Angeles *alcalde* Jose Antonio Carrillo. The combined posse was made up of 75 men, 225 horses, and a makeshift armory of 49 rifles and muskets, 18 pistols, 19 spears, and 22 swords and sabers.[8]

The Chaguanosos had several day's head start on Carrillo's posse, but the pursuers steadily closed in on the slower moving herd. With so large a herd only a fraction of the horses could be adequately watered at Bitter Spring before the thristy beasts were driven out onto the jornada del muerto to Death Valley. The desiccating trail took a terrible toll as the herd trudged across the southern end of the valley. Animals were dropping every few hundred feet, and the trail was stewn with their carcasses. There was insufficient water at Salt Spring, so no halt was made until they reached Resting Spring. By then Carrillo was close on the heels of the last straggling ponies.[9]

The posse reached Bitter Spring on the morning of May 24 and found the tracks of the herd so fresh that Carrillo decided to press on as soon as fresh mounts could be readied, leaving the spent horses and pack animals behind. Late that afternoon the Californians saw in the distance dust clouds from some of the straggling horses. But the Chaguanosos's scouts saw the posse, too, and brought word to Thompson and the others camped at Resting Spring. Shortly before sunset the following day Carrillo's posse charged into the camp at Resting Spring, only to find it abandoned and all but a few spent horses gone. The Chaguanosos had beat such a hasty retreat that they left saddles, clothes, and cooking utensils scattered about the camp. In one of the coats the Californians even found a list of the names of some of the thieves—all Americans. His own horses now exhausted, Carrillo decided to give up the pursuit. Many years later, Calvin Jones, who also claimed to have been one of the raiders, suggested that Carrillo's decision may not have been entirely voluntary. Jones boasted that he and Bill Williams had crept back at night into the posse's camp and driven off their horses, which they held hostage until Carrillo agreed to abandon the chase.[10]

Whatever the case, in his official report Carrillo expressed satisfaction that, since the thieves had already lost at least fifteen hundred horses— roughly half the herd—on the jornada, and would doubtless lose most of the remainder on the trail ahead, the raid would prove so unprofitable that it would not soon be repeated.[11]

The Chaguanosos, however, had just moved up the trail a short distance, most likely to Stump Spring, where they allowed their surviving horses to rest for several days. Satisfied that the Californians would pursue them no farther, they then proceeded at a more leisurely pace, with little further loss in horseflesh. The following year Thompson sold the last of the herd on the Missouri River. In all they probably got close to $100,000 from the raid—a profit that did little to discourage later raids, although none of these was ever as large.[12]

The Southern Paiute around Resting Spring must have enjoyed many feasts on the horseflesh bonanza left in the wake of the 1840 raid. Nor could they have failed to notice how the Chaguanosos and Californians played fast and loose with one another's horses at Resting Spring, which may have encouraged them to make an overt raid of their own a few years later. The annual caravans and the herds of raiders were generally so large that the Paiute merely picked off a few stray horses and scavenged the carcasses of those that dropped along the trail. But their big chance came in the spring of 1844, when half a dozen New Mexicans with about thirty horses ventured out ahead of the main caravan to get the first pick of the grass at the springs.

The New Mexicans—Andreas Fuentes and his wife, the Hernandez family, and Santiago Giacome, their guide—reached Resting Spring in mid-April. There they decided to wait for the caravan trailing about two weeks behind them. After a few days several Paiute came into camp and seemed friendly enough to allay any fears the New Mexicans may have had. Thus they were taken by surprise on April 23 when the Paiute suddenly surrounded the camp and attacked in a hail of shouts and arrows. Fuentes and the Hernandez boy, Pablo, were mounted, circling the horses at the time. The two drove the herd into the attacking Paiute hoping to rout them, but then kept on going, fleeing for their lives and leaving the others to their fate.[13]

Fuentes and Pablo rode all that night back across the jornada del muerto, pausing only long enough to shift their saddles to fresh mounts. The following day they left the herd at Bitter Spring and continued down the trail until they happened upon John C. Fremont's exploring party at the Mojave River. The next morning the two New Mexicans returned to Bitter Spring with the exploring party, only to find that the Paiute had taken the horses. Kit Carson, Fremont's guide, and Alex Godey volunteered to go with Fuentes in pursuit of the thieves. Fuente's horse, already nearly exhausted from the ordeal, gave out after 20 miles, so he returned to camp, but Carson and Godey continued. From Fremont's description of the pursuit, it appears that on reaching the south end of Death Valley the tracks of the horses led away from the Spanish Trail, through the low hills to the east, and up Beck Spring Canyon in the Kingston Range to the Paiute village of Moqua, at what is now known—perhaps not coincidentally—as Horse Thief Springs.[14]

Fearful of losing the track in the dark as they entered the canyon, Carson and Godey made a cold camp late that night, wrapped in sweaty saddle blankets. At dawn on April 26 they spotted the horses at the Paiute camp, just beyond the ridge at the head of the canyon. Several horses, already skinned and butchered, were being cooked for a feast. Carson and Godey crept toward the herd until a startled horse alerted the Indians. Then with a war whoop they opened fire on the village. The Moquats returned a volley of arrows but then scattered up the slope behind the camp with the women and children, apparently fearing a larger attack. Carson stood guard as Godey rushed forward to scalp two Indians who had fallen from the shots. It was a blood-chilling sight, for the second Indian that Godey scalped was still alive and let out a hideous scream. As he leaped to his feet, blood streaming from his head, Godey shot him dead.[15]

Late that afternoon Carson and Godey returned victorious to Fremont's camp at Bitter Spring with fifteen of the horses and the two bloody scalps dangling from Godey's gun. Fremont had trouble finding words enough to praise their heroic deed, proclaiming it "the boldest and most disinterested which the annals of western adventure, so full of daring deeds, can present." Another member of the party, Charles Preuss, detected such envy in Fremont's praise that he suggested Fremont might gladly have traded all the results of his explorations just "for a scalp taken by his own hand." Preuss himself found "such butchery disgusting."[16]

Traveling at night over the jornada del muerto, easily marked even in the moonlight by the bleached bones of spent horses, Fremont's party arrived at Resting Spring on April 29, six days after the attack. They found the arrow-pierced bodies of Giacome and Pablo's father with one hand and both legs cut off. Only a little dog belonging to Pablo's mother was alive to greet the grief-stricken boy. They concluded that the two women had been taken captive, although Carson and Godey had not seen them at Moqua. Later, Carson heard that the caravan had found the bodies of the women staked to the ground and mutilated.[17]

Fremont renamed the place Agua de Hernandez, but the name didn't last. Only the skull of one of the men, hung on a pole, told travelers of the tragedy. Fremont took the orphaned Pablo back to Washington, D.C., where the eleven-year-old boy was left for Fremont's father-in-law, Senator Thomas Hart Benton, to raise. But things went badly and Pablo eventually returned to the West. The last Fremont ever heard of him was a curious rumor that he had turned to a life of banditry in the California mines, under the name of Joaquin Murieta![18]

The horse trade to New Mexico began to decline during the Mexican War and came to an end in 1849, as the gold rush created a bonanza market for horseflesh in the California mines; however, horse raiders kept herds moving over the Spanish Trail for at least another decade.[19]

Despite increased vigilance by Mexican authorities after the 1840 raid, Pegleg Smith mounted a successful raid the very next year, and others followed his path. Military patrols of Cajon Pass and the Mojave River caught a few thieves and retrieved several hundred horses, but many of the Chaguanosos only shifted their rendezvous back to the San Joaquin Valley and made for the Spanish Trail by way of Walker's cutoff through the south end of Death Valley.[20]

When California became part of the Union after the Mexican War, patriotic American trappers claimed that they abandoned the horse raids because, as Pegleg Smith avowed, "I never make war on my own people." But the trappers still had plenty of horses to sell, so they let Walkara and his Utes be the middlemen. Walkara became chief of the Timpanogos Utes as a result of his accumulated wealth in horses and was known to whites as the "Napoleon of the Desert" for the skill with which he carried off horse raids against them. He seems to have gotten his start in the early 1840s, demanding tribute from the annual caravans on the Spanish Trail as they passed through central Utah. Despite latter-day rumors that he took part in the great raid of 1840, Walkara's first raid on the California ranches was probably in October 1845, when he came posing as a peaceful trader and left three months later with more than a thousand stolen horses. Thereafter Walkara and his lieutenants made regular raids on the ranches of southern California, until his death in 1855.[21]

The demise of the horse traders and horse raiders did not mean the end of horsemeat for the Death Valley Indians, however. The Paiute along the Amargosa still picked off strays from trail-weary travelers, and Shoshone such as Panamint Tom and Hungry Bill made furtive raids on ranches near the passes to San Bernardino and Los Angeles on into the 1870s.

The Trail to Gold

The gold seekers of 1849 gave Death Valley its name and won for themselves a prominent place in its history. In getting there, however, many lost not only their way but their wagons, animals, belongings, and in some cases even their lives. The few tantalizing nuggets of gold and silver that they found in the valley were no compensation.

Their story has become the most repeated, though frequently garbled, tale in the history of Death Valley. It is in reality several separate stories only loosely intertwined, for the argonauts who trekked into Death Valley and the Amargosa came like a routed army in retreat—in scattered bands, demoralized and confused, each on their own course. Their stories are those of the jornada del muerto through Death Valley, the quest for Walker's cutoff, the gold at Salt Spring, the tragedy of Pinney's eleven, the ordeal of the Jayhawkers and Bugsmashers, the gunsight silver and Goller's gold, the triumph of the Wades, and the heroic rescue of the Bennetts and Arcans by Manly and Rogers.

The ragtag argonauts who stumbled into the depths of the valley were but a small part of that army of westering emigrants who struggled through Death Valley and the Amargosa en route to the goldfields of California. Nearly a thousand men, women, and children, over two hundred wagons, and a couple of thousand horses, mules, oxen, cattle, and dogs started down the Spanish Trail south from Salt Lake in the fall of 1849.[1]

Not one had originally intended to take that trail; they had all started for the northern route to the mines, which led west from Salt Lake along the Humboldt and over the Sierra to the diggings. But for one reason or another—late starts or delays along the way—they had each reached Salt Lake too late in the season to get to the Sierra before the snow closed the passes. The Spanish Trail was not an inviting route: it was little more than a pack trail and was unsuited for wagons—only one wagon had ever been taken over it. It was poorly watered and foddered, with some jornadas of more than a day without any water or grass at all; and, if all this weren't bad enough, it took the gold seekers about 500 miles out of their way! But it was the only alternative to wintering at Salt Lake. For eager argonauts anxious to get to the diggings before the gold was gone, there was no other choice.

Two former trappers, Jim Waters and Charley McIntosh, guided the first band of gold seekers down the trail—130 men and boys with pack horses and mules. They left Fort Utah, now Provo, on August 15, 1849, and reached Death Valley and the Amargosa early in October. Doubtless at their guides' insistence, they refrained from raiding the Indian gardens they found along the trail—though the thought of fresh food must have sorely tempted them—and were in turn well treated by the Indians. In fact, while camped at or near Resting Spring, the Paiute gave them fresh melons and corn, to which they responded with gifts of red flannel shirts and silk handkerchiefs. Waters learned that, through the influence of the Mormons, the Ute chief Walkara had sent word to the Paiute along the trail not to molest the argonauts. To formalize this, one enthusiast, Judge Harvey S. Brown, immediately took it upon himself to draw up a treaty—festooned with a great glob of sealing wax—between the argonauts and the Paiute, who were most likely represented by Tecopa, guaranteeing safe passage to all passing down the trail. Unfortunately not all the adventurers who followed kept their hands off the Paiute gardens, so the Paiute indulged in the travelers' livestock in return. The desert itself, of course, was not even temporarily amenable to such persuasion, and on the jornada del muerto across the end of Death Valley, even the packers lost a quarter of their animals, "abandoned under the scorching sun for food for the PiUte." But they lost not a single man and reached Isaac Williams's Chino Ranch in late October.[2]

By then, the whole army of argonauts was on its way down the trail. Those with wagons and stock had waited for the weather to cool before starting in late September and early October. The largest train, which styled itself the San Joaquin Company, soon corrupted to the Sand Walking Company, consisted of 400–500 souls, about 110 wagons, and roughly 1,000 oxen, cattle, and pack animals. Jefferson Hunt, a former captain of the Mormon Batallion in the Mexican War, agreed to be their guide, for a fee of $10 per wagon. Hunt was well qualified, for he had been down the trail and back in the winter of 1847–48 getting seed and stock for the struggling new settlement at Salt Lake. But about a third of those heading down the trail had refused to join Hunt's train—some for lack of money to pay his fee, but most simply because they feared that there would not be enough water and grass for so large a crowd. They had formed two smaller trains and pulled out onto the trail several days ahead of Hunt. The first party was made up of about two dozen wagons with a Mexican guide familiar with the trail; the second party had about three dozen wagons led by a Captain Hooker, who was relying on Fremont's map and report.[3]

Unlike the pack train led by Waters and McIntosh, the wagon trains soon broke up into a dozen or more parties, each determined to go at its own pace and even its own separate way. These parties in turn fragmented into even smaller bands. By the time the first wagons reached the Amargosa the trains were thoroughly disintegrated, scattered back along the trail for nearly 200 miles and out onto the trackless desert to the north for over 100 miles.

The breakup of the Hunt train came when, as one of its victims termed it, "a hearsay delusion seized the camp." The wagons had been on the trail for a couple weeks when a party of packers led by a twenty-year-old New Yorker, Captain Orson K. Smith, overtook them. Smith was determined to take a shortcut to the mines by way of the Walker cutoff, which he had learned of from Barney Ward, a former trapper who had settled at Salt Lake. Ward claimed to have been over the cutoff three times, apparently on horse raids, and he had even traced out the route for Smith on a crude map, but his geography was faulty. Word of the map and Smith's plan spread quickly through the train, and the cutoff became an obsession with most. Indeed, who could doubt it? Even Fremont's great map of the West, published just the year before, showed a grand but imaginary east-west "dividing range" at about that latitude, and along its stream-fed base a good trail was sure to lie.[4]

On November 3, the Hunt train reached the point near Meadow Valley Creek in Utah, where Fremont's imaginary range started and where Smith said the cutoff began. There a grand council of all the wagons was convened. The first speaker was James Welsh Brier, a tall, raw-boned Methodist preacher with a ready opinion on every subject. He fired the crowd with "zeal for the cutoff," vowing that "go it he should, sink or swim, live or die, he should take the cutoff—'go it boots.'" Others echoed the call. That night, a hundred wagons voted to follow Smith over the cutoff; only seven chose to stay on the Spanish Trail.[5]

The next morning they parted company, for Hunt refused to take the cutoff, stating that he had been hired to guide them down the Spanish Trail and that as long as any of the wagons wanted to go that way, he was honor-bound to guide them. He further warned those who wanted to take the cutoff that it might only lead to hell. But once they had parted he openly expressed his joy at being rid of them, especially a set of "mobocratic spirits" who blamed him for every mishap and inconvenience on the trail and even threatened his life. Thus Hunt and his seven remaining wagons set off as fast as possible to "get out of their way" in case they turned back to the trail. In the course of a month, most did just that.[6]

Barely 25 miles off the trail, the wagon train following Smith came to a halt before a deep canyon at the head of Beaver Dam Wash. Smith and the pack trains had gone down the canyon, but it was impassable to the wagons. After several days camped at what they dubbed Mt. Misery, exploring the possible detours, most of the wagon train recognized their mistake and headed back to the Spanish trail to try to catch up with Hunt. Only about two dozen wagons—the Jayhawkers, the Bugsmashers, including the Reverend James Brier, and several smaller groups—took their wagons on around the head of the canyon to make their own trail right into the heart of Death Valley.[7]

Smith and the packers struggled west for a couple of weeks, covering only about 90 miles to Coyote Spring, at the foot of the Sheep Range north of Las Vegas, before most of them also decided to turn back. They initially called the place Dead Horse Spring because they started killing horses there to eat when their provisions ran out, but after splitting up they renamed it Division Spring. The first to turn back was a party of Mormons led by Charles C. Rich, who headed south, striking the Spanish Trail at the Muddy River just as Hunt arrived. A second party, led by Jacob Stover, followed them to the Muddy a couple days later and met the tail end of the Hooker train, which had fallen behind Hunt.[8]

Still eleven brave but foolish souls, led by a hulking redhead named Pinney, were determined to continue ever westward against all odds. With only a scant ration of dried horsemeat in their backpacks they set out on foot over the Sheep Range to keep a rendezvous with destiny in the Death Valley country. O. K. Smith, who had so valiantly vowed to die facing west rather than turn back, was not among them. With the remainder of the packers he retraced his steps all the way back to Meadow Valley Creek, where he had first left the trail. Destitute and nearly dead from starvation, Smith and his companions were rescued by the Huffaker train—the last wagons down the trail that winter.[9]

The first of the wagons to reach the Amargosa country were those led down the Spanish Trail by the Mexican whose name no one could recall. They were nearly out of food and living on their cattle, which gave out when they got to Resting Spring in the latter part of November, so their guide and five others rushed on to the settlements for relief. The wagons waited at Resting Spring for about a week, hoping that the Hooker train might catch up to give them aid. Finally abandoning several wagons and other belongings to lighten their load, they moved out onto the jornada del muerto for the Mojave River. They just missed Hunt's wagons and the Mormon pack train, which arrived at Resting Spring before their campfires were cold.[10]

Hunt and the packers didn't linger long at Resting Spring or elsewhere in the Death Valley country. Yet even in their haste, it was they who discovered the first gold in Death Valley. It seems a whimsy of fate that with all the gold seekers trudging down the Spanish Trail in the fall of 1849, the discovery of gold was made by two Mormon missionaries bound

The imaginary east-west "dividing range" on Fremont's 1848 map (opposite) helped lure shortcut-seeking Forty-niners off the trail and into Death Valley.

for the South Seas! But they were, after all, the only men who really knew what to look for, because they alone had already been to the California goldfields.

James S. Brown and Addison Pratt were both called by Brigham Young to carry on the Mormon mission in Tahiti. Brown had joined the Mormon Batallion in the Mexican War, arriving at Sutter's Fort in the fall of 1847. He spent the winter there and was helping to dig the mill race when James Marshall found the first flake of gold. Pratt, who had

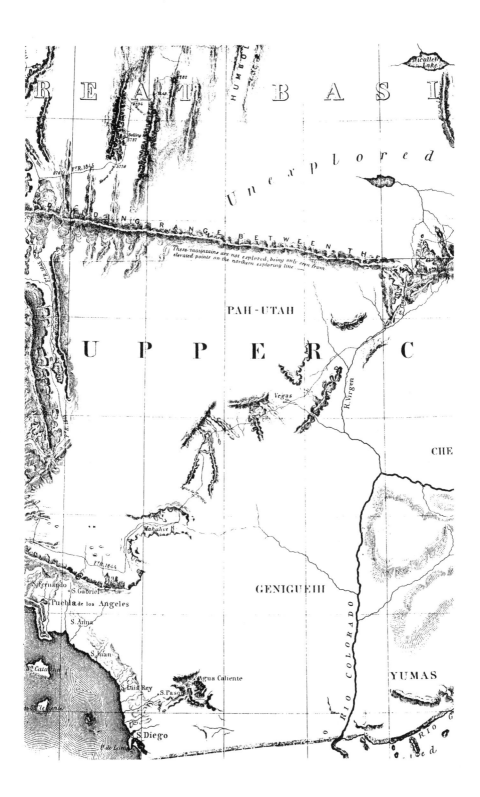

founded the mission in Tahiti, returned to California and went to the diggings in the spring of 1848. Both crossed the Sierra to Salt Lake later that year; then, called to renew the mission, they were accompanying Hunt back to the coast.[11]

On the afternoon of December 1, Hunt turned the wagons south from the Amargosa toward Salt Spring, which lay just beyond a low rocky point. Then he and four companions—Brown, Pratt, a man named Rowan, and a boy named Forbes—rode ahead to check the spring where they planned to camp, taking a shortcut through a notch in the rocks. As they led their horses up the narrow pass, Pratt noticed bits of loose quartz and suggested that there might be gold nearby. At that they all started searching. Soon several flakes of gold were found in the sand. Then Rowan called out "Here is gold!" The others crowded around him to see the 4-inch quartz vein in which he had found several pea-sized grains of gold. After chipping out a few samples, they hurried on over to the spring a mile ahead, where the teams were already gathering. The discovery caused quite a stir, as several of the argonauts scrambled back to the spot to have their first look at California gold. Grabbing a cold chisel and hammer, Brown set to work, taking out more gold from their original strike while others prospected the surrounding slopes. The jornada del muerto still lay before them, however, and when Hunt gave the call to move on, the would-be miners reluctantly fell in with the train. But the first gold had been found in Death Valley, and it was not to be forgotten.[12]

From the time the first wagons reached Resting Spring in November of 1849 until the last wagon was abandoned in Death Valley in February of 1850, scarcely a day went by when one or more struggling bands of argonauts could not be found in some part of Death Valley or the Amargosa.

Hunt arrived at Resting Spring just after the first wagons had left, and just before he left, the lead wagons of the Hooker party pulled in, along with Stover's packers. In almost continuous succession they were followed by the straggling wagons of the Sand Walking Company, which had turned back to the trail from Mt. Misery, and by others who had gotten a later start—Egan's pack train, Pomeroy's wagons, and finally the Huffaker train, bringing the now infamous O. K. Smith, which passed through in early January 1850. Long before that, the scattered bands of die-hard cutoff seekers, who had refused to turn back to the known trail, began to blunder into the upper reaches of the Amargosa. The last of them—the Bennett and Arcan families—didn't leave Death Valley until February.[13]

"Into the Jaws of Hell"

When the argonauts left the Spanish Trail in pursuit of O. K. Smith and the illusive shortcut to the goldfields, Jefferson Hunt had warned them, "If you want to follow Captain Smith, I can't help it, but I believe you will get into the jaws of hell." None heeded his words at the time, but the farther they got from the trail the louder those words echoed in their minds. And for Pinney's band of eleven backpackers, the words took on a grotesque significance.[1]

Pinney's men were the first of the cutoff seekers to reach Death Valley and the Amargosa. They must have wandered into the Amargosa Desert, 60 miles or more north of the Spanish Trail, and blundered on into Death Valley about the first of December, while Stover and the rest of their former companions were camped at Resting Spring. Stover had almost gone with Pinney's party when they set out from Division Spring a couple of weeks earlier. But at the last minute he decided against it because two others, Wiley Webster and John Adams, who had been "on the wrong side every time" a crucial decision was made in the past, decided to go with Pinney. Stover gambled that they had made the wrong decision again. Only Pinney and a man named Savage survived to tell their tale.[2]

When Pinney first reached the mines, he said that he and Savage had left the other nine in a disagreement over which way to go—he and Savage had headed west while the others headed northwest. But later, when he and Savage chanced to meet Stover at Nevada City, they confided in him, telling quite a different story. When Pinney's band reached the Amargosa Desert, they were close to starvation: their horsemeat rations were exhausted, and they had seen no game to shoot. That night Wiley Webster announced that[3]

> we would have to draw cuts in the morning who should be killed to eat. As we did not want to be killed to be eaten or eat anybody, when we thought they were asleep we got up and traveled till day; then we took our butcher knives and dug holes in the sand and covered up all but our heads till night when we would come out and travel all night again. By this time we did not fear them and were recruited. This sand was what saved us.

Pinney and Savage were finally rescued by the Paiute at Owens Lake, nursed back to health, and guided over the south end of the Sierra and up to the Mariposa mines. Some thirteen to fourteen years later, Slate Range miners found the skeletons of nine men, lying together with a little rock wall built around them—right in the heart of Death Valley, just north of the dunes, Brier claimed. When the band had left Division Spring they had feared they might not make it out alive. So that their families would know what became of them, they had given Stover's party their names— G. Wiley Webster, Charles McDermot, John Adams, Deacon Moore, T. Ware, J. Ware, Baker, Samore, and Allen—and, of course, Pinney and Savage.[4]

Close on the heels of Pinney's band came the rest of the cutoff seekers, all inexorably gravitating to the lowest spot on the continent, but each by slightly different routes. On November 11, after Smith and the packers had gone down the canyon at Mt. Misery, the Jayhawkers, Bugsmashers, and scattered followers who refused to turn back to the Spanish Trail started cutting a new trail for their wagons north around the head of the canyon.

The Jayhawkers—some three dozen men mostly from Knoxville and Galesburg in Illinois—had a dozen wagons and were led by Captain Edward Doty. The Bugsmashers, headed by Captain Town and Jim Martin, numbered over a dozen men, including three blacks; they were mostly from Georgia and Mississippi and had about half a dozen wagons. The vociferous Reverend Brier, his wife Juliet, and their three sons attached themselves to the Bugsmashers. Three other families—Asabel Bennett's, John Arcan's, and Harry Wade's—trailed along behind, together with an assortment of stragglers, including the ailing Richard Culverwell and Bennett's friend William Lewis Manly. In all, there were over eighty men, four women, and eleven children, two dozen or more wagons, and over a hundred oxen. Jim Martin was elected captain of the whole group shortly after they left Mt. Misery, but within a week they began to break up.[5]

The wagons headed northwest across the First Muddy, now Meadow Valley Wash, to the Second or Ward's Muddy, the White River, looking for Fremont's mythical east-west dividing range, along the base of which they expected to find the Walker cutoff. But as the days passed, it became clear that no such range existed. Manly and the stragglers gave up the quest after a week and headed west. Martin and the rest continued north for a couple of more days before they too gave up and soon overtook Manly again. Turning southwest into a sterile valley they now pursued a new illusion—a shimmering mirage of a vast lake, which proved to be only a few muddy alkaline pools that they named Misery Lake. With the aid of a captured Paiute, they finally found good water near the foot of the Timpahute Range, and camped there for a few days to recuperate.[6]

They split up again there, when they couldn't agree on which way to go next. About December 1, Jim Martin and the Bugsmashers, impatient with the slow pace, abandoned their wagons, made packs for their oxen, and headed west toward a high snowy range they saw far ahead. The Briers tried to follow in their wagon. Sixteen years later the local Paiute women salvaged the great iron tires from the abandoned wagons and rolled them 25 miles to the mining camp at Pahranagat. A blacksmith there paid well for the iron, which, it was rumored, the desert's furnace had forged into tempered steel![7]

The rest of the argonauts continued south for another week, before the Jayhawkers also decided to turn west, although they kept their wagons intact, at least for a while. Only Bennett and the other stragglers, guided by Manly, still held their course to the south, steering for the snowy peak of Mount Stirling, at whose base Manly hoped to find water.[8]

The Jayhawkers trudged for five days over a waterless route, with only a light snow to slake their thirst, before they reached the Amargosa River "just in time," one wrote, "to save our cattle." For them it was indeed Relief Valley, and they rested for a week at the seeps of that bitter stream about a dozen miles northwest of what is now Death Valley Junction. Here too they started cutting up their cumbersome wagons to make two-wheeled carts, which were faster and more manageable in the rough terrain. Some of the wagon iron they hammered into new shoes for their oxen. Back on the move, the Jayhawkers too split up. Some headed west over the Funerals while the rest continued south around the end of the range to the head of Furnace Creek Wash. There, on December 20, they found a horse trail which they imagined was Barney Ward's "old pack trail," although it was probably just the tracks of a few horses run off by the Indians from the Spanish Trail.[9]

The coming of the Jayhawkers with their strange horned beasts and odd rolling contraptions disrupted the quiet life at the village of Tumbisha near the mouth of Furnace Creek. The women and children retreated to the mesquite thicket to the west while the men kept a distant but careful watch on the intruders. Only a lame old man remained in the village, buried in sand up to his neck, trying to hide. The argonauts were as startled as he when they discovered him, but they treated him kindly, allaying the fears of his watchful companions and saving themselves from reprisals.[10]

After an unsuccessful attempt to cross the salt flats to the west, the Jayhawkers moved up the east side of Death Valley to a point on Salt Creek that is now known as McLean Spring. There they rejoined those who had come over the Funerals. But with the Panamints now clearly barring their path, the Jayhawkers too finally concluded that they could take their wagons and carts no farther. They spent the next three days making pack saddles from the wagon spokes and canvas, slaughtering the weaker cattle, making moccasins for themselves and the surviving oxen from the rawhide, and burning the rest of the wagons to smoke and dry the meat to jerky. Then they divided up their scant remaining provisions, which, with the jerky, were to last them until they reached the settlements. Each man got half a dozen crackers, a few teaspoonfuls of rice, coffee, and dried apples, and a bit of flour and bacon. They also agreed that "thereafter every one must look out for himself and not expect any help from anyone," although their compassion would temper this dictum.[11]

At this melancholy camp, in what they called Salt Valley, Martin's Bugsmashers caught up with the Jayhawkers. Heading west from Timpahute the Bugsmashers had found the country so rough that they were forced to turn south again down Forty Mile Canyon to the Amargosa, where they picked up the trail of the Jayhawkers. They passed a dreary Christmas in Furnace Creek Wash with the Briers, who had also abandoned their wagon by then. "The men killed an ox for our Christmas," Juliet Brier recalled,[12]

> but its flesh was more like poisonous slime than meat. There was not a particle of fat on the bones, but we boiled the hide and hooves for what nutrient they might contain. We also cooked and ate the little blood there was in the carcass. I had one small biscuit, but we had plenty of coffee, and I think it was that which kept us alive.

In the meantime, the Bennetts and the other families had stopped short of Manly's snowclad peak at a hastily abandoned little Indian village, most likely Hugwap at Cane Spring. They stayed for nine days, devouring the winter's store of squash which they found there and fattening their oxen on the stubble in the cornfield. The Paiute would later trail them all the way across the Amargosa, seeking revenge on their oxen, but to no avail. Meanwhile Manly scouted on ahead. Climbing to a snowy pass just east of Mt. Stirling, at the northwest end of the Spring Mountains, he saw smoke from several campfires some 30 miles to the south. These must have been the camps of the last of the straggling wagons of the Hunt train, which had turned back to the Spanish Trail from Mt. Misery and were camped at Stump Spring and Resting Spring at the time. Ironically, Manly didn't realize that after more than a month of wandering he was only two days' travel from the Spanish Trail and that relief was in sight. Instead, he concluded that the smoke was from Indian camps, so he decided that he and the families should also head west. Thus they followed the Jayhawkers and Bugsmashers into Death Valley, but at the mouth of Furnace Creek they turned south again, away from the others and into the very sink of Death Valley, to camp at the springs west of Badwater.

There, on the verge of starvation, the Bennett and Arcan families would remain for over a month.[13]

The Shoshone from Ohyu had watched the Jayhawkers' camp closely. "When it came night," George Hansen, then a boy of ten or twelve, later recalled, "we crawled close, slow like when trailing sheep. We saw many men around a big fire. They killed cows and burned the wagons and made a big council talk in loud voices like squaws when mad. Some fall down sick when they eat the skinny cows. . . . After they go we found many things that they left there." Apparently believing that the wagon burning was a mourning ceremony for dead companions, he adds, "because some died, we did not touch these things"—not for a while, at least.[14]

The Bugsmashers spent only one night in the Jayhawkers' dismal camp on the floor of Death Valley before they moved on west. But there they too began to split up. Jim Martin led the Georgians up a steep canyon in a spur of the Panamints where sparkling snowbanks beckoned. The Mississippians and the Briers, led by Captain Town, drove their weary oxen around the spur and up Emigrant Wash toward the pass that now bears Town's name. As the Jayhawkers finished packing their animals they too set out in splinter groups, following Town toward the pass. At least one bunch of Jayhawkers turned up what is now known as Jayhawker Canyon, on the south side of Emigrant Wash, to camp at an inviting snow patch near its head. It was late at night on New Years' Eve when they finally reached the snow and found Jim Martin's Georgians huddled around a fire, melting snow for the thirsty newcomers.[15]

Near this camp, on the slopes of what they later called Silver Mountain, now Tucki Mountain, Jim Martin and some of the other Georgians had found some fabulously rich silver ore. "One of the boys," Jayhawker John Colton later recalled, "showed me a chunk of black rock he held in his hands, and told me it was half silver, and that nearly all the rock we were walking over was very rich in silver, and if we only had provisions and water and knew where we were, that there was all the wealth in sight that we could ask."[16]

At the time, neither the Georgians nor the Jayhawkers cared much about making a fortune; they were worried only about making it out alive. Indeed, they left more wealth than they took. Instead of digging up a fortune in silver, they buried a small fortune in gold! For here on the rim of Death Valley the Georgians decided to leave their failing pack animals and strike out on foot, taking only what they could carry on their backs. After slaughtering a couple oxen and jerking the meat, they emptied their packs of everything not absolutely essential for survival. One man with $2,500 or more in gold coin offered half to anyone who would carry it out, but got no takers. So they pooled their money; each took what he

FREMONT'S IMAGINARY "DIVIDING RANGE"

MISERY LAKE

MT. MISERY

TIMPAHUTE

MUDDY

WARD'S

VIRGIN RIVER

DIVISION SP.

HUGWAP

OWENS RIVER

N

FORTY MILE CYN.

DEATH

TRAIL

COLORADO RIVER

SIERRA NEVADA

TOWNE PASS

TUMBISHA

SPRING MTNS.

LAS VEGAS

BENNETTS WELL

AMARGOSA RIVER

HAUTA

VALLEY

SPANISH

RESTING SP.

WALKER PASS

SALT SP.

WALKER'S CUTOFF

BITTER SP.

MOJAVE RIVER

TRAILS
OF THE
FORTY-NINERS

—— SPANISH TRAIL
--- WALKER'S CUTOFF

APPROX. ROUTES OF

—— JAYHAWKERS
– – BUGSMASHERS
---- BENNETT - ARCAN
········ WADE
–·– SMITH
–··– PINNEY - SAVAGE
–···– RICH - STOVER

CAJON PASS

RANCHO SAN FRANCISQUITO

LOS ANGELES

WILLIAMS' RANCH

wanted and they buried the rest in a blanket under a greasewood bush. So far as is known no one has ever found the money, although several are known to have tried.[17]

Most of those who later came seeking treasure, however, were not looking for a paltry few thousand dollars in gold; they were hunting for the mountain of silver. Only a few small pieces of the silver ore were packed out of Death Valley by the Georgians just as souvenirs. One particularly rich piece, which Jim Martin took to Mariposa and had made into a gunsight, eventually captured the imagination of miners throughout the West and sent them scurrying into the Death Valley country in search of this "Lost Gunsight Lode." It could never be found—at least not to everyone's satisfaction—but the search would do much to open up Death Valley's mineral wealth.[18]

When they broke camp at the snow patch, the Jayhawkers went on south, down Panamint Valley, where they rejoined the others from their party who had come through Towne Pass. The Georgians pushed on to the west across the upper end of Panamint Valley through Darwin Canyon toward Owens Lake. From there the Paiute directed them south along the foot of the Sierra Nevada to the long sought Walker Pass. The Jayhawkers later heard rumors that all but a couple of the Georgians and the Mississippians who followed them were killed by Chowchilla Indians in San Joaquin Valley. But Jim Martin and at least twenty others struggled into the camp of Agua Fria at the Mariposa mines in late January and early February. The miners, hearing their story, promptly sent out a well-intended but unsuccessful relief party to find the Briers and other stragglers left behind.[19]

Yet one of the Georgians, it would seem, never got out of the Panamints. Many years later, Hungry Bill told how his father, following the trail of the departing argonauts over the mountain to pick up whatever they discarded, found the body of a man. He had a badly broken leg, and a bullet hole in his head! None of the argonauts mentioned this incident.[20]

Most of the Mississippians followed the Georgians west from Panamint Valley through Darwin Canyon, but Captain Town and four other Mississippi boys, the Briers, and the Jayhawkers all turned south down the valley. In a mesquite thicket near the center of the valley they discovered the Shoshone camp of Hauta, temporarily abandoned except for one old woman who scolded them from a doorway. The camp was littered with horse bones, which raised false hopes that the ranches of California were finally close at hand. Inspired anew, Captain Town and the remaining Mississippi boys decided to head west and catch up with their companions. The night before they left, Juliet Brier baked the last of their flour for them and was rewarded with some of the biscuits for her family. The smell of baking was torture to the rest of those in camp, who had eaten nothing but jerky for days. Jayhawker Asa Haynes offered a $5 gold piece for just one biscuit, but was refused. He wept, "I have the best 160 acres in Knox County, Illinois, 100 stock hogs, and 2,000 bushels of old corn in the crib and here I cannot get one biscuit for love or money." At this young John Colton, who had spent most of the evening gathering firewood for Mrs. Brier in the hopes of also getting a handout, went silently and sadly to his blankets.[21]

By the time Town left, most of the Jayhawkers had moved on south toward a pass in the Slate Range to Searles Lake. The Briers trailed along behind with several other stragglers, including Old Man Fish and his teamster William Isham, who had separated from Culverwell in Death Valley when he decided to follow Manly to the south. Isham's fiddle had been the only bright spot in many dreary evenings on the trail. But both men were rapidly failing and on January 13 the climb up to the ridge of the Slate Range proved fatal. Fish reached the summit only by clinging to the tail of an ox. Perhaps it was the hope of seeing ranches with cattle on a thousand hills that had kept him going that far, but atop the ridge, with only a vision of endless wastes of salt and sand ahead, he fell, to rise no more. That evening Isham didn't come into camp and two men went back to look for him the next morning. He had crawled on his hands and knees for 4 miles toward their campfire before they found him "there in the alkali among the boulders—stone dead." For the Jayhawkers, this was Death Valley.[22]

At the briny edge of Searles Lake the Jawhawkers and their followers turned sharply west. They reached the foot of the Sierra near Indian Wells and found the old horse trail that could lead them at long last up into Walker Pass. But fearing that by then it would be choked with snow they continued south instead, over a fainter trail through Red Rock Canyon, across Antelope Valley by Willow Spring to Soledad Pass, and then down Soledad Canyon to salvation at the Rancho San Francisquito. They were "nothing but skeletons" when they reached the ranch on February 4, 1850—three awful months to the day since they had left Hunt and the Spanish Trail. But they were overjoyed just to be alive.[23]

In that purgatory between Death Valley and salvation the Jayhawkers had lost two more men and found a few gold nuggets. William Robinson died in Soledad Pass on January 28 from "drinking too much cold water" at the first spring they found after leaving the desert. Two days later an old Frenchman—some say his name was Coverly—disappeared when the oxen stampeded in Soledad Canyon. The Jayhawkers thought he had gone crazy and wandered away to die, but it is said that he was found fifteen years later, traded as a slave to the Paiute east of Death Valley. It was two young Germans, John Goller and a companion whose name is now lost, who found placer gold somewhere out there—Goller could never remember exactly where. The two usually traveled a little apart from the others, and one day when they had stopped to rest in a dry wash, Goller's partner hollered, "John, come here and see what I have found—gold!" But Goller snapped, "I want water; gold will do me no good," and so they moved on. His partner did, however, pick up a few nuggets, which later sent men searching for the "Lost Goller" all the way from the slopes of the Panamints to Willow Spring in the Mojave.[24]

Although the Jayhawkers were finally out of the desert, the last stragglers still hadn't left Death Valley. When the Bennetts and others trailing behind them reached the mouth of Furnace Creek two days after Christmas, they learned that they would have to abandon their wagons if they were to follow the Jayhawkers out of Death Valley to the west. So they decided to turn south instead, heading down the valley in hopes of finding a wagon pass.

There were at least thirty of them, including three women and eight children, who headed down into the bottom of Death Valley with seven wagons. They were an odd assortment, thrown briefly together by chance and circumstance, with no bond other than convenience. The most cohesive were the Bennett and Arcan families—Asabel Bennett, a thirty-five year-old-Wisconsin trapper and lead miner, his wife Sarah, their two daughters and a son; and John B. Arcan, a French immigrant in his mid-thirties, his wife Abigail, and their infant son. They traveled with Bennett's friend William Lewis Manly and his companion John H. Rogers, both in their late twenties, and with four teamsters they had hired to drive their four wagons. The Wade family—Harry, nearly fifty, and his wife Mary, both English immigrants, with their three sons, a daughter, and a teamster named Charles, who drove their wagon—always camped apart from the rest. Of the two remaining wagons, one belonged to the Earharts—two brothers, Jacob and Henry, and a grown son, John—who had started from Iowa with Stover's party. The other wagon belonged to Anton Schlogel, who was traveling with another Alsatian named Schaub and perhaps two others. In addition there were three packers: two Germans—Louis Nusbaumer, a thirty-year-old jewelry store clerk and avid diarist, and his companion Hadapp—and the ill-fated Richard I. A. Culverwell, an ailing forty-eight-year-old government clerk, who had left his wagon when his oxen died on the Amargosa and whose companions, the equally ill-starred Fish and Isham, and a black, Joe Smith, had left him at Furnace Creek to join the Jayhawkers.[25]

On January 6, after resting for over a week at Travertine Springs near the mouth of Furnace Creek, the Bennetts and Arcans headed south across Death Valley to the base of the Panamints. The others followed the next day. In crossing the flats, Manly led the way, probing the wet salt crust with a mesquite stick in an attempt to find ground strong enough to support the wagons. In spite of his efforts one of the wagons broke through the crust and mired in the mud beneath. The teamsters eventually got the wagon out but it must have been a frustrating task, for all five quit a day or so later and set out on foot to follow the Jayhawkers.[26]

The wagons slowly made their way from one spring to the next along the foot of the Panamints until they reached a small, sulphury water hole south of Bennetts Well. There, seeing what looked like a good pass at the head of a canyon to the west, they suddenly decided to try to take their wagons over it without first waiting to explore it. They struggled for two days working the wagons up the canyon before they saw that they could not get through.[27]

Upon returning to the water hole they debated long into the night over what they should do next. Finally Bennett suggested that their best bet was for two of the younger men to go on ahead to the settlements for help. Manly and Rogers agreed to go and the following day, January 15, taking about ten days' rations of jerky and some $60 in coin with which to buy food to bring back, they started off on foot for the settlements. The rest moved back north several miles to the fresher water at Bennetts Well to await the boys' return.[28]

Not everyone agreed that waiting was a wise policy, however. They argued that since "they had nothing to live on but their oxen, it would be certain death to wait here and eat them up, and that it would be much better to move on a little every day and get nearer and nearer the goal before the food failed." Bennett countered that only by waiting for the boys to return could they be sure to "get out successfully." But the rest had little faith in their return, maintaining that "if those boys ever get out of this cussed hole, they are damned fools if they ever come back to help anybody."[29]

Harry Wade, who had previously been content to follow along behind the rest, now took the lead in searching for a wagon pass farther south. None realized that if, instead of crossing the mountains to the west, they simply followed the valley to the south they would come to the Spanish Trail at Salt Spring. Wade, however, found a pass to the west through Wingate Wash, and about January 22 he and his family set out in their wagon, accompanied only by Schaub, one of the Alsatians, whom Wade hired as a teamster to replace the man who had left. Working their way easily through Wingate Wash, they turned south, possibly following an Indian trail by way of Lone Willow Spring and Granite Wells—a good wagon route that was later used by the first borax wagons from Death Valley to Daggett. In less than a week they reached the Mojave River and the Spanish Trail, near present-day Barstow. Two days later, on January 29, they met some men heading out to Salt Spring to look for the gold Hunt's party had discovered. They gave the Wades a bucket of flour—the first they had had in weeks—and the news that the first ranches were just 60 miles on down the trail. After resting their animals for a few days on the Mojave River, Wade brought his wagon into Rowland's Ranch at Puente on February 10.[30]

By then, all but the Bennetts and Arcans had set out to follow Wade's trail. They had started less than a week after the Wades, but they were so crippled with scurvy that after three painful days they had to turn back. Nusbaumer's feet were so swollen that he had to cut his shoes open to the toes just to get them on, only to find that even then his feet hurt too much to walk far. While they recuperated, a couple of others, probably some of the Earharts, scouted ahead and reported back that Wade's trail did in fact look like a practical route. Thus all but the Bennett and Arcan families started out again on February 7, with what scant provisions as they had loaded onto the Earhart's wagon.[31]

After just one day on the road Culverwell realized he was still too weak to travel and turned back again for Bennett and Arcan's camp at Bennetts Well. He died several miles short of the camp, barely a day before Manly and Rogers returned to rescue the remaining members of the party. They found him, Manly recalled, lying "upon his back with arms extended wide, and his little canteen, made of two powder flasks, lying by his side." Culverwell is the only argonaut known for certain to have died in Death Valley, although there are eleven others who might have—Wiley Webster and his companions, the unknown man with a bullet hole through his forehead, and possibly young John Earhart. Stover later heard that Earhart died there, but no evidence has been found to confirm or deny it.[32]

Following Wade's trail to the Mojave River and the Spanish Trail, the Earharts and their companions finally reached the ranches and safety about February 26. The Wade and Earhart wagons were the only two to make it through out of more than two dozen wagons that had started west from Mount Misery: the scrapped and burned remains of the rest were scattered all the way from Timpahute to Death Valley.[33]

Back in Death Valley, the Bennetts and Arcans were also beginning to think that waiting was a mistake. They had expected Manly and Rogers to return within two weeks, but when two and then three weeks passed with no sign of the boys, they finally decided that they must try to move on, for they would die for sure if they stayed. They had stripped the canvas off their wagons and were making packs and harnesses for the oxen while they gloomily contemplated what would be their fate on the unknown road ahead. Then suddenly they heard a rifle shot and all came alive with joyous shouts, "The boys have come! The boys have come!"[34]

Manly and Rogers had been gone twenty-six days on their heroic rescue mission to the ranches and back. They had come upon the Jayhawkers' trail crossing the Slate Range several days ahead of them. Traveling light and fast they caught up with some of the Jayhawkers at Indian Wells, passed the rest near Red Rock Canyon, and reached the San Francisquito ranch on January 26, nine days before them. There, with the aid of Tejon rancher Darwin French, Manly and Rogers bought three pack horses, a poor little one-eyed mule, and sacks of beans, wheat, good meat, and oranges for their return trip. But trying to make time retracing their route, they rode the animals too hard. One horse dropped dead in the Argus Range and the other two gave out trying to climb the Panamints. Only the desert-wise little mule came through. Finding Culverwell dead on the floor of Death Valley, Manly and Rogers feared that they had returned too late and that the others were also dead. Their fears grew as they neared the camp and saw the wagons stripped of canvas and no sign of life. Manly imagined that Indians had raided the camp and might still be waiting to ambush them. Fearing to approach closer than a hundred yards, they fired a warning shot, and their fears fled as their friends suddenly emerged from under the wagons.[35]

It was a joyous reunion lasting late into the night, as the Bennetts and Arcans ate their first real meal in months. But after the initial elation came the sobering realization that they were still more than 200 miles from the nearest ranches. In a couple days everything they could take with them was packed. Leaving their wagons and most of their belongings behind, they set out once again on the afternoon of February 13.[36]

Rogers led the march with his ox and the mule; Bennett and Manly guided the other pack animals; the women each rode an ox; and Arcan followed leading Old Crump, a slow, steady old ox that carried the children—the older two on his back and the younger ones in bags slung on either side. But they had gone only 4 miles when a pack on one of the oxen slipped over to one side and the animal went wild, bawling and bucking and kicking and thrashing to get free of the thing. The others joined the rampage, all but the little mule, and soon packs and a couple riders were scattered in the sand. It was more comic than tragic, for no one was hurt, but thereafter the women decided to walk. It was late in the afternoon before the packs were all gathered up and the harnesses mended, so they made camp right there and Rogers and Bennett went ahead with a shovel to bury Culverwell. Early the next morning they climbed up Six Spring Canyon, and by nightfall they were nearly out of Death Valley. They camped high in the Panamints at a spring just short of the crest. From the summit the following morning, February 15, Manly, Bennett, and Arcan took a long look back and uttered those parting words, "Good-bye Death Valley!" which have cursed the place ever since.[37]

Their trek to the settlements was a twenty-three day ordeal over rugged, desiccating terrain. But all survived and on March 7, 1850, they struggled into the San Francisquito ranch: four months from Mount Misery, the last of the argonauts emerged from the jaws of hell.[38]

And what became of them all? None, of course, found the fortunes they had dreamed of in the diggings, and most returned home in disillusionment. Even those that stayed left the diggings for the rich farmlands or rising commercial centers. But none ever forgot the awful ordeal that brought them into Death Valley and the Amargosa. The Jayhawkers even held annual reunions to celebrate their deliverance. A few later wrote down their memories of that terrible trek, but none did so as thoroughly or as eloquently as William Manly in his now classic *Death Valley in '49*. Yet even Manly didn't tell it all, or tell it quite straight. Worst of all, he never mentioned that the Wades and Earharts had simply taken their wagons out to the south. Perhaps he feared that that would have spoiled the heroic climax of his rescue of the Bennetts and Arcans.[39]

But long before Manly and the others ever got around to writing of their ordeal, the cursed name they had left on the land and all of the sensational rumors of riches and horrors that had grown out of their ordeal had already transformed that lonely piece of desert into the deadliest, richest, and most mysterious spot in America.

A Hard Lesson

Late in January of 1850, even before the last argonauts had left Death Valley, would-be miners were heading out there to look for gold. They got little precious metal but they did get a hard lesson in the realities of mining economics, laid bare as only desert mining can. It was a hard lesson, indeed, for men to learn that rich mineral alone did not make a paying mine. Equally essential were an abundance of water and wood, or cheap transportation. For once the ore was removed from the ground it still had to be crushed, or perhaps smelted, before it could be refined to metal. This required steam-driven stamps and charcoal-fed furnaces, whose boilers and blasts consumed wood and water at gluttonous rates. If these were not available at hand, the ore had to be taken to where they were. Even placer deposits, already milled by countless eons of erosion, required water for the rockers and sluices that saved the gold from the sand.

That the Death Valley and Amargosa country was essentially waterless and treeless, and clearly remote, was obvious even to the unperceptive. Yet in the excitement of a rich strike, these realities were all too often forgotten, only to be learned again and again, sometimes at enormous cost in capital, energy, and even life.

The first gold found in Death Valley was that picked up just off the Spanish Trail at Salt Spring on December 1, 1849, by the two Mormon missionaries James Brown and Addison Pratt, and by the argonaut Rowan, all of whom were traveling with Hunt. The hardships of the trail didn't permit them to linger long, but when they moved on they did take a few nuggets with them. Three days before Christmas they reached Isaac Williams's ranch at Chino and spread the word of their discovery. The following month Williams led the first expedition back up the trail to investigate. They brought back more rich rock and reported a "whole mountain" just like it! In the meantime, Rowan had gone on to Los Angeles, where his nuggets created more excitement. Benjamin D. "Don Benito" Wilson, Los Angeles's first mayor, organized the Salt Spring or Margose Mining Company and fitted out a second expedition in February to open the mine. But they soon found that "the expense and difficulty of getting there and taking out the gold was more than it would pay for." Thus the argonauts went on to the northern mines, where they still

Benjamin D. "Don Benito" Wilson, the first mayor of Los
Angeles, organized Death Valley's first mining company to work
the gold ledge at Salt Spring in 1850. (*Courtesy of UCSD Library*)

expected to pick up nuggets from the top of the ground, and the missionaries sailed off for the spiritual riches of Tahiti.[1]

Even if the original discoverers had lost interest, one young Angeleno,
John B. Reill, who had gone out in Wilson's expedition, still had faith in
the mine. He felt that they had failed only because their operations were
too primitive, and he was certain that with proper machinery, the mine
could be made to pay a very handsome profit. He realized, of course, that
this would first require a very heavy outlay of capital, and so, gathering
up a number of rich ore samples, he left for San Francisco. There Reill

induced several "gentlemen of wealth and enterprise" to outfit another expedition to the mine. Upon their return to San Francisco in July 1850, thoroughly convinced of its worth, they organized as the Los Angeles Mining Company and dispatched Reill with a crew to take formal possession of the mine. They reached Los Angeles in the latter part of August. But while they were outfitting for the desert trek, another party arrived in town from the northern mines.[2]

One of Williams's original party, a man named Davis, now awakened from the dream of easy riches in the placers, had taken a renewed interest in the gold he had seen in Death Valley. He told the story to a Colonel Lamb at Grass Valley in July, and the Colonel offered to finance an expedition. On reaching Los Angeles, Lamb learned of the impending departure of Reill's crew before they learned of him. So Lamb hastily but quietly refitted his party, which was back on the trail to the mine several days ahead of Reill. Davis had no trouble locating the lode, and Lamb laid claim to the richest ground. When Reill's crew arrived, they were furious at having been beaten to the scene. But Lamb hadn't hogged the whole lode, so the latecomers staked out the rest and bloodshed was averted.[3]

The Salt Spring lode is a 6- to 10-foot-wide quartz belt running north and south across the tip of the ridge. It carries free gold, mostly well-distributed fine gold but with occasional pockets of coarse. The largest of these pockets yielded about $11,000 in rock, paying a few hundred dollars a ton. Most of the surface rock, however, averaged only about $60 a ton and decreased in value with depth. It would be many years before the building of railroads could make this grade of rock even marginally profitable. But this fact had yet to be learned.

Colonel Lamb, who had gained some practical knowledge of the economics of quartz mining at Grass Valley, soon seemed to perceive the difficulties of developing the lode. Within a few months he sold his interest to a group of would-be entrepreneurs in Los Angeles, including former mountain man Andrew W. Sublette. They formally organized as the Desert Mining Company, with Sublette as superintendent of the mine.[4]

Both companies began work in the fall of 1850, and by spring one had sunk a shaft 30 feet. The Desert company had also constructed two arrastras to crush the ore, and the Los Angeles company had one. The arrastra was a primitive, slow, but effective machine with an ancient tradition, long used by the Spanish throughout Latin America. It consisted simply of a large boulder that was dragged by mule, horse, or ox around a circular rock-lined pit into which the ore was placed. By relentless friction it ground the ore. A cleanup was made periodically and the pulverized rock was either panned or amalgamated with quicksilver to extract the gold. Since it could be cheaply constructed of local materials, the arrastra earned the nickname of "poorman's mill." It was commonly used to work small quartz claims throughout California from the 1850s through the 1880s. Decades later, the crumbling remains of these and other arrastras in the desert often prompted the romantic speculations that they had been built centuries before by Spanish padres or even conquistadores to work some ancient lost mine![5]

Working the coarse gold from a few rich pockets, the arrastras proved the worth of the Salt Spring ore. But Reill and the Los Angeles company had grander plans. In January 1851 they shipped a steam-powered quartz crusher from Los Angeles, although it was a long time coming to the mine. The ill-fated machine got only halfway out on the Mojave when the wagon carrying it broke down, leaving it mired in the sand beside the trail for many months. This misadventure turned tragic when the two teamsters, Patrick McSwiggen and a Creek Indian named Sam, were murdered on January 27, apparently by horse raiders, in Cajon Pass en route back to Los Angeles. Old hatreds led to the arrest on murder charges of the two young sons of Jose Maria Lugo, a prominent San Bernardino rancher. A lynch mob laid seige to the Los Angeles jail, but justice was upheld. The charges were shown to be unfounded and the case dismissed.[6]

Supplying the mining camp at Salt Spring with even the barest essentials of food and provisions for man and beast was an immediate and costly obstacle to development. The scant acre or two of salt grass and tule that grew around the spring was insufficient to support the stock, and the ground was too salty to cultivate. It was a hard and desolate 200 miles to Los Angeles and teamsters refused to make the haul for less than $260 a ton. The only essential that the area did provide was drinking water, but even this was not an unqualified blessing. Although the water welled up from the spring in the arroyo bottom at a rate of several hundred barrels a day, it was noxious smelling and brackish, and required some getting used to. Moreover, it was rumored that the water contained arsenic and that several men had died from drinking it. Nonetheless after a few days most of the miners did acquire a taste for the stuff. A few enthusiasts even claimed to prefer it to fresh water, which they said tasted "insipid and flat" by comparison. Analysis has failed to turn up even a trace of arsenic in the water, but has traced its unpleasant taste to its being saturated with Glauber and Epsom salts. Although the water seems to have done no harm to the thirsty miner or mule, it would prove to be the death of steam engines.[7]

Shipping costs were cutting heavily into the assets of both companies, and without a prompt return in bullion, these soon became a weightier burden than most of the stockholders wished to bear. In May 1851 the Desert Mining Company called its first assessment of $2 a share. This was compounded by an additional levee of $1 a share each month thereafter. As the stockholders forfeited some of their shares at auction to cover the assessments on the rest, the value of shares dropped and the company spiraled into bankruptcy. It was dissolved in August 1851. The Los Angeles Mining Company succumbed at about the same time. unable even to get its quartz crusher to the mine.[8]

The lure of gold in Death Valley still tempted others, however. Within a month both properties were bought up by their Los Angeles merchant creditors, led by Don Benito Wilson and his partner Alfred Packard. Wilson, who had been the first to work the mine, had learned once that it would not pay. But now, perhaps tempted by having a monopoly on the property or by that little steam-powered quartz crusher already half-way to the mine, he plunged in again. Wilson reorganized once more as the Salt Spring Mining Company and kept Sublette as superintendent, but he swept out all the skeptics and pikers. Such was the faith of the new investors that they unhesitatingly put up as much as $100 a share on a single assessment. Such too was the measure of the high operating cost.[9]

Teams were promptly put on the trail to rescue the quartz crusher from its resting place on the Mojave and to set it up at Salt Spring. At the same time Sublette headed straight to the mine with a crew to start stockpiling ore for crushing. But when the little crusher finally started up in the spring of 1852, the real trouble began. It took all the mesquite and creosote bush within haul of the mine just to get the little boiler roaring. No sooner was this accomplished than the Glauber and Epsom salts began to cake in the boiler and stuff and clog the pipes and valves, until suddenly the whole miserable machine shuddered to a halt.

Work at the mine was suspended and, while Wilson was pondering what to do next, a few "troublesome" Paiute descended on the camp. They smashed up part of the evil-looking machine, then ran off with some shovels and other loose tools. If Wilson hadn't already decided to quit, this was all he needed to convince him. He officially "stopped their machinery" in July 1852. Ostensibly he was lining up foreign capital to finance a much larger quartz mill, but it never materialized. Sublette was killed a year later in Malibu Canyon by a grizzly bear.[10]

What was left of the boiler and engine was sold to Charles Crisman, a San Bernardino lumberman, that same July. His son George hauled it back from Death Valley to Mill Creek in the San Bernardino Mountains. There, after considerable cleaning out and rebuilding, Crisman used it to power the first sawmill in those mountains. The rest of the equipment was left in Death Valley, but even the Paiute had no further interest in it and it lay undisturbed, to puzzle and entice occasional visitors, one of whom noted wistfully that the "amalgamator, mining instruments, spades, blankets, rough furniture and a small block house with its door open wide, invite in vain a renewal of the enterprise." This old stone and adobe house was the first building in Death Valley and it is still occasionally used today.[11]

In the spring of 1854 the Reese brothers, John and Enoch, opened a shortcut on the Spanish Trail through Kingston Spring, bypassing Salt Spring and the Death Valley–Amargosa leg of the old trail. Thereafter there weren't many travelers on the old route to be enticed by that open door at Salt Spring. Even for those who might have been tempted, the obvious failure of the camp seems to have cooled their ardor, at least for a while.[12]

Then with the excitement that swept the Pacific Coast after the discovery of silver in the Comstock, prospectors swarmed into the desert country east of the Sierra, and the glitter of gold at Salt Spring caught the eyes of some. In the fall of 1861 an inexperienced but eager group of young Angelenos set out for Death Valley to reopen the mine. They spent about a year working it, but found, as had their predecessors, that they couldn't make it pay good wages by crushing ore in the tediously slow arrastras, so they disbanded. But again, one enthusiast in the party, a drugstore clerk named St. Charles Biederman, had faith that the mine would pay if he could only raise enough money to put up a stamp mill.[13]

Like Reill a dozen years before him, Biederman collected a sack of picture rock and set out for the city. In the giddy mining stock frenzy that had seized San Francisco he found a ready market. Biederman sold the idea first to grocer Ebenezer H. Shaw, who in turn convinced several of his friends in the fruit and produce trade, as well as an old friend in the shipping business, Thomas E. Trueworthy, to help him raise the capital. On February 16, 1863, they floated the Amargoza Gold and Silver Mining Company, with a paper capitalization of $1.2 million in shares of $500 each. Although the shares sold at closer to $100, that still represented an investment of almost a quarter of a million dollars: Shaw was president and Biederman was named superintendent.[14]

In a further curious parallel to earlier misadventures, some of Biederman's previous associates had succeeded in raising a more modest amount to reopen the mine. When they returned to Los Angeles en route to the mine, they learned that Biederman's company was already on the ground, so they grubstaked themselves and went off to prospect.

Three months after its inception the Amargoza company shipped a five-stamp mill and a 12-horsepower steam engine from San Francisco, but some of the parts turned out to be missing, so five months dragged by before it was set up at the mine. When everything was finally ready, in October, Shaw came out to Death Valley to watch. For a solid month

Biederman and his crew cursed and coaxed the steam engine through its first run of ore, before it too choked up with salt. Shaw, taking the amalgam back to San Francisco for refining, shouldn't have been too surprised to learn that the yield didn't match the cost. Still, he seems to have given Biederman one more chance. Financed by a string of assessments totaling about $20 a share, the mill was enlarged early the following year, but all in vain. By June 1864, the San Francisco mining bubble had burst, and with it stockholder indulgence. Nearly half the shares of the Amargoza company were delinquent on assessments, and the company folded.[15]

Shaw and his grocer friends returned to the business they knew best. So did a disheartened Biederman, who surrendered his dream, dropped the "St." from his name, and retreated to San Francisco to become a drugstore clerk once again. Only Thomas Trueworthy saw clearly that the way to make money in desert mining was in shipping, and he put a steamboat on the Colorado River under contract to supply mines at Eldorado Canyon.[16]

In the course of fifteen years, the Salt Spring mine had been opened to a depth of only 120 feet. The vein had been cut by several tunnels and shafts that showed a large amount of ore, but all of low grade. The value had dropped from $60 a ton at the surface to only $20 or less at depth—far too poor to pay. Three miners nevertheless were kept on at the mine to hold the property for its creditors, but they came to a tragic end early in October 1864, when a roving band of Chemehuevi raided Salt Spring, setting fire to the mill and killing Cook, one of the men. The other two, Joseph Gordon and a man named Plate, fled "in a fright and committed suicide upon the desert while suffering or famishing with fatigue and want of water." Their bodies, horribly mangled by coyotes, were found by Salt Lake emigrants 20 miles to the south on the jornada del muerto. That winter the salvageable mill machinery was moved to Eldorado Canyon to work ore from the Techatticup mine.[17]

To bring the story full circle, James Brown, one of the original discoverers, finally returned to Salt Spring in the spring of 1867 with a crew of Mormon miners. Returned at last from his Tahitian mission, Brown had chanced to show Brigham Young the little Salt Spring nuggets he had treasured for years, and Young sent him out to have another look. But a quick survey of the now decrepit mine convinced him that the little nuggets had promised much more than they were ready to deliver. There were still others, however, who were to learn that lesson the hard way, and with every new mining boom in Death Valley, at least one of them would come out to reopen the Salt Spring mine again.[18]

Gunsight Silver and the Wonderful Bailey Ore

The little piece of silver-lead ore that Jim Martin brought out of Death Valley in January 1850 and made into a gunsight had an impact on the history of the valley out of all proportion to its value. It became the lodestone for the early exploration of Death Valley. This lost lead of the Panamints exerted a pull on men's minds that the found gold at Salt Spring could never approach. The Salt Spring gold remained a known and measurable quantity, even for those who hoped to make their fortune from it. But the Gunsight silver grew with every telling, until it became the embodiment of elusive, immeasurable wealth. For decades this bit of rock drew men into the Death Valley country. Although they never found the riches they hoped for, some did discover real wealth. The wonderful Bailey ore was something else entirely.

The Death Valley argonauts led the search for the Gunsight silver. Turner, one of the Mississippi boys, was the first, then Jayhawker John L. West, and later Asabel Bennett, Reverend Brier, and others. They were men who had been close enough to the discovery to catch their imaginations afire, but not close enough to know the spot or sensibly measure its worth. So far as is known, neither Jim Martin nor any of the Georgians who actually found the ore ever bothered to return. Perhaps they knew enough about the practicalities of mining to realize that a few pieces of rich float, or even a rich pocket of ore in a remote and arid land, were good for a campfire story but not for a mine.

Turner and the other Mississippi boys had followed Captain Town out of Death Valley through Towne Pass. When they later caught up with the Georgians, Turner saw the ore, heard tales of the Silver Mountain from which it had come, and decided to try to find it. Martin's silver gunsight created quite an excitement in the Mariposa mines, and Turner, confiding that he was the actual discoverer, had little trouble rounding up a party to outfit him and accompany him in his quest. They set out before the snow was off the passes of the Sierra, so they came south to Darwin French's Tejon Ranch before turning northeast toward Death Valley. They suffered so on the long waterless stretches that half the party turned back. Turner and half a dozen determined souls, carrying all the water they could, continued to the edge of Death Valley. But once there, Turner was unable to find even a piece of ore, let alone the silver mountain.[1]

West met with similar disappointment and came close to losing his life. Most likely he was in that little band of Jayhawkers who had camped with the Georgians at the snow patch right after they had found the ore. He was certain that he could find the spot again, and he saw it as his one chance to become "a millionaire in a few days." Soon after he reached Los Angeles he got together a party to go back to Death Valley. But when he got there and couldn't find the silver, some of his companions, furious at having come 250 miles across the desert for naught, threatened to hang him on the spot. Cooler heads prevailed, sparing his life, if not his chagrin.[2]

The failure of these first quests seems only to have added to the lure of the Gunsight silver in the minds of others, making its search an even greater challenge to them. Indeed, the failure of one party seemed certain to spur another to try, until the quest became irrepressible. Thus it was that in the fall of 1850, Judge Ricard and three other Mariposans, who had gone with Turner in the first search, were ready to try again. They were joined by Darwin French, now drawn by the challenge too, and an Indian guide, Ignacio. Learning more about the country from Captain Town, they set out from Tejon Ranch in September with two months' provisions and three 10-gallon water kegs, so that they could explore some distance from the springs. In the Coso Range they found a Paiute who showed them the argonauts' trail, leading them to Darwin Canyon, which French later named for himself. There they made a base camp and, three at a time, searched the hills to the east around Towne Pass. They found oxen tracks and signs of campfires, but not a trace of silver.[3]

No one knows how many other prospectors attempted to find the Gunsight silver in the decade that followed, for few records survive. Half a century later a surveyor in the Panamints found the weathered corner post of a mining claim with the date 1852 carved in it, apparently left by some long-forgotten prospector. And George Hansen, in his youth, earned his name, Boy-who-runs-away, from a start he got coming suddenly upon a Mexican prospector on a trail near Emigrant Spring some time around 1852–53. Legend also has it that in 1857 the Mormons mined and smelted lead at Furnace Creek to make bullets during the Mormon War. But this notion seems to have come from the confusion of a Mormon mine in the Spring Mountains with the little furnace later found at Furnace Creek.[4]

This Mormon mine too was linked to a quest for a Silver Mountain. In mid-May of 1856, Nathaniel V. Jones led a party of Mormon prospectors into the upper Amargosa and possibly even into Death Valley. Brigham Young had sent them from the mission at Las Vegas to search for a mysterious "Silver Mountain" and to investigate some more mundane Indian reports of lead deposits northwest of Las Vegas. This might have been the same silver mountain that the Georgians found, but more likely it was a mountain veined with wire silver, which had been found in November 1849 by some of the Stover party following O. K. Smith just before they reached Division Spring northeast of Las Vegas. Wiley Webster, a Dr. William McCormick, and a few others picked up enticing ore samples there. Webster's ore vanished with him, but McCormick and the rest took bits of the silver to California, and word of the discovery may somehow have reached Brigham Young. In later years this silver was often confused with that of the Gunsight.[5]

Jones's party made a very hasty trip, trekking 400 miles in just seven days through what he described as "one continuous stretch of dry, burnt-up mountains and arid sand plains." They failed to find any silver mountain, but they did discover gold at the north end of Spring Mountain and lead at the south end. At that time lead was far more important to the Mormon economy, which was still struggling for self-sufficiency, so it was the lead deposit at Potosi Spring, just south of the Spanish Trail, that Brigham Young wanted to develop. By January 1857 Jones had opened the mine, built a small smelting furnace, and produced over 9,000 pounds of lead. That apparently supplied the Mormon demand, at least for a time, and operations were suspended. This lead, found to contain paying amounts of silver, gave rise to tales of the Mormons using silver bullets.[6]

It was the discovery of the Comstock silver lode in the fall of 1859 that gave renewed impetus to the quest for the Gunsight silver. Asabel Bennett led the new wave of prospectors into Death Valley. He had seen hard times since he had come to California. Working in the mines with Manly and another Hunt party friend, William M. Stockton, Bennett had accumulated a small pile and bought a little farm at the mouth of the Salinas River, where he eked out a living until his wife died. Then, giving his youngest child to friends, he moved to southern Utah, married a Mormon girl, and ran a dry goods store for a year or two until that too failed. After a brief fling in the Fraser River rush to British Columbia, he was back in southern California—by then in his mid-forties and flat broke—staying with his old friend Stockton, who had taken up a ranch in San Gabriel. Suddenly news of the great silver discoveries on the Comstock, east of the Sierra, brought to mind the stories Bennett had heard of the Gunsight silver, and with them a new chance for wealth.[7]

Early in April 1860 Bennett and Stockton, with several friends—Charles Alvord, John Shipe, and some Mormons—headed for Death Valley to seek the elusive Gunsight. Bennett had no real idea where to look, only that it was somewhere in the Panamints. So they made camp at the south end of the range, apparently at Anvil Spring, and began to prospect. Close to camp Alvord and Stockton found two brilliant metallic veins which looked like "pure silver." To test the richness of the rock Bennett built a small air blast furnace, like he had once used to heat his pick for sharpening when he was a lead miner in Wisconsin. The furnace was little more than a rock chimney about a foot high, open at the base, with wings to draw in the air. In a good steady wind it could burn charcoal hot enough to smelt lead, but not silver. To everyone's delight the ore samples survived the fiery blast of the furnace, although Bennett was not sure he had gotten a strong enough draft. Just to make certain, they moved down into Death Valley to the mouth of what would soon become known as Furnace Creek. There, on a windy point facing the valley, Bennett built a second little furnace. The ore still refused to melt, and Bennett was now certain that it was in fact pure silver. Jubilantly they headed home, confident that they had at last found the Gunsight lode and that it would prove to be the richest mine in the world. But their joy faded when assays revealed that they had only found some very refractory lead ore. At that point they began to take an interest in some gold nuggets that Alvord had picked up, but that's another story.[8]

In the meantime, the Comstock silver discovery had also started others thinking about the Gunsight silver. Darwin French had left his ranch at Tejon, but he hadn't forgotten his quest for silver in Death Valley, and the thought of it now drew him back again. French reached the Coso Range in mid-April of 1860, leading about a dozen eager prospectors from Oroville and Sacramento. They found traces of silver in the Cosos, and most of the party stopped right there to look for more. But French and three others—James Hitchens, John H. Lillard, and William McIntyre— continued eastward to seek the Gunsight in Death Valley. They came close to the trail of the elusive silver, stopping at Jayhawker Spring, just below the long-vanished snow patch where the Georgians had camped after they found the ore. Hitchens scratched his name and the year—still visible today—on a lava boulder nearby. But instead of climbing up the waiting slopes of the Georgians' silver mountain, they headed on down into Death Valley. There they found the Jayhawkers' burned wagons and scattered belongings, abandoned a decade before. Then at the mouth of the canyon near Travertine Springs they discovered the little furnace that Bennett had built only weeks before and for which French named the canyon Furnace Creek. They also named the Panamint Range and Towne Pass, but they didn't find the silver mountain they sought.[9]

On returning to their camp in the Coso Range, however, French and his companions found that the others had struck some very rich silver leads right there, so they christened that camp Silver Mountain! On May 28 they chose the name Coso—"fire" in Paiute—for the mining district as a whole. Coso ore, assayed in Visalia, ran over a thousand dollars a ton, and a rush to the new district began. By the fall of 1860 there were hundreds of prospectors in the surrounding hills. That same summer a prospecting party from the Comstock, working its way south toward the Colorado River, had discovered the abandoned Mormon lead mine in the Spring Mountains to the east of Death Valley. Some of the lead ore assayed as high as $750 a ton in silver. The Potosi Mining District sprang into existence, and a stage line was started from Visalia over the old Walker cutoff. These new silver strikes further spurred the Gunsight quest, and more prospectors converged on Death Valley. By early 1861 miners in the Panamints had organized the Telescope Mining District bordering the valley on the west, while others in the Amargosa Range on the east formed the Washington district. At the south end of the valley, St. Charles Biederman and his friends reopened the Salt Spring mine. But for all of the excitement, few of the Gunsight seekers would even find metal; some would stake claim to a talc deposit, thinking it was silver; and seven would lose their lives in the desiccating valley that summer.[10]

It was a party of Gunsight seekers from Visalia, led by Dr. Samuel G. George, who opened the first mine in the Panamints. Tracing the route of the argonauts out of Death Valley, they camped at Wildrose Spring in December 1860. Three miles to the southeast, on Christmas day, Dr. George and William T. Henderson discovered a massive, silvery looking lode over 25 feet thick, which they christened the Christmas Gift. Back in Visalia, assays showed the rock to be mainly antimony sulphide, but there was just enough silver in it that George and his partners returned to the Panamints in April 1861. They collected a quarter of a ton of ore, staked some more claims around the Christmas Gift, climbed and named Telescope Peak, and formally organized the Telescope Mining District. This time they sent the ore to San Francisco for assay, but again it proved to be mostly antimony. Still, there was an enticing fraction of silver, and Dr. George was convinced that the antimony would give way to silver at depth. So the Combination Gold and Silver Mining Company—with no mention of antimony—was formed on July 24 with a paper capital of $990,000 to open the Christmas Gift and adjacent claims. Henderson, as superintendent, put a crew of six to work sinking a shaft about 50 feet to test Dr. George's idea that the ore should get richer with depth. When the shaft failed to find paying silver, they started a tunnel to tap the lode at even greater depth. The tunnel was in 155 feet by April 1863, when the Panamint Indians attacked the camp, killing the four miners then at work there and burning the company's cabin. Henderson and others, who had gone to Visalia for provisions before the attack, were driven away by the Indians when they tried to return. But Henderson, said to have been the man who killed Joaquin Murieta, swore vengeance. A short time later

The Combination was the first mine opened in the Panamints, but it was rich in antimony, not gold or silver, so it took half a century and a world war before it could be made to pay. (*Courtesy of Wells Fargo Archives*) he led an attack on a party of Panamint Shoshone, killing nine, including their *pakwinavi,* dubbed Thieving Charley by the miners. The Christmas Gift, however, would not be reopened for over a decade.[11]

The Panamint and other Indians throughout the desert country had been tolerant of the first prospectors, although they sometimes found their actions curious. As one Panamint Indian noted, "mostly they come in pairs without their women; this we thought was strange for it is not a custom of our people to go that way." But when the miners began to take over the springs and cut down the pinyon, it was clearly time to put an end to their intrusion. Starting with the Coso rush, the Paiute and Shoshone throughout the Death Valley and Amargosa country made sporadic attacks to drive the whites out. Such efforts continued into the late 1860s, until their futility became obvious to all. Indian hostility only briefly slowed the tide of miners sweeping into the country, for the lure of the Gunsight and other storied wealth drew men there with an irresistible pull.[12]

For those who tried to work its minerals, the remoteness of Death Valley was a much greater problem than were occasional Indian raids. But to those who chose to work the stockholder instead, Death Valley's remoteness was a vital ingredient for success. The first to make this discovery was Lieutenant Robert Bailey of Oroville. Bailey first came to the Death Valley country in the spring of 1860 with Darwin French, chasing the elusive Gunsight. He held a share in a number of good leads in the Cosos, but it was in the Amargosa Range on the eastern edge of Death Valley that he claimed to have made his big discovery.[13]

In January 1861, Bailey appeared in San Francisco. News from Coso was creating a lot of excitement, what with reports of rock assaying over a thousand dollars a ton. But these paled to insignificance when Bailey produced a strange new rock, heralded as "the richest that has ever been found," yielding a prodigious $16,342 to the ton! Reporters and would-be investors flocked around him, wanting to know more about the wonderful ore and the lode from which it came. Bailey assured them that his lode was "inexhaustible" and that the country around it abounded in rock just like it. But he preferred to keep the location of his find a secret, saying only that it was in the Washington Mining District—an area twice the size of Rhode Island that stretched more than 70 miles along the Amargosa Range from Daylight to Saratoga springs. Bailey's evasiveness further piqued the interest of his would-be partners, who were willing to buy a mine they had never seen nor even knew the location of, if Bailey would only go and get a little more rock to show them. Bailey readily agreed and left early in February for his wonderful lode. No less than seven "exploring companies" organized in San Francisco just to follow him, but he gave them all the slip.[14]

By the time Bailey returned in April with three or four bags of rock and a newly acquired partner, Dr. Benjamin Franklin Dewey of Stockton, his investors were more anxious than before. Even though his new rock assayed only $4,200 a ton, real estate broker O. B. Bagley and a few others eagerly paid him $12,000 "cash on the nail" just for a half interest in what Bailey said was the "first southeast extension" of his claim. They promptly organized the Bailey Silver Mining Company with a paper capital of $180,000 divided into 900 shares at a par of $200. Bailey apparently got close to half of the shares for his remaining interest in the claim and proceeded to sell them off quickly at bargain prices of $50 or more a share. When he had sold them all and buyers still called for more, he and Dewey suddenly remembered that they also owned a second extension. With a flair for timeliness they christened this newly recalled bonanza the Comet, after Thatcher's comet, which had just begun nightly displays in the skies of San Francisco. Taking in a few more heavy investors, Bailey and Dewey floated the Comet Silver Mining Company, offering an additional 1,600 shares at only $500 apiece to those who still wanted to be let in on this wonderful lode.[15]

Meanwhile, Bailey's original investors were becoming anxious to see returns on their money, so they put up an assessment of $2 per share to outfit a crew to go to the mine and bring back a ton of the wonderful ore. Bailey, who was of course the company's superintendent, took charge of these arrangements and of the money. He signed up several workmen and ordered a stock of picks, shovels, and groceries. The crew was to travel by way of Los Angeles on the steamer *Senator* on July 18. Bagley and other investors, who wanted to see the fabulous Bailey Lead for themselves, also booked passage on the *Senator,* and Bailey thoughtfully gave each of them a sturdy new canvas sack to fill with the wonderful ore.[16]

When the date of sailing came, Bailey was nowhere to be found. One rumor had it that he had several matters to attend to in Los Angeles and had gone ahead to meet the party there. Thus Bagley and the others confidently steamed off for Los Angeles, although the workmen Bailey had hired were left standing on the dock because he had somehow never gotten around to paying for their passage. When the company reached Los Angeles they seem to have been genuinely surprised that no one there had ever heard of, let alone seen, Bob Bailey. For two weeks the cry of "Where's Bailey?" rang through the dusty pueblo, and posters and placards everywhere asked his whereabouts, while the saddened members of his company sweltered in a 105° heat wave. Most of the investors finally conceded that they'd been "sold" and returned to San Francisco. But a few diehards hung on for a full two months, doggedly singing their rallying song, one verse of which went:

> Oh, Bailey's the man to put us through,
>   Du da, du da;
> We'll stick to him and Dewey, too,
>   Du da, du da day.
> Let Frisco men say what they will,
>   Du da, du da,
> We believe all's right with Bailey still,
>   Du da, du da day.

In November the Bailey Silver Mining Company finally disbanded with the auctioning of its equipment, provisions, and canvas sacks at Los Angeles.[17]

Back in San Francisco, Bailey's wonderful ore had attracted attention not only from prospective investors, who ogled at its richness, but from geologists and mining men who were interested in learning the processes of its origin. Some had noticed earlier that instead of the usual matrix rock associated with silver ores, several of Bailey's specimens had loose dirt and sand fused to them! But Bailey had casually explained that a volcano had opened directly on the line of the lode and that "the fire had smelted the ore," causing it to flow out over the countryside. This explanation satisfied the faithful, but not the former geologist for the Pacific Railroad Survey, William P. Blake, who managed to get hold of some of the "unsmelted" rock shortly after Bailey's departure. Blake made a thorough analysis and reported his findings to the California Academy of Natural Science early in August. Not only did he show that the ore was unlike any known mineral but he found a chunk of charcoal in the middle of a piece of the "so called ore"—clear evidence that the stuff was artificially and rather sloppily concocted in a backyard furnace![18]

With this news the Bailey bubble was undeniably burst, but the mystery of his whereabouts lingered on. It was rumored that on the day before the *Senator* left for Los Angeles, Bailey and Dewey had left on the steamer *Salinas* for Watsonville, where they purchased two horses. Then in mid-September, a startling discovery was made. Travelers crossing the sandy marshes between Tulare and Buena Vista lakes in the south end of the San Joaquin valley came upon a deserted camp spattered with blood. Following the trail of gore into the tules they discovered the grisly body of a man, tied by the heels, his head and face mutilated with buckshot, and burned beyond recognition. They promptly buried the body, but bits of the clothes and a knife found on the body were taken to Visalia, where some identified them as belonging to none other than Robert Bailey.[19]

Thus the mystery remained. Had Bailey and Dewey quarreled, and one of them murdered the other, or had they murdered and mutilated some innocent traveler and dressed him in Bailey's clothes? The only certainty was that at least one of them had gotten away with at least $25,000—and some said as much as $100,000.[20]

Thirty years later, an aging bartender in San Diego occasionally entertained his patrons by recounting a few adventures of his younger days. He would start with the hardships of his trek across the plains in 1849 and then tell of his luck, good and bad, in the placers at Bidwell's Bar and Shasta; of his fights with the Indians in the Pit River war, where he earned the rank of Lieutenant in the volunteers; and of his quest with Darwin French for the famous Lost Gunsight. Here he would lapse into cataloging the perils of crossing Death Valley and would mention only in passing that they failed to find the elusive silver lode and that in the summer of 1861, he sailed away to Tahiti on the aptly named brig *Sûreté*. In old age Bob Bailey had become a master of understatement. He might also add that when he returned a year later, he mined for a time in Idaho and Montana, and hired out as an Indian scout in Wyoming and the Dakotas, before he finally settled down in 1869 to tend bar in San Diego. Bailey was a changed man by the 1890s—a man who had held one job for over twenty years and who spoke with pride of having been appointed a deputy sheriff for eight months. Indeed, those who once sought him would probably have never recognized him, and thus he remained a successful fugitive from justice to the day he died.[21]

So whose mutilated body had been found in the tules? That is another story.

Alvord and Breyfogle

As if the lost Gunsight and Goller were not enough to lure men into Death Valley, the quest for these elusive leads led to even more elusive and alluring gold, which soon outshone them in the minds of most. For in the crowd of lost-ledge seekers that came into the valley in the early 1860s were two men, Charles Alvord and Charles Breyfogle, who each emerged with a handful of gold-specked rocks and a faulty memory of whence they came. Alvord's gold became the catalyst in the naming of Death Valley. Breyfogle's became an obsession—the best known, most sought-after "lost mine" in the West, as "breyfogling" became synonymous with the quest for lost mines everywhere.[1]

Charles Alvord came to Death Valley first. He was an energetic and entertaining, bald, medium-weight, sixty-year-old New Yorker. He was college educated, with an avid interest in horticulture and a book knowledge of geology, but no practical experience in mining—hardly the popular image of the grizzled western prospector. He came to Death Valley to seek the Gunsight silver with Asabel Bennett's party early in April 1860. He and William Stockton found what they thought were the silver lodes they sought right near their camp at Anvil Spring, up in the south end of the Panamint Range. While the others in the party explored the lodes and Bennett tested the ore in his first little furnace, Alvord went looking for Goller's gold. He was gone so long that his companions began to fear that he had been killed by Indians. But after a couple of weeks Alvord came trudging back into camp, his saddlebags filled with rich-looking rock. None of this rock seemed half as rich as that from the wonderful silver lodes near their camp, however, so it was quickly forgotten.[2]

But Alvord had held back from his partners a few choice rocks, which Manly later described as "dark as stone-coal and speckled with gold." On his return to Los Angeles, Alvord secretly sent one of these specimens to San Francisco for assay with his friend Isaac Hartman, a lawyer. The assay showed the rock to be fabulously rich, and Alvord finally confided the news to Bennett and Stockton. They made plans to secretly return to locate this new bonanza, but their former partners learned of Alvord's ore and demanded their share. Some of Bennett's other Mormon friends also cut themselves in for a share, apparently in exchange for provisions, horses, a wagon, and equipment, including a small blacksmith's outfit and anvil. In addition Stockton wrote to William Lewis Manly, with whom he and Bennett had worked in the mines, asking him to join the party, but Manly didn't arrive in time.[3]

By the time they set out from San Bernardino in late August 1860, there was considerable friction, for Alvord was not at all happy with the prospect of sharing his potential fortune with so large a crowd. Returning to Anvil Spring, the men waited anxiously while Alvord began searching for the source of his fabulous ore. While they waited, prospectors from the Coso mines occasionally drifted into their camp—dubbed Mormon Camp by the Coso miners—and Bennett delighted in playing the old pioneer, telling any visitor who would listen all about his perilous journey across the desert in '49, and about his long camp at what they thereafter called Bennetts Well in the great, as yet unnamed, valley to the east.[4]

Alvord searched the Panamints for weeks, but for one reason or another he failed to find the spot. Some of his Mormon companions began to suspect that he was holding out on them again, and a few even threatened to hang him if he didn't show them where he'd found the gold. But after two months they finally gave up and left Alvord in disgust, wishing he would starve to death as he deserved. With so many other prospectors around, however, there was little real chance of that. In their disgust the Mormons threw the little anvil into the spring rather than haul it back to San Bernardino. Anvil Spring got its name seven years later, when Lieutenant Charles Bendire's party found the anvil there.[5]

Bennett and Stockton left with the others, after secretly assuring Alvord that they would return to continue the search. When they reached Stockton's ranch at San Gabriel, they found Manly waiting and eager to join them. To provision the return trip they cut in Caesar Twitchell, a local merchant, and late in November 1860, Bennett, Manly, and Twitchell headed back to Death Valley and Alvord. In later years Manly remembered the trip as a noble reenactment of his and Rogers's heroic rescue of the Bennetts and Arcans. At the time, however, the thought of gold seems to have been foremost in his mind—and not just Alvord's gold, for despite what he subsequently described as the urgency of getting back to Alvord, Manly took time to go to Los Angeles and talk to John Goller in hopes of learning where he had picked up his nuggets. But Goller had already hunted for that spot twice with no luck, so Manly got no clues from him. That didn't prevent Manly from looking, of course, and he and his companions took the long way back to Death Valley, retracing their route of 1850, so that they could prospect for Goller's gold all the way from Antelope Valley to the Argus Range.[6]

Finally reaching the Panamints, they made camp the first night in the canyon where Manly and Rogers had abandoned their horses on their return to Death Valley early in 1850. After they had settled down for the evening they were startled by the sound of footsteps, and out of the twilight came Charles Alvord. He had seen their tracks and found them. Manly, certain that Alvord would have perished had they not arrived just in the nick of time, later prided himself in having thwarted "the Mormon ghouls who had left him to starve in the desert."[7]

They made a base camp down in Panamint Valley while Alvord continued his search. By then it was late December and winter snows heavily blanketed the Panamints. Now, try as he might, Alvord could not find the source of his wonderful nuggets. He could only vaguely point out where he thought it was, near the snowy crest of the range.[8]

Questionable as this effort was as a rescue mission—and unsuccessful as it was as a prospecting venture—it was nonetheless pivotal in Death Valley history, for it gave the valley its name. Reminiscing by the campfire, Manly and Bennett must have recalled their half-forgotten naming of Death Valley over a decade before. And when they met others in the Panamints and later in the Argus and Coso ranges, they proudly recounted their earlier exploits and passed on the awesome name as well. It spread like a plague. Twitchell, returning home to San Gabriel, gave the name to a *Los Angeles Star* reporter, who first put it in print. At the same time the California boundary surveyors picked the name up from the Coso miners and within weeks carried it to San Francisco. Before the end of the year Coso mining promoter Minard Farley had the name on his map, and it has been Death Valley ever since.[9]

Even though their grub was running low and it was obvious that they couldn't get back into the Panamints before spring, Alvord and Manly wanted to prospect some more in the Argus Range. Bennett and Twitchell agreed to return to Los Angeles for more provisions. Just as they reached the San Gabriels a blizzard struck, and they barely got over the mountains alive. By the time the storm ended they decided it would be foolhardy to go back, for the storm would surely have driven Manly and Alvord out of the Death Valley country as well. Their partners had indeed left, but only after waiting until the end of January, when their provisions were exhausted. Fortunately, they were picked up by Dr. George's party and taken to Visalia. Manly was a long time in forgiving Bennett for leaving him "to perish"—a curious gratitude for Manly's rescue of Bennett and his family.[10]

Manly and Alvord headed back to Death Valley as soon as spring came, but they dallied at Coso, prospecting there so long that the summer heat drove them out before they ever got to the Panamints to look for Alvord's gold. Perhaps they kept waiting around, hoping to get away without being followed, and simply waited too long. Whatever the reason, they made plans to return again that fall. But during that summer of 1861, Alvord went over to the west side of San Joaquin Valley to prospect for coal with a man named Jackson and was never seen alive again. Dr. George became suspicious when Alvord's shotgun and mule were discovered in the possession of a man who said he bought them from Jackson. George led a party to their abandoned camp and found the unrecognizable body of a man nearby—the top of his head blown off by a shotgun and his face mutilated. They buried the body, but took a pocket knife and some scraps of clothing back to Visalia. At first they were thought to have belonged to Bob Bailey, who had recently disappeared from San Francisco, but George finally determined that it was Alvord's knife. He concluded that Jackson must have killed Alvord because he wouldn't show him the source of his gold.[11]

Although Alvord would never return to Death Valley in quest of his elusive gold, others soon did. The Searles brothers, Dennis and John, got hold of at least one piece of Alvord's rich float and searched for its source in the Slate Range in the fall of 1861, until they found some leads they liked better. A short time later John Shipe, who had been with Alvord and Bennett on their first trip into the Panamints, found what may have been Alvord's lost gold. He caused quite a stir in Visalia when he began showing up with gold from a secret mine. Several parties tried to follow him, but he always succeeded in losing them. Most thought his mine was somewhere on King's River, but before they could find out for sure, Shipe was killed while resisting arrest during a drunken hoot in Visalia. His squaw later went to live with a rancher named Prewett, and she eventually took him to Shipe's mine somewhere out in the Coso country or beyond. At least that's what Prewett told David and Luther Burton when he sold them the property in 1891.[12]

Then there was Joseph Clews, a Mormon from San Bernardino, who claimed to have been one of those with Alvord when he went back to the Panamints in the late summer of 1860, and to have won Alvord's everlasting gratitude for having persuaded the others not to hang him. Clews said Alvord had promised him a share in the ledge but never told him where it was. He made a number of trips searching for the gold after Alvord's death, but with no result. In his old age Clews is said to have finally come to the enigmatic conclusion that Alvord found his gold in some low hills just north of the Mojave River and more than 50 miles south of their camp in the Panamints. This notion may have grown out of the discovery of gold in those hills in 1881 by J. D. Potter, a misinformed or perhaps just overly optimistic prospector who claimed it was Alvord's lost gold and named the mine for him. This Alvord mine actually produced about $150,000 in gold and as a result, those low hills that Charles Alvord probably never saw still carry his name.[13]

If anyone ever did find the source of Alvord's gold, it was most likely

E. H. Edwards and Henry Dunlap, who were prospecting around Anvil Spring in February 1876, during the Panamint boom. In a little gulch northwest of Striped Butte, they discovered some rich float and traced it up to a little 2- to 3-inch-wide vein that pinched out at a depth of 12 feet. That may have been all there ever was to Alvord's gold.[14]

Breyfogle's gold was more enigmatic than Alvord's, and perhaps just for that reason, it had a far greater hold on men's minds. Charles C. Breyfogle was a stout, balding New Yorker in his mid-fifties. He was hardly a veteran prospector but he seems to have picked up some of the tricks of the trade quite quickly. Unlike the amiable Alvord, Breyfogle was gloomy, irritable, and taciturn, at least by the time he came to Death Valley. He hardly spoke except when spoken to, and then only with a gruff reply.[15]

Breyfogle had come to California in the summer of 1849 over the Humboldt route, along with his brother Joshua. After a brief stint in the Yuba mines and a fling at farming in San Jose, he turned to politics. He was elected Alameda county assessor in 1854, and two years later he became county treasurer. But his career was cut short when auditors discovered a shortage of $8,107.37 in August 1859. Leaving his bondsmen to pay the deficit, Breyfogle and his wife joined the rush to the Comstock that winter of 1859–60 to try to make a new start. From there he drifted to the Reese River country of central Nevada, and in 1863 was running a hotel in the promising new camp of Geneva in the Great Smoky Valley, a dozen miles south of Austin. But by the end of that year Geneva's boom was past, and Breyfogle was again looking for new prospects.[16]

Several years before, Breyfogle had met one of the original Death Valley argonauts, who had told him of a vast ledge of gold-bearing quartz that they had discovered near Death Valley. The argonaut may have been referring to the Salt Spring gold, or possibly to Goller's. Whatever its source, Breyfogle got a piece of gold-specked quartz and a vague description of the spot where it was found.[17]

In late January 1864 Breyfogle and four companions headed south for Death Valley to try to find that gold again. When they reached the Amargosa Desert they split up to prospect the surrounding hills. On one of these excursions Breyfogle was gone for a number of days. When he finally returned to camp, exhausted and half-starved, he told of finding a place that fit the old argonaut's description, and a rich-looking quartz lode that he thought must be the "lost ledge." Breyfogle had gathered up a few pieces of ore and, hurrying back to join his companions, had somehow lost his way. His partners were eager to see the bonanza for themselves. But as luck would have it in such stories, they were out of grub and the

Indians had run off most of their animals, so they were hard pressed just to get out alive. Unable to make it back to Austin, they continued south to the Spanish Trail and Los Angeles.[18]

When Breyfogle finally got back to Austin by way of San Francisco in mid-March, the *Reese River Reveille* editor was eager to hear all about his adventures and promised readers a full account. But when Breyfogle told his tale and the editor saw assays of the ore—said to have run $4,500 a ton in gold—he decided to keep the story to himself and help grubstake a party to go back with Breyfogle to claim the lode. Not until several years later did the editor finally tell the story. By that time he had squandered $700 on Breyfogle's prospecting ventures, with nothing to show for it but a little piece of ore Breyfogle said he had found.[19]

Summer heat delayed the departure of the first party until the fall. Then before Breyfogle and his companions had gone far, they had to turn back because of Indian troubles, of which the Salt Spring mine attack was a part. It was not until mid-March of 1865 that Breyfogle's second party finally reached Death Valley, but this venture was equally abortive and came to a tragic end. South of Austin, four Gunsight seekers, led by Joseph Todd, had fallen in with Breyfogle's party, and they all camped at Furnace Creek. Breyfogle had started prospecting in the Funerals to the northeast when he suddenly got into a quarrel with one of the interlopers and swore he wouldn't reveal the location of the lode as long as the "obnoxious member" was there. In a curious parallel to Alvord's misadventure, Breyfogle's partners at last decided to return to Austin, leaving him to prospect on his own. They left him with two months' provisions early in April at Summit Spring—about 10 miles north of Daylight Spring—on the east side of the Funeral range.[20]

In May 1865 Breyfogle was found nearly dead at Las Vegas Springs by F. R. Granger's wagon train from Los Angeles. His head was badly lacerated and Granger reported that he had been half scalped and left for dead by the Paiute. Granger brought Breyfogle to Salt Lake City, where he stayed with Pony Duncan until he regained his strength. Breyfogle could recall only that he had been attacked by Indians, but many years later the Ash Meadows Paiute told more of the story. From Summit Spring, Breyfogle eventually wandered south along the Amargosa, and there a young Paiute became fascinated by his shoes. They were much bigger than any he had ever seen, and he vowed to have them. He and a few companions followed Breyfogle for days, all the way to Stump Spring on the old Spanish Trail. Ash Meadows Charlie—who later admitted to being one of the party, if not its principal—told how, when Breyfogle was leaning over cooking his dinner, they clubbed him on the head and stole his marvelous shoes and all of his g.ub.[21]

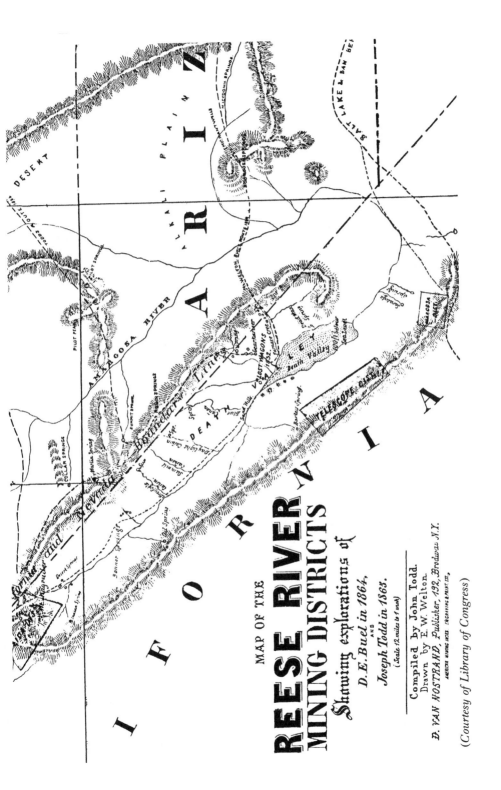

MAP OF THE

REESE RIVER MINING DISTRICTS

Showing explorations of

D. E. Buel in 1864,
AND
Joseph Todd in 1865.

(Scale 12 miles to 1 inch)

Compiled by John Todd.
Drawn by E. W. Welton.
D. VAN NOSTRAND, Publisher. 192, Broadway N.Y.
AMERICAN MINING DISTS. ENGRAVING & PRINT STS.,

(Courtesy of Library of Congress)

The gash from this blow on his already balding, sunburned, and blistered head made it look as if Breyfogle had been scalped. But the Paiute denied scalping him; indeed, a couple of them apparently felt sorry enough for him that they carried him to the springs at Las Vegas. Granger, however, also reported that Breyfogle had been shot twice, and the Paiute are silent on that point.[22]

While Breyfogle was still lying in Salt Lake City, recovering from his ordeal, his Austin grubstakers decided to continue the search in Death Valley without him. In September 1865 they sent William Gearhart and A. A. Simmonds, who had been with Breyfogle that spring, and two other men, William McBroom and C. C. Sears. These men came to a truly tragic end.

Camped at what they called Gearhart's Spring, just north of Furnace Creek, they had been prospecting for about a week when a few Indians and their squaws came into camp and told them to "vamos." But as they were packing to move, three friendlier Indians came, offering to show McBroom "oro stone" in exchange for a pair of red blankets he had. Thinking they might at last find Breyfogle's lost ledge, McBroom and Sears eagerly followed the Indians while their partners waited in camp. They were supposed to return in two days, but they never did. After four days Gearhart and Simmonds began to fear for their own safety and packed up to leave the next morning. Just before dawn they heard the bark of a coyote and an answering howl. As the sun came up they were attacked by a hail of arrows and scattered gunshots. Both men were wounded, but they held off their attackers long enough to saddle their horses and make their escape. Tom Wilson, Panamint Tom's son-in-law, later told how some renegade Paiute from the south fork of the Kern River had come to Furnace Creek while four white men were there asking for gold rock. These Paiute lured two of the men over to Breyfogle Buttes, killed them for their guns, and came back to kill the other two, who got away. The Panamint Shoshone drove the intruding Paiute out and buried the two white men. When Gearhart and Simmonds reached Austin, a punitive force was organized to chastise the Indians. Former Texas Ranger George Wilson led ten armed men to Death Valley early in November, but they found no one to shoot at, nor any trace of McBroom and Sears. The Kern River Paiute had gone, and the Shoshone had taken refuge in the mountains.[23]

By this time the *Reveille* editor had decided that Breyfogle's whole story was either "an absolute hoax or at least a gross exaggeration." The editor was convinced that Breyfogle's ore had come not from Death Valley but from the Gold Hill mine on the Comstock. Breyfogle might well have gotten the ore samples when he first went to the Comstock in the winter of 1859–60. He could also have obtained them up on his way back to Austin after his first trip to Death Valley, perhaps after learning that the rich-looking rock he had picked up in the valley wasn't that rich after all. It is easy to imagine how he might have thought that he had simply grabbed some poor samples, because he knew the gold was there—after all, the Death Valley argonauts had seen it too! So what was the harm in passing off a few rich substitutes, just to show people what the ore was really like, so they would help him go back to find and claim the real "lost ledge"?[24]

Then again, it is possible that Breyfogle came by the ore samples in quite a different way. In 1878, an Arizona rancher recalled how in the early years of the Civil War he and several other Southerners on the Comstock decided to return home secretly to join the Confederate forces. On the pretense of prospecting they went east to Austin, then headed south for the Colorado River, where they planned to turn east to Texas. But at a camp south of Austin a man started following them. They feared that he might be a Union spy who had discovered their plan, so after several days one of the Southerners waited behind on the trail and confronted the man, demanding to know what he was after. The man confessed that he was following them because he thought they would lead him to some secret new strike. The Southerner thought for a moment, then pulled out a rich piece of rock he had picked up in California and gave it to the man, confiding that it had come from a very large, rich mine that they were heading for. He pointed out where it lay in the saddle of a range far to the south. But he warned the man not to try to follow them just then, because his partners didn't want outsiders there yet, and it would be dangerous for him if he followed. The man, heeding the warning, turned back toward Austin. Years later, when he heard of Breyfogle's quest, the rancher was certain that Breyfogle had been that man.[25]

Whatever the origin of Breyfogle's ore, as soon as he recovered from his wounds in Salt Lake City he was determined to resume the quest. Having exhausted his credibility in Austin, Breyfogle headed for San Francisco to find grubstakers and converts for another expedition to Death Valley. He seems to have had little trouble finding them, and about April 1, 1866, he was back at Furnace Creek, having come by way of Los Angeles with ten new followers and a couple of wagons full of provisions. Breyfogle prospected in the Funerals and neighboring hills for over a month, but somehow he still couldn't find the wonderful lost ledge. Late in April the party was joined by Nevada Governor Henry Blasdel's expedition, which was searching, among other things, for a route to the new Pahranagat mines. When the governor's party moved on east early in May, Breyfogle and most of his now disgruntled companions followed, doubtless anxious to see some real mines again. Three others, who had already seen enough, headed back to Los Angeles to catch a steamer for home. At Pahranagat the remainder of the party broke up. Breyfogle stayed there to prospect and to round up some new followers for another try at Death Valley. His former followers, tired, ragged, and dirty, returned home by way of Austin, "cursing all the Breyfogles that ever lived."[26]

As soon as the summer heat was past, Breyfogle and a flock of new hopefuls set out from Pahranagat to see the elephant in Death Valley. Standish Rood, a Pahranagat mining promoter, wrote an entertaining but fictionalized account of this trip for a Milwaukee magazine a few years later. He claimed to have gone with the party, but most likely he only heard tales of the trek from those who had gone. Rood tells us that Breyfogle took an erratic route, climbing nearly every mountain in sight, going way south to the abandoned Salt Spring mine and then back up north beyond the head of the Amargosa before he finally made camp at Furnace Creek. From there he led prospecting excursions out to one little butte after another along the east side of the Funerals. But the Pahranagat prospectors were less patient than Breyfogle's San Francisco followers. After only a couple of weeks of fruitless searching and aimless wandering, they mutineed and headed home. Breyfogle grumbled and protested that the lost ledge was somewhere within 10 miles of their camp, but the Pahranagaters were willing to leave its discovery to the "next batch of fools" he brought out there.[27]

Rood also tells us that Breyfogle's mood grew darker on the way back to Pahranagat. Just east of Ash Meadows he was hit in the knee by a Paiute arrow, causing him more pain than injury, but he had to be carried on a litter between two mules the rest of the way, and he smarted for vengeance. While camped at Timpahute he suddenly drew his revolver and fired wildly at a few friendly Paiute, killing one instantly. The party spent a sleepless night and beat a hasty retreat in the morning, before the Paiute tried to seek vengeance of their own. Rood's account of this incident is apocryphal, but several weeks later Breyfogle was in fact shot just below the knee by Indians during an abortive prospecting expedition led by William Hamlin into the Hualapai country south of the Colorado River. Breyfogle was laid up for a month thereafter at Pahranagat suffering from the wound.[28]

How many more fruitless treks Breyfogle made to Death Valley are lost to memory. Pony Duncan, who had nursed him back to health after his "scalping" in 1865, accompanied him on at least one more trip, and one of Breyfogle's cousins who had settled in San Francisco helped grubstake another try in the fall or winter of 1868. Though every trip ended with the lost ledge still lost, Breyfogle's persistence in wanting to look one more time always won him another grubstake and a few new followers, who hoped to be the lucky ones that would be with him when he made the big strike. Breyfogle was last heard of in August 1869, prospecting in Secret Canyon, some 60 miles east of Austin. No one recalls his ultimate fate. Popular legend has it that he ended his quest a "raving maniac." The tradition among his relatives is that he died of blood poisoning from an arrow wound on yet another trip to Death Valley.[29]

Even though Breyfogle finally ceased his pilgrimages to Death Valley, the Breyfoglers would not—they had become a self-perpetuating breed. Just seven years after Breyfogle's first trip to Death Valley, the editor of the *Territorial Enterprises* was confident that "every mining prospector in Nevada has heard of Breyfogle's lost mine." And each had heard his own unique version of Breyfogle's gold, told to him by a man who knew "the man" and had seen the gold. It mattered not that they knew him as Anton, Henry, Jacob, or John—hardly anyone knew Charles. Nor did it matter when or where he had found the gold. Some swore he was one of the original Death Valley argonauts who had found the gold in 1852, while others knew for certain that he was a Southerner heading back to join the Confederacy when he stumbled on it in 1862. All that really mattered was that, like Breyfogle himself, none doubted the existence of the gold. Why should they? Breyfogle's nuggets were turning up everywhere from San Francisco to New York City, in the hands of penniless prospectors and in the fancy mineral cabinets of Senator George Hearst and Governor Leland Stanford.[30]

The search was the thing. Even if Breyfogle himself couldn't find the gold again, his persistence was proof enough that the gold was there. Only a few lamented all the money, time, and lives wasted in the search. One Fresno man was said to have squandered $25,000 in the quest, but no one will ever know how much was spent altogether, how many looked, and how many died. Risk was part of the lure and the challenge. By 1893, it was said that the search had taken sixty lives, and in 1907, sixty men were said to have died in just one season's quest. One innocent journalist even reported that Death Valley had been named because of all the Breyfoglers who had died there![31]

Yet the quest was not a complete loss: in the half century and more that Breyfogle and the Breyfoglers combed the Death Valley and Amargosa country, they did find some real mines—but that's still to come.

Camels, Frauds, and Lost Guides

Not everyone who came to Death Valley and the Amargosa came looking for lost ledges that lay hidden in the land. Some came just to learn the lay of the land itself—to map and study it. They were surveyors, topographers, geologists, mineralogists, zoologists, botanists, meteorologists, and astonomers. They measured and sampled the land, discovered its great heights and surprising depth, and assayed its mineral and agricultural potential. They made the first maps of Death Valley and the Amargosa, locating for all who would follow the mountains and valleys, the passes and trails, the vital springs and ephemeral streams. In so doing they should have dispelled some of the lore and mystery that shrouded the land, but in fact they only added to it. They are best remembered not for what they contributed to the knowledge of the land but for the frauds a few pulled, for the camels they brought, and for the guides they lost—especially for the guides.

The first of the surveyors came into Death Valley in the fall of 1853 looking for a railroad route across the continent. It was an abortive quest. Earlier that year Congress had authorized surveys of five separate routes west from the Mississippi River to span the nation. The federal surveys, with good logic, stayed close to the proven overland trails, and none would pass through Death Valley or the Amargosa country. But in August, some Californians, questioning the adequacy of these surveys, held a mass meeting in San Francisco to consider alternate routes. One of the more entertaining speakers, and certainly the most opinionated, was none other than the Reverend James W. Brier. He awed the crowd with his heroic tales of '49, and none guessed it was his wife who brought him through alive, as he pronounced their blundering trail to be the ideal route for the railroad! So the meeting ended with the organization of a Pacific and Atlantic Railroad Committee to finance an expedition to survey the route—and, of course, to find a suitable connecting pass over the Sierra.[1]

Such was the enthusiasm of San Franciscans that funds were raised and the expedition was outfitted in little over a month. The party of seventeen was guided by "Major" John Ebbetts, who had come to California in 1849 as captain of the Knickerbocker Exploring Company. The chief surveyor was Lieutenant Tredwell Moore, a twenty-eight-year-old career army officer, apparently on temporary leave. He was assisted by a British artist, cartographer, and amateur naturalist, George H. Goddard. They set out from Stockton on October 7, heading for the Vegas de Santa Clara on the old Spanish Trail at Meadow Valley Creek, where Brier and the other Death Valley argonauts had left Hunt. But they took a wandering course and never reached their goal. Crossing the Sierra over the Sonora Trail, they turned north along the Walker River to Walker Lake before heading southeast toward their intended destination. The quest for water, however, brought them much farther south, to Fish Lake Valley at the base of the White Mountains, and from there they continued down into the desiccating basin of Eureka Valley, just missing numerous springs in the Sylvania Mountains.[2]

On November 7, 1853, after two waterless days, they crossed eastward in desperation over the Last Chance Range and into Death Valley. As they entered the valley, Moore saw the verdant signs of water and salvation at Last Chance Spring. There they camped for two days, recuperating from their ordeal. They had already lost several mules, and many of those remaining could barely carry their own weight, so most of the men were on foot. While they rested, they killed and skinned a crippled mule and made moccasins to replace their worn-out boots. They also discarded everything they could possibly do without in order to lighten the load on the animals.

Their second day at the springs they found an old Indian whom they plied with food and a few gifts and quizzed about the prospects of water farther to the east. He indicated that the only springs were on down Death Valley to the southeast. Ebbetts favored going that way, but Moore, probably pointing out that they were already south of their destination, convinced him that they should at least try to head east. When the old man wanted to return to his own camp that evening, they kept the gifts they had given him, hoping to ensure that he would come back the next day and guide them. He had been much more impressed by the mule carcass, however, than with any of their offerings.

When they awoke the next morning, Ebbetts and Moore found that the old man had indeed returned, but not to guide them. The old man and a friend had come quietly during the night to shoot several of the mules, killing one and wounding three others so badly that they too had to be killed. In their rage, Ebbetts and Moore burned the old man's gifts and all of the discarded equipment that they could, then buried the rest, rather than let the Indians get it. And when they broke camp, three men were left to wait in ambush for the Indians to come back for the dead mules. The rest of the party headed up Oriental Wash to the east. It was a slow, hard trek and, after losing two more mules and failing to find water, they had to make camp that night in the dry wash just short of the ridge of Gold Mountain. That evening those who had stayed behind to ambush the Indians rejoined the party. They reported that within an hour the old man and a companion had arrived to butcher and skin one of the mules, but in their eagerness for revenge they had opened fire too soon and succeeded only in scaring the Indians away.

At dawn the next day, November 11, Ebbetts and Moore scrambled on to the head of the wash and the rim of Death Valley to scout the country beyond for any sign of water. They saw nothing but a seemingly endless wasteland and finally decided it was time to turn back. That evening they returned to the spring, and left Death Valley by way of Last Chance Canyon the next morning.[3]

Ebbetts and Moore had failed to find a railroad route, but Goddard had collected over six hundred geological and botanical specimens, and they had mapped much new country—including, for the first time, the upper reaches of Death Valley. Goddard showed the results of their exploration on his map of California, which was published in 1857. On the map their trail leads rather enigmatically to their camp of November 10, which Goddard called "East Camp." As other mapmakers borrowed from this map, the trail, the springs, and other natural features along the trail faded in confusion, but East Camp remained. A decade later this fleeting camp of a day appeared for all the map-reading world like a boomtown in the midst of an unknown desert, enticing and mystifying would-be adventurers.[4]

The quest for a transcontinental railroad route also lured John C. Fremont through the hills just north of Death Valley in March 1854, just four months after Ebbetts and Moore. This—Fremont's fifth, last, and nearly forgotten expedition—was financed from his own pocket, apparently on the rebound from the disappointment of his having not been chosen to lead one of the federal surveys. Fremont hoped to show that a perfect railroad route existed along the base of that great east-west "dividing range" he thought he had glimpsed from afar on his earlier explorations, and that he had placed so confidently on his great map of the west in 1848. But he learned, as had the Death Valley argonauts before him, that these mountains were pure fiction. Fremont, however, soon set out on another futile quest as the fledgling Republican Party's first candidate for president of the United States.[5]

The next surveyors came just a few years after Fremont with contracts to run the township lines for the General Land Office, and subdivide the land into 160-acre quarter sections for the settlers who might come someday. William Denton and his crew of axmen, chainmen, and a compassman—among them the infamous Joel H. Brooks—surveyed the south end of Death Valley and the Amargosa in the latter part of 1856. At the same time Allexey von Schmidt surveyed Panamint Valley to the west. Early the following year Brooks hired on with "Colonel" Henry Washington to extend the surveys into the heart of Death Valley and up the Amargosa until they reached what they judged to be the state line. Their surveys, published in the surveyor general's map of California in 1857, gave the first detailed topography of Death Valley, although the valley itself was marked only as an unnamed "Dry Lake." Denton's survey of the curious twin basins on the southwest edge of Death Valley, which appear to form the eyes and face of an owl, gave rise to their current name, the Owlshead Mountains.[6]

Although this map showed the Death Valley and Amargosa country better than any that would follow for over three decades, the surveys fell under a cloud of suspicion and their results were generally ignored. The surveyors had contracted only to subdivide land that was suitable for farming or ranching. But since they were paid essentially by the number of acres they subdivided, some couldn't resist stretching the definition of "suitable." Thus they filed surveys of such unlikely farmland as salt flats, sand dunes, and mountainsides so steep and rugged a man could hardly climb up them.

Henry Washington, a self-styled colonel from Virginia, was the most unabashed in his exaggerations, claiming nearly a million acres from the sink of Death Valley to the crest of the Amargosa as potential farm and ranch land. For subdividing it, he submitted a bill of $40,811.82. This overran the surveyor general's budget for the year, but Washington was able to get his money before his claims were challenged. Denton and von Schmidt were more cautious in their claims, but it was von Schmidt's subdivision of Panamint Valley that first drew fire in 1861, when the cartographer of the California Boundary Commission denounced it as a shameless fraud. Although the topography shown on the survey plats was generally quite accurate, at least in the Death Valley and Amargosa country, and the fraud came only in claiming that it was suitable for settlement, the ensuing scandal cast such suspicion on the whole business that the surveys were discredited and ignored by later mapmakers. It took over three decades of further surveying to rediscover what was already known.[7]

By the time they had finished making the township surveys, most of the surveying crew wanted no more to do with Death Valley or the Amargosa, but Joel Brooks was the exception. In June 1860 he was back again as guide of the first military expedition into the heart of Death Valley. In March of that year a Salt Lake teamster, Thomas Williams, and his brother-in-law Jehu Jackman, had been attacked by Indians at Bitter Spring while coming down the Spanish Trail. Williams was killed outright and Jackman was mortally wounded. A cattleman had been killed by Indians on the Mojave River two months before, and this second attack spurred demands for immediate military action. Just two weeks

Township surveyor Henry Washington made the first reliable map of much of Death Valley in 1857, but it was discredited and ignored because of frauds.

after the Bitter Spring killings, Joel Brooks had killed a man on the Mojave while in a drunken rage, and there was some agitation for his arrest. But the troops who went after the Indians took Brooks as their guide instead![8]

Major James H. Carleton was dispatched from Fort Tejon with two companies of dragoons to punish the Indians. He reached Bitter Spring in mid-April, but finding no Indians, he searched on over the Avawatz Mountains, across the tip of Death Valley to Salt Spring, and up into the Kingston Range before returning to the Mojave River. There he set up a base, Camp Cady, from which to launch further forays to almost every point of the compass. The first success came on a sortie to the southwest, where Lieutenant Benjamin Franklin Davis captured two unsuspecting Indians. They were promptly taken to Bitter Spring and hung as a grim warning on a makeshift gallows next to Williams's grave. Then, to the east near Kelso Dunes, three more Indians were killed, their heads cut off and added to the trophies at Bitter Spring. This gory display—though not the random butchery—was more than Carleton's commander General Newman Clarke could stomach, and he ordered it removed "from public gaze."[9]

Carleton, however, was frustrated with not having found more Indians. He even hid some soldiers in a couple of wagons and sent them up the Salt Lake Trail as far as Mountain Springs in the hopes of enticing the Indians to attack, but to no avail. Finally he concluded that the Indians must have fled into the Panamint Range. So early in June he sent Lieutenant Davis and thirty-five men to hunt them there. Joel Brooks was their guide, but his services were of questionable worth. Heading north from Camp Cady, Brooks failed to find a spring he knew of north of Granite Mountain, so they had to turn east to Saratoga Springs for water. Marching back west toward the Panamints, Brooks again failed to find water, so they followed the "Agua Margosa" on down into the sink of Death Valley until they reached what Davis called "Ponamint Springs"—probably Bennetts Well. Davis probed the neighboring canyons for a couple of days but found no Indians, just a few abandoned rancherias. Brooks assured Davis that he could find plenty of Indians just to the north at Furnace Creek, but the Lieutenant decided that the Indians he was after must be farther west, on the other side of the Panamints. Since these Indians were out of reach and rations had been nearly exhausted while searching for water, Davis headed back to Camp Cady. With the failure of the expedition to Death Valley, Carleton concluded that he had done all that he could. He abandoned Camp Cady and returned to Fort Tejon.[10]

With the onset of the Civil War the following year, Davis, a Southerner, stayed with the Union and rose quickly to the rank of colonel before he was killed on the Rappahannok in June 1863. In the meantime, Joel

Brooks had finally faced murder charges for the Mojave killing, and had been acquitted. Since he had only shot the man in the arm, it was decided that death had resulted from "mal practice." Within a year Brooks was back in Death Valley, this time as the guide for the U.S. and California Boundary Commission party.[11]

The U.S. and California Boundary Commission was a fiasco of the first order. The discovery of rich mineral deposits east of the Sierra in 1859–60 had finally made Californians interested in determining the location of the eastern boundary of the state, which had been defined by Congress in 1850 but never surveyed. Furthermore, prompt action was called for because miners and settlers had begun agitating for creation of the Nevada Territory with its boundary moved west to the crest of the Sierra, thus annexing that long-neglected but now seemingly rich eastern edge of California. In the spring of 1860, after an unsuccessful bid to extend California's boundary east to include all of the new mines, California Congressman C. L. Scott finally settled for a bill creating the Boundary Commission, which was to reassert and survey the old line. But when the newly appointed U.S. commissioner, Lieutenant Sylvester Mowry, arrived in San Francisco that fall to begin surveying, he found that there was no California commissioner, because the state legislature had never gotten around to passing the necessary legislation.[12]

Undaunted, Mowry organized a preliminary reconnaissance party to look over the route in anticipation of a survey the following spring. The newspapers, calling for quick legislative action, bubbled with "magnificent anticipation" of new riches to be found, and envied Mowry's "glorious privilege . . . to be the first to unveil the secrets of those mysterious regions to the gaze of civilization." But Mowry was deprived of that privilege, too, for when the time came for the party to start, the state legislature still hadn't acted and he had to stay in Sacramento to lobby for the bill. The honor should then have fallen to Mowry's second in command, Lieutenant Joseph Christmas Ives, but Ives's first duty was to accurately determine the southeastern end of the line, where the Colorado River crossed the 35th parallel, and two months of clouds and wind had kept him from doing so.[13]

Thus the command of the boundary reconnaissance party fell to Dr. J. R. N. Owen, an Oroville physician, amateur geologist, and Coso mine owner, who saw it as an opportunity for a government-financed prospecting expedition. He was joined by several other Coso miners, including J. H. Lillard and James Hitchens from Darwin French's party, who signed on to do odd jobs for the chance to prospect. No bona fide prospecting venture could have been better staffed, for Owen also recruited

Federico Biesta, an experienced assayer, to make on-the-spot assays of anything they might find.[14]

The reconnaissance also became the last government test of Jefferson Davis's dream of a western camel corps. In 1856 Davis, then Secretary of War, had some three dozen camels brought to the southwestern United States from the Near East, to see whether they might prove to be more economical than mules. After a few unsuccessful tests, most of the camels ended up in the charge of Edward Beale at Fort Tejon. When he learned of the expedition, Beale persuaded Mowry to take along four camels, to be matched in one final test against about a dozen mules. Hadji Ali, a Syrian more popularly known as Hi Jolly, was in charge of the beasts. He drove Touli, an enormous, temperamental male that was half-Bactrian and half-Arabian, and that could carry more baggage than three mules. Maya and Catchouk, two smaller Bactrian females, each packed as much as two mules. The fourth camel, a white dromedary named Seid, never got to Death Valley. Touli killed him in Los Angeles in a fight over the females, so Mowry had his bones shipped to the Smithsonian, for exhibit.[15]

Finally, of course, there was the official purpose of determining the route for a boundary survey. This detail was left to just two of the fourteen men in the party—an astronomer, J. M. McLeod, and a topographer, Aaron Van Dorn, who became the unofficial chronicler of the expedition.[16]

Starting from Ives's camp on the Colorado, the reconnaissance party worked its way northwest by way of the Potosi mines, reaching Resting Spring late in February 1861. It was there that Joel Brooks, hearing of the relatively low altitude of the place, announced that the great valley to the west must be well below sea level. Scoffs turned to bets, and it is not likely that many sided with Brooks. Only a few days before, he had led the party to a great lake in the middle of Ivanpah Valley that proved to be a mirage, and in the days that followed some of his companions had even more cause to doubt him as he led them through a new comedy of errors.[17]

On March 4, at the lower edge of the Amargosa Desert, Brooks reached the limit of his previous explorations, and though he scouted ahead with one of the camels he was unable to find water. Amid much grumbling, the party had to make a dry camp near the later site of Lee. But one of the Coso miners, Sam McClelland, claimed that he knew of a spring just a half a dozen miles to the southwest, so he and a companion set out to find it that evening. When they hadn't returned the next morning, Brooks, Lillard, and Van Dorn went looking for them, while Owen took the rest of the party back to the last water they had left on the Amargosa. Brooks lost the trail of the missing men on the crest of the Funerals, but continued on down to Travertine Springs near the mouth of Furnace Creek, expecting that they would be there. They weren't. Leaving his two companions at the springs, Brooks departed the next morning for Owen's camp to guide the main party back to Furnace Creek. But he took the wrong fork near the head of Furnace Creek, lost his way, and finally had to return, quite embarrassed, to his two companions. The following day all three of them started out. Following the wagon tracks of the forty-niners, they found the right fork this time, but just beyond the head of Furnace Creek they took a shortcut over a low spur to the north. When they reached the Amargosa just at sunset, they found that Owen and the others had left earlier that day, going around the other side of the spur. Without food or water the three had to turn around and head back to Furnace Creek in the dark. About 2 A.M., cold and hungry, they stumbled back into Travertine Springs, finally catching up with the main party again. Owen and the rest were relieved to see them alive, since they had been missing for three days and the two men they had gone looking for had returned just after they left.[18]

For all of Brooks's ineptness, when McLeod took a barometer reading at Furnace Creek he found that they were almost exactly at sea level. With the great valley still below them it was clear that, at least this time, Brooks had guessed right about its incredible depth. On March 11, 1861, McLeod and Van Dorn lugged the barometer out onto the salt flat and made the crucial reading. At half past nine in the morning, with the sky clear and the air a pleasant 69° F, the barometer read 30.462 inches of mercury—well below the sea-level value. Here in the midst of the great western desert, flanked by snowy peaks towering 2 miles above them, they calculated that they were standing more than 377 feet below the level of the sea! Brooks had won the bet.[19]

The reconnaissance party had reached the depths of Death Valley, but it had also reached the end of the trail. That same evening, camped amid the debris of the Jayhawkers' burned wagons, trace chains, broken pots, and scattered ox bones, the men took a somber look at their own faltering animals, with their bony frames and distended bellies. Provisions were running out and the alkali was beginning to take its toll, so they decided to quit and head for Coso and home.[20]

The reconnaissance had proved a failure on all counts. They hadn't gotten more than a third of the way along the boundary toward their destination at Lake Tahoe. They had also failed to find the wonderful bonanzas they dreamed of—indeed, they were so disgusted with the mineral prospects of the country that they even concluded the Gunsight silver must have been talc! And the camels, too, proved wanting. Although they seemed superior to mules in sand and an even match in gentle terrain, the balky beasts could not be made to carry anything up steep slopes, on which the mules went faithfully ahead. Thus Jeff Davis's dream of a camel corps was finally ended, although by then Davis himself was pursuing a new dream.[21]

The whole idea of a federal boundary survey was abandoned in May, when it was discovered that the abortive reconnaissance had already cost $71,967.40—much more than Congress had appropriated for the entire project. Mowry, charged with squandering the money, was promptly fired, and Congress passed a bill creating the Nevada Territory with its western boundary on the crest of the Sierra, apparently deciding to leave settlement of the dispute up to the local governments.[22]

Joel Brooks seems to have had his fill of Death Valley at last, and so far as is known, he never went back there again. Instead, he joined partners with a man named Hart, staked claim to Coso Hot Springs, and announced that they were going into the brimstone business. That must not have lasted long, however, for early the following year the two were having a shoot-out in the Tehachapis.[23]

The boundary dispute was finally settled in February 1865, when the Nevada legislature officially recognized the original California boundary. Three months later James Lawson and William McBride surveyed the line down into the northern tip of Death Valley. But it was not until 1873 that Allexey von Schmidt returned to the Death Valley country to run the first complete survey of the boundary line from Tahoe to the Colorado. By then, the country had been more thoroughly explored by a number of other government expeditions.[24]

The first official expedition into Death Valley after the Boundary Commission party was that led by Nevada Governor Henry G. Blasdel, although he ended up there only by accident. In the spring of 1866, during the rush to the newly discovered Pahranagat mines in southeastern Nevada, Blasdel organized a party to find a shorter route to the mines and to determine whether they were in fact in Nevada and not in neighboring Utah or Arizona, as some suggested. Accompanied by State Mineralogist Richard H. Stretch and an assortment of some twenty state officials and would-be prospectors, Blasdel set out from the new camp of Silver Peak early in April. He doubtless expected to make a quick trip, because the Pahranagat mines were little over 100 miles nearly due east of Silver Peak. But failing repeatedly to find water in that direction, they drifted farther and farther south and into Death Valley, like Ebbetts and Moore before them.[25]

In Tule Canyon at the head of Death Valley, Blasdel picked up the two-year-old wagon tracks of some Gunsight seekers from Austin. This Gunsight party, curiously enough, had been led by David E. Buel, who had been Blasdel's opponent in the race for governor. Blasdel followed Buel's tracks all the way down the valley to Furnace Creek. By that time the party was growing mutinous. They had traveled for three weeks, gone over 100 miles, nearly exhausted their provisions, and were no nearer Pahranagat than when they had started. Before Blasdel could decide how best to proceed, six of the men quit and hastily set out on their own. When they ran out of water at Ash Meadows, they began to have second thoughts, but one of them, G. Gillis, headed on toward Eagle Mountain with a shovel to look for water. When he didn't return, the others turned back to Furnace Creek. They later found Gillis dead of dehydration 4 miles from the mountain. They buried him with his own shovel, hitting water just 2 feet below where he lay.[26]

At Furnace Creek, Blasdel and his companions had met Breyfogle's party from San Francisco, and although Breyfogle wouldn't part with any of his provisions, he eventually agreed to rent Blasdel one of his wagons and a large water cask. With this, Blasdel and four companions set out for Las Vegas ranch to replenish their provisions. Stretch and the others waited at Furnace Creek, whiling away their time hunting doves and lizards for supper, prospecting the nearby hills, and probably keeping a watchful eye on Breyfogle in the hope that he might finally find something. By the time the relief party returned two weeks later, Breyfogle's followers were ready to leave too, so most of them followed Blasdel on to Pahranagat. None of them had accomplished anything in Death Valley.[27]

As a shortcut to Pahranagat, Blasdel's Death Valley route was an obvious failure. He had wandered for 300 miles to end up barely 100 miles from where he started—it would have been hard to find a longer route if he had tried. On the way back to Carson City he did find a shorter route, but it wasn't by way of Silver Peak. Stretch claimed success for showing that Pahranagat was indeed within the bounds of Nevada, but even that had become a moot point, for while Blasdel's party was still in Death Valley, Nevada's congressmen had gotten a bill passed extending the state's boundaries farther east and south, just in case. The *Reese River Reveille* summed up Blasdel's exploits: "they left with a grand flourish, a grand company of State dignitaries . . . creating grand expectations, and have made a grand fizzle."[28]

The search for a route between Silver Peak and Pahranagat brought one more expedition through Death Valley the following spring. This party was led by Cavalry Lieutenant Charles E. Bendire from Camp Independence, established in Owens Valley during the Paiute War. Bendire set out with twenty-nine men on April 6, 1867, under orders to scout the country east of Coso, through Emigrant, now Redlands, Canyon in the Panamints and across Death Valley to the Amargosa and beyond, returning by way of Silver Peak.[29]

They were gone over six weeks, exploring much of southern Nevada and mapping a practical, if circuitous, route from Pahranagat to Silver Peak. But they did very little exploring in Death Valley itself. Finding Redlands Canyon impractical for pack mules, Bendire dispatched Sergeant Neale and several men through it, while he took the main party on south through Windy Gap, now Wingate Pass, at the southern end of the Panamints. In the spring, near Alvord and Bennett's old camp, Neale found their discarded anvil and thus christened Anvil Spring. He rejoined Bendire at the abandoned Salt Spring mine; from there they followed the Amargosa River until they crossed Blasdel's trail and then headed east to Pahranagat.[30]

Despite 110° heat, long waterless treks, and "poisonous" wells, Bendire lost only one animal out of forty-six in all that time—an accomplishment he credited entirely to the "indomitable energy and shrewdness" of his guide. A German by birth, Bendire had hired a colorful fellow country-man, Charles Fredrick Reinhold Hahn, to guide him. A veteran pros-pector from Cerro Gordo with a wealth of campfire tales, Hahn also had a reputation for selecting the most difficult route when much easier courses were at hand. Nonetheless, Bendire enthused, "as a mountaineer Mr. Hahn had few equals and no superiors." It was perhaps on the strength of this recommendation that Hahn was subsequently hired by Wheeler's survey party for what proved to be his last trip to Death Valley.[31]

George M. Wheeler's extensive topographic and scientific surveys west of the 100th meridian during the 1870s made an invaluable contribution to the knowledge of the West and earned him national recognition. Wheeler was still in his late twenties, a first lieutenant just launching his career, when he came to Death Valley in 1871. This was his first major expedition, coupling scientific investigations with topographic surveys, and it was the success of this expedition that enabled him to get con-gressional support for the extensive program of exploration that would continue through the end of the decade. But for a brief moment, the mysterious loss of two of his guides put it all in jeopardy.[32]

Wheeler started at Halleck Station on the Central Pacific Railroad on May 3, 1871, to survey all the way from northern Nevada to southern Arizona. He had roughly eighty men in the party, including geologists, mineralogists, and naturalists as well as the necessary corps of topog-raphers, surveyors, astronomers, and meteorologists. Keenly aware of the value of publicity, Wheeler also brought along that talented pioneer pho-tographer, Timothy H. O'Sullivan, and an able young writer and poet, Frederick Wordsworth Loring, who was heralded in Boston as "the most promising of all the young American authors." Loring contributed sketches to *Appleton's Journal* detailing some of his adventures with the expedition.[33]

To cover more territory, Wheeler divided the expedition into two parties that rendezvoused periodically. One party was under his direct command; the other was commanded by Second Lieutenant David A. Lyle. Wheeler had wanted his West Point classmate and fellow topographical engineer Daniel W. Lockwood to be his second in command, but because of delays in Lockwood's transfer, he had grudgingly taken Lyle, an even younger but enthusiastic artillery officer just returned from Alaska.[34]

Although the expedition was well planned for the most part, it was certainly poorly timed: at the peak of the summer heat, in July, they converged on Death Valley and their troubles began. The two parties had divided again at Belmont, Nevada. Wheeler circled east by way of Pahranagat, then back to the Amargosa to cross Death Valley to their next rendezvous at Camp Independence. Lyle, hiring Hahn as a guide, headed west through Silver Peak and the new mining camps at the north end of Death Valley. Reaching Independence on July 18, well ahead of Wheeler, Lyle decided to try to meet Wheeler and guide him across Death Valley. It was an ill-starred endeavor.[35]

Rounding up eight volunteers, including Hahn, Lyle headed directly east over the Inyo Mountains for Death Valley. On the other side of the range, Hahn asked Lyle to wait for a day before taking the pack animals farther, so that he could scout ahead for water and grass between there and Grapevine Springs. Hahn set out at 8 A.M. on July 23, accompanied by an Indian, Sam, and naturalist John Koehler, who wanted extra time to collect specimens at Grapevine Springs. Hahn led them over the broken hills to the northeast, across the dunes in Termination Valley, and up a spur of the Last Chance Range before he backtracked to find a pass late that evening at the head of what Lyle later named Breakneck Canyon, leading down into Death Valley.[36]

At eight that night, Koehler said, Hahn suddenly left him without saying a word. None of the party ever saw Hahn again, and his fate remains a mystery. Koehler thought Hahn was returning to Lyle, but two days later Lyle found Hahn's trail continuing on into Death Valley. Rumor had it that, after traveling all day without finding water, Koehler had vowed to "make him find water or kill him." Lyle later thought he saw the tracks of Hahn's mule at the north end of Death Valley, but he didn't follow them. He concluded that Hahn, "having led us into a dilemma from which he could not extricate us, had deserted and gone for the White Mountains." Privately, Lyle swore that if he had had the time, he would have hunted Hahn down and shot him.[37]

Lyle had more immediate problems, however. Following Hahn's erratic, waterless trail, Lyle and his men reached Death Valley almost dead from thirst. Abandoning all hope of getting to Grapevine Springs, they turned north toward a beckoning green patch that they named Last Chance Spring—the same spring that had saved Ebbetts and Moore nearly two decades before. After a day's rest they made their way to the nearby fledgling mining camp of Gold Mountain. There Lyle persuaded miner Thomas J. Shaw to go down to the Amargosa to find Wheeler and guide him back to Pigeon Spring at the north end of the Last Chance Range, where Lyle would wait for him with fresh provisions. By the time Wheeler reached the spring, his party was suffering from privation, and he must have been grateful for Lyle's initiative in coming to meet him. But when they finally got to Camp Independence, David Lockwood was waiting and Wheeler promptly gave him command of Lyle's party, making Lyle his own executive officer.[38]

On August 12 Wheeler set out again to explore Death Valley. Lockwood had left a few days earlier for the south end of the valley, which he would cross without incident by Walker's cutoff. But new trouble awaited Wheeler. He sent Lyle with the main party directly to Wildrose Spring, to wait till he arrived with a side party by way of Cottonwood Canyon, some 20 miles to the north. Lyle recruited a new guide, William Egan, a quiet, studious man from Cerro Gordo. After a few days' wait at Wildrose Spring, Lyle dispatched Egan to guide O'Sullivan and a packer to Wheeler's camp in Cottonwood Canyon to take some photographs, and then guide them all back to Wildrose. The three left on August 19 and camped that night in Death Valley at Emigrant Spring. The weather was unbearably hot, and all of the animals but Egan's mule were close to collapse by the end of the first day. When they started out again the next morning, O'Sullivan and the packer were unable to keep up with Egan, so they decided that he should ride on ahead and mark the trail. O'Sullivan also decided that if he didn't reach Cottonwood Canyon by eleven o'clock that morning he was turning back. At eleven there was no sign of either the canyon or of Egan, so O'Sullivan and the packer headed back toward Wildrose Spring. Like Hahn, Egan was never seen again, although it took some time for his companions to realize that he was lost.[39]

When Wheeler arrived at Wildrose on August 21, Lyle wasn't surprised that Egan hadn't reached Cottonwood Canyon before Wheeler left. Nor was he concerned, because Wheeler had left a few men behind, and Lyle expected that Egan would join them. It wasn't until several days later, after the main party had moved on across Death Valley to Ash Meadows and the remaining men from Cottonwood Canyon had arrived without Egan, that Lyle realized that Egan might be lost. Even then, Lyle wasn't certain, and he eagerly seized on a rumor that Egan had been seen in the Clarke District, more than 100 miles to the southeast. Wheeler, however, wrote to Captain Harry Egbert, commander of Camp Independence, "I am afraid that we have lost another guide," and asked to be informed of any news about either Hahn or Egan.[40]

Lieutenant George M. Wheeler lost two guides
and left new mysteries in Death Valley in the
summer of 1871 while surveying for this map.
(Portrait from *Harpers New Monthly,* May 1876)

As word of the disappearance of the two guides spread through Owens
Valley, four separate search parties formed to seek some trace of the men,
and in their wake came a wave of condemnation of Wheeler and the
survey. The local paper, the *Inyo Independent,* began printing rumors of
Koehler's threat to kill Hahn, intimations of a dispute between Wheeler
and Egan over mining claims, and harsh criticisms of the imperious
attitudes of "Wheeler's sophomores." The "delicate" Mr. Loring's attempt
to minimize the tragedy in a sketch for *Appleton's Journal* only intensified
the rage of the Inyoites, and Loring's own murder by Indians in Arizona
didn't temper their feelings. Burlesquing Egan as an offensive, boorish
fraud of an old mountaineer who spat on everything in sight, Loring had
coldly rejoiced that "he did not come back and never will come back
again," and portrayed Egan's disappearance as some sort of comic justice![41]

Captain Egbert finally came to Wheeler's defense and suggested that
such charges would injure the development of the region. He pointed out
that "it is exceedingly difficult to obtain appropriations from Congress to
survey and examine countries supposed to be desert," and warned that if

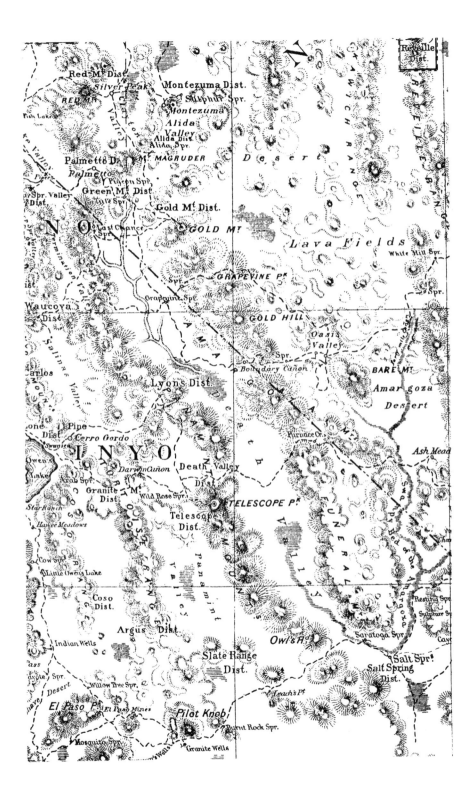

the charges were reprinted in other newspapers they "will be enough to prevent the granting of an appropriation on the one hand, or the Engineer Office from asking for it on the other." To help quiet matters, Lyle finally gave Egbert a lengthy account of the affair, which he had printed in the *Inyo Independent*. With this, the Inyo editor was content to let the matter rest "until the sea shall give up its dead and the mysteries of the Valley of Death are unravelled."[42]

The mystery would not die, however, and every new clue, real or imagined, breathed new life into it. One of the search parties had found Hahn's saddle, his blankets, and some of his clothes and papers in a box canyon at the north end of Death Valley, near Gold Mountain. Two years later an Indian found a pair of field glasses, believed to be Hahn's, out in the middle of the valley between Breakneck Canyon and Grapevine Springs. The glasses created a brief sensation of their own, because the lenses had what were thought to be perfect images of sagebrush burned into them by some mysterious photographic process. This mystery was dispelled when a San Francisco optician pointed out that this was a common result of crazing of the cement between the segments of the lenses. That same year a body reported to be Egan's was found in the borax beds north of Furnace Creek. The following year a dismembered leg, also imagined to have been Egan's, turned up at the north end of Panamint Valley—and so it went.[43]

The most intriguing clue—and one that may in fact solve half the mystery—was a letter from A. J. Close in the spring of 1875. Close wrote that his partner Fred Fink had talked to a rancher on the Arkansas River near Pueblo, Colorado, who claimed to have met Hahn just two years before. Hahn told the rancher that when he failed to find water he was afraid to return to the others, so he left his saddle and a few belongings to throw them off the track and set out bareback on his mule for Arizona. A short time later he had joined the rush to the San Juan country, and at last settled on a ranch on the Arkansas River. There he had been killed in a drunken quarrel with a neighbor on December 20, 1873.[44]

Although Wheeler's survey shed new light on Death Valley, the loss of his guides also shrouded it in new mystery. The only certainty is that Hahn and Egan are now dead, but how and when they died remains a matter of speculation.

Wheeler did nonetheless get the continuing appropriations that he wanted and went on to make the first extensive surveys of the West. But he had had his fill of Death Valley and never returned there, although he did send two detachments back to the valley in the summer of 1875. Lieutenant Rogers Birnie led one into the heart of Death Valley after bonanza ore was discovered in the Panamints. Lieutenant Eric Bergland led the other, from the south edge of the valley to the Colorado River, after Nevada State Mineralogist Richard Stretch suddenly turned into a visionary reclamationist. Stretch wanted to divert water from the Colorado at Callville near Las Vegas and run it into Death Valley to tame the savage climate, reclaim the wasted desert, and cash in on its "exuberant fertility." He believed that the entire "Colorado once flowed into Death Valley, and from thence through a chain of lakes . . . to the Gulf of California," and that the collapse of the "Aztec civilization of Arizona . . . dates from the time when the great Colorado had cut down its bed in the big canyon so deep that its course was diverted . . . and the lakes which once existed in Southern California gradually evaporated." At the insistence of his superiors, Wheeler dutifully dispatched Bergland to look into whether the diversion was possible. Bergland reported back with a resounding "no," which killed the notion, at least for a while. That was the last that Wheeler had to do with Death Valley.[45]

THE POCKET MINERS

The last third of the nineteenth century saw the coming of the pocket miners and the first profitable mining ventures in Death Valley and the Amargosa. They found and worked rich pockets of ore, or sometimes refined metal, from which a few men could extract a profit, at least fleetingly. Some found pockets so rich that the ore paid a profit even though it had to be shipped hundreds or even thousands of miles for reduction. Others found pockets that were not quite so rich but were fortunately situated near a spring and a stand of pinyon, so that the ore could be profitably worked close by. Still other clever souls found that they could turn an even bigger and quicker profit if they just took the rich assays and worked quite different pockets of coined metal on the streets of San Francisco, Chicago, or New York! Yet no matter how rich the pockets were, each of them, whether of ore or coin, inevitably petered out, the venture was abandoned, and the pocket miners moved on. But while they lasted, these miners also opened rich pockets of history in the story of Death Valley.

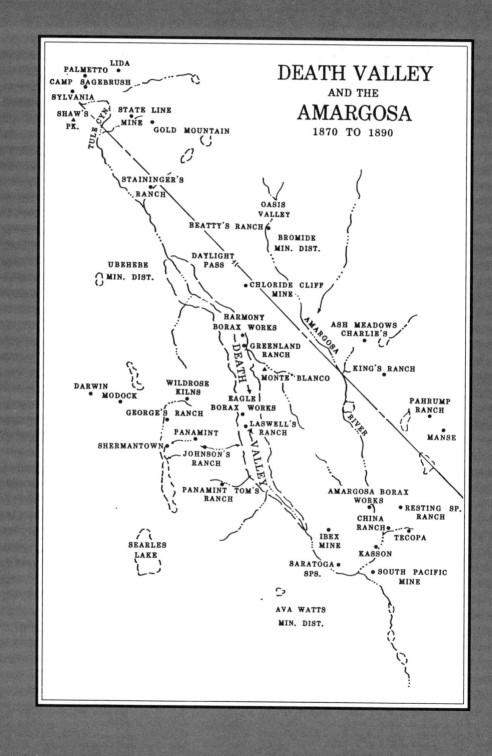

DEATH VALLEY
AND THE
AMARGOSA
1870 TO 1890

LIDA
PALMETTO
CAMP SAGEBRUSH
SYLVANIA
SHAW'S
PK.
STATE LINE
MINE
GOLD MOUNTAIN
TULE CYN.

STAININGER'S
RANCH

OASIS
VALLEY
BEATTY'S RANCH
BROMIDE
MIN. DIST.

DAYLIGHT
PASS
UBEHEBE
MIN. DIST.
CHLORIDE CLIFF
MINE

HARMONY
BORAX WORKS
ASH MEADOWS
CHARLIE'S
AMARGOSA
GREENLAND
RANCH
DEATH
KING'S RANCH
MONTE BLANCO
DARWIN
MODOCK
WILDROSE
KILNS
EAGLE
BORAX WORKS
RIVER
PAHRUMP
RANCH
GEORGE'S RANCH
LASWELL'S
RANCH
MANSE
PANAMINT
VALLEY
SHERMANTOWN
JOHNSON'S
RANCH

PANAMINT TOM'S
RANCH
AMARGOSA BORAX
WORKS
RESTING SP.
RANCH
CHINA
RANCH
SEARLES
LAKE
IBEX
MINE
TECOPA
KASSON
SARATOGA
SPS.
SOUTH PACIFIC
MINE

AVA WATTS
MIN. DIST.

Tom Shaw's Country

The first successful pocket miners started in the north end of Death Valley in the late 1860s. In the decade that followed they found several rich pockets of gold and silver, and around these mines sprang up the ephemeral camps of Gold Mountain, Palmetto, Tule Canyon, Lida, and Sylvania. But the opening of profitable mines was slow and erratic, and the failures far outnumbered the successes.

More than anyone else's, this end of Death Valley was Tom Shaw's country, from Shaw's Spring, seeping from the side of Gold Mountain on the east edge of Death Valley, to Shaw's Peak, crowning the Last Chance Range on the west. Lieutenant Wheeler put those names on the map in gratitude for Shaw's aid in getting his party out of the country alive in that tragic summer of 1871. The names stuck until after the turn of the century, when the U.S. Geological Survey resurveyed the region and left them off its new map.[1]

Thomas Jefferson Shaw deserved better than that. He was not the most successful miner in that part of Death Valley, but he was certainly the most persistent. A thirty-year-old Texan and veteran Nevada miner when he first came to the valley in the summer of 1866, Shaw kept trying when no one else would, until he had shown that despite their remoteness, mines in Death Valley could in fact be worked at a profit. For he had discovered the first profitable ore pocket in Death Valley—the State Line Mine, the pride of Gold Mountain.[2]

Tom Shaw was not the first to find gold on Gold Mountain, however. That honor goes to Leander Morton and two companions from Austin, who chased Breyfogle's elusive ledge in the fall of 1865. They located several rich-looking croppings of gold on the great quartz ledges that ribbed the sides of Oriental Wash, and to secure their claims before they left, they organized the Gold Mountain Mining District on November 20. But when they got back to Austin, they found that most of the rock didn't assay more than $50 a ton. That certainly wouldn't pay to mine, so they never returned. Morton drifted on, looking for quick riches elsewhere; perhaps out of frustration, he tried his hand at robbing the Central Pacific Railroad train at Pequop station in November 1870. He had no better luck at that, was quickly caught, convicted, and sent to the Nevada State Prison at Carson City. Unrepentant, Morton led a massive prison break in September 1871, and headed back toward Death

Valley to hide out until spring. He never made it. In Long Valley, near what is now known as Convict Lake, he and two other escapees were captured by a posse and hung. Such was the fate of the discoverer of Gold Mountain.[3]

Tom Shaw wasn't the first to try to make the rich ore pockets of northern Death Valley pay, either. There were dozens of men who had tried that and failed. The most spectacular failure was Colonel Edwin C. Catherwood. If it hadn't been for Shaw's success, Catherwood's failure could have set Death Valley mining back for a decade or more. Catherwood, a former colonel of the volunteer Thirteenth Missouri Cavalry in the Civil War, had come west to the boom camp of Silver Peak in the winter of 1865–66. He was sent as agent and superintendent for the newly formed New York and Silver Peak Mining Company, an innocent bunch of New York investors who had bought half a dozen claims, sight unseen, from an itinerant mining promoter. The colonel, brother of one of the bigger investors, Robert B. Catherwood, had dutifully commenced assembling an expensive mill that the company had sent with him, when he suddenly discovered that the only ore on the company's claims was in a six-ton boulder and a few other rocks that had rolled there from a nearby ledge! Before he returned east to break the news to the other investors, Catherwood went searching for other claims the company might buy. He met H. W. Douglass, who had just discovered a rich silver ledge he called the Champion, 20 miles south of Silver Peak, in the new mining district of Palmetto.[4]

The Palmetto district, formed in April of 1866, owed its name to the fact that its discoverers had never seen a Joshua tree before. They concluded that the Joshua must be a relative of the Southern palmetto, and so named the district. Others poked fun at this idea, insisting that Joshua trees are related to the date palm instead—albeit a "bitter date." Both were wrong, but the name stuck nonetheless.[5]

Douglass, one of the organizers of the district, had discovered the Champion on April 16. Catherwood was so impressed by the assays of rich surface rock, laced with hornsilver and running as high as $2,427 a ton in silver and $800 a ton in gold, that he bought the claim before it was a month old. Not only were the assays extraordinary but the Champion was ideally located. Even though it overlooked the dreaded Death Valley, it was high on the pinyon-covered western slope of Palmetto Mountain and was surrounded by several springs. Despite these advantages, Catherwood must have had some trouble convincing the other investors to undertake this new venture, because it was nearly a year before he returned to Palmetto to begin work. He had also learned one thing from the misadventure at Silver Peak, for this time he vowed not to put up a mill until he was certain that he really had ore in the mine.

Thus in the spring of 1867 he brought in a crew of about thirty to sink three inclined shafts at intervals along the Champion and thoroughly prospect the lode. By working three shifts around the clock, two of the shafts were down 310 feet—and still in ore—by the following spring. Although the ore was much more refractory than that at the surface, it assayed as high as $600 a ton, which could still pay a handsome profit.[6]

Catherwood was finally convinced that they couldn't lose. Doubling the size of the crew, he began construction of a splendid mill in Palmetto Wash, 2 miles west of Pigeon Spring and just 3 miles down the slope from the mine. He spent $90,000 on the mill, sparing no expense, and assembled an impressive array of equipment—twelve stamps driven by a steam engine, six roasting furnaces, and a full complement of the latest design in amalgamating pans. The mill buildings were all of solid brick, as were his office, his residence, and even the stables! It was an awe-inspiring enterprise, the dawn of the industrial age in Death Valley. By the time the mill was completed, Catherwood had roughly two hundred men working at the mine and mill, and the company had sunk $155,000 into Palmetto. But there was promise of an immediate return of double their money, because Catherwood had already mined and stockpiled over a thousand tons of first-class ore, which was expected to return from $300 to $400 a ton.[7]

The mill started up on November 20, 1868, and in two months most of the ore on hand had been worked. But despite all his planning and modern machinery, Catherwood's mill produced only $83,000 in bullion from all that ore, recovering barely $100 a ton—not even a third of its value. The ore was just too refractory to be worked efficiently with the technology at hand.[8]

Defeated, Catherwood abandoned the whole works in May 1869 and headed east, never to return. His brother held onto the mine until the end of the century in the hope that it might some day be made to pay, but not even a watchman was left to look after the wonderful mill, and it all quietly vanished: picks, shovels, pans, stamps, and engine—even most of the bricks—were "spirited away." Only the company's well, which no one could figure out how to dig up and carry off, seemed secure. Within a few years it and the crumbling chimney were all that remained as a reminder of what still-hopeful prospectors liked to think had been "New York mismanagement." There was of course truth to that, but as they too inevitably learned, the problems of profitably working Death Valley's ores were as complex as the ores themselves.[9]

It was Tom Shaw who first happened upon a solution. His was a modest solution, but that was the secret: it was all a matter of scale. In each rich pocket there was only a fixed amount of ore and a fixed amount of bullion that could be extracted from it. By definition, then, a pocket could pay a profit only if the costs of working it were less than the value of that ore. If the pocket was small, that meant working it on a modest, economical scale, with as small a capital investment as possible. On too large an investment it couldn't even return the outlay, let alone pay a profit. But what was too large an investment could really be known only in retrospect, for who could see into the rock to know how big or how small the pocket was and what it would pay? Current technology has greatly improved the guesses, but this remains the essential gamble of mining. For Death Valley's early miners and investors, it was only a game of trial and error.

Tom Shaw was the first to win the game. He didn't have the option of investing too much money, but he did make a heavy investment in time and effort. He and two companions, George Ayer and Grand Rhodes, first ventured onto Gold Mountain in July 1866. There they found some rich croppings of gold quartz. When the Shoshone killed one of their horses, they took it as a signal to get out, but the rock was too good to forget, so they patiently waited for over a year until they felt it was safe to go back.[10]

In January 1868 Shaw and his partners returned to explore the district more thoroughly. On the barren ridge that marked the north side of Oriental Wash, Tom Shaw found the "monster lode" he named the State Line—a bold outcropping of gold-bearing quartz, 12 feet thick and several thousand feet long. They promptly set to work, sinking two incined shafts along the foot wall of the lode. On one, at a depth of 20 feet, they cut into the lode, opening a dazzling crystal grotto with gold-studded walls that rivaled the fabled cave of Aladdin. Tom Shaw was so awed by it all that he leveled the floor, knocked a chimney through to the surface, and made it his cabin! Although it measured only 9 by 10 feet, it was warm in the winter, cool in the summer, and an inspiration year-round as he sat each evening with fire and candlelight mirrored in myriad golden flashes from every wall.[11]

It must have taken that to make Shaw keep coming back to Gold Mountain for four more years, even after the rest of his partners had all abandoned hope. Their first disappointment came when they hauled a third of a ton of hand-crushed, selected ore over 100 miles to Belmont for amalgamation and found that it paid them only $58.86—not three days wages for the six of them. But the ore did yield nearly $180 a ton, and since most of their time had been spent crushing and hauling it, they could have made a profit if they had milled it near the mine. They tried briefly to find investors to put up a small steam-powered stamp mill, but nothing came of it. Shaw's partners turned elsewhere to seek their fortunes, but Shaw persisted. Although the Shoshone began to take a toll of his horses again, and it was rumored that two prospectors had been killed nearby, Shaw kept coming back to probe the lode for richer pockets that might be shipped out to a mill at a profit. He found nothing quite rich enough, however, so he finally decided to try working the ore on a small scale himself. By then trouble from the Shoshone had been ended by the establishment of a small military outpost near the old abandoned Palmetto mill. Captain Harry Egbert, commander of Camp Independence, sent a detachment of fifteen men from Company B of the Twelfth U.S. Infantry, under Sergeant Remsnyder, to set up the outpost in December 1870. Known informally as Camp Palmetto or Camp Sagebrush, it was maintained for sixteen months, until the Shoshone curbed their appetite for horseflesh—temporarily, at least.[12]

In April 1871 Shaw and a new partner, James Ruth, built a mule-powered arrastra at Shaw's Spring, the nearest water, located 5 miles east of the State Line mine. The following month they worked the first ore, and it paid them well. Their arrastra could grind a tenth of a ton of ore a day, and while one of them ran it, the other could easily mine and haul that much more ore from the lode. On $180-a-ton ore they were each making $9 a day—an excellent day's pay at a time when even the best miners could earn only $4 a day working for wages. Thus the first of Death Valley's rich ore pockets had begun to pay a profit—Death Valley finally had a paying mine![13]

As the word got out, others headed for Tom Shaw's country to hunt for rich pockets of their own, and a mining boom was on. The rush soon centered not on Gold Mountain, but in Lida Valley to the northwest, just beyond the head of Death Valley. The ores there were even richer than those from Gold Mountain, and the country was also a bit more inviting, being surrounded by several springs and some scattered stands of pinyon. William Scott and William Black found the first rich pocket there. Prospecting on the hill just south of Lida Spring, they discovered a rich ledge of silver-lead ore, the Cinderella, in July 1871. Scott and Black organized the Alida Valley Mining District the following month. Alida Spring, corrupted to Lida, had been named by Dave Buel for his wife when he passed through in January 1864 in his futile quest for the Gunsight silver. Buel should have stopped right there, for Black and Scott began taking out $1,000-a-ton ore right from the surface croppings. This soon attracted a whole crowd of hopefuls who rushed in to try their luck. Even George Ayer, one of Shaw's old partners, had second thoughts and came back, and he did well. In February 1872, on a rugged ridge of Palmetto Mountain a few miles west of the Cinderella, Ayer and Sam Halsey struck a large pocket of $700-a-ton rock, which they christened the Lida Belle. That same month, in the low hills just east of the Cinderella, another lucky prospector, W. J. Brown, found an equally good pocket that he named Brown's Hope. These two mines would be the mainstay of the Lida boom.[14]

Lida became the Death Valley country's first real mining town—it was the first place with a saloon. Lida even had its own coinage for a while in 1873, when a scarcity of cash forced the use of little silver bullion bars stamped in odd denominations, ranging from $1.50 to $7. The town was conceived on March 1, 1872, with the platting of the townsite at Lida Spring; was born in May, with the opening of "two richety whisky shops and a half-starved store"; and was baptized in blood on the Fourth of July, with its first shooting scrape, when a drunken six-shooter accidentally nicked Guadalupe Ochar in the arm. With that first mark of urban violence, a neighboring editor predicted, "a great future for Lida is now assured." By fall it had acquired three well-stocked stores, a bakery, an eating house, numerous tents and cabins, and a weekly stage and mail line from Independence. By the time Lida was one year old, it had reached its prime and boasted a hundred residents, nearly two dozen businesses, a new stage line running 190 miles from Austin, and a stamp mill. A Mexican barrio had also sprung up half a mile to the south, around some small smelting furnaces. Known as Lida Valle to its inhabitants and as South Lida to its gringo neighbors, it sported a couple more stores, a few saloons, and a lively dance hall. Both towns rallied together on Cinco de Mayo and the Fourth of July, or whenever two horses could be found for a race. The Shoshone made their camp between the two towns, working odd jobs and watching.[15]

Outwardly, Lida had a raw look of rough-hewn logs and flapping canvas roofs that reminded old-timers of the rowdy gold-rush camps. But it was actually a remarkably quiet place. There was no jail, and they didn't need one: Justice of the Peace W. J. Brown simply banished offenders. Cornelius Buckley's was a typical case. Accused of shamefully maltreating a squaw and otherwise making himself obnoxious, he was given a small amount of cash, some crackers, and some advice, and was sent packing to Owens Valley. There was only one fatal fray, and that too was handled in a summary fashion. George Chiles, an itinerant gambler who fancied himself something of a desperado, was hassling a couple of seven-up players in Scott and Fitzgerald's saloon late one afternoon in May 1873, when one of them told him to "dry up." Chiles reached for his pistol and was knocked to the floor. He got up firing wildly, killing two bystanders at the bar. Several men then jumped Chiles, and in the scuffle he was shot and killed.[16]

The rise and fall of Lida, however, was the rise and fall of the Lida Milling and Mining Company, one of the most profitable early ventures in the Death Valley country and the creation of two men—John B. Hiskey and David Conkling. Hiskey, a talented, hardworking, practical Washoe mill man, put the Lida Milling and Mining Company together and made it pay. Under this management it was a model of profitable, conservative mining. With a small initial investment, Hiskey made the mines pay their own way and generate their own additional capital by reinvesting a portion of their profits in expansion and development. To get that initial capital, Hiskey had relied on Conkling, a San Francisco bookkeeper turned tobacco importer and would-be entrepreneur. Conkling would eventually be the venture's undoing.[17]

Hiskey and a partner, Josiah Walker, had run a custom mill on Wyman Creek in Deep Spring Valley, 35 miles west of Lida Spring, and it was there that Black and Scott had taken their first batch of Cinderella ore for assay and milling. In January 1871 Hiskey and Walker had leased and remodeled the idle mill, which belonged to the failing Deep Spring Mining and Milling Company, in the hope of doing a profitable custom business milling ore from various small mines in the White Mountains at a charge of $50 a ton. Most of the local ores had proved too refractory for successful milling, so Hiskey and Walker were about to quit when they saw the Cinderella ore—good milling rock that paid as much as $1,000 a ton! Hiskey promptly got an option to buy the lode. He and Walker had exhausted what capital they had by renovating the mill, so they turned to David Conkling, one of the stockholders of the foundering mill company. Along with his two associates in the tobacco trade, George Parker and Samuel Wattson, Conkling put up the necessary money. The five men became the Lida Milling and Mining Company, and in December 1871 they bought the Cinderella.[18]

Hiskey put several men to work extracting ore, and with a twenty-two mule pack team he began shipping it to the Deep Spring mill in February 1872. Within a month they had produced $6,000 in bullion, but the rich ore pocket in the Cinderella was nearly exhausted. Hiskey, however, had already arranged to purchase a more promising lode, the newly discovered Brown's Hope. They bought it in March for $5,000, and began steady shipments of $500-a-ton ore. The mill recovered 80 percent of that value, so even though mining, milling, and packing costs ran about $100 a ton, the mine paid for itself in a month—and ultimately paid back the cost twenty-fold.[19]

By the fall of 1872 the Lida Milling and Mining Company had produced $60,000 in bullion, and Hiskey was ready to enlarge the operation. The little water-powered mill at Deep Spring was unable to keep up with the output of the mines, so Hiskey had added a 12-horsepower engine from a steam-vibrator threshing machine for more power. Even with this makeshift arrangement, they could keep the mill running only about a fifth of the time, so Hiskey had no intention of renewing the lease. Instead, he bought a secondhand mill on Walker River and moved it to Lida. At the same time he bought Lida's other bonanza mine, the Lida Belle. The Lida Milling and Mining Company paid a handsome price—$16,000—for this mine, because George Ayer and Sam Halsey had already proved its worth, shipping several tons of $700-a-ton rock and exposing the ore body to a depth of 50 feet. Although it pinched out the following spring, much sooner than expected, the Lida Belle more than repaid its cost.[20]

Hiskey set up the mill on the south edge of town and started it up in March 1873. It was an eight-stamp, steam-powered affair, equipped with two reverberatory furnaces for "chloridizing" some of the more complex ores, and it recovered better than 80 percent of the assay value of the ores. By the end of the year Hiskey had milled some 480 tons of ore and produced a little over $100,000 in bullion. This brought the company's total bullion production to $162,646, of which roughly half must have been clear profit, even after paying back all the mining and milling expenses, the property and equipment costs, and all of the capital invested. The return on the latter was manyfold.[21]

By then the dream was over, the rich pockets of bonanza ore were exhausted, and David Conkling had mired the company in debt and litigation. As fast as the money had come in, Conkling had found ways to spend it even faster, and borrowing heavily against his seemingly endless future profits, he had signed away the mines and the mill as collateral, unbeknownst to his partners. They first learned of his debts in June 1873, when one of his creditors, John D. Teller, brought suit against the company for money Conkling either couldn't or wouldn't pay. After two months' closure of the mill, Hiskey and Walker won a temporary postponement until the end of the year, during which they feverishly worked out the last of the high-grade ore in their mines. Taking the proceeds, they let the property go toward settling Conkling's debts.[22]

Hiskey took his share north to Candelaria, where new mines were opening up, while Walker put his profits into a ranch in Owens Valley. Having demonstrated his financial ineptness—or adeptness, as the case may be—Conkling plunged ahead to become a mining stockbroker. The failure of the Lida Milling and Mining Company left the town and the mines in a state of shock. One stunned miner claimed it paralyzed mining, crippled business, and cut the population by 200 percent! Yet despite the exodus, there were those who knew that there was still good ore to be found in the mines, and they stayed to keep the town alive. The confidence of others was restored temporarily that spring when General Addison Page bought all of the company's property and began remodeling the mill to work ore not only from Lida but from Gold Mountain as well.[23]

Over at Gold Mountain, Tom Shaw's early success had brought in scores of prospectors to locate nearly every foot along the trace of the great quartz ledges for 10 miles or more. Even George Ayer, after his own success at Lida, came back to Gold Mountain to have one more look, and once again he was richly rewarded. In August 1872, just beyond the edge of Death Valley in the deep-cut canyons on the east side of Gold Mountain, Ayer, Sam Halsey, Jim Ruth, and Tom Coates found a magnificent boulder "alive with golden nuggets." Pieces chipped from the rock assayed $64,000 a ton, and word quickly spread that this was in fact the Lost Breyfogle. And the ledge from which it came was even richer, with assays reaching $107,000 a ton! One enthusiast reported that it "excels anything ever seen in the United States of America for richness and size!" They named this bonanza the Oriental, and the name is still preserved in Oriental Wash. Within two months Ayer and Halsey had sold the Lida Belle so that they could spend all of their time exploring the Oriental.[24]

Despite such fabulous ore, Gold Mountain had one dreadful handicap— an awful scarcity of water. This proved to be an almost insurmountable obstacle to the working of its mines. The miners who rushed to the incipient town of Gold Mountain quickly found that there wasn't even enough water for their mules. An urgent mass meeting, called to seek solutions to the problem, broke up in despair when the only proposal was a $30,000 pipeline from the nearest good spring. It would be nearly a decade before water would finally be brought in. Until then Gold Mountain was no more than a one-store town. That store was a combination saloon, restaurant, and butcher shop run by a German immigrant, P. Benson, and his wife, who was the only woman in the camp. It did, however, have the dubious honor of being the first store in Death Valley proper.[25]

Even Tom Shaw was becoming painfully aware of the scarcity of water on Gold Mountain. In the heady excitement of the rush that he had created, he too began to grow impatient with the slow but steady profits he was making from his arrastra, and to yearn for quicker returns. So in February 1872 Shaw sold an interest in his mines to Robert H. Stewart and Benjamin Franklin Higgs, who planned to put up a small, steam-powered stamp mill. Even a little two-stamp mill would be able to work twenty times as much ore in a day as the plodding arrastra. First, however, they had to find an adequate source of water, so Frank Higgs started sinking a well. When he got down 80 feet and still came up dry, he gave up. By May 1873 Shaw had at last decided to sell the State Line and move on. W. T. "Joggles" Wright, an experienced mining superintendent from Belmont, took a one-year option to buy the mine for $30,000. After he had sunk $5,000 into further exploration of the ledge, he backed out, realizing that the pocket of $180-a-ton ore just wasn't big enough to pay back the costs of bringing in water and putting up a mill. Although there was an estimated $1 million in lower-grade ore in sight on the monster ledge, it averaged only about $30 a ton, and it would be a long time, if ever, before it could be worked at a profit. Shaw finally sold the State Line in the spring of 1874 for $6,500 to General Addison Page.[26]

In the meantime, Ayer and his partners had discovered that the Oriental was a very "pockety vein." Despite the fantastic assays of selected samples, the ore averaged only $40 a ton, so they sold out to Allen A. Curtis and John A. Paxton, the kingpins of Austin. Curtis and Paxton, owners of Austin's bank and principal mines, bought up some forty other Gold Mountain claims in addition to the Oriental, and talked of putting up a twenty-stamp mill near Lida to work the ore. But after a year of exploratory work on the ledges, they too concluded a mill wouldn't pay, and sold out to General Addison Page.[27]

At forty-four, Addison L. Page had been a mill owner in Austin, a mine operator in White Pine, and a railroad builder in Pioche. He was also an erratic sort who, having served as a volunteer captain in the Civil War, affected the title of General and seemed obsessed with winning the Nevada Republican gubernatorial nomination. In the spring of 1874, flush from the sale of his Pioche and Bullionville railroad holdings, he came to the north end of Death Valley and bought up most of the promising mining property. His plans for resuming operations on a grand scale breathed new life into the moribund camps. In a fever of activity that summer, he acquired additional water rights, ordered wagonloads of lumber, renovated the Lida mill, started it up on rock from the dump, and brought in machinery for a five-stamp mill at Gold Mountain. But then everything stopped—the mill at Lida closed down again, and the mill at Gold Mountain was never set up.[28]

Page seems to have suddenly turned his full attention to his quixotic quest for the gubernatorial nomination, even going so far as to stuff the ballot box in the primary election at Lida. Rejected once more, he retreated to San Francisco—suffering, it was said, from an enfeebling attack of "softening of the brain." Frank Higgs and two partners finally hunted him up and persuaded him to lease the Lida mill to them. They started it up as a custom mill in May 1875, to the relief of Lida's remaining miners. This seems to have jogged Page's memory of his neglected Lida and Gold Mountain properties, because that same month he suddenly incorporated the two groups of mines as the Alida and the Golden Slug mining companies, offering the public a total of $6,000,000 in stock. Six months later he was dead, and the litigation over his estate closed the Lida mill once again.[29]

Tom Shaw, in the meantime, had temporarily gone back to prospecting. As soon as he optioned the State Line to Joggles Wright, he and Jim Ruth struck out from Shaw's Spring across Death Valley to the hills just north of Shaw's Peak. William F. Kincaid had discovered a pocket of rich argentiferous galena there, which he called the Liberal, and Shaw and Ruth found other promising ledges. On June 14, 1873, they organized the Sylvania Mining District, and a short-lived little camp sprang up at Log Spring. Being rich in lead, the ore was easily smelted, and several blastless "basso" furnaces were built at the springs. A Columbus, Nevada physician, Dr. A. Marotte, and his brother Louis fired up the first furnace in June 1874, followed soon after by Kincaid. But these small, makeshift furnaces could hardly run for more than a day before they would either heat up and collapse or choke up and "freeze." Even when they were working, the melt from most of the ore was 98 percent lead. There was so little silver in the resulting bullion that it was worth only about $200 a ton. This wasn't as rich as the shipping ore from the Lida mines, and the bullion still had to be shipped all the way to San Francisco for refining. One by one these would-be bonanza kings realized it wouldn't pay, and moved on. But Scott Broder and Solomon Moffat, who fired up their furnace in January 1876, learned something from the misfortune of their predecessors. They worked only the lower lead ores from surface croppings of the Uncle Sam ledge, and succeeded in turning out bullion worth $500 to $600 a ton, which would pay enough to ship. They produced $11,000 worth of bullion before the exhaustion of the surface pocket and a drop in silver prices brought an end to the operation that summer, and the district was abandoned.[30]

By then Lida and Gold Mountain were also "distressingly quiescent," for the litigation over Page's estate was just beginning, and it would be three more years before that was resolved. Still, a handful of miners kept patiently at work, content with making a modest profit, as Tom Shaw had done. They took high-grade ore from rich pockets either to work in an arrastra of their own or to stockpile until they had enough that they could afford to lease the old Lida mill for a short run.[31]

Others made good wages working the placers down in Tule Canyon, which cuts its way into Death Valley just south of Lida. Placer gold had been discovered there in May 1869 by some forgotten Mexican prospector. Thereafter the ground was worked almost continuously until well past the turn of the century. There were at least two dozen miners there year-round. They were mostly Mexicans in the 1870s, Chinese in the 1880s, and a mix of Chinese, Shoshone, and Anglos in the 1890s. At the upper end of the canyon there was water enough for sluicing, but most of the miners worked the dirt dry in rockers and various other "dry washing" contraptions. Although much of the fine gold doubtless slipped through, they recovered nearly all the coarsest grains and nuggets—one of which weighed 5 pounds. The placer miners would take out over a million dollars worth of gold from Tule Canyon by the end of the century, just working the ground in a modest way, as Tom Shaw had first done at Gold Mountain.[32]

Long before that, Tom Shaw had moved on. He had bought a ranch with his savings in the mid-1870s, intending to settle down. But the excitement of the Bodie rush to the north soon drew him back to the mines, where he squandered his money on poker and then started all over again. Shaw finally found another remote but promising prospect way up near the Oregon line in the Disaster Peak country. He built another arrastra and worked the claims for several years, but all he got this time was pneumonia. He was found dead alone at his camp in September 1884.[33]

Panamint—The Wonder of the World

Just before the first snows fell high in the Panamint Range in the winter of 1872–73, Richard Jacobs and his partners discovered a great silver lode they called the Wonder of the World. For a time many believed it was just that—a giant bonanza so large and so rich that it could eclipse the Comstock. It would prove to be only a shallow pocket of rebellious ore, but few could see beyond those wonderful surface croppings—and who wanted to? It was a grand delusion, and it was, after all, a real wonder in its own way: thousands of people would come there; hundreds of thousands of dollars would be spent there; and tens of millions in stock would be offered there—on the very brink of Death Valley. That was the real "wonder of the world.[1]

The fabled Gunsight silver had remained a persistent lure, drawing prospectors to the Panamints to try their luck, long after the Coso excitement of the early sixties had been forgotten. William B. Rood, one of the Jayhawkers, had come back in the spring of 1869. He found a boulder in Emigrant Wash on which he scratched his name, but he didn't find the Gunsight silver nor the buried gold, although he hunted hard for both. The following winter a Los Angeles party led by Richard Fuller did find some rock in the Panamints that ran to $900 a ton. On the strength of such assays they sold the ledge to a San Diego insurance salesman, W. H. Creighton, who was certain it was the Gunsight, and so named it. No one else believed that, of course, so the search continued. Even the Reverend James Brier finally came back to Death Valley, lusting for the Gunsight silver, early in 1873. He led a small party to all of the scenes of his heroic ordeal, and they did find some silver in the Panamints, but nothing that measured up to what Brier recalled of the wonderful Gunsight ore.[2]

Among the most persistent seekers of silver in the Panamints, however, were Robert P. Stewart and William L. Kennedy. They had come to Coso in 1860, and to the Slate Range in 1862, and they had prospected the Panamints on and off for over a decade thereafter—whenever Stewart could talk Kennedy into leaving his store at Kernville, and, of course, supplying the grub. But for all their searching, they had little luck until they teamed up with Richard C. Jacobs in the fall of 1872. Jacobs, a gregarious, thickset forty-niner with sandy whiskers and blue eyes, had spent most of his life in the mines of California and Mexico and had a

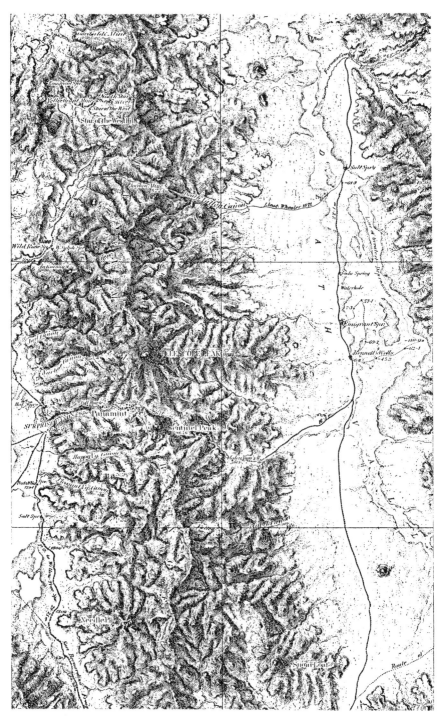

Panamint and Death Valley from Wheeler's map of 1875. (*Courtesy of Bancroft Library*)

keen sense for mineral. It was Jacobs who led the way up that deep gorge in the Panamints that they would soon call Surprise Canyon. He had spotted some rich float washed down the canyon and was determined to find its source. They had climbed for miles, almost to the crest of the range, when to their surprise the canyon widened out a bit into an idyllic little valley, and there, another thousand feet up on the precipitous, pinyon-dotted slopes, were the great quartz lodes they sought. But by then it was early December and the winter storms had gathered, so Jacobs and his partners barely had a chance to grab a few samples from the wonderful lodes before a heavy snow blanketed everything and drove them out.[3]

Returning to Kernville, they found that the rock assayed even better than expected, so late in January 1873 they hurried back to the Panamints with several months' grub to wait out the winter until they could return to Surprise Canyon to stake claim to their bonanza. It was a long and anxious wait, for when they left the Owens Valley road at the Little Lake stage station, they discovered they were being followed by a disreputable looking gang with wide-brimmed hats, and "enough guns to stock a hardware store." The expectant bonanza kings must have suddenly felt their fortune slipping away, because they feared that the gang intended to jump their claims as soon as they located them.[4]

They wouldn't have rested any easier if they had known more about the gang either. There were six in all, mostly young toughs in their late twenties: Henry Gibbons, the leader, Dan G. Tipton, James Dempsey, James Bruce, William M. Cannin, and Louis O. Hudon. They had fled to the Death Valley country from Pioche, a rough, raw camp in eastern Nevada that was known for good reason as the "wickedest place west of the Rocky Mountains." Hank Gibbons and his pals had felt quite at home in Pioche, at least until they had run short of cash. Then late in October 1872 they had held up the Hamilton to Pioche stage for Wells, Fargo and Company's treasure box, and had headed for the Panamints to hide out for a while. They must have been about ready to move on, and they may have come out to Little Lake station to look over the prospects for hitting the stage there before they left. But when they saw the three eager prospectors heading back to their wonderful bonanza, Gibbons and the boys decided to stick around a little longer.[5]

Jacobs, Stewart, and Kennedy made their winter camp at the south end of the Panamints rather than at the hot springs near the mouth of Surprise Canyon, most likely to try to throw their followers off the track. They also posted notices all along the foot of the range, calling for a meeting at their camp on February 10 to form a new mining district and adopt a set of laws. But apparently the three of them were the only ones who attended. Gibbons and his friends didn't seem to have much interest in the law. Undaunted, the three elected Kennedy chairman of the meeting, Jacobs secretary, and then formally organized the Panamint Mining District, with Stewart as recorder. With that they settled down for the winter, hoping they could outwait their rivals.[6]

But in April, when the snow had at last receded from the slopes and Jacobs and his partners headed back up Surprise Canyon, Hank Gibbons and his gang were close behind. Outnumbered two to one, Jacobs realized that their only hope was to show the toughs that there was enough rich ground for all. There may have been some tense moments, but the sight of those great silver quartz lodes that ribbed both walls of the canyon finally won the day. Without further ado, they scrambled up the slopes to stake their claims. On the north side of the canyon Jacobs located his Wonder of the World claim, on the west end of that lode; Stewart claimed Stewart's Wonder on the east end, and Gibbons took up the Challenge between the two, where the lode was cut by Wonder Gulch. Kennedy, Gibbons, and the rest of the gang then scaled the opposite side of the canyon to stake out the Wyoming, Hemlock, and other claims on some equally promising lodes that paralleled the Wonder of the World on the south. The Wyoming would in fact become Panamint's biggest producer.[7]

Just eighteen months later, a crowded, raucous town would be crammed into that once tranquil little valley at the head of Surprise Canyon. But the Panamint boom grew slowly at first. Word of the new finds drew prospectors up the canyon, and by the fall of 1873 a hundred claims and a townsite had been located, but only twenty men had taken up residence there. The ever-enterprising Jacobs had pushed steadily ahead in opening his claim, but he created no great excitement. He had sold a share in his Wonder of the World for a modest sum to James Palache, a San Francisco shipping agent, and to a couple of druggist friends. Together they incorporated the Panamint Mining Company on November 24, 1873, with a relatively conservative paper capital of $2 million. Jacobs, retaining one-sixth of the stock, became the superintendent. That winter he put a crew of about three dozen to work sinking exploratory shafts and grading a mill site. Nearly all the Panamint ore was too complex to yield much by simple milling, so Jacobs planned to crush the ore and concentrate it ten to one, so that it would run about $1,000 a ton. Then it could be shipped to San Francisco for reduction, and still pay a good return. In March 1874, he purchased an inexpensive but serviceable old mill at Soledad, over 100 miles to the south, tore it down, and started hauling it to Panamint that summer. By then there were over a hundred men in the camp, living on free meals served up by Jacobs's company in a large tent known as Hotel de Bum. Yet the camp had still not attracted even one saloon or a store of any kind. All that was about to change.[8]

Suddenly that summer the great Panamint rush began, sparked by the electrifying news that Nevada Senators John P. Jones and William M.

Stewart had bought the Panamint mines for a quarter of a million dollars or more! It was the biggest rush that Death Valley country would see for the rest of the century. Panamint! Panamint! Panamint! was the sound on every tongue, the gleam in every eye, as a couple of thousand hopeful and curious souls rushed up Surprise Canyon to see the new wonder of the world.

Eliphalet P. Rains was the man behind this Death Valley carnival, this Panamint pandemonium. Rains was a smooth-talking Southerner in his late forties who lived by his wits and usually managed to stay at least one step ahead of the law. He had plied his skills most recently in Pioche, and he may well have been the man who cased the Hamilton-Pioche stage job for Hank Gibbons and the boys. In the fall of 1873 he followed the gang to Panamint to become their agent in finding a buyer for their claims. He also secured an option on Stewart's Wonder. Armed with an alluring assortment of picture rock, Rains set forth in December on an odyssey that would take him to Los Angeles, San Francisco, and all the way to Washington, D.C. before he finally arranged a deal for the mines with Senator John P. Jones.[9]

Jones, Nevada's new silver champion and an extravagant spender, was the "hero of the hour" in Washington. A former Comstock mining superintendent turned instant millionaire in 1871, he had bought a seat in the Senate the following year, and still seemed to be having trouble finding enough ways to spend his money. Jones brought Nevada's senior senator, William M. Stewart, into the deal. Stewart, a lawyer who had made a more modest fortune in the early legal battles for the Comstock mines, had recently turned to supplementing his income by mining promotion abroad. With Stewart came his partner in the mining promotion, Trenor W. Park, a fellow lawyer who had first struck gold in the litigation over Fremont's Mariposa mines, and who had built on that by dealing in railroads and steamships.[10]

Jones, Stewart, and Park became equal partners in the Panamint deal, although Jones may have bankrolled Stewart. In June 1874, they sent Jones's brother Henry back to Panamint with Rains to look over the mines, and on the basis of his favorable report, Stewart and Park followed in August to close the deal. They apparently bought almost everything Rains had to offer: Stewart's Wonder and the Challenge, both on the Wonder of the World lode; and the Wyoming, Hemlock, and others to the south. They paid somewhere between $113,000 and $200,000 for these claims, and two months later they bought Jacobs's Wonder and his still uncompleted mill from the Panamint Mining Company for a comparable amount.[11]

The news that these claims had sold for over a quarter of a million dollars thrust Panamint into the headlines and started the big rush for the camp. Extraordinary as the selling price was, it was not the most important

Nevada Senators John P. Jones and William M. Stewart created
Death Valley's first big mining bubble at Panamint. (*Courtesy of
UCLA Library*)

part of the deal as far as Hank Gibbons and the boys were concerned.
They were still fugitives from the law; they didn't just want money, they
wanted the freedom to enjoy it, and they got it. At first, of course, they
denied any knowledge of the stage robbery, but when a Wells Fargo
detective found that one of them was wearing an engraved watch known
to have been in the treasure box, they grudgingly admitted some acquaintance with the affair, although muttering among themselves about anyone
fool enough to carry a stolen watch. Many years later Senator Stewart
claimed that he personally negotiated a secret deal between the robbers
and Wells Fargo, whereby some $12,000 to $20,000 of the purchase

money for the Panamint claims was paid directly to the express company to cover the loss of its treasure, probably with interest. In exchange, the company simply forgot that the robbery had ever occurred.[12]

The real secret of the Panamint deal, however, known only to Jones, Stewart, and Park, was how to make a profit from the mines. They had come in like greenhorns, buying almost everything in sight and paying outrageous prices. But they were shrewd mining men who must have expected an even more outrageous return.

A close look at the mines revealed that there wasn't that much showing in the ore pockets themselves. If Jones and his partners were to make a profit, it was clear they would have to work other pockets as well. To be sure, the Panamint lodes were heralded as a "California Comstock" that

Nature in her kindness had already opened to great depth to display its wondrous wealth. How could anyone doubt that, when the deep gulches, which cut the lodes as much as 600 feet below the highest croppings, showed rich rock at the very bottom? What one must not notice, of course, was that the rock at the bottom was rich float that had fallen in from above, and that the underlying quartz was barren. One had to dig a little to see that, but it didn't go unnoticed by the senators' methodical mining expert, Carl A. Stetefeldt. He was, of course, quite circumspect in his public report on the property. There he marveled at the massive surface croppings of silver, copper, and antimony sulphides that averaged nearly $100 a ton and ran as high as $919.57; deplored the "lack of judgement" that had pushed exploratory tunnels into barren ground; and expressed his overall confidence that the ore value would continue undiminished at depth.[13]

There was, in fact, roughly half a million dollars worth of ore exposed, and that was about all there was—but oh, how wonderfully exposed it was! What Jones and his partners had bought was a promoter's dream, and they knew how to work it. With these wonderful pockets of ore they hoped to draw much more from the pockets of investors. They would play every angle, but the one thing they didn't reckon on was that their own pasts would return to haunt them.

As soon as they got hold of the claims, they started incorporating each as a separate mining venture with a capital stock of $5 to $6 million. It's very likely that big parts of those startling purchase prices were also paid in such stock, but even then they must have put up nearly $100,000 in cash. In all they formed nine mining companies to offer the public an unconscionable $50 million in stock! For themselves they also formed the Surprise Valley Mill and Water Company, with capital of only $1 million, to mill all the ore for the mining companies—a clear imitation of the Comstock mill rings, which milked the mines and took all the cream. Under the Comstock plan they could skim off what profits there were by controlling the mining companies just long enough to elect the directors and sign favorable long-term contracts with their mills, assuring a profitable return for themselves. Then they could unload most of the stock in the mining companies and let the stockholders foot the bills for developing and operating the mines. Jones and another partner were running just such an operation on the Comstock—the Nevada Mill and Mining Company—but they didn't have a monopoly there.[14]

In Panamint the Surprise Valley Mill and Water Company was "the Company," dominating the mining companies and the camp alike. For a time, the Company's notes, in denominations of $1 to $500, were, in fact, the only currency. Henry A. Jones, the senator's brother, was named general superintendent, and Isaac G. Messic, an old gold-rush friend of the senator, was manager. They were also temporarily the superintendents of the various subsidiary mining companies. The Company began operation on a mammoth scale, with seemingly profligate expenditures. As soon as it was organized in September 1874, Henry Jones returned to Panamint and put roughly three hundred men, nearly half Chinese, to work opening the mines; building offices, boardinghouses, warehouses, and a company store; cutting pack trails up the steep slopes to the mines; and grading sites for the mill and ore concentrators. On the road behind him were over 1,500 tons of machinery, equipment, supplies, and provisions. Who could doubt that Panamint was there to stay?[15]

To help make a market for their mining stock and bring some immediate return on their investment, Jones, Stewart, and Park started shipping their best high-grade ore to England. This was a proven promotional device that Park and Stewart had used three years before in working a Utah mine, the Emma, on the English market. But it may have worked too well, for the eager British investors had paid so much for the Emma mine that it was unable to pay back more than a fraction of the cost, and they had started to cry foul. Nonetheless, in October 1874 the Company began stripping out the richest ore from the surface croppings for shipment to the smelters at Swansea, Wales. The shipping ore averaged $300 a ton, and despite the great distance it was shipped, it paid back over $200 of that in profit. Ironically, the most expensive part of the operation was hauling the ore some 200 miles to Los Angeles, which cost about $40 a ton—nearly twice what it cost to ship it the remaining 9,000 miles to England on the Pacific Mail Company's steamers. Park, who was also a director of the steamship company, arranged that rate. More than $150,000 worth of ore was shipped abroad, bringing further publicity to the mines and paying back most, if not all, of the cash spent in buying the mines.[16]

As soon as they started shipping ore, Senator Jones began making overtures to British acquaintances to help sell the mines in England. At least one, J. Barr Robertson, was willing to take the bait until he learned that those "objectionable" gentlemen, Stewart and Park, were behind the scheme; then it all seemed just too transparent. Some of the press also noticed "the shapes of the Emma and Mariposa speculators flitting about in connection with Panamint," and warned of "a new Emma looming up."[17]

Although it was Stewart and Park who were eyed with suspicion, Jones's reputation was equally unsavory. He had made his fortune by cheating the stockholders of a company that employed him in a position of trust. As superintendent of the Crown Point mine, Jones kept secret from directors and stockholders alike the discovery of a fabulously rich ore pocket until he and a partner, Alvinza Hayward, had quietly bought up a majority of the company's stock at bedrock prices of only a few dollars per share. After the discovery was revealed, the stock skyrocketed to $1,825 a share; the bonanza paid $11 million in dividends; and Jones's fortune was made. Comstock cynicism also made Jones something of a folk hero, since in addition to the stockholders, he had also deceived William Sharon's much-hated mill ring. Some of the stockholders, who for one reason or another had held onto their Crown Point stock, did of course make money along with Jones, which couldn't be said for any of the investors in the Emma. Still, potential Panamint investors might well have been just as wary of getting an honest deal from Jones as from Stewart and Park.[18]

Nonetheless, it was the lurking ghost of Emma that seems to have forced major changes in Jones, Stewart, and Park's scheme for promoting and unloading their Panamint stock. During the winter of 1874–75 they shifted their attention from British to American investors, and changed their mining operations from surface stripping of high-grade ore for shipping abroad to deeper mining of bulk ores for local milling. They also tried to show faith—or at least the appearance of faith—in the worth and permanence of the mines by increasing the capital investment to include not just a mill but a furnace, a tramway, and even a railroad. Finally, to make the whole deal seem like a bargain they consolidated most of their original companies into just two, so that investors could get four or more promising mines for the price of one, and they offered the first of these shares for only a fraction of par.

In December 1874, Jones, Stewart, and Park merged most of their companies to form the Wonder Consolidated and Wyoming Consolidated companies, which controlled 3 running miles of the richest lodes in Panamint. The $12 million in combined capital of the two companies was a bargain price compared to the $50 million in stock originally offered for the same mines. The following month, Jones and Park and some Los Angeles businessmen incorporated the Los Angeles and Independence Railroad to build a line from Santa Monica to the mouth of Surprise Canyon. Park predicted that their mines would ship 500 tons of ore a day, giving the railroad an annual income of $1 million, and giving their mines an income of over $50 million a year! Jones estimated twice that.[19]

Amid this heady talk, the Wonder Con and Wyoming Con stocks were placed on the San Francisco Stock & Exchange Board, and the papers were flooded with ads for a special limited offer of the stock at a discount price of only $15 for a $100 par share on the first 20,000 shares sold. Who could resist? In the flush of excitement the specter of Emma was temporarily forgotten. Half of the shares offered were taken within three days, and the rest were gone within two weeks. Even the miners at Panamint were said to have bought 3,000 shares, with one half down and the remainder in payroll deductions. How much additional stock they sold is unknown, but it was reported that one unfortunate investor, who got in too late for the initial offer, offered $20 a share for 500 shares, but was granted only 100. These sales, amounting to over $300,000, gave the Company ready cash for further developments, on which they expected even greater returns. The ads for the Wonder and Wyoming Con stock had promised that the money from the sale would go solely to "building mills, roads, etc., to make the property available." What they hadn't said was that these mills would belong to the Surprise Valley Mill and Water Company, not to the mining companies![20]

During the next six months the Company spent some $350,000 in Panamint. They built a reservoir, and laid nearly a mile of pipe to supply it; completed several miles of road and trail to the mines; built an aerial tramway up to the Wyoming mine a thousand feet above the floor of Surprise Valley; and finally finished Jacobs's five-stamp mill. But most of this money went into the construction of the Company's wonderful new twenty-stamp mill, which had four Hendy concentrators and a Stetefeldt furnace. With this they could reduce even their most rebellious ores right there in Panamint. It was a magnificent structure, built of half a million bricks at a cost of $210,000. It surpassed even Calderwood's extravaganza at Palmetto. It was an inspirational monument that instilled an overwhelming faith in the wealth of Panamint everlasting. It was the closest thing to a church Panamint ever had.[21]

By that winter of 1874–75, Panamint had become the biggest town for more than 100 miles around. It had grown within a season from a struggling camp of a hundred to a boisterous boomtown of two thousand. Men had come on foot, by mule, and on horseback, in creaking wagons and in fancy buggies, but they had all come with hope. A few came with money, hoping to buy themselves a bonanza. Others had wagonloads of goods they hoped to sell. Some even brought their families, hoping to settle down for a while. But most came with no more than they could pack into their saddlebags—and holsters—hoping to find a good ledge, a little work, or at least some action. Many came with nothing but hope, without a blanket or even a cent to their name, hoping against hope. The entrepreneurs bought 25- by 100-foot lots on Main Street for $100 to $350—a few paid as much as $1,000 for a choice spot—and hauled in lumber at 35¢ a board foot to build some two hundred stores and houses. But back of Main Street the bulk of Panamint's citizens were squatters, holding title only "by virtue of a good shotgun." They camped in open tents or under the stars until the first snow. Then they scrambled to throw together bark shanties or scrape out rock-and-canvas dugouts. If they felt flush they could dine on oysters and imported wine at Galeron Hypolite's French Restaurant and Saloon, or for a dollar they could get a square meal at the San Francisco Chop House or one of the other, more mundane eateries. But most made do with coffee, beans, and salt pork—and an occasional free lunch in the saloons.[22]

To the casual visitor it might have seemed that it was the saloons, not the mines, that made Panamint. The saloons were certainly busier than most of the mines, and they were also more profitable. Almost every other business in Panamint was a saloon: there were over two dozen scattered for three quarters of a mile down Main Street, all the way to Louis Munzinger's brewery at the lower end of town. Dave Neagle, a young Nevada tough, advertised his Oriental as the "Palace Saloon of Panamint," but his rivals boasted equally elegant crystal chandeliers, beveled mirrors, and gilded satin wallpaper. Most of Hank Gibbons's gang—Dempsey, Tipton, Cannin, and Hudon—with their newly bought respectability, also went into the liquor business. Next to drinking, poker was the favorite pastime at the tables, with pots sometimes running into the thousands. In one highly publicized game, a $10,000 pot was taken by two pairs—sixes and aces. Others found their sport back of Main Street in the cribs of Martha Camp's girls in Little Chief Canyon.[23]

Panamint was not lacking in more respectable enterprises, however. Three stage lines provided almost daily service. Buckley's stages ran three times a week to Bakersfield, connecting with the Southern Pacific trains to San Francisco; Dodge's ran twice a week to Lone Pine; and Hughes's had a weekly stage to Los Angeles. There was daily mail service from Lone Pine, as well as Jones and Stewart's "Panamint Poney Express" to Los Angeles. Panamint's lucrative freighting business sparked heavy competition between Meyerstein's Panamint Transportation Company and Remi Nadeau's Cerro Gordo Freighting Company. Panamint boasted two banks, three doctors, four lawyers, several large general stores, and a variety of specialty shops: butcher shops and barbershops, bakeries, booteries, and apothecaries, assayers and jewelers—even Mrs. Zobelein's hat and ribbon boutique. But most important, Panamint had a newspaper—the Death Valley country's first. Thomas Spencer Harris, an itinerant printer and dancing teacher, started the triweekly *Panamint News* on Thanksgiving Day, November 26, 1874. It began as a bantam sheet—barely 5 by 9 inches of printing to a page—scorned by some as a mere "nose rag." But it grew with the camp, and Harris made it a feisty champion of the camp's interests, campaigning for a local hospital, a fire company, a telegraph, and even a new county of Panamint.[24]

Yet the most urban thing about Panamint was probably its homicide rate, which earned it the reputation of being a "new fighters' paradise."

Five men were murdered in Panamint within five months—a per capita homicide rate that rivaled such notorious camps as Pioche and exceeded the worst of today's cities. William Masterson, Francisco Gonzales, Phillip DeRouche, Edward Barstow, and Robert McKinney were the unfortunate victims. The last two were killed by James Bruce, apparently not yet fully reformed, even though editor Harris praised him as "one of our most charitable and public spirited citizens." Bruce shot Barstow, who had come gunning for him, in Martha Camp's bedroom; he shot McKinney when an argument over a gun ended in a wild shoot-out in front of the Bank of Panamint. Not one of the murderers was tried; Panamint's justice of the peace, William Cassius Smith, a popular young notary public, dismissed them all on grounds of self-defense.[25]

Most of those who came to Panamint found that its mineral deposits were already thoroughly picked over by the time they arrived. More than six hundred claims had been located by the end of 1874, covering a combined area of 20 square miles! That included every bit of ground that showed the least bit of promise, and a lot more that didn't. So those who still hoped to stake claims of their own had to seek new lodes elsewhere along the range, or reopen old ones.[26]

Among the late arrivals was Dr. Samuel George of Visalia, who had done the first real mining in the Panamints at Wildrose over a decade before. When Dr. George came back to see the new Panamint mines in 1874, he found to his chagrin that he had just missed discovering them himself years before. In January 1861 his Indian guide, later known as George Hansen, had led him up Surprise Canyon. But Dr. George, becoming suspicious of the guide, had turned back just short of finding the great lodes. Now there wasn't a piece of quartz unclaimed within miles of Surprise Canyon. So George returned home and dusted off the ledger books of the old Combination Gold and Silver Mining Company. In December 1874 he started levying a couple of 10-cents-a-share assessments on the stock to reopen the Christmas Gift for one more try at finding pay rock. He and his partners probed the lode again for over a year, but all they ever found was more antimony.[27]

Other prospectors also drifted north to Wildrose, and organized the Rose Spring Mining District. By the summer of 1875 they had staked out more than 150 claims. The most successful were two young Italian immigrants, Joseph and Jasper Nossano. They discovered some rich pockets of free-milling silver ore—the Garibaldi, North Star, and Maria—high on the Death Valley side of Tucki Mountain. The Maria showed masses of native silver, and some were certain that this was, in fact, the long-lost Gunsight. It was a likely candidate, since Jim Martin's Georgians had crossed Tucki Mountain somewhere around there in their exodus from Death Valley a quarter of a century before. Even if this claim wasn't the Lost Gunsight, with all of the claims staked on Tucki Mountain that season, it seems inevitable that one of them must have been the source of that wonderful ore. By then, of course, no real ore pocket could come close to fulfilling the expectations of most Lost Gunsight seekers.[28]

Whether or not the Nossano brothers had found the Lost Gunsight, they did a lot better than anyone else at Wildrose, for they succeeded in selling their claims for $70,000, at least $30,000 of which was in cash. William H. Lent, a shrewd stock operator affectionately known as Uncle William, bought the claims in February 1876, and immediately incorporated them as the Garibaldi and Inyo mining companies, with a combined stock issue of $20 million. Lent worked the ore pockets with a flourish, and talked grandly of building a mill and of piping water all the way across Death Valley from Furnace Creek. In the meantime he tried to work the stock in San Francisco, but apparently met with little success, for he abandoned the mines that summer to move on to bigger game in the new Bodie boom.[29]

Charcoal, however, not silver, proved to be Wildrose's biggest product. In May 1875 Jerome Childs discovered a bonanza of smelting ore in the Lookout district, just across Panamint Valley to the west of Wildrose. Three months later the claims were bought by George Hearst and organized into the Modock Consolidated Mining Company. Hearst, a practical mining man who had gotten into the Comstock early and made his first fortune opening the famous Ophir, was more an investor than a speculator, seeking good mines to buy for long-term development—his Homestake mine in the Black Hills has now been worked for more than a century. Under Hearst's direction the Modock company erected two furnaces, which started up in October 1876, producing about 10 tons a day of silver-lead bullion that ran $500 a ton. But the furnaces also consumed 3,000 bushels a day of charcoal. By the end of the year they had nearly exhausted the scant timber in the district, and Hearst turned to the pinyon stands of the Panamint Range. There in the spring of 1877, under the direction of S. B. Morrison, the Modock company built the ten great charcoal kilns that still stand near the head of Wildrose Canyon. They were modeled after a couple of smaller beehive kilns built near Owens Lake for the Cerro Gordo mines. The Wildrose kilns stand about 25 feet high, measure 30 feet in diameter, and held 42 cords of pinyon, which burned for a week to yield about 2,000 bushels of charcoal. James Honan, a former Panamint saloon keeper, contracted to supply wood for the kilns and kept a crew of forty or more cutting pinyon for a mile or two around. Remi Nadeau's Cerro Gordo Freighting Company hauled the charcoal to the furnaces. Most of the charcoal was produced in the spring and summer of 1877, while the Modock furnaces turned out

Panamint News.

VOL. I.   PANAMINT, CAL., NOVEMBER 26, 1874.   NO. 1.

PANAMINT NEWS.

PUBLISHED TRI-WEEKLY BY THE

Panamint Publishing Company,

AT PANAMINT, INYO COUNTY, CAL.

T. S. HARRIS, MANAGER.

SUBSCRIPTION RATES :

One Copy one week, by Carrier, - - 50 cents
One Copy one month, by Carrier, - - - $2 00
One Copy one month, by Mail, - - - 1 50

ADVERTISING RATES :

Business Cards, four lines, one month, - - $4 00
"   four lines, three months, - 10 00
Special Notices, four lines, one time, - - 2 50
Each additional line, - - - - - 75 cents

☞ No Bills will be honored unless purchased by or on the written order of T. S. HARRIS, Manager.

☞ Subscriptions and Advertising invariably in advance.

Business Cards.

Inyo Items.

We find the following items in the Inyo Independent of the 14th instant. Independence is referred to as a "Deserted Village" as follows :

That's the name of our town about these times. A few remain here ; some because they are attached to the place much as a rat is to a steel-trap when he can't get away, others because they like a quiet decent time, the remainder because they think this is going to be the best place of all of them after awhile. The main cause may be summed up in one word—Panamint.

The Nevada papers may do some of their readers a favor by announcing the fact that passengers from that section, bound for Panamint, can count on good, comfortable stages all the way through from Carson via Aurora, Benton, Independence, Lone Pine to Panamint. From Lone Pine they have the chance of two routes, twice a week by stage via Coso, or three times a week via Indian Wells.

We are pleased to know that a mail contract has been let to Wm. Buckley, of the Bakersfield and Lone Pine stage line, to connect Panamint with this line at Indian Wells. It is to be tri-weekly, and make close connection with the Lone Pine and Bakersfield stages at the Wells.

There are now no less than six stations being put up on the Coso-Panamint or new road, and the longest stretch is only thirteen miles.

A number of heavy teams are loading at, or on the road from Bishop Creek, with flour, grain, etc., for Panamint.

The Great Race.

The result of the great four-mile and repeat race in San Francisco is thus briefly stated in the S. F. Bulletin of the 19th instant :

Two heats decided the contest. In a field of eight, with seven starters, the Eastern four-year-old, "Katie Pease," was a waiting and easy winner. The time made was not extraordinary—7:13½ and 7:36¼. Her dangerous competitors, "Joe Daniels" and "Thad Stevens," failed to meet the expectations of their backers. "Stevens" was nowhere in the contest, and comes out of the race with a crippled off fore leg. "Daniels on the last half of the mile of the second heat, utterly broke down and quit. His injuries—which are strains of sinews in a fore leg—are such that it is doubtful if he will ever be fit to again appear on the turf. It is also doubtful if "Stevens" will ever again secure backers should he be entered for a race. Of those selling in the field, "Henry" made the best performance, coming in second on the last heat. In the first heat "Hardwood" took the place of "Thad Stevens," after the latter was pumped out, and tried to save the day, unsuccessfully, but with an amount of determination and speed not looked for in the animal. "Hockhocking," although trailer to "Thad Stevens" in the first heat, made no place in that heat, and "Alpha" was so completely blown at the finish that she was drawn, and did not start in the second heat. Although the attendance was immense, and the start showed the most brilliant array of horses ever started in California, yet the race lacked that interest which it would have possessed had the favorite not so overmatched her competitors. But for "Daniels'" break-down he might, possibly, have won the second heat, and thus given those who bet on the sorrel mare an opportunity to hedge out. That is, had it been in the programme. But as it was the ancient comparison of the jug-handle painfully suggests itself. "Katie Pease" won easily, and in little better than a gallop, never coming to the front until on the last half mile of each heat. "Stevens'" defeat was utterly humiliating. Never was a horse, of any pretensions, so ignominiously beaten.

AT the sale of the Lick property in San Francisco, on the 17th instant, the sum of $1,959,925 was realized, and the Los Angeles ranch and Santa Catalina Island were withheld from sale. The Lick House block was bid off at $920,000, but the trustees refuse to confirm the sale. It will be again offered at auction, when it is expected over a million dollars will be obtained for it.

The Garibaldi mine at Wildrose was only one of the grossly inflated stocks of the Panamint boom.

$630,000 in bullion. During that time Wildrose boasted a population of nearly a hundred. Honan put up a boardinghouse; M. Scheeline opened a store; Ed Hall, for whom Hall Canyon was later named, started a blacksmith shop; and Morrison, who remained to run the kilns, even moved his wife and children up there. But the coal camp began to decline that fall, when the Modock ore turned rebellious, and the company shut down the furnaces and the kilns in the summer of 1878. Several years later new ore bodies were opened in the Modock, but the charcoal kilns at Wildrose were apparently never fired up again.[30]

During the Panamint boom, Wildrose was also the hangout of a pair of incompetent stage robbers—John Small, a short, red-faced blowhard, and his taller, quiet partner, J. McDonald. They came to the Panamints in August 1874 after a spate of abortive holdups of the Austin and Eureka stages. They had consistently picked the coaches with empty treasure boxes, and got only $18 cash out of three robberies. But they made such nuisances of themselves that Wells, Fargo and Company posted a reward of $500 each for their capture, and thereby drove them out of Nevada. In the Panamint Range they found refuge among kindred spirits and such casual law enforcement that they could walk into the express office and tear their wanted poster off the wall without fear of arrest, or even protest. They camped just out of Wildrose Spring, and busied themselves posting location notices, apparently more for past and future alibis than for any actual mineral discovery. Then, early in December 1874, they quietly revisited Eureka to try once more to pull off a successful holdup. Wells Fargo detective James Hume got wind of the impending robbery and put a guard, Jim Miller, on the coach. Small and McDonald stopped the stage 8 miles out of Eureka. When they started to open the box, Miller drew a shotgun on them, and after exchanging a few shots, the bumbling bandits fled for Wildrose, leaving the unopened treasure box behind. Although they had failed again, Wells Fargo raised the price on their heads to $2,000 apiece. This finally brought letters from some of Panamint's more enterprising citizens, revealing the fugitives' whereabouts, and in May 1875 the Eureka sheriff came to Panamint to get them. But when he confronted Small and McDonald, they produced location notices to show that they were at Wildrose on the dates of the robberies, and Dave Neagle and a few of Panamint's other solid citizens swore to their claims. The sheriff left in disgust, and Small and McDonald returned to their Wildrose "mines," at least for a while.[31]

Two other new districts were formed in the Panamint Range during the boom. Northeast of Wildrose, William L. Hunter and John L. Porter discovered two enormous copper ledges, the Piute and Cohee, and on July 8, 1875, they organized the Ubehebe Mining District. That euphonious name, said by the discoverers to have been that of an "Indian princess," still survives on the neighboring peak and on the volcanic crater farther north. However, the joy of the discoverers soon vanished when they began to study the economics of copper mining. Although some of the ore was seductively rich in copper, averaging about 24 percent by weight, it couldn't be made to pay a profit: with copper at 20¢ a pound, the ore was worth barely $100 a ton, which wouldn't pay to ship, and with wood and water so scarce, it wouldn't pay to smelt it locally either. Then at the far south end of the range, Panamint shoemaker Eliphalet Harris and a couple of companions stumbled upon some nice-looking ore not far from where Bennett and Alvord had made their first strikes in 1860. The new discoverers formed the Silver Spring Mining District on February 20, 1875, but it died again when the assays didn't live up to expectations.[32]

In the meantime other prospectors had stopped short of Panamint in the old Coso district to the west. There, late in October 1874, Raphael Cuervo, "Professor" William D. Brown, and his brother Robert had found massive deposits of easily smelted silver-lead ore that assayed as much as $700 a ton. Within six weeks of their discovery there were a hundred and fifty men in the new camp of Darwin, and an exodus from Panamint began as most of the floating population started drifting back down Surprise Canyon.[33]

By the spring of 1875 the first flush of the Panamint boom was past, and the camp had settled back to a population of around six hundred, nearly half of whom worked for the Company and its subsidiary mines. The myriad rainbow-chasers had moved on. Mining stock sales were also lagging as the more cautious investors waited for a little more development before risking their money. But Panamint was still full of promise, as the Company pushed steadily forward and other new ventures were launched. Richard Jacobs had joined with J. S. Niswander and several other San Francisco investors in organizing the Sunrise Silver Mining Company to work the district's only pocket of free milling ore, the Sunrise mine at the head of Surprise Canyon. They brought in a new five-stamp mill, which started up later that summer and produced as much as $900 a day in bullion. But scarcity of both water and high-grade ore made its operation intermittent. Several other independent companies were also opening mines and talking of mills. One optimistic bunch of speculators, led by San Francisco haberdasher William Sherman, organized the Panamint Mining and Concentration Works, which staked out 800 acres of sagebrush down in Panamint Valley, at the imagined railhead of the Los Angeles and Independence Railroad. They subdivided the sagebrush as Shermantown, to sell both town lots and company stock in the future milling center of the Panamints. Former Virginia City Mayor Rufus Arick joined in the speculation, seeking a franchise for an aerial tramway line all the way down Surprise Canyon to carry ore to those promised trains and mills.[34]

It was the solid developments of the Surprise Valley Mill and Water Company that carried the camp, however, and made it look better and better with each passing day. The Company's great stamp mill was completed late in June; the tramway to the Wyoming mine was finished; and the furnace was fired up at the end of July. Tests by Stetefeldt showed that the mill recovered up to 96 percent of the value of the most rebellious ore on hand and produced bullion that was 98 percent pure silver. The success of the mill, the Company boasted, "puts the blush on all Panamint croakers and its enemies generally." The mill began steady operation on August 27. Running around the clock, it worked about 15 tons a day of $90-a-ton rock, turning out bullion at a rate of $1,300 a day, $40,000 a month, or $500,000 a year.[35]

All of that wonderful bullion created a serious new problem. Wells Fargo, wanting nothing more to do with that den of thieves, had refused to open an express office at Panamint, thus leaving Jones, Stewart, and Park to ship their bullion at their own risk. The Gibbons gang, of course, had squared accounts with Wells Fargo and had even promised safe passage to the bullion. But Stewart feared that with all that silver around, they just might be tempted back to their old ways. Even if they weren't, there were others congregated in the hills, like Small and McDonald, who hadn't made any such promises—and weren't about to, either. At last Stewart hit upon a solution that was as simple as it was effective: cast the silver into ingots so heavy and so unmanageable that no thief could possibly get away with one. In that way the Company eventually shipped over one third of a million dollars in fine silver bullion down Surprise Canyon as ordinary freight, without so much as a single guard. Even Small and McDonald could figure out which wagons the treasure was on, but they couldn't do a thing about it. Stewart took seemingly endless delight in recounting how he outsmarted the would-be thieves and how they cursed him for it. With the telling and retelling, the bullion bars grew in his mind to 750-pound silver cannonballs! But the records show that 400-pound cubes, each nearly a foot on a side and worth about $6,200, were the effective deterrent to thievery.[36]

By the beginning of 1876, Jones, Stewart, and Park had developed their Panamint property into a very solid and prosperous-looking operation with steadily producing mines and a highly efficient mill. And they must have been ready to make a final push to unload the rest of their mining stock, when suddenly the ghost of Emma returned to haunt them once again. Until then the scandal had been confined pretty much to the British courts and the British press, but in February 1876 the U.S.

Congress began an investigation into the involvement of the American ambassador to England, Robert C. Schenk, who had aided Stewart and Park in the scheme. The House Committee on Foreign Affairs opened hearings in Washington in March, and soon the whole "dark and devious" deal was exposed to public scrutiny and condemnation. Although it was only a congressional hearing, not a trial, Park and Stewart, by then retired from the Senate, were repeatedly called to answer allegations of unethical, deceptive, and downright fraudulent practices. The two consistently denied any wrongdoing, but the committee chairman denounced their dealings as a "little short of robbery." The inquiry into the "Emma Mine Swindle" made pithy news from coast to coast, and by the close of the hearings in May it is doubtful that there was an investor left in the country who could have been persuaded to put money into any scheme of Stewart and Park's.[37]

Thus any hope of unloading the rest of the Panamint stock was shattered, and by then the surface pockets were nearly exhausted, so Jones, Stewart, and Park ended the charade. The hearings closed on May 4, and two days later, after months of encouraging reports from the mines, word suddenly came from the Company that the "outlook is not so bright"—the ore in the Wyoming and the Hemlock had pinched out. The mill shut down, and the last bullion was shipped ten days later. The deal had collapsed, and Panamint was all but dead.[38]

It would have been fitting, considering its spectacular rise, if Panamint had come to an equally dramatic end. Popular lore indeed has it that a cloudburst swept the whole town down the canyon in one grand catharsis on July 24, 1876. But fickle Nature was not so obliging. The storms that wrought havoc elsewhere in the Great Basin that day hardly touched the failing camp, so Panamint was left to end not with a bang, but with a whimper.[39]

Well before the Company shut down, most of Panamint's businesses had closed. Editor Harris had cut the *News* back to a weekly, then finally suspended it and moved to Darwin. The Bank of Panamint and the Panamint Brewery had closed their doors. The stagecoaches had begun to come only weekly and then not at all. One by one the saloon keepers had packed up their stock and headed down the canyon; Martha Camp followed with her girls. The Gibbons gang had dispersed. Eliphalet Raines, adding the "e" to his name for class, had gone to San Francisco and declared himself a stockbroker, but in the fall of 1876 he was arrested in a goldbrick scam. Even Small and McDonald had moved on. At last getting their act together, they had stopped on their way out at Harris and Rhine's combination store and bank in Panamint one morning in

April 1876, tied up the clerks and a few customers, and robbed the safe of over $2,000.[40]

Still, the camp lingered on for a time after the big mill closed. Company Superintendent Isaac Messic kept a couple of dozen men at work, sinking shafts on the Wyoming and Hemlock lodes to be sure there wasn't a real bonanza lurking below. By the end of 1877, however, after sinking over 700 feet through "perfectly barren" rock, the Company finally quit. In the meantime, Stewart and Park had turned their full attention to the continuing Emma litigation, and Jones had returned to the Senate, where he would stay for a near-record thirty years.[41]

Although the Panamint mines had proved to be the most productive that the Death Valley country had yet seen, producing roughly half a million dollars in precious metal, the Panamint deal was an undeniable failure, especially of expectations. Who lost how much is less certain. Whenever it served their purposes, Jones, Stewart, and Park claimed large losses. During the promotional boom they talked of spending $1 to $2 million to purchase and develop the Panamint mines—talk aimed at supporting the asking price of the stock they were pushing. After the failure of the deal, they publicly claimed losses of a million dollars or more, blunting possible suits by destitute stockholders. Park even had the chutzpah to cite his Panamint losses in later Emma litigation, apparently to show what a risky business mining was and to counter claims by British investors that they had suffered unusual losses. And thirty years later, with uncharacteristic candor, Stewart conceded that the operation had cost about a million dollars, and maintained if they could have continued a few months longer they would have at least gotten back all of their expenditure "without loss."

No balance sheet was ever published, of course, but their obvious cash expenditures did total close to $800,000, including at least $100,000 for the purchase of the mines, about $290,000 for development and operation of the mines, and $385,000 for construction of the mill, tramway, roads, buildings, and other improvements. Their known returns totaled almost the same—about $150,000 from shipping ore, $340,000 from bullion, and over $300,000 from stock sales. In view of the uncertainties, it's quite possible that Stewart was correct in his recollection that only a few more months' work, with the mines paying about $40,000 a month, were required to balance the books, and that he, Jones, and Park actually lost only about $100,000 among them. Later operations showed that there was just about that much left exposed in high-grade ore, so the trio must have decided to leave it as window dressing to draw some future purchaser. But even if they had broken even, it was the loss of all those expected millions that smarted, and caused Jones, Stewart, and Park to truly curse the whole deal. But all those aspiring Panamint investors might well have given a prayer of thanks, because those expected millions would surely have come from their own pockets, not from the mines. Those who had already bought stock proved that, for they were the only certain losers, being out at least $300,000. Such was the wonder of the world.[42]

The Education of Jonas Osborne

Like many who had come to the desert before him, Jonas Osborne had to learn the hard way that without wood and water the seeming richness of ore he saw near Resting Spring was just another of the desert's mirages. Unlike most, Osborne was not easily discouraged. He doggedly pursued every avenue trying to reach the unreachable, and in so doing he again laid bare the hard lessons of desert mining. Once he had learned those lessons, Osborne wasn't reluctant to cash in on them and fill his own pockets at the expense of those less wise. Still, he had faith that the Resting Spring ore could someday be made to pay, so he held the ground for three decades, until he finally found the answer that only time and change could bring.

Many, of course, had preceded Osborne into the Amargosa country east of Death Valley. A few Breyfoglers were found there every season, and in the winter of 1867–68 exciting rumors reached the outside settlements that Breyfogle's gold had actually been found. Somewhere around the Amargosa a party of Mexicans from Owens Valley were said to have discovered placers that paid as much as $100 to the pan. Rumor had it that they had taken out $11,000 worth of dust and nuggets before hostile Indians drove them out. Armed expeditions set out from surrounding towns all the way from Lone Pine to Austin, but none ever found the wonderful ground again.[1]

More tangible discoveries were made a year later farther to the southeast, just beyond the Amargosa. Early in the spring of 1869 Johnny Moss—a buckskin-fringed prospector with a powerful gift of gab and a keen eye for minerals, which earned him the title of the "mining Kit Carson of the Coast"—brought a mule load of trinkets to the Paiute *pakwinavi* Tecopa and secured a treaty opening the country to prospectors. Leading an expedition from Visalia, Moss searched for several months until they found some rich copper and silver ledges on what is now Clark Mountain. They formed the Clarke Mining District in July, naming it for one of their party, Visalia saloonkeeper William H. Clarke. The mountain took its name from the district, but eventually lost the "e." A rush to the new mines began in the fall of 1869, more wagons rolled across the Walker cutoff and by the end of the year there were nearly a hundred men in the camp of Ivanpah on the northeastern slope of Clark Mountain. The mines flourished for over a decade, producing roughly $3,000,000 in silver and inspiring prospectors to comb the hills for many miles around—even back over into the Amargosa country.[2]

Latecomers to Ivanpah reopened the old Salt Spring mine in the latter half of 1870, but still couldn't make it pay. Then in November 1871, Johnny Moss and Sam Strong discovered more copper and silver leads in the mountains southwest of Salt Spring, where they organized the Ava Watts Mining District. The mines there, though worked for a few years, never amounted to much. The name, however, evolved through Eva Watts and Ivawatz to the present Avawatz, and fastened itself onto the mountains before the excitement fizzled out. Strong later moved across the tip of Death Valley to Saratoga Springs to prospect the scattered hills to the north, but he met with no better luck there.[3]

Farther north, three more hapless prospectors from San Bernardino—August J. Franklin, Eugene Lander, and a man named Hanson—discovered rich-looking ore high up in the Funeral Mountains near Daylight Pass. While killing a rattlesnake, Franklin spotted the promising float, and the next morning, August 14, 1871, he and Hanson followed it up to its source on the crest of the range. It was a great quartz belt, laced with what they thought was silver chloride, so they named it the Chloride Cliff. Crude assays made in San Bernardino suggested that the rock contained anywhere from $200 to $1,000 per ton in silver, so their friends eagerly bought into the claim—among them Manly's and Bennett's old partner, William M. Stockton. Styling themselves the Chloride Cliff Mining Company, they worked the ledge until the fall of 1873, sinking a shaft 150 feet and taking out 100 tons of "ore" before they found that what they had thought was silver chloride was really only lead chloride, averaging less than $28 per ton. The company disbanded in disgust, but Franklin couldn't believe that the mine wouldn't someday pay. He returned each year until his death in 1904 to do the necessary work required to hold the claim, and his son George took up where he left off. Even though the mine never did pay, their faith was eventually rewarded when George finally sold it to a stock promoter for $110,000. Ironically, in all those years they never noticed a real bonanza just a mile away—the Keane Wonder, which was to produce over $1 million in gold.[4]

Although Lander quit the Chloride Cliff, he too still believed that there were riches to be found in the surrounding hills, so he continued to prospect the upper Amargosa for nearly a decade. In November 1879 he found the Blue Monster, an immense ledge of argentiferous "black metal" on Bare Mountain, some 15 miles northeast of Chloride Cliff, in what he called the Bromide Mining District. Assays were said to run as high as $25,000 a ton, and it was rumored once more that the long-lost Gunsight had at last been found. Once again William Stockton and others eagerly joined in forming a new company. They eventually opened several shafts on the ledge, built a couple of arrastras, and even constructed a little furnace on the banks of the Amargosa. By 1886, however, most of the company had concluded that the ore was just too rebellious and too pockety to pay. Like Franklin, Lander and his partners had also missed some real bonanzas just across the Amargosa in what would be known as the Bullfrog district, which was destined to produce over $2 million in gold.[5]

It was a rich strike of silver-lead ore in the Resting Spring Mining District, however, that brought Jonas Osborne to the Amargosa country. Having found good smelting ore at Darwin, west of Death Valley, in the fall of 1874, and having faith in the natural balance of things, the systematic "Professor" William D. Brown and his brother Robert D. headed for the Amargosa country east of Death Valley in the spring of 1875 to look for more ore. They found what they were looking for in the hills just south of Resting Spring on the old Spanish Trail. It was an "immense body of splendid ore," which they naturally named the Balance. It ran more than $60 a ton in silver, plus a large percentage of lead, and they promptly sold an interest to George Hearst, who had missed a chance at their Darwin discoveries. Together they formed the Balance Consolidated Gold and Silver Mining Company, which began work that fall. In anticipation of the rush that followed, the enterprising Brown brothers laid out a townsite—modestly christened Brownsville—on Willow Creek, 6 miles southeast of Resting Spring. They also started a potato and vegetable ranch and a fruit orchard at Resting Spring, and set up a sawmill 35 miles to the east, up among the yellow pines on Spring Mountain. For good measure they even opened up a subsidiary mining district called Brown's Treasure about 20 miles north, near what is now known, coincidentally, as Brown Peak, named for a later resident, Charles G. Brown.[6]

Jonas Osborne was one of the first to come into the Resting Spring district. In his mid-forties, he was the superintendent of a British mining company at Eureka, Nevada, but he was looking for new ground, and he found it at Resting Spring in the winter of 1875–76. The ore there was rich by Eureka standards, so he promptly bought an interest in several of the Brown brothers' claims and moved to the new camp. Some selected ore, running over $600 a ton, was rich enough to ship—and it even attracted a few ore thieves or high-graders, who had to be shipped out as well. But the great bulk of the ore needed smelting, so Osborne built a small furnace and began experimenting with ways to work it.[7]

By the beginning of 1877, Osborne was convinced he had found a way to profitably work the bulk ores, but he needed additional capital to build a large smelting furnace. George Hearst, however, had lost faith in the mines and was unwilling to take the gamble, so Osborne began looking

George Hearst

George Hearst soon lost faith in the Tecopa silver leads, but
they eventually became Death Valley and Amargosa's
biggest metal producer. (*Courtesy of UCLA Library*)

for new investors. He found them in Los Angeles in banker Jonathan S.
Slauson, James F. Ward, and other adventurous businessmen. With
Osborne, they formed the Los Angeles Mining and Smelting Company
in May 1877, with a paper capital of $960,000, and bought up the
principal mines in the district. Operating as middleman in the deal,
Osborne purchased the Balance Company's mines for $10,000; he also
bought the Noonday and four other mines from the Brown brothers for

$500. He sold them all to the new company for $42,000, in exchange for which he took exactly half of the stock and became superintendent. The company also paid $9,000 to a group of miners for several other claims, including one called the Gunsight. This and the Noonday proved to be the most productive mines in the district.[8]

Even before these deals were completed, the rumor of the consolidation of the mines had triggered a new rush to Resting Spring. There were some four hundred men there by the spring of 1877. Osborne, who had purchased the Brownsville townsite for $100 and renamed it Tecopa for the local *pakwinavi*, was happily selling town lots for $50 to $75 each. By the time his big smelting furnace was completed in January 1878, some two hundred hopefuls had settled in the bustling camp. Tecopa boasted a daily pony mail from San Bernardino and a semimonthly stage, three "gin mills," a like number of merchandising houses, a boarding-house, a livery stable, and an assortment of miners' adobes, shanties, and tents. The prospect of collecting taxes from its citizens excited both the Inyo and San Bernardino county supervisors to such a degree that they ordered a joint survey of their common boundary to determine within whose realm the camp lay. Inyo County took the honors—by barely 300 yards—and the Inyo surveyor, named deputy assessor for the occasion, collected $400 in poll, road, and hospital taxes for his trouble.[9]

Osborne had designed his big furnace to smelt over 20 tons of ore, yielding $900 worth of bullion, each day. In practice, however, it averaged only a fraction of that, so that the cost per ton exceeded the yield. Forty-four men were needed to keep the furnace going—cutting and hauling wood, making charcoal, sorting and hauling the ore, and feeding and repairing the furnace—especially repairing the furnace. Lack of water to keep the cooling jacket around the furnace full was a chronic problem. Every time the water ran low, the furnace overheated, the cooling jacket cracked, the water burst in to quench the fire in a blast of steam, and the whole mess "froze up." Worse yet, as they went deeper on the Gunsight lode, the ore changed from galena to carbonates which, although richer in silver, were so poor in lead and natural fluxes that they would no longer smelt even when the furnace was running.[10]

In the fall of 1878 Osborne at last decided to abandon the smelting furnace and try milling the carbonate ores. With 1,000 tons of such ore on the dump, he persuaded the company to buy a newfangled rotary mill, known as the Davis Pulverizer. This contraption, invented by San Francisco wool merchant John T. Davis, was advertised as being much better than a conventional twenty-stamp mill and requiring far less power. It was also much lighter and cheaper to transport, which made it seem like a bargain indeed. In a new flush of enthusiasm Osborne began setting up the machine and building a new road and tramway from the Gunsight mine. But with an eye for a little real estate business on the side, he decided to locate the pulverizer not at Tecopa, but back at Resting Spring, 6 miles away.[11]

There Osborne laid out a new townsite and began selling town lots again. By February 1879 Tecopa was abandoned and the new milling camp of Resting Spring was on the boom. A flurry of construction produced a large stone hotel, several adobe stores and saloons and, of course, a commodious new house for Superintendent Osborne and his wife. The post office moved too, but it kept the name Tecopa, for the Post Office Department refused to recognize the peripatetic whims of its citizens. The department, in fact, was still confused over which county the camp was in. It did realize, however, that since the number of hopefuls willing to gamble on the new camp had declined to less than a hundred, they only needed triweekly mail. William Godfrey extended his stage line from San Bernardino. But Remi Nadeau's Cerro Gordo Freighting Company stole much of the freight business away from that town by running his teams over the old Walker cutoff across the south end of Death Valley to Mojave station on the Southern Pacific Railroad.[12]

When the wonderful pulverizer finally started up at Resting Spring, however, it was found to be a "most expensive bilk," completely incapable of working the ore. In protest, Osborne and his partners apparently balked at making the final payments on the contraption. But when the manufacturer threatened to attach the mines, they reluctantly began levying assessments on their stock to pay off the debt, while the pulverizer itself was being torn down for scrap.[13]

Osborne was not defeated, however, and he tried once more to make the mine pay. This time he contracted with the San Francisco mining machinery firm of W. O. M. Berry and J. F. Place to put up a conventional ten-stamp mill, with the understanding that the firm would work the mines until the cost of the mill was repaid. Under the direction of Berry and Place's agent, J. S. Sherburne, the mill was erected and began pounding away on Gunsight ore in August 1879. The mill had a capacity of 40 tons a day, but since most of the ore was too refractory for simple milling, it recovered only $40 a ton from rock that assayed at least twice that. Nonetheless, Sherburne managed to clear enough to pay for the mill from the ore already on the Gunsight dump, but when Osborne and his partners took over the mill that fall and began extracting more ore from the mine, they found that the inefficient operation would not pay for the added costs of mining.[14]

In hopes of reducing mining costs and perhaps even striking richer ore, Osborne next commenced a little Sutro tunnel at the base of the hills to tap the Gunsight lode 800 feet below the surface croppings. This would eliminate the costs of hoisting the ore out of the mine and at the same time allow for increased production, because ore could be taken out more rapidly. But the tunnel had to run 1,000 feet through barren rock to strike its mark, and since only four men at a time could work at the tunnel face, progress was slow. By the time he began the tunnel, Osborne had learned most of the lessons of desert mining and had begun to realize it was going to take some time and many costly stock assessments before the mine could be made to pay a profit. So while his partners anxiously looked forward to the tunnel's completion, Osborne sold off nearly all of his stock and gave up being superintendent. His partners, who had apparently begun to think that their problems lay not so much with the mine as with an inept superintendent, were not unhappy to see him go.[15]

The company appointed as their new superintendent a prominent San Francisco mining engineer, Caesar A. Luckhardt, in the hope that he could quickly put the mine on a paying basis. His arrival at Resting Spring in May 1880 temporarily galvanized the camp into new life, but after three months he too quit. Foreman Everett L. Smith, a practical Comstock miner, was left to push the tunnel to completion. It took over a year and stock assessments totaling $72,000 before the job was done, although Smith helped defray some of the cost by running the mill on selected high-grade ore from the upper workings of the mine.[16]

Well before the tunnel was completed, even the camp's most hopeful citizens had begun to leave, one complaining simply that it had just been "too long a dry spell between drinks." The exodus was given a further push in April 1880, when the camp was briefly threatened with "complete annihilation" by a rumored five hundred Shoshone warriors! In a curious turn of events, it seems that a man named Rockwell had stolen a mule from the Shoshone in Ash Meadows, 30 miles north of Resting Spring. The Indians caught up with him as he was making jerky of the animal. They stripped him of everything he had, then turned him loose unharmed. Rockwell, however, crept back into the Shoshone camp that night, clubbed to death four sleeping Indians with a miner's pick, and then escaped. The enraged Shoshone came to Resting Spring and threatened to attack the camp if the murderer wasn't brought to justice. Rockwell was not in the camp, so one of the miners and a Shoshone were dispatched as a posse to hunt him down. The rest of the miners waited uneasily for several days, fearing the threatened attack if Rockwell was not found. Some grew jittery and even called for an arsenal of Springfield rifles from San Bernardino and a detachment of troops from San Francisco. But by the time the posse had returned tempers had cooled, even though Rockwell had not been seen. The Shoshone retired peacefully to Ash Meadows, and Resting Spring continued to decline.[17]

In February 1881 the tunnel finally struck the lode, and with great expectations Smith started up the mill. But the new ore at the tunnel level was not as rich in free-milling values as that above, so even with the reduced mining costs, it still wouldn't pay a profit. A few months of further exploration failed to uncover any better rock, and in July, when the stockholders refused to pay another stock assessment of $16,800, the Los Angeles Mining and Smelting Company closed down. The Gunsight had produced an estimated $260,000 in bullion, but except for some early profitable shipments of high-grade ore, the inefficient smelting and mining had consistently cost more than they had produced. The last hangers-on left that fall. Resting Spring and Tecopa were dead—at least for a while.[18]

Jonas Osborne in the meantime had turned his attention briefly to the old Salt Spring mine, which he sold for $22,500 to Caesar Luckhardt and a partner from New York, but that's yet another story. Osborne then turned farther south into the Mojave, where he became quite an operator, working some sharp deals with a number of mines during the latter years of the nineteenth century. But he still had a soft spot for his first love, the Resting Spring mines. He bought back the idle property from the Los Angeles Mining and Smelting Company early in 1883, and spent considerable money and effort over the next two decades experimenting with traction engines to find a cheap way to get the ore to a smelter. He even designed and patented his own "self propelling steam wagon" to try to haul the ore to the railroad at Daggett, but that didn't prove profitable, either. Still he held on, and finally in the summer of 1906, when the Tonopah and Tidewater laid its tracks within half a dozen miles of the mines, Osborne's faith was at last rewarded, as he sold his interest in them for $175,000. The new owners built a railroad spur to the mines and eventually shipped around $4,000,000 worth of ore. It was, in fact, the biggest metal mine in the whole of Death Valley and the Amargosa.[19]

On the New York Exchange

By the end of the 1870s the mining sharps of San Francisco found the pockets of California investors were nearly picked clean, so they began to turn east for new pockets to pick. California voters also gave them a hard push in 1879, by enacting a new constitution that sharply curtailed speculation of the local exchanges. But the dream merchants were eagerly embraced by Easterners only newly awakened to the wonders of western mining by the instant fortunes of the Comstock's Big Bonanza. In the wave of mining speculation that swept across the country, the wrecks of a myriad western mines were floated anew—and none bobbed up more prominently than those of Death Valley.

The romance and remoteness of the dreaded valley gave a special aura to the stock of its mines; indeed, for the promoter of gilded insecurities, their lore and inaccessibility were their biggest assets. So when the new speculative wave crested in 1881–82, the biggest stocks on the New York Mining Stock Exchange were those of two mines at opposite ends of Death Valley—the old State Line and Salt Spring mines. In those two effervescent years before all the bubbles popped, these Death Valley stocks dominated sales on the New York exchanges and paid their promoters millions of dollars—much more than all of the ore pockets in Death Valley and the Amargosa had yet done.

Before any of the Death Valley mines were launched in New York, however, a few were floated on smaller pools in the Midwest. In the spring of 1877 Frank Miller, one of the few remaining miners at Gold Mountain, sold some "very promising ledges" to a group of Illinois investors headed by Colonel Obed H. Foote, a Civil War volunteer. When they incorporated as the Gold Mountain Mill and Mining Company, Foote also volunteered as superintendent and dutifully put a crew to work building a five-stamp mill about 3 miles south of Lida. But in April 1878, just as the mill neared completion, either Foote's fellow investors got cold feet or Foote himself hot-footed it with their cash, for they forfeited the mill at a sheriff's sale on a mechanic's lien for a paltry $541.43. This proved to be a philanthropic gesture, and local miners ran it for years thereafter as a custom mill.[1]

Over at Panamint, a slippery operator, styling himself Professor James Cherry, floated the windy Leota Consolidated Gold and Silver Mining, Smelting, and Water Company in May 1879. Trying to push a puffed-up

143

$20 million in stock on Chicago investors, the enterprising "professor" announced that he had bought the great Panamint mill and all of the big mines. In August he started up the mill for a short run, sending out the word that the camp was "born again." It's hard to say how many Chicagoans joined the revival, but it's certain that little if any of their money ever got up to Panamint, for the miners' wages and merchants' bills went unpaid. In December the miners seized the property long enough to make the mill run on their own account for $5,000 in back pay. They were lucky; the other creditors, out a total of $18,000, tried attaching the mill and mines only to discover that the professor had just leased them. By then the slippery Cherry had moved on to new ground in Colorado, before the law finally caught up with him.[2]

Down at the south end of Death Valley two other ventures were floated for the sake of Midwesterners. In the Mineral Basin district, just across the Amargosa to the west of Resting Spring, Barton O'Dair had a claim called the Vulture, which he had opened with financial aid from Los Angeles attorney and city councilman John S. Thompson, among others. When they found the ore wouldn't pay, they decided to look for a buyer back East. They found just the man in Amasa C. Kasson, a Milwaukee sewing-machine salesman. Together they organized the Gladstone Gold and Silver Mining Company in June 1879, with $12 million in stock for sale. Talking fancifully of a water-powered, sixty-stamp mill on the Amargosa River, a bullion production of nearly $2 million a year, enough ore to run for twenty years, insured dividends, and very limited offers of bargain-priced stock, Thompson sold Kasson's Milwaukee acquaintances a sizable share in the paper dream. He also sold the postal authorities on establishing a post office at the paper town of Kasson, and he sold Rand McNally on putting the town into their new *Indexed Atlas of the World.* The post office was abolished within a few months, when word got back to Washington that there was "not a soul living within twenty-five miles of the place." The Milwaukee investors were only a little slower in learning that they too had been sold. But the ghost of Kasson haunted maps for over a decade.[3]

Not all of the Death Valley promotions worked in the Midwest, however, were pure scam. The Ibex Mining Company of Chicago made an honest if quixotic effort to work their mine before they too learned the hard lesson of desert mining. They were so persistent that the name Ibex is now ubiquitous, marking a mountain, a peak, some hills, two passes, a wash, and a spring in the south end of Death Valley. Two young prospectors, Frank Denning and Stanley Miller, found the silver-copper croppings they named the Ibex in 1881. The lode lay on the east slope of what is now ironically the Black, not Ibex, mountains, about nine miles north of Saratoga Springs. With little proven worth but much promise, they sold

the Ibex in May 1882—for a startling $48,000—to a novice promoter,
the Reverend Calvin A. Poage, publisher of the San Francisco *Occident,*
"the Presbyterian Weekly of the Pacific." That fall the reverend persuaded
a group of eighteen Chicagoans to join him in forming the Ibex Mining
Company, a closed corporation with a modest capital of $1 million. Poage
took a quarter of the stock in exchange for the mine, and the Chicagoans
put up the money for development. They opened the lode to a depth of
80 feet on a 15-inch pay streak assaying $300 a ton, and they put up a
solid little five-stamp mill at what was subsequently known as Ibex Spring,
located in the Ibex Hills 3 miles southeast of the mine. The mill began
running in May 1883, but lack of wood and water made its operation
erratic and the rebellious ores demanded the addition of a small roasting
furnace the following year, which further taxed the wood supply.
Moreover, Death Valley's record heat forced suspension of work each
summer. But whenever enough good ore, wood, and water was accumulated, the little mill could turn out $60,000 worth of bullion in a month;
unfortunately for the reverend and his friends, those were rare months.
They persisted, however, working the mine and mill on and off each
season for seven years. It is possible, although not likely, that they got
their money back before they finally quit in 1889.[4]

Even before the Ibex was found, the big show had already gotten under
way in New York City at the mining exchanges, appropriately located on
Broadway. There the Death Valley mines took the spotlight in three
elaborate plays for the confidence of Eastern investors. Imaginatively written, lavishly staged, and convincingly portrayed, these charades captured
the hearts and dollars of a spellbound crowd, paid their producers well,
and took a terrible toll of shattered dreams for the deadly valley.

The first and most elaborate scenario was set at Tom Shaw's old State
Line mine, against the backdrop of Gold Mountain. Its props included
the largest mill ever built in Death Valley, a 12-mile pipeline, a pliant
press, a celebrated array of thirty knowing experts, and an unsuspecting
cast of hundreds—all to sell exactly forty-eight reams of colorfully engraved paper! It was an awful farce that cost Eastern investors and
speculators over three million dollars, most of which ended up in the
pockets of one man, George D. Roberts.

Roberts was at the peak of his career, and the State Line deal is said
to have been his most profitable con. He was an unpretentious little man
with a big round head, a quick eye, and a pleasant smile that belied the
hard edges of his soul. He had come to California about 1852, a trusting
Kentucky farm boy in his twenties. Thirty years later he had hardened
into one of the most unscrupulous operators in the West. His was a
thorough transmogrification. It is said that he had worked hard in the

goldfields for eighteen months accumulating his pile, only to lose it all in an hour to a Nevada City poker shark. Roberts vowed then and there to learn the game, and learn it he did. He may have never done another honest day's work, for he went on to learn every angle of the mining and stock games as well. Indeed, he was subsequently credited with inventing the shotgun system of salting placers; with salting Comstock drilling samples right under the rose of the crafty Bonanza King Jim Fair; and with masterminding that most infamous salting of all, the great Diamond Swindle of 1872. He also became a master of the stock deal on the San Francisco exchanges, ballooning mining shares to fancy prices on nothing but hot air, skillfully unloading, selling short, and then popping the balloon to fleece the lambs both going up and coming down. In 1879 he joined the exodus to the East, and with Senator Jones and other sharps, he opened the new American Mining Stock Exchange at No. 63 Broadway to exercise the wildcats. But Roberts worked his biggest schemes across the street at No. 62, on the ostensibly more conservative New York Mining Stock Exchange—the mining affiliate of the staid old New York Stock Exchange.[5]

By the fall of 1880, when Roberts began casting the State Line deal, quite a number of Eastern investors had already seen some of his work— his puffing, gutting, and dumping of the Chrysolite and a few other promising Colorado silver mines. In fact, New York *Engineering and Mining Journal* editor Rossiter W. Raymond, who was among those taken in on the Chrysolite deal, loudly denounced Roberts's "disgraceful and criminal" operations. But there were still many naive new investors ready to pay the price of admission. There were also a number of sharp brokers who thought they knew Roberts's script and could share in the take by getting out before the final curtain. But the ever-versatile Roberts had a different scenario in mind.[6]

Roberts bought the old State Line mine in September 1880 for a highly publicized $100,000 from Austin bankers Paxton and Curtis, into whose hands it had passed after Page's death. Roberts never bothered to visit Death Valley, but he sent his old Diamond Swindle crony Asbury Harpending and a terse Comstock mining superintendent, Isaac M. Taylor, out to the valley to look at the mine for him. They knew what he wanted in a mine, and despite such obvious drawbacks as the generally poor ore, utter lack of water, and exorbitant asking price, they reported back favorably. Roberts paid out $33,333 in cash and gave notes for the rest. He then promptly incorporated the property for $20 million and divided it into four separate companies named the State Line Gold Mining Company No. 1, No. 2, No. 3, and No. 4—one for each of the claims on the lode. Roberts held absolute control over the companies, taking

California con man George Roberts got away with roughly $3 million from New York speculators through his scandalous manipulations of these Death Valley shares.

199,994 of the 200,000 shares in each company for title to that part of the mine. His six token directors, including "Deacon" Stephen V. White, president of the New York Mining Stock Exchange, were each given just one share to satisfy the law, so all of the sellable stock was Roberts's. But he wasn't ready to sell any yet. First he had to set the stage.[7]

The State Line deal opened with an impressive chorus of experts singing the praises of the wondrous lode, with a flurry of earnest actors bearing mining and milling machinery and water pipe to make a mine, and with a crowd of extras eagerly rushing in to build a new metropolis in Death Valley. The experts, ranging from practical miners to learned professors, were portrayed as respected and disinterested critics, but they were in fact either obliging confederates or easily bought pedagogues like Benjamin Silliman, Jr., a Yale chemistry professor who traded on his father's famous name and cranked out fatuously extravagant appraisals of any mine—even the infamous Emma. These "experts" gave Roberts just what he wanted, of course: startling pronouncements of the extraordinary value of this immense—nay, inexhaustable—lode. They saw choice ore that ran to $15,000 a ton, and swore that the whole lode averaged $50 to $100 a ton; it was Midas's own, with "not a pound of waste rock in the entire mine." They even accused one another of being too conservative, while concurring that it was nothing less than the "greatest gold mine on this continent."[8]

In the meantime, Roberts was setting up the other props. He put the taciturn Isaac Taylor to work as the companies' general manager, purchasing machinery for a giant forty-stamp mill and enough pipe to bring water 12 miles from Magruder Mountain at the northern tip of Death Valley. Water had always been Gold Mountain's most obvious drawback, so Roberts's pipeline would play a leading role in the scheme. Some 65,000 feet of 6-inch, spiral-riveted iron pipe was shipped from New York in November 1880 to the Nevada Central railhead near Austin and then hauled the remaining 120 miles by team. The first pipe reached Lida in December, but one delay after another tied up the rest for four months. Then things finally got moving as a crew of twenty began digging the ditch and laying the pipe from Mammoth Springs on the south side of Magruder.[9]

Most of the machinery for the forty-stamp mill came from the old Highbridge mill at Belmont, which Taylor had dismantled and hauled to the State Line mine that winter. He had also begun work on a large double-compartment shaft and steam hoisting works just above the mill site, on the dividing line between the claims of companies No. 2 and No. 3. He confidently predicted nearly million-dollar-a-year profits once the mill started up in May, and that the speedy construction of a second mill would double that by July. Roberts meanwhile had set two more investor traps in March by incorporating the Oriental and Miller gold mining companies, which generated an additional $10 million in paper on some of Frank Miller's claims at old Gold Mountain, 6 miles east of the State Line mine.[10]

All of this ballyhoo drew the inevitable crush of hopefuls in from the wings, and the new camp of Gold Mountain sprang up on the barren slope just below the mill. Taylor sold town lots for $50 to $500 a piece, and Ed Shumway sold water for $4 a barrel, hauled over from Shaw's Spring at the old camp. In December, Cal, Lou, and Wilkes Brougher opened the State Line Saloon—the first in the camp—and dispensed drinks for two bits. Within two months they had five rivals, so to stay ahead of the competition they added a club room for "lovers of a social game." By March the camp had taken on a "townlike appearance," with a population of nearly two hundred and some seventy stores, houses, and dugouts lining Main Street and its byways. In addition to the saloons there were two over-stocked general stores, a couple of boardinghouses, a restaurant, chophouse, butcher shop, bakery, livery stable, and two blacksmiths. There was even a hurdy house under construction, so the future looked bright indeed. George Bowers, son of the Paiute *pakwinavi,* promised to bring in watermelons from his ranch in Deep Spring Valley, and Urial Gates packed down five to six hundred tons of snow on the shady north slope of Magruder Mountain so they would have ice come summer. Frank Clugage and Greek George both ran weekly stages from Columbus, and there was talk of two railroads, the Carson and Colorado and the Nevada Central, both coming within just a few miles of the camp that fall. By that time, some predicted that Gold Mountain would rival Virginia City![11]

Despite continued warnings by Raymond and a few other responsible editors that a new swindle was being staged, Roberts's opening act attracted a wide audience of potential investors. They were all the more enticed by Roberts's insistence that the "mine is not on the market," although they must have known that the genial little man would eventually relent. Late in March, just as work on the pipeline and mill was about to begin, Roberts finally began to make his move with the stock, letting in a few brokers at "hard pan" prices of about $1 a share on about 10 percent of the stock, to form a pool. Then Roberts and his new confederates, trading mostly among themselves, carefully worked the quoted sale prices up toward their $25 par, going a little higher with every new verse from the chorus of experts. Roberts also packaged the shares into three combinations of two companies each, suited to the tastes of his audience. For the conservative investor he offered the combination of State Line Nos. 2

and 3, which held the center of the lode, the mill, and the pipeline, and commanded the highest prices per share. Speculators had their choice of two cheaper long-shot combinations: Nos. 1 and 4, which had the tail ends of the lode and only the promise of a mill; and Oriental and Miller, which had only the promise of a promise. As the pipeline and mill neared completion in mid-May, State Line Nos. 2 and 3 were quoted at $14 a share, and the others were up to $4.[12]

But then, when Roberts really put the shares on the market and began unloading, the prices naturally began to fall. Within a week, with less than 20 percent of the stock out, State Line Nos. 2 and 3 had dropped by half, to $6.50 a share. It was now time for the most crucial part of the con game—the stall, that unexpected occurrence that seems to temporarily block the goal, that annoying trifle that would appear to momentarily thwart the startup of the mill and the opening of the door to expected riches, blocking it just long enough for Roberts to unload and quietly slip away before that door was finally opened and the dream of riches shattered. Roberts was a master of the stall. He had worked it perfectly in the Chrysolite deal a year before, and he was ready this time with sudden news from Gold Mountain that the pipe leaked and would have to be replaced. Although that appraisal was privately disputed by a disinterested party at the mines, it found a believing audience in the East—even among critics, for Raymond had already questioned the adequacy of the pipeline.[13]

Together with this news, of course, Roberts ushered in a new chorus of experts to reaffirm that the worth of the mine was still just as enormous, undiminished by the "failure" of the pipe; the realization of that worth would simply be delayed briefly—a few months at most. The experts sang this refrain again and again, not only in the "subsidized press"—the mining and stock journals—but in the popular dailies as well—the *New York Tribune* and the illustrated *Graphic,* which filled a full page with maps and views of the mine and mill. The blame for the "failure" was obligingly shouldered by Taylor, who stepped down to make way for a new manager.[14]

With these reassurances, stock prices climbed back to $9 by mid-June, as investors and speculators alike hoped to take advantage of the temporarily depressed values. They were joined by a number of knowing brokers to whom Roberts sold large blocks of stock at less than market price, supposedly letting them in on a new pool to work up the price again, so that they could all unload in the flush of excitement when the mill finally started up. What the knowing didn't know was that Roberts had no intention of starting up the mill; he had the price he wanted, and while they helped keep it up he was assiduously divesting himself of all the stock he could. By the end of July Roberts appears to have dumped about 80 percent of the stock in State Line Nos. 2 and 3 at prices averaging around

$7 a share, and most of the other State Line, Oriental, and Miller shares at about a fifth of that. He must have gotten away with roughly $3 million in all—definitely his biggest con.[15]

Roberts slipped out so quickly and quietly that few brokers or investors realized he was gone until they read it in the papers in August. On word of his departure some of the brokers suddenly saw Roberts's script more clearly and immediately worked up a small rally in order to liquidate their own holdings. Asbury Harpending, however, had lined up some new Boston directors for the mines, headed by former Massachusetts Congressman and Union Pacific Railroad Manager John B. Alley, so the other large holders apparently decided to pool with the Bostonians and stay with what still looked like a workable script: support the price until the mill started up and get out with a profit on a rise then. But someone got anxious, and they ended up falling all over themselves trying to slip out just ahead of one another.[16]

In September 1881 Alley hired a practical new superintendent, William A. Farish, with the promise of a large block of stock if he sent back word that the mine looked good. Farish got the idea, sent the message, and got the stock. With some new pipe and a large crew he suddenly brought new life to Gold Mountain, which had been all but deserted since the pipe "failure" and shutdown in June. By November he sent word that he had the mill ready to go, had stockpiled a six-month supply of ore on the dump, and expected to finish the pipeline and start up the mill on December 15. In the meantime, however, he reportedly telegraphed to his wife to sell his stock. Whether or not Farish sent such a telegram, the rumor got out, and in a mad rush of selling State Line stocks fell to barely $1 a share. Farish denied the rumor, but Alley called him back to New York the first of December. There he caused a new flap with assays indicating that, contrary to the reports of Roberts's thirty previous experts, the State Line ore averaged less than $10 a ton—not $100, as touted. The directors demanded his immediate resignation and sent out a new superintendent, John Selover, brother of one of the New York brokers, to make a mill run and show that it would pay. Selover finished the pipeline and started up the great mill early in February 1882. In two weeks he had the answer and telegraphed the insiders: Farish was right. But they lacked Roberts's finesse, and in the frenzy of selling, as each tried to cut this own losses, the stock plummeted again. The long-anticipated boom was a bust, and before the year was out the once-proud State Line could be had for about a nickel a share.[17]

It was time to bring down the curtain, but a few of the actors still refused to quit. Early in 1882 Gold Mountain merchants Seth Squires and Samuel Tallman won an attachment suit on all of the property for $17,702 in unpaid bills, and the sheriff inventoried everything for sale,

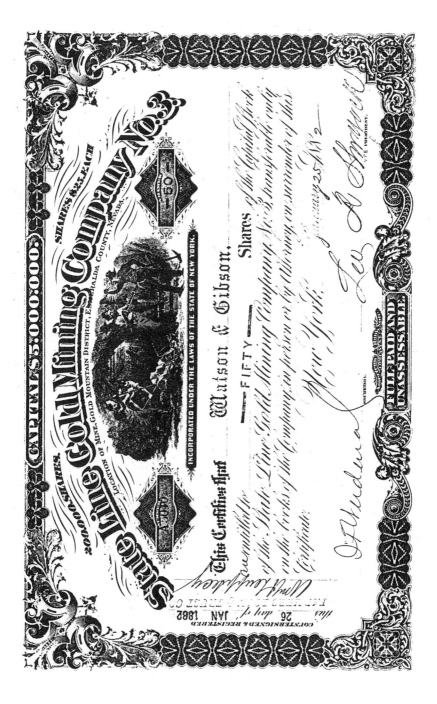

State Line Gold Mining Company No. 3

CAPITAL $5,000,000.

200,000 SHARES.

SHARES $25 EACH.

LOCATION OF MINE, GOLD MOUNTAIN DISTRICT, ESMERALDA COUNTY, NEVADA.

INCORPORATED UNDER THE LAWS OF THE STATE OF NEW YORK.

This Certifies that ———— Watson & Gibson ———— is entitled to ———— FIFTY ———— Shares of the Capital Stock of the State Line Gold Mining Company No. 3, transferable only on the books of the Company in person or by attorney on surrender of this Certificate.

New York ———— January 25 1882

VICE PRESIDENT.

SECRETARY.

FULL PAID AND UNASSESSABLE

COUNTERSIGNED & REGISTERED this 26 day of JAN 1882

FARMERS LOAN & TRUST CO.

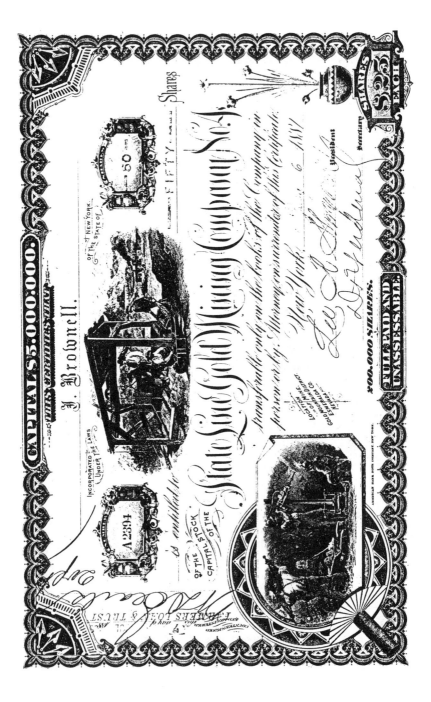

from the mine and mill to the cutlery and chamber pots. Then other creditors appeared with bills totaling $175,000 and threw the property into litigation for several years.[18]

It was the diligent work of the stock pools propping up prices and those awful scrambles to get out before the last curtain that ran up record sales for the State Line stocks. By the end of 1881 over 6 million shares of State Line, Oriental, and Miller had changed hands again and again in the New York mining exchanges—more than a sixth of all the shares traded that year. State Line was thus the largest and, one financial editor concluded, "the most barefaced operation of the year, if not the late mining boom." Rossiter Raymond called it "downright robbery."[19]

The genial little George Roberts had worn out his welcome in New York City, and after a short time in Mexico he moved to Philadelphia to play the exchange there. But nothing went quite as well again after State Line, and trying to diversify, Roberts eventually lost his ill-gotten gains in a cable scheme and a wheat deal. He went back to mining scams, but never made it big again; his last deal was a Siberian fiasco—a far cry from Death Valley. He died in a New York hotel on Christmas Eve of 1901.[20]

The Panamint mines, in the meantime, also made a play on Broadway, to the same end but in a different way. They were brought out as the Inyo Consolidated mines in the spring of 1881 by George M. Pinney, another San Francisco expatriate. Like Roberts, Pinney had already gained an unenviable reputation. Beginning as the purchasing clerk at the Mare Island Navy Yard, just up the bay from San Francisco, he was said to have issued fraudulent government warrants to finance a string of mining schemes that suddenly came to an end in 1875, when the stockholders sued him for fraud and the government charged him with forgery. Pinney fled to South America—some say all the way to the South Seas—while he pondered a course of action. After two years he suddenly returned to San Francisco to announce that he had been ordered to issue the fraudulent warrants by a gang of powerful Republican politicians and that he had left half a million dollars with a friend to pay back his part of the money—a claim even his wife denied. He was promptly indicted on numerous counts of forgery and embezzlement and brought to trial. But after two more years, a mistrial, and an acquittal, the remaining charges were dismissed and he headed east to make a new start.[21]

Pinney still held three Panamint mining claims—the Ida, Eureka, and Independence, which he had acquired in 1875. In New York in the spring of 1881, he formed the Inyo Consolidated Mining and Milling Company around these claims and issued $500,000 in stock. The titular president of the company was Henry A. Mott, Jr., a pudgy young chemistry professor at the New York Medical College and Hospital for Women. But

Pinney was general manager and directed the play from his new offices next door to the stock exchanges on Broadway. Although he seems to have improvised the script as he went along, the basic plot was simply to put on an appearance of running a steady, dividend-paying venture, which he then hoped to unload on even the most conservative of investors.[22]

The star attraction in the play was not Pinney's untried claims, in which one of his overly enthusiastic experts saw profits of as much as 43 percent per year, but that seasoned old actor, the great Panamint mill. Pinney puffed the proud old mill in a centerfold pictorial spread in the New York *Daily Graphic* in July. He claimed that the mill and the mines together had cost $500,000, so that the stock was solidly priced at no more than the value of the property. In fact, Pinney had bought the mill from Senator Jones the month before for only $50,000, and the three claims for much less. Pinney also set about showing what a profitable investment Inyo Con could be, declaring his first dividend even before he had milled a pound of ore. In July he proudly announced a profit of 1 percent, or 5¢ a share, and paid himself $5,000, at least on paper. He confidently predicted regular dividends of 1 percent per month thereafter, with an extra dividend come October, and he paid them just like clockwork, out of one pocket and into the other.[23]

Pinney seems to have gotten so carried away with showing how profitable the operation was that he almost forgot to put anybody to work in the mines and mill. But in September he finally lined up a larcenous former Pioche mining sharp, Thomas B. Pheby, to take the role of superintendent. In the belief that he was to be an equal partner in the deal, Pheby played his part with gusto, sending Pinney a steady flow of glowing reports on the weekly progress of the mines. He arrived at Panamint in October, with talk of hiring 150 men; he started up the mill for a run in December, with talk of shipping $40,000 a month in bullion. Pheby apparently did such a good job of talking that by June of 1882 Pinney was able to claim that, in less than a year, the mill had shipped $107,400 in bullion and the company had paid $45,000 in dividends. That sounded good, if you didn't mind that most of the dividends had been paid before an ounce of bullion was produced. But then most of the bullion wasn't from the company's ore anyway—it was from custom ore Pheby worked for local miners at bargain rates to swell the bullion output.[24]

Such subtleties went unnoticed by those who eagerly took shares. Indeed, Pinney apparently found enough takers that in the spring of 1882 he formed a second venture, the Richmond Mining and Milling Company, around Jacobs's old Wonder of the World, renamed the Wall Street, and issued another $500,000 in shares. The gullible new editor of the *Inyo Independent* praised "Pinney's pluck and hard common sense management" of the Inyo Con, but others were not so easily conned and began to question Pinney's wonderful showing. By the summer of 1882 the San Francisco *Alta California* was blasting the operation as a fraud and its editor, recalling Pinney's earlier exploits, wondered how any sane man could buy stock in anything he was connected with. By the fall a couple of Broadway brokers had started passing out pamphlets in front of the company's office, exposing Pinney's past. Pinney filed charges of criminal libel, but he realized that it was time to make one final push of the stock and get out.[25]

In the spring Pinney had temporarily suspended dividends, ostensibly to pay for repairs and improvements on the mill. This was basically a stall, however, because it was becoming more and more costly to pay dividends as he unloaded more and more stock. With one delay after another, the repairs obligingly dragged on through the summer. For the final push, Pheby announced in October that the mill was at last completely over-hauled and would require no further expenditures for a long time. With 500 tons of ore on hand, he started up the mill in a flash of activity, predicting a steady bullion output of $6,000 a week. At the same time Pinney doubled the Inyo Con capital, offering another $500,000 in new shares and putting out a new prospectus. By December 19 Pheby had nearly completed the mill run and had turned out $26,000 in bullion, when a fire accidentally broke out in the retort room. In minutes the grand old Panamint mill was gutted—"An Inyo Monument Gone," mourned the local editor.[26]

But was the fire an accident, or was it too part of the script—the final stall to defer once more those expected dividends until a new mill was built and Pinney was gone? It served that purpose either way, and it also provided an additional source of quick cash, for Pinney had thoughtfully just increased the mill's insurance. Pheby talked confidently of rebuilding the mill by spring and of keeping a full crew at work in the meantime taking out more ore. But in fact he took all the cash on hand—nearly $11,000—and headed for San Francisco, where he sold the bullion and collected $33,500 from the insurance adjuster. Pheby then spent a few months at the Bay paying off the mortgage on his house in Oakland and making up a set of books to show that of the $70,238.46 of the company's funds that he held, only $336.53 were due the company because he was owed the rest for various expenditures.[27]

Early in May 1883 Pheby arrived in New York to deliver the books and the pittance to the company and to settle his private accounts with Pinney, dividing up the take from both the mines and the stock sales. But Pinney balked at turning over Pheby's share, or so Pheby later claimed, and when he couldn't persuade Pheby to let him put it all into a new scheme, he had Pheby arrested on charges of defrauding the company of $50,000. Pheby, stunned at being made the fall guy, blurted out the whole story to the press. He revealed that, contrary to his weekly reports, the company's mines had produced a total of only $55,000 and had "never paid expenses," let alone earned dividends. He had been able to keep them going only by using his share of the profits from the boardinghouse and the company store. With these revelations Pinney's Inyo Con was over, although litigation would stalk the stage until the summer of 1885.[28]

Even after all the revelations and litigations had been aired, a few of the unshaken faithful tried to reopen the mines. They reorganized as the Surprise Mining and Milling Company and sent one of their number, Nelson G. Fairman, to Panamint to build a new prefabricated mill. The task was nearly completed one Sunday afternoon in November 1886 when a great wind burst down the canyon. Fairman's mill "filled like a balloon," was lifted from its foundation, and scattered for a mile. Undaunted, Fairman and his backers started all over again, and in December 1887 a new mill was finally finished. But it was a hollow success, for try as he might, even Fairman had to concede at last that Pinney's mines really wouldn't pay after all.[29]

Long before State Line and Inyo Con had completed their runs on Broadway, yet another Death Valley play had opened. It was the last and most frivolous, a light fantasy verging on comedy of the absurd, and the creation of San Francisco, mining expert Caesar A. Luckhardt and New Yorker speculator James M. Seymour. It was set in the old Salt Spring mine at the south end of Death Valley. Luckhardt, a German-educated metallurgist and a San Francisco-educated mine puffer, had visited the property while he was at Resting Spring for the Los Angeles Mining and Smelting Company. Jonas Osborne, who had acquired title to the property, touted it as a long-lost treasure trove of the argonauts, and sold it to Luckhardt on its promising promotional prospects. Early in 1881 Luckhardt sold it to James Madison Seymour. Seymour was a slim, dapper operator in his mid-thirties. He had speculated in cotton in Texas and grain in Chicago before coming to New York to buy a seat on the New York Stock Exchange and stage a run of stock manipulations.[30]

Together, Luckhardt and Seymour dressed up the old Salt Spring mine until it became the new speculative favorite of Broadway. They bought the mine for $22,500 and gave it the exotic stage name of the South Pacific Mining Company. Staying behind the scenes themselves, they gave their creation a conservative-looking paper capital of $500,000 in $1 shares and a respectable-looking paper directorate that included New Jersey Lieutenant Governor Garret A. Hobart and several New York brokers who were distinguished by the fact that they had "not before been identified with any mining scheme." Posing as a disinterested expert, Luckhardt then came forward with a wonderfully romantic report on the mine—that it was first discovered by Spaniards, that it had produced the richest gold quartz ever found in California, and that it was abandoned only because the Indians attacked and burned the mill. Further fantasizing a 1,200-foot fall of water from the Amargosa River to power a fifty- or more stamp mill, Luckhardt envisioned profits running into millions a year. In the glow of Luckhardt's praises, Seymour put the South Pacific stock on the exchanges in October 1881, and within a month he and his broker friends had "washed" the price up from its $1 par to $14.63 a share! No other mining stock on the New York exchanges had ever been so far above par, and none had ever been more fictitious. Even when Seymour began to unload, the stock only fell to around $4 a share by mid-December, and the light trading over the Christmas holidays gave that price the appearance of solidity. Thus when Seymour made his final play early in 1882 he was able to keep the price above par until late April, by which time he had dumped all of the stock he could for something over a million dollars. By then too, the volume of real and imaginary trading of the stock on the New York exchanges had passed three million shares. South Pacific was well on its way to becoming the most active, if not the most popular, stock of 1882.[31]

For the final act Seymour brought out a comic trio of experts to entertain reporters from the New York dailies—the *Graphic,* the *Tribune,* and even the *Times.* The first expert, "Professor" George A. Treadwell, who later gained notoriety as a mining sharp in his own right, adorned the mine with a line of old stone forts to fend off the Paiute and sharpened the imaginary profits to precisely $145,800 a month. The second expert, one George Glendon, Jr., magically perceived millions in gold not only in the vein itself but in the granite on either side and swore that "the whole gulch, 40 feet wide, would pay." The third expert, aptly named Dr. G. Wiss, recalled a visit to the mine eleven years earlier, when he had been assured by the great Baron Von Richthoffen that it was only a matter of time before that little range of hills at Salt Spring "would surpass California and Nevada combined in the production of the precious minerals!"[32]

Many a seasoned investor must have howled with laughter over such foolishness, but there were some credulous souls who kept a straight face even when Seymour's buffoons misplaced the mine 180 miles west, not north, of San Bernardino, thus locating it in the Pacific Ocean—at least that began to make a little sense of its name. Those who failed to see the humor in Seymour's jokes, however, paid the price of many a share. Only after the show was over did some of them think back on what they had heard and start writing frantic letters to friends or even strangers in California, trying to find out what was up. And even then, they must have had a hard time seeing anything funny about it.[33]

Stock sharp James Seymour pulled off an outrageous swindle of Eastern investors with this Death Valley stock.

Not all of the newspapers had been as easily conned by Seymour's troupe as had the *Times* and the *Tribune*. The western press had panned the play from the start, and some eastern mining papers like the *Engineering and Mining Journal* and the *Mining Record* had done the same. But the most damning blasts came from the editor of the New York *Daily Stockholder,* who summed it all up when he wrote:

> There is no investment nonsense about Seymour. He can't wait for dividends. He doesn't calculate interest on the money he puts into mining stocks—multiplying the principal by 500 and pocketing the product is good enough for him. He isn't going to travel 4,000 miles to see if the South Pacific mine is good for anything—he can demonstrate its value *to him* right here in New York . . . he can buy a mine for less and sell it for more; he can get more of the public's money and hold it better; he can look you square in the face and talk less truth and more taffy; he has the most cheek and the least conscience; he can profess more sincerity and possess less; he has brought less to the mining interests and taken more from them—well, than any other schemer on a large scale who has made a big bank account and lost only a small reputation![34]

The curtain finally came down on South Pacific in May, when its stock crashed from 65¢ to 5¢ in two weeks. Soon after, Superintendent Everett Smith and his four-man token crew brought suit to try to get their unpaid wages, but they only got the mine. The stock, which shuffled on, mine or no mine, was finally pulled off the exchanges in 1883. And what became of Seymour? He went right on staging more cons for nearly a decade, opening nineteen branch offices to push all his paper, before he finally retired to New Jersey. And one of his paper directors, Garret A. Hobart, went on to become vice president of the United States.[35]

"Starving to Death on a Government Claim"

"Starving to death on a government claim" was the western homesteaders' frequent refrain, and many did go broke trying to eke out a living on homestead claims throughout the West. But in the very midst of the Death Valley and Amargosa country—that seemingly most sterile of lands—there were little oases, rich pockets of ground, that could become for a time more profitable bonanzas than most of the surrounding mineral lands. These mother lodes of fertile soil and perennial springs could produce bonanza crops of $200-a-ton beans and hay, or fatten a herd of $600-a-ton beef cattle, which meant quick fortunes for the homesteader as long as the neighboring mining camps boomed. Even a hay ranch could pay startling profits. With as many as eight alfalfa cuttings a year, each acre could produce 10 tons and a modest 40-acre plot could yield up to $80,000 worth of hay per year—provided there was a boom camp nearby. Thus a good ranch could be worth as much as, if not more than, a good mine. Their proximity to one another determined the profitability of both, but ultimately it was the size of the ore pocket that limited the size of the salable crop, so as the mines went from boom to bust, so did the ranches.[1]

The natural fecundity of watered land in Death Valley and the Amargosa had long been demonstrated by the Southern Paiute and the Shoshone, who raised abundant crops of corn, beans, melons, and squash around some of the springs and seeps. Then, in the late 1860s, Mormon Charlie, a progressive Paiute, started a stock ranch in Pahrump Valley with animals left to him by the miners at Potosi. The homesteaders were soon to follow.[2]

In the popular lore, Death Valley's first homesteader was an enigmatic cuss known as "Bellerin" Teck. The original story came from Amargosa rancher Cub Lee in 1891, while he was showing New York writer John Spears the sights of Death Valley. Cub told the city slicker how "'Bellerin' Teck took a ditch full of water out of Furnace Creek and made a small ranch on which 'he raised alfalfa, barley, and quails.'" But, Cub added solemnly, "'Bellerin' Teck got a reputation for being a bad man. He traded a part of his ranch to a Mormon named Jackson for a yoke of oxen, and then within a week ran the saint out of the valley with a shotgun. Then 'Bellerin' moved out himself and, sad to say, faded out of Death Valley history." It was a colorful anecdote, and an appreciative Spears made good use of it in his 1892 paperback, *Illustrated Sketches of Death Valley*—the first popular book on the valley. Indeed, he only wished that Cub could have told him more about the bellicose Teck, for Spears was certain that "a man who rejoiced in such a name, who was handy with a shotgun and who withal was the first citizen of Death Valley, must have had an interesting biography."[3]

Later writers were also intrigued by the colorful Teck but, frustrated by the meagerness of Spears's account, they inevitably fell into the temptation of inventing a few new "facts" to help flesh out Bellerin's elusive biography. They conjured up a properly early date of 1870 for his arrival and concocted a last name of Bennett, and then an initial, until he was finally christened "Bellerin V. Tex Bennett." Other enthusiasts made him a Confederate Army deserter, or at least a vigilante escapee, and gave him a fine adobe with a wide veranda, a duck pond, a rare green thumb, and a bellering claim to the whole of Death Valley. All this hot air has already filled many pages in many books, and doubtless someone will eventually find enough wind to blow a whole book on Bellerin Teck![4]

But behind all this puffery there really was a "Bellerin Teck"—in deed, if not in name—a man who did just about what Cub Lee said he did, a bullheaded Kentuck named Andrew Jackson Laswell who was, in fact, Death Valley's first homesteader.

Andy Laswell first came through Death Valley from Pioche in the summer of 1874 with a partner, Cal Mowrey, who may or may not have been a Mormon. They came in the rush to the Panamint mines, although they sought their fortunes not in the rock but in the soil. They struck pay dirt when they got a contract with the Surprise Valley Mill and Water Company to supply hay for about $200 a ton. Late that summer they headed back over the Panamints into Death Valley to start a hay ranch at Bennetts Well. They built a shelter, seeded a field of alfalfa, dug an irrigation ditch, and in just a couple of months Laswell was packing their first bonanza load of hay up to Panamint. But with that first sale sprouted the seeds of trouble, for the two partners couldn't agree on how to divide the proceeds, and the more they argued, the more stubborn and angry the two became. So by the time Laswell set out with the second load, Mowrey swore that if he didn't settle up on his return, there would be a "shooting match." Laswell got back to the ranch on December 5, ready to shoot it out. Before Mowrey could draw his gun Laswell opened fire, hitting his partner three times in the arm and once in the temple. Then in a fit of remorse Laswell headed to Panamint to get a doctor and turn himself over to the deputy sheriff. Mowrey recovered, but their partnership did not—Laswell kept the ranch, and Mowrey moved on.[5]

Laswell did well during the Panamint boom and even started a second hay ranch on the east side of Death Valley at the mouth of Furnace Creek. But as Panamint began to decline in the fall of 1875, he abandoned his

Death Valley ranches and moved east to the foot of the Spring Mountains, just beyond the Amargosa basin. There he bought the Paiute rancheria at Indian Springs and made it a popular way station on what had become the main road from Pioche to the Death Valley camps. By then he had acquired a wife, but he had not yet lost his penchant for trouble. He got into another shooting scrape at Ash Meadows, where he was rumored to have been killed, and was nearly lynched at Ivanpah after he or a partner killed a man in a gambling dispute. Laswell finally reformed after that, settling down with his family at Calico.[6]

The boom market at Panamint early in 1875 attracted one other settler to Death Valley—William Johnson, also a Kentuckian in his early thirties. He started a truck garden up in the canyon that now bears his name. Moving in on the spring at the Shoshone camp of Puaitungani, just 6 miles east of Panamint, Johnson terraced a piece of ground, ran a ditch, and planted a variety of vegetables that eventually brought him several hundred dollars a ton in the hungry boom camp. In the expectation that Panamint would last, he even set out some fruit trees, but the boom was over before they could bloom. Johnson then moved across the Sierra to the Long Tom district on the Kern River. There he became involved in a bitter mining dispute with the Yoakum brothers, and he and a partner were killed in ambush on April 13, 1878. Public sentiment was so inflamed against the murderers that, when the state supreme court set aside their conviction, a mob stormed the Bakersfield jail and hung the Yoakums in their cells.[7]

At the north end of the Panamints, Ubehebe discoverer William Hunter started a seasonal ranch where he left his pack animals to graze while he tried to open his new copper claims. A few ranchers had also settled in the hills at the far north end of the valley during the Lida boom. The most persistent was a Nova Scotian named Charles Murphy, who squatted at Pigeon Spring about 1873 with his aged mother on a little ranch he called the Home Rule. He stayed long after the boom collapsed, supplementing his meager earnings by working little high-grade pockets in the neighboring mines and selling a little whiskey to the Indians. But the whiskey business soured in 1891, when several of his customers laid seige to his cabin and had to be turned away with a rain of buckshot. Soon after that the authorities arrested him in a crackdown on the liquor trade with the Indians. Rather than risk going to prison, Murphy finally gave up everything, jumping bail and abandoning his ranch and his mother for parts unknown.[8]

The best ranch lands, of course, were not in Death Valley: they were over on the Amargosa at Resting Spring, Ash Meadows, and Oasis Valley, and farther east at Pahrump, where more than a dozen ranchs were started

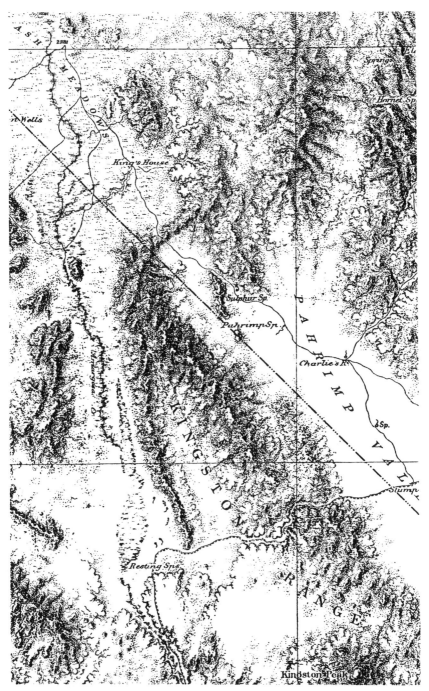

Charles King's pioneering cattle ranch in Ash Meadows and Mormon Charlie's ranch at Pahrump from Wheeler's map of 1873. (*Courtesy of Bancroft Library*)

during the Ivanpah, Panamint, and Tecopa booms of the 1870s. Some of these ranches are still going today, sustained after the booms by a few scattered mines and persistent prospectors, until cheap transportation finally opened a far wider market.

Charles King was the first of the ranchers to settle on the Amargosa. He came early in 1873, and in the years that followed many others came as well—the Lees, the Bennetts, the Browns, the Younts and the Winters, Lander, Stockton, the Longstreets and the Beattys.

King was a down-east Yankee who had joined the gold rush to California in 1850. By 1870 he had tried his hand at just about everything but ranching. He had been a lighterer on San Francisco Bay, a merchant in Sacramento, a lumberman at Yankee Jim, a sheriff in Placer County and, of course, a miner all over California and Nevada. In the summer of 1871 he was mining at Timpahute when Wheeler's survey came through, and he signed on as one of the guides. King did much better than the others. He was camped with Wheeler on the Amargosa when Hahn disappeared trying to reach them, and he was scouting ahead in Furnace Creek when Egan vanished. He not only survived that awful summer but used the survey to look over the business prospects of the country, and he liked what he saw. With the Ivanpah, Chloride Cliff, and other mines opening up in the neighboring hills, King saw his chance for a fortune on the range land at Ash Meadows. Amid the scattered ash trees that gave the meadow its name were dozens of perennial springs and seeps that watered thousands of acres of virgin grasslands. There he could fatten up cattle, bought in California for a few cents a pound on the hoof, and sell them at the mines for 30¢ a pound, slaughtered. The land was there for the taking; all he needed was a partner with enough money to buy a herd. He found just the man in Pioche mining superintendent Charles Forman.[9]

With Forman's backing, King went into the cattle business on a grand scale, buying 1,300 head in southern California and driving them to Ash Meadows in January 1873. He gave the cattle free range, and at the foot of a small butte from which he could keep an eye on them, he built a solid stone house at what is now Point of Rocks Spring. In his enthusiasm, King plunged ahead on far too grand a scale, without reckoning either on the limited market that the neighboring mines provided or on the deadly toll that alkali, black leg, and occasional Paiute arrows would take on his stock. But he would succeed in spite of himself, for the great Panamint rush was about to begin, giving him all the market he could ever hope for. The following year King started running his cattle across Death Valley to his new butcher shop at Panamint. There his beef bonanza was worth even more per ton than the high-grade ore that the Surprise Valley Company was shipping all the way to England. But by the spring of 1875, King had apparently had his fill of the Death Valley country, and he had learned enough about the cattle business to decide that he should get out before the Panamint boom collapsed. Thus he sold his half of the partnership to Gold Hill butcher L. T. Fox at boom prices and moved on again to try his hand at something new.[10]

The oases of the Amargosa also beckoned others, who began arriving even before King left. The Lee brothers, Philander and Leander, known as Phi and Cub, came during the Panamint rush in the winter of 1874–75 with a herd of cattle from San Joaquin Valley to stake out a spring near King. They were still in their early twenties, but they came to stay, taking Paiute wives and settling in to grow with the country. In the years that followed they became both the source and the subject of much local lore—especially Cub, that "tall, thin and solemn storyteller," who told countless tales of that queer country and his oddly named brothers, Meander and Salamander.[11]

On down the Amargosa in the spring of 1875 the Brown brothers, William and Robert, after discovering silver at Tecopa, started the first ranch at Resting Spring. The Tecopa mines boomed for several years, providing a market for ranchers all along the Amargosa. But the Browns soon moved on, and Phi Lee eventually took over the Resting Spring ranch. Back up that stream in the fall of 1879, Eugene Lander had found the pockety ores of the Bromide district and started a ranch in Oasis Valley near the present town of Beatty. When Lander moved on a few years later, that ubiquitous "Old Man of the Desert," William M. Stockton, took over the ranch as a base for his all-consuming quest for the Gunsight silver and Breyfogle's gold. By the end of the 1870s, most of the remaining springs and seeps along the Amargosa had been taken up by homesteaders, among them Aaron Winters and his wife, Rosie, who would gain brief fame and fortune with their borax discoveries in Death Valley. Ash Meadows Charlie was also expanding his own ranch just east of Longstreet Spring.[12]

Farther east, Charles Bennett and his family moved in next to Tecopa's rancheria at Pahrump Spring in 1875, starting what would become the biggest ranch in the whole Death Valley and Amargosa country. Seven years later Bennett sold that ranch for $20,000 to Aaron Winters, who was flush from the sale of his Death Valley borax claims. Mormon Charlie's pioneer ranch just to the east was taken over by the Jordan brothers in 1876 and sold to Joseph Yount and his family early the following year. The Younts, who were wintering a herd of cattle at Ash Meadows en route from eastern Oregon to Arizona, suddenly decided to stay when a Paiute renegade, Horseshutem, shot all their draft horses near the springs that now bears his name. With their son-in-law, Harsha White, the Younts spent most of their lives on that ranch, known as the Manse, before they finally sold it in 1910 for $50,000.[13]

With the decline of the Ivanpah and Tecopa mines in the early 1880s, about half the ranchers on the Amargosa had to pull up stakes and move on for lack of a market. But there were still a few new settlers who came in to try their luck. Among them was John Howell, the first black, who took up a ranch in Oasis Valley in 1895, and Ah Foo, who farmed for a few years on Willow Creek, at what has since been known as China Ranch.[14]

The most notable of the later settlers, however, were "Old Man" Beatty and Jack Longstreet. Both settled in Oasis Valley, took Shoshone wives, and left their names on the land, but there the similarity ended. Montillion Murray Beatty, a former Gold Mountain miner and Amargosa borax worker in his late fifties, took over the original Lander ranch in the spring of 1896, soon after Stockton's death. Beatty was a generous, hardworking family man who made his ranch a welcome home to all who passed that way. He lived a quiet life until the discovery of the Bullfrog mines; then bitten again by the mining fever, he sold his ranch for $10,000, gave his name to the town, started a new ranch at Cow Creek over in Death Valley, and dabbled in mines until his death in December 1908.[15]

Andrew Jackson Longstreet, another hot-blooded Kentuck, was cut from different stock. He was equally renowned for his long hair and his bad reputation. His hair hid ears that had been cropped as punishment for cattle rustling in his youth, while his reputation showed that the punishment had failed to reform him. One newspaperman later called him "the most perfect typification of the Old West's gunmen." Before Longstreet settled on the Amargosa in 1889, he had run a saloon in the Mormon settlements over on the Muddy River near the Utah line. He killed one man there in a squabble over a horse race and was said to have bushwhacked a Singer Sewing Machine salesman in a row over a hired horse. While he lived in Oasis Valley, he got into a scrape at Sylvania "administering Indian justice" to an unpopular mining superintendent. A few years later, after he moved to a ranch in Ash Meadows near the spring that now bears his name, Longstreet was involved in a claim-jumping shoot-out at the Chispa mine just to the east. He finally left the Amargosa around the turn of the century and survived many another scrape before death caught up with him in 1928, at the age of 90.[16]

Almost all the Amargosa ranchers held 160-acre homestead claims, but they were usually able to irrigate only a fraction of that, while what stock they had ranged free for miles beyond. During the mining booms they were mostly hay ranchers, with their cultivated acreage in alfalfa, since that paid the biggest return for the least work. They got four big alfalfa cuttings a year on the Amargosa, with a yield of about 6 tons an acre, worth from $70 to $200 a ton in the camps, depending on the market. Some ranchers also raised barley, which was always worth nearly $200 a ton, but yielded only a couple of tons per acre. They all had a vegetable patch with corn, beans, potatoes, beets, cabbages, onions, squash, and melons. Those who planned to stay a while planted small orchards with apples, peaches, pears, figs, plums, apricots, nectarines, almonds, and walnuts. Any surplus could usually be sold in the mines at over $200 a ton for vegetables, and over $500 a ton for fruit and nuts. A few ranchers even set out vineyards and made wine, for which there was always an insatiable market. Joseph Yount had the largest vineyard—2.5 acres in seven varieties of grape—and those who drank his Chateau Manse swore that it was superior to California's finest.[17]

All of the ranchers kept some stock, but except for King, none had even a hundred head. Most kept about two dozen cattle, a dozen or so stock horses and mustangs, a couple of work horses, and some hogs. A few, like Yount, also raised chickens, turkeys, ducks, and geese. The horses and cattle grazed the open range on bunch- and saltgrass from spring till fall, and were fed hay, barley, or even mesquite beans in the winter. Alkali and locoweed were perennial problems, and local lore added another affliction, said to have been caused by some strange mineral in the water, that weakened the cattle's legs so that they couldn't stand and had to crawl around on their knees![18]

The size and value of the ranches varied greatly, of course. The smaller hay ranches, worth only a few hundred dollars, were two-man operations with little irrigation and all of the cutting and baling done by hand. The largest ranches—Bennett's and Yount's—each had several hundred acres in crops, miles of irrigation ditches and fences, and were highly mechanized and worth $20,000 or more. Bennett was the first to mechanize, buying a "mammoth self-binding harvest machine" in the spring of 1880. He and Yount later brought in a variety of mowing, reaping, and threshing machines for the fields, and fruit cutters, parers, and dryers for the orchard harvest. They employed several permanent ranch hands and a large seasonal crew of Paiute.[19]

Amargosa ranch houses ran the gamut from brush and mud *jacals* to comfortable, thick-walled adobes with wooden floors, shady verandas, and cool cellars. Aaron Winters's house on Ash Meadows, the old King place, was typical of most. A visitor gave a poignant description:[20]

> Close against the hill, one side half-hewn out of the rock, stood a low stone building, with a tule-thatched roof. The single room within was about fifteen feet square. In front was a canvas-covered addition of about the same size. The earth, somewhat cleared of broken rock

originally there, served as floor for both rooms. There was a door to the stone structure, and directly opposite this was a fire-place, while a cook-stove stood on a projecting rock at one side of it. At the right was a bed, and at the foot of the bed a few shelves for dishes. A cotton curtain was stretched over some clothing hanging on wooden pegs in the corner.

On the other side was the lady's boudoir—a curiosity in its way. There was a window with a deep ledge there. A newspaper with a towel covered the ledge, in the center of which was a starch box supporting a small looking-glass. On each side of the mirror hung old brushes, badly worn bits of ribbon and some other fixings for the hair. Handy by was a lamp-mat, lying on another box, and covered with bottles of Hogan's Magnolia Balm, Felton's Gossamer for the Complexion, and Florida Water—all, alas, empty, but still cherished by the wife, a comely, delicate Spanish-American woman with frail health and little fitted for the privations of the desert.

The shelves about the room and the rude mantel over the fire-place were spread with covers made of notched sheets of newspaper. Two rocking chairs had little tidies on their backs. The low flat pillows were covered with pillow shams and the bed itself with a tawny spread. In place of a library there were a number of copies of the *Police Gazette*. There was a flour barrel against the wall, a small bag of rice near by, and two or three sacks of horse feed in a corner. The sugar, coffee, and tea were kept under the bed.

The water of the spring ran down the hill and formed a pool in front of the house, and here a number of ducks and chickens, with a pig and a big dog, formed a happy group, a group that rambled about in the house as well as romped beside the water of the spring. A few cattle grazed on the bunch-grass of the valley that stretched away before the house, gray and desolate.[21]

The homesteaders' life on the Amargosa was indeed a lonely one. The scattered ranches, one to a spring, were usually several miles apart, so neighbors were rarely seen. For most, the only contact with the outside world was the infrequent arrival of a prospector, an occasional trip to Tecopa to sell produce and buy a few necessities, and, of course, the annual, 200-mile pilgrimage to the county seat to pay taxes. The latter could be a risky undertaking, as Winters learned in November 1884 when he headed for the Nye County courthouse at Belmont. He hid his tax money in the jockey box on his wagon, but when he stopped to rest at San Antonio station, a man there, B. E. Kennan, saw where the cash was kept and grabbed it while Winters was saying good-bye to the station keeper. Winters spotted Kennan near the wagon and, discovering the loss, drew his gun and demanded the money back. Kennan refused and started to reach for his own weapon. Winters shot him dead. The money was found on the body. Two days later Winters paid his taxes, and the coroner's jury promptly acquitted him on grounds of "justifiable homicide."[22]

During the long years of the 1880s and 1890s, while they prayed for a new mining boom, some of the Amargosa ranchers tried their own luck at prospecting. For all of their looking, both Lander and Stockton missed the big bonanza just west of their ranch, although Winters did strike it rich with his borax finds, and Phi Lee and Yount's son, William, likewise found some rich borax ground. Lee and Yount's sons also played a part in the later gold discoveries in the Funeral and Spring Mountain ranges. Others looked for what they thought was a more certain treasure—that said to have been buried by the Death Valley forty-niners. After years of telling and retelling, legend had made those argonauts one of the wealthiest parties ever to cross the desert, and had them burying as much as $200,000 in gold and jewels somewhere in Death Valley or the Amargosa. Who could doubt it, when Mary Scott, one of the Ash Meadows Paiute, sold a prospector an old solid gold watch that her father had found? It was rumored that she even had a diamond bracelet and other fine jewelry. Phi Lee and Old Man Beatty both spent many a day digging up the old campsites in search of this wonderful treasure. They never struck anything except wagon iron and broken china, and finally decided that the Indians must have already found it all. Others, however, kept looking.[23]

Visions of a railroad down the Amargosa briefly brightened those dull days of the late eighties and early nineties. Union Pacific officials had talked of extending a branch from Utah to southern California as early as 1882, and in the winter of 1887–88 they finally sent crews out to survey a route. They ran a line from the Utah Central terminus at Milford southwest past Pioche and Pahranagat to Ash Meadows, then down the Amargosa into the south end of Death Valley and out along the old Walker cutoff to connect with the Southern Pacific at Mojave. With the surveyors came prospectors and speculators, who took up old mining claims in the neighboring hills and new homestead claims all over Ash Meadows and Pahrump Valley. They had high hopes for a few years, while surveyors adjusted and readjusted the line and grading crews worked sporadically at the Utah end of the track. But little work was actually done, and even the most hopeful speculators at last gave up their tracts for taxes after Union Pacific went into bankruptcy in the Panic of 1893.[24]

In the meantime, back in Death Valley, there were also a few new ranches. Hungry Bill had moved onto Johnson's abandoned ranch and replanted the garden. With the help of George Hansen and other relatives, he also terraced and irrigated several more acres and set out more peach trees. At the south end of the valley, his brother Panamint Tom did the same, starting a ranch at Pabuna near Warm Spring. At the opposite end of the valley was another new ranch, that of Jacob Staininger, a none-too-hospitable sort who came to be known as the Hermit of Death Valley. Staininger was a green young Pennsylvania farm boy in his late twenties when he came west with his brother right after the Civil War and settled in central Nevada, starting the first ranch in Monitor Valley. But the Stainingers quickly earned themselves a hard reputation, killing a neighbor, Tom Andrews, whom they accused of jumping their land, and then suing his estate for title to the land. Jake and his brother finally went their separate ways in 1880. Jake, drawn by Roberts's State Line bubble, came to Death Valley and started a couple of hay ranches, one near the hot springs in Grapevine Canyon, and the other a few miles west at Grapevine Springs down in Death Valley. After the bubble burst he stayed on, hoping for another boom, raising mustangs and quail, and tending a vineyard of native grapes. From these tart little berries he made a potent wine that eased the passage of the lonely years while he dreamed of the day when his hot springs ranch would become a "famous pleasure resort." He never saw that day, but long after his death his dream did come true, when Death Valley Scotty's partner bought the ranch to build Scotty's Castle.[25]

But the biggest and most profitable ranch in Death Valley was the Greenland Ranch at the mouth of Furnace Creek, started in 1883 as part of the great borax operation, and that story is next.

Borax Bonanza

Although it was the lure of gold and silver that drew most men to Death Valley and the Amargosa, the country's greatest mineral wealth was not in the precious metals that lay hidden in the surrounding hills, but in the lowly salts that lay right underfoot. Those salts were the inexorable product of eons of evaporative concentration of soluble minerals, leached from the hills by the scant rains that slowly etched the land. Of all the salts that accumulated in the crucible of Death Valley, the most prized was borax— that miracle of the laundry, that friend of jewelers and potters, that preserver of meats and mummies. A hundred different uses made a market for that versatile salt, and thus made Death Valley a treasure vault.

The first to profitably tap this treasure was William Tell Coleman, a respected but controversial San Francisco commission broker and vigilante leader. Coleman showed that borax was Death Valley's most profitable product. He shipped roughly a million dollars worth of the salt out of the valley in the mid-1880s—more than all of Death Valley's gold and silver mines had yet produced. But he barely scratched the surface, working only the pockety playa deposits at the edge of the great salt flat. Later operators have taken out more than thirty times that value, and the known reserves of Death Valley borate are worth at least thirty times more than that—over $1 billion at today's prices.[1] Borax was first recognized in the salt beds of Death Valley a decade before Coleman began mining it. The deposits he would work, not far from the Jayhawkers' burned wagons, were discovered in the spring of 1873, at the height of the great borax fever that sent prospectors scouring every salt pan from eastern Oregon to southern California. One enthusiast wrote excitedly of "acres and acres" of borax in Death Valley, "sparkling and glittering . . . as white and immaculate as a shirt done up by the What Cheer Laundry." Borax then sold for over $700 a ton, but even at that price the commercial worth of Death Valley's deposits was hastily discounted because of the remote and inhospitable locale. Instead, work was begun at the more accessible deposits on Searles Lake to the west. Death Valley's borax lay all but forgotten until the fall of 1881, when Aaron Winters and his wife Rosie rediscovered it.[2]

Talk that fall of extending the Carson and Colorado railroad south through Owens Valley and the Southern Pacific railroad east across the Mojave had revived interest in the borax deposits of the adjacent country

173

and sent a handful of prospectors back to the dry lakes. One, Henry Spiller, chanced to stop for a night at Winters's meager ranch in Ash Meadows. In the course of the evening Spiller showed his host a sample of borax and how to test for it by pouring sulphuric acid on the salt, then alcohol, and striking a match to it. If it burned with a green flame, it was borax. Winters watched attentively, for he recalled seeing salts that looked like that over in Death Valley. When Spiller left, Aaron and Rosie headed for the valley. Aaron Winters was a chubby little man with a round, ruddy face and a bushy goatee, a middle-aged Midwesterner and former hotel keeper of failing fortune. In those salts he saw a new chance.[3]

Down on the salt flat a few miles north of Furnace Creek, "wabbling about" in excitement, Winters gathered up likely looking samples. Then he and Rosie went back up to the springs in the canyon, made supper, and waited for nightfall to make the faint flame test. At last, when the shadows had closed in around them, Winters put some of the salts into a saucer, poured the acid and alcohol on them, and with trembling hand struck a match. It was an anxious moment. Then he shouted, "She burns green, Rosie! We're rich, by God!"[4]

Winters quietly got word of his wonderful discovery to the two best-known borax men in the country: William Tell Coleman, who had a virtual monopoly on the distribution of American borax, and Francis Marion Smith, who was already the biggest producer and on his way to monopolizing American production. Together they quickly dispatched agents to examine the deposit and to secure and purchase the claim. Smith sent Rudolph Neuschwander and a crew of practical miners from his works in Nevada, and Coleman sent his lawyer, John A. Robinson, and a surveyor from San Francisco. They found Winters's claim to be every bit as rich as he had imagined. On November 21, 1881 they formally organized the Death Valley Borax and Salt Mining District, electing Winters district recorder. Then they started systematically staking out the ground with placer claims, named simply No. 1, No. 2, and so on, all the way up to No. 27. The locations covered roughly 4,000 acres of borax land along the east edge of the salt flat. When they were through, Winters signed over his title to Coleman for $20,000.[5]

Flush from this triumph, Winters and two cronies, Gordon Ellis and S. J. Parks, headed for the Amargosa to look for new deposits. They soon found another, poorer borax bed just 6 miles west of Resting Spring. Some of Coleman's men rushed over from Death Valley and on March 6, 1882 they formed the Eagle Mountain Borax and Salt district. They again bought out Winters and his partners, and neatly located another set of claims, this time named A through U, that covered another 3,000 acres.[6]

Winters spent most of his money almost immediately, buying Charles Bennett's big Pahrump Ranch for $20,000 in May 1882. But his good fortune didn't last. Rosie died a short time later, and although the crops remained bountiful, the market vanished. Winters took in partners to try to keep the ranch going, and turned to prospecting again, but to no avail. In 1887 he lost all but a small part of the ranch for back taxes, and by the end of the century he had become a virtual hermit in the Shadow Mountains. Gordon Ellis got $5,000 for his share of the Amargosa discovery, but he didn't enjoy it for very long. He got into a poker game with a man named James Center at Winters's ranch in August 1882. The game ended in a heated argument over the magnificent sum of $1.50, and the two started shooting at each other. Ellis shot first, but wound up dead anyway. Parks quietly took his share and returned to his home in the East.[7]

The biggest Death Valley borate discovery, however, was made late in 1882 by Winters's neighbor, Phi Lee, and two companions. They found a whole mountain of the white salts, which they named Monte Blanco. Coleman and Smith's borax experts couldn't have missed seeing it, jutting out of the south side of Furnace Creek Wash—it can be seen for miles. But the experts had studiously ignored it, confident in their knowledge that borates could only be found out on the salt flats. But Phi Lee and his friends didn't know any better when they tried the flame test on some of the salt and found that it, too, burned green. They had in fact discovered a new borate mineral, a calcium borate, which fickle fate would name colemanite. It had formed from borates in ancient salt flats laid down millions of years before and subsequently thrust up and exposed along the fault scarp that is Furnace Creek Wash. The Monte Blanco Borax and Salt Mining District was formed on November 3, 1882, and Coleman's men began combing the hills for other deposits of the new mineral. They found several others, most notably the Biddy McCarthy claim. Phi Lee and his brother Cub, prospecting some 30 miles to the east, found still another colemanite deposit the following winter, named the Lila C. Those two claims would later produce some $30 million worth of borates. But neither compared in potential wealth to that original mountain of salt, the Monte Blanco, which still holds roughly three million tons of borates. Phi Lee and his partners sold their claim to this great bonanza for only $4,000. But Lee was a man of simple needs. He bought a slightly larger ranch—the one at Resting Spring—and it supported him and his family for the rest of their days.[8]

Coleman bought up just about every borate deposit in the Death Valley and Amargosa country—every one, that is, except the Eagle deposit, over on the west side of the valley. This little borax crust of barely 320 acres had been discovered by a hopeful young Frenchman, Isadore Daunet, who was determined to work it himself. Daunet was the first to ship borax out of Death Valley, but his was a tragic story. Born in the Basses-Pyrenees

Former San Francisco vigilante leader William Tell Coleman formed the Harmony Borax Company to open Death Valley's borax bonanza. (*Portrait courtesy of UCLA Library*)

in 1850, Daunet had come to San Francisco with his family at the age of ten. His father died soon after; his brothers went to work as waiters to be sure to get something to eat; and he ran away to the mines to seek a fortune. He had roamed the West for more than half his life, with nothing to show for it, when he first wandered into Death Valley in October 1880. He had left the old camp of Panamint with five other hapless fortune seekers, heading for Arizona to try their luck. But they ran out of luck the first day, losing their way as soon as they got into Death Valley. Two

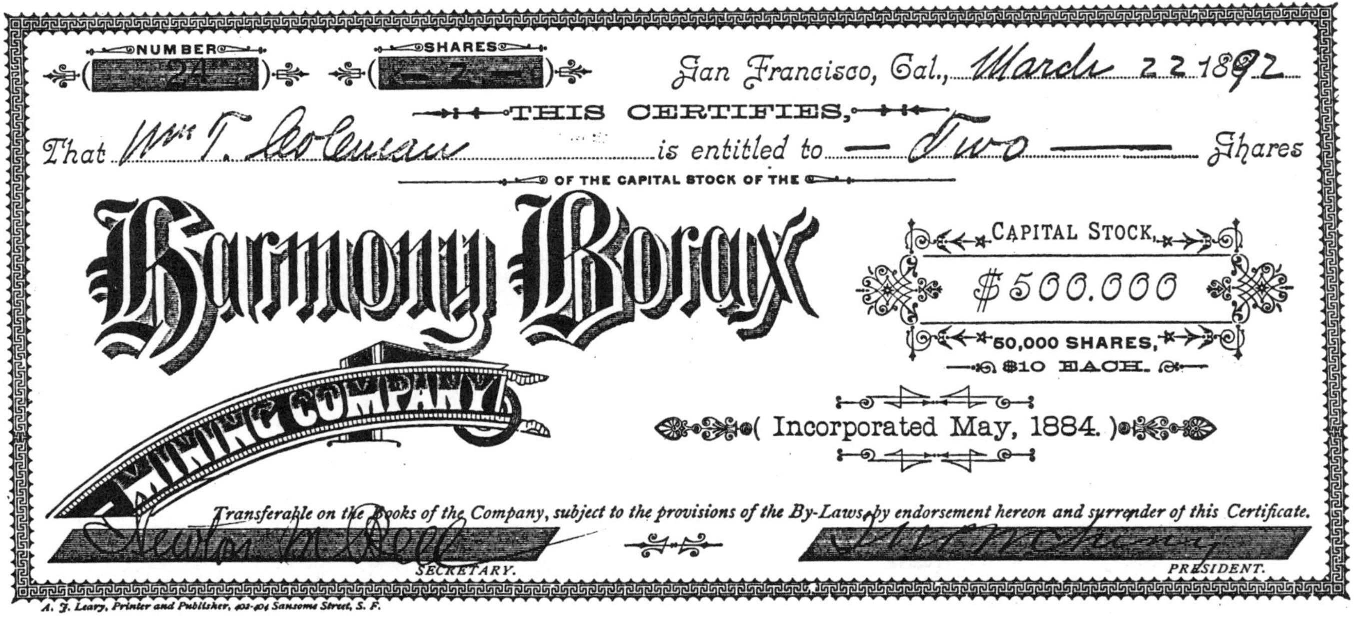

NUMBER 21

SHARES

San Francisco, Cal., March 22 1892

THIS CERTIFIES,

That Mrs. L. McLennan

is entitled to —— Two —— Shares

OF THE CAPITAL STOCK OF THE

Harmony Borax

MINING COMPANY

CAPITAL STOCK,

$500.000

50,000 SHARES,
$10 EACH.

(Incorporated May, 1884.)

Transferable on the Books of the Company, subject to the provisions of the By-Laws by endorsement hereon and surrender of this Certificate.

SECRETARY.

PRESIDENT.

A. J. Leary, Printer and Publisher, 421–423 Sansome Street, S. F.

turned back immediately. Daunet turned back the second day, after they started killing their mules and horses to drink the blood. Panamint Tom went out to rescue the others. He found one alive, one dead, and never did find the third man.[9]

That awful experience was still vivid in Daunet's memory a year later, when he heard of Winters's discovery. But it wasn't strong enough to keep him from going back. Daunet was certain that he too had at last found his fortune, but had just not realized it, out there on those blinding salt flats. With two companions, Christian C. Blanch and J. A. McDonald, he hurried back to Death Valley early in May of 1882, and located the Eagle borax ground just north of Bennetts Well. With borax then selling at 17¢ a pound, he and his partners thought that all they had to do was scoop up the crude salts, ship them to San Francisco, and their fortune would be made. The following month Al Robinson's pack mules carried Daunet's first load of borax out of Death Valley by way of Wildrose. But that first shipment of 37 tons of crude salts brought them only 8¢ a pound in San Francisco. This barely paid the shipping costs, so they realized that they would have to refine the salt and ship it more cheaply if they were to make a profit. In August they took in a new partner, Myron Harmon, a Darwin merchant who put up $4,000 to construct a simple refinery.[10]

The Eagle Borax Works, built that winter of 1882–83 about 2 miles north of Bennetts Well, was designed simply to separate the borax from the other salts by recrystallization. The core of the works was a 1,200-gallon iron dissolving tank, $20 \times 3 \times 2$ feet on a side, heated by a firebox that ran under it to a stovepipe at one end. Each day a few tons of crude salts were thrown into the tank of water and heated until the borax dissolved. Then the liquid was drawn into one of a dozen 1,000-gallon crystallizing tanks and left to slowly cool for ten days while the borax crystallized out. At the end of each day the insoluble waste was cleaned out of the dissolving tank, readying it for the next day's run. Blanch superintended the operation, keeping ten or so men at work gathering salt for the tank and mesquite for the fire. When everything ran smoothly they could produce 22 tons of concentrated borax per month. Daunet also found a cheaper way to ship the borax, contracting with former Nevada freighter James McLaughlin to haul the salt by wagon more than 100 miles south to Daggett, on the new Atlantic & Pacific line. Roughly following the Wade's route, Blanch broke the road from the works through Wingate Pass, to Lone Willow Spring, where it connected with the former Panamint to San Bernardino road, running by way of Granite Wells and Black's Ranch to the Mojave River. Ed Stiles hauled the first wagon load of borax out of Death Valley for McLaughlin with a twelve-mule team late in 1882; it took him eleven days to get to Daggett.[11]

By June 1883, Daunet was on top of the world. He and his partners had produced over 130 tons of borax and had officially incorporated the Eagle Borax Mining Company, with an optimistic capital of $100,000 and Daunet as its president. In a whirlwind of romance, Daunet had married an attractive French-Canadian seamstress, Clotilde Garand. But Daunet's world was about to crumble, for as the warmer weather arrived, he found that the tanks wouldn't cool enough for the borax to crystallize efficiently, so he was forced to close down for the summer. By the time he started up again that fall, the price of borax had dropped to less than 10¢ a pound. Daunet felt that Coleman was trying to freeze him out. He struggled on through the winter and spring, trying to work the richest patchs of salt, but by May 1884 he was on the verge of bankruptcy.[12]

In the meantime, Daunet had discovered that his wife had been married before, but hadn't told him—and when she learned of his impending financial failure, she secretly filed for divorce. On May 28 Daunet returned home to find his wife gone and divorce papers awaiting him. Everything and everyone seemed to have turned against him. He sat up all that night composing a long and rambling letter, berating Coleman and spilling out his life's dreams. Then at a few minutes past seven in the morning Daunet went down to the parlor, pulled a chair up in front of a mirror, sat down, tied a white handkerchief around his head, and "quietly and impassively . . . blew his brains out."[13]

By the early 1880s, William Tell Coleman had more wealth and power that Daunet ever dreamed of. Coleman was a preeminently successful businessman, leader of San Francisco's vigilante committees in 1856 and 1877, and soon-to-be touted for the Democratic nomination for president of the United States. Coleman was a quiet, self-confident Kentuckian in his late fifties, balding, with a walrus mustache, keen eyes, and a genial countenance that masked an iron will, rigid principles, and an obsession with monopolistic control. He controlled an extensive wholesale business with offices in New York, Chicago, and San Francisco, a line of clipper ships, and a score of lesser enterprises. Usually tight-lipped about his business affairs, he did tell one tale on himself—about how, in the winter of 1850, he had cornered all of the flour in Placerville and could have swiftly doubled his investment. But he held out for even bigger profits and wound up selling at a loss when his monopoly was broken. He said he had learned a lesson on that deal: to take his profits when he could get them. Yet he kept on trying to corner every market he could, and that would eventually be his undoing. He had cornered the marketing of western borax in the early 1870s and had helped finance the Nevada producers. When the Pacific Borax Company failed in the late seventies, Coleman took over the operation for a couple of years, but sold the company to Francis M. Smith in 1880. Now with Smith's help, Coleman went back into borax mining again.[14]

Coleman set up an elaborate corporate hierarchy around the Death Valley and Amargosa properties. Early in 1883 he formed three firms—the Harmony, Henry Clay, and Meridian mining companies—each with a capital of just $500, to hold the borax claims; and two others—the Greenland and Amargosa borax companies—with a capital of $50,000 each, to work the claims and refine the borax. Fourteen of Coleman's clerks and one of Smith's served as nominal directors of these firms. The following year Coleman reorganized the business, consolidating the playa mining and refining operations of the Greenland and Amargosa companies into a new firm, the now famous Harmony Borax Mining Company, incorporated on May 15, 1884 with a capital of $500,000. In November of that year he formed two additional companies: Meridian Borax, apparently for the purpose of mining and refining the colemanite deposits, although it did only enough work to hold and patent the claims; and California Chemical, which took over the final purification and packaging of the borax in a reconverted soap factory in Alameda, just across the bay from San Francisco.[15]

Despite these corporate intricacies, all of the Death Valley and Amargosa operations were, from their beginning in 1881 to their end in 1888, under the direction of just one man—Superintendent Rudolph Neuschwander. A forty-five-year-old Swiss immigrant and innovative mechanic, Neuschwander had worked in the Nevada borax fields since the early 1870s and had served as superintendent of the Pacific Borax Company's works under both Coleman and Smith before coming to Death Valley in the winter of 1881–82 to set up the operations there. He was assisted by John W. S. Perry, a former San Francisco druggist, who served as foreman.[16]

Coleman began sending mining and refining equipment to Neuschwander in the winter of 1882–83. He also sent seeds and seedlings for what would become the Greenland Ranch, at the mouth of Furnace Creek. Neuschwander designed and built two refining works, one at Winters's Death Valley deposits and the other at the Amargosa deposits. The Amargosa works, which were smaller and were completed first, began shipping borax in the summer of 1883. The Death Valley works, at what came to be known as Coleman, began operation that fall. Just south of Coleman, Neuschwander laid out the Greenland Ranch—tradition places it on the site of "Bellerin" Andy Laswell's last alfalfa patch. A mile-long irrigation ditch brought water from Furnace Creek for 40 acres of alfalfa—plus melon, sweet potato, and vegetable gardens and a small orchard of fruit trees to help feed the men and animals at the works. Neuschwander also built the comfortable ranch house with double roof, 4-foot-thick adobe walls, and encircling veranda that some later credited to "Bellerin Teck." With persistent irrigation, the ranch began producing alfalfa before the works began producing borax. Eventually as many as nine crops a year were cut at Greenland Ranch, and it remains the most bountiful oasis in Death Valley.[17]

The Harmony Borax Works at Coleman, which Neuschwander modeled after the earlier Pacific Borax Works at Fish Lake Valley in Nevada, had two enormous dissolving tanks, each holding about 3,000 gallons; eight 2,000-gallon settling tanks; and fifty-seven 1,800-gallon crystallizing tanks. These works made Daunet's operation look amateurish at best. Neuschwander designed the plant not only to extract whatever borax there was in the crude salts but also to convert the more abundant ulexite, or cottonball borate, into borax by the addition of soda, thus greatly increasing the yield. In addition he steam-heated the tanks and crushed the crude salts so that they would dissolve more quickly. The great steam boiler, 17 feet long and 4 feet in diameter, which heated the tanks and powered the crusher and pumps, still stands at the site today. Neuschwander also increased the efficiency of the crystallizing tanks by wrapping them with many layers of felt, which when soaked with water helped cool the tanks by evaporation. Even so, the Death Valley works were only able to function for about eight months of each year, suspending operations early in June and resuming in October. During the summer months only two men were left at the ranch, and the borax operations were shifted to the Amargosa works. The weather there was just enough cooler that the borax crystallized even in the summer, but the deposits there were not rich enough to work year round.[18]

Neuschwander ran the borax operation with a crew of about forty men. Three-quarters of them were Chinese who gathered the salt out on the playa for $1.50 a day. Coleman got most of that back over the counter of the company store for such staples as tea, rice, and dried cuttlefish. It was hot, dusty, backbreaking work out on the playa, scraping the salt into windrows, shoveling it into handcarts and then into wagons for the works. But jobs at the works, stirring the boiling brine and scraping the crystals and mud from the tanks, weren't much more inviting, even though Coleman paid $50 a month for them. Nor were the legendary horrors of Death Valley an inducement. One later visitor even fancied that the works had finally closed down because everyone who went there either died within six months or left a broken-down invalid! Several men recruited at Daggett however did quit as soon as they saw the valley, claiming they had been deceived. Complaining of the cost of hauling such men out and back, Coleman instructed his agent at Daggett to screen the men carefully thereafter and send only those who would "stick—I want nothing to do with tramps."[19]

Charles Bennett, who had gone into the freighting business at Daggett after selling his ranch to Winters, took a year's contract with Coleman in 1883 to haul the borax to the railroad. That summer he took the first wagon loads from the Amargosa works to Daggett by way of Saratoga Springs, Cave Spring, Garlic Spring, and Coyote Well. In the fall he began running his wagons across the Devil's Golf Course on a road that had to be graded by sledge hammers to the Eagle Works, then followed their route to Daggett. But that was a difficult road, and Bennett soon found a better route to the railroad, leaving the Daggett road at Granite Wells and heading west to the station at Mojave. By the spring of 1884 he had a total of nine eighteen-mule teams on the new road from Coleman to Mojave. When the work shifted to Amargosa again in the summer, the borax was still hauled out to Mojave, reopening part of the Mojave to Tecopa road along the old Walker cutoff from Saratoga Springs to Granite Wells via Owl Hole and Leach springs.[20]

The drop in borax prices that helped push Daunet to suicide also forced economies on Coleman, and when Bennett's contract ran out Coleman decided it would be cheaper if they did their own freighting. Neuschwander's foreman, Perry, had been studying the freighting business, and he soon organized the teaming operations with the same efficiency with which Neuschwander had set up the works. He built ten giant wagons at Mojave and selected five teams of eighteen mules and two horses to pull them. Teams that size and larger had been used at various times and places throughout the West, but it was these five teams that the Pacific Coast Borax Company would later immortalize with its advertising campaign for "20 Mule Team Borax."[21]

Perry's borax wagons nonetheless were of giant proportions, weighing nearly 4 tons each and dwarfing the men who handled them. The wagon beds measured 4 by 16 feet and were 6 feet deep, holding over 10 tons of borax. The rear wheels stood 7 feet high, the front 5, and the iron tires, 8 inches wide and 1 inch thick, weighed a quarter of a ton apiece. Each wagon cost at least $900—some say $1,200. The wagons were hitched in pairs, with a water wagon carrying a 500-gallon tank attached behind. Fully loaded, the ensemble weighed over 30 tons—an awful load to pull through deep sand and up steep grades. But the teams and teamsters were equal to the task. The teams were hitched up with the two horses at the wagon tongue, but not because they were smarter than the mules—far from it. As one mule fancier claimed, "A dumb mule—if there is such a thing—is smarter than a smart horse." Two draft horses were used simply because they had the weight to handle the wagon tongue on quick turns. Ahead of the horses were the mules. The "most civilized" pair were put in the lead; the next most intelligent pair were in the back, just ahead of the horses; and in between were all "the sinful, the fun-loving and the

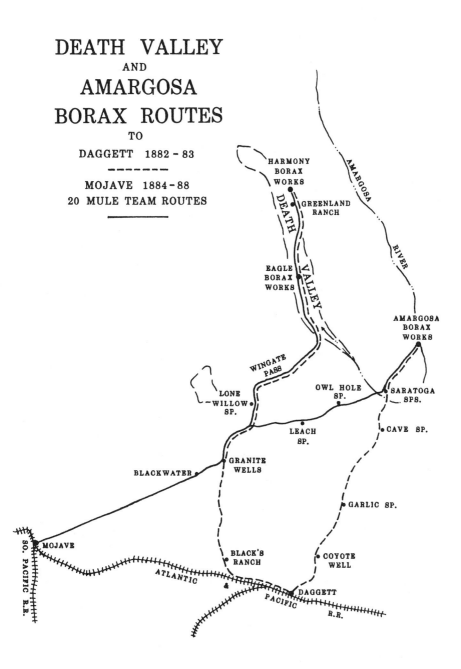

DEATH VALLEY
AND
AMARGOSA
BORAX ROUTES
TO
DAGGETT 1882 - 83

MOJAVE 1884 - 88
20 MULE TEAM ROUTES

HARMONY
BORAX
WORKS

AMARGOSA

DEATH

GREENLAND
RANCH

RIVER

EAGLE
BORAX
WORKS

VALLEY

AMARGOSA
BORAX
WORKS

WINGATE
PASS

LONE
WILLOW
SP.

OWL HOLE
SP.

SARATOGA
SPS.

CAVE SP.

LEACH
SP.

GRANITE
WELLS

BLACKWATER

GARLIC SP.

MOJAVE

SO. PACIFIC R.R.

ATLANTIC

BLACK'S
RANCH

COYOTE
WELL

DAGGETT

PACIFIC

R.R.

raw-hides." It took skillful teamsters to handle such teams, and they earned every cent of the $100 to $120 a month that Coleman paid. The teamsters were each assisted by a swamper, whose most important duty was to handle the rear wagon brake on a downgrade.²²

The teams ran almost like clockwork. The round trip from Death Valley to Mojave and back—some 330 miles—took twenty days. One team loaded and left the borax works every four days; they were constantly on the road. The teamsters were paid when they arrived at Mojave, and had only the afternoon and evening for a fling. But that was usually all it took, for there was a skillful faro dealer in town. "It was a good thing for us," Perry noted, "for the teamster could go broke in one night and be ready to go out over the road in the morning." The teams were only run nine months out of the year, from mid-September to mid-June, and the borax company claimed that they never lost an animal. But they did lose a man.²³

That happened on October 25, 1886, just after the teams had started up for the season. Teamster Al Bryson and his swamper, Sterling Wassam, were hauling the summer's borax from the Amargosa works to Mojave. The mules had been balky that morning, and Bryson was in a bad mood by the time they stopped for lunch at Saratoga Springs. He was opening a can of beef with a butcher knife when he started cussing out Wassam for not keeping the knife sharper. Wassam made some obvious reply, and Bryson lunged at him, knife in hand. The swamper jumped back and ran behind a wagon, with Bryson in pursuit. When the teamster rounded the corner, Wassam whacked him with a shovel, "splitting his skull open and killing him instantly"—at least that was Wassam's story. He buried Bryson in a shallow grave, then stayed there for the night. Soon after starting the next morning, he overturned the wagons and broke his leg. Unhitching the animals, he rode on for 60 miles, until he overtook the next team and accompanied them to Mojave. There he was arrested and brought to San Bernardino, where he was tried for murder and acquitted.²⁴

The Harmony Borax Mining Company was producing about 2 million pounds of borax a year from the Death Valley and Amargosa deposits, and in 1886 the company started shipping a comparable amount of cole-manite from beds discovered near Calico. This essentially doubled American borax production from what it had been before Winters's discovery. This increase also broke the price of borax, since Coleman was unable to create a comparable increase in demand. In 1883, he and Smith had successfully lobbied for a protective tariff on borax of 3¢ a pound, which cut off most foreign competition, but that didn't prevent the glut from domestic production. By 1887 the price had fallen to less than 6¢ a pound in San Francisco, from a high of nearly 15¢ a pound just four years before, when Coleman shipped his first borax from Death Valley. Coleman, Smith, and the other producers couldn't afford to let the price go any lower. Late that year they all agreed to cut back production to bring the price back up. It was a successful plan, but for Coleman it was too late.[25]

In 1886 Coleman, then in his early sixties, had turned over the management of most of his business to his two junior partners—Carlton, his younger son, and Frank S. Johnson, whom he treated just like a son. With Coleman's blessing these two tyros set out to build new empires. In 1887 they tried to take over the Pacific canned salmon industry and corner the American raisin market. It was the raisins that did it. "The market was high here and we purchased heavily," Coleman later lamented, "lower prices followed; a dull market, bad handling, and the bad results of our Eastern correspondents did the rest." They lost over $1 million on raisins that year, and Coleman started negotiating the sale of the Death Valley borax operations to bail them out. Coleman said he was "on the eve" of closing the sale with an English syndicate for $2 million, when Congressman Roger Q. Mills of Texas introduced a tariff reform bill to remove the duty on a number of commodities, including borax. Coleman's buyer backed out, his creditors demanded payment, and the house of Coleman collapsed on May 7, 1888.[26]

The Harmony Borax Mining Company promptly shut down, never to resume. Death Valley's twenty-mule team days were over, and the great wagons and teams dispersed. Two of the teams hauled colemanite at Calico for a time; two others were sold off to freighters; and one of the remaining wagons was left at the north end of Death Valley in 1890, when it got mired in the sand en route to Nevada. Only two men stayed on at Greenland Ranch to look after the property. One soon changed his mind and tried to walk out. He took a 5-gallon canteen and traveled 40 miles before he died. The other, James Dayton, remained caretaker for over a decade, making the ranch a lifesaving oasis for desert travelers. He died less than 20 miles from the ranch on a trip to Daggett in July 1899.[27]

Coleman never rebuilt his financial empire, but he did retain his uncompromising adherence to principle. Although his creditors agreed to write off his debts at 40¢ on the dollar, he was determined to pay them in full. It took him four years, but he did just that. He also bought back the defunct shares of Harmony Borax. But that was his final triumph; he died soon afterward on November 22, 1893, from what his doctor described as "a general breaking up of the vital forces."[28]

Francis M. Smith bought all of the Death Valley, Amargosa, and Calico property from Coleman's assignees on March 12, 1890 for $150,000 in cash and $400,000 on time. With that, Smith truly became the "Borax King," and he consolidated all of his holdings to form the great Pacific

Coast Borax Company that September. He also saw that the profitable days of the playa borax deposits had passed and concentrated his resources on the full development of the Calico colemanite beds. Within a year Smith made the Calico mine the principal borax producer in the United States, and for the next fifteen years it was virtually the sole producer. Not until 1906, when the Calico deposits were nearly exhausted, did Smith at last return to open the great colemanite beds of Death Valley— but that story is yet to come.[29]

GOLD AND GAS

Gold and gas fueled Death Valley's greatest mining boom, which raged for two decades at the turn of the century: gold produced the spark, and gas did the rest. The final collapse of silver prices in the 1890s had made it clear that silver was just another commodity, like borax or hay, and had sent prospectors back into the hills in search of that one last standard—Gold! Gasoline propelled them; it drove their wheels, their pumps, and their mills. Newfangled automobiles crowded out the Concord stages and even threatened the burro. Gasoline and diesel engines powered the hoists that brought up the ore, the mills that crushed it, and the pumps and generators that provided water and electricity. Scalding steam drove the locomotives that brought in all the mining machinery and hauled out more ore. Behind it all, gas of a different sort blew the bubbles that brought in the money that made it all run—and much, much more.

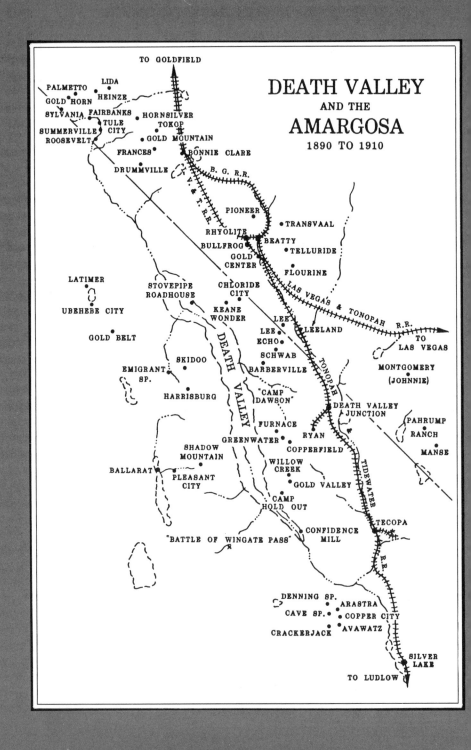

DEATH VALLEY
AND THE
AMARGOSA
1890 TO 1910

TO GOLDFIELD

PALMETTO
LIDA
GOLD HORN
HEINZE
SYLVANIA
FAIRBANKS
SUMMERVILLE
TULE
ROOSEVELT
CITY
HORNSILVER
TOKOP
GOLD MOUNTAIN
FRANCES
BONNIE CLARE
DRUMMVILLE
B. G. R.R.
V. & T. R.R.
PIONEER
TRANSVAAL
RHYOLITE
BEATTY
BULLFROG
TELLURIDE
GOLD
CENTER
FLOURINE
LATIMER
STOVEPIPE
CHLORIDE
ROADHOUSE
CITY
LAS VEGAS & TONOPAH R.R.
UBEHEBE CITY
KEANE
WONDER
LEE
TO
GOLD BELT
LEE
LEELAND
LAS VEGAS
ECHO
SKIDOO
SCHWAB
MONTGOMERY
EMIGRANT
BARBERVILLE
(JOHNNIE)
SP.
HARRISBURG
CAMP
DAWSON
DEATH VALLEY
JUNCTION
FURNACE
PAHRUMP
RANCH
SHADOW
GREENWATER
RYAN
MANSE
MOUNTAIN
COPPERFIELD
BALLARAT
WILLOW
CREEK
PLEASANT
GOLD VALLEY
CITY
CAMP
HOLD OUT
TECOPA
"BATTLE OF WINGATE PASS"
CONFIDENCE
MILL
R.R.
DENNING SP.
ARASTRA
CAVE SP.
COPPER CITY
AVAWATZ
CRACKERJACK
SILVER
LAKE
TO LUDLOW

DEATH VALLEY
TONOPAH
TIDEWATER

The Montgomery Brothers

It was the Montgomery brothers who started Death Valley's great gold boom. They found the gold that started the rushes; they brought in the first gasoline engines; they opened the first big mines; and they stayed with it for over twenty years—all the way to the end—eventually making over a million from it. Few would make more from the great boom, although no one would have predicted that from the way the Montgomery brothers started. Their first two ventures in the Death Valley and Amargosa country were terrible disasters, ending in bankruptcy and bloodshed.

There were seven brothers in all; three came to Death Valley—George, Frank, and Ernest Alexander, known as Bob. The eldest and the youngest, George and Bob, played the largest roles in the valley's history. George, in his late thirties when he first came to Death Valley, was a man of unassuming build with dark hair and blue eyes. But he was an enthusiastic and extravagant talker and, as it turned out, an impulsive and extravagant spender, especially of other people's money. Bob, eleven years his junior, was prematurely grey, shrewder, and reserved—some would say pretentious—and he learned from George's mistakes. Frank was just hardworking. They stayed together through hard times, but good fortune would finally break them up. Born in Canada, they had come with their parents to a farm in Stuart, Iowa after the Civil War and had come west with the rush to the mines on Wood River, Idaho in 1884. They worked in the mines of the Northwest for the rest of the decade before coming to Death Valley.[1]

George led the way in the winter of 1890–91. Like many others before him, he came to look for the wonderful Lost Breyfogle; unlike most, he would soon tell the world that he had found it. Late in 1890, he and five companions set out from Calaveras County on the Mother Lode to scour Death Valley for the legendary ledge. By the New Year they were just about to give up when George Montgomery made the discovery. They had camped at the north end of Pahrump Valley on the east edge of the Amargosa. George was returning to camp at about sundown across a low ridge. He had paused to rest when, as he recalled,

> within a few steps of my resting place I saw a quartz ledge, and sticking out boldly were scattered nuggets of gold. I was so startled by the sight that I thought I must be dreaming, and walked away a

short distance. On returning the gold was still there, and what was more I could break it out of the rock; and then I knew my find was not a dream; but a reality.[2]

George staked out the lode as the Chispa, Spanish for "a nugget," and he and his partners promptly went to work sinking a prospect hole. In the next few weeks before their grub ran out, they took out over $800 worth of gold. Leaving his partners to hold the ground, George took a yeast powder can full of nuggets and went to Daggett for supplies, and then to San Francisco to spread the word—the Lost Breyfogle was "Found At Last." He caused quite a stir with his can of nuggets, his stories of rock studded with gold "like plums in a pudding," and his claim that the new camp of Montgomery would rival Virginia City.[3]

A new "Breyfogle Fever" seized credulous miners in scattered towns throughout California and Nevada, and they all started for the Amargosa. By April there were a hundred men and one woman camped at the mines. The good ground was quickly taken; even Bob Montgomery, who was among the first of the newcomers, found poor pickings. But a couple of good strikes were made 4 miles to the north, where Pahrump *pakwinavi* Tecopa's son, John, found the rich Johnnie ledge—the best in the district. Close to it, Joseph Yount's boys found another rich cropping, the North Belle. The rest staked out the intervening ground and waited for George Montgomery's return.[4]

After two months of high living off his can of gold, George returned from San Francisco with a new partner, M. B. Bartlett, and in a flurry of excitement, he began spending money right and left. First, he bought a little one-stamp Kendall prospecting mill to set up at Horseshutem Springs. Then he bought a marvelous new Huntington Centrifugal Roller Quartz Mill to set up at the mine and 6 miles of pipe to bring water from the springs. He hired a crew of thirty-five at a prime $4 a day to sink three shafts on the Chispa, set up the mills, lay the pipe, and put up a bunkhouse, blacksmith's shop, and other works. At the same time George began buying up the Johnnie and other outlying claims. With all this excitement Montgomery was a promising looking camp that summer of 1891, boasting some sixty settlers, two rival stores, the necessary number of saloons, and plans for a hotel. There was also a regular freight line from Daggett 160 miles away, talk of a 200-mile stage line from Candelaria, and the dream of a railroad connection, if the Utah Central continued west. The Post Office Department, overreacting to the boomlet, established an office not only at Montgomery but also at each of the two big ranches, Pahrump and the Manse, just a dozen or two miles to the south.[5]

Then suddenly in February 1892, the bubble popped and work came to a halt, amid charges that George Montgomery's "extravagant management has threatened to ruin his backers." George and his partners had in fact run out of money, most of which they had squandered on a mill that couldn't work the ore efficiently. The marvelous contraption recovered less than $30 a ton on ore that assayed $70. Since most of the ore assayed much less than that, it simply did not pay to work it. Once again, George headed for San Francisco, and the camp was virtually abandoned. The nation was entering a depression, and George had no immediate luck finding new investors. It was not until the winter of 1894–95, when the economy had begun to recover, that the camp of Montgomery revived.[6]

That winter, George found new backers in a prosperous group of Salt Lake Mormons, led by Hugh J. Cannon, one of the sons of Hunt party forty-niner and church leader George Q. Cannon. The Mormons had formed the Sterling Mining and Milling Company to work several claims just over the north end of Spring Mountain in the old Sterling district, which had been organized twenty years before, during the Panamint rush. They had hastily put up a ten-stamp mill, only to discover that the ore was too poor to pay, so they decided to try to recoup their losses by throwing in with Montgomery. With their backing, George resumed work with a flourish early in 1895. He moved the Sterling mill over to the Chispa, started a crew of forty to work in the Chispa and Johnnie, bought yet another Huntington roller mill to set up with the old one on the Johnnie, and bought a couple 40-horsepower gasoline engines to run them all. Dozens of new tents sprang up at Montgomery, and a new boom was on. By August there were hundreds of tons of ore on the dumps, and the mills were running.[7]

The prospects looked so good that Angus McArthur, a disgruntled ex-foreman from the Chispa, decided to get a piece of the action. Claiming that Montgomery had failed to do the assessment work on the Chispa for 1894 as required to maintain title, McArthur staked claim to the property. When George ignored his claim, McArthur offered a half interest in the claim to one Phil Foote, if Foote would take possession of the mine. "Nervy Phil" was just the man to take a fighting chance. A sometime gambler from Colorado who had once held up a Salt Lake gaming house when his luck failed, he was now down on his luck again, working as a blacksmith on the Johnnie. Foote promptly recruited Jack Longstreet, a couple of other drifters, and several adventuresome Paiute. Armed with Winchesters, they quietly seized the Chispa mine at daybreak on August 28, while the crew were still asleep in the bunkhouse below. Foote then fired a round to announce his presence, but the startled miners offered no resistance. By the time word of the seizure got to George Montgomery at the Johnnie, Foote had brought up a wagon-load of supplies and was ready for a long siege.[8]

George telegraphed to Los Angeles for two cases of rifles and to Salt

Lake to alert his partners. Hugh Cannon's half brother, a lawyer, headed for the Nye county seat at Belmont to take legal action. But by the time he arrived in Belmont, the rifles had reached Montgomery and George was ready to take direct action. At seven o'clock Sunday morning, September 8, George, his brother Bob, a friend named Harry Ramsey, and a number of loyal miners were lying in wait atop a cliff overlooking the mine when Foote and his men confidently came out to eat their breakfast on the dump. As soon as Foote sat down a single shot rang out and he fell back mortally wounded, a bullet through his chest. Longstreet and the others scrambled for cover and soon surrendered without much of a fight. Foote, given a dose of morphine to ease the pain, died that afternoon, and was the only casualty. A Colorado newsman wrote his obituary: "He lived for the reputation of a dead game man and he played the string out."[9]

Who fired the fatal shot is unknown, but the best marksman in the group was probably Harry Ramsey, a brash Texan then in his mid-thirties who had already put more than seven notches in his gun in avenging the murder of his father and the ransacking of his border saloon. No one was ever charged with killing Foote—quite the opposite, George Montgomery was honored soon after by a dance at the Odd Fellows' Hall in Belmont. Longstreet and two companions were convicted of claim jumping and fined several hundred dollars, which they worked out in the county jail. Deciding not to press his claim further, Angus McArthur moved on.[10]

With what they termed the "late unpleasantness" resolved, the company resumed work in the Chispa and Johnnie, but George Montgomery turned his energies to a new mine, the Confidence, right in the heart of Death Valley. Mary Scott, an Ash Meadows Paiute, had picked up some interesting rocks on the Death Valley slope of the Black Mountains about 8 miles northwest of the old Ibex mine. When she happened to show them to her cousin, Bob Black, he immediately saw that they were gold float and, it was said, for "twelve bottles of desert wine," he persuaded her to show him the source. It was indeed a rich-looking ledge, but Bob had found gold once before and had learned how hard it was for a Paiute to get a fair deal. He had discovered the rich ledges at Vanderbilt, south of Ivanpah, in 1891, but had received next to nothing for that discovery. This time he hoped to do better, for he had his eye on his brother-in-law Jack Longstreet's ranch at Ash Meadows, which Jack wanted to sell for $4,000. So Bob showed the rock to the millwright at the Johnnie, Frank Cole, and a friend, James Ashdown, offering to lead them to the ledge if they would promise to pay him the necessary $4,000. They agreed, and on April 24, 1895, they staked claim to the ledge, naming it the Confidence. For good measure they staked an adjacent claim, the Mendocino, the following day. The Confidence was an enormous quartz lode that was

50 feet wide and said to average $45 a ton, with pockets running as high as $250 a ton. When they showed the great lode to George Montgomery, he immediately agreed to buy Ashdown's half for $7,000. George then arranged the sale of both claims to Hugh Cannon and his partners for $81,000, of which George was to get $57,000 and Cole $24,000. Most of this was apparently in shares of the Confidence Mining Company, which Cannon formed. Out of all these transactions, Bob Black got a note from the company for $4,000 with which to buy Longstreet's ranch.[11]

George, of course, became superintendent of the new Confidence company, and he plunged ahead in a new rush of activity in the winter of 1895–96. He bought a string of pack mules at $100 a head, a China pump, a rock crusher, a 20-horsepower gasoline engine, and still another newfangled machine—a Bryan Roller Quartz Mill, with three great 3,000-pound wheels that rolled around on the ore. He also put crews to work opening the ledge, building a bunkhouse, sinking a well, erecting the mill, and grading a wagon road 7 miles from the mine down to the mill site on the floor of Death Valley. He is said to have spent between forty and fifty thousand dollars on the mill alone.[12]

Early in February 1896 the Confidence mill started up and the trouble began. The mill returns showed that the ore was much more rebellious than George had supposed, so once again the whole expensive contrivance recovered only a small fraction of the gold in the ore. The Chispa and Johnnie mills weren't doing much better, so Hugh Cannon suddenly decided to cut his losses and not pay out another cent. No one bothered to tell the men at the mine, however; they had to figure it out for themselves when no paychecks came in February or March. They finally quit on April 4, and headed for the settlements to try negotiating their time checks. They had little luck, for the company had already accumulated $15,000 in unpaid bills.[13]

By then a great smell had surrounded both of George Montgomery's operations. Once again he was denounced for gross mismanagement. The Confidence Mining Company was branded the "Lost Confidence," and the few remaining residents of the camp of Montgomery, taking a sudden dislike to the name, started calling it The Deuces.[14]

In August 1896 Hugh Cannon finally sent a practical milling man, Thomas P. Gillespie, out to the mines to try to find a profitable way to work the ore. Gillespie might have succeeded if he hadn't been shot dead through the head by an unseen gunman at The Deuces on Sunday afternoon, October 25. No real evidence was ever turned up as to the identity of the murderer, but local suspicions pointed to Bob Black, for among the Confidence company's unpaid accounts was Bob's $4,000 note. Bob had signed the note over to Longstreet, but since the company hadn't honored it, Bob still didn't have the ranch. In an attempt to placate him, George

Montgomery had let Bob draw freely on the company store, but when Gillespie arrived he ended that. It seems to have been a fatal decision. For Bob it was the final straw; he'd been cheated again—all that was left was revenge. And things only got worse after Gillespie's murder. In 1905 Bob Black killed his wife, his brother, and two others, in a drunken rage. He then hid out with Longstreet for several years until Jack finally killed him in a quarrel in 1910. Such was the fate of a Paiute prospector.[15]

In all, Montgomery and his partners had taken out about 4,000 tons of select ore from the Chispa and Johnnie mines, but the mills had recovered only about $100,000—less than half the value of the ore—and the profits were lost in the tailings. So after Gillespie's murder they tried to sell the mines. They lined up a group of Pittsburgh investors and were just about to close the deal in November 1898, when the Chispa mill burned to the ground and the deal fell through. Still, Hugh Cannon ultimately retrieved $12,000 from the Confidence, selling it to his father's estate in 1901 when he became the executor.[16]

The Montgomery brothers in the meantime had found yet another gold mine. This one they called the World Beater. They discovered it in the fall of 1896 way up in the Panamints, south of the famous old silver camp. In this new bonanza, George offered his Mormon partners one more chance to recoup their losses. They took the gamble, and the town of Ballarat was soon born.

Others had been working gold ledges in the Panamints for some time, but it took a natural publicist like George Montgomery to work up a boom. Tales of Goller's elusive nuggets and Alvord's lost ledge had enticed a number of prospectors to hunt for gold among the silver leads of the Panamints, but they did little more than leave a few names on the land. In June 1883, Milo Page thought he had found Goller's gold in what has since been known as Goler Wash, south of Anvil Spring. Page organized the Butte Valley Mining District and made wages for a few seasons working high-grade ore from the ledge in a little arrastra. In April 1889, two other prospectors, grubstaked by Riverside banker Robert B. Taylor, located the Gold Hill ledge on a spur of the Panamints that still bears that name. Taylor formed the Death Valley Mining Company and explored the lode on and off for a decade while he debated whether or not it would pay to put up a mill. He finally decided he would do better to sell. Royal McIntyre, a Redlands carpenter, could have used some of Taylor's caution. When he found gold in April 1894 in what is now Redlands Canyon, he rushed back home with a few specimens of "fabulously rich gold ore" and quickly talked his neighbors into forming the Redlands Gold Mining Company. Within four months of his discovery he had set up a ten-stamp mill just below the mine. Only then did he begin to probe the extent of the pay rock and find that all he had was a tiny pocket of ore amounting to just about one day's mill run![17] What brought the Montgomery brothers to the Panamints, however, were the gold strikes in Pleasant Canyon, just above old Post Office Spring. There in 1893 Charles Anthony, a sixty-year-old storekeeper and part-time prospector who had come with the great Panamint rush and stayed on at Darwin, found a gold ledge he called the Mineral Ranch, high up on the south wall of the canyon. In September 1895 he sold an interest in his "Ranch" to a group of Los Angeles investors, who formed the Golden West Mining and Milling Company and set up a five-stamp mill just below the mine. It was a promising mine, but the venture foundered on poor management. With no thought to water supply, the mill was erected on a ledge 600 feet above the streambed. A well sunk at the mill was dry, so they tried pumping water up from the stream, which proved to be both costly and inadequate. Then, when the mill finally started up, it recovered only $5 a ton from $45 ore! While the company bumbled along by fits and starts trying to improve the mill, most of the men took off to prospect for mines of their own. The most successful was a gray-eyed Kentuckian, Henry C. Ratcliff, who located the Never Give Up just 2 miles above the Mineral Ranch in May 1896. It was to become the district's biggest producer. This strike attracted the Montgomery brothers, and that September, just half a mile above Ratcliff's claim, Bob and George found their World Beater. The South Park Mining District was formed that same month, George sent out the word, and a new rush to the Panamints began.[18]

With characteristic enthusiasm George Montgomery rallied Hugh Cannon and his other Mormon backers and plunged ahead. Before the end of the year he had dismantled the Confidence mill and moved the machinery to a spring in the mouth of Pleasant Canyon. With added backing from two San Francisco promoters, Charles Fish and George Wells, Montgomery formed the South Park Development Company, added a rock crusher and a concentrator to the old Bryan mill, and put a crew of forty-five to work on the mine and mill. The mill started up in March 1897, on free-milling ore from surface croppings which paid as much as $40 a ton.[19]

This burst of activity brought the merchants and whiskey dealers. Three rival camps sprang up: Pleasant City, in the canyon near the mines; Post Office Spring, at the foot of the great fan at the mouth of the canyon; and Ballarat, out on the flat, half a mile north of the spring. Ballarat, named for the great Australian gold-rush camp of the 1850s, became the boss camp, with Pleasant City a distant second. The townsite was laid out in March 1897, and lots were snapped up at anywhere from $10 to $75 apiece. By the end of that month Ballarat had two saloons, dispensing whiskey at a rate of 15 gallons a day, plus a general store and a dozen tents. Two months later it boasted four saloons, two general stores, two restaurants, three feed yards, an assay office, a hotel, and a population of over a hundred. On the Fourth of July, another hundred miners came down from the canyon to take part in the foot and burro races, hammer throwing, and informal drinking bouts that were capped off with a grand tug-of-war. By the end of the year the camp had added a post office, two rival weekly stages, and two little gasoline-powered custom mills with a total of eighteen stamps, running on sample lots of high-grade ore from mines opening up in nearly every canyon up and down the Panamint Range.[20]

The Montgomery brothers led the development of the district with large payrolls and steady bullion production. By the fall of 1898 they had taken out about 2,500 tons of ore, turning the surface croppings of the World Beater into an "immense quarry" and producing over $50,000 in bullion. They had also opened the lode at depth, blocking out fully 16,000 tons of ore. The mine's future seemed bright, but the prospects weren't quite what they appeared. The mill had saved only two-thirds of the assay value, even for the easily worked surface ores, and the bullion production thus far had left little if any profit. Moreover, most of the deep ore that they had blocked out was much more rebellious than that on the top and simply wouldn't pay without costly improvements on the mill. The easiest way to make money out of the mine at that point was to sell it, and they soon did just that.[21]

With proven production and large reserves, the World Beater was an attractive-looking mine, and in the spring of 1899 the South Park Development Company sold the property to Los Angeles investors. At the same time they sold the mill tailings separately to Pridham, Dineen, and Quinn, who styled themselves the P.D.Q. Cyanide Company, set up the Death Valley country's first cyaniding plant at the tailings, and recovered around $20,000 worth of gold from them within a couple months.[22]

The new owners of the World Beater were James P. Flint, a young Angeleno who had dabbled successfully in oil promotion; his father, the Reverend Frederick W. Flint; and Tracey N. Stebbins, a practical miner who became superintendent. Stebbins immediately moved the mill 6 miles up the canyon to the mine, remodeled it, and started it up again in July 1899, running on the richer portions of the rock that the Montgomerys had blocked out. Even though the mill recovered barely $15 a ton, Stebbins managed to turn out several thousand dollars' worth of bullion every month on into the new year.[23]

By September of 1898, Henry Ratcliff had opened the great ore body of the Never Give Up enough to sell it for $30,000 to several Michigan investors, led by the brothers Albert J. and William W. Godsmark, who

Crowell's map of 1903, showing the beginnings of Death Valley's gold boom at Montgomery and Ballarat. (*Courtesy of Henry E. Huntington Library and Art Gallery*)

had built up prosperous grocery and creamery businesses in Battle Creek. They formed a closed corporation, the Ratcliff Consolidated Gold Mines, Ltd., with an experienced mining man, Robert F. Harrison, as superintendent. Harrison commenced work that winter with a burst of energy, erecting a ten-stamp mill just below the mine and running a 4,200-foot aerial tramway and a 10,000-foot pipeline to carry the ore and water. The first stamps dropped in February 1899, but there were problems. The stationary cable tram kept breaking down, and the mill barely recovered half of the value of the ore. Undaunted, Harrison shut down and thoroughly overhauled the operation. He put in a new double-traveling cable tramway, enlarged the mill to twenty stamps, and added a 50-ton cyanide tank to work the tailings. When he had finished, he had doubled both the capacity and the efficiency of the plant. Harrison started up the mill again in January 1900, turning out $15,000 a month in gold to make the Ratcliff the new boss mine of the Panamints.[24]

On up the canyon at Panamint Tom's old Stone Corral, two more mills started up. There James Fenimore Cooper, a seasoned old miner with a borrowed name, had found a little high-grade deposit that he was content just to work himself—"like drawing money from the bank," he said. Cooper made it a model of pay-as-you-go mining. He worked the first ore in a hand mortar until he had saved up enough to buy a two-stamp mill in the fall of 1897. With this little mill he eventually accumulated enough to buy a four-stamp mill, which was just about all he could handle. Cooper sold his old mill in March 1899 to J. R. Dover and his son, who were following his example and developing their own mine, the Mountain Boy.[25]

In the meantime, Charles Anthony had at last gained control of the Golden West mill after a lengthy litigation with his former partners. In the spring of 1898 he moved the mill down to the canyon floor, where he could get water, and started crushing ore again that summer. The ore was still just as refractory; the yield was still low; and the production was erratic, as Anthony spent most of his time trying to find a new buyer for his mine, but he is said to have taken out over $100,000 in gold before he finally sold out.[26]

Although the Pleasant Canyon mines were Ballarat's biggest producers, there were a few hopeful contenders in the neighboring canyons. The richest of these was the Oh Be Joyful, discovered in February 1897 by Bob Montgomery and a couple of partners who named it for their favorite whiskey. It was located near the mouth of the canyon now known as Tuber, a corruption of *tuba,* the Shoshone word for pinyon nut. Bob and his partners systematically opened the lode, blocked out the ore to reveal its extent, made sample runs on the custom mills at Ballarat to demonstrate its worth, and got $48,000 for their trouble in the spring of 1899, when they sold the mine to Flint and Stebbins. They put in a Bryan roller mill that fall, but it broke down after just a few months—the rock was too hard—and was finally replaced by a six-stamp mill. That did the job, and by the summer of 1900 the Oh Be Joyful was turning out about $10,000 worth of gold bullion every month. In neighboring Jail Canyon, Jack Curran found the Gem mine and gave a half interest to Ballarat storekeeper Charles Weaver in exchange for a three-stamp mill. They rigged up the little mill to run from a waterwheel—the first in the Death Valley country—and started shipping several thousand dollars in bullion monthly in the winter of 1899–1900.[27]

Most claims, however, produced little more than a brief flurry of excitement. One eager Los Angeles promoter, Richard Day, following in the footsteps of the Redlands company, acquired a few claims a couple of miles north of Redlands Canyon and rushed in with an enormous milling plant that rivaled that of the Ratcliff: then he discovered he didn't have a mine! Day formed the Mineral Hill Gold Mining Company in the fall of 1899 and began putting up a Merrill mill with a capacity of 60 tons a day, a 40-ton cyanide tank, and a 6,400-foot aerial tramway. He talked grandly of building a hydroelectric plant at the mouth of Surprise Canyon to run the whole operation, but settled instead for an old steam engine. He at last started up the mill in the fall of 1900, promptly exhausted the paying ore, and closed back down within just a couple months.[28]

Then there was the wily Phil Ginser, who discovered a nice pocket of high-grade ore not far from Mineral Hill. He worked it himself for a year or so, sending small batches of select ore to the custom mills at Ballarat, but by the summer of 1900 he seems to have grown tired of manual labor and headed for Salt Lake City to work the "dying miner" con. There, within three weeks, claiming he was "wasting away under the dreadful effects of consumption," Ginser unloaded his little prospect on a prosperous furniture-store owner, Charles Freed, and retired with $10,000 in cash—some said $50,000. Freed formed the Ballarat Gold Mining Company and sent a mining engineer, Fred H. Vahrenkamp, to the mine to put up a thirty- or even forty-stamp mill. But after taking out what little high-grade Ginser had left, Vahrenkamp advised Freed not to waste another cent.[29]

By 1900 there were nearly three hundred men working in the mines around Ballarat. The Ratcliff, World Beater, Oh Be Joyful, and Gem were all turning out bullion, and by the end of that year their total production had reached $500,000. Ballarat was at its peak, and its citizens proudly proclaimed it "*The* Mining Camp of the Desert." After all, it now had a fine two-story hotel with a shady veranda; a school with thirty-one pupils, including eight Indians; a red-light district with half a dozen cribs; an impromptu "Shake-em-up Band"; and a jail. There was even talk of a railroad. It lacked a church, of course, but to many it seemed that the only thing Ballarat really lacked was a little excitement. The town was so tame that the high point of the Fourth of July celebration was a burro race featuring several young ladies from Bakersfield competing for a quarter interest in a claim called the Hot Cake.[30]

In three years there had been only three deaths in Ballarat, and they had all been from incurable diseases contracted elsewhere. But one disgruntled customer of Porter Brothers' general store—rumor said it was George Montgomery—did shake things up by placing a stick of giant powder on their bedroom window ledge late one night in protest of price-gouging markups of as much as 700 percent. Although one wall of the house was blown away, its occupants escaped unscathed, and the town promptly returned to its slumber. It was left to the lawmen to provide Ballarat's only homicide, but that didn't happen until October 1905, when Justice of the Peace Richard Decker was gunned down in his office by the Constable Henry Pietsch. In the meantime, John Calloway, the Ballarat Hotel keeper, could only pretend it was a rowdy camp, posting warnings in all the rooms that the management was "not responsible for either their lives or their valuables," nor would it bear any part of their funeral expenses.[31]

The real excitement came that fall of 1900, when the news got out that a Nevada rancher named Jim Butler had made an enormously rich strike at a spring called Tonopah, 150 miles north of Ballarat, way beyond Death Valley. By the spring of 1901 the new Nevada camp was the center of the largest mining rush the desert country would ever see, and Ballarat was almost deserted. Almost all the mines in the Panamints were shut down as miners and mine owners alike went off "to see the elephant," the Montgomery brothers included. The great rush drew new prospectors from all over the West to try their luck in the desert country, and it drew new investors from all over the country to take a fling in mining ventures. The Panamint mines eventually shared in this excitement, but Ballarat never fully recovered.[32]

The exodus of 1901 dealt Ballarat a crippling blow, and the elements tried to do the rest. A terrible storm ripped through the town that summer, smashing several houses, killing one woman, and kiting off everything loose. Up in the Panamints it unleashed a cloudburst that sent flash floods down the canyons to the north, destroying the little Gem mill in Jail Canyon and sweeping away many of the abandoned buildings in old Panamint. A year later, just as Ballarat was starting to recover, another cyclone wrought even more havoc, tearing the roofs from Calloway's hotel and other adobes and leveling every frame building that was left. Then came a rush of water down Pleasant Canyon, demolishing Anthony's old mill, which he had fortunately just sold to a Boston company, and flooding the battered town. But as the mines resumed, Ballarat rebuilt again.[33]

First to resume was the Ratcliff Consolidated Gold Mines, Ltd., which started up again in January 1902, with owner William W. Godsmark replacing the departed Harrison as superintendent. Godsmark soon got together a crew of fifty and had the mill running night and day, making it once again the mainstay of Ballarat. By the summer of 1903 he had turned out another $250,000 in bullion, bringing the total production of the mine to roughly $450,000. But by then all of the remaining ore was so refractory that it couldn't be worked profitably, and Godsmark was forced to close down again. He stayed on for another year, experimenting with roasting and smelting furnaces and trying to make the base ore pay, before he finally gave up.[34]

By that time, the irrepressible George Montgomery had returned. Late in 1903 George and his brother Frank had found a rich chute of free milling high-grade in the abandoned World Beater, and George staked claim to the old mine again, renaming it the Republican. He then hustled up new backers in Los Angeles, formed the Republican Mining Company, put up an aerial tramway to the mine, and refurbished the old Bryan mill. In April 1904 he started it up on $75 to $100 rock, recovering 80 percent of value, and by the time the high-grade was exhausted in the summer of 1905 he had produced $107,000 in bullion. J. P. Flint had also formed a new company, Inyo Gold, in the summer of 1902, to reopen the Oh Be Joyful, but he only recovered about $20,000 by cyaniding the tailings, then returned to Los Angeles to go into the liquid air business.[35]

A few other new companies joined in the Ballarat revival, but they produced little for anyone but their promoters. Such was the Cecil R. Gold Mining and Milling Company, named for the late mining mogul Rhodes of Africa, and floated by a hawkish-looking stock promoter, James Monroe Graybill, with offices in Los Angeles and Plattsburg, Missouri. Graybill had acquired the Santa Rosa—a run-of-the-mill claim that had miraculously been puffed up in value ten-thousandfold in the course of five years without producing more than a handful of gold. The talented Phil Ginser had first located the claim 3 miles south of Ballarat in 1897, but promptly disposed of it for a paltry $25 to a young miner, Ed Cross. Cross probed it on and off until 1901, when he passed it on to Frank Howard for a tidy $2,800. Howard bought Dover's little two-stamp mill, moved it down to the claim, ran a sample lot of ore and, seeing that it wouldn't pay, sold the lot to Graybill for $15,000 in the fall of 1902. Graybill subdivided it into a million shares and set out to sell them for $250,000 or more, if he could get it. In the style of George Pinney, Graybill immediately declared a series of monthly dividends of 1 percent each and started advertising the Santa Rosa as a "dividend paying mine" even before his superintendent reached the property. Stock sales apparently went well enough that Graybill stopped the dividends early in 1903 and started to stall, putting the little mill through a series of remodelings, increasing it to eight stamps, and adding a gasoline engine. That cost little but kept hopes up—and the mill shut down for most of the year—while Graybill tried to unload the rest of the stock. When he had sold all he could, all the work stopped.[36]

Fred Vahrenkamp, who had also come to realize that there was easier money in promotion than in mining, suddenly saw new potential in the original Ginser mine, which the Ballarat Gold Mining Company had abandoned. Vahrenkamp formed the Gold Crown Mining Company in the summer of 1903 to reopen it, and put up a mill and a tramway the following spring. He apparently got rid of his stock before the other stockholders discovered that there was nothing left in the mine that was worth going after. The stockholders then bought Dover's Mountain Boy and Cooper's mine up in Pleasant Canyon, but found them pretty nearly exhausted too.[37]

By 1905, when George Montgomery finally ran out of high-grade in the old World Beater, the mines around Ballarat had produced nearly a million dollars in gold, becoming the Death Valley country's most productive hard-rock district. But that was to be a fleeting honor, for Bob Montgomery and a few fellow Ballaraters had already found new bonanzas at Bullfrog, on the other side of Death Valley, that would soon surpass any around Ballarat. The great Death Valley mining boom was on, and Ballarat would soon be all but deserted again.

Bullfrog!

The Bullfrog excitement was the biggest thing of its kind ever seen in the Death Valley and Amargosa country. Ed Cross and Shorty Harris found the green-stained ore that gave a name to the excitement. Bob Montgomery, with a little help from his friends, opened the great mine on which it grew. Then the infamous George Graham Rice puffed it and puffed it until at last it got so big that even "Steel King" Charley Schwab couldn't support it. By then, thousands had rushed into the desert just to see it; railroad, telephone, and power lines had followed; a dozen boom towns and a modern metropolis had risen in its honor; its name had spread across the nation; tens of thousands had sunk millions into its slippery promises; and Bob Montgomery had emerged as Death Valley's first mining millionaire.[1]

It was in the summer of 1904 that the two Ballaraters made the Bullfrog strike. Frank "Shorty" Harris had dreamed of such a day for over a quarter of a century. Born in Rhode Island on July 21, 1857 and orphaned at the age of seven, he had ridden the rails west in the late 1870s to seek his fortune in the mines. He had chased his luck from Leadville to Tombstone, from the Coeur d'Alene to the heart of Death Valley. That summer of 1904, he got as close as he would ever come. He had it within his grasp, but it slipped through his fingers. The gabby little man, barely five foot four, with big ears, blue eyes, and a bushy moustache, had a weakness for the Oh Be Joyful that got the best of him. But Shorty's partner, Ernest "Ed" Cross, a quiet, sober young newlywed, held on long enough to get full measure for his share.[2]

Shorty picked up Ed at fellow-Ballarater Jack Keane's new gold strike in the Funerals. They had arrived too late to get any good ground, so they headed for the low hills to the north where Shorty had previously seen some good indications. There on the south side of a little brown hill, now known as Bullfrog Mountain, they found the wonderful ore on the morning of August 9. They never could agree on who picked up the first piece. Ed said that he spotted that glistening rock, about the size and color of a bullfrog, and called to Shorty, who only smiled skeptically at first. But as Shorty began to examine it, his cheeks flushed with excitement and he finally let out a war whoop, jumped up and shouted: "Hellfire, Eddie, we've struck the richest jackpot this side of the Klondike!" But Shorty insisted that he broke that first piece off a big boulder and called to Ed, who had wandered away, "Come back, we've got it!" He later stretched the story a bit, claiming he found the ore while rounding up his burros when Ed was cooking breakfast back in their camp at Buck Spring, and let out a yell that brought Ed running—from 2 miles away![3]

One thing they did agree on was that they wasted little time staking the Bullfrog claim and rushing to Goldfield to have the ore assayed. That first rock showed $665 a ton in gold, and other samples reached $3,000. Shorty headed for the saloons to celebrate. Ed promptly lined up a sale for $10,000, but it fell through because Shorty couldn't be found to close the deal. Shorty sobered up six days later to find that in his drunken stupor he had signed away his half of the claim to one J. W. McGalliard for a paltry $1,000. He is said to have blown that sum in disgust, treating his friends to a few more rounds. By then Ed had realized he could get much more by joining with McGalliard to form a stock company, the Original Bullfrog Mines Syndicate. He eventually sold his interest to a San Francisco broker for a reported $125,000, and he and his wife bought a big ranch near Escondido.[4]

In the meantime, word of the Bullfrog strike had electrified Tonopah and neighboring Goldfield, and the stampede was on. A quarter of a century later Shorty still vividly recalled:

> I've seen some gold rushes in my time that were hummers, but nothing like that stampede. Men were leaving town in a steady stream with buckboards, buggies, wagons and burros. It looked like the whole population of Goldfield was trying to move at once. Miners who were working for the big companies dropped their tools and got ready to leave town in a hurry. Timekeepers and clerks, waiters and cooks—they all got the fever and milled around, wildeyed, trying to find a way to get out to the new "strike." In a little while there wasn't a horse or a wagon in town, outside of a few owned by the big companies, and the price of burros took a big jump. I saw one man who was about ready to cry because he couldn't buy a jackass for $500.00. A lot of fellows loaded their stuff on two-wheeled carts—grub, tools, and cooking utensils, and away they went across the desert, two or three pulling a cart and the pots and pans rattling. When all the carts were gone, men who didn't have anything else started out on that seventy-five mile hike with wheelbarrows; and a lot of 'em made it alright—but they had a hell of a time![5]

Thousands of other hopefuls came trekking in from more distant camps all over the west. The Bullfrog Mining District, organized on August 30, just three weeks after the discovery, was the new Golconda, and everyone wanted a piece of it. Most looked for good surface indications, or at least proximity to them. Others sought the aid of psychics, like the Long Beach faith healer who claimed in her visions to find ore deep under ground,

The Bullfrog mine, discovered by Ed Cross and Shorty Harris in 1904, started the great rush, but Shorty only got $1,000 for his share when he sold out, drunk, to the organizers of this company.

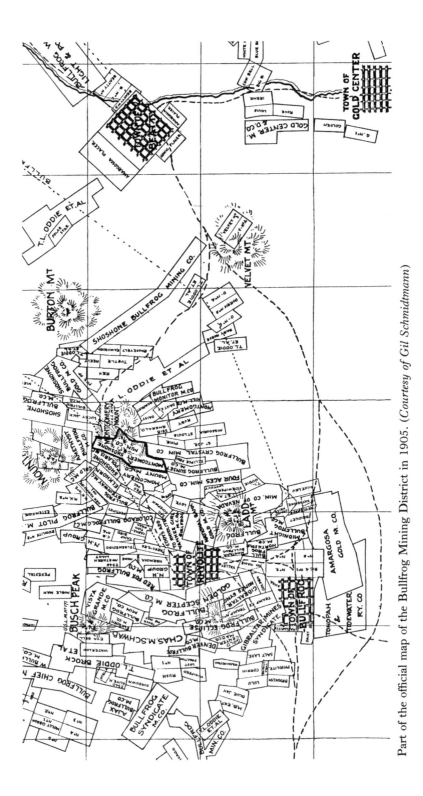

Part of the official map of the Bullfrog Mining District in 1905. (*Courtesy of Gil Schmidtmann*)

and the Montana rancher who professed to be a "human divining rod," his whole body quivering whenever he got near gold. Before the stampede ended they had staked over two thousand claims covering every hill and gulch for 30 miles, from the foot of the Funerals all the way across the Amargosa into the old Bromide district. The only showing on most of these claims was the gleam in the locator's eye. But several did show promising pockets of picture rock that rivaled or even surpassed the original Bullfrog ore. Among these were the Gold Bar and Homestake, a few miles north of the Bullfrog; the Tramp and Denver, on Bonanza Mountain to the east; and the Mayflower and Pioneer, up near the head of Oasis Valley. But the most promising of all was Bob Montgomery's Shoshone.[6]

Bob Montgomery was one of the first to join the stampede from Goldfield. He had left Ballarat in the rush to Tonopah three years before. But he had found romance rather than wealth and had gotten married and settled down there as a jeweler and optician. He caught mining fever again, however, in the fall of 1903 during the Goldfield excitement, and in the summer of 1904 with the Bullfrog stampede. He first came to Bullfrog early in September on a $75 grubstake by three Goldfielders. He stayed only a couple days and found nothing of great value, but he dutifully staked several claims in his partners' names.[7]

It was heading home that Bob's luck began to change, although it wasn't obvious at the time. Stopping at Howell's ranch in Oasis Valley, he met a young Shoshone known as Hungry Johnny. Johnny claimed to know something about ore, so Bob took a gamble and hired him to scout out a couple of good claims, giving him a store order for grub and a promise of more later. Bob wrote out for Johnny two location notices for claims to be called the Shoshone and the Indian Johnnie. He made out the notices in his own name and that of Thomas E. Edwards, a Tonopah merchant and friend whom he figured would be willing to pay for the grub, and dated them for the following day, September 6, 1904.[8]

When Bob returned to Bullfrog almost three weeks later, Johnny met him at Beatty's ranch and proudly led him to the new claims on what is now Montgomery Mountain, 3 miles to the west. Johnny had staked an unlikely looking deposit of crumbly pink talc that showed no free gold at all, but he assured Bob it was "all the same" as rich ore found on the Denver farther west. Bob located two more adjoining claims, the Shoshone Nos. 2 and 3, then hurried back to Goldfield to have some of the rock assayed. The Denver ore had paid way up into the hundreds of dollars per ton, but to Bob's disappointment his Shoshone samples didn't even run as high as $5![9]

Still hopeful, Bob went back again and again to sample different parts of the mile-long talc deposits covered by his claims. But he had met with no luck when along came Al James, a grizzled old veteran who confidently offered to show Bob and his partner where the pay rock was in exchange for an interest in the claims. They agreed, and James took them to a spot on the Shoshone No. 3 where the talc ran $300 a ton in gold. Edwards immediately put up the money to run a tunnel below that point to cut the deposit at depth. Any doubt that the values were only surface enrichment vanished in February 1905, when the tunnel struck the talc in bonanza ore 70 feet thick, with assays running as high as $16,000 a ton! When Bob Montgomery first saw the great bonanza, tears filled his eyes and he sobbed with joy, "I have struck it; the thing that I have dreamed about since I was 15 years old has come true; I am fixed for life and nobody can take it away from me." Bob immediately set about getting control of more of the mine. He and Edwards promptly bought out James's newly acquired interest for $20,000. Then Bob bought Edwards's half for $100,000 and sold a quarter interest for the same price to Tonopah mining engineer and promoter Malcolm L. Macdonald and associates in order to pay off Edwards.[10]

In a whirlwind of puffery Montgomery's Shoshone was suddenly touted as the new wonder of the West. It was heralded as "the greatest discovery ever made on the desert," "richer than the mines of King Solomon." Its enormity was said to make even old mining men "gasp for breath." One old-timer became positively giddy, estimating the total worth of the ore at no less than $165,766,700! No words seemed too extravagant to describe it. Indeed, this ballyhoo quickly blew the whole Bullfrog excitement out of all proportion.[11]

Behind it all, blowing harder than anyone else, was a skillful, unscrupulous young publicist and scoundrel known as George Graham Rice. He was an intense, confident, cosmopolitan little man with a friendly air that gave no hint of his sordid past. Born Jacob Simon Herzig, the son of a respectable New York furrier, he had begun betting on the horses in his teens and stealing from his father to cover his losses. He was sent to the New York State Reformatory, but emerged unreformed and was soon back to gambling and forging checks. These reached $40,000 before he was locked up again, this time for six years, in the New York State Prison at Sing Sing. After he got out again, he assumed the name George Graham Rice, got a part-time job as a newspaper reporter in New Orleans, and started a racing tip sheet on the side. When the Post Office Department stopped his tip sheet on a fraud order, he headed west to the boom camps of Nevada for a new start. There he formed the Goldfield-Tonopah Advertising Agency and turned his talents from touting horses to touting mines. One of his first jobs, in the spring of 1905, was the promotion of the new Rhyolite townsite and two mines just west of Montgomery's

Shoshone, in exchange for seven corner lots and 20,000 shares of stock. Rice sensed that if the Shoshone boomed everything around it would follow, so he generated reams of puffery on its seemingly incalculable wealth. He eventually cleared $20,000 for his work, and claimed it was his publicity that attracted Steel King Charley Schwab to the Shoshone.[12]

Montgomery's Shoshone instantly became the new boss mine of Bullfrog, and nearly everyone in the district rushed to settle at its feet. At the time of the great Shoshone strike there were half a dozen rival camps, each with its own special claim for public favor: the first and largest camp, Amargosa, originally called Aurum, was located half a mile below the Original Bullfrog mine and boasted the first saloon and, naturally, the first shooting scrape; Bullfrog, laid out at the mine, had a good name but little else, and it soon lost even that; Bonanza, near the mountain of that name, was closer to the center of the district, had the Miners' Union, Local No. 235 of the Western Federation of Miners, and hoped to become the lunch-bucket town; Gold Center, farther east at the mouth of Oasis Valley, had enough water to supply the first brewery and nurture the dream of becoming the railroad and milling center; Beatty, located a few miles farther up the Amargosa, just west of old man Beatty's ranch, had the most attractive location and an abundance of water; and Rhyolite, named for the rosy country rock, was the newest camp. Frank Busch had staked claim to the site just north of Bonanza in November 1904, and his brother Pete put up the first tent in January. Rhyolite had only one thing to recommend it, but that proved to be enough—it was the closest camp to Montgomery's Shoshone.[13]

Everything started hopping once they struck bonanza ore in the Shoshone and the great consolidation began. When they heard the news, the residents of Bonanza—Miners' Union and all—packed up and moved en masse to Rhyolite, where the Busch brothers gave them free lots. The excitement of the move proved to be too much for one onlooker, who dropped dead of heart failure, becoming the Bullfrog district's first fatality. The promoters of the Amargosa townsite, fearing a similar exodus of their own citizens, laid out an identical new town just below Rhyolite and transplanted the whole of Amargosa there, lot for lot, early in March. They also transplanted the name of Bullfrog for their new town, over the protests of the few remaining inhabitants of the original Bullfrog. But this only forestalled the inevitable, for one by one the new Bullfroggers hopped on up to Rhyolite. Beattyites might have joined the rush too, if Bob Montgomery hadn't bought into that townsite, vowing to build a grand hotel and make the town his milling center. Only a few stalwarts stayed on at Gold Center, waiting for a railroad and smarting under their new nickname, "Dead Center."[14]

Rhyolite's population had leapt to 1,200 in two weeks, and it had topped 2,500 by June 1905, before the camp was even six months old. By then it sported fully 50 saloons, dispensing 15¢ shots of whiskey and 75¢ bottles of beer; 35 roulette, faro, and card tables, raking in coin of every denomination; and an untold number of cribs, turning a couple of dollars a trick. There were also 19 lodging houses, providing a blanket and a cot for $1 a night; 16 restaurants and hash houses, dishing out meals for 75¢; and half a dozen barbers, giving 25¢ shaves and 50¢ haircuts. There was just one public bath, Mrs. Hill's Stockholm Bath House, offering "all kinds of baths, massage, manicuring, etc." for $1.75 a dip. There was also the camp's biggest booster, the *Rhyolite Herald,* an eight-page, illustrated weekly begun on May 5, 1905 by two young printers from Wyoming, Earle R. Clemens and Guy T. Keene.[15]

Golden, Rhyolite's main street, was choked with traffic and dust, and crammed with a confusion of pedestrians, pack mules, burros, dogs, horses, autos, stagecoaches, and freight wagons. There were four daily concord stages from Goldfield, making the 60-mile trip in two days for $18 a person. For the more affluent and adventuresome, there were the rival auto lines, which ran seven-passenger Pope Toledos and White Steamers from Goldfield in just 5 hours for $25 and from the new rail station at Las Vegas, 120 miles to the east, in 14 hours for $40. The most famous of the auto drivers, or "mahouts," was "Alkali Bill," William F. Brong, who held the record time of 3 hours and 40 minutes on the Goldfield-Rhyolite run in his specially built Columbia. By summer he claimed to have logged 20,000 miles on that run.[16]

Although Rhyolite became the unchallenged "Queen City" of the Death Valley country, Beatty and Bullfrog continued to squabble over who would be the runner-up. The contest was made all the more lively by the fact that each had its own newspaper, both of them claiming the name *Bullfrog Miner.* C. W. Nicklin of Las Vegas was the first to stake claim to the name, getting a sample *Bullfrog Miner* printed for Beatty early in March 1905 for use in rounding up prospective advertisers and subscribers. But while Nicklin was waiting for his printing plant to arrive, the Bullfrog Townsite Company asked former Colorado newspaperman Frank P. Mannix to start a paper to boost their camp. Seizing the opportunity and the name, Mannix began his *Bullfrog Miner* on March 31, printing it in Tonopah until he could get a press of his own. Nicklin started his *Bullfrog Miner* at Beatty the following week and charged Mannix with "bald-faced plagiarism." Amused readers referred to the papers as *No. 1* and *No. 2,* but none could agree as to which was *No. 2.* Mannix proudly proclaimed his to be the pioneer paper of the district, while Nicklin self-righteously proclaimed his to be the first paper actually printed there. Both refused to give up the name, but Nicklin finally ended the confusion after six weeks of mutual vituperation by changing his masthead to the *Beatty Bullfrog Miner*. Then his brother, T. G. Nicklin, took over the paper and the fight. He temporarily got Mannix's *Miner* banned from the mails, charging it was not a real newspaper, just an advertising circular for the Bullfrog Townsite Company. But Nicklin's coup de grace was a clever Bullfrog-shaped map of the district, with Beatty at its very heart and both rivals, Bullfrog and Rhyolite, in the armpit![17]

The fabulous strike in Montgomery's Shoshone was heralded nationwide and followed by reports of bonanza assays from surrounding claims. This combined to generate the kind of excitement over the Bullfrog district that made it a promoter's paradise. Before the excitement ended, more than 200 Bullfrog mining companies had been floated to unload over 200 million shares of stock on the public—at least a couple shares for every man, woman, and child in the country! Almost every company had the magic word "Bullfrog" in its name and a vignette of the fat little amphibian stamped, lithographed, or engraved on its shares. There was every kind of Bullfrog company one might want—a Little Bullfrog, a Greater Bullfrog and a Giant Bullfrog, a United Bullfrog and a Bullfrog Alliance, a Bullfrog Merger and a Bullfrog Combination, a Bullfrog Apex and a Bullfrog Annex, a Bullfrog Gold Dollar and a Bullfrog Greenback, a Bullfrog Broker and a Bullfrog Wall Street, a Bullfrog Daisy and a Bullfrog Mayflower, a Bullfrog Swift and a Bullfrog Rush, a Bullfrog Moonlight and a Bullfrog Starlight, a Bullfrog Puritan and a Bullfrog Tramp, a Bullfrog Chief and a Bullfrog Outlaw, a Bullfrog Croesus and a Bullfrog Mogul. And reigning over them all a Bullfrog King and a Bullfrog Queen with a Bullfrog Golden Sceptre. There was even one Bullfrog Winner—or so they hoped.[18]

Most of these companies were promoted by a newly festering breed of mail-order broker-tipsters who advertised the Bullfrogs with banner type and huge grinning frogs smiling out from the pages of metropolitan dailies, mining and investment weeklies, and popular monthlies. They touted the district as "THE GREATEST GOLD DISCOVERY OF MODERN TIMES," "A NATURAL INCUBATOR OF THE MINING MILLIONAIRE." They claimed vast fortunes were being made in Bullfrog stocks—profits of $3,592,500 in sixty-two days! They challenged readers to "BUY BULLFROGS AND WATCH THEM JUMP." They flooded the mails with Bullfrog prospectuses, free maps of the Bullfrog mines, lithos of big heaps of Bullfrog rock, folksy letters from their man at Bullfrog, laudatory clippings from the Bullfrog press, fatuous reports from Bullfrog experts, even little bags of Bullfrog ore. Each pushed his own pet pollywog, but they all promised fortunes at bargain prices of anywhere from ½¢ to 25¢ per share on $1 par stock. Some even "guaranteed" price advances and phenomenal profits of as much as 800 percent in four months. And just as they promised, they indeed raised their selling prices every month or two to turn a paper profit for their customers, while promising even greater profits on the next raise. It was a great ride for the Bullfrog investors, until they tried to cash in.[19]

Only a fraction of the Bullfrogs were floated in the traditional way on the stock exchanges. But investors there didn't fare much better, for those prices too were manipulated to fictitious values by wash sales and concocted reports of rich strikes in the mines. By the spring of 1906 eight Bullfrog stocks were selling at better than par, but only the Original Bullfrog and Montgomery's Shoshone had yet shipped any ore. The Original Bullfrog had made the district's first ore shipment at the end of February 1905, accompanied by an enormous stuffed bullfrog, four shotgun riders, and a brass band playing "There'll Be a Hot Time in the Old Town Tonight." McGalliard took the seven tons of high-grade to the smelters at Salt Lake City at a cost of $652, and it returned $5,148. Bob Montgomery began shipping ore two months later.[20]

Montgomery's Shoshone had been making a spectacular showing. Bob and his new partners—Malcolm Macdonald and associates—had organized as the Montgomery Shoshone Mines Company early in April 1905, with Bob holding three quarters of the 1.25 million shares and the presidency. Par value of the shares was $1, but as soon as Bob offered the stock for sale the price was bid up to $3, and 25,000 shares were sold in two hours. And why not? For at the same time, Bob began shipping high-grade by the 50-ton carload to the Salt Lake smelters. He and his wife accompanied the first bonanza shipment, which was rumored to have averaged $2,300 a ton, and he boasted that he could take out $10,000 a day from the mine. He also talked of putting up a twenty-stamp mill and a cyaniding plant at Beatty and a 3-mile aerial tram to the mine. But Macdonald was already trying to line up a purchaser for the mine. He first approached Philadelphia financier John W. Brock, who had bought Jim Butler's great Tonopah mine, but Brock's agent advised against the Shoshone purchase because he felt it was only a superficial deposit. Macdonald then turned to Pittsburgh "Steel King" Charles M. Schwab, who had recently bought into a Tonopah mine adjacent to Brock's and made a few quick millions in paper profits as the stock price skyrocketed on news of his purchase alone.[21]

Schwab's agents, John McKane and Donald Gillies, reported favorably on the Shoshone, and in August 1905 the Steel King offered about $1.5 million in cash for 51 percent of the stock—a price consistent with the market value of the shares. Bob could have cleared $1 million from the deal and still kept half of his shares, but at that point his wife, Winnie Aubrey, stepped in. She was a big, gregarious woman, weighing fully

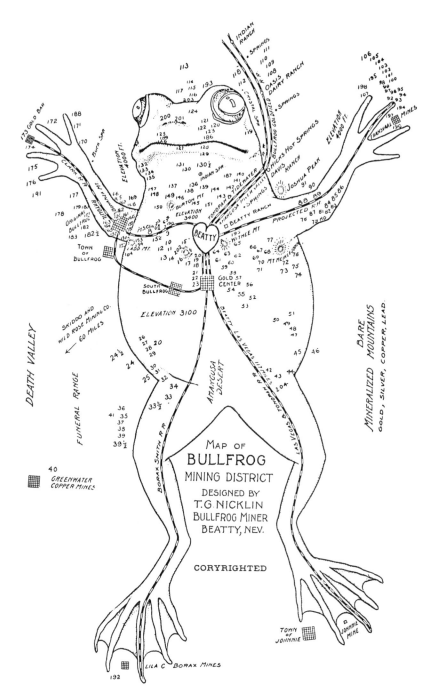

(*Courtesy of Nevada Historical Society*)

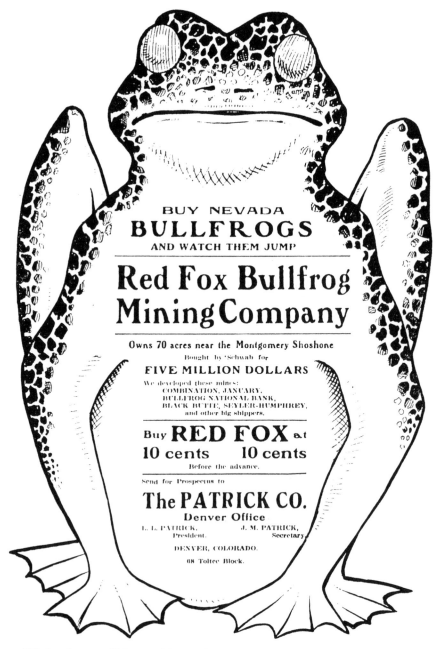

(Mining Investor, February 26, 1906)

240 pounds, with a robust enthusiasm that often overwhelmed her more reserved husband. But she was also levelheaded and determined. When Bob told her of the deal, she roared, "Go and tell Mr. Schwab that you have changed your idea about the value of the mine. Tell him that the $1,000,000 is for you, and that I want $1,000,000 for myself out of this deal." That reply brought the Steel King out West to have a good look at both the mine and the lady, and it also brought results.[22]

New problems arose, however, that clouded the title to the mine and temporarily blocked the deal. That summer two of Bob's grubstakers on his first trip to Bullfrog, Louis Finnegan and Pat O'Brien, filed suit for a share in the mine. They each asked for a quarter interest in the Shoshone, claiming that Bob had located the mine on their grubstake. They had gotten a rather confused statement from Hungry Johnny suggesting that he and Bob had located the Shoshone on Bob's first trip. But when the case came to trial early in November, Johnny suddenly disappeared just before he was to testify. Both O'Brien and Montgomery offered rewards for Johnny's return, and the trial was postponed for several days while the sheriff and others scoured the desert looking for the vanished Indian. Johnny was eventually found hiding in Owens Valley, apparently fearing that he would be jailed for not being able to remember the exact date that he and Bob went to the claim. But the trial had resumed without him when Bob's attorneys, led by that ever-flexible ex-Panamint promoter, ex-Senator William M. Stewart, offered to let O'Brien take the stand as Johnny's proxy to testify to what he thought Johnny would have said if he had been there! It was a very effective ploy, because the judge gave no credence whatever to such hypothetical testimony. Then the plaintiff's collaborating witness, a young man named Harris who claimed he had seen Bob and Johnny make the location during that first trip, was discredited by Stewart, who revealed that O'Brien had promised Harris $20,000 if he and Finnegan won. Bob's defense brought forth several witnesses who testified that he had indeed returned to Goldfield, thus ending the grubstake before he ever saw the Shoshone claims. Early in January 1906 the judge ruled in Bob's favor, clearing the title to the mine, and the following month Charley Schwab bought control of Montgomery's Shoshone.[23]

The Montgomery-Shoshone deal was trumpeted by enthusiastic boosters as the "largest mining deal ever made in the state of Nevada," and it was reported that Bob got anywhere from $2 to $6 million out of the transaction. No precise dollar value could in fact be set, because the terms included not only a cash payment but also an elaborate exchange of shares in the original company and adjacent properties for shares in a new Montgomery Shoshone Consolidated Mining Company, organized by Schwab. Bob claimed he got about $1 million in cash plus about a fifth of the 500,000 shares in the new company. These shares had a par value of $5, but they sold for as much as $23 when first marketed, and they sold above par for nearly two years thereafter. Thus Bob could have made as much as $2 million more from their sale, if he had not held onto them for too long.[24]

Whatever additional money he got, the Shoshone sale made Bob an instant millionaire, and he and Winnie headed for San Francisco to celebrate. If it hadn't been for Winnie, Bob might not have lived long enough to enjoy his good fortune, for they were staying on the tenth floor of the St. Francis Hotel that fateful April morning when the great quake struck. The hotel withstood the shock, and Bob was soon fast asleep again. But Winnie saw the approaching fire, and she had to wake Bob twice to get him out of bed before the hotel was engulfed in flames.[25]

Bob soon put much of his money into the purchase and development of a group of twenty-three claims up in the Panamints, which Winnie named Skidoo. These mines eventually produced another million. But Bob also sank a lot of money into unprofitable speculations in California oil and Nevada mines. Like other nouveau riche, Bob went in for some more conspicuous consumption too, purchasing an elegant home in Los Angeles and taking Winnie on the grand tour of Europe. For her part, Winnie bought Bob a big gold bullfrog scarf pin with emerald eyes and diamond spots all over its back. She bought herself a flashy new De-Detriech automobile in which she darted around fearlessly at up to 60 miles per hour. When the thrill of fast driving wore off, she took to the air in 1908 in Roy Knabenshue's propeller-driven inflatable airship. As a business venture she bought a Mexican alligator and pheasant farm, which helped keep her in fancy shoes and feathered hats.[26]

Bob's good fortune didn't extend to his brothers, however, and may in fact have helped to end what remaining ties there were between them. The closest George ever came to the Montgomery Shoshone fortune was the name, when for luck, a joke, or a scam, he bought a worthless claim in the Searchlight district because it was called the Shoshone, just so he could have one of his own. Frank at least got odd jobs in Beatty wall-papering Bob's new Montgomery Hotel.[27]

Bullfrog's new kingpin, Charley Schwab, just a year older than Bob, hadn't really gotten accustomed to his new wealth, either. He had had a few more years to do so, but he also had many more millions to which to adjust. With a little help from his friends, Schwab had skyrocketed from an engineer's helper at the age of eighteen to president and part owner of the Carnegie Steel Company at age thirty-five. The disarmingly chubby, boyish looking Schwab was a quick study who had mastered each job assigned to him so rapidly that he attracted the attention of Andrew

Carnegie himself. The aged Carnegie steadily advanced the young fireball until he finally gave him a share of the business and presidency of the company. Soon after that, when financier J. P. Morgan set out to consolidate the steel industry in 1901, Carnegie's empire was the key, and Schwab arranged the deal between Morgan and Carnegie. He was rewarded with the presidency of the great new trust, the billion-dollar U.S. Steel Corporation. With this, Schwab reportedly became "the highest salaried man in the world," drawing over $2,000,000 a year, and his stock holdings were counted in the tens of millions.[28]

Charley Schwab had become the new saint of the American Dream of rags to riches, the epitome of upward mobility, a giver of pious lectures on the rewards of hard work, and the benefactor of a trade school and a few churches. But his was an intoxicating rise to enormous wealth, and he had trouble finding extravagances enough to spend it on, such as great houses, racing yachts, regal tours of Europe hosted by kings, rumored indulgences at Monte Carlo, and many guileless speculations. It was the latter two activities that most tarnished his saintly image and ultimately brought him down a notch. For although he still preached Carnegie's gospel of industry, Schwab saw that the greatest riches were to be had not in industry but in finance. Thus Schwab turned, in Carnegie's words, "from the manufacture of iron to the manufacture of securities," endeavoring by the magic of combination to "turn water and wind into gold."[29]

In the summer of 1902 Charley Schwab had joined in the attempted flotation of a new trust, the U.S. Shipbuilding Company, a windy effort to sell the public $71 million in highly watered stocks and bonds on assets valued at barely $10 million—namely, half a dozen scattered shipyards and a little steel mill at Bethlehem, Pennsylvania that had been discarded by Morgan's steel trust. Schwab was also president of this waterlogged venture, so when it sank amid cries of fraud and falsification, he lost his halo.[30]

Morgan and Carnegie promptly dumped Schwab from the U.S. Steel presidency for reasons of "health." As the bankruptcy litigation over the sunken trust worked its way through the courts, Schwab worked hard to defend his role in the affair and to retain control of its biggest asset, the Bethlehem mill. He was successful in the latter effort and thus emerged in 1904 with his fortune intact, including the Bethlehem steel mill, on which he would ultimately rebuild his reputation. Although chastened by the shipbuilding trust debacle, Schwab was still eager to take new gambles. He found them out in the desert boom camps, where he also found an admiring if mercenary crowd of promoters who would wine and dine him again as the "Steel King," interested not in his past indiscretions but in how much cash he would put into new mining ventures and how much more cash his name would bring in. It was a buyer's market, and buy

Schwab did. On the advice of his agents, McKane and Gillies, he bought heavily in Tonopah, Goldfield, and Bullfrog. But the Montgomery Shoshone was his biggest purchase, and it was the showpiece of his western holdings.[31]

As soon as he took control of the mine in February 1906 as president of the Montgomery Shoshone Consolidated Mining Company, Schwab commenced development on a grand scale. He appointed Gillies general manager, hired a crew of a hundred, began the systematic opening of the deposit through nearly 2 miles of tunnels and drifts, and started construction of a mammoth mill with a capacity of 300 tons per day. It was the biggest, most modern mill yet built in the Death Valley and Amargosa country. Consisting of a crusher, three giant rollers, over a dozen cyaniding tanks, and a reduction furnace, it was designed to profitably work ore that paid as little as $6 per ton. For water, Schwab bought the Bullfrog Townsite Company's 11-mile pipeline from Goss Spring; for power, he contracted with the Nevada-California Power Company to run a line across the north end of Death Valley to deliver electricity from their hydroelectric plant at the foot of the Sierra, more than 100 miles to the west. Schwab also contracted with the Las Vegas and Tonopah Railroad, then building through the Bullfrog district en route to Tonopah, to run a spur to the Shoshone dump so that he could bring in heavy machinery for the mill and haul out high-grade ore for the Salt Lake smelters.[32]

Rather than selling the company's treasury stock to finance all of this development, Schwab sold his own stock and loaned the company money as it was needed—ultimately about half a million dollars. This arrangement—one thing he had learned from the shipbuilding fiasco—allowed him to sell off as much of his own stock as he chose and still retain first claim on the property, as its principal creditor. It also assured him of the first earnings of the mine, through repayment of his loans before any dividends could be paid out to other stockholders. Publicly, however, Schwab's loan was advertised only as a measure of his great faith in the mine, and it was that, too. After all, everyone who had examined it agreed there was at least $5 million in sight.[33]

The first Las Vegas and Tonopah train reached Rhyolite late in December 1906, and the spur to Montgomery Shoshone was completed the following March. Mill machinery began to arrive, and the mine began shipping high-grade to the smelters at a rate of three carloads a week. The mill was finished in August, and the electric power lines were completed a few weeks later. Finally, on September 23, 1907, the great roller wheels of the Montgomery Shoshone mill started to turn. Although no official figures were released, the *Rhyolite Herald* editor estimated the first month's mill run at 3,000 tons, yielding $75,000, and high-grade shipments at 1,000 tons, paying $100,000—a combined rate of production of over $2 million a year. The Bullfrog district had a big producer at last, and everyone was so confident of the district's future that even the national financial panic that fall passed with little notice in the continuing excitement of the boom.[34]

By 1907, Rhyolite had become the model of a modern metropolis, with four thousand citizens, three-story skyscrapers, concrete sidewalks, electric lights, water mains, telephone and telegraph lines, daily and weekly newspapers, a monthly magazine, three railroads, police and fire departments, and a hospital, school, opera house, and stock exchange. Rhyolite even had two churches—the first in the Death Valley country. But its civic services were financed by licensed prostitution.[35]

Rhyolite's pride and joy was the John S. Cook & Co. Bank on Golden Street. This modern three-story, four-floor office building of concrete, steel, and glass was completed in January 1908. It cost over $90,000, much of it lavished on fancy time locks for the vaults, Italian marble stairs, imported stained-glass windows, and Honduran mahogany trim. But such extravagances helped break the Cook bank, which folded within the year, surrendering its business and its luxurious offices to the rival First National Bank of Rhyolite. The upper floors were crowded with brokerage offices, while the basement, complete with a second vault, held the post office, run by M. J. Moore, who had succeeded his wife Anna as postmaster. Boosters saw this impressive edifice as the symbol of Rhyolite's maturity— solid evidence that the city was there to stay. But Panamint Joe saw it more clearly. After watching the construction for a while, he squinted over his spectacles and shrugged, "Someday white man gone—Indian sleep here." Now no one sleeps there; only its crumbling walls remain as a reminder of Rhyolite's dreams.[36]

Rhyolite boasted other impressive buildings as well. The Las Vegas and Tonopah Railroad's California-mission style depot, which cost its builder, Montana Senator William A. Clark, about $130,000, is still occupied. There was also the three-story Overbury Block, built of rock that assayed as much as $16 a ton, and the solid concrete, two-story, eight-room school, built on a $20,000 bond issue after wind blew the first school off its foundation. But Rhyolite's most curious building was the famous Bottle House, built in February 1906 by a resourceful miner, Tom T. Kelley, from 50,000 beer and liquor bottles all emptied in the intoxicating excitement of those first boom years. Restored by Paramount Pictures in January 1925, the Bottle House remains a popular tourist attraction.[37]

Much less impressive architecturally than the bank or the Bottle House, but more important in its own way, was the Rhyolite Mining Stock Exchange. Stock certificates, not bullion bars, were the chief product of most Bullfrog mines, after all, and the spartan little storefront on Golden,

E. A. "Bob" Montgomery became Death Valley's first true mining millionaire in 1906, when he sold his Shoshone mine to "Steel King" Charley Schwab, who made the Montgomery Shoshone Consolidated the mainstay of the boom. (Sketches by Buel from the *Tonopah Sun*, October 3 and November 8, 1905)

CAPITAL STOCK $2,500,000.

MONTGOMERY SHOSHONE CONSOLIDATED
MINING COMPANY.
INCORPORATED UNDER THE LAWS OF THE STATE OF SOUTH DAKOTA.

This Certifies that

LADENBURG, THALMANN & CO.,

is the owner of

SHARES SHARES SHARES

shares of the
Capital Stock of the Montgomery Shoshone Consolidated Mining Company in
transferable only on the books of the corporation by the holder hereof in
person or by attorney upon surrender of this certificate properly endorsed.

subscribed their names and caused the seal of the corporation to be hereto affixed.

APR 19 1907

SECRETARY.   PRESIDENT.

SHARES $5.00 EACH.

AMERICAN BANK NOTE COMPANY, NEW YORK.

The Grand Company of America,
TRANSFER AGENT.
ASSISTANT SECRETARY.
APR 19 1907

equipped only with telephones, blackboards, a railing and a platform for the caller, was the "mill" that helped put fleeting value into that paper. The exchange opened for business on March 25, 1907, with a hundred twenty-five members, including brokers in New York, Philadelphia, Denver, Butte, Spokane, Salt Lake, San Francisco, and Los Angeles. Seventy-four Bullfrog companies and a comparable number from surrounding districts were listed. Sixty thousand shares changed hands the opening day, and over three-quarters of a million shares had been shuffled by the end of the second week, as Rhyolite brokers feverishly worked up prices for their wares and phoned out the news of every rise.[38]

Telephone service had been the first of the modern conveniences to reach the district. The Tonopah, Goldfield, Amargosa, and Bullfrog District Telephone and Telegraph Company's line reached Amargosa in February 1905, and was extended to Bullfrog and Rhyolite with the consolidating rush the following month. Running water came that summer, when three rival companies completed pipelines from Beatty, Indian, and Terry springs. Prior to that, water hauled in by burro from Beatty sold for up to $5 a barrel and tasted of the whiskey barrels in which it came. The pipelines brought running water into every business and home, fire hydrants on every corner, and the opening of public swimming pools. Next came an ice plant. Ice brought down from Goldfield had been more precious than high-grade, selling for $400 a ton. Drinks with ice had sold for twice the price of those without, and one sharp saloon keeper had even tried substituting chunks of glass for the prized cubes. Relief came in August 1905, when a gasoline-powered compressor made the first ice at Bullfrog. As others got into the business, a "Hot War Between Icemen" ensued, chopping the price to just a few pennies a pound, to the delight of man and beast. Then in the spring of 1906, Countess Morajeski opened the Alaska Glacier Ice Cream Parlor. Electricity came last in April 1907, when the Rhyolite Light, Heat, and Power Company started up their gasoline-powered generators. Service was greatly expanded in September, when the Nevada-California Power Company completed the line from their hydroelectric plants on Bishop Creek. They put up streetlights on every corner and brought electricity to every house, not only for lights but for every newfangled home appliance, from electric toasters and coffee-makers to electric bedwarmers and vibrators.[39]

Three rival railroads tied the desert metropolis more closely to the outside world. The combined boom of the Tonopah, Goldfield, and Bullfrog districts attracted several railroads into southern Nevada, each seeking a share of the bonanza profits. The first to reach the Bullfrog district was Senator Clark's Las Vegas and Tonopah Railroad, built to connect with his San Pedro, Los Angeles, and Salt Lake road. Clark began running regular trains from Las Vegas to Rhyolite on December

The Bullfrog Goldfield and two other railroads raced into the Bullfrog district in 1906–07. (*Courtesy of Ken Prag*)

14, 1906. He got the lion's share of the inbound freight, and he secured the ore-shipping contract with the Montgomery Shoshone. The Bullfrog Goldfield Railroad, an offshoot of John Brock's Tonopah and Goldfield road, began regular service from the north the following June. Borax King Francis M. Smith's Tonopah and Tidewater Railroad, designed not only to tap the gold camps but also to open the great Death Valley colemanite beds, reached Gold Center in October. Two months later, Smith began train service to Rhyolite over the tracks of the Bullfrog Goldfield road, which he leased the following spring. The railroads opened up the Bullfrog district for high-grade shipment, as a "price war" for ore cut shipping rates to the Salt Lake smelters to as little as $5 a ton. The railroads also cut heavily into the auto and stage business, slashing passenger fares from Goldfield to less than a third that of the autos and trimming at least 45 minutes off even Alkali Bill's best time. Still more impressive was the fact that the grueling three-month trip the Jayhawkers had made from Salt Lake City to the Amargosa could now be completed in the comfort of a Pullman car in just nineteen hours. The autos were there to stay, however, and Rhyolite became the hub of new stage lines to the new pollywog camps springing up all around. Standard Oil and a rival independent opened gas stations in Rhyolite, and Alkali Bill even formed a company to manufacture special autos for desert travel.[40]

Newspaper competition was lively, too. Frank Mannix of the *Bullfrog Miner* had given up on the Bullfrog townsite and moved his plant up the slope to Rhyolite in March 1906 to challenge the *Herald's* monopoly. Then on September 23, 1907, while the two weeklies were still sparring with one another, three young tyros—John App, Richard Carr, and Charles Peterson—started a fiesty little daily, the *Bulletin,* to take them both on. The daily was barely the size of a letter sheet, but they packed it with gossipy items and the latest stock quotations, which won it a faithful following. The trio had a relaxed attitude toward the business, however, and blithely suspended the *Bulletin* for a four-month summer vacation in 1908 while App visited his mother. In the meantime, Deputy District Attorney Paul DeLaney had entered the fray in November 1907 with a sixteen-page illustrated monthly, the *Death Valley Prospector,* renamed the *Death Valley Magazine* with the new year. DeLaney filled his pages with colorful local features on the flamboyant Scotty, the Panamint Indians, and the horrors of the dread valley, and he hunted up old argonaut John Colton to do a serialized story on the Jayhawkers' trek of '49.[41]

Rhyolite was also a strong union town. The Bonanza Miners' Union, whose membership reached nine hundred in the spring of 1907, maintained wages at $4.50 a day, opened the district's only hospital, and spent $30,000 on a two-story, stone union hall. The Miners' Union Hospital provided full health care to union members for a monthly fee of $1, and offered the same to the public for $2. The miners also encouraged other workers to organize the Carpenters' and Joiners' Union of American Local 1581, the International Brotherhood of Electrical Workers Local 557, the Rhyolite Typographical Union Local 665, the Rhyolite Newspaperboys' Union and, of course, the Wobblies, the Industrial Workers of the World Local 258. The Wobblies boasted a membership of six hundred, second only to the miners in numbers. They staged Rhyolite's only labor dispute, such as it was, by posting placards all over town in 1907, proclaiming:[42]

THE UNIQUE AND ADOBE CONCERT HALLS
ARE UNFAIR HOUSES

We request all Union men not to patronize said halls. The unfair girl workers are:

TESSIE ALFRED	KITTY LA BELLE
LITTLE FAY	MAZIE
SKIDOO BABE	FAY

Signed by

THE CONCERT GIRLS

Just about everyone in Rhyolite must have belonged to some sort of organization. In addition to the unions there were fraternal organizations: the Eagles, Elks, Woodmen, Masons, Odd Fellows, and Knights of Pythias—even an Ornery Men's Club of the World and an Ancient and Honorable Order of the Gumph Grabbers. There were also Republican and Democratic clubs, the exclusive Rhyolite Club and its posh rival, the Shoshone Club, the charitable Ladies' Aid Society and Rhyolite Relief Corps and, of course, the First Presbyterian and St. Mary's Catholic churches.[43]

Rhyolite offered a wide range of general amusements, from the saloons, gaming tables, and cribs of Amargosa Street to the Saturday night movies and variety shows at the Arcade Opera House, pool and tennis tournaments, high-school basketball games between Rhyolite and Tonopah, and Sunday afternoon baseball games that matched the Rhyolite Stars, the Railroad Bullets, the Teddy Bears, and the Sixty Six Club for the Bullfrog district championship at Pastime Park. Impromptu horse races, occasional cockfights and prizefights, and a traveling circus complete with elephants and sword swallowers provided additional diversion. There was also a circulating library run out of Goodrich's Book Store.[44]

Rhyolite's early boosters had claimed that it was one of the "best behaved" towns in Nevada, but as it grew, so did the crime rate. Rhyolite never matched Panamint's record of a murder a month, but by 1908 the desert metropolis had witnessed eight homicides and at least a dozen robberies. None of the killings aroused the community more than that of a young prostitute, Isabelle Heskett, known locally as Mona or Norma Belle. She was murdered by her pimp, a tinhorn gambler and morphine addict named Fred Skinner, alias Fred Davis and L. L. Felker. Mona had been talking of quitting the line. The night of January 3, 1908, she and Skinner got into a drunken quarrel in which he beat her then shot her four times as she begged for mercy. Skinner was arrested and quietly taken to Beatty, because an angry crowd of Rhyoliters threatened to lynch him, fearing he would go free in the courts, since no one had yet been convicted of any homicide in the district. Justice finally prevailed, however. After two years and two trials, prosecuted by Pat McCarran at a cost of $35,000, Skinner was convicted and sentenced to fifty years in the state prison. In the meantime, indignant Rhyoliters had rallied to try to drive all the other "macques, pimps and hop fiends" out of town—but not the girls, of course.[45]

Like other places at the end of the rainbow, Rhyolite had a high per capita rate of suicide. There were losers like Martin O'Toole, who had come with his wife and five children from Colorado to try to make a new start, but got to drinking again, lost his job, and ended it all with a dash of cyanide in his coffee. And there were winners like Fred Mason, who sold a claim for $1,600, sent $100 to his sister, and blew the rest on a grand spree that he capped with a lethal bottle of carbonic acid behind the Turf Saloon.[46]

City government—or the lack thereof—was Rhyolite's most persistent problem. Its citizens tried more than once to form a municipal government, but were thwarted each time by the Nye county commissioners. They finally tried to secede and form their own county. Concern over lack of fire protection, sanitation, and schools prompted Rhyoliters to create a Town Board in August 1905, but their actions were repudiated by the county commissioners. The townspeople then countered by organizing a private Board of Trade to carry out the necessary work. Raising money by donations, dances, and box socials, the board hired a night watchman and set up a volunteer fire company and a grammar school. The board also turned out en masse to settle claim-jumping disputes and formed a "Joint Committee on Red Light Affairs" in conjunction with the Miners' Union to establish boundaries for the red-light district and "keep the women on their reservation." After a year had passed with the county commissioners still ignoring Rhyolite's need for local government, the board finally resolved late in 1906 to promote the creation of a new Bullfrog County out of the southern half of Nye, and former Senator Stewart drafted a bill to present in the state legislature. This at last brought a promise from the commissioners to set up some form of city government. In anticipation of this, the board drafted a long list of ordi-

GRAND CELEBRATION ON THE

4TH = AT BEATTY

1776 Once a Year the Hearts of Patriotic Americans beat high as they Celebrate their Independence. This year, July 4th, 1905, Beatty Celebrates with Horse Racing, Baseball Game, Footraces, Pie-eating Contest, Decorations, Fireworks, Oratory, Music, Dancing and a **1905**

GRAND BARBECUE

Under the personal supervision of Mr. Carl Brown, reputed to be one of the finest barbecue men in the State of Nevada, with beef, mutton, chickens, chuckawallas, etc., etc. The following is a list of the games, sports and prizes. Everybody Come. All invited to enter. See program or address Fourth of July Committee at Beatty for particulars. Begins in the morning, lasts all day.

$300-PRIZE HORSE RACE-$300

Slow Burro race, owners to change mounts. Last burro in takes the money. Prize $25, entrance fee $1. 100 yard dash for all comers; prize $50. 50 yard dash, prize $25.
Ladies race, 1st prize $10; 2nd $5
Little Girls race (under 12) 1st prize $3; 2nd $2; 3rd 1.

Boys race, under 12, 1st prize $3; 2nd $2; 3rd $1.
Indian saddle pony race, 1st prize $25; 2nd $10. Squaw Horse Race, prize $25.
Pie-eating contest 1st prize $2; 2nd $1.
Ladle egg race, 1st prize $3; 2nd $2.
Wheelbarrow race, 1st prize $20; 2nd $10.
A dancing platform 32x48 will be erected for the dance in the evening.

Baseball Game in the Morning between the Beatty and Bullfrog Teams

Fireworks in the Evening COME EVERYONE COME Dancing in the Evening

Let Everybody Come to Enjoy and Celebrate American Independence Day at BEATTY, the Southern Nevada Oasis, the Heart of the Bullfrog District.

1905   **JULY 4**   **1776**

(*Beatty Bullfrog Miner*, June 24, 1905)

PATRIOTISM, SPORTS, PARADE

....On the....

FOURTH OF JULY

....AT....

Prospectors, Mining Men, Merchants, Bankers,
Statesmen and their wives, daughters and sweet-
hearts will unite in a glorious celebration of America's great day on the Fourth at RHYOLITE.

At four o'clock in the morning all the mines of this
wonderful Mining District will whistle their salute
to the day.

At nine o'clock there will be a general parade led by
prospectors of the camp.

At ten a. m. a prize drilling contest, single and
double handed, between brawny Sons of the West
will begin.

In the afternoon at one o'clock will commence the horse and
foot races and field sports, and the greased pig will be turned loose.

At four p.m there will be a Baseball game between the Rhyolite and Goldfield teams for a prize of $500.

Fireworks will be displayed from the mountain in the evening at seven, and the great day will be closed by an oration
by the famous statesman SENATOR Wm. M. STEWART,
with a beautiful musical program, band music and dance.
There will also be a Grand Raffle in the evening of a town
lot for the benefit of the hospital building.

nances, including one establishing a Town Committee. The commissioners voted that one down, but then passed all the others, creating a fire department, a police department, and a chain gang, and outlawing gasoline storage and hog raising inside the city limits, and prostitution outside the red-light district. The city's services were financed through two additional ordinances, licensing dogs for $3 a year and prostitutes for $5 a month. A license on gaming tables was added later, but the state legislature outlawed gambling soon after that. The Bullfrog County bill, in the meantime, had passed the state assembly but died in the senate.[47]

Of Rhyolite's early rivals, only Beatty was still alive; Bullfrog and Gold Center were dead. In February 1906, Charley Schwab had bought part of Bob Montgomery's Beatty interests, including the Montgomery Hotel, which was the largest in the district. But Schwab had no time to waste promoting the town, and soon after the arrival of the Las Vegas and Tonopah Railroad he sold his holdings for a reported $100,000 to one Dr. William S. Phillips. The "Doctor," a dapper young con man heralded as the "little millionaire hustler from Chicago," announced his intention of making Beatty the "Chicago of Nevada." He staged a big publicity blitz to celebrate the arrival of Beatty's second railroad, the Bullfrog Goldfield, in April 1907, posting signs on vacant lots all over town to mark them as future sites of a new $100,000 hotel, a hospital, a city hall, a church, and so on. As soon as he had sold all the lots he could, he skipped with the cash, leaving a pile of unpaid bills, not the least of which was that due to Charley Schwab. Phillips next turned up in Los Angeles, selling lots in an imaginary new town of Velma, supposedly located on the banks of the Amargosa south of Gold Center in the midst of what Phillips called the "Amargosa Oil Fields!" The law finally caught up with him for mail fraud in 1908, and he was sent to prison for three years. In the meantime, Beatty still struggled along, boosted by Nicklin as best he could through the columns of his *Miner*.[48]

Bullfrog had died after Mannix moved his *Miner* to Rhyolite in late March 1906. Six weeks later the last merchant followed, and Clemens of the *Herald* happily proclaimed that "verily Bullfrog croaketh." The few faithful who had remained at Gold Center awaiting the coming of the Las Vegas and Tonopah line were joined by a hopeful printer, G. Harold Ellis, who started the *Gold Center News* in anticipation of the big event in September 1906. But their hopes were soon dashed when the railroad built right on through to Rhyolite.[49]

Although Rhyolite's early rivals had succumbed, a few new camps did spring up elsewhere in the district to take up the challenge, at least briefly. The first of these was Transvaal, in the northeast corner of the district over a dozen miles from Rhyolite. Late in February 1906 George Probasco located a claim in the hills just east of Oasis Valley, which he named the Transvaal for the famous South African mining country. Assays of $182 a ton from the grass roots started a rush. One enthusiast returned to Beatty claiming enough gold had stuck to his boots to buy dinner. Within two months the new camp of Transvaal boasted a population of over seven hundred, tents and rag huts numbering in the hundreds, a daily stage from Beatty, and two weekly newpapers! Clemens created the *Transvaal Tribune* at his Herald plant in Rhyolite for distribution by auto to the new camp, and Nicklin started the rival *Transvaal Miner* by running off an extra edition of his Beatty *Miner* under the new masthead. But the whole bubble burst when miners found out that the rich rock didn't go down—it was only shallow surface enrichment.[50]

Two other brief excitements in the southeast part of the district sparked the camps of Flourine and Telluride in the spring of 1908. A rich strike by leasers on a claim called the Diamond Queen attracted a few hundred curious souls to the east side of Bare Mountain. Among the first was an enterprising promoter, John Doser from Beatty, who laid out the townsite of Flourine to sell prize lots for $50 a piece. Within weeks of the first strike, another was made on Meiklejohn Mountain to the north, and Doser planted a second townsite there. He held a contest to name this one, offering a corner lot on Main Street for the best suggestion. He got responses from as far away as New Jersey, but a local miner won the lot with the name Telluride, a gold-bearing mineral in the ore. But both strikes proved to be only small pockets and the camps disappeared by summer, before anyone even thought to start a newspaper.[51]

The only new camp in the Bullfrog district that really came close to equaling Rhyolite was Pioneer, but then its big mine, the Bi-Metallic, was the only one that ever came close to equaling the Montgomery Shoshone. The three Bi-Metallic claims had been purchased in 1905 by a couple of Denver promoters, William J. and Richard F. Tobin, and floated as the Bullfrog Pioneer Gold Mines Company for a paltry 2¢ a share. After a few years of desultory exploration that exhausted what little funds the company had, the Tobins joined with a practical miner, J. Ruben Bryan, to form a second company, the Bullfrog Pioneer Leasing and Milling Company, which took a lease on the most promising claim, the Bi-Metallic No. 3, early in 1908. After working for nearly a year without success, Bryan was about to give up, when suddenly he struck pay rock on November 1. It was not only rich but there was a lot of it, and within the month Bryan began shipping out $100 ore by the carload. The Bi-Metallic was the biggest thing in Bullfrog since the Montgomery Shoshone strike. Pioneer stock leaped to over 30¢ a share, and the stampede to Pioneer was on.[52]

By February 1909 there were twenty-five hundred rainbow-chasers at the instant camp of Pioneer, and in numbers, at least, it momentarily surpassed Rhyolite, which it helped to deplete. Town lots were selling for as much as $1,350, and two townsite additions had been appended to the original to keep up with the demand. In the flurry of excitement nearly three hundred buildings had been put up. They ranged from stores covered with corrugated iron for fire protection to the ubiquitous ragtop cabins. Many structures were simply moved in from Rhyolite and Beatty— not all with the owners' permission, however, for at least two would-be Pioneers were arrested on their way out of Rhyolite for house stealing! Even the big Montgomery Hotel was dismantled and moved to Pioneer, where it was renamed the Holland House. Stories of a $10,000 poker game at the hotel attracted one of Nevada's most flamboyant gamblers and promoters, George L. "Tex" Rickard, to the new camp to open a gambling hall and speculate in mining leases.[53]

Bill Brong monopolized the 2-mile, fifteen-minute auto-stage run to the Bullfrog Goldfield Railroad, connecting with the trains twice a day at Springdale Station, while five other "mahouts" vied for the business on the longer run from Rhyolite. Telephone lines had already reached the camp, and electric lines were close behind. The miners had formed a new local, No. 218 of the Western Federation of Miners, and the carpenters followed. The camp boasted two rival weeklies, started within a day of one another, the *Pioneer Topics,* commenced on February 17 by Theodore Lowe and delivered by train from his *Columbia Topics* plant near Goldfield, and the *Pioneer Press,* begun the following day at Rhyolite by the ever-ready Clemens of the *Herald.* Lowe soon moved a printing plant to Pioneer, but Clemens was more cautious.[54]

For a time it looked as if nothing could stop Pioneer. Gold seemed to be everywhere. One irrepressible booster reported that when the first man died there, his friends who gathered at the graveside had no sooner finished reading the last rites than one of them spotted a rich-looking rock from the hole. A quick assay showed it to be so rich that they dug up the body and started sinking a shaft. A new grave was started half a mile away, but the last round of shots uncovered a new ledge spotted with gold. With that they decided to ship the body to Goldfield "so he could rest in peace."[55]

Everything was hopping again. The Pioneer leasing company's high-grade shipments reached $60,000 a month, surpassing the Montgomery Shoshone's monthly output. New leasing companies were at work on the other two Bi-Metallic claims and all of those surrounding them. A little five-stamp mill, hastily put up on the Mayflower mine just west of the camp, started up on March first, turning out bullion at a rate of $10,000 a month.[56]

Not even an $80,000 fire that gutted the main business block on May 7—despite the corrugated iron—could stop Pioneer. Editor Lowe happily observed that the bank and the red-light district were spared, and rebuilding began two days later. By the Fourth of July the block was rebuilt, and Pioneer celebrated with festivities and prizes of cash and stock that topped Rhyolite's. That same day Lowe commenced the *Pioneer Daily Times,* proudly proclaiming it the "Only Daily in the Bullfrog District," since Rhyolite's *Daily Bulletin* had folded. By then the Pioneer lease, which had shipped some $350,000 worth of ore in half a year, was closing fast on the great Montgomery Shoshone, which had thus far produced barely twice that amount. Not only that but the Pioneer leasing company had just declared the Bullfrog District's first dividend![57]

Before the end of July, however, the whole Pioneer boom collapsed in a tangle of litigation. In January the Tobins had acquired the Conservative, an undeveloped claim adjacent to the Bi-Metallic No. 3. With it they formed a new company, Gold Hills Mining and Milling, and promptly prepared to sue their original company, the Bullfrog Pioneer, for all the ore taken out, arguing that it came from the ledge claimed by the Conservative. The other Pioneer stockholders brought suit against the Tobins, claiming that they were being defrauded of their property. In the meantime, the Tobins sold their new company to Goldfield mining operator George Wingfield and David R. C. Brown of Aspen, Colorado. The new owners, forming yet another company, Pioneer Consolidated Mines, announced their intention of merging both Gold Hills and Pioneer. Wingfield and Brown offered to exchange stock share for share in the new consolidation, but they held back an equal amount of watered stock for themselves, so that the consolidation would cut the original Pioneer stockholders' interest in the mine to just a quarter. To pressure "troublesome" stockholders into going along with this merger scheme, Wingfield and his partner brought suit in the name of the Gold Hills company against both the original Bullfrog Pioneer and the Pioneer Leasing companies. None of these arcane maneuvers, however, had interrupted the steady ore shipments from the mine. That happened when yet another litigant, the Indiana Nevada Mining Company, joined the fray. This company was organized in May when W. B. Milliken, owner of the Indiana, which was adjacent to both the Bi-Metallic and Conservative, saw his chance to get a piece of the action. He brought suit, claiming that it was really the Indiana that had title to the gold-bearing ledge, and on July 24 he got an injunction against the Pioneer Leasing company. This not only shut down the mine but also halted payment of the first dividend, and that killed Pioneer.[58]

The Indiana suit kept the Bi-Metallic shut down for three years. Few

Pioneers waited for the revival; most left in a hurry that summer of 1909. Only a few days after the injunction, Lowe was arrested on a bad check complaint from his landlady. The charges were soon dismissed, but she gave him a sound thrashing with her handbag and sent him packing on the next train to Los Angeles. That was the end of the *Topics* and the *Times*. Clemens never bothered to issue the *Press* again, either.[59]

Only the little Mayflower mill continued a while longer. But it too was at last shut down when the president of the company tried to grab the mine. In the heady excitement of the boom, soon after the mill had started up, Goldfield speculator Gus Eisen, titular head of the Mayflower Bullfrog Consolidated Mining Company, suddenly realized that it might actually become a paying mine, and wanted it all for himself. He promptly fired the superintendent without the approval of the company directors, put in his own man, and enlarged the mill to fifteen stamps. Then he shut it down, blatantly announcing to the stockholders in December 1909 that, despite the profitable production of over $82,000 in bullion, the company was suddenly in debt to him for over $50,000 in concocted loans. He further informed them that he had remedied this situation by signing over a twenty-five year lease on the property at a paltry 5 percent royalty to a new leasing company that he had just formed, and happily offered to sell them shares. The outraged stockholders revolted, and after protracted litigation, they eventually dumped Eisen.[60]

The Mayflower reopened under new management in 1911, but produced only $30,000 more before exhausting the pay ore. The last of the Pioneer Consolidated litigation was finally untangled in November 1912, and the Tobins took over the management again. They had pretty well gutted the mine of high-grade during the boom to maintain high production and correspondingly high stock prices. Still, there appeared to be a lot of milling ore, so they put up a ten-stamp mill, which produced only a disappointing $50,000 worth of bullion over the next few years.[61]

Aside from Pioneer's Bi-Metallic, no other mine in the Bullfrog district even came close to rivaling the Montgomery Shoshone. The wonderful Original Bullfrog and the highly touted Gold Bar, Homestake, Denver, and Tramp all proved to be awful disappointments to their investors and terrible embarrassments to nearly everyone else in the district, for they fell so far short of expectation.

The Original Bullfrog had been the first to fall from grace. The phenomenal surface pocket that put the district on the map was quickly exhausted, and exploration at depth revealed nothing of value. Even Ed Cross, who stayed in for all he could get, at last sold out in 1907, and the company ceased exploratory work that summer. After that the Bullfrog

W. J. TOBIN

William Tobin's Pioneer mine hit pay rock in 1908, to become Bullfrog's second
biggest producer before a tangle of litigation shut it down. (*Portrait courtesy of
Nevada Historical Society*)

was worked only sporadically, mainly to supply Rhyolite jewelers with
specimens of that famous green rock to cut into little bullfrogs for watch
fobs, cuff links, and stickpins.[62]

The Denver, showing rich talc like that of Montgomery's Shoshone,
had been combined with the Tramp and other claims by Tonopah mining
operator Tasker L. Oddie to form the Tramp Consolidated Mining Company in the spring of 1906. Touted as a sure bet to become "one of the
biggest and foremost producers in the state," its shares sold for as much
as $2.75 and held above $1 par for over a year. Although it never produced

more than $50,000 worth of ore, it remained a great favorite among Eastern speculators, who worked it for much more on the exchanges.⁶³

Two of the biggest disappointments of all the Bullfrog mines were the Gold Bar and Homestake, considered to be two of the safest and most conservative enterprises in the district. These twin mines shared the same ore body, had remarkably similar types of management, and eventually came to the same sad end. The Bullfrog Gold Bar Mining Company had been organized in the spring of 1905 by two of Goldfield's instant millionaires, James P. Loftus and James R. Davis. The neighboring Homestake Consolidated was organized that fall by Dallas real estate man B. D. Milam. Systematic development at depth opened ore pockets said to average over $500 a ton, and their stocks climbed to over $2 a share in the spring of 1906. That summer Davis reported to the Gold Bar stockholders that development work had exposed some $2,347,000 worth of ore, and the following year Loftus told them that further work had increased that amount to $4 million. At the same time the Homestake company announced that they had also opened an estimated $2,350,000. By this time stockholders were getting anxious to see some return, so both companies at last decided it was time to put up mills. Like Charley Schwab, both managements declared that they had such faith in their mines that they would personally put up construction money for the mills rather than sell the company treasury stock.⁶⁴

At this point the two companies took slightly different courses. Loftus and Davis not only loaned the money for their mill but contracted with themselves to build it, charging the Gold Bar company about $50,000 for an ineffective little ten-stamp mill that couldn't recover even 40 percent of the assay value of the ore. But they kept that fact a secret, publicly declaring the mill to be a splendid success, while dumping the rest of their stock and then selling the treasury stock to pay off part of their loan. On June 1, 1908, Loftus suddenly announced that the mill had shut down; the pay ore was exhausted, and it had yielded only $5,238.97 in bullion! The mine, he said, was an "empty shell"—the wonderful $4 million had vanished! But Loftus and Davis didn't even leave the stockholders the shell; instead, they attached the property for $36,000 still due on their loan. Shocked stockholders, who had paid Loftus and Davis an estimated $350,000 for their shares, cried fraud, and the Rhyolite papers denounced the shameless pair for "giving . . . mining a black eye."⁶⁵

In the heat of the condemnation, Loftus brushed aside all criticism with the classic "public be damned." A quarter of a century later the world had turned upside down, as a benevolent Loftus recalled how an overly eager investor had once offered him $1.50 a share for his Gold Bar stock when it was selling for only 50¢. But he had steadfastly refused to sell even a share until the mine had proven its value. He just couldn't let the man "take a chance on losing a fortune," Loftus said. "It might have given the mining business a black eye."[66]

In the meantime, Milam of the Homestake had built a much grander twenty-five-stamp mill, at a much grander cost of $170,000. This mill was said to recover over 90 percent of the assay value of the ore. The problem, of course, was that there just wasn't much value in the ore. So after nearly a year's run the Homestake mill too shut down in April 1909, having produced only $70,000. All of those millions once in sight had vanished again. Milam also attached the property for the mill construction costs; the investors who had bought his stock sued and lost; and mining got one more black eye.[67]

Through all of this, the great Montgomery Shoshone had remained the one steady producer, the bulwark of the Bullfrog district. In three years of grinding, the great mill had turned out over a million dollars in bullion. Yet as an investment the great mine had to be the district's greatest disappointment, for out of all that bullion not one cent was ever paid out to any of its stockholders, save one. Even that one—Charley Schwab, of course—insisted in the end that he was the most disappointed of all, and he probably was, for he had expected much more than most.

The early profits in his Montgomery Shoshone stock had spurred Schwab into further speculations on the advice of Gillies and Macdonald in neighboring districts. But after the "Schwab stocks" had steadily declined for over a year, some of the Steel King's acquaintances, whom he had "let in" at top prices, began to complain. When it got so bad that they snubbed him at his club in Pittsburgh, Schwab finally admitted in October 1907 that he too had been "sadly disappointed" in his mining investments—all except the Montgomery Shoshone, that is. Although Schwab singled out the Shoshone as the one exception, it too had already disappointed him when he learned that the wonderful high-grade that had brought it fame was confined to only a few stringers and that what he had actually bought was a large low-grade mine. Schwab took none of the blame for any of these disappointments, insisting that he had been "deceived" by his engineers, who had "exaggerated to me and . . . lied to me." But other western promoters, already suffering from a market crippled by the nationwide financial panic that fall, quickly rallied to counter Schwab's charges, and gadfly George Graham Rice branded Schwab as a lowly "welcher who pleads the baby act" in trying to make patsies of his partners.[68]

Despite Schwab's continued public praise of the Montgomery Shoshone, its other stockholders had watched their stock shrink steadily from $23 a share to less than $3 in the course of three years. So even though Superintendent Bryce Turner reported at the annual stockholders' meeting in February 1908 that there was now $5 million worth of ore blocked out in the mine and that the mill would soon be turning out $75,000 a month, some of the stockholders couldn't help wondering if they too were being deceived, and they demanded a second opinion. The result was disastrous.[69]

A committee of the minority stockholders selected A. Chester Beatty, an eminent British mining engineer who worked for the Guggenheims, to examine the mine, and Beatty sent an associate, Henry Krumb, to do the actual work. Krumb turned in his report to the committee on April 29. The text was not released, but the committee immediately announced that the report was "distinctly unfavorable," and word was telegraphed across the country: "SHOSHONE BIGGEST SWINDLE IN MINING WORLD...NOT $400,000 NET IN SIGHT!" Shoshone stock crashed from $3 to 75¢ in just two days' trading, cutting the market value of the more than $1 million, to only $375,000. Somebody clearly could have made a tidy profit by selling short, but just who that might have been is not as clear.[70]

Just before the crash, while Krumb was still writing his report, the price of the stock had been worked up on tips that Bernard M. Baruch, the budding financier who had speculated in Goldfield stocks, was now quietly buying Shoshone stock for the Guggenheims. Subsequent rumors had it that the Guggenheims had grabbed up over 200,000 shares when the price broke. It was also reported that Bob Montgomery had sold at least half of his remaining 100,000 shares to Baruch and others for $2, although Bob denied the specifics, and that Malcolm Macdonald had sold 70,000 shares. Rhyolite papers claimed the crash was a "freeze out" of the Westerners. Macdonald even intimated that there had been "a change in control" of the mine. Baruch, however, disclaimed either "having or contemplating" an interest in the company, although that would have been true even if he had sold short. Charley Schwab, of course, said he was the "heaviest loser" in the crash and was "getting tired of mining ventures."[71]

When the Krumb report was finally made public, it was revealed that although Krumb hadn't agreed with Turner's estimate of $5 million worth of ore blocked out, he also hadn't said there was only $400,000 in sight, as was widely reported. He had given that figure as the expected profit, but since the company was still in debt to Schwab for $432,000 in loans, that wasn't exactly good news either. In response Schwab quickly brought in John G. Kirchen from his Tonopah property to replace Turner as superintendent, and at the next stockholders' meeting, in February 1909, Kirchen reported that the annual production of the mine had reached $535,763 and that there was still $1 million in sight. This time no one rose to question the superintendent's estimate. Montgomery

Shoshone stock, which had slowly recovered, reached $2 a share after Kirchen's report, and investors were again "scrambling to buy."[72] The bulk of this production was now coming from ore averaging only $9 a ton. But Kirchen had trimmed mining and milling costs to only $3.72 a ton, so that with losses of about 75¢ a ton in the tailings the company was now making a 50 percent profit on every ton milled. It would have been profit, that is, if only the mill had been financed by treasury stock sales rather than by Schwab's loan. But no new ore was being discovered, and the value of that remaining steadily decreased. The production for 1909 slipped to $446,224, and for 1910 it dropped to only $246,661. Worse yet, the profit for that year was down to a bare 1 percent! The mine had in fact been running at a loss most of the year. So on March 14, 1911, the directors finally closed it down. The stock, which had already declined to 10¢ a share, dropped to 4¢ and was taken off the exchanges.[73]

Editor Clemens of the *Rhyolite Herald,* hoping against hope, waited for over a week after the closure before he at last announced "Montgomery Shoshone is dead!" It had been a good mine, producing a total of $1,418,636.21 in bullion, but it had never paid a dividend, because all of its "profits" had gone "a glimmering," toward paying back the $432,000 in loans from Schwab. Over $100,000 of that was still unpaid, so the mill and other machinery were sold to pay off Schwab, leaving the other stockholders with nothing at all. George Graham Rice called Montgomery Shoshone "one of the sorriest failures in Nevada," claiming that the public's losses mounted into the millions. But Clemens summed up its sorry history as just "a case of trying to make a world beater out of what would be considered ordinarily a 'mighty good little mine.'"[74]

Both Rhyolite and the Bullfrog were on the decline well before the final closing of the Montgomery Shoshone. The shutdown of the other once-promising mines—Tramp, Gold Bar, Homestake, Pioneer, and Mayflower—and countless lesser prospects had, one by one, taken their toll on what Clemens had once called the "Camp of Confidence." In 1910 the census taker found only 611 residents in the once bustling city of 4,000. Bank failures and newspaper suspensions had also marked the steady decline of the desert metropolis from its peak in 1907–08. The John S. Cook and Co. Bank went under in the fall of 1908; the Bullfrog Bank and Trust Co. closed its doors the following spring; and the last survivor, the First National Bank, failed on March 21, 1910. DeLaney's *Death Valley Magazine,* which issued its last in October 1908, was the first casualty in the fourth estate, followed by the little *Daily Bulletin* on June 8, 1909, and Mannix's *Bullfrog Miner* on September 25. In May 1909 Nicklin had

Bullfrog's newspaper bonanza.

sold his *Beatty Bullfrog Miner* to Clemens, who shut it down in July. At the same time Clemens gave up on the *Pioneer Press,* which left his *Rhyolite Herald* as the district's only paper.[75]

The closure of the Montgomery Shoshone was the last straw for Clemens, as well as many others who had stood by the declining town. Clemens sold the *Herald* just a few weeks after the Shoshone closed and gave up the mining camps entirely to settle in the quiet little farm town of Terra Bella in the San Joaquin Valley. His former assistant editor, A. B. Gibson, kept the paper going for another year before he too gave up, laying it to rest on June 22, 1912. By then hundreds of houses and whole business blocks were deserted, and more were vacated every month. The post office closed in November 1913; the last train pulled out of the Rhyolite Station the following July; and the Nevada-California Power Company turned off the lights and took down their lines in 1916. A visitor the following year found Rhyolite all but abandoned. The offices, stores, and houses stood silent and empty, their windows smashed and doors battered down. Even the wonderful Cook bank building was but an empty shell, the big steel vault doors taken off and sold, the floor strewn with canceled checks and worthless stock certificates. The desert metropolis had become a "graveyard of blasted hopes."[76]

The Bullfrog excitement was at last a thing of the past. Only the debris and memories remained. All of the movers and shakers were gone. Shorty Harris had gone on across Death Valley to new strikes in the Panamints. His one-time partner Ed Cross had turned to ranching in southern California. Bob Montgomery, who was pursuing another million at Skidoo, sent back a few bucks now and then to Shoshone Johnny. George Graham Rice, awaiting trial for mail fraud, had just enough time to write his *memoires, My Adventures with Your Money,* before he was sent back to prison again. Charley Schwab had finally returned to the business he knew best, and with the coming of the First World War he built his Bethlehem Steel corporation into much more than the shipbuilding trust could ever have hoped to be. Even Rhyolite's first settler, Pete Busch, was gone, but not by choice. He had stayed on after nearly everyone else had left, only to die in Death Valley's record heat wave in July 1913.[77]

Mysterious Scott

In the heat of the gold fever, on Sunday afternoon July 9, 1905, a three-car special, the "Death Valley Coyote," dashed out of the Santa Fe railroad station in Los Angeles on a record-breaking run to Chicago. In the rear car, waving a fat roll of gold backs, whooping and hollering, was a flamboyant cowboy-prospector who claimed he had struck it rich in a secret mine in Death Valley. With this spectacular stunt, Death Valley Scotty burst into headlines across the country. He grabbed the imagination of the nation, and he held it for decades, becoming the personification of Death Valley's hidden riches. He remains today better known in his own peculiar way than any other man in the valley's history.[1]

Death Valley Scotty was a ham actor, a conscienceless con man, an almost pathological liar, and a charismatic bullslinger. For all his ruddy-faced bluster and bravado, he had a ready smile, a colorful gift of gab, and an ingratiating manner that disarmed even his sharpest critics. But behind the engaging showman could be sensed a furtiveness in his steel blue eyes and a tension that sometimes set his jaw to granite. He was an insatiable attention-seeker, a reckless publicity hound, willing to say or do almost anything for one more moment in the limelight. Yet he carefully shrouded most of his actions in studied mystery. Almost everyone knew of him, but hardly anyone really knew him. Those who tried to gain his confidence came away poorer and not much wiser for their efforts. Death Valley Scotty was also the consummate grubstake-eater, the quintessential moocher, who perfected the prospector's homely come-ons and string-alongs to an art form. He conned a small fortune out of his backers, and squandered it all in his compulsion for notoriety.[2]

Death Valley was the key for Scotty. "I will never forget the first time I saw Death Valley, and the impression it made upon me," he recalled:

> I had ridden from Wells across country and had been on the lookout for a view of the place for two days. Finally I came in full sight of it. I was on the summit of the Grapevine Mountains, when I saw Death Valley yawning down beneath.
>
> Now, no one has ever accused me of being superstitious, or believing in spirits, or other things of a like nature, but when I saw Death Valley for the first time a strange feeling came over me. I felt that I had found what I was looking for. I had heard a great deal

about the place and had regarded the name with horror, but now when in plain view of it I felt good . . . This place so avoided by everybody, whose very name made so many shudder, attracted me. To be plain, I felt that it was to be, some way, instrumental in bringing about a great fortune for me.

That fortune, however, was still quite distant that day in 1895 when Scotty first came to Death Valley.[3]

Walter Edward Scott was born on September 20, 1872, near Cynthiana in the bluegrass country of Kentucky. His father, George, bred trotting horses and made whiskey on the side. Scotty was the youngest of six children. He felt neglected and unwanted in his childhood. His mother died when he was an infant and after his father remarried, Scotty was sent to be raised by a stepsister. At the age of fourteen he ran away, heading west to Wells, Nevada, where his brothers, Bill and Warner, were working as cowhands. Within a few years he had become a skilled broncobuster, competing in the local rodeos, and in the early 1890s he landed a job with Buffalo Bill Cody's Wild West show. There he learned the tricks of the showman and the huckster and became addicted to the roar of the crowd.[4]

Scotty worked in Buffalo Bill's show nearly every season for a decade, riding the bucking broncos and acting in melodramatic skits of the Pony Express and an Indian attack on the Deadwood stage. But it was only seasonal work, touring from late April through October. Between tours he got odd jobs in the West, on the range in Nevada and in the mines of Arizona and Colorado. Once, in the summer of 1895, lured by tales of Breyfogle's gold, Scotty dropped out of the Wild West show for a season to join a survey party under C. H. Sinclair, who was running a new California-Nevada boundary line across the north end of Death Valley and the Amargosa Desert to Pahrump. Scotty later claimed that he first glimpsed his mysterious mine that summer. He did glimpse the possibilities, but that glimpse wasn't enough to keep him from going back to the Wild West show the next season.[5]

In the spring of 1900, Scotty met a young widow who was clerking in a candy store in New York City. Her name was Ella Josephine McCarthy Milius, but he called her Jack. They were married in Cincinnati that November. But after a nine-day honeymoon in Kentucky, Scotty put his bride on a train back to New York and headed for Cripple Creek to get a job in the mines for the winter. He didn't see Jack until the next spring, when the Wild West show started in New York again. After the tour disbanded that fall, Scotty took Jack with him when he returned to Cripple Creek. It was that winter of 1901–02 that the superintendent of the mine Scotty was working in chanced to take Jack on a tour underground, pointing out a vein he claimed was "the finest ore in America today." "I was thrilled," she recalled,

> and I begged him to give me a chunk of the rock that I might carry back to New York in the spring to show the girls at the Broadway confectionery store. Instead of one bit of rock, the superintendent gave me two. Later, when we were packing to leave for New York, after the winter grind in the mine was over, I showed the specimens to Scott. His eyes popped out a foot, but he said nothing.[6]

Things happened quickly after that. They arrived back in New York on April 21, 1902, the day the Wild West show opened at Madison Square Garden, but Scotty missed the opening parade down Broadway. When Cody threatened to dock him a week's pay for being late, Scotty quit and stubbornly refused to return, even after Cody relented. Instead, Scotty took those two bits of picture rock Jack had gotten in Cripple Creek and headed down Fifth Avenue to see Julian M. Gerard, the third vice president of the giant Knickerbocker Trust Company.[7]

Gerard, three years younger than Scotty, was a Yale graduate, and a rising young banker with old and influential family ties, and he had a soft spot for the West. As a boy he had spent a few months on a ranch in Arizona for his health, and he later delighted in telling people that he had once been a cowboy. When Buffalo Bill's Wild West was in town, he occasionally dropped into the Putnam House bar, where the cowboys hung out after the show. It was there he had met Scotty. He also had a strong interest and a bit of experience in mining. He had studied mineralogy at Yale, and after graduating in 1897 went prospecting briefly in the Southwest before returning to New York to commence a career in finance. He was the perfect mark for what Scotty had in mind.[8]

When Scotty showed him those little pieces of picture rock, Gerard saw at once that they were free milling high-grade and was anxious to learn where they had come from. Scotty made up a wonderful story of how he had picked them up on a great bonanza that he and an old desert rat, "John Berryman," had discovered way out in the sinister reaches of Death Valley, how there was an immense fortune waiting there, and how all he needed was a grubstake to open it up. Gerard hesitated only long enough to have the rocks assayed. They ran over a dollar a pound in gold— $2,248.89 a ton—and Gerard was hooked. On April 23 they signed a grubstake agreement. Scotty gave Gerard a half interest in his marvelous "mine," and in any others he might happen to discover within the next six months. When pressed for a legal description of his bonanza, Scotty fancifully located it "about one hundred and thirty miles southwest of Fenner on Santa Fe R.R. and about one and one-half miles north of Furnace Creek Mountain and about five hundred yards east of what is known as Burro Trail running to Alkali Spring, which is about a quarter of a mile from the mine." That first direction would have put it near Mt. Palomar, more than 150 miles south of Death Valley! But that may have been just a typo, for it didn't seem to bother Gerard, who happily gave Scotty $1,500, half in cash right then, and the rest to come later. That was as much as Scotty could earn in a whole season with Buffalo Bill—and so much easier, too. And it was only the beginning, for he eventually got many times that amount out of Gerard before the young banker, in Scotty's words, "got wise."[9]

The transformation from part-time cowboy to full-time con man had begun. "Walter wasted no time once he had his grubstake," Jack recalled. "He rode the cab of the first westbound engine out of New York heading for the sands of Death Valley." There he commenced a long but winning string of letters and telegrams to Gerard that are minor classics of the grubstake-eater's art. Though clumsy and erratic at first, Scotty dedicated himself to his new role with the single-mindedness of the broncobuster, and one by one he mastered all the come-ons and string-alongs, all the baits and stalls. He worked every dip, angle, and spur as he slowly put together his elaborate charade—his one-man show—to keep the money coming.[10]

Leaning hard on the perils of Death Valley, Scotty set the stage with incredible tales of the heat, hardships, and hazards. "I am about burnt up fearful," he wrote Gerard under a Death Valley dateline on the Fourth of July, 1902. "The heat is terrible. For ten straight days it has been 140° in the shade. . . . Bad water and the heat has got me all to the bad." Again he wrote, "Hot, great God! Got in the lower end of the Valley—liked to die. . . . I am sick—my head is all out of shape. The extreme heat has got me crazy." By Scotty's telling the heat and bad water also took a devastating toll on his burros and jacks, which dropped like flies by the wayside, while others were spirited away by wanderlust or Indians, so that he was often left on foot to get out or die. Once, when the water holes dried up, he had to go 116 miles without water, he said, but it was cooler then—only 134°. Even when it rained, things were no better. He wrote from Barstow, "I got here today at noon. I walked 145 miles. Had no jacks. Lost two outfits in a cloudburst. I never saw such mountains of water in all my life. . . . I got caught in a long canyon and about four in the morning a wall of water came down and took everything. I just barely got out myself. I had jacks scattered all over Death Valley." Such tales discouraged Gerard from rushing out to see the mine for himself and made him content just to send his money.[11]

Against this awful backdrop Scotty wrote enticingly of the prospects and development of the "mine." He had quickly dispensed with Berryman by simply writing Gerard that the old man was now "out of the game entirely." And when Gerard later began to worry that Berryman might try to get back into the game, Scotty conveniently wrote that he had found Berryman's bones at the southwest end of the Funeral Range. Scotty also gave the "mine" some semblance of reality by recording a location notice in the Inyo County Courthouse in his and Gerard's names. He called it the Knickerbocker Quartz Mine Claim, and gave it the same fanciful location he had described to Gerard. By the Fourth of July 1902, Scotty wrote that he had already opened up a lead 30 inches wide and had taken out a ton of that precious $1-a-pound rock, and another 3 tons of lower grade ore worth only $700 a ton! A year later he claimed he had "at least $5,000,000 in sight." But he wryly cautioned Gerard, "don't stagger and don't tell no one for they would say you and I was crazy." Finally, early in 1904, he wrote that he had hired two young miners to help him and that he had bought a power drill and an ore crusher. By then he had reported striking a rich new ledge 14 feet wide and had stopped even trying to estimate the worth of the ore in sight. He even recorded sixteen more paper claims to secure the ground all around this wonderful "mine." News of Jack Keane's gold strike in the Funerals early in 1904 and the Bullfrog rush that fall helped lend credence to Scotty's claims.[12]

All of this imaginary work and all of those lost burros, of course, provided a ready excuse for more money. So just before he signed his letters with a "Your true amigo" or an "Adios," Scotty usually got to the point of the whole thing with a simple, blunt, "You send me some coin," "You send me $200," or "I need some money." It worked, too, at least for a few years.[13]

Gerard was slowly growing skeptical of the deal, however. Despite the glowing reports and endless promises, Scotty had never let Gerard or anyone he knew see the mine, nor had he ever sent Gerard another piece of ore. Once Scotty had told Gerard that he was heading East with a satchel full of gold amalgam. But when Scotty got to Philadelphia, he reported that the bag had been stolen from him on the train from Pittsburgh, so all Gerard ever got to see were newspaper clippings of Scotty's claim that he had been robbed of $12,000 in gold. When Gerard wrote that he was sending a mining engineer, E. M. Wilkinson, to look at the mine, Scotty protested, "You cannot make me believe in an expert. They can't see through the ground." And when Wilkinson arrived at Daggett in August 1903, Scotty scared him off, telling him he would have to face 150° heat under "a broiling sun with absolutely no shade whatever" and drink water "not fit for the jacks." Scotty explained to Gerard that he hadn't dared to take Wilkinson for fear that if the engineer died, he would be accused of murder. Unimpressed, Gerard sent Wilkinson back in October together with an old friend, Rufus King. Scotty again

Location Notice. Quartz Claim

Notice is hereby given, that we the undersigned, citizens of the
United States, over the age of 21 years, do hereby locate and claim
1500 feet on this vein, lead or lode of mineral bearing quartz,
together with 300 feet on each side of the center of the vein,
and all timber growing within the limits of the claim, and all
water and water rights thereon or appurtenant thereto are hereby
claimed. The exterior boundaries of the claim are distinctly
marked and are more particularly described as follows, to-wit:-
Commencing at monument at S.W. corner of claim where
this notice is posted thence 600 ft. north-westerly to monument;
thence 1500 ft. North-easterly to monument; thence 600 ft south-easterly
to monument; thence 1500 ft south-westerly to place of beginning.
Said claim is about 1½ miles North of Furnace Creek Range, and
about 500 yds. East of the Burro Trail, situate in the
County of Inyo, State of California. This claim is named and shall
be known as the Knickerbocker Quartz Mining Claim.
Located June 17th. A.D. 1902.
　　　　　　　　　J. M. Girard, and
　　　　　　　　　W. E. Scott　, Locators.

Received at the Request of W. E. Scott ⎫
Aug 16th. 1902 at 30 minutes past 8 o'clock a.m. ⎭　J. E. Murooney,
　　　　　　　　　　　　　　　　　　　　　　　　Recorder.

Death Valley Scotty filed this bogus claim in 1902 to con Knickerbocker Trust
Vice President Julian Gerard out of another grubstake. (*Courtesy of Inyo County
Recorder*)

refused to take them claiming this time that they had "instructions to locate everything in sight" and cheat him out of his mine. With injured innocence, Scotty complained to Gerard, "You could not expect me to be a knight of the desert and let some bum mining engineers come . . . and hand me a bum package. . . . I will have nothing to do with Wilkinson." Gerard hired another engineer, W. H. Ferguson, but Scotty turned him away, too.[14]

All this time Scotty had insisted that he would show the mine only to Gerard, confident that his tales of the terrors of Death Valley were enough to keep Gerard away. But when all else had failed, Gerard decided to brave those awful terrors and call Scotty's bluff. Scotty met him at Needles in the spring of 1904 and took him to Manvel, on the California Eastern Railroad about 30 miles north of Fenner. Then Scotty disappeared for most of a day and at last returned to tell Gerard, "We can't go. We can't get any burros." Gerard protested, but he finally returned to New York in disgust.[15]

As Gerard began expressing fears that he was being conned, Scotty tried everything he knew to regain his confidence. He joked, "Now look here Gerard . . . when I get ready to rob a man I will take a gun and do it in a business way." Next he barked, "The nerve of you to say I was trying to razz you and there was no mine . . . and you was only wasting your valuable time and money. . . . I have some valuable ground and I will hold onto it, see! And no one can gain my confidence with money—it will not buy me." Then he purred, "Hope you have no ill feelings toward me—I certainly have none against you." At last Scotty conceded, "You may think me crooked and trying to do you. Don't give a damn what you think. I will clean up a bunch of money—you just wait." By the spring of 1905 all reason told Gerard that he was being conned, but he still wasn't absolutely sure.[16]

In three years Scotty had taken Gerard for nearly $10,000, and he had gone through it as fast as he had gotten it. Jack had come out to Los Angeles in June 1902, and Scotty set her up in a little apartment. But he spent little time with her and neglected to give her enough to live on, so she left to get a job in Stockton. Scotty managed to spend most of the money just keeping himself in food and drink—and cigars. What was left he spent on occasional attention-getting sprees, setting up the house at Rol King's Hollenbeck Bar in Los Angeles. There he began to develop a new role as the spendthrift prospector, encouraged by King and aided by a young sports reporter for Hearst's *Examiner,* Charles E. Van Loan, who with generous exaggeration made him into a colorful local item. Scotty even attracted the attention of the Los Angeles police in December 1904, when he happened to appear with a big bank roll right after a Wells Fargo express messenger had been robbed and killed near Daggett. Scotty was hauled in for questioning, and was so mysterious about the source of his money that he wasn't released until Van Loan and King came to vouch for him.[17]

Out on the desert at the railroad towns of Daggett and Barstow, Scotty also created a stir now and then, flashing a big roll every time Gerard wired him more money. The rest of the time Scotty tried to impress the locals with a big carpet bag wrapped in dog chains and padlocks. He said it was full of high-grade from his secret mine, but it drew more snickers than awe. When it had outlived its usefulness there, Scotty hauled it to Redlands to make a show of depositing it in a bank vault. This was the bag that was last seen en route to Philadelphia.[18]

When Scotty did occasionally venture into Death Valley, he spent most of his time in a hideout he called "Camp Hold Out," in the Black Mountains on the east side of the valley opposite Wingate Wash. His hideout was near a spring a few miles up what is now Scotty's Canyon, described by some as "the wildest and most inaccessible canyon in the range." Scotty made his camp on a narrow shelf under an overhanging ledge and furnished it with a couple of mattresses, a steamer chair, a tin bathtub he'd stolen from the old Confidence mine, silverware from various railroad dining cars, and towels from a Los Angeles hotel. Rumor had it that he kept the camp provisioned with slabs of bacon, cured hams, fancy French canned goods, mackerel, sardines, caviar, and after dinner mints, plus a fine stock of whiskey and champagne. The rock wall was decorated with pictures of actors, actresses, and Wild West show performers, in addition to two signs. One invited, "Eat all you want, stay as long as you want, but don't take anything away." The other cautioned, "Look out for the pet rattlesnake. Don't kill her. She won't kill you——Walter Scott."[19]

As Gerard had become increasingly tightfisted with his money, Scotty began looking around for softer touches on whom to work his con. With the help of a Chicago acquaintance, Obadiah Sands, he found his mark. In the fall of 1904 Sands introduced Scotty to Edward A. Shedd, who had turned to finance after making a fortune in cold storage, and his partner, Albert M. Johnson. Scotty hooked them with his wonderful tale of the fabulously rich lode he had discovered in Death Valley, and how he just needed a grubstake to work it. They bit, apparently without even getting a piece of picture rock to assay. They put up $2,500 in cash, but wrote a grubstake contract on November 2, demanding a two-thirds share in all mining property Scotty might find prior to January 1, 1906. Scotty, playing the complete rube, then gave Sands half of the remaining third for arranging the deal, leaving only a sixth for himself. The Chicagoans may well have congratulated themselves for driving such a hard bargain. But who was taking whom became clear a few weeks later. When Scotty and Sands, heading for Death Valley to claim the bonanza, stopped at Goldfield to outfit for the trip, Scotty disappeared with most of the cash— $1,850. No wonder Scotty was especially vague about where his money came from when the police chanced to pick him up in Los Angeles a couple weeks later for questioning about the express robbery. When Sands returned to Chicago, however, both Shedd and Johnson were too embarrassed to prosecute. That should have been the end of any dealings between them, and it doubtless would have been, had it not been for the "Death Valley Coyote."[20]

By June 1905 Scotty had about run through the Chicago money and was at loose ends again. With the imaginative aid of reporter Van Loan, however, his little sprees had begun to attract not only a crowd of freeloaders but some more affluent Angelenos as well. Among them was E. Burdon Gaylord, a sharp but impulsive mining promoter. In July 1904, following Jack Keane's gold strike in the Funerals, Gaylord had rushed in to bond a nearby claim, the Big Bell, for a giddy $250,000, with $25,000 down and the balance in a year. In the intervening months, however, with the Bullfrog and southern Nevada camps attracting all of the public's attention, Gaylord was unable to interest anyone in purchasing the property. So by June 1905, with barely a month to go before he would have to forfeit his $25,000, Gaylord was desperate. He suddenly saw in Scotty's antics a chance to work up enough Death Valley excitement to unload the property, or at least to recoup his losses. Gaylord saw through Scotty's charade better than anyone else and quietly made him a proposition he couldn't refuse. Although the details were never revealed, Gaylord basically offered to bankroll Scotty in much more extravagant publicity stunts, in order to make him "living proof" of Death Valley's riches, in return for Scotty's aid in promoting the mine. It was the chance of a lifetime for Walter Scott—and it was the making of Death Valley Scotty.[21]

On June 23, 1905, Scotty burst onto the front page of the *Los Angeles Examiner* in headlines proclaiming:

HIGH ROLLER IS DEATH VALLEY CROESUS

WINE FLOWS LIKE WATER WHEN WALTER SCOTT,
LOADED DOWN WITH GREENBACKS, COMES TO
LOS ANGELES FROM MINE

$2600 IN THREE DAYS JUST SEEING THE SIGHTS

EVERYBODY IS THE FRIEND OF THIS MYSTERIOUS
STRANGER, WHO TARRIES A WHILE AND THEN
DEPARTS AS QUIETLY AS HE CAME.

"The Man from Death Valley," Charlie Van Loan continued,

is as much of a mystery as the cruel stretch of desert from which he says he comes. Nobody knows anything about him. Whence he comes and where he goes, are riddles which certain shrewd financiers would give much to read.

The only thing certain is that at stated intervals of several months, Walter Scott, miner, turns up in Los Angeles loaded with a great bundle of yellow-backed gold certificates. During his brief stays in the city, his only serious business seems to be that of distributing the sort of money which the average citizen finds it hard to change.

Clad in his familiar old light ulster—for Scotty never wears a coat and hates suspenders with an undying hatred—a high black slouch hat, pinched up to the regulation Texas peak, a blue flannel shirt and shoes with the high vaquero heel, this strange man from nowhere goes down the line shedding money like the only son of a deceased pork packer.

Cartoons of Scotty lighting his cigar with a $10 bill, tipping a porter with $100, and throwing money to the birds all followed, together with an exclusive inteview with the "mysterious Croesus" himself.

"I ought to be saving this money?" Scotty asked.

Well, what's the use of that? I tell you, there's plenty more where it comes from. You save money when you don't know where the next roll is coming from. I know, I don't have to worry about that. It's out there waiting for me. It won't get away. . . .

I've got a big thing out there—one of the biggest you ever heard of. I've got rock that runs between $40 and $50 a *pound*. A lot of fellows want to know where that is. Don't I know that I've been followed several times? I know that desert country like a book, and that's where I've got the bulge on the other fellows. I tell you, this playing for big money is a mighty interesting game; it keeps you moving some.

I've got six different pack trains and I never make up my mind which one I'll use until the last minute. I don't want to tip this thing off to anybody, but the money's there and lots more where it comes from.

These fellows come to me when I'm around town and they say to me:

"When you going out to the desert, Scotty?" I always tell 'em "Tomorrow." And you can bet that when I do go, I slip out without anybody finding out.

There are a lot of men who would kill in cold blood for a mine like I've got; lots of men who wouldn't think anything of shooting a man in the back for a tenth part of what I've got. But they've got to get the drop on me before they can shoot, and that's a game I know a little about myself. . . .

Do you believe everything you hear? . . . Because if you do, I'm
mighty bad people. I've been accused of killing no less than eight
men to keep them from cutting in on my private snap out there. . . .
I haven't shot anybody yet, but men have taken a pot shot at me. I've
got a gun here that shoots about two miles. . . . I got it in Germany
and it's a pretty good gun. I may have use for it some day.

"Many a wise man," Van Loan added, "has tried to pump this guileless
Croesus as to that property. Scotty never tells the same tale twice. Sometimes that mine is on the desert; sometimes it is located in the Funeral
Mountains; sometimes he says it is in the Panamint country. The wise
ones are still guessing about it, but the money is always in that big ulster
pocket. . . . A fool and his money, is he? Well, try to take some of it away
from him and you'll find him the wisest fool that ever wore high heels." [22]

In the days that followed, Scotty became an almost daily feature in the
Examiner, as his antics quickly built toward a climax in the Coyote special.
He bought a bright red tie so everyone would be sure to recognize him.
He tore up $100 bills to make change. He bought dollarino cigars by the
fistful, champagne by the case, and rented suites in two hotels to dodge
the handout seekers. Then on June 26, as a preview of things to come,
he suddenly took the train to Daggett, got off, had a few drinks, and hired
a nonstop special back to Los Angeles—just on a whim, he said. [23]

In between spending sprees, Scotty spun more tales of his wonderful
mine. He flashed an assay return, running $88,250 a ton in gold, from
ore so easily worked you could "jar it on your open palm and rattle out
. . . an ounce or two of gold in small grains like wheat." He said he had
a whole ledge of it too, 40 feet wide and averaging $20,000 a ton, located
high up in the Funeral Range. He even revealed that he had staked sixteen
claims, called the Knickerbocker in honor of his partner, New York
banker Gerard, who had put up $12,000 to help him get started. At times,
he said, he employed as many as ten men—all paid top wages but sworn
to secrecy and bound by oath not to stake claims nearby for at least a year
after they quit. His first shipment, he confided, had netted $38,000, and
he was now ready to make regular shipments, running $75 to $150 a
pound! The *Examiner* reporter was sure Scotty must have found the
Breyfogle, and maybe the Lost Pegleg too! [24]

Then on July 1, Scotty pushed himself into newspapers across the
nation, announcing that he would hire a special train to make a record-
breaking run from Los Angeles to Chicago. It was a guaranteed attention-
getter. In the summer of 1895, Benjamin P. Cheney, Jr., son of the Santa
Fe Railroad's largest stockholder, had made a dramatic 79-hour dash over
the same tracks, rushing to his dying father's bedside. Rudyard Kipling

promptly immortalized that run in his novel, *Captains Courageous,* but cut the fictional time to 57 hours 54 minutes. That spurred other nabobs to trim the real time to just under 53 hours. Now Scotty offered the Santa Fe Railroad $5,500 if they could make the run in less than 48 hours, and to sweeten the deal he offered to pay an additional $20 for every minute under that time. After several days of haggling, railroad officials finally agreed to a deal, and on July 8 Scotty made a big show of peeling off $5,500 from the fat, new roll Gaylord had quietly given him to pay the Santa Fe passenger agent, John J. Byrne.[25]

The following day a crowd of fifteen hundred or more gathered at the Santa Fe station to see Scotty off, and at 1 P.M. they let out a wild cheer as his "Death Valley Coyote" started on its mad dash to Chicago. The train itself consisted only of an engine, a baggage car, a Pullman sleeper, and a Fred Harvey diner, which served such specialties as Porterhouse Steak à la Coyote and Caviare Sandwich à la Death Valley. The engine and crew were switched every hundred miles or thereabouts, so that nineteen engineers and nearly fifty men took part in the record run.[26]

With Scotty was his wife Jack, whom he had dragged back into the act, his *Examiner* buddy Charlie Van Loan, and a magazine writer, Frank N. Holman, hired by the railroad. A reporter for the *Los Angeles Times,* G. E. Towle, temporarily stowed away in the baggage car, but was put off the train at Barstow. In a last minute piece of showmanship, Scotty had a friend rush out and get a homeless, hungry, "yaller pup" for $1 at the pound for him to take along as proof that his "heart's in the right place." Claiming that the pup, dubbed Goldbug, was the only friend he had, Scotty indulged him with squab on toast and a $1,000 gold collar set with diamonds—or so he said, for detractors swore it couldn't have cost more than 25¢.[27]

Crowds turned out at towns all along the route for a fleeting glimpse of the Death Valley Mystery. The Coyote sped through most stations and didn't stop for more than a couple of minutes even to switch engines. That was just long enough for Scotty to toss a $10 bill or two to the crowd, and for Van Loan to put out up-to-the-minute dispatches to be telegraphed to the Hearst papers across the country. Between stations the engineers pushed the Coyote to as much as 106 miles per hour—faster than any train had ever run before. In his eagerness to set new records, one engineer nearly derailed the train near Albuquerque, when one of the drive wheels jumped the track. He was able to stop before the others went, however, and within a minute the crew got the wheel back on the track and the Coyote was running again. It was a wild ride for all on board, and the lurch and sway of the cars wrought special havoc in the diner. One lunge swept the dinner table clean, dumping a stuffed tomato in Van Loan's lap and shattering the glasses and china, while Scotty howled, "That's the dope. That engineer's all right." On another lurch, Scotty was thrown head first into a window, but emerged from the shower of glass uncut to crow that "We are busting this old railroad record all to pieces." By the end of the trip he claimed that every glass and most of the windows in the diner had been smashed.[28]

At last, at 11:45 A.M. on July 11, Scotty's Coyote raced into Dearborn Street Station in Chicago, 2,265 miles from Los Angeles, with a new time of 44 hours 54 minutes, breaking the old record by 8 hours! A riotous crowd of thousands carried Scotty and his pup off the train. Scotty was an instant celebrity. He had captured the railroad speed record and front page headlines all across the country. Death Valley Scotty had arrived.[29]

The lucky, daredevil cowboy-prospector that Scotty portrayed captured the imagination of the nation, inspiring poets, preachers, paperback writers, and even a popular playwright. The cowboy poet E. A. Brininstool dashed off a lively ballad of "Scotty's Ride," and other rhymers eagerly joined in the homage to the "Lochinvar of Death Valley." Preachers also found lessons in Scotty, praising his push, pluck, and perseverance, and condemning his "modern American money-mad spirit" of wicked wastefulness and vulgar display. Pulp publishers put out instant paperbacks on *The Story of "Scotty"* and *"Mysterious Scott," the Monte Cristo of Death Valley,* while the Santa Fe Railroad issued its own promotional pamphlet on the *Record Breaking Run of the Scott Special.* Even the "Master of Melodrama," Charles A. Taylor, creator of such cliché classics as "Through Fire and Water" and "From Rags to Riches," joined the circus, writing a new play, "Scotty, King of the Desert Mine," for the Death Valley Mystery himself to star in.[30]

Scotty also inspired numerous imitators, who appeared briefly in Rhyolite and Bullfrog, San Pedro and Los Angeles, claiming to have made rich strikes "right next to Scotty's." A couple of them even donned red ties and blue flannel shirts, pretending to be the real thing. Most tossed $20 gold pieces around, bought two-bit cigars for $10, or left mining stock for tips. But one piker Croesus with a hole in his pocket amused himself by kicking nickels and dimes out of his trouser leg to the street urchins, until a couple of them grabbed for his pocketbook. Another would-be Scotty was drugged and robbed of $1,000, then jailed and fined $10 for drunkenness. Buffalo Bill even hired a Scotty impersonator for his Wild West show to come out of the audience and ride a bronco.[31]

Others were inspired simply to put the touch on the Death Valley spendthrift. They beseeched Scotty and besieged him. They wrote letters by the basketful; they waited for hours outside his hotel room; they mobbed him in the streets. There were beggars and fakers, charity workers and missionaries, circus managers and patent medicine manufacturers,

THE STORY OF Price 25 Cents.

"Scotty"

AND HIS
GREAT
WESTERN DRAMA

BY
CHARLES A.
TAYLOR.

WALTER SCOTT
SPHINX OF THE AMERICAN DESERT

KING OF THE DESERT MINE

Scotty grabbed nationwide publicity in 1905 with his record-breaking
run from Los Angeles to Chicago in a train called the Death Valley
Coyote. "Master of Melodrama" Charles Taylor helped spread his fame
with a stage play and this paperback. (*Courtesy of Automobile Club of
Southern California*)

airship promoters and submarine builders, widows and orphans, and grafters with a thousand flimsy schemes. But they came away empty-handed, for instead of the simple prospector, they found the steely-eyed con man. The Death Valley Croesus did, however, let go of $100 to a woman who named her baby after him.[32]

While Scotty was fending off these fast-talking handout seekers, he was doing some mighty fast talking of his own to Albert M. Johnson, who had grubstaked him the previous fall. Johnson met Scotty as soon as the Coyote got into Chicago, eager to forgive him for disappearing with the money and anxious to hear all about *their* mine. Johnson, like Gerard, had a fascination for mining and the West that made him an easy mark for Scotty. A tall, frail, teetotaling Quaker, Johnson also had a peculiar fascination for the robust and rowdy cowboy just a few months his junior. The son of an Oberlin, Ohio banker, Johnson had graduated in engineering from Cornell University in 1895 and had begun amassing his own fortune speculating in the Missouri zinc mining boom with $40,000 borrowed from his father. Then in December 1899, while they were looking into some mining ventures in Colorado, he and his father were in a train wreck. His father was killed, and Johnson barely escaped death with a broken back, which laid him up on a waterbed for a year and a half. When he was finally able to walk again, he gave up mining speculation for a more sedentary life and moved to Chicago to join an old family friend, Edward Shedd, in various financial manipulations. Through these he acquired control of the National Life Insurance Company in 1902 and became its president.[33]

Scotty's stunts had convinced Johnson and Shedd that he did have a mine after all, and Scotty assured them that they would share big in its profits. But first, Scotty explained, he had to settle with Gerard, who had grubstaked him previously and still had an interest in some of his claims. Scotty insisted, however, that Gerard had backed out before he made his big strike and thus had no claim to that.[34]

After just a few days, Scotty announced he had tired of Chicago, and leaving Jack to follow, he headed for New York with his dog and bank roll to see Gerard. "I am going to show him that he is not so much after all," Scotty roared. "I intend to land in New York and go to his blooming old bank and then I'll keep shoving rolls of money into the teller's wicket until I play them to a standstill. I'll show them what going some with money is." Gerard was intrigued by Scotty's extravagant show of wealth, but a bit skeptical nonetheless. When Scotty first wired that he was hiring a train to come East, Gerard had suggested that Scotty just send a little money instead. But Scotty snapped back, "Can't see why I should send you a few thousand dollars to show you I am right. You never flashed a bankroll to me. . . .You passed me up like a yellow dog."[35]

Scotty offered the New York Central Railroad $12,000 to take him to New York in a record thirteen hours—five hours under the regular time of the Twentieth Century Limited. But the offer was declined, so he took the regular train. Nonetheless, there was a crowd of a thousand to greet him when he arrived at Grand Central Station on July 14 with his yellow dog and his roll. Others surrounded him wherever he went, expecting him to shower them with gold nuggets. His appearance in the gallery of the New York Stock Exchange even brought trading to a temporary halt. The brokers gave him a loud cheer, and one shouted, "Hey, you King Opulence of the blooming West! Burn your money here if you're game." But all he threw them was his hat. Other New Yorkers were also disappointed that Scotty wasn't throwing money away, and it took the police to rescue him from one unhappy crowd.[36]

Scotty's extravagant antics once again convinced Gerard that he really did have a mine; moreover, they attracted other Easterners eager to be let in on wealth. With these new prospects and Johnson hooked again, Scotty had little further use for Gerard, except for the perverse satisfaction of making him think that he had really missed out by not keeping up the dole. Scotty's only concern now was that Gerard not make trouble, so for a token $100 Scotty obligingly signed over to him full title to the Knickerbocker claims. Scotty was as evasive as ever in revealing their location, however, knowing that he could keep Gerard busy for some time just trying to find the claims. The Death Valley Croesus, of course, announced publicly for Johnson's benefit that he had settled all accounts with Gerard. He then slipped back to Chicago on July 25 to hit Johnson up for a loan, just to tide him over until he could get back to his mine, of course.[37]

Scotty's antics were raising suspicions in some quarters, however. As the editor of the *New York Times* wrote:

> We would all like to believe that Mr. Scott is the long missing link between Western realities and Western romances—that he is a simple child of nature, son of the plains and the mountains, who, exhilarated by sudden wealth and incidental strong waters, has come East under the grotesque delusion that he can amuse himself more violently here than in his native wilds. But the man does not fit the theory. The Death Valley Live One's naivete is all too obviously a somewhat laborious pose, assumed for reasons not yet revealed.

Others also suspected that Scotty was not "simply a fool and his money" and searched for the "method to what seems his madness." Some were convinced that he had been hired by the Santa Fe Railroad in a grand publicity scheme that netted them $100,000 worth of free advertising. Others concluded that he wore a "Hearstcollar" and had been hired to stir up circulation for the newspaper chain. But most suspected that there was a gigantic mining stock swindle at the bottom of it all. Such speculation had first surfaced just before the Coyote left Los Angeles, when Scott was seen secretly meeting with mining promoter Gaylord. At the first rumor Scotty had indignantly vowed, "I have no stock jobbing scheme in view. . . . I haven't got a thing in this world that's for sale . . . no man in this country can buy in with me. This deal is my own little private show and I'm running it to suit myself." But the suspicion wouldn't die, and editors across the country cautioned their readers to look out for a big stock push at the end of the show. Such warnings, of course, didn't hurt Scotty at all, since his personal game was a subtler one, and in fact they gave him an easy excuse to refrain from any overt promotion of Gaylord's Big Bell.[38]

Nonetheless, Scotty's whirlwind trip across the nation did help stir up a Death Valley mining excitement, just as Gaylord had hoped. One Eastern mining journal openly praised Scotty for having "done more toward booming Death Valley and the surrounding country than any of the Goldfield and Bullfrog men have yet attempted." As a result, some miners did find it easier to raise money. But things didn't happen quickly enough to save Gaylord from the forfeiture of his $25,000. He tried to recoup his loss, however, by taking a more modest bond of $20,000 on a neighboring claim called the Indian.[39]

Scotty returned to Los Angeles early in August, denouncing New York as "one big con" and commencing new antics designed to keep himself in the papers. He made a splash by buying a new red tie for $100, and claimed he bought diamonds for the shoes of his mule, Slim, to cheer Slim out of melancholy. He even covered a temporary lack of cash by declaring that he hadn't been getting his money's worth from his spending sprees, so he "got wise" and was "taking lessons on the millionaire business from John D. Rockefeller." He also threatened to sue the Santa Fe Railroad for using his picture in their ads. But mostly he talked of setting new railroad speed records—repeating his Chicago run in 40 hours, making an even longer run from San Francisco to Chicago in 38 hours, and completing a transcontinental dash in 56 hours.[40]

In the meantime, Scotty's mystery mine had taken on a life of its own, as all sorts of stories circulated around the campfires and through the press. In the West it was knowingly said that the mystery mine was situated in such an awfully hot and waterless spot that even Scotty himself could stay there only a few days at a time and could work the ledge only at night. The crafty miner was also said to have eluded those who tried to trail him by padding his burro's feet so that they wouldn't leave tracks and by traveling only at night during the dark phase of the moon. In the eastern press, in contrast, it was grandly written that Scotty worked his mine with a full crew of thirty-seven trusted men under a sixteen-year-old foreman, all of whom were paid premium wages with $500 bonuses every two or three months. The mine itself was said to be a fortified camp surrounded by a stockade and patrolled night and day by armed guards with Krag-Jorgensen rifles and powerful spyglasses. Rumormongers east and west agreed on only one thing—that the ledge was incredibly rich, worth somewhere between $23 and $33 billion![41]

Suddenly, late in August, the telegraph wires buzzed with the startling news from Bullfrog that a wandering prospector had actually found Scotty's mine, that hundreds were rushing in, and that all the ground for a mile around would be located within seventy-two hours. The news brought crocodile tears to the eyes of the *New York Times* editor, who lamented,

> There is about that rich and mysterious repository an interest of romance and wonder which it would be a pity to have dissipated by turning a flood of commonplace daylight on it. . . . While it is known solely to its original discoverer, it will continue a province of the land of fancy and dream, kindling bright pictures in the imagination. . . . Once located on the map . . . it would quite likely be found out that its treasure had a limit—that it was not the vestibule of Plutus's bullion chambers or propylaea of God Mammon's vaulted crypts, but just a hole in the ground, capable of petering out like the rest of them. . . . Its chief interest is in the mystery which surrounds it, and that will much abate if it should at any time be thrown open to the public with admission on the ground floor or any of its more elevated levels.

But the awful news proved false. The hapless prospector had only stumbled upon Camp Hold Out—just one of several caches, Scotty assured the press—so his mystery mine was still safely a mystery.[42]

There was, of course, one thing that was even more important to Scotty than keeping himself in the headlines: keeping the money coming in. The very success of the former, in fact, posed a problem for the latter—namely, how to continue mooching money now that he claimed to have a virtually inexhaustible mine of gold. The inventive con man, however, was equal to the challenge. Indeed, he had already set the stage before his departure on the Coyote, by talking of the risk he ran from men who would kill for his mine. Upon his return, he revealed to the press sinister plots being hatched to murder him and take his mine. First there was a "gang of thugs" in Bullfrog who planned to trail him to his mine and kill him.

Then there were two men from Kansas who intended to kidnap him, drug him and make him tell where his mine was, and leave his "bones on the desert sands." Finally, there was a "whole band of Apache Indians" sent out by a "New York crowd" to grab his mine and do God knows what to him. This last menacing band was conjured up around a Harvard-educated Indian, Antonio Apache, who was sent by Gerard to find the elusive Knickerbocker claims that Scotty had signed over to him. Apache and Scotty exchanged a few verbal shots, but nothing more.[43]

These fancied dangers allowed Scotty to stall for a while, mooching loans and stringing out creditors until he could safely return to his bonanza. Although this ploy started out harmlessly enough, complications arose and it eventually got out of hand, almost becoming his undoing. For at the same time Scotty was working up another scam on a would-be mining promoter, named Azariah Y. Pearl, whom he had met on his Coyote run to the East. Pearl, a forty-year-old carpenter from a quiet little New Hampshire town, had suddenly "blossomed" as a novice financier after inventing an auger that he claimed could bore a square hole. Scotty had promised in a New York bar to let Pearl in on some good ground near his mine, so Pearl had eagerly followed him back to Los Angeles, bringing several thousand dollars as a measure of good faith.[44]

Thus in September, when Scotty announced that he was at last ready to brave the murderous thugs and go back to his mine, he agreed to take Pearl along and even let him bring a camera. Scotty also took along his brother, Bill, who had come down from Wells to join in the fun, and two other scouts, all armed with six-shooters and high-powered rifles. They headed for Camp Hold Out and, although Scotty naturally refused to show them his secret mine, he did show Pearl some real claims that he swore were "just as rich," about a mile farther up the canyon. These claims had been located by a half-Cherokee cowboy from Stinking Water Creek, Nebraska, who called himself Bill Key. Nearly everyone else, however, kept calling him Keyes, so he eventually changed his name to suit them. Scotty told Pearl that he had a share in Key's claims and, for the chance to make big money using Scotty's name, Key in fact later gave Scotty a share, hastily scribbling on a scrap of paper under a boxcar at a railroad siding.[45]

Scotty only let Pearl get a quick look at Key's claims. Then he had one of the scouts, Shorty Smith, stage a little "gun play" to make Pearl think the thugs were after him, and they all beat a hasty retreat to Barstow. Scotty left the others, however, to go by way of his mine, and arrived in Barstow with a 100-pound bag of rock that he said was so rich it would "startle the world." Naturally he couldn't let anyone see it, but he did pose for a photograph with the bag and his mule Slim—apparently to answer critics who charged that he had never shipped even a pound of ore. Pearl at least was properly impressed and headed East to line up capitalists to buy the claims.[46]

Scotty returned to Los Angeles, vowing to set a new record train run across the continent at a mile a minute. When the railroads turned him down, he turned his attention to automobiles to set new speed records. But he ended up in the hospital with a fractured pelvis, after a White Steamer he was in crashed into a wall just trying to make a 28-mile run to Pasadena and back in a modest 38 minutes. That was fast enough, however, that Scotty and his driver were fined $75 for speeding. Concluding that you should "order a coffin before you start out for an auto record," Scotty swore off auto racing after that.[47]

Next, Scotty grandly announced that he was going after "some theatrical records," putting $100,000 into the new play that Charles Taylor was writing about him. He was tired of being "looked at as a freak," he confided, and wanted, "to show that I am not as bad as some of the newspapers have pictured me." He was also going to star in the play, of course, along with his pet mule, Slim, his trusted Indian companion, Jack, and his dour bodyguard, a bullet- and knife-scarred character named Sam Jackson. It would be a great play, Scotty promised, "absolutely faithful to fact," with no "flubdub." Taylor was also confident that the play would be a "money maker" that would boost his own sagging finances, and booked a ten-week engagement at the Grand Opera House in New York.[48]

Some of the press, however, were growing tired of Scotty's antics the second and third times around. A *Los Angeles Express* writer waxed poetic as he complained:

> Of Scotty's strikes, of Scotty's scads,
> Of Scotty's fakes, of Scotty's fads;
> Of Scotty's drinks, of Scotty's drunks,
> Of Scotty's thinks, of Scotty's thunks;
> Of Scotty's friends, of Scotty's folks,
> Of Scotty's jibes, of Scotty's jokes;
> Of Scotty tender, of Scotty tough.
> Mein Got in Himmel! we've had enough.

But the ever-resourceful Death Valley Mystery still had a few new tricks left, and they were surefire headline-grabbers.[49]

In late November, Scotty dropped out of sight, and a few weeks later newspapers across the country carried the startling headline that he had apparently been murdered. Scotty and his brother Bill had quietly slipped off to Death Valley, and about the first of December, while camped at Salt Wells with several prospectors, Scotty complained that he was being followed by a man on a red mule and that he was going to put a stop to it. That night Scotty started back over their trail toward Wingate Pass. Seven days later his mule Slim returned riderless, with a bullet hole through the back of the saddle and blood spattered on the saddle blanket. Bill followed Slim's trail until it was obliterated by sand, finding no trace of Scotty. The word went out that Scotty was missing and probably murdered. Rol King of the Hollenbeck Bar sent scouts to search for Scotty, and offered a thousand-dollar reward for his body or any evidence that he had been killed.[50]

The press speculated for days about the possible fate of the Death Valley Mystery, while his wife, sick with worry, was taken to a sanitorium in Glendale. Then, on Christmas day, King received a letter from Scotty, and announced to the world that Scotty was alive and well—refusing, however, to say anything about what had happened. But Scotty's no-nonsense brother, Bill, soon told others that the whole thing was a simple accident, that Scotty had shot a mountain sheep, and while loading the bloody carcass onto his mule, his rifle discharged, putting a bullet hole through the saddle and frightening off the mule. Other prospectors, returning from Death Valley, confirmed that Scotty was unharmed.[51]

Early in January 1906, just as it seemed the mystery had been solved, Scotty arrived in Barstow with a 30–30 steel-jacketed bullet in his right thigh and a fantastic tale of an ambush in Wingate Pass just two days earlier, on New Year's Eve. Ignoring the sheep story, Scotty claimed he had been ambushed twice. He hadn't been hit in the first affray on December 7. His Indian scout, Jack, had been riding Slim at that time and was only "winged" by the bullet that went through the saddle. The second ambush was the one in which Scotty said he got shot.[52]

It was a cold, stormy evening, with sleet blowing in their faces, Scotty said, as he and two companions came into the wide pass about sundown, where the ambushers waited behind rocks along the trail:

> Jackson, my old desert man, was riding ahead, when z-z-zip, I heard a bullet sing by him; and then another and another. Then I heard someone call, "You're shooting the wrong man; Scott is second in the line," and ping! ping! the lead began to whistle about me. I rolled off the saddle, and by the great horn spoon, what d'ye think of that—I had failed to load the magazine of my gun. Ought to have been killed, hadn't I?
>
> I know a bit about guns, and I heard five shots from my man, and then I knew his magazine was out, and I started to run him down, but, happily, I thought better of it and made for a little arroyo and threw myself flat in it and plunked my magazine full of those long Mauser cartridges. Those are the boys I can get a man with at five miles range. I raised up a bit and let drive at the puff of smoke where

my man had fired at me, when bang! another fellow let drive at me and I got it in the thigh.

Say, you've heard the snare drummer at the theatre start off a roll and keep it up? Well, that's the way our rifles and the other fellows' popped for a time. . . . When it was all over I climbed on Slim and started for Barstow, only 135 miles away.

There were three hired ambushers, Scotty added, "I know who they are. I know how much they were paid. . . . I know their orders. These read: 'After you know where his claims are, get the man.'"[53]

How Scotty really got shot remained a mystery for some time. It was later reported that the doctor who examined Scotty's wound found powder burns, suggesting it was self-inflicted. Would Scotty have gone so far as to shoot himself in the leg, as one Los Angeles paper charged, just to try to bluff through his claim that thugs were after him, or was it accidental? The bullet through the back of the saddle couldn't have gone through his thigh, too. Then two Arizona prospectors revealed that a man they thought was Scotty had shot himself in the leg trying to draw a rifle to scare them off some ground in Death Valley. Many years later Bill Key essentially confirmed that story, placing the incident at Cave Spring in the Avawatz Mountains.[54]

Whatever happened, the bizarre affair captured more press coverage for Scotty than anything since the Coyote. Scotty was so pleased with it all that he wanted Taylor to add the gun battle as a new act in his play. As soon as Scotty was back on his feet, he headed for New York to talk to Taylor about the addition—it even had ready-made parts for Slim, Jackson, and the Indian Jack. He had other business to attend to there as well.[55]

Pearl, with the help of a Boston broker, Edwin D. Mellen, had been surprisingly successful in lining up capital to buy Key's claims. Introducing himself as the only man Death Valley Scotty had even taken near his mysterious mine, Pearl had enticed select Easterners with the prospect of getting in on some nearby ground which was "just as rich," and which he said Scotty and his partner Key promised to sell for only $60,000. Foremost among this coterie was the six-foot-four powder giant, T. Coleman du Pont, who by a series of shrewd manipulations had just consolidated American powder manufacturers into a $50,000,000 trust, the I. E. du Pont de Nemours Powder Company. Amazingly, du Pont and several others eagerly agreed to put up the money, if Pearl could prove his claims. Thus, as soon as Scotty arrived in New York he met with the would-be investors to confirm that everything Pearl had said was indeed true. Scotty further reassured them that he would personally keep an eye on Pearl and wire them immediately "if Pearl should not act on the square." As a final formality, the Easterners wanted an expert's report on the claims, but Scotty apparently told them that they would have to act swiftly before his partner sold to someone else. Thus it was agreed that Daniel E. Owen, a Boston mining engineer already in Nevada looking at other property for Mellen, would accompany Scotty and Pearl to the claims and wire his report to the Easterners to complete the deal.[56]

Before he left, Scotty also tried to mollify Gerard again. Antonio Apache had reported to Gerard that Scotty had never been seen shipping ore from any mine, that the newspaper stories of Scotty's spending sprees were grossly exaggerated, and that what money Scotty had spent was obtained from Los Angeles men under false pretenses. Apache concluded that the only way Gerard would learn the location of Scotty's mine, if there was one, was to bring a suit against Scotty for an accounting. Finally disgusted when he heard of Scotty's latest antics, Gerard had publicly threatened to expose Scotty "if he didn't stop getting shot!" So after denouncing Apache as a yellow dog, Scotty once again promised to be friends with Gerard and to really show him where the mine was—a little later.[57]

In the meantime, Johnson was beginning to worry about his share of Scotty's wonderful mine. In a melodramatic moment Scotty had once told Johnson that if Gerard ever got his mine he would kill himself! Johnson now feared that Scotty was so determined to keep Gerard from getting the mine that he might lose it instead to relocators. Johnson finally decided that the only way to secure his own interest was to go out to the mine and see that it was properly located. In February 1906, soon after Scotty returned from New York, Johnson also arrived in Los Angeles, determined to go the mine.[58]

The stage was set for Scotty's most elaborate charade. Although Taylor had refused to add the fanciful "Battle of Wingate Pass" to the play, Scotty was now going to present it himself on an even grander scale—a full dress ambush designed to scare off both Owen and Johnson. It seemed the perfect solution to the problem that now faced him, since Scotty of course had no claims to show Johnson. Even though Key's claims did have a good showing of rock—running as high as $1,000 a ton—it was hardly as rich or extensive as people expected from Scotty's fabulous mystery mine, and both Scotty and Pearl had promised the Easterners claims "just as rich as Scotty's were cracked up to be." Scotty's experiences with Gerard had shown him that as long as he could keep the experts scared off, the Easterners would keep putting up more money, at least for a few years, for fear of losing out. Now that hundreds of prospectors were roaming Death Valley, however, the valley had lost most of its terror, so the simple ploys he had worked on Gerard's men wouldn't work on Owen and Johnson. But some lively gunplay that put them in fear for their lives should still do the trick, and Bill Key and Scotty's Indian, Jack Brody, agreed to take part in the game. Scotty may also have let Pearl in on the plan to scare Owen, but that isn't clear.[59]

The party assembled at Daggett late in February. They were an odd lot, nine in all—Scotty; his brothers Bill and Warner, who had now joined the show; Key; Brody; Pearl; Owen; Johnson, who, not yet wanting to risk his reputation by having his name associated with Scotty's, introduced himself as Jones; and an enigmatic fellow with the imposing name of A. W. DeLyle St. Clair, hired as a teamster and later rumored to have been a spy sent by Gaylord to learn whether Scotty really did have any property. With $2,500 from du Pont and perhaps another $1,000 from Johnson, Scotty outfitted one of the fanciest private expeditions that ever set out for Death Valley. There were two wagonloads of provisions and firearms, hay and water, and extra animals—even two cameras to document it all. To set a mood of lurking danger, Scotty talked ominously of past attempts on his life and of the likelihood of more trouble on the trail ahead. For added effect, shortly before they left, Scotty suddenly disappeared amid rumors that he had been kidnapped. He reappeared just as suddenly a few hours later with Daggett's constable, hired as a bodyguard until they were ready to leave.[60]

After posing for photos the party at last set out late in the afternoon of February 23 and camped at Lone Willow Spring, just west of Wingate Pass, two days later. The following morning, February 26, Key and Brody left on the pretense of going to Ballarat for more hay. As soon as they were out of sight they cut back toward the Wingate Pass road to take up their positions for the ambush. Scotty and the others started several hours later, leaving brother Bill behind to rest the extra animals. Coming through the pass, they headed down Wingate Wash into Death Valley, with Scotty and Pearl in the lead riding mules, followed by Warner and Owen in the first wagon and St. Clair and Johnson in the second. Everything was going as Scotty had planned. Owen, a nervous, overweight man, was already so ill from alkali water surreptitiously put into his canteen that he had to be tied into the wagon seat; it wouldn't take much more before he wanted to turn back.[61]

About dusk, however, just as they neared the spot where Key and Brody were waiting, things started to go awry. Suddenly, two shots were heard on the trail ahead, and a man came riding hard toward them. He was J. J. Hartigan, a former deputy sheriff at Bullfrog, who had happened along at the wrong time, so the lurking ambushers fired a couple shots in his direction to get him out of the way before Scotty and the others arrived. Scotty and Pearl rode ahead to meet him and find out what had happened. Hartigan warned Scotty that gunmen were waiting in ambush ahead. Scotty only laughed, offered him a drink, and told him not to say anything to the others. By then the wagons had caught up, and they continued on down the wash, with the first wagon now in the lead. Hartigan waited to see what would happen next.[62]

Moments later shots rang out, and Scotty's "Battle of Wingate Pass" began. Confusion reigned, and when it ended there were contradictory versions of what had happened. One thing is certain: it hadn't gone according to the script. Key later blamed Brody for sloppy shooting, claiming he was drunk. Owen and Hartigan recalled only two or three shots being fired, and Owen insisted that Scotty fired first into the air—apparently as a signal. Scotty and Pearl said that the ambushers fired first, at Pearl, and that they had returned the fire for at least ten minutes, emptying their Mausers and six-shooters in heroic fashion. Scotty, of course, also maintained that "all of the shooting except for the first shot at Pearl was intended for me." He showed two bullet holes in his coat, and Pearl showed one through his hat, which only missed his head because his mule bucked, he said. That was the kind of harmless gunplay Scotty had in mind, even if he had to make it up after the fact. But then a bullet hit Warner in the groin, causing what Pearl described as "the most painful wound that a man can receive." He went down shrieking in agony, and Scotty jumped up, swearing, "Stop firing you god damned fool, you have hit Warner!" Those words stopped the shooting instantly, but they also "tipped off the whole deal," Key complained.[63]

The ambushers having suddenly vanished, Pearl and Johnson temporarily sewed up Warner's wound, then camped right there for the night. The next morning they dumped all of their provisions in a pile by the side of the road, to make bed space in the wagon for Warner, and headed back to Barstow. On the way back, Scotty badgered Owen to give his wounded brother some money as "recompense," and the frightened expert finally signed over a note for $1,000. But once he was safely back in Boston, he refused to honor it.[64]

As soon as they reached Barstow, Scotty fired off a telegram to Los Angeles announcing, "Ambushed us in Windy Gap. One shot fired at my head, missed and struck Warner in the hips." The *Examiner* headlines proclaimed the next morning, "'SCOTTY' AMBUSHED BUT ESCAPES DEATH," and for a few days the papers were filled with thrilling details derived solely from Scotty and Pearl, and enlivened with photos, maps, and diagrams. Then others began to speak out, and suspicions turned toward Scotty. Owen, corroborated by Hartigan, swore that Scotty hadn't fired a single shot at the ambushers, and Owen concluded that he, not Scotty, was the intended victim. Even Warner agreed that the bullet that hit him must have been aimed at Owen, and missed only because the wagon lurched. These stories prompted San Bernardino County Sheriff

John C. Ralphs to make a thorough investigation of the affair—an investigation that would ultimately lead to criminal charges against Scotty. At the same time, the editors of the *Los Angeles Evening News,* sensing a chance to embarrass the rival *Examiner,* launched their own exposé of the making of the Death Valley Mystery.[65]

Scotty, meanwhile, had hurried off with Slim and Jackson to Seattle, where his play opened on March 11. Standing-room-only crowds packed the Third Avenue Theater on opening night to see the "real original" himself, and they were surprised to find he was a much better actor than they had expected! The play itself, however, was a "perfect measles of melodrama," ending with Scotty's dashing to New York in his special train to rescue a kidnapped waif from the clutches of a scheming banker. One critic, captivated by the snake-oil magic of it all, raved,

> For the blues take "Scotty." For broken heart, bankruptcy, chronic coughs and all wasting diseases, take "Scotty." It builds up the flesh and promotes digestion. It strengthens, soothes and heals. It cures when all else has failed. Dr. Osler recommends it for the worst cases of "forties." And if you have not the money, borrow it. If you cannot borrow it—get it anyway. But don't miss "Scotty."[66]

The great attraction of the play was the mystery that surrounded the man, and much of that was about to be stripped away. On March 17, St. Clair signed a sensational statement for the San Bernardino sheriff, charging not only that Scotty planned the fake ambush to frighten off Owen but also that on the way to Death Valley, he decided to kill Owen instead and get his telegraphic code book to send a fake report to the Eastern investors. Warrants were issued immediately for Scotty's and Key's arrests, on charges of assault with a deadly weapon. Confident that he could pick up Scotty at any time, the sheriff set out for Death Valley to find Key and arrest him first. But Pearl left just ahead of the sheriff, got to Key first, and they slipped out of Camp Hold Out just before the law arrived. Returning empty-handed from an eleven-day trek through the valley, the sheriff threatened to charge Pearl with aiding a fugitive, or perhaps complicity. Meanwhile, a friend of Key's, Lillian Malcolm, the "Lady Prospector," convinced that Scotty planned to frame Key in order to get Key's claims, hired a lawyer for his defense and headed for the valley herself to try to find him. But it was Hartigan, deputized by the sheriff, who finally found Key and arrested him early in April at Ballarat, where he had just signed over an option on his claims to Pearl. A few days later Pearl was arrested for complicity.[67]

By then, Scotty had also hired an attorney, William W. Wideman, who

"SCOTTY" NO LONGER IS A MAN OF MYSTERY

Now comes the truth, with stern unyielding force,
This base pretender ruthlessly detecting;
His swindling games, so impudent and coarse
No longer shall deceive the unsuspecting.

Various papers exposed Scotty as a fraud, but the dauntless con man went right on with his chicanery. (*Los Angeles Evening News,* March 19, 1906)

promptly got himself arrested trying to bribe St. Clair. To further complicate matters, brother Warner filed a damage suit against Scotty, Pearl, and Key, claiming his injury resulted from their "wicked and unlawful conspiracy" to scare off Owen. He asked for $2,000 for medical expenses, $100,000 for mental suffering, and $50,000 in punitive damages. This prompted two of Scotty's creditors to bring suits, too: the doctor who had treated Scotty's leg wound from the first fanciful affair at Wingate Pass tried to collect $77.50 due for his services, and a boardinghouse keeper claimed $584.50 in unpaid rent and loans.

When the play reached California, Scotty was arrested on criminal charges and hauled into court in San Bernardino, where he had to admit he was penniless and unable to raise $2,000 in bail—even his old friend, Rol King, refused to aid him. He was at last released, but only after Taylor came up with the money and pleaded that, since Scotty had failed to put up any of the much-publicized $100,000 for the play, he had had to finance it entirely with his own money, even mortgaging his home. He was deeply in debt because of this, and would be ruined for sure if Scotty were not able to remain in the play.[68]

All of this made headlines for Scotty that were as big as ever, but it was devastating news for the Death Valley Mystery, as the press exposed him as "Scotty, the Faker," "The Death Valley Humbug," and "The Death Valley Freak." The *Los Angeles Evening News* led the pack, spreading its exposés and cartoons of the "Desert Vulture" all over the front page, day after day. Even the *Examiner* joined in the debunking, headlining every new revelation of Scotty's fakery. Editorial writers had a heyday. The *San Bernardino Sun* editor reflected the sentiments of many when he wrote,

AN IDOL SHATTERED

The Scotty boom has been as thoroughly punctured as that of any faking pretender who has flashed in and out of public view. . . . Just what the courts may make out of Scotty is yet to be developed, but nothing additional is needed to establish the fact that he is utterly discredited; that he has been a shining example of "all cry and no wool." For he has failed to "come through" at any stage of the game. He is a false alarm, a penny-ante bad man, who is in his element when shooting blank cartridges and flashing stage money in a bum play.[69]

In the eyes of the public, Scotty had been exposed as the fraud he was, so it didn't much matter that he escaped the harsh judgment of the law on a technicality. The charges were dismissed on April 27, after Scotty's lawyer showed that the shooting took place just over the line in Inyo County—and thus outside the jurisdiction of the San Bernardino courts. That was the end of the case, because the Inyo authorities decided not to waste the taxpayers' money on further prosecution. With the mystery stripped away, the public was quickly losing interest in Scotty, and the play drew ever-diminishing audiences until it folded in some forgotten Midwest town in May. The press was finally exacting the cruelest punishment of all by purposely ignoring Scotty—at least for a time.[70]

Pearl, meanwhile, had hurried East as soon as he was released, protesting his innocence and convincing du Pont and the others to go ahead with the option on Key's claims, despite the Wingate Pass affair. Late in May they formed the Key Gold Mining Company and sent a new expert, with a crew of thirty-five men, to Death Valley to thoroughly examine the property. The men were so apprehensive of Key and the rumored "Scott gang" that they took along a whole case of rifles. Key did nothing to allay their fears in showing them the skeleton of some luckless prospector and deliberately behaving in a suspicious manner. They imagined Scotty spying on them in the night, and finally so scared themselves shooting at shadows that the expert abruptly decided that the claims were too remote and left. But with surface assays running as high as $1,500 a ton, du Pont and his friends were so sure that they were onto something big that they went ahead and bought Key's claims for $25,000 without further examination. After that, just so they wouldn't miss anything, they bought up fifty surrounding claims, which gave them over 2 square miles of ground. They probed their vast estate on and off for the next half-dozen years. Their superintendent, J. K. Brockington, built roads, sank shafts, ran tunnels, even struck a rich pocket on one of the claims, the Desert Hound, and shipped at least $12,000 worth of rock, before they finally gave up, realizing that they too had been conned by Scotty's tales.[71]

Despite everything that had happened, however, Scotty wouldn't admit to a thing. In the face of all the evidence, all the scorn, and all the snickers, he still stubbornly tried to keep up the pretense, doing anything he could just to try to "keep 'em guessin.'" Scotty doggedly repeated the same overworked routines that had once drawn such crowds and made such headlines. He still flashed a fat roll whenever he could get his hands on the money, still boasted of secret ore shipments, still talked of hiring more trains for new records, still claimed hired assassins were out to get him for his mine, and even staged a little more gunplay. But there was little audience for such antics anymore.[72]

Yet Scotty did somehow manage to keep a few guessing, and foremost among them was Albert Johnson, who still couldn't shake the crazy hope that Scotty really did have something after all. However, Scotty finally worked that hope dry, too, after a few more years—but not before Johnson had, by his own meticulous accounting, given up a total of $22,921. Johnson also took great care to secure title to his share of Scotty's fabulous mine, obtaining quit claims from his own partners, Shedd and Sands, and getting Scotty and Gerard to seemingly settle their differences with a new agreement that gave Gerard 22½ percent of everything Scotty ever had or would discover. Scotty meanwhile revealed that his real bonanza wasn't on those elusive Knickerbocker claims after all, but was over on the west side of Death Valley, near Wingate Pass. He even dutifully located some new claims, the Sheep Head and the Robbers' Roost, southeast of the pass at Hidden Spring in the Owlshead Mountains. Scotty also took Johnson on a few more wild goose chases through Death Valley that never quite got to the mine, of course. On one occasion in June 1907, he even concocted another shooting to put Johnson off. He claimed that he and his man Jackson had been ambushed by two would-be assassins, and produced a bloody bullet that he said he had cut from poor Jackson's back. Although he refused to take Johnson out that time, he produced a piece of ore that he said was from the mine. It assayed $10,174.40 a ton—enough to hold Johnson's interest a little longer.[73]

By the beginning of 1908, however, Johnson was becoming impatient, and dispatched a young employee from his insurance company, Alfred MacArthur, to try to learn the location of the mine. Johnson paid Mac-Arthur $125 a month plus expenses, so MacArthur persisted, dogging Scotty for months. First, Scotty just stalled MacArthur before even agreeing to take him to Death Valley. Then he and Key took the greenhorn to Surveyor's Well, where they tried to scare him with some gunplay in the middle of the night. Next, claiming that their animals had been stolen, they sent him back to Rhyolite, while they searched for the beasts. Mac-Arthur waited patiently for a few more weeks, and when they returned without the animals, he set out with them again to continue the search, to Mexico if need be. Scotty even bummed money off MacArthur, hoping that would drive him off, but still he stayed. In disgust, Scotty at last found the missing animals and took MacArthur to Wingate Pass. There he finally unveiled the "mine"—a 30-foot shaft with a stringer of $5 ore in the bottom—and MacArthur pretended to be impressed.[74]

As soon as they reached Barstow the cagey tenderfoot told Scotty that the game had gone far enough and demanded that Scotty make restitution for all of the money he had conned out of Johnson. Scotty obligingly let him have the horses, saddles and all, without protest; then he quietly got the local hotel keeper to attach the whole outfit for an unpaid bill. When the constable tried to serve the attachment, MacArthur resisted and was hauled off to jail in San Bernardino, to Scotty's delight. Key, however, had taken a liking to the spunky kid and went after him to get him released. When they returned to Barstow, they found that Scotty had already left with the outfit. They rode hard and caught up with him 25 miles from town. "Then," Key recalled, "Scott tried to make up with the kid. He even got down on his knees and cried like a baby. I never saw a man do such a trick, but the kid was through with him."[75]

MacArthur reported everything to Johnson, concluding that there was no longer any question about it: Scotty had no mine. But Johnson still wasn't ready to hear that. "I don't care what happened out there," Johnson insisted, "where there's smoke there's fire!" So the following year Johnson spent a whole month following Scotty around Death Valley, again to no avail. Scotty finally ditched him by sending poor Slim back to camp riderless with a bullet wound in his shoulder.[76]

After MacArthur's trip, Johnson did become tightfisted with Scotty, putting up just enough to outfit a trip to the valley every year or so, when Scotty would promise once again to show his Golconda. With each successive disappointment Johnson slowly had to face the fact that Scotty really didn't have a mine. But Scotty still had a few other would-be partners he could work for occasional loans and grubstakes. He also seems to have taken up a new game for quick cash—fencing high-grade ore stolen from Goldfield's bonanza mines, claiming that it was rock from his own mystery bonanza. With phenomenally rich ores running as high as $100 a pound, highgrading was rampant in Goldfield, and mining men there suspected that Scotty was part of the fencing business. One bonanza king, Alva D. Myers, the "Father of Goldfield," even accused him publicly. Scotty blustered, and after a few stiff drinks he tried to bully Myers. But Scotty was shamed again, coming away with a black eye and a further diminished reputation.[77]

Scotty soon got cheap revenge on Myers, and on others as well. With the aid of his old friend, Rol King, Scotty pretended to make friends with Myers; then, announcing that he was tired of desert life and was ready to sell his great bonanza, he offered to let Myers have the first look at it. Against his own better judgment, Myers agreed to outfit an expedition, but he brought along a friend, Sidney Norman, the mining editor of the *Los Angeles Times*. Scotty also invited King to come along, apparently still nursing a grudge against him for failing to put up bail after the Wingate Pass fiasco. For reasons of his own, Scotty let his long-suffering wife Jack come, too. Early in June 1908, Scotty led them into Death Valley and made camp at the old Eagle Borax Works, where they immediately got sick on alkali water and then discovered that all but one of their animals had mysteriously disappeared. The next morning Scotty left on the remaining mule to track down the missing beasts. The rest of the party waited "for seven days and seven nights," Norman recounted, "in that hell on earth . . . eaten alive by mosquitoes at night, fighting horseflies as big as bats by day." Finally realizing that they had been suckered by Scotty's "old bunco game," Myers and Norman walked 25 miles across the center of Death Valley to Furnace Creek Ranch for help. Scotty returned to the camp as soon as they left. He had apparently been relaxing in the shade and comfort of Hungry Bill's ranch up in the Panamints just to the west, where he could keep an eye on them.[78]

Norman in turn got revenge on Scotty by exposing the whole shabby affair in a widely copied story in the *Times*, and just for good measure he reprinted it as a booklet, *Chasing Rainbows in Death Valley.* "Poor Scotty," he wrote, "I pity him. The strain of nursing an attenuated and feeble wraith of his former mystery has told upon him and even he can only see suggestions of its existence through the magnifying glass of a bottle." But he concluded, "He is nothing short of a public nuisance and a menace to the legitimate mining industry," and he urged state officials to take "some drastic action towards ridding the valley of Scott and his band."[79]

Myers may have succeeded in doing just that, by hiring detectives to hound Scotty in hopes of catching him with stolen ore, because that fall Scotty left Death Valley to take up a lease on a mine in the Humboldt Mountains of northern Nevada, and he stayed there off and on for the next three years. Scotty claimed that he found a rich ore pocket on the lease, but rumor was that it was just a new cover for fencing stolen ore from the new highgrader's delight, the incredibly rich National mine, just a short ride to the north. The Goldfield detectives followed him there, too, even arresting him on occasion. But they never caught him with the goods, and Scotty boasted, "If I am a thief, I'm certainly a smart one—to beat 38 arrests." In later years he did claim that he had been in "cahoots" with the highgraders, but of course Scotty might claim anything. One thing is certain: as soon as the high-grade ores at National were exhausted early in 1912, Scotty returned to Death Valley.[80]

In May 1912 Scotty made a last-ditch bid to regain the public eye as the Death Valley Mystery—a bid that led instead to his final humiliation. He dramatically announced that at long last he had sold his mystery mine for $1,000,000. Scotty talked grandly of dividing his fortune with Jack and using his half to "continue to fool around Death Valley and monkey with new mining ventures." He also confided, "I am telling you this story because for many years people—some people—have been calling me a fakir and said I had no mine." The sale was his proof. The purchasers, three mining promoters by the names of Thomas A. Watt, Frank E. Sharp, and F. C. Goodwin, were to pay $40,000 down and $50,000 a month until Scotty was paid in full. They naturally organized a $2,500,000 stock venture, the Death Valley Scotty Mining and Developing Company, and printed up fancy certificates, adorned with a portrait of the mystery himself, to push on a waiting public at a dollar a share.[81]

The news was a headline-grabber that even attracted the attention of a movie company—a fast outfit called Kalem, which cranked out four movies a week! They signed up the "only and original" Scotty to star in a picture to be called, naturally, *Death Valley Scotty's Mine*. Even though it was only a single-reeler and Scotty's role was less than heroic—as it was the heroine who rescued *him* from the villainess and her gang—there was money in it; there was even more publicity; and Scotty would be a movie star. What more could he have asked for?[82]

The news also attracted the attention of one Dr. C. W. Lawton, however, and that was Scotty's downfall. Lawton, who had treated Warner's wound after the Battle of Wingate Pass, had never gotten paid. But he had gotten a judgment against Scotty for $1,200, and he now took Scotty to court to collect. Scotty casually testified that he had really been paid only $25,000 and that he had simply thrown the money away and was now broke. When he refused to be more specific, the judge threw him in jail for contempt of court. This time there was no one to bail him out.[83]

In the course of his testimony, Scotty had revealed that he hadn't actually sold the promoters a mine, just the "knowledge" that some prospects existed. This drew the attention of the district attorney, who was interested in learning more about a mining company with stock to sell but no mine. Thus he hauled Scotty and the company secretary, Goodwin, before the county grand jury on June 18. There, an embarrassed Goodwin admitted that they had only bought the use of Scotty's name and picture and whatever knowledge he might have of a "mineral proposition." Then Scotty was asked again what had become of the $25,000. This time he blithely swore that he had given $50 to his wife Jack, who was sick, and then put all but $100 or so in a tin box, which he gave to an Indian to bury out in the desert. "You had $25,000 and you only gave your sick wife $50?" he was asked in disgust. Scotty sat quietly for a moment, as tears welled up in his eyes. Then he blubbered, "No. I'm a liar; I'm a liar. I'm ashamed to tell you how little I did get." He was so ashamed that he couldn't name the figure; he just held up two fingers. "Two hundred?" he was asked. "That's all," he murmured. Then like "a bad boy caught playing hookey," he blurted out everything, confessing that his mine was a myth and that most of the money he had spent came from Gerard, Johnson, and Gaylord, who paid for the train. It was a great catharsis, and when it was over he laughed and said he hadn't felt so good in years. But the Death Valley Mystery was a mystery no more.[84]

"Death Valley Scotty has admitted that he is a faker," the editor of the *San Francisco Call* wrote sadly.

> So the Scotty bubble has burst. . . . It was once reported that this kingfisher in a sea of gulls was a highwayman and that he secured his fabulous returns by robbery. But even that dubious fame is to be denied him. He appears, from his testimony before the Los Angeles grand jury, to be a cheat and nothing more.[85]

The movie was a flop, too, and little more was heard from Scotty for several years, until Albert Johnson came back to Death Valley and stirred up a new mystery. But that is yet another story.

Heart of Gold

Jack Keane's wonderful gold strike high on the Death Valley slope of the Funeral range had been the jumping off place for the great Bullfrog rush. But Keane's Wonder was all but forgotten in the first flush of that rush. It was not until the boom had grown so big that Bullfrog could no longer contain it that the excitement spilled over into Death Valley again. By then the furor had revived all the old dreams of hidden wealth, and the mysterious Scott and other dream merchants were busy selling even grander dreams. One new dream-spinner even imagined untold gold— more than all the world had ever seen—buried right in the heart of Death Valley.

Thus a new throng of hopefuls rushed into the valley to seek its riches, and a score or more died in the quest. Most eventually gave up in disgust, but many did find gold, at least in traces, and high up on the Panamint slope two actually found a giant ledge, the Skidoo, that would pay out over a million in gold. Jack Keane's Wonder did almost as well. These two mines were at the heart of the Death Valley rush, Clarence Eddy's dream was its soul, and then, of course, there was B. X. Dawson.

It was the prospect of silver, not gold, that had first brought Jack Keane and his partner, Domingo Etcharren, into the Funerals. In January 1904, Keane, a quick-tempered Irish miner out of work in Ballarat, had talked Etcharren, the camp's one-eyed Basque butcher, into joining him—and, of course, bringing the grub—on a prospecting trek across Death Valley to the old Chloride Cliff district. There, halfway up the Funerals toward the old mine, they located a little silver-lead prospect, the Whip Saw. It seemed promising enough, at least to Keane, that they returned to do more exploratory work in the spring. Although Etcharren's enthusiasm quickly waned, Keane insisted on staying on alone until the grub ran out.[1]

Just before Etcharren left, he noticed a quartz cropping a couple of hundred yards below their claim and suggested that Keane take a look at it before returning to Ballarat. A few days later, on April 5, Keane did just that, and found it wonderfully rich in free gold. He hastily scribbled out a location notice, dubbing it the Keane Wonder, then grabbed up a few ore samples, took the pack animals to the Furnace Creek Ranch, and borrowed a saddle horse to rush to Etcharren with the news. From Ballarat word of the strike was quietly telegraphed to an old mining man, Joseph R. DeLamar, in New York, and he summoned his expert, Hartwig

275

Cohen, back from Alaska to examine the property. Within twelve days De Lamar's man was on the ground, and within five weeks of the discovery Keane and Etcharren had De Lamar's check for $10,000 as down payment on a one-year option to buy the claim for $160,000.[2]

That blitz of excitement unleashed a rush to Chloride Cliff that it might have seemed nothing could stop. But it turned out to be an abortive affair that barely got going before it flopped. By July, five hundred men were there, staking the ground all around. Ballarater "Johnny-behind-the-Gun" Cyty and his partner Mike Sullivan had just made a rich strike nearby, called the Big Bell, and had collected $25,000 on a $250,000 option from the impulsive Burdon Gaylord. But by the time Shorty Harris and Ed Cross got there in early August, all the promising ground had been taken, so they drifted on to the north and soon made the strike that started the great Bullfrog rush and evacuated the Funerals. Thereafter, the Keane Wonder was looked upon by nearly all but those on the ground as just one more pollywog in the great Bullfrog pond. In August 1905 even those on the ground at last conceded the second-class status of their district, renaming it South Bullfrog.[3]

Attempts to attract capital also received a temporary setback. Cohen had estimated that there was as much as a quarter of a million tons of $30 ore, totaling $7.5 million, in the Keane Wonder ledge, and De Lamar had put a crew of thirty miners to work to test that estimate. By the time the option was due to expire in May 1905, De Lamar had spent over $35,000 in opening the mine and had found only $600,000 in ore. After trying unsuccessfully to talk Keane and Etcharren into lowering their price, he forfeited the option. A Goldfield promoter, Lucien Patrick, then took an option and opened the lode further to reveal fully $1 million worth of ore, but he couldn't get the price he wanted and dropped his option that winter. Cyty's sale of the Big Bell had also fallen through when the luckless Gaylord failed to raise enough money, even after bankrolling the Scotty Special in a desperate attempt to work up some excitement. But the saddest blow was dealt to poor old A. J. Franklin, who, after faithfully holding the Chloride Cliff mine for thirty years, died in 1904—just as the revival he had waited for at last began. His son George, however, did manage to cash in on the boom, selling an interest in the old derelict to a Los Angeles promoter J. Irving Crowell the following spring for a reported $110,000.[4]

Things didn't begin to move again at the Keane Wonder until early 1906, when another Goldfield speculator, John F. Campbell, took an option on the property for $250,000. He formed the Keane Wonder Mining Company, with Keane as president, Etcharren as secretary, and 1.5 million shares, half of it treasury stock. By spring Campbell had worked the shares up to 50¢ on the strength of the ore blocked out, and

Jack Keane's Wonder was the first big gold producer in Death Valley proper, but Keane ended up in an Irish prison.

in August he sold a controlling interest in the mine to Homer Wilson. Heralded as "one of the boldest and most successful operators" on California's Mother Lode, Wilson, a fifty-year-old Midwesterner, was in fact a quiet, hardworking, practical mining man whose success rested on his personal management of his mines. He saw the Keane Wonder, not as "a big mine or a high grade mine, but as a nice little proposition that will clear good and dependable money every month of the year." He would, in fact, make it do just that. Wilson moved to the mine with his family, putting a crew to work on a twenty-stamp mill at the foot of the Funerals and on a mile-long aerial tram to bring the ore to it. Development of the Keane Wonder was at last under way.[5]

For their part, Keane and Etcharren apparently got $50,000 in cash and a lot of stock. Jack Keane returned to Ballarat to celebrate his good fortune with two prostitutes on a drunken binge. But, ending up in a quarrelsome mood, he shot and seriously wounded the constable and his deputy. When he was finally released from the county jail, Keane decided to return to the "old sod." But he returned to his old ways again, too, and in less than a year he was in another shooting scrape. This time he killed a man and was sentenced to seventeen years in an Irish prison. Etcharren simply used his share of the money to buy a bigger store in Darwin.[6]

By then, Cyty had bonded his claims to another mining promoter, Walter O'Brien, who incorporated the Death Valley Big Bell Mining Company, proclaimed it another wonder, and pushed the stock in San Francisco at 25¢ a share with talk of more tramways, mills, and $60-a-ton ore. Several other would-be wonders had also appeared with shares for sale, and two townsite ventures had been laid out. The towns, however, were doomed from the start, since both were located on the other side of the ridge from Keane's Wonder. Keane Spring, calling itself the "Gateway to Death Valley," was platted in April 1906 at a spring 4 miles north of the Wonder, where the Death Valley Mercantile Company had opened their store. It briefly boasted a saloon, a post office, and a weekly stage from Rhyolite. The rival Chloride City was laid out up near the old Chloride Cliff mine. By summer both camps had already begun to fade.[7]

In the meantime, the Bullfrog excitement was spilling over into all of Death Valley, carrying a new wave of gold seekers far beyond the old Chloride Cliff district. They chased the ghost of Breyfogle all over the Funerals, trailed the Lee boys on down the range, followed Shorty Harris across the valley into the Panamints, and even tracked Scotty up and down the valley.

The excitement at Bullfrog had drawn two of Phi Lee's boys, Richard and Gus, up from the ranch at Resting Spring to try their hands at the mining game. In November 1904, with the help of septuagenarian Breyfogler Henry E. Finley, they found two nice little gold ledges, the

Hayseed and the State Line, some 30 miles south of Bullfrog at the eastern foot of the Funerals. When rock running $40,000 a ton was brought to Bullfrog, the word went out once again that the long lost Breyfogle had been found at last. A stampede began, and the Lee Mining District was organized in March 1905. Though greenhorns, the Lee boys were quickly catching onto the mining game—perhaps too quickly. In May they optioned the Hayseed to Goldfield speculator W. F. Patrick for $75,000 with 10 percent down, and when Patrick died suddenly two months later, they found that they got to keep both the Hayseed and the $7,500. This certainly beat selling the mine, so they eagerly optioned it again, and again, and yet again, collecting another $7,500 to $10,000 on each round. The only problem was that they didn't bother to wait for one option to expire before letting the next one, so they soon found themselves on the wrong end of lawsuits that took over a year to sort out.[8]

The rich ore in the Hayseed and the ghost of Breyfogle had drawn hundreds of men into the district to stake the ground all around. Some had even gone with Dave M. Poste into the low hills a few miles to the north just across the line in Nevada, found gold there too, and formed the Poste Mining District. Others had climbed on up into the Funerals and over into Echo Canyon on the Death Valley side to find more gold and start the Echo District. A Mormon prospector, Chet Leavitt, made the first strike in Echo Canyon in January 1905, while chasing his pack animals, which he found on a big quartz ledge. He and his partner, Moroni Hicks, a silver-bearded giant of a man, grabbed a few samples for assay. But the rock failed to show any gold, so they didn't get around to taking a second look at the ledge they had dubbed the Stray Horse until March. This time they found a lot of rich rock just a little farther up the ledge, and they plastered it with nearly twenty claims.[9]

The litigation over the Hayseed was finally settled in February 1907, and the Hayseed Mining Company was formed by Rhyolite promoters. With assays reported to run as high as $123,000 a ton, Hayseed was an instant favorite with speculators. The initial stock offering of over 50,000 shares sold in less than two hours at 50¢ a share. Within two months the price reached 75¢ on reports that the company was taking out over $1,000 worth of shipping ore a day from the mine. Over in Echo Canyon, Chet Leavitt had joined with Mormon friends from Provo, Utah to buy out Hicks and form a closed corporation, the Inyo Gold Mining Company. At a depth of 65 feet, they were into $300-a-ton ore. Even the Steel King, Charley Schwab, had bought into the district. Close to the Stray Horse, a gold-bearing talc deposit had been found that was said to rival that of the Montgomery Shoshone, and Malcolm Macdonald and Donald Gillies persuaded Schwab to buy it in May 1906. Schwab incorporated it as the Skibo Mining Company in honor of the Scottish castle retreat of his former patron, Andrew Carnegie—perhaps with an eye toward getting the old man to invest in it.[10]

The Lee boom reached its peak in 1907. The population topped 600 that spring; dozens of mines were being opened up; and before the end of the year the Tonopah and Tidewater Railroad would come within a few miles of the district, enroute to Rhyolite. There was even a lively townsite rivalry raging in the district, with five contenders—three of them named Lee—within a radius of 4 miles. The eventual victor was Lee, California, located near the Hayseed. At its peak in the spring of 1907, it claimed a population of 300 men and 20 women, plus more saloons and cribs than any of its rivals. Lee also boasted a post office; a board of trade that dutifully delineated the red-light district; the Death Valley Miners' Union, Local No. 258 of the Western Federation of Miners, with a big union hall; and the district's first and only newspaper, the *Lee Herald,* a six-page weekly started on October 15 by Earle Clemens as a spinoff of his *Rhyolite Herald.* A telephone line plus rival daily Concord and auto stages ran to Lee from Rhyolite, and when the Tonopah and Tidewater established Leeland station 6 miles to the east in October, a stage started running there to connect with the trains twice a day. The burgeoning town even attracted the attention of the Inyo County supervisors, who appointed a justice of the peace and, of course, made him a deputy tax collector.[11]

The rival town of Lee, Nevada, in the hills 3 miles to the north, had only two things to recommend it: a baseball team that could beat Rhyolite, and legalized gambling. But the illegality of their gaming tables didn't seem to worry the California Leevites. The third Lee, locally known as the North Addition, sat halfway between the other two, just inside the California line, but had nothing going for it. None of the Lees, of course, had any water of their own, but the Ash Meadows Water Company was promising to pipe it in. Until then the Leevites had to rely on Adolph Nevares to haul water 13 miles from Rose Well for $5 a barrel. At that price even the townsite promoters went to Rhyolite for a bath.[12]

Over in Echo Canyon was the rival town of Schwab, laid out just below the Steel King's Skibo mine. It was a wonder of the modern age, a complete canvas town shipped in five boxcars from Los Angeles by the Clark line to Rose Well, and hauled up into the Funerals in January 1907. Within two months it had a population of two hundred, its own post office, and its own Echo Miners' Union, plus telephone and daily stage connections through Lee to Rhyolite. Then the townsite company was taken over by three women—Gertrude Fesler, a young blue-eyed blonde stockbroker from Chicago; Mrs. F. W. Dunn, a San Bernardino matron; and her daughter, Helen H. Black. The attendant publicity of "A Mining Camp Built by Ladies . . . one of the most unique wonders of the new

West" gave it a new boost. But as they sat taking their afternoon tea under a big, striped Arabian tent at the head of Main Street, the women started worrying about the morality of their new offspring. They soon sealed its fate when they started frowning on saloon men, asking gamblers to get out, and putting a ban on "sporting women." Only Schwab's name misspelled, now remains, attached to a neighboring peak by the Geological Survey. The last contending settlement, Echo townsite, on the crest of the Funerals halfway between Schwab and Lee, never attracted more than a couple of tents.[13]

Just across Furnace Creek to the south, however, there was one more camp, or so it was said—the mythical Camp Dawson. No one seemed to know exactly where it was supposed to be located—not even its imaginative creator, B. X. Dawson, a thirty-two-year-old mining promoter from Colorado, who proudly billed himself as "a bold and intrepid mining engineer . . . clean cut, finely educated . . . strictly temperate and reliable . . . the personification of energy, intelligence and experience!" That was nothing, however, compared to the extraordinary things he said about Death Valley and his marvelous mine, the Hidden Hell.[14]

It all began in November 1905 when the intrepid Dawson returned to Denver to recuperate from a harrowing ordeal in Death Valley and told the world of his amazing discovery there—of how, "like the dying dragon of the fairy tale, Death Valley has at last surrendered its golden treasure so long withheld." Before giving up its secrets, the dread valley, that "abiding place of death-dealing agencies lurking at every turn," had sorely tested him. But with a cool head he had finally outwitted the demon valley, saving not only himself but one, or maybe two, others from its awful maw. It was only then, camped one night at Furnace Creek, that he met the mysterious "Yogi," an "unsavory, uncommunicative" old Indian whose trust and friendship the bold Dawson somehow won with "coins, firewater and bacon." If anyone should doubt his story, Dawson even published a photo of "Yogi" glowering from behind a Navajo blanket somewhere in New Mexico! By that campfire in Furnace Creek, "Yogi" told his new friend of the "yellow rock mines of his fathers, mines so old that even Indian traditions had lost their origin," and the next day he led the "young pale-face" to them.[15]

There on Furnace Creek, Dawson said he had found prehistoric mining tools and an ancient arrastra—"a monument to a people perhaps vanished before Columbus ever dreamed of a western world." His "experienced eye" quickly assayed its riches, and he realized that this ledge was "the very one which tradition has accredited with having enriched many men for many centuries and eventually led them all to their death!" Dawson claimed it all for himself, dubbing it the Hidden Hell. And he vowed that once the mine again began to give up its riches, he would reward the "loyal Indian" with "more tobacco, more bright, silk handkerchiefs—more corn juice, if he wishes—than his fondest hopes for immense wealth have ever led him to dream of."[16]

The "yellow rock," of course, was fabulously rich, and news of its discovery, the bold B. X. claimed, unleashed such a rush that fully five hundred claims were staked all around his Hidden Hell within a fortnight. Even whole families came "crazy with the gold fever . . . not thinking nor caring for the horrible suffering they would endure before they reached the new strike" and, he added sadly, "many lost their lives, and their bodies were left for the buzzards."[17]

It was a bizarre tale, made all the more curious by the fact that not a soul in Death Valley knew a thing about it. Late in December, Dawson did mail location notices to the Inyo County recorder in Independence. But that was just a technicality he attended to after he and his brother, I. F., had incorporated the "mine" as the Death Valley Gold Mining and Milling Company and launched a lavish promotional campaign to sell its 3 million shares.[18]

Dawson's promotional style was every bit as bizarre as his story—no one, in fact, capitalized on Death Valley quite like he did. He sent out stories of his Death Valley fantasies to newspapers across the country. He gave interviews to Colorado mining and financial papers on his notions of scientific mining and his theory of how Death Valley was once a "lake of fire" that "purified our gold." He ran double-page ads in mining and investment magazines with little skulls and crossbones scattered about and ghoulish cartoons of skeletons beckoning investors to riches. He filled the ads with the tales of his trials in the death-dealing valley, his meeting with the mysterious "Yogi," his discovery of the ancient "Aztec" mines, and his wonderful new Camp Dawson, toward which Borax Smith was building his railroad. He even started his own magazine, *The Death Valley Dawsonian,* a twelve-page illustrated semi-monthly published in Denver, "devoted to the Treasure Vault of the Nation and the Drug Store of the World." He also gathered a lot of his stuff together into a free, thirty-two-page "History of Death Valley," entitled *Death Valley of Superstition and Imagination, The Gold Valley of To-day.* The cover of this little masterpiece was a photo of "The Camp Dawson of the Future," a pastiche model of a smoke-belching mill with heaping ore cars of the Death Valley G. M. & M. Co. in the foreground and a sprawling city of skyscrapers and tree-lined avenues stretching off to the hills beyond. And, of course, there was the company prospectus: *DEATH VALLEY RE-CLAIMED, What Modern Science & Scientific Mining Engineering Has Accomplished,* by B. X. Dawson, "mining engineer and one of the most successful and prominent mine owners of Death Valley."[19]

Even Dawson was impressed by it all, as he assured his readers, "it is

Now
Is
Your
Oppor=
tunity

DEATH VALLEY

Gold Mining and Milling Co.

Property Located on Furnace Creek,
in Funeral Mountains, Near
Death Valley.

Denver News, Oct. 9, '05

Scotty Returns With More Gold

Death Valley Croesus, Under a Heavy Guard, Packs Into Barstow,
California, With Seven Burros Loaded With the Auriferous.

LOS ANGELES, Oct. 8.—With seven burros loaded down with
pure gold and valued at $165,000, Walter Scott, the so-called Croesus
of Death Valley, arrived at Barstow yesterday, escorted by a body
of seven heavily armed men. The trip in from the mysterious
mine of the desert was accompanied by much hardship and "Scotty"
looked tired and worn to an unusual degree when he arrived here.

Read the description of
the property and the story
of finding it on the opposite page and
it will interest you.

Colorado con man B. X. Dawson made a killing with ghoulish ads like this.
(*Mining Investor,* December 4, 1905)

the most wonderful story that you have ever read. And the most remarkable part of it is that it is true . . . No buncombe, nonsense or fraud." Through it all, his message was clear: "I want small investors. Investors with from $50 to $1,000. I want them to believe in me." He promised them profits of 500 to 5,000 percent; he guaranteed their investment; and he quoted them Emerson on luck and Huxley on science. But he cautioned them, too—"YOU MUST ACT QUICK . . . Now is the time to enter Death Valley. Yesterday was too soon. Tomorrow may be too late." He started selling the stock at 3¢ a share on December 1, 1905, and as his advertising began to pay off, he steadily raised the price to 5¢ in February, 10¢ in April, 20¢ in June, 50¢ in October, and all the way to $1.00 on New Year's Day, 1907. In June 1906, just to sweeten the pot, Dawson even bought the stockholders a little silver-lead mine way out in the Mojave Desert. It actually shipped nearly $24,000 worth of ore before B. X. either skipped out or was thrown out of the company in September 1907—it isn't clear which. He never had done anything in Death Valley, of course, but he had sold 1,862,407 shares of Death Valley stock, from which he probably took in around a quarter of a million dollars.[20]

In the meantime, the pied piper of Bullfrog, Shorty Harris, was leading new rushes to the other side of Death Valley. After losing the original Bullfrog in a drunken stupor within days of its discovery in the summer of 1904, Shorty was back to hustling grubstakes again. That fall, with another promoter, George Pegot, and a grubstaker, Leonard McGarry, he headed for the Panamints. There, in mid-December, on the north side of Hunter Mountain, they found a little pocket just "lousy" with free gold. While his partners staked out the claims, Shorty rushed to Goldfield with sacks of rock he said would assay at least $260 a ton. He diligently made the round of the saloons with his sacks, trading news of his new strike for a free drink or two until he had exhausted its value. By then he had worked up enough excitement to start a New Year's rush across the valley. But it lasted just long enough to organize the Gold Belt Mining District and generate talk of a townsite, before the rainbow-chasers found there wasn't enough paying ore to spit at. Only the name remains on the nearby spring today.[21]

That summer, Shorty returned to the Panamints. But that was only after he had worked his fame as the Father of Bullfrog for all it was worth in free setups in the saloons of Rhyolite during the district's first Fourth of July celebration—a two-day affair the likes of which the Death Valley country had never seen before and would never see again. When he finally sobered up, Shorty rustled up another grubstake and set out for Death Valley to dry out. At Furnace Creek Ranch he fell in with a lanky young Basque greenhorn named Jean Pierre "Pete" Aguereberry, who had just been bluffed out of Echo Canyon by Chet Leavitt and was heading for Ballarat. They took the short trail straight across the valley, up Blackwater Canyon and over to Wildrose Spring. Not one to linger on the trail, Shorty was a mile ahead by the time Pete reached the flat at the head of the canyon and paused to pick at the big "barren" cropping, passed up by every traveler on the trail for a couple of decades. But Pete, not knowing it was supposed to be barren, spotted flecks of gold and gathered up a bunch of rocks to test in camp that evening. Shorty scoffed at first and didn't even want to look at the samples, but Pete finally convinced him that the rock was rich indeed.[22]

The next morning, July 11, the two hurried back to the big ledge and staked several claims apiece. Pete claimed the north half as the Eureka. Shorty took the south, calling it Providence. Then they continued on to Ballarat to record their claims and assay some of the rock. Shorty, of course, had to tell everyone he met on the way all about his wonderful new mine—nothing less than "the biggest strike ever made in the Southwest"—and in all the telling and retelling Pete's name was mentioned less and less.[23]

Word of the strike with assays going over $500 a ton electrified the old camps of Ballarat and Darwin as everyone, it seemed, bolted off to see the new Bullfrog. Shorty and Pete barely got back to their claims in time to fend off jumpers. Within ten days there were 300 men on the ground; within two months there were over 500. The old Wildrose District was resurrected; a townsite was platted; and wishful rumor even had it that a newspaper plant was on the way. The new town was christened Harrisbury in an attempt by its promoters to honor its discoverers, Shorty and somebody called "Ogerbury." Before anyone could correct it to Harrisberry, the "y" turned into a "g," making it Shorty's town alone, and Harrisburg it would remain.[24]

Taking full advantage of the first rash of excitement, Shorty's two grubstakers, William P. O'Brien, a Bullfrog promoter, and William Corcoran, a young Rhyolite mine owner and Inyo rancher, hustled him off to San Francisco. There they quickly found backers to form the Cashier Gold Mining Company on September 12, 1905, just two months after the discovery. Shorty ended up with nearly 50,000 shares of stock, plus four times that on margin and, he said, $10,000 in cash. It was the biggest sale he ever made, and he took a trip back East to celebrate. Aguereberry's grubstakers, Frank Flynn and Tom Kavanaugh, lining up backers in Los Angeles, formed the Midas Panamint Mining Company the following January, and Pete too got a lot of stock, but very little cash.[25]

O'Brien had promptly put a couple of dozen miners to work opening the Cashier that fall, but as the feverish excitement abated not many others remained. After all the hoopla, Harrisburg ended up with a single saloon and store, dependent on water hauled in from Emigrant Spring—not much of a town for Shorty to boast about. Things cooled down even more that winter, and by the time spring came there was a wonderful new strike just over the hill that drew all the praise.[26]

In late January 1906 there were only two prospectors, John L. Ramsey and John A. Thompson, camped at the springs in Emigrant Canyon northwest of Harrisburg, and even they didn't plan to stay long. Legend has it that they had stopped there because they were lost in a rare Death Valley fog. In fact, they were just waiting for someone to come along who could tell them how to find the next water hole to get across Death Valley. While they waited Ramsey poked around in the wash below the spring, and late in the afternoon he came across some rich float from a slide. The next morning he and his partner traced its source to the ridge a couple of miles to the east. There they found a gigantic lode they called the Gold Eagle—one so big they eventually staked thirty claims to cover it all.[27]

In the days that followed, Ramsey and Thompson tried to keep their find a secret until they could prospect it thoroughly and be sure they got the richest ground. They did indeed get the best ground, but they couldn't keep it a secret. Nonetheless, word of the strike didn't get out of the Wildrose district for several weeks, because everyone who happened along stayed to stake claims of their own. One piggish prospector reportedly staked 150 claims before he simply ran out of names with his last claim, the American Hog. Finally, Shorty Harris came along, claimed some outlying ground, dubbed it the Eagle's Tail, and headed for the saloons of Rhyolite to "tell the world."[28]

In mid-March Ramsey and Thompson signed a sixty-day option on their best twenty-three claims for $23,000 to George M. Ottis, one of Aguereberry's Midas Panamint backers, and his partner, E. Oscar Hart, a flamboyant New York mining promoter who had made a big splash in Los Angeles by tearing up $100 bills and throwing them to the crowd, trying to outdo Scotty. Hart hurried back to New York, where he lined up a sale with Charley Schwab's bankers. But late in April, before Hart returned, Bullfrog's new millionaire, Bob Montgomery, heard of the strike, came over with Ottis to sample the ground, and liked what he found. Fresh from the sale of his own Shoshone, and with over a million dollars seemingly burning a hole in his pocket, Bob made a persuasive offer with a big cut for Ottis, who immediately wired Hart that the option had been extended because of the San Francisco quake-fire, thus causing Hart to delay sending the money and unknowingly forfeit the option. By the time Hart sent the money to close the deal, Bob Montgomery had already hustled Ramsey and Thompson off to Los Angeles in his speedy new car and bought all twenty-three claims for himself. Furious over his partner's betrayal, Hart threatened to prosecute them all. He ended up just suing Montgomery for restitution, but to no avail. Ramsey and Thompson are said to have netted $30,000 apiece from the sale. Ottis walked away with at least $40,000, but felt he was entitled to even more. He too later sued Montgomery and lost, claiming Bob had promised him an eighth of the mine.[29]

Bob's purchase of the Gold Eagle, claiming it "beats the Shoshone," started a new stampede to the Wildrose District. But it was Bob's wife, Winnie, who gave the stampede a name. On hearing that Bob was buying twenty-three claims, she quipped, "23 Skidoo," a catch phrase of the time, and the Skidoo mines they became. Lore now has it that the name was inspired by a "23 mile" pipeline Bob later built to the mine, but the pipeline hadn't even been conceived of when the mines were named, and it wasn't that long anyway. The phrase itself is said to have originated with a Kentucky racetrack owner, whose track accommodated only twenty-two horses, so he turned away further entries with a shout of "Twenty-three for you, Skidoo!" Picked up by others, it was popularized by a vaudeville performer at the turn of the century. The word is an offshoot of the equally whimsical "skedaddle," a Civil War creation loosely drawn from the Greek *skedannumi,* meaning a "riotous retreat." In Death Valley, Skidoo quickly came to mean just the opposite, as hundreds of miners rushed in to see the new marvel.[30]

The Skidoo mine was indeed a marvel, with more exposed ore than any other metal mine in the Death Valley country. One enthusiast even claimed it was the biggest mine on top of the ground, ever found. Bob's first sampling, at least, had convinced him that there was half a million dollars just in the top five feet, and that was what made him decide right then that he had to have the mine. With all of that ore exposed, Bob was so certain of profitable returns that he was even willing to develop the mine entirely on his own money. But anxious to enjoy his new fortune, he was not willing to devote much of his own time. So he started the Skidoo Mines Company as a partnership, keeping three-quarters for himself and letting in two friends to run the operation. Matt Hoveck, his former superintendent on the Shoshone, became the general manager of the mine, and W. R. Wharton became the business manager. When Bob eventually incorporated in 1907, he also offered stock on a cooperative plan to the miners.[31]

Bob spared no expense in opening the Skidoo, ultimately putting some $550,000 into it before it began to produce. Within weeks of the purchase, he had shipped in nearly $30,000 worth of supplies and equipment and had nearly a hundred graders, carpenters, and miners at work. By fall Bob estimated that fully $3 million worth of ore had been opened, and he talked of eventually taking out $10 million! The key to working this

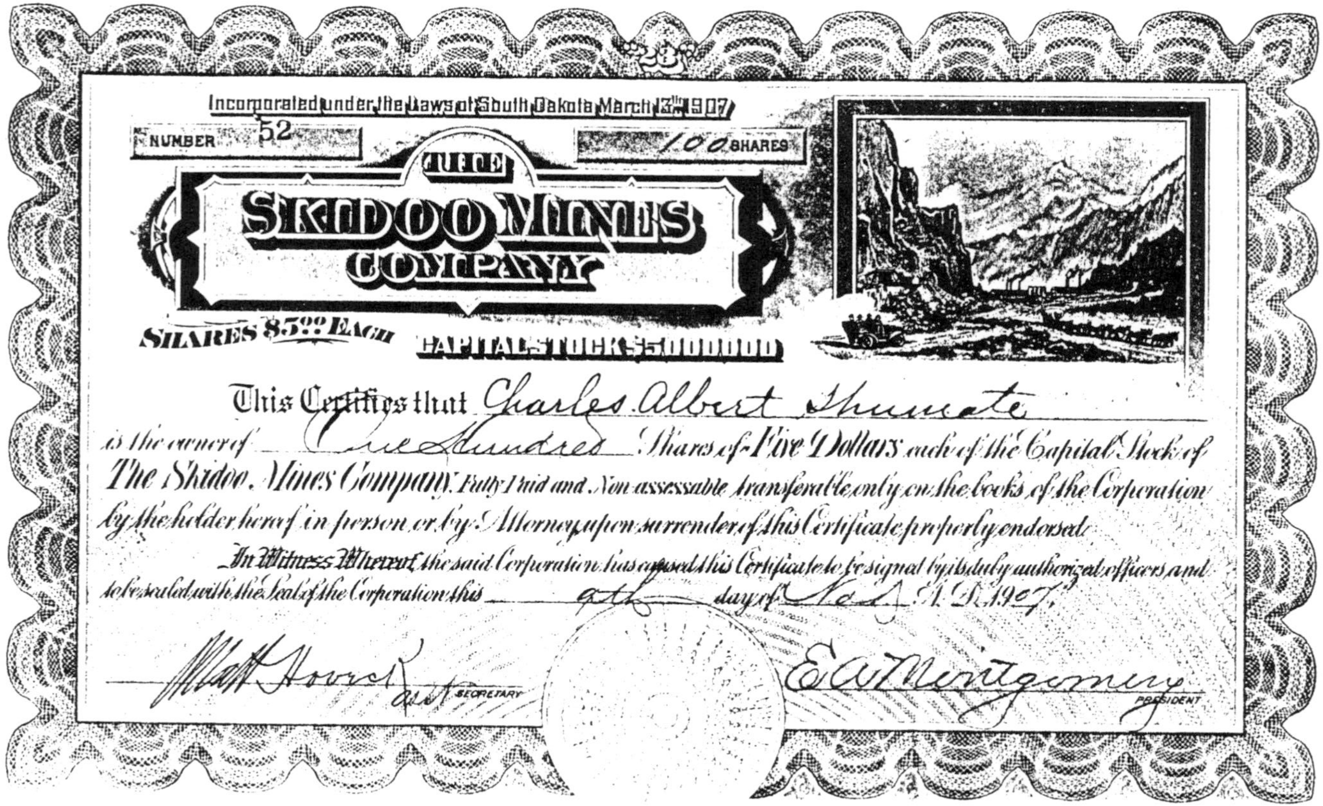

NUMBER 52

Incorporated under the laws of South Dakota March 12th, 1907

THE SKIDOO MINES COMPANY

100 SHARES

SHARES $5.00 EACH   CAPITAL STOCK $500,000.00

This Certifies that _Charles Albert Shumate_ is the owner of _One Hundred_ Shares of _Five Dollars_ each of the Capital Stock of The Skidoo Mines Company Fully Paid and Non assessable transferable only on the books of the Corporation by the holder hereof in person or by Attorney upon surrender of this Certificate properly endorsed.

In Witness Whereof the said Corporation has caused this Certificate to be signed by its duly authorized officers and to be sealed with the Seal of the Corporation this _10th_ day of _Feb_ A.D. 19_07_.

Matt Shumate, Secretary

E.A. Montgomery, President

Bob Montgomery's Skidoo was Death Valley's only dividend-paying gold mine, but even its investors lost money. (Courtesy of Albert Shumate) bonanza was a grand pipeline, designed to furnish not only the water for the mill but the power as well. It was an impressive engineering feat, costing $250,000 and running 21 miles, skirting high ridges and spanning deep gorges from Birch Spring up near Telescope Peak. Bob expected impressive things from it, too—water enough to generate 7,500 horse-power on a Pelton wheel, enough to run a fifty-stamp mill.[32]

Bob not only expected great things but expected them quickly, and it was Matt Hoveck who bore the brunt of his frustration with inevitable delays—especially those in the construction of the pipeline. Bob had talked of completing the line in three months, but with delays in pipe delivery, heavy snowfall, and countless minor problems, the work dragged on for eighteen months. By the time it was finally finished, in December 1907, Hoveck had become a physical wreck. Crippled by nervous pros-tration and insomnia, he resigned as manager on doctor's orders to rest quietly on a southern California beach. It was Bob's money and grand hopes and Hoveck's hard work and dedication that made Skidoo boom.[33]

The first rush in May 1906 had brought about two hundred miners to Emigrant Spring, where a saloon and store were started to rival Harris-burg. Within weeks another rival, Wild Rose, was platted midway be-tween them. Then in July Bob laid out a town of his own in a little cove just north of his mine. It was an ideal site, not like that of most camps, which, like tin cans, just landed where they were thrown. But most important, it was situated closest to the action at the Skidoo mine, and thus it quickly became the boss camp of the district. Bob called the town Montgomery, but nearly everyone else was calling it Skidoo—everyone, that is, except the Post Office Department. Rejecting both names on the ground that the first was already in use and the second was simply unusable, the postal authorities called it Hoveck. The self-styled Skidoo-vians, however, were determined to make their name stick, despite Bob Montgomery or the postmaster general. Bob capitulated in November 1906, filing a new town plat as Skidoo, with exactly twenty-three blocks. The postmaster reluctantly followed suit, officially renaming the post office Skidoo on April Fools Day, 1907.[34]

By the spring of 1907 exuberant Skidoovians were predicting the camp would soon surpass Rhyolite and reach a population of ten thousand within two years. Lots in the original twenty-three blocks had been snapped up in days, prices had tripled in three months to as much as $1,000 apiece on Skidoo Street, and Bob had surveyed more lots to meet the demand. Over a hundred wood and canvas structures were up, and more were being built. Two Wyoming printers, James Sterrett and Edwin Drury, had rushed in with type cases and a press to start the *Skidoo News*—the first and only newspaper actually printed within Death Valley. It debuted on December 21, 1906, with a yellow banner headline blazing

"CALIFORNIA GOLD!" A prosperous-looking H. Lawson McNew had arrived with a valise containing $2,000 he had borrowed in Los Angeles, and had opened the Southern California Bank of Skidoo in one corner of the general store. He took in $10,000 in deposits the first day and loaned it all back out just as quickly to a mining company he was in with. He was bankrupt two months later when his $2,000 note came due, but his Los Angeles creditors came to the aid of the Skidoovians and reopened the bank.[35]

Bob, in the meantime, had formed the Tucki Consolidated Telephone and Telegraph Company, which ran a line around the mountain of that name and across Death Valley to Rhyolite, replacing a heliograph which had flashed Skidoo news to the *Rhyolite Herald* office by mirrors, with a relay atop the Funerals. So that they would have a place to stay, Bob and Hoveck had also organized the aristocratic Tucki Club, which signed up members at $100 apiece from as far away as New York and Alaska. It offered members elegantly furnished rooms and a well-stocked sideboard. The Inyo County supervisors had appointed a popular merchant, James Arnold, as justice of the peace, and he started holding court in one of the saloons. At the same time the citizenry formed a Board of Trade to see to it that women and children were kept out of the saloons. The miners, who had organized the Wild Rose Miners' Union with twenty-three charter members the previous summer and then disbanded, reorganized in the fall of 1907 as the Skidoo Miners' Union, Local No. 211 of the Western Federation.[36]

By then there were stages running in and out of Skidoo almost daily. A twice-a-week Concord from Rhyolite competed with a triweekly coach and weekly auto from Ballarat. Moreover, rumor had it that two railroads were assured within a year—an extension of the Santa Fe from the south, and a branch of the Tonopah and Tidewater across Death Valley from the east. The first stage and freight teams into Skidoo had come up by way of Ballarat from the Santa Fe railhead at Johannesburg, 110 miles away. But Rhyolite merchants eager for a share of the trade had raised a subscription to build a 56-mile road to Skidoo over Daylight Pass and across the south end of the Death Valley dunes. James R. Clark started the grading from Bullfrog in the fall of 1906, and Bob put on a crew to build east across the valley from Skidoo. They met at the dunes, where they had to corduroy several miles of sand with mesquite. Freight wagons, stages, autos, and motorcycles were running over the road even before it was finished, and Clark and a couple partners set up the Stovepipe Road House at the well to serve the weary pilgrims. Death Valley's first "resort" was no more than a dugout, but by the spring of 1907, as traffic increased, they had added several tents for a grocery, eatery, bar, lodgings, and bathhouse. Clark also tapped into the Skidoo telephone line to install Death Valley's first telephone.[37]

Suddenly, in the midst of the Skidoo excitement came sensational reports of an incredible find up in the wilds of the Panamints—a "band of bloodthirsty redmen," hiding in a stone fortress, guarding a secret mine, and preying on emigrants and prospectors—the real killers of all those victims thought to have died in the valley of heat and privation! The author of these revelations, claiming to have barely escaped with his life, was a big, friendly, pudgy fellow in his early thirties who called himself "The Poet-Prospector," Clarence E. Eddy. He was nothing if not imaginative, even outdoing B. X. Dawson. A farm boy from Oregon, educated at the University of Idaho, he had worked as a printer, reporter, and editor on papers in the Northwest. Spurned by his first love for a wealthy Klondiker, he had turned to prospecting to seek both wealth and revenge. With passion he vowed, "I want to find tons of gold and then tell her NO!" By the time he came to Death Valley he had located over a hundred mines, including, he said, the long-sought Lost Packer in Idaho; and he had published a book of poems, *The Pinnacle of Parnassus*. But wealth and vengeance had continued to elude him.[38]

Grubstaked by a Salt Lake newsman, Eddy arrived at Rhyolite in March 1907, picked up a few extra bucks writing sketches and doggerel for the local papers, and then—on a mysterious tip from Death Valley Scotty—he headed for the Panamints with a partner, Edward Gould. Clambering up Johnson Canyon, Eddy was startled to discover the stone terraces at Hungry Bill's Ranch and then to come face-to-face with Bill himself. The Shoshone, who had finally gotten a government patent on his land to keep off jumpers, told the trembling intruder, "This is the Indian's country. The white man has taken all the rest; this is ours. We give you warning." His imagination afire, the Poet-Prospector beat a hasty retreat back down the canyon to tell his tale in Rhyolite.[39]

Old-timers simply grumbled, "Bosh!" at the story. But a few greenhorns ate it up and followed after Eddy when he returned, armed to the teeth, to "oust the warlike band" and find their secret mine. In the weeks that followed, Eddy and his followers located a string of gold claims in Johnson Canyon, set up a camp called Shadow Mountain, and floated a couple of stock companies. Taking a leaf from Dawson's book, they announced the discovery of an ancient Indian mine that they dubbed the Lost Inca, complete with crude implements and the ruins of a furnace. But after John Larson, one of the innocents headed for Eddy's fantasyland, died crossing Death Valley that summer, Rhyolite's deputy district attorney, Paul DeLaney, denounced it all as a "rank fake"—a concatenation of imagination and fraud. Eddy, puzzled by the "inexplicable spite" of his detractors, retreated to Salt Lake to recuperate from his Death Valley ordeal. When he returned that fall, he came with even more startling revelations—of a secret dream of wealth untold.[40]

Death Valley, the Poet-Prospector had come to believe, was the "treasure basin of creation," filled with gold enough "to make every poor man in the world richer than Croesus; to make King Solomon's mines and Monte Cristo's treasure look like penny savings banks!" Death Valley was an immense mining, milling, and reduction plant, nature's own gold factory! Eddy proclaimed:

> For ages, the rains and snows have been beating these mountains down into Death Valley. They are filled with precious metals. Gold, silver, copper and lead abound here. The great quartz rock, on account of their weight go down. Down, down, down they have rolled for centuries! The melting snows and rains of winter keep the surface of the basin damp throughout the season. The entire surface of the valley is composed of the highest chemical matter. There is salt, saltpetre, iron—every chemical known to science, in one form or another. Vats of vast areas have formed which are perfect quagmires of chemicals under constant action. Well, these highly mineralized rocks, largely impregnated with the precious metals, are constantly rolling down into this cauldron of chemicals. They have been doing it for ages and centuries. The dampness of winter set the processes to work. The hot suns of summer follow. No druggist's graduate nor assayer's crucible ever performed more scientific functions! The quartz may be seen there in all stages of decomposition. It melts under these processes like the snows in the burning sunshine above. In a few years the ore is part and parcel of the bed of this great sink—a mixture of strong chemicals in powdered and liquid form that work on and on with the centuries, filling higher and higher the great basin that has become one of the seven wonders of the world.[41]

Eddy had first glimpsed this vision on his first trip into the valley with Ed Gould, when they chanced to find a flash of coarse gold in a handful of dirt they panned out on the salt flat. To the prospector in Eddy it seemed unbelievable, and rightly so, but to the poet it was an instant revelation. Gould grew wild-eyed, Eddy said, as the poet confided his dream, and they grabbed up more samples for Gould to take to Berkeley for analysis. But then Eddy got caught up in his Shadow Mountain fantasies and, hearing nothing more from Gould, he all but forgot about the valley floor.[42]

Not until the fall of 1907, when Eddy returned from Salt Lake, did he discover that Gould had returned to locate some 25,000 acres of placer claims between Furnace Creek and Bennetts Well, allegedly financed by the notorious John A. Benson, whose land-grabbing schemes were being widely publicized by muckraker Lincoln Steffens. Eddy further heard that the assays had shown over $2 in gold per cubic yard, that Gould and his partners had formed the Death Valley Gold Placer Mining Company, and that they had a gold dredge waiting at the Ballarat to be hauled into the valley. Moreover, a rival outfit, camped near Wingate Pass, was rumored to have claimed another 18,000 acres of placers in the south end of the valley. Eddy was suddenly certain that his fabulous visions of Death Valley's riches must indeed be true. By the time he got back to the valley to stake his own Sub Sea placers, he found only 1,200 acres of placer ground left. Yet even this was enough ground, he felt, to yield a billion dollars![43]

Eddy imagined that fortune at last was within his grasp, if only he too could raise enough money for a dredge. Then James Edmonds, an experienced dredging man who had heard of the discovery, came to look over the prospects. Eddy, bubbling with enthusiasm, took him to Death Valley, where Edmonds bored a 12-foot hole to test the stiff, sticky clay beneath the salt crust. That was enough for Edmonds. The clay was fine for pottery, he concluded, but there wasn't a trace of placer gold in it. Eddy protested that the test was only superficial, and with "child-like faith" he clung to his dream. The gold really was there, he insisted. "It may be 100, 1,000, 10,000 feet below, but it is there, and when the process is discovered by which it may be reclaimed, all the world will be rich, and gaunt poverty will cease its weary journey in the land!" His newspaper friends in Rhyolite, however, spread the word: the Death Valley placers were a hoax![44]

The Poet-Prospector went back to Salt Lake and eventually put together two more books of poems, *Ballads of Heaven and Hell* and *The Burro's Bray,* which fondly recalled the "golden schemes and golden dreams" of his Death Valley days. He never did get to say "NO!" to the woman who spurned him, but he found a new love, a less mercenary lass named Juanita. They spent their honeymoon in 1912 hiking across Death Valley.[45]

By October 1907 the Death Valley gold boom was in full swing, and optimism ran high. At the Keane Wonder, $750,000 worth of ore had been blocked out, the tramway was completed, and the mill was just starting up. At Lee, the Tonopah and Tidewater Railroad had come within just a few miles of the mines, machinery was arriving by the carload, and the Hayseed was starting to ship out high-grade. At Harrisburg, a merger and sale of the Cashier and Midas properties was pending to Eastern capitalists who promised rapid development. At Skidoo, the great pipeline was nearly finished, mill construction was under way, and ore was being stockpiled for its completion.[46]

Elsewhere in the country, there was much less optimism: interest rates were climbing rapidly, and money was getting tight. Then, on October 23, the giant Knickerbocker Trust of New York closed its doors, depositors rushed to the banks, and financial panic swept the nation. In the depression that followed there was little money left for mining speculation. The boom was over, many small mines closed, and the Death Valley camps began to decline, even though the big mines at last began to produce.

The Skidoo mine was barely affected by the panic, which only forced Bob to trim back slightly. On May 10, 1908, after two years of work and an outlay of over half a million dollars, the Skidoo finally came into production. Hoveck had finished the pipeline the previous December, and Bob's new general manager, H. W. Squire, completed a ten-stamp, water-powered mill five months later. Bob made a flying trip up from Los Angeles in Winnie's new French car to watch the first ore run through the mill and see the first returns on his investment.[47]

With free water power, the mining and milling costs of the Skidoo ore ran under $6 a ton—almost as cheap as Schwab's big electric-powered operation on the Shoshone. But the pipeline didn't provide as much power as Bob had expected—ten stamps, not fifty, was all it could handle. So when Bob enlarged the mill to fifteen stamps the following year, he had to bring in gasoline engines for additional power. The pipeline wasn't all that dependable, either, as it nearly froze solid in the winters, cutting the flow of water and power to a trickle. Despite such problems, the Skidoo started turning out from $15,000 to $20,000 worth of gold a month, at a profit of over 50 percent. Although the monthly output inevitably declined, the Skidoo remained a nearly steady producer for almost a decade, nearly matching the total output of the great Montgomery Shoshone. Moreover, the Skidoo did what no Bullfrog district mine ever did: it actually became a dividend payer.[48]

The camp of Skidoo didn't fare as well, however. The panic was taking its toll, although there was still joy in the camp in December 1907, when the first water from the pipeline began running free in the streets. Tomato-can baths became a thing of the past. There was now water enough for swimming pools and skating rinks, Bob proposed. The Skidoovians even tried laughing off the panic at the end of the year with a "Hard Times Frolic." "In a burst of defiance against the solemn depression thrust upon our beloved Death Valley region by the heartlessness of Wall Street and high finance generally," they announced, there would be eats, drinks, and good cheer for all, plus the most "freakish exhibition ever devised by man on the ragged edge of Death Valley"—a colored-light dance by Shacknasty Nell from Ballarat, a herd of marvelously trained goats from Emigrant Spring, and a colony of educated fleas from Stovepipe Wells.[49]

In the weeks and months that followed, hard times settled down to stay. Most of the little mines in the district had already fallen in the panic, laying off their crews. With the completion of the pipeline and mill, Bob cut back his payroll to less than half, letting the construction men go. So even though the Skidoo mine was finally producing, the camp withered as businesses closed, tents came down, and the Skidoovians skedaddled. The *News* folded in August of 1908, and the press was removed to Keeler that winter. By spring there was only one store left in the once lively camp—a combination general store and soft-drink parlor.[50]

Not all of the Skidoovians got out alive, however. Joseph L. "Hootch" Simpson was one of the pioneers of the camp, and a quarrelsome fellow with an unenviable reputation. He held several promising claims, but by questionable title. With a partner, Fred Oakes, he ran the Gold Seal saloon and restaurant, which had paid him well during the boom, and he was Skidoo Babe's pimp. Some say he was slightly deranged from syphilis. There is no question that he was a hard drinker and a mean drunk. With a head full of hootch he fancied himself a gunfighter—the boss bad man of Skidoo—and amused himself with menacing gunplay. But one man had called his bluff, and Hootch got part of his nose shot off. The Skidoo Mines Company doctor, Reginald Macdonald, had patched him up as best he could, but Hootch was left disfigured. Then came the panic, and his saloon business was hard hit by the decline. The worse business got, the drunker and meaner he became.[51]

On Easter Sunday morning, April 19, 1908, Hootch had been on a roaring drunk for several days, brandishing his gun and threatening anyone who crossed his path. That morning he went out looking for more amusement. He staggered across the street into Jim Arnold's Skidoo Trading Company store and lunged over to the Southern California Bank counter in the corner. There he leveled his gun at the cashier, Ralph Dobbs, and under threat of instant death loudly demanded the magnificent sum of $20! Before Dobbs could reach into the cash drawer, Dr. Macdonald and another customer grabbed Hootch and disarmed him. Arnold then unceremoniously kicked the would-be bank robber out of his store. Constable Henry Seller wanted to handcuff Hootch to a telephone pole until a warrant could be obtained to take him to the county jail in Independence, but he was persuaded to let Hootch's partner Oakes guard him instead. Hootch soon fell asleep in the back of the saloon, so Oakes hid his gun and left him. When Hootch awoke early that afternoon, he was in a black mood. Still smarting from his humiliation that morning, he thrashed around until he found his gun and then headed back across the street to get the storekeeper for kicking him. He found Arnold in the back of his store, and with few words shot him just below the heart.[52]

The sound of the shot was heard all over the town, and by the time Hootch emerged from the store both Constable Seller and the doctor were on the scene with guns drawn. Another drunk, Gordon McBain, stumbled into the middle of things trying to arrest Hootch, but ended up just giving him cover to get back across the street to his restaurant. Seller, however, was in hot pursuit and, after threatening to blow McBain's head off to get him out of the way and narrowly missing being shot in the stomach himself, he finally subdued Hootch. This time the constable handcuffed his prisoner and locked him up in a corrugated iron shed under constant guard. He also arrested McBain for interfering.[53]

In the meantime, Arnold was failing fast. The bullet had severed the spinal artery, and he died that evening, despite the efforts of Dr. Macdonald. He was buried Tuesday on a hill above the town. A little wreath of wildflowers brightened the black pall covering the coffin; but it was a gray, overcast day, and as his mourners sang "Rock of Ages" and "Nearer My God to Thee," their thoughts were on Hootch Simpson. Arnold's was the town's first death, but not its last.[54]

Hootch, far from repentent, was gloating over the killing—he could finally put a notch in his gun—and laughingly proclaimed that he was a "Hero," a "True Blue," and a "Bohemian." His boasting enraged Arnold's friends, and just before midnight Wednesday, some fifty masked Skidoovians broke down the door to the makeshift jail and, holding Seller and his deputy at gunpoint, took their prisoner out. The next morning, April 23, Hootch Simpson was found hanging from a telephone pole. No one seemed to know anything about the lynching, although one wag said he had been awakened twenty-three times during the night to be told of the hanging, and he was "surprised every time." Someone had also awakened McBain that night, telling him that Hootch had been hung and that he had better "run like hell." He didn't wait to be told a second time. His iron-riveted boots echoed down the gulch "like ghostly thunder," and by morning he had passed Stovepipe, a little lame but still going at a dog trot.[55]

The editor of the *Skidoo News* summed up local sentiment when he wrote:

> Had the murderer been sent for trial it would have cost the county thousands of dollars, which would have been nothing short of an imposition on long-suffering ratepayers. It would have cost some of the citizens of this community considerable inconvenience and expense, and, maybe, before it had dragged its way through, another case might have come up, perhaps involving the death of other

SKIDOO NEWS.

VOL. II, NO. 18   SKIDOO, INYO COUNTY, CALIFORNIA, SATURDAY, APRIL 25, 1908   TEN CENTS

MURDER IN CAMP
Murderer Lynched
WITH GENERAL APPROVAL

Joe Simpson Shoots Jim Arnold Dead and Is Hanged By Citizens

The disturbance which has shaken the community to the roots, in the past few days, opened on Sun'ay morning last, at about eleven o'clock, when Joe Simpson, familiarly known as Joe 'Hootch' (that being his favor te bever ge) held up the Southern Calif. Bank here, for its alnable sum of twenty dollars, that being the sum of his immediate need. He was overpowered before he could collect, and his gun taken from him. He returned to the bank (which is located in the store) again and became very abusive Jim Arnold, managing partner in the store, finally put him out. Three hours later, he returned again with his gun and deliberately shot Arnold, who was unarmed. He turned, and covered the bank er, Ralph E. Dobbs and would probably have killed him had not his...

Arnold died the same evening. An Inquest on Arnold's body was held on Monday, the jury returning a verdict, "killed by gun shot wound inflicted by Joe Simpson." Sometime on Wednesday night an armed body of citizens overpowered the sheriff and seized prisoner and hanged him to a telephone pole. On Thursday, inquest was held on Simpson's body, the jury finding that "he died by strangulation by persons unknown." The body was disposed of...

THE TRAGEDY

The comparative quiet of Sunday morning was broken by a wild disturbance that resulted in the brutal murder of James Arnold, one of the most prominent citizens of the camp—the father of the camp in fact, inasmuch as he located the townsite, and ended in the lynching of his assailant, Joe Simpson, a local saloon keeper and gun fighter. It will go on record as one of the most remarkable lynchings that has taken place in the United States for many years...

THE CAPTURE

THE LYNCHING

The lynching took place on Wednes day night Irving Nefers, when Inte...

(Courtesy of Eastern California Museum)

innocent people. Further, a conviction might not have ensued, resulting in the prisoner being turned loose upon some other community. That such a man should be at large, is not only a national shame, but a national crime.

The method of disposing of such, in the way that happened here, is JUST,—CHEAP and—SALUTARY in the lesson it conveys. Local gun men are already in a chastened frame of mind. Would-be bad men, as they bowl along the road on their triumphal entry of Skidoo, will note the number, the stoutness, the great convenience of the telephone poles, and reflect thereon.

It is a matter of deep regret, but it was the will of the people.

So far as Skidoovians were concerned, Hootch had simply "died by the visitation of man."[56]

There is a popular story now that Hootch's corpse was dug up and strung up on the telephone pole again for the benefit of photographers from the Los Angeles dailies. It's a good story, but it's not quite accurate. What did happen was much more macabre, and photographs were the least of it. The Los Angeles papers were quite content to take their accounts of the lynching from a wire service dispatch, and none bothered to send a reporter, let alone a photographer, to Skidoo. There were, nonetheless, two photographs taken of the late Hootch. Dr. Macdonald took them as morbid momentos the morning after the lynching—one of the corpse laid out on a table in a tent that doubled as a morgue, and the other hanging up again from a crossbeam of the tent. They were never published in the papers, but when the hanging photo turned up years later it spawned the story of the newspaper photographers.[57]

It was what happened to Hootch's corpse, not a photo of it, that's the grisly story. First, the Skidoovians' sense of justice rebeled at the idea of burying Hootch in their newly started cemetery beside the man he had murdered, so the corpse was put in a cheap pine box and dumped without ceremony into an abandoned prospect hole. Then Dr. Macdonald, perhaps pondering whether Hootch's brain might have been damaged by syphilis, decided to do further work on his skull. In the dead of the night he went out to the prospect hole with a helper and a sharp scalpel and cut off Hootch's head. Back in his office he cut open the skull and apparently satisfied his curiosity. Then he left the mess on an anthill until most of the flesh was picked off, and finally boiled the skull for three days to remove the remaining meat from the bone.[58]

The doctor kept Hootch's skull in his office as a curiosity for a while, but when he quit Skidoo he left it hanging in a canvas ore bag under the floor of his cabin. Years later another desert doctor retrieved the skull, and it has since passed from one curious hand to another. One of its keepers tried to give it to a local museum but was refused because it was against their regulations to display the skull of a white man—only Indians' skulls were permitted! What happened to the rest of Hootch's remains is uncertain. One former Skidoovian claimed that several years later the headless skeleton was unearthed by a startled prospector poking around in the hole looking for gold. Other old-timers claimed that a couple ladies of the evening, perhaps including Skidoo Babe, came over from Beatty with a wagon and dug up Hootch's remains to take them back for a decent burial. But on that long, hot wagon ride through Death Valley, the stench overpowered their sentiment, and they ditched Hootch along the way. Whatever happened to the rest of him, there's at least one thing all agree on—he didn't rest in peace.[59]

Meanwhile, in neighboring Harrisburg, the financial panic had only aggravated an already bad situation. The hoped-for merger and sale of the Cashier and Midas in the summer of 1907 had fallen through, but the panic wasn't to blame for that. Shorty later claimed that Aguereberry had blocked the sale for $115,000, doggedly holding out for a million. Pete, however, claimed it was because of litigation with a dog-in-the-manger promoter from Los Angeles who tied up his title for two years, and there was certainly some truth to that. O'Brien and his San Francisco partners had let their interest in the Cashier go the previous fall for only $20,000 to a former Montana rancher, Thomas E. Crawford, who thought it was the Lost Breyfogle. Shorty, still hoping for a bigger sale, held onto his shares. He and Crawford thus became the biggest stockholders, but it was an uneven arrangement. Crawford worked hard, putting all of his time and much of his money into blocking out the pay ore, while Shorty worked only his jaw, telling everyone what a great mine it was. Yet all went well until the merger and sale fell through, and then the panic hit. To continue work, Crawford finally levied an assessment of 1¼¢ a share. Shorty couldn't pay and lost his stock on the auction block in March 1908. He later claimed it was just a "freeze out game" designed to do him out of his share. There was still a lot of work to be done before the mine could even begin to pay, and that took money. It also took time, for the rock was so hard it yielded only half a foot per shift in the tunnel and drifts. But Crawford persisted.[60]

By the spring of 1909, Crawford had finally blocked out enough $50-a-ton ore to warrant putting up a mill. By then he was also broke and owed the miners back pay. Undaunted, the determined cowboy lassoed a stray horse, rode it to Johannesburg, and sold it for the price of a ticket to Oakland. There he talked the Best Manufacturing Company out of $15,000 worth of milling machinery on credit. He rode back to Johannesburg on the freight with the machinery, because he couldn't afford a return ticket. Then he worked as swamper for a teamster who agreed to haul the machinery to the mine on credit. At least that's the way Crawford said it all happened. One thing is certain: he did set up a little three-stamp mill with a 25-horsepower engine in July, and by early August he had produced his first gold brick.[61]

Pete Aguereberry, in the meantime, had finally gotten clear title to his mine again—with the aid of a friend who secretly relocated it for him after Pete had refused to do the annual assessment work for his troublesome partners. Pete had also found some good-paying ore, but had no money to develop it, so for a share of the debt on the mill and machinery, he joined partners with Crawford. Together they turned out as much as $10,000 a month in bullion, paid off their debts, and started taking a profit.[62]

Crawford decided the partnership had gone too far, however, when Pete started making passes at his wife the following spring. The partners got into a free-for-all that ended when a bullet creased Pete's scalp. He charged Crawford with attempted murder, but the judge concluded, "Pete got what was coming to him." That should have settled the matter, but it didn't. As soon as they stepped out of the courtroom they were back at each other, and Pete again came out second-best as Crawford chewed up his face. Needless to say, that was the end of the partnership. Crawford sold out that winter, taking his wife to Los Angeles. Half a century later Crawford referred to the affair cryptically as a dispute "over the boundary of my claims."[63]

On the other side of Death Valley, over in the Lee district, the panic was discounted at first in all the excitement over the railroad's arrival and the Hayseed's first shipment. There was even a new cause for excitement that fall, when C. E. Barber, a tenderfoot from Denver, came into camp claiming he had found $4,700 ore in a secret gold ledge on the west side of the Funerals. When he started back to his claim, a herd of Leevites were on his trail, and he led them on a merry chase for three days before he lost them. Several tantalizing weeks passed before outsiders finally found the mystery bonanza, just a couple of miles southeast of Old Man Beatty's and Adolph Nevares's ranch on Cow Creek. By then Barber had guards posted with shotguns to keep anyone from even getting a sniff of the ore. But the newcomers feverishly staked the ground all around, organized a new Breyfogle district, and started two rival camps, Barberville and Kenyon, before the mystery ore was found to be practically worthless, and the whole thing was revealed as just another wildcat scheme.[64]

By the beginning of 1908 the deepening depression was starting to make itself felt in Lee. But optimistic Leevites turned out one last time in a "grand la pageant de burro," parading the "desert canaries" with costumed ladies and decorated floats up and down Nevada Street until one surefooted beast stumbled, dumping a buxom beauty in the dust. Lee itself was about to come down just as hard. And there were other signs that the wolves would soon be at the door, as when stage driver Ed Hitchcock rushed into Lee having just beaten off two big, hungry, gray wolves that had attacked his coach just a mile east of town. That was enough to send newly arrived psychic mining expert, palmist, phrenologist, and telepathist, "Mrs. Dr." Sellier packing.[65]

The railroad had cut shipping costs, but not by enough to make Lee ores profitable. Nothing less than $50-a-ton ore would even pay costs, and there wasn't much of that in the district—all the wonderful big assays had been from little pockets. Even the marvelous Hayseed had made just one shipment of 18 tons worth only $1,314. The best of the remaining ore ran barely $15 a ton, and there was little of that, so the superintendent closed down that summer. The *Lee Herald* had suspended in February, and other businesses folded soon after. By summer there was only one saloon left in the district.[66]

William H. Lillard was the last to give up. He kept a store at Lee until 1912, hoping each new year would bring back the boom times. The closest he got was in 1910. Early that year F. S. Harding, a former Calaveras physician, took a three-year lease on the Hayseed and set up a little secondhand three-stamp mill 4 miles east of the mine at a well near Leeland. But after he produced his first gold bar in September, he too realized it wouldn't pay, and he quit.[67]

The big mine in the Funerals was Homer Wilson's Keane Wonder. He started milling ore the very day the Knickerbocker Trust failed, and turned out a steady flow of bullion despite the panic and depression. The ore wasn't any richer than that in the Hayseed; there was just a whole lot more of it—enough to induce Wilson to put up a $150,000 mill and tramway, and enough to maintain $15,000 to $20,000 a month in bullion shipments, month after month, year after year, just as he had predicted.[68]

Despite its remoteness, Wilson claimed to operate the Keane Wonder just as cheaply and economically as either the Shoshone or the Skidoo, with mining and milling costs under $6 a ton. Thus the surface ores running over $15 a ton paid a generous return, at least in the beginning. Certainly mining costs were low for the surface rock, which was simply quarried from the side of a cliff. Just a few men could knock down enough ore to keep the mill running to capacity. Its twenty stamps, run by a 126-horsepower, oil-burning steam engine, worked about 75 tons a day and, augmented by a cyaniding plant in the spring of 1909, the recovery was 94 percent of assay. But lack of water, as always, was a persistent problem. The well at the mill provided only enough water to operate the plant about two-thirds of the time, even with scrupulous recycling of steam from the boiler and water from the slimes. Heat, of course, was a chronic problem, and the whole camp suffered through 124° days and 100° plus nights because Wilson, unlike most Death Valley operators, refused to shut down for the summer. He was, however, forced to run the mill only at night during the hottest months, because he lost all the amalgam into the slimes otherwise. Wilson paid higher wages to compensate the men, at least until the panic. Then, in the summer of 1908, while the Rhyolite miners' union was struggling to maintain a uniform $4 a day wage there, Wilson used the opportunity to cut his wages to that same figure. A few men quit in protest, but jobs were scarce enough that their places were quickly filled.[69]

But Wilson's aerial tram, proclaimed Death Valley's "sky railroad," was a bigger attraction to visitors than the mine itself. It was gravity-powered and ran for nearly a mile up the rocky slope of the Funerals. The weight of the descending ore buckets, each carrying nearly half a ton of rock to the mill, raised the empties back up to the mine, and Wilson cleverly rigged the cable to run a rock crusher, too—the only such thing in the world, one enthusiast vowed. Wilson, his wife, and daughter lived down at the mill with a few mill hands, while the miners and muckers all lived in a boardinghouse perched up at the mine. They all rode the tram on occasion to get back and forth between the mine and the mill. The twenty-minute ride was an exciting experience, especially for visitors, seated on a little iron bench, clinging with a death grip to a side bar while their legs dangled in space hundreds of feet above the jagged rocks. It was an experience only a few cared to repeat. In addition to ore and passengers, the tram carried all sorts of supplies—occasionally even fresh pastries, whenever the mine cook, Radio Tadich, made cream puffs and sent some down.[70]

Small and isolated as it was, the Keane Wonder nonetheless had a few amenities: electric lights from a gasoline generator, a telephone, the second in Death Valley, and triweekly stage service as a stop on the Skidoo-Rhyolite line. For a time the camp even had its own train service—not a railroad, but Lane's traction train. This quixotic venture, known as the Keane Wonder Traction Company, was the creation of Rhyolite merchant Joseph R. Lane. In the summer of 1909 he got the supply contract for the mine and bought an old steam traction engine for the job. The giant 110-horsepower tractor, previously used by Borax Smith at Calico, made its first trip to the mill late in July. It was a 26-mile haul over Daylight Pass, and the monster machine, pulling two trailers with 20 tons of freight, barely crawled along at 3 to 4 miles per hour, consuming 3,000 gallons of oil and water in the course of the trip. But Lane made $200 a trip, and by fall he was planning two trips a week. Then on November

6, chugging up Daylight Pass, the old beast died of a ruptured boiler; too many years of hard desert water had clogged the boiler tubes until they burst. Dubbed "Old Dinah," the derelict remained where she had stopped beside the road in Daylight Pass, a landmark and a curiosity for over twenty years. Then the borax company spirited her down to Furnace Creek Ranch one night, and there she can still be seen.[71]

Although the panic didn't curtail operations at the Keane Wonder, it did precipitate a lengthy and labyrinthine legal battle for the control of the mine—a battle that ultimately outlived the mine itself. The trouble started the day the Knickerbocker Trust failed. Within hours the State Bank and Trust Company of Nevada also closed its doors. But its president, Thomas B. Rickey, assured depositors that not a man, woman, or child would lose a dollar because their money was amply covered by the bank's assets, which included no less than 975,000 shares of Keane Wonder stock—65 percent of the total issue. Rickey, then in his seventies, was considered both one of the safest bankers in the state and one of its shrewdest speculators. He was a pioneer cattleman who had amassed a fortune during the heydays of the Comstock and had built up a financial empire that included not only his banks and vast land holdings in Nevada and California but irrigation projects, the Nevada-California Power Company, and mines in the southern Nevada boom camps. He was the man who had bankrolled Homer Wilson's purchase of the Keane Wonder and who had made the money available for its development. He and Wilson jointly owned the 975,000 shares, which had been given to the bank as security for $150,000 in loans for the mill and tramway construction.[72]

Despite his assurances to his depositors, Rickey had no real intention of giving up his Keane Wonder shares to satisfy their claims. Soon after the bank failed, Rickey arranged a deal with Donald Mackenzie, president of the Frances-Mohawk Mining and Leasing Company, the bank's largest depositor. It was simply a fast shuffle. Mackenzie wrote a check on the bank for $150,000, which he gave to Wilson as a loan. Wilson handed the check to Rickey, repaying the bank's loan; Rickey handed Wilson the Keane Wonder stock held by the bank as collateral; and Wilson gave the stock to Mackenzie as security for his loan. It would even have been legal if the bank's assets hadn't been frozen. Indeed, when the bank's court-appointed receiver discovered the stock was gone, he charged them with conspiracy to defraud the depositors and brought suit to recover the stock.[73]

Rickey's scheme didn't stop there, for he had no intention of giving Mackenzie control of the mine, either. Thus at a cozy meeting in August 1908, the majority stockholders—Rickey and Wilson—voted to give Rickey a trust deed to the entire property as collateral for a $45,000 loan he had made sometime before. When that loan came due in October, Rickey slipped into the Inyo County Courthouse to foreclose on the property. That would have left Mackenzie with nothing but worthless stock. But Mackenzie learned of the foreclosure in time to stop it, and realizing the vulnerability of his collateral, he too demanded a deed to the property as security, instead of the stock. Thus a new deed was written jointly to Mackenzie and Rickey for their combined loans of $195,000, and foreclosure proceedings were begun on this deed in April of 1909.[74]

Then Rhyolite editor Earle Clemens entered the fray as a stockholder, petitioning to stop that foreclosure on the grounds that Mackenzie had no legitimate claim against the company for his personal loan to Wilson. Although Clemens filed his petition on behalf of minority stockholders, cynics saw in his action the fine hand of "sly old Rickey:" now that Rickey had the controlling block of stock back, he had little to gain and a whole lot to lose by foreclosing. These suspicions became widespread when money was suddenly raised to pay off the company's debt to Rickey, leaving only the "personal" debt to Mackenzie unpaid. Rickey then publicly "admitted" that his trading of the bank's accounts, which gave Mackenzie his claim against the Keane Wonder, was illegal.[75]

Mackenzie, furious at these maneuvers, filed suit against Wilson for mismanagement of the company's affairs and asked that the Keane Wonder be put in the hands of a receiver. The courts quickly rejected that bid, however, since the mine was steadily shipping bullion and paying its daily bills. But what still had the courts confused was who should receive the profits. So while the courts tried to untangle the mess, a trust fund was set up to which Wilson and the Keane Wonder were to repay their loans. There was nearly $100,000 in the fund before the case was finally settled by splitting the money four to one between Mackenzie and the other bank creditors.[76]

In the meantime, the Keane Wonder kept right on turning out a quarter of a million dollars a year in gold. Its continuing bullion output and a brightening economic outlook nationwide even inspired optimists to put up mills on a few neighboring mines, but not one of them paid. The old Chloride Cliff was the first to benefit from the revival. Los Angeles promoter J. Irving Crowell, who had purchased an interest from George Franklin before the panic, rounded up a couple of Pennsylvania investors and formed the Penn Mining and Leasing Company in the fall of 1909 to reopen the mine. In among the lead ore they discovered some gold-bearing rock that assayed over $35 a ton, and in a flurry of excitement the following spring they set up a little one-stamp Ideal mill right at the foot of the mine dump. Only after the mill was in place did they seem to discover that they didn't have enough water to even make a trial run! Crowell talked grandly of piping in water and enlarging the mill, but the single stamp still stands atop the Funerals, untried to this day—a true monument to folly. Crowell eventually shipped about 300 tons of high-grade, apparently to establish the mine as a "producer" before he sailed for England to try to sell it. Despite a few hopeful rumors, he had no luck at that either, so he ended up just holding it for a decade or more, as Franklin had done before him.[77]

Next came a little mill at the Indian mine in what is now Monarch Canyon, 3 miles north of the Keane Wonder. Johnny Hughes, a Shoshone, had discovered a gold ledge there in 1903 while out hunting mountain sheep, and after the mining boom started he showed the ledge to A. K. Ishmael, who located it as the Indian in December 1904. Scotty's hapless backer, Burdon Gaylord, eagerly bonded the claim for $20,000 the following year, in a last ditch effort to capitalize on the excitement he had helped to generate with Scotty's record run. But Gaylord failed even to recover his earlier losses. For four years after that Ishmael did little more than the annual assessment work on the mine, until he found a partner, Richard E. Clapp, who had enough money and enthusiasm to develop the mine. Opening a vein of $25-a-ton ore, they piped in water about a quarter of a mile and erected a two-stamp Nissen mill in the summer of 1910. They cast their first gold bar in September, but closed down just a couple of months later because the ore simply wouldn't pay costs.[78]

Little "Johnny-behind-the-gun" Cyty put up the third mill. He had watched his hopes of riches vanish one by one, and this little mill was his last hope. His future had looked bright when he sold the Big Bell in 1905 for 295,000 shares of stock in the Death Valley Big Bell Mining Company and several thousand dollars in cash. He put the money into the Unique Dance Hall in Rhyolite, hoping it would grow with the boom. But he refused to hire union girls, and the Wobbly boycott killed his business. Then the panic wiped out most of the paper value of his stock, which broke from 30¢ to 4¢ a share. Hoping to recoup a fortune, he turned to the gambling tables with his stock, but he lost it all—$10,000 worth—one night in April 1908 on Dick Jones's roulette wheel in the Stock Exchange Bar.[79]

He had just one hope left, another claim just below the Big Bell, and he set out to work on it again. But there was a smoldering dispute over its title. C. Kyle Smith, the district recorder, claiming the annual assessment work hadn't been done, had relocated the ground himself in 1906. The showdown came in the fall of 1908 when Cyty resumed work on the claim, vowing that if Smith came on the ground he'd never leave it alive.

On Saturday afternoon, November 21, Smith went to the claim armed, and the two men shot it out alone. Smith was mortally wounded in the leg and stomach; Cyty was hit in the arm. Cyty claimed that Smith came up, shouted, "What are you doing on this ground you son of a bitch," and started shooting. All Smith said before he died was "the Dago shot me when I wasn't expecting it." Cyty was tried for murder and convicted of manslaughter. He appealed for a new trial and was finally acquitted in April 1910, after serving a year and a half in the county jail.[80]

That winter Cyty went back to work again on the disputed claim, and within months he hit a pocket of some of the richest rock ever found in the Funerals. Certain that he again had a fortune within his grasp, he got Homer Wilson to work some of the ore at the Keane Wonder mill, and with the returns from that he bought the Hayseed mill at the sheriff's auction for $500. He set up the little three-stamp mill at a spring about a mile west of the mine, and in October 1911 he turned out his first gold bar. But before the year was out the little pocket was exhausted, and with it Cyty's last hope.[81]

By the end of 1911, over $800,000 worth of gold had been taken out of the Keane Wonder. A crew of seventy-five was taking out another thousand or two dollars a day, and it seemed that the surface had barely been scratched. Wilson, enthused over rich new strikes not only in the Keane Wonder but in the newly acquired Big Bell as well, envisioned fully $20 million more to come. But while Wilson talked loudly of bringing in electric power and enlarging the mill to forty or fifty stamps, he was quietly looking for a buyer for his and Rickey's shares in the mine—all 975,000 of them. He found just the man in W. H. Wells, a mining engineer and promoter who took a quick look at the mine and persuaded a wealthy group of Philadelphians to buy it. They closed the deal in May 1912. Rickey boasted that the sale price was $600,000, or more than 60¢ a share, but that's undoubtedly a generous overestimate because, even after a sharp rise on news of the sale, Keane Wonder stock still sold on the exchanges for only 35¢ a share. Wilson agreed to stay on as manager for a short time to help enlarge the mill. But that never happened, for in August, just three months after the sale, the Keane Wonder closed down: the pay rock was exhausted.[82]

Wilson doubtless hadn't expected it to end that soon, or in that way, when he and Rickey took control of the mine in 1906. But the ore—rich, easily worked, and highly profitable at the surface—had grown poorer, more pockety, and more costly with depth, until finally it wouldn't pay to work. Even though the mine produced nearly $1 million before it shut down, almost all of the profits from the early years had gone toward paying off loans, purchasing additional machinery, and financing extensive exploratory work in an unsuccessful search for more pay rock. The highly touted strikes had all proved to be just small pockets. So even Homer Wilson finally realized that the mine had reached a point where it was only good for selling. On a solid record of production and earnest promises of more of the same, he did just that.[83]

The closure of the Keane Wonder came as a shock to many. The press quickly charged sly old Rickey with "handing a lemon" to the innocent Philadelphians, but at the same time they exonerated Wilson with their silence. Wells and the Philadelphians weren't all that innocent, either. They worked the stock up and down on the Eastern exchanges all the way to the end of the decade, even though they lost all title to the property in 1914! In November of that year Mackenzie and the long-suffering creditors of the State Bank and Trust Company finally foreclosed on their deed for the unpaid debts, which had grown, with interest, to $215,000. In the hope of making up some of their losses, the creditors reopened the mine briefly in 1916. But they produced little and shut down for good that summer, letting the property go to the Porter Brothers for unpaid grocery bills. That was the end of the gold boom in the Funerals. Only Johnny Cyty remained, hired as a watchman at the Keane Wonder.[84]

With the closing of the Keane Wonder, Bob Montgomery's Skidoo became the last survivor of the Death Valley gold boom. It alone just kept on turning out gold bars, despite a burst water pipe, a disastrous fire, lawsuits, and amalgam thieves. The year of 1913 was the worst; a severe cold snap in January burst the great pipeline in several places, shutting down the mill until the spring thaw, and no sooner was the pipe repaired than the mill burned down. But Bob immediately began rebuilding. Salvaging ten stamps and half of the cyanide tanks from the ruins, he had the mill running again by September. Then came another round of mining litigation. When Ramsey and Thompson had first staked the Skidoo, they inadvertently left several worthless slivers of unclaimed ground in between their claims. These "fractions," later located by others, were all purchased in 1909 by a neighboring mine owner, William B. Gray, who saw a chance for a shakedown. He promptly brought suit against the Skidoo Mines Company to expel them from the ground, apparently hoping for a cash settlement out of court. But after three years in the courts, all Gray got was a quit claim from Bob acknowledging Gray's title to the worthless ground. Bob did, however, insist on his right to continue passing over and through the ground in the course of working the Skidoo. That gave Gray cause for a new suit in the fall of 1914, in which he demanded $168,950 in restitution for ore he claimed Bob and the company had taken from one of his claims, Fraction No. 5. After two more years of haggling in the courts, Gray was thwarted once again when the case was dismissed in January 1917, and he was ordered to pay all the costs.[85]

In the meantime, others had found a more direct way of sharing Bob's wealth—simply stealing the gold-laden amalgam from the Skidoo mill and selling it in Grass Valley on the other side of the Sierra. Bob's superintendent became suspicious, and in April 1915 when one of the thieves, James L. Seymour, came back for more, he was arrested with 18 pounds of stolen amalgam worth $950. Seymour made a full confession, named the amalgamator at the mill as his accomplice, and turned state's evidence at the latter's trial. But the case ended up in a hung jury and charges of bribed jurors.[86]

By the time the pay ore was at last exhausted and work stopped in September 1917, the Skidoo mine had produced $1,344,500 in gold, becoming the second largest gold producer in the whole Death Valley and Amargosa country—just 5 percent short of the Montgomery Shoshone's record. The Skidoo also became the first and only real dividend-payer in the Death Valley gold boom, paying out $385,000 to stockholders. But even with dividends, the Skidoo too was still a loss for most of its stockholders. They had paid $1 or $2 a share, got back only 38½¢ a share in the course of ten years, and were left with worthless stock in the end.[87]

Only Bob Montgomery seems to have come out ahead, and not by much. As near as can be figured, Bob put about $640,000 into the Skidoo venture: three fourths of the $115,000 purchase price, for which he received 450,000 shares; an additional $400,000 for all of the treasury stock at $1 a share; and $150,000 in development loans. He apparently got back about $700,000: around $250,000 from sales of a quarter million shares during the boom; at least $230,000 from dividends on the remaining 600,000 shares he still held; $150,000 from repayment of his loans; and a final $60,000 from the sale of his remaining stock at 10¢ a share, shortly before the mine shut down. Even that was a poor return on his investment—less than 1 percent per annum over the decade. He could have done much better if he had just left the money in the bank.[88]

Poor investment that it was, the Skidoo mine was still much better than anything else he had put his money into, for by 1917 Bob Montgomery, the mining millionaire, had lost most of his fortune. None of his other mining ventures had paid, and he had lost heavily in oil speculation in Mexico. His personal life was also in a shambles. He had divorced Winnie to marry young Antoinette Schwartz aboard the *Mauritania* in July 1912, but after a whirlwind honeymoon in Europe, they too divorced. Bob never married again and, estranged from his brothers, lived alone thereafter. But he did manage to hold on to enough money to keep on speculating in mines for the rest of his life. He was working on yet another mining deal shortly before he died in Clovis, New Mexico, on August 15, 1955, at the age of 91.[89]

The Skidoo had been Bob's last Death Valley venture. After a quarter of a century, the Death Valley gold excitement ended just as it had begun—with the Montgomery Brothers. George had taken out the first gold from the Chispa in 1891, and Bob took out the last from the Skidoo in 1917.

A Copper Frenzy

In the midst of the great gold excitement, Death Valley was seized by a copper frenzy. It was an awesome and awful thing to behold. The word went out that a whole mountain of copper had been found right on the brink of Death Valley, at a place called Greenwater. Thousands of prospectors rushed in to stake it, and all the big mining operators in the country, it seemed, wanted in, or were taken in. In a whirlwind of excitement Greenwater was heralded as "the greatest copper belt the World has ever known!" A quarter of a billion dollars in stock was offered to the public in the name of Greenwater, and tens of millions of dollars were taken from them. But when it was all over, only one mine had even shipped ore, and the total recorded production of the district amounted to exactly $2,625.09. George Graham Rice called it *"the monumental mining-stock swindle of the century."* It may well have been. There was certainly no bigger, more vacuous bubble in the whole history of Death Valley and the Amargosa.[1]

At the height of the frenzy there was a lively dispute over who had in fact discovered Greenwater. Who should receive the laurels? A Los Angeles reporter even wrote a jingle:

> Who found Greenwater?
> Who was first on the hill?
> Was it Birney or Creasor,
> Or Furnace Creek Bill?
> Pick out the hero
> Who made the first journey—
> Was it Kunze, or Creasor
> Or Tenderfoot Birney?

The answer, of course, was none of the above. They were all latecomers, although they were certainly the ones who stirred up the excitement—all but "Furnace Creek Bill," that is, who was just added for the rhyme. Greenwater's copper had been known for a quarter of a century before anyone got excited about it.[2]

The first indications of copper had been found in 1880 by Nicholas Kavanaugh, an old miner from Resting Spring. He and a partner, remembered only as Tony, dug out the little spring that slowly filled with green-tinged water and gave the place a name. A couple of miles to the

310

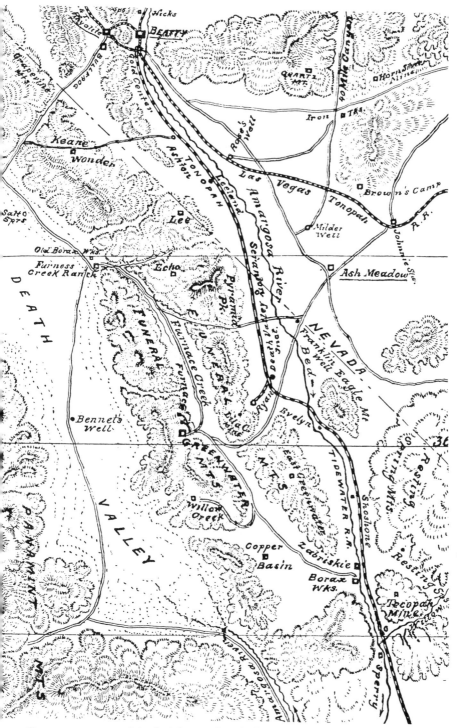

Greenwater, scene of the "mining-stock swindle of the century," from the
California State Mining Bureau's map of 1908.

(*Death Valley Chuck-Walla,* March 1, 1907, *courtesy of Bancroft Library*) north, they staked the first copper ledge and sank a shallow prospect-hole. But they soon realized that the ledge was too remote even to sell, so they let their claims lapse, only to be rediscovered and relocated by others again and again.[3]

Foremost among these later relocators was a trio from Ballarat—Frank McAllister, John Wesley "Doc" Trotter, and Robert Warnock. They relocated the ledge on March 3, 1898, as the Copper King and Copper Queen. Failing to find an interested buyer, they too let their claims lapse. But one by one they came back. Doc Trotter was the first to return in the winter of 1901–02. He had lost interest in copper by then and was chasing the Bryfogle. He didn't find it, of course, but he posted a claim just the same—a shaggy-dog classic of the locator's art:

> Notice is hereby given that we, the men that wrote this notice, are over the age of 31 years and are citizens of the United States, Cuba and the Philippines; we do this day locate one gold mine. Known as the Bryfogle, and more particularly described as follows:
>
> Commencing at this big monument of stone on a cold and rainy night and running 35 hours with Indians after him, come to a big canyon that leads up to the north with two big rocks on one side of the mouth of the canyon, the one on the right round and smooth, and the one on the left rough and rugged. These rocks stand 20 feet high. Follow up this canyon about five hours on burros or one and one-half hours on horseback you will come to the forks of the canyon. Take the left hand one and ride hard for two hours and you will come to an old stone corral. Go to the right of this about 9,000 feet and you will come to a small gulch leading up to the right. Go up this about a quarter of a mile you will come to a small hole. Sometimes it's a Dry Hole. If it's a water hole when you get there, water your animals, fill your canteen and then go on until it forks again, and then take the right hand one until it forks, then lead up the left one just a little ways and you will discover the find we have been unable to locate. The canyon is [undiscovered] yet, and we take this means of locating the big find. The map of the above described property will be furnished to anyone on application to the undersigned. Located this first day of January, 1902.
>
> Locator, J. W. TROTTER
>
> P.S.—Don't look for this mine in the summer time, as it is dangerous. DOC.[4]

In the meantime along came Shorty Harris, hearing of the copper ledge from Phi Lee. He too relocated the old ground, apparently just to have something to show for a grubstake from Judge Decker of Ballarat. Shorty gave the Judge the notices to record in Independence and thought no more of them until he heard the first news of the excitement at Greenwater.

Then Shorty rushed to the Judge to tell him of their good fortune, only to find that he had gotten drunk and forgotten to record the claims. At least that's what Shorty said, but then he claimed that the ledges eventually produced a million dollars, too![5]

Finally Frank McAllister came back. Talk of a railroad through the Amargosa country stirred memories of the abandoned copper ledges. So in the spring of 1904 McAllister and a partner, Allen Cook, got a grubstake from a Tonopah mining superintendent, Arthur Kunze—the man who would eventually claim the title of "The Father of Greenwater." They relocated the old ledges again as the Copper Queen and Copper Glance on May 22, 1904, covering the ground with sixteen claims and five fractions. But they still had trouble finding anyone willing to put money into an isolated copper prospect. That's where Birney and Creasor came in.[6]

Fred Birney and Phil Creasor had come from Spokane to the southern Nevada boom camps, and they had continued south from Goldfield hoping to find some place where no white man had ever gone before. At Ash Meadows in January 1905 they met that ill-fated Paiute Bob Black, who pointed the way to the Greenwater country. Just two days later Black went on the murderous rampage that ended in the killing of his wife, his brother, and two others.[7]

By then Birney and Creasor were camped in a dry wash north of Greenwater Spring. In the early morning light the glint of a little piece of copper float caught Birney's eye, and he was soon scrambling up the wash to find its source. Half a dozen miles above, almost to the crest of the Black Mountains, he found a great ledge he called the Copper Blue, "standing out like a wall," he said, just 3 miles northwest of McAllister's claims. He and Creasor staked half a dozen claims. Then they set out across Death Valley for Independence with a bunch of rich samples to send to an old acquaintance and prosperous Spokane mining man, Patrick Clark. Patsy, as he was generally known, was a quick-witted, practical man who had come west in 1870 and had risen from miner to mine owner in Butte and the Coeur d'Alene.[8]

The Greenwater samples were richer in copper than anything ever found on the surface at Butte, so Clark hastily dispatched a mining engineer, James P. Harvey, to investigate. It was a comedy of errors. Setting out from Daggett, Harvey lost his outfit in a cloudburst in the Avawatz Mountains and had to turn back. Refitted, he set out again and got to Greenwater Spring. But try as he might, he couldn't find Birney and Creasor's claims, and he finally returned to Spokane in disgust. The two prospectors couldn't imagine why they hadn't heard from Clark, but they persisted, sending him more rich rock. Clark at last came to Rhyolite in

March 1905, and sent his brother Dennis with another engineer down to Greenwater. They found the claims and brought back such glowing reports that Clark immediately bought a controlling interest. Greenwater copper finally had its first buyer.[9]

Patsy Clark incorporated the property on May 15, 1905, as the Furnace Creek Copper Company, with a paper capital of $1.25 million. Within the month he sent his brother Dennis out with a crew to set up camp and start exploratory work. They made surface cuts and sank a 100-foot shaft, reporting several streaks of very rich shipping ore and a massive body of smelting ore. Clark also sent out carefully picked mining engineers from Spokane, Butte, and New York, all of whom dutifully praised the property in the most extravagant terms, proclaiming it a veritable "mountain of ore and one of the most wonderful veins in the country."[10]

In the spring of 1906, Clark made his move. He brought back his engineer James Harvey as general manager to begin large-scale development; he put over $100,000 into the company treasury to finance it; and he took out nearly all of the 250,000 shares of treasury stock at half their $1 par value. Then with an active mine, rich showings, and glowing expert reports, he started talking of plans for a 300-ton-a-day smelter and of offers from both Borax Smith and Senator William Clark to run railroads to the mine "upon request." The Furnace Creek Copper Company, still little more than a prospect, suddenly became a thing to be reckoned with. And Patsy Clark, with some skillful help, began to let out the shares on the New York Curb and the mining exchanges of San Francisco, Los Angeles, Spokane, and Butte. They were snapped up instantly, and prices skyrocketed. That was mostly the work of John "Bet-A-Million" Gates, who made the market on the New York Curb. Gates, having made a fortune in the barbed-wire business in the Midwest, had gone to New York and made a reputation for reckless and unscrupulous speculation that would eventually cause J. P. Morgan to drive him out of the market. Gates took a block of 400,000 shares of Furnace Creek Copper at about 50¢ each; Patsy spread the word that Gates had paid a whopping $3.25 a share for them; and by June they were selling on the exchanges all across the country for $4.25, rising eventually to $5.25. The Greenwater copper frenzy had begun.[11]

The frenzy started so quickly that most of those in Death Valley and the Amargosa didn't know a thing about it until they suddenly heard that there was a bunch of barely scratched copper claims out on the brink of Death Valley with stock selling from coast to coast at a market valuation of over $5 million! There hadn't even been enough men out there to warrant forming a mining district. But all of that quickly changed. It didn't take long for veteran prospectors and promoters to see that there was quick and easy money to be made in Greenwater copper, and they rushed in for a piece of it. They had already learned that it was just as important—if not more so—to have a market as to have a mine, and Patsy Clark and "Bet-A-Million" Gates had clearly shown there was a market for Greenwater copper.[12]

Copper had, in fact, become the most profitable metal in Western mining. The rapid growth of the electrical industry had created a seemingly insatiable demand for the metal. By the end of 1905 Western copper mines were producing roughly $100 million a year and paying annual dividends of some $26 million—surpassing that of all the gold, silver, and other metal mines combined. It was no wonder that investors and speculators were "crazy over copper stocks" and went into a "frenzy" over the news that a new copper bonanza had been found in Death Valley.[13]

The first outsiders to cash in on all the excitement that Patsy Clark was generating were Arthur Kunze and his partners. In December 1905, raising a few thousand dollars from Tonopah lumberman-promoter Jack Salsberry, Kunze hired a crew of five to set up a camp and do a little exploration of their claims. They soon opened a network of surface fractures with ore shoots carrying up to 25 percent copper. But it was not until Patsy got the stock excitement going that they too finally found a buyer—none other than Steel King Charley Schwab, fresh from his purchase of the Montgomery Shoshone. Malcolm Macdonald and Donald Gillies made a hasty auto trip down from Rhyolite and bonded the property in June 1906, giving Kunze and his partners at least $180,000 in cash and a promise of about 10 percent of the stock. The following month Schwab organized the Greenwater and Death Valley Copper Company, with a capital offering of 3 million shares at $1 par. Gillies was general manager. Following Patsy's plan, Schwab and his associates put a quarter of a million dollars into the company treasury to finance large-scale exploratory work in three shafts, and they took out at least a quarter of a million shares of treasury stock. In the growing frenzy they easily worked the stock up to over $2 a share, and before the end of the year they were unloading it at over $3.50. By that point Schwab, like Clark, had all of his money back out of the company, plus a profit, and he still had most of the stock to sell.[14]

The stampede to Greenwater began in the scorching days of late July and early August 1906. By July 29 there were seventy men gathered at the little spring to belatedly organize the Greenwater Mining District. Hundreds more arrived each week. Within a month there were nearly a thousand men on the ground. Close behind, in autos chartered at $100 a day, came the laced-boot crowd of mining engineers and promoters, all shopping for claims. There were plenty to choose from. Every piece of ground was staked, it seems, just because it was there. Some 4,500 claims were filed, covering roughly 150 square miles! Yet there wasn't a mine in the whole lot.[15]

There was easy money in some of those claims for the locators, and a lot more for the promoters who bought them. Even the rankest greenhorns, such as teenagers Ed Bahten, dubbed the Furnace Creek Kid, and C. M. Wandell, known as the Greenwater Kid, made quick money. But they lost it nearly as fast. The Greenwater Kid picked up $12,000 for his share of some ground he helped to locate, but he dropped most of it within a few days at the gaming tables in Rhyolite's 66 Club. He then had the chutzpah to sue the club owner for $10,000, claiming his loss was illegal because he was underage! A sympathetic jury awarded him $2,762.50, which was more than the whole Greenwater district produced. The Furnace Creek Kid, who had earned his name working at the borax company's ranch, got somewhere between $5,000 and $30,000 for a group of claims he staked. He promptly set himself up in Greenwater as an expert on real estate and mining investments, but he is said to have lost everything within six weeks on bad deals and a fling in San Francisco. At the other extreme there was a skillful but unnamed mining engineer who worked one deal both ways, or so the story goes. He grubstaked a prospector to locate a few claims, took a nice profit on their sale, then turned around and collected a fee from the buyer for telling him they were no good. In all, Greenwater boosters claimed that roughly $3 million was paid out for the purchase of claims. Only a small part of that was in cash; the bulk was, as always, in stock. Of course that's where the big money was to be made, but the seller's stock was generally locked up in a "pool" while the promoters worked up the price and unloaded theirs.[16]

The rush to Greenwater sparked the inevitable townsite war. Within the first two weeks of August, three towns were born. Kunze laid out the first town, naturally called Greenwater, in the wash just below his camp where most of the early arrivals had taken up ground. Clark also surveyed a townsite, dubbed Furnace, near his camp, but he was too busy selling stock to take much interest in town lots. Then came Harry Ramsey of the Chispa mine war fame, who had bought out McAllister's mining interests. He located a rival town, Copperfield, halfway between Kunze's and Clark's, and the townsite war began in earnest.[17]

Kunze's Greenwater had not only the magic name but most early advantages as well: the first store, the first saloon, the first post office, and the first newspaper, the *Greenwater Times*. It was launched on October 23 by two former Butte newsmen, James Brown and Frank L. Reber. They had started Las Vegas' first paper, also called the *Times,* the previous year, but gave that up for a chance in what they hoped would become

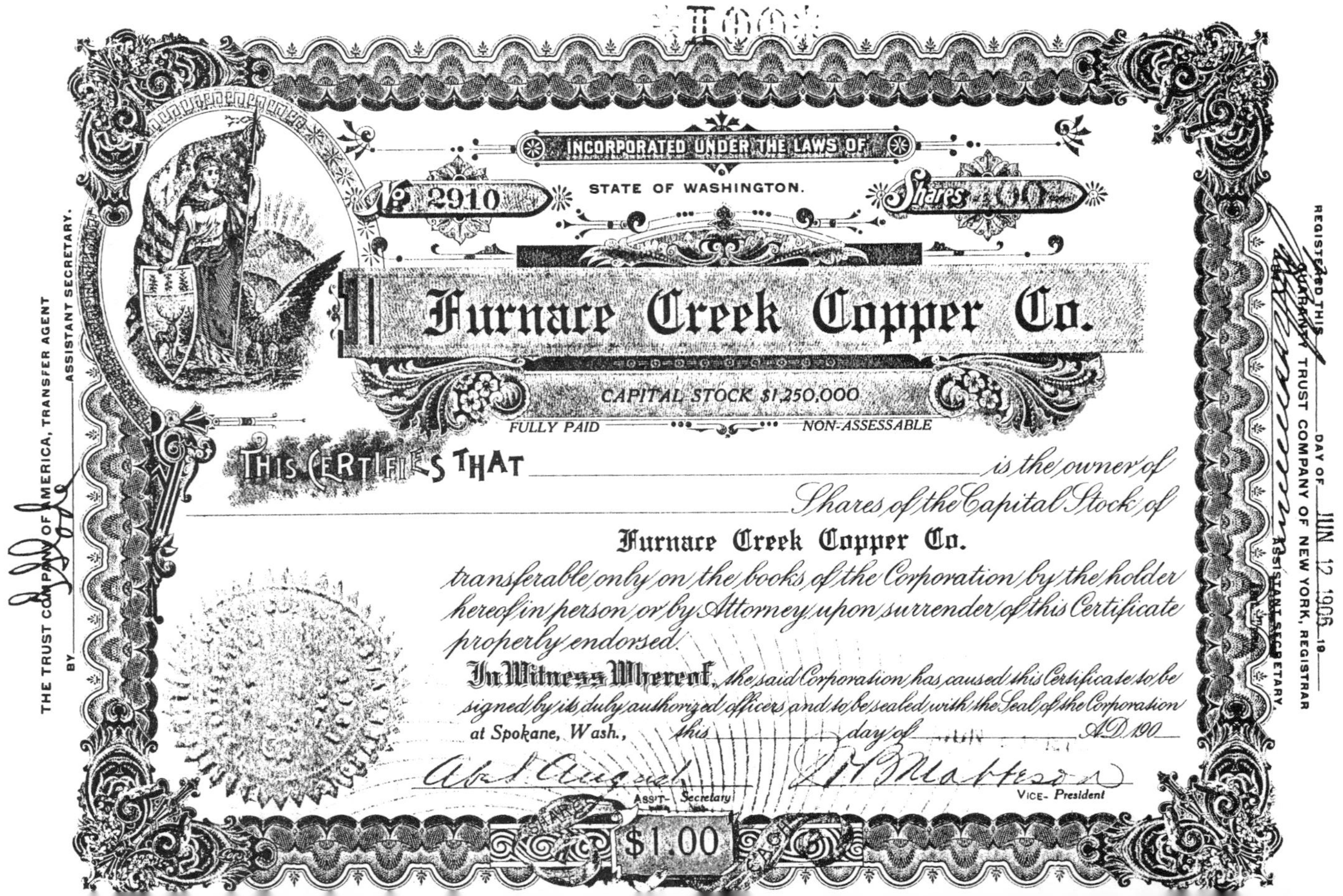

No. 2910

INCORPORATED UNDER THE LAWS OF

STATE OF WASHINGTON.

Shares

Furnace Creek Copper Co.

CAPITAL STOCK $1,250,000

FULLY PAID — NON-ASSESSABLE

THIS CERTIFIES THAT ______________ is the owner of ______________ Shares of the Capital Stock of

Furnace Creek Copper Co.

transferable only on the books of the Corporation by the holder hereof in person or by Attorney upon surrender of this Certificate properly endorsed.

In Witness Whereof, the said Corporation has caused this Certificate to be signed by its duly authorized officers and to be sealed with the Seal of the Corporation at Spokane, Wash., this ______ day of ______ A.D. 190__

ASS'T-Secretary — VICE-President

$1.00

REGISTERED THIS ______ DAY OF JUN 12 1906 19__

GUARANTY TRUST COMPANY OF NEW YORK, REGISTRAR

BY ______ ASSISTANT SECRETARY.

THE TRUST COMPANY OF AMERICA, TRANSFER AGENT

BY ______ ASSISTANT SECRETARY.

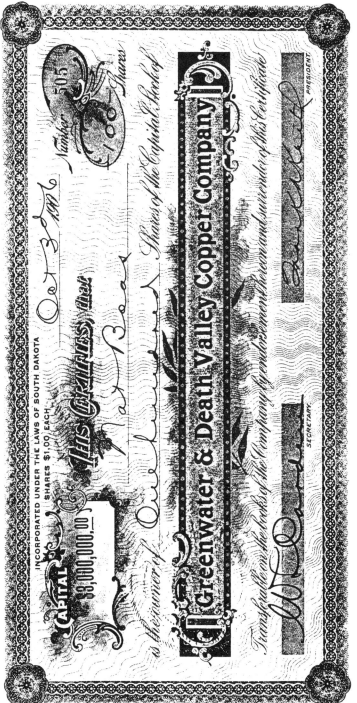

Investors lost tens of millions in the Greenwater bubble. These shares, promoted by Patsy Clark and Charley Schwab, were the biggest cons.

"The Greatest Copper City of the Century." The rapid growth of Kunze's town, however, pointed up what boosters saw as its greatest fault—the wash in which it sat was too cramped to hold even the burgeoning camp of a thousand, let alone the city of five thousand expected by spring, or the metropolis of ten thousand predicted within a year![18]

Harry Ramsey had envisioned that need for elbow room early in September when he moved his fledgling townsite of Copperfield a few miles to the east, out into Greenwater Valley, where there was room enough for a hundred thousand fools if need be. Charley Schwab blessed the new site, and Nevada banker turned U.S. Senator George S. Nixon gave it his blessings as well, setting up the district's first and only bank in a corrugated iron building Ramsey had hauled down from Rhyolite. Other dreamers followed, among them Major John F. A. Strong, former editor of the *Nome Nugget,* who came down from Alaska to start the *Greenwater Miner* at Ramsey's town late in December.[19]

Kunze answered Ramsey's challenge with a lawsuit. He claimed Ramsey was squatting on his ground, and he produced the mining locations to prove it. Ramsey, unabashed, added insult to injury by renaming his town Greenwater too. The dispute was finally resolved late in November, when Jack Salsberry and three partners bought out both Kunze and Ramsey. Salsberry gave the citizens of Kunze's Greenwater comparable lots in the rival town, and in early December he began moving them in a mass exodus to merge the two Greenwaters at Ramsey's site. A carnival atmosphere prevailed en route.[20] As one exoduster wrote

> Pandemonium reigns. Saloons and boarding houses, stores and brokerage firms are doing business on the run and trying to be on both sides of the mountain at one time. A barkeep puts down his case of bottles on a knoll en route from the old camp to the new and serves the passing throng laden with bedding and store fixtures. A shot of skee or a glass of lager lightens the load, and the burden is taken up to the next station. The butcher kills a cow en route and deals out steaks and roasts to the hungry multitude hurrying back to the old camp to get the necessaries for the new. The grocer opens a case of coffee and a can of cream and catches the business going both ways. Those who remain in the old camp are walking two miles to the new to get the eggs for breakfast. Those who have journeyed to the new are walking two miles to the old to get their mail, and a pair of socks, which the travel has made necessary, but which the new town does not yet afford.[21]

Growing room was really the least of Greenwater's problems. Next to the lack of pay rock, water was its biggest shortcoming—and certainly the most immediate need for all the hopefuls who had rushed out there.

Greenwater Spring itself was useless, no more than a seep of a few gallons a day—hardly sufficient for a man or a burro. The water for Greenwater had to be hauled at least 18 miles from springs in Furnace Creek Wash. Several teams pulling 500-gallon tank wagons were busy full time just trying to keep up with the demand. But they often drank as much as they delivered. One particularly hot day, so the story goes, the teams drank the whole load and struggled into the camp thirsting for more. Water rarely sold for less than $7.50 a barrel in Greenwater—half again as much as the top price in any other Death Valley camp—and at the height of the rush prices climbed to $15 or more. During one "water famine," when the teams had broken down, thirsty Greenwaterites drank up everything in sight that would pour, even making a run on canned tomato puree. One go-getter is said to have dashed off to Furnace Creek with a borrowed team and brought back two barrels of the precious fluid, giving one to the owner of the team and selling the other by the canteen and pailful for $30. Even in less trying times some recycled their water as many as three times—first to bathe in, then to wash clothes in, and finally for the mules to drink! Other necessities were nearly as scarce, or as dear. Jackrabbit was usually the only fresh meat, and gasoline at $1 a gallon or greasewood at nearly $300 a cord was all there was to keep warm by when the first snow fell in December.[22]

Nonetheless, by the spring of 1907 "Greater Greenwater," as the merged camp came to be known, had at least the appearance of a prosperous mining town. Boosters claimed a population of two thousand; even Clark's fledgling Furnace was said to have attracted five hundred. Greenwater town lots were selling for up to $5,000 a piece. There were twenty frame buildings and hundreds of tents. A quarter of a million dollars worth of construction contracts had been let, and Jack Salsberry couldn't haul in the lumber fast enough, even with a giant twenty-two-horse team. There was every essential: restaurants and lodging houses, general stores and a bank, barbershops and a shoe repair, doctors and a dentist, assayers and surveyors, telephones and telegraph—even lawyers, brokers, and an undertaker. Greenwater, in fact, temporarily surpassed Rhyolite in newspapers and with two weeklies, the *Times* and the *Miner,* and its own semimonthly magazine, the *Death Valley Chuck-Walla,* begun on New Year's Day. The Greenwater Miners' Union, organized even before the mining district as Local No. 207 of the Western Federation, was building a hall and raising money for a hospital. Civic-minded Greenwaterites had formed a town committee to attend to sanitation and squatters, and the Inyo County supervisors had appointed a justice of the peace and constable. There were even promises of ample water. The townsite company was sinking a well. The Ash Meadows Water Company, organized by Rhyolite Judge L. O. Ray with Scranton, Pennsylvania money, had started work on a 30-mile pipeline from Longstreet Spring and a 15-million-gallon reservoir in a canyon above the town. A rival visionary talked of a 25-mile pipeline across Death Valley from Telescope Peak and a giant hydroelectric plant in the valley to electrify the mines and the town.[23]

Two stage lines were running, and there were predictions of three railroads by summer. The Kimball Brothers ran daily stages 50 miles from Johnnie siding on the Las Vegas and Tonopah Railroad—an $18, two-day trip with a night at Ralph Fairbanks's Ash Meadows ranch. A rival stage ran every other day, 40 miles from Dumont, the railhead of the Tonopah and Tidewater, for only $10, also taking two days, with a night at the old Amargosa borax works. That famous mahout "Alkali Bill" Brong outran them both, making the trip in just three hours with his Death Valley Chug Line auto, which he also chartered for $100 a day. Preliminary surveys had been run for short line railroads connecting with the Las Vegas and Tonopah, the Tonopah and Tidewater, and the Bullfrog Goldfield. Borax Smith had even gone so far as to incorporate a Tonopah and Greenwater Railroad Company, which he said would start building a 37-mile line to Greenwater from the old Amargosa borax work just as soon as his Tonopah and Tidewater railhead reached there.[24]

Greenwater didn't lack for amusement, either. There were more saloons than anything else, and they packed in the thirsty crowds in such stylish spots as the Greenwater Club and such homely dens as the Do Drop In and the Cozy Retreat. Although it was illegal in California, the saloons also sported faro layouts and roulette wheels, which were discreetly tucked out of sight the one time the law came over from Independence. And, needless to say, Greenwater had a lively line of cribs. The most fondly remembered was that of Tiger Lil, "a tall, willowy, slightly wilted gal, with flaming red hair, flaming disposition, and enough freckles to complete justification of the name." Legend also brightened her smile with four sparkling diamonds in her teeth![25]

The would-be metropolis had even been baptized in blood in December 1906, with two inglorious shootings, one fatal. The first started with a dispute over a momentous debt of $2.50. It ended with the debtor shot in the leg with a 38-caliber Smith and Wesson, and his trigger-happy creditor run out of the camp by an impromptu citizens' committee. Just a few days later, Donald Chism was hit in the head by a load of birdshot from an "unloaded" shotgun in the hands of a friend, Billie Waters. Chism died instantly. Waters, a popular bartender, said his friend had been examining the gun when the trigger jammed and had handed it to him to fix, which he did, with deadly results. Local gossip had it that they were jokingly menacing one another over the payment of a drink. It was a stupid accident either way, but it was Greenwater's only homicide.[26]

Greenwater's real claim to fame, however, was the pungent little *Death Valley Chuck-Walla,* "A Magazine for Men—Published on the desert at the brink of Death Valley, Mixing the dope, cool from the mountains and hot from the desert, and withal putting out a concoction with which you can do as you damn please as soon as you have paid for it." It measured barely 4 by 6 inches and was printed on brown butcher paper, but it had a sharp bite. "If you don't like it, don't read it," its editors snapped:

> If you do read it remember these facts. What it says is true; what it does is honest; it will call a liar a liar, a thief a thief, or an ass an ass, as is justified, and if you don't like it you may kick and be damned. Its editors are its owners, and will do as they see fit with their own, restricting themselves only in so far as they are restricted by their demand for the truth, and their wish to give the devil his due.[27]

Even though the *Chuck-Walla* wasn't quite as independent or as high principled as it pretended to be, it was without question the liveliest, most entertaining little paper that ever came out of the desert country. It was a curious mix of sophomoric macho, prospector yarns, and huckster pitches. Its forty or more pages were filled with lost mine lore and perilous and mysterious tales of Death Valley; with poems, fables, and a two-act play; and with windy puffs of Greenwater men, mines, and stock. Greenwaterites eagerly ate it all up, and so did ten thousand others, so its editors claimed, all the way to Wall Street and the White House.[28]

The *Chuck-Walla* was the creation of two brash young newspaper cubs, Curt E. Kunze and Carl Burgess Glasscock, each with barely a year's experience on the *San Francisco Examiner.* Glasscock liked to say that they had started the magazine with just $35.35 between them. But Kunze's brother Arthur, Greenwater's founding father, put up the real money. Glasscock's brother Harry also joined in to do the printing. A few critics claimed the magazine was just an imitation of Eastern satirist Elbert Hubbard's freewheeling *Philistine,* "A Periodical of Protest." But there was no protest behind the *Chuck-Walla's* creed, just pure promotion. "The game on the desert is to make money," the *Chuck-Walla* preached. "Bet your stack against fortune. . . . You can't break the dealer. God Almighty is holding the bank roll in the shape of the minerals which he placed in the desert. He won't break. There's no limit. The game on the desert is to make money." Brokers swore such talk "really sold stock," and the young tyros were "very proud of it." But years later Glasscock confided he was "a little ashamed now."[29]

The *Chuck-Walla* was, in fact, the Greenwater bubble's biggest puffer. It was aptly named, too. Its cold-blooded namesake is best known for its peculiar defense. When threatened, it takes a stance between two rocks and puffs itself up until almost nothing can dislodge it. The little "maglet"

The Death Valley Chuck=Walla

A MAGAZINE FOR MEN

Volume 1, Number 1.
Greenwater, California
January the 1st, 1907.

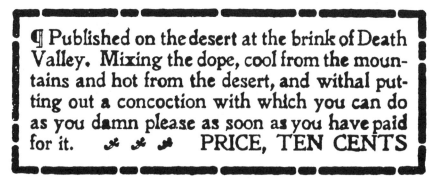

❡ Published on the desert at the brink of Death Valley. Mixing the dope, cool from the mountains and hot from the desert, and withal putting out a concoction with which you can do as you damn please as soon as you have paid for it. ✄ ✄ ✄ PRICE, TEN CENTS

(Courtesy of Bancroft Library)

did the same, puffing furiously whenever Greenwater came under attack, and it held on until the last, too—until nearly all the air had leaked out of the bubble.

The stock frenzy that Patsy Clark had started was still far ahead of any excitement on the ground. His Furnace Creek Copper shares had sky-rocketed, and the public still clamored for more, so Clark created a new company on neighboring ground, Furnace Valley Copper, with 1.25 million shares at $5 par; then another, Kempland Copper, with 1.25 million more shares at $5; and finally, as the demand at last began to slacken, one more, Clark Cooper, with yet another 1.25 million shares at a bargain $1 par—until he had turned out fully $15 million in paper. Not to be outdone, Charley Schwab, the great consolidator, merged his Green-water and Death Valley Copper with four other worthless companies in December 1906 to form a grand consolidation, the Greenwater Copper Mines and Smelter Company, watering his original $3 million par shares to $25 million![30]

All the while, of course, Clark and Schwab fed the speculative fever with telegraphic dispatches of more wonderful ore strikes, more expert appraisals of "a mountain of ore," more talk of railroads and smelters, and even rumors of a deal with the Guggenheims. That must have been what feverish buyers wanted to hear, for none seems to have noticed, much less cared, that the only thing these multimillion-dollar companies had done to develop their enormous bonanzas was to hire a few dozen miners and buy a little gasoline hoist or two. Nor did investors seem concerned that, despite all the talk of wonderfully rich ore, not a ton of it had yet been shipped, nor had any outsiders ever been allowed underground to see it. Even if Clark or Schwab did believe that there was a chance of striking pay ore at depth, they were in no hurry to find out for sure—not as long as there was easy money to be made just selling stock.[31]

Such was the frenzy for Greenwater stock that by the fall of 1906 hundreds of promoters all across the country had eagerly joined in to get a piece of the action. They patted each other on the back, claiming among their ranks "all the Copper Kings, and many of the Copper Princes," "the greatest collection of millionaires and mine makers ever interested in any single mining camp." High in the ranks, of course, were Patsy Clark, "Bet-A-Million" Gates, and "Steel King" Charley Schwab. They were joined by Montana's "Copper King" and railroad-building Senator William A. Clark; Utah's copper baron, Samuel Newhouse; and two popular princes of copper finance—F. Augustus Heinze, the hard-driving boy wonder of Butte, who had just emerged victorious from a David and Goliath bout with the giant Rockefeller trust, the Amalgamated Copper Company; and Thomas W. Lawson, the wily Boston speculator whose muckraking exposé, *Frenzied Finance—The Crime of Amalgamated,* had made him the instant hero of the little investors, though critics would call him a "Billy Sunday of Finance." The Greenwater boosters even claimed in their legion the powerful Guggenheims and the whole Amalgamated crowd, including John D. himself, but that was pure hype—Greenwater was too raw a deal for their tastes. Among the legion of boosters, however, were many of Death Valley and southern Nevada's most successful operators—Bob Montgomery, Malcolm Macdonald, George Graham Rice, Donald Mackenzie, Thomas B. Rickey, George Wingfield, Tasker Oddie, John W. Brock, Senators George Nixon and Francis Newlands, and Governor John Sparks—all of whom joined the push of Greenwater stock. But the biggest pushers of Greenwater paper were the brokers of Goldfield, Tonopah, Butte, Los Angeles, and New York, who also created their own offerings for the occasion.[32]

More than a hundred mining companies were formed in the name of Greenwater to push on the public nearly a quarter of a billion dollars in stock. Some actually put crews to work on their claims, at least long enough to dig a shallow hole to call a shaft and pose for promotional photos. Most were much cruder. Two-thirds of them didn't even bother to file incorporation papers in California, as was expected if they intended to do anything at all in Greenwater. But, their sole business, of course, was selling stock elsewhere. In the blind frenzy of speculation then raging, they didn't need a mine; any worthless piece of ground was more than sufficient. Some didn't even bother with that. All they really needed was the magic word "Greenwater" on their stock and an ad in a newspaper.[33]

A name, in fact, was all that some companies seemed to offer—in addition to their stock, that is. Such was the Guggenheim-Greenwater Copper Company, a penny-a-share mail-order stock that blatantly advertised, "YOU HAVE HEARD of the Guggenheims . . . YOU HAVE READ about Greenwater . . . BUY INTO BOTH," when in truth you got neither! Others played subtler name games. Imitating Schwab's Greenwater and Death Valley Copper Company, one promoter dubbed his creation Greenwater Death Valley Mining Company. Another mimicked Clark's Furnace Creek Copper Company with a Greenwater Furnace Creek Copper Company. The latter even had the cheek to publish a "WARNING" to investors to beware of a nonexistent Greenwater Furnace Creek Copper *Mining* Company, confiding, "It is an old trick among mining promoters to organize a company with a name much similar to some well-known property, thereby gaining advantage from the advertising thus cheaply obtained."[34]

No boast, no promise was too outrageous for boldface headlines in the ads that shouted, "GREENWATER . . . the GREATEST COPPER CAMP the World has ever known!" "An inexhaustible deposit of Copper," they cried, "in the rapacious maws of this Man-devouring monster"—Death Valley. "IMMENSE PROFITS AND IMMENSE DIVIDENDS" were sure to follow. "A minimum profit of 100%" within a month, 700% in less than a year, total returns of "A HUNDRED FOR ONE," "fortunes . . . that will stagger the imagination, and make the millions produced yearly from the great Superior mines, Butte, Montana, United Verde and Jerome sink into insignificance"—all would flow from Greenwater stock bought today! There wasn't even any risk; Greenwater was "AS SAFE AS A BANK," "guaranteed against loss." But hurry, "get on board a Good Thing . . . take passage with us for the Port of Wealth . . . MILLIONS UPON MIL-LIONS WILL BE MADE . . . by those who dared." [35]

The awful frenzy over Greenwater even stirred up fleeting copper excitements elsewhere in Death Valley, at Ubehebe, Willow Creek, and Crackerjack.

Copper had been found at Ubehebe, on the other side of Death Valley, by William Hunter and John Porter in 1875—well before the first Greenwater strike. They and others had tried everything they could think of to make it pay, with no success. Hunter, however, never gave up, holding his claims until his death in 1902. Like Greenwater, the Ubehebe ore simply wasn't rich enough to ship, and there wasn't enough of it to warrant putting up a smelter. During the Greenwater frenzy, however, none of that mattered, so Ubehebe finally had its boom, although it too was only on paper. [36]

One resourceful group of promoters, led by A. D. Whittier, a cartoonist from the *Bullfrog Miner* who said he was a nephew of the poet, even romanticized the failures of the past to help sell stock. In the fall of 1906 Whittier and his friends happened upon the ruins of a couple of arrastras, a little ore roaster, and a few stone walls—the remnants of Hunter's futile efforts. Staking claim to the ruins and some nearby ground, they grandly announced that they had discovered a fabulous "Lost Spanish mine" that had been sought for fifty years. Although they lacked the flair of B. X. Dawson, they too imagined that the mine must have been worked by Indians before the Spaniards, and speculated on what awful fate might have befallen the Spanish miners. Had they been driven off by hostile Indians; had they perished on the desert; or had they simply given up because there was so much copper in the ore that it couldn't be worked by their primitive methods? Whatever the case, it made enticing stuff for a mining promotion, so they obligingly formed the Ubehebe Mining Company around its "ruins and romance," offering $1 shares for 15¢ and advertising, "IT'S NEW, IT'S OLD, IT'S RICH . . . GET IN NOW." [37]

Several other Ubehebe companies formed during the boom, including the Ulida Copper Company, organized by Salt Lake operators on Hunter's actual claims. Ubehebe's biggest operator was Jack Salsberry from Green-

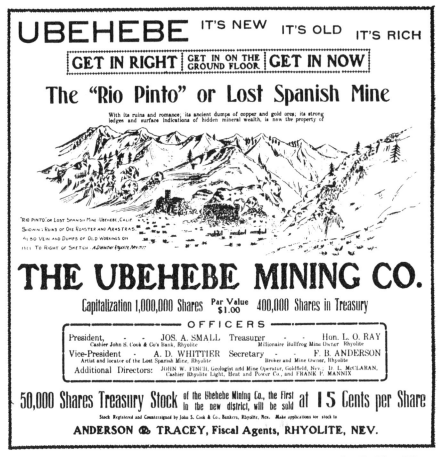

Ubehebe promoters invented a "lost mine" to help sell their stock. (*Bullfrog Miner,* May 24, 1907)

water. Salsberry first came in August 1906, and took up, some said, as many as 500 claims! Then in partnership with a Baltimore speculator, Henry G. Merry, he formed the Ubehebe Copper Mines and Smelter Company, with 3 million shares at $1 par, which he started pushing at 25¢. To hear Salsberry tell it, Ubehebe too was a veritable mountain of copper. By the time he had two shafts down barely 85 feet, he claimed to have "in sight fully 50,000,000 tons" of ore running anywhere from 10 percent copper to the pure metal—at least a billion dollars worth of copper! Like Clark and Schwab at Greenwater, Salsberry talked grandly of building a railroad and a smelter. He even printed up a $1 million bond issue for the railroad, which was to run 60 miles across Death Valley and up Grapevine Canyon to connect with the Las Vegas and Tonopah line. He actually built an auto road over that route to bring in several carloads of Eastern investors. A couple of miles northwest of Racetrack dry lake, Salsberry laid out a little townsite, which he first called Salina City and renamed Latimer to flatter a heavy investor, Cleveland traction magnate Jay E. Latimer. It was a questionable honor, however, for even at its peak the camp never had more than twenty tents, and its business was limited to the company store, a lodging tent, feed yard, and two saloons. It didn't even rate a post office. A rival Ubehebe City was started at the south end of the Racetrack, but it amounted to even less.[38]

Willow Creek, although organized as a separate mining district, was little more than a suburb of Greenwater, lying over on the Death Valley side of the Black Mountains just 10 miles to the south. Its biggest attraction was not its copper but the creek itself—an inch deep, a foot wide, a mile long, and the only live stream in the whole barren range. Prospectors fanning out from Greenwater discovered the little oasis in July 1906, and convinced themselves that there were enough copper indications thereabout to justify a camp. That fall Chet Leavitt from the Echo district established the first town, Copper Basin, near the springs that give rise to the stream. Soon after that, Ernest Mattinson, who styled himself Death Valley Slim, started a second town, Willow Creek. Slim quickly got the edge of his Mormon rival by opening a saloon, and by the end of the year Copper Basin was dead. The following spring, however, some of the boys sitting around the saloon played a joke on a stranger that backfired and nearly depopulated Willow Creek.[39]

It had been a standing joke. Whenever a tenderfoot arrived in camp asking where to find some good ground, the boys would helpfully direct him to three little hills of couple of miles to the south which they all knew were barren. After a day or two the tenderfoot would return sheepishly, realizing that the boys had gotten a good laugh and that the drinks were on him. So it was when Joe Witherell arrived in May 1907. The boys eagerly directed him to those little hills. As the days passed, however, and he failed to return, they began to wonder. Was he so dense he couldn't see that he had been joshed, or was he just so embarrassed that he was ashamed to return? At last they saw him trudging back into town, and all gathered around him to watch him blush. To their surprise, the joke was on them: on the side of one of those little hills, Witherell had discovered a ledge of quartz specked with gold, and scattered all around were immense boulders "as large as a house and filled with gold"—each one, it seemed, worth a fortune in itself. There was an instant stampede, and the word went out that the strike was so rich that this time there could be no doubt the "Real and Only Breyfogle" had been found at last. Even a rusty old gun barrel and a broken watch found nearby were displayed in Rhyolite as "BREYFOGLE'S." For a time men guarded their ground with guns, and a man couldn't even leave long enough to bathe in the creek without his claim being jumped. Gold Valley, a grand new town of ninety-six city blocks laid out by the Goldsworthy brothers, quickly became the new boss camp of the district.[40]

Willow Creek withered, and with it Slim's fortunes. Instead of moving on with the others he just sat in his saloon and watched Willow Creek die. In a peevish fit, he finally smashed all the glasses, set his wet goods on the counter, and let the few remaining boys go at it. When they had finished, Slim tossed the cash register, money and all, into the sagebrush and set fire to the saloon. Then he lit out for Greenwater, where he made more mischief before the deputy sheriff, Charlie Brown, finally locked him up.[41]

A little farther south near the old Ibex mine, Otto Donnell and a couple partners heading for Greenwater happened upon a vein of copper-, gold-, and silver-bearing ore in June 1906. They named it the Rusty Pick and immediately set to work picking out the high-grade. But Donnell fell victim to the desiccating heat a month later, while trying to haul out their first load of ore, and his partners sold out to the Busch Brothers. They organized the Rusty Pick Consolidated Mines Company and succeeded in getting out a few shipments of high-grade while they tried to unload the mine on Eastern investors.[42]

Others, meanwhile, were stirring up a little excitement nearby with the invention of new "lost mines," the tragic legacies of two more Death Valley victims, Albert Rhodes and Judge Bethune. In the winter of 1885 Rhodes had found a pocket of silver ore that he called his Black Metal mine, 7 miles south of the spring that now bears his name. During the next year or so he packed out enough shipping rock to attract a prospective buyer. But he died, it is said, en route to the mine with the would-be purchaser, and the deal fell through. Then in 1894 his cousin, a man named Spegler, relocated the mine, but reportedly went out to work it and was never heard from again. In November 1905 three greenhorns discovered the old shaft and proudly announced that the "famous" lost mine was found at last. Then they found that Rhodes had cleaned out nearly all the paying rock before he decided to sell.[43]

Lawrence Bethune, a tireless septuagenarian, had discovered a silver and copper ledge near Ibex Spring in 1901. Some of the rock ran into the thousands per ton, but because of its remoteness he did little more than the annual assessment work needed to hold the claim for the next few years. In June 1905, however, he was finally heading back to thoroughly explore the claim when he died in the north end of Death Valley, apparently trying to rescue two lost tenderfeet, Titus and Weller.

Even before Bethune's body was found, an eager bunch of promoters led by A. G. Cushman of Rhyolite, relocated the ground as the Lost Bethune. Then forming a mining company of the same name, they started pushing 1.25 million shares of stock with a string of stories capitalizing on the tragic fate of its discoverer. They stretched the stories a little more with each telling, until they had finally made poor Bethune into a latter-day Breyfogle, dying in a whiskey-crazed quest for a fabulous ledge whose location he could no longer recall. When that was nearly worked out, they started shrouding the "Great Lost Bethune" in mystery. With the help of a few arrowheads and other artifacts, they transformed the crumbling walls of the old Ibex mill into mysterious ancient ruins that antedated the coming of even the Spaniards! Finally they succeeded in stripping out over $13,000 worth of high-grade to help unload the last of the stock before they finally abandoned the mine. Even that was a lot more than all the Greenwater mines ever produced.[44]

Down in the Avawatz Mountains at the south end of Death Valley, other prospectors discovered a couple of old arrastras dating from Johnny Moss's activities in the early 1870s. Like Whittier at Ubehebe, they too imagined that they had stumbled upon some lost mines worked by Spanish miners nearly a hundred years before. In the surrounding rocks, they envisioned bonanzas of gold, copper, silver, and lead. It was a crackerjack find, so in October 1906 they organized it as the Crackerjack Mining District. The copper showings alone were said to be richer than Greenwater's. Rumor had it that Schwab and Clark were buying up the ground, and the Furnace Creek Kid, Ed Bahten, squandered his Greenwater pile on Crackerjack claims. The Tonopah and Tidewater Railroad was already completed along the east side of the district, and the Crackerjack Auto Transit Company started running a Pope Toledo daily, 20 miles from Silver Lake station. Five hundred hopefuls flocked in. Townsites appeared everywhere. Crackerjack and Copper City were the leading camps, but Arastra, Avawatz, Cave Springs, Copper Center, and Denning Springs were eager contenders. Copper City claimed a population of one hundred by the time it was ten days old, and it was the scene of the district's first and only homicide, when Fremont Cole shot John Ward over a claim dispute in April 1907. But Crackerjack had the name and succeeded in getting the post office in February and a printer, Herbert Stanton, to start a paper, the *Crackerjack News,* in May.[45]

By the winter of 1906–07 the Greenwater stock excitement had turned into a feeding frenzy for mining sharks. Swarms of gudgeons and minnows had been lured in with the simple bait of big names and big talk, and the ensuing carnage was awful. By the end of 1906, it was said, small investors had sunk $18 million into Greenwater stock. By the time the slaughter was over, George Graham Rice claimed that the smallfry had lost fully $30 million![46]

It had turned into such a frenzy that sharks were even attacking sharks. First the Greenwater sharks attacked one another, then other Western sharks attacked them, and finally the Wall Street sharks attacked them all—each and every one battling for a bigger bite of the gudgeons. It began on November 30, 1906, when George Graham Rice, through his Chicago agent, brought suit against a rival shark, Dr. John Grant Lyman, for fraudulent misrepresentation of Boston-Greenwater Copper Mining Company stock and misappropriation of $200,000 from the sale of it. The debonair doctor had a tainted past—albeit hardly as tainted as Rice's. He had specialized in diseases of the ear at the New York Homeopathic College, but after a few years selling patented gold eardrums in Chicago, he had returned to New York City to turn his talents to mining stock promotions. His grandest scheme had been the flotation of the International Zinc Company, Ltd., on a few claims in Joplin, Missouri in 1900. The good doctor was said to have culled about half a million dollars from that operation, with which he acquired a stable of racehorses, several fast cars, and a seat on the New York Stock Exchange. He was soon forced to sell the later, however, when the zinc promotion was exposed as a fraud. Lyman then turned his attention to the racetrack, until the Bullfrog excitement brought him West.[47]

Lyman and Rice had crossed paths before, first at the track at Saratoga and then at Bullfrog, and rumor had it that an old grudge—or perhaps just "professional jealousy"—was behind Rice's suit. Whatever the reason, Rice would soon regret the decision. But for the moment at least, he eagerly publicized the fraud charges against Lyman with sensational press releases from his Goldfield news agency. Lyman condemned himself by slipping out of his hotel room in the middle of the night to escape arrest. Pinkerton detectives finally captured him in Boston, but Rice quietly dropped the suit for a small cash settlement, because he was suddenly in serious trouble of his own.[48]

The attack on Lyman was just what the Wall Street sharks needed to launch a much wider-ranging attack of their own through the Eastern press. At least that's the way the Western press saw it. The Lyman exposé was "received with the utmost relish by the Eastern press," one Goldfield editor claimed, as proof positive of the inherent fraud of mining stock speculation, not just in Greenwater but throughout the West. Moreover, the muckraking magazines quickly dispatched special correspondents to the West to ferret out more frauds. Western mining editors were nearly unanimous in claiming that Wall Street sharks were behind these attacks. They charged that Eastern sharks, covetous of the millions being poured into Western mining stock, were out to discredit all mining ventures in order to scare the small investor back into their own jaws. Whatever the motives of the Eastern press, that was indeed the net effect of their exposés.[49]

The first and most effective of the muckrakers to hit the mines was Lindsay Denison, who wrote a blistering series that ran for six weeks in *Ridgways, A Militant Weekly for God and Country.* Denison focused not on Lyman but on his accuser, George Graham Rice, revealing his real identity and exposing his whole seamy past, from Elmira Reformatory to Sing Sing Prison. Then he lit into Rice's mining stock schemes, which were being conducted under the seemingly dignified name of the L. M. Sullivan Trust Company, and which listed no less than Nevada's Governor John L. Sparks as a director. The other directors, Denison revealed, were an "unsavory crew" at best. Sullivan, the company's titular head, had earned the name "Shanghai Larry" on the Portland waterfront before coming to Goldfield to start a protection racket in the red-light district and to run the gaming tables at the Palace Bar, just across the street from the company's office. Rice, although officially only the vice president, was clearly the brains of the operation; he was also, of course, a convicted criminal. The other two directors were John D. Campbell, a mining engineer of pliant scruples who wrote favorable reports on the company's mines for a share of the take, and Peter Grant, an unpretentious fellow who managed the games for Sullivan and doubled as company treasurer.[50]

Behind this curious facade, Rice had set up an elaborate operation. It was, Campbell once candidly observed, "a manufacturing plant": Rice's trust manufactured mining company stock; his news agency manufactured publicity that was planted in the Eastern papers; Rice himself quietly manufactured fictitious stock prices with wash sales on the San Francisco exchange; and on the basis of all this, his trust advertised and sold the stock all across the country. It was big business, too, employing half a dozen bookkeepers and as many as thirty stenographers, spending $60,000 a month on advertising, and taking in, it was said, as much as $1.25 million a month! Denison's exposé brought all of that to a swift end. Early in January 1907, even before the series ended, the Sullivan Trust Company closed its doors, and its stocks, including the Furnace Creek South Extension and Greenwater Sulphide copper companies, tumbled.[51]

By then other Western sharks were already slashing away at the whole Greenwater crowd. "What madness is it that prompts you to place your cash in an undeveloped, unknown country such as Greenwater?" asked Parmeter Kent, a feisty Goldfield shark, in his tip sheet, the *Gossip:*

Why do you do it? Why when you can get investments that are sure and sound do you show such asinine stupidity? . . . In God's name what is it you are buying . . . a bunch of names? . . . Our biggest men are simply the biggest money-makers. But because they can add to their capital by exploiting a new district is no argument that you can add to yours by buying what they have to sell. You are not on the inside. You are not in their class. You are paying for their properties—that's all the use you are to them.[52]

"Parmeter Kent is just an ordinary ass," huffed the *Chuck-Walla* tyros, who charged he was only knocking Greenwater to lure readers to his own wildcat promotion, the South Nevada Copper Syndicate, at Cuprite near Goldfield. Kent playfully agreed that he might indeed be an ass. He even revealed that Kent was only an alias; his real name was Sydney Flower, and he had previously promoted stock in a number of questionable schemes—a nicotineless "Health Cigar," a chain of milk sanitariums, and a magnetic ore separator—all through a Chicago magazine called *New Thought,* until the postal authorities had shut him down with a fraud order. Kent nevertheless swore that he was dead right in his attack on Greenwater and on the sharks who would "sell sagebrush to the public . . . and call it a copper mine."[53]

Even George Graham Rice, resurfacing in Reno with a new batch of promotions and a new cover, the *Nevada Mining News,* finally began lashing out at what he called the "Crime of Greenwater." Nor were the sharks alone in their attack; others with untainted reputations and no other stock to sell had also joined the fray. Early in 1907, Thomas A. Rickard, the eminent mining engineer and editor of the San Francisco *Mining and Scientific Press,* had started publishing lengthy articles on the vacuousness of the Greenwater boom, concluding that no other district had been "used so recklessly for irresponsible mine promotions." Furthermore, Rickard raised the question of whether some of his estimable colleagues, such as Pope Yeatman and Seeley W. Mudd, who had privately reported unfavorably on Greenwater, didn't have an ethical duty and a civic obligation to warn the public at large of the notorious stockjobbing being perpetrated at Greenwater. One Greenwaterite, however, did claim that rumors of Yeatman's adverse report on the Clark property were responsible for the break in stock prices.[54]

Under attack from the Eastern press, Western mining stocks in general had started to fall in early 1907, and Greenwater stocks in particular, beset from all sides, fell much faster than most. Patsy Clark's Furnace Creek Copper, the price leader, fell off steadily to barely 50¢ a share by the end of June—down 90 percent from its $5.25 high. Even Clark's highly touted ore shipments that spring—Greenwater's first and last— failed to halt the decline, but then they only amounted to $2,625.09. The Greenwater frenzy was over. By summer, the district was all but dead.[55]

The only Greenwater companies still working by the summer of 1907 were Clark's and Schwab's. All the others had given up even the pretense of activity. It was now obvious to everyone that no pay ore had been found. All those "rich strikes" had been in little stringers that wouldn't pay to work. Yet there was still one last remaining hope that, somewhere down below, there was a great mother lode of copper sulphides like those found in the great mines of Arizona and Montana. Both Clark and Schwab had stopped work on their shafts at a depth of about 500 feet, spending their time on crosscuts to tap all those little stringers and titillate stock prices. But finally in the fall of 1907, both men vowed to start sinking again, down to 1,500 feet if necessary, in quest of the hoped-for "sulphide level." And why not? There was still enough money left in the treasuries of both companies, since they had been careful not to expose too much—or, more precisely, too little—too soon, while the stock was selling. The only alternative was to distribute the money to the stockholders and declare the companies bankrupt. By sinking the rest of the treasury money into exploration, however, both Clark and Schwab could continue to declare their undaunted faith in the mines and spare themselves the wrath of public indignation over the collapse of the Greenwater bubble. In addition, there was always a chance, slim as it was, that they might actually strike sulphides. That could pay both men even more than they had already made on stock sales, and it might even pay back some of the smallfry.[56]

Thus work on the two mine shafts resumed in the winter of 1907–08. It resumed at a snail's pace, however, sinking less than 2 feet a day, since neither company put more than about a dozen men to work.[57]

In the meantime, the once-booming metropolis of Greenwater had been all but abandoned. The exodus had begun in the spring of 1907 after the stock had started to fall. Jack Salsberry sold out his Greenwater interests to concentrate on Ubehebe in May. At the same time Major Strong unloaded the *Greenwater Miner* on the *Chuck-Walla* boys and returned to Alaska, where he eventually became governor. The demise of the camp was further hastened by fires. The worst, on June 22, started in the *Miner* and *Chuck-Walla* office and wiped out a whole block. With water still selling at $8 a barrel, no attempt was made to quench the flames. The little *Chuck-Walla* never resumed, and its fire-warped press was left standing amid the ashes. But Glasscock and Kunze did keep the *Miner* going for two more months, until they took over the *Greenwater Times*.[58]

One by one, even the saloons closed, until at last one saloon keeper walked into his rival's establishment and announced, "Nichols, two saloons on this side of the street are too many. I'll shake you dice to see whether you take mine or I take yours." Without saying a word Nichols reached for the dice box and threw sixes. The challenger threw aces. Nichols stepped out from behind the bar, put on his hat and caught the next stage out—at least that's the way old-timers tell it. But the surest sign that Greenwater was a goner came when Tiger Lil resorted to taking chickens in trade. Greenwater was buried symbolically that summer with an out-of-work printer, Billy Robinson, who died of delirium tremens and was laid to rest holding 5 aces.[59]

A faithful few stayed on, still hoping for boom times once again if Clark's or Schwab's shafts struck the fabled sulphides. But as time dragged on, even the most dedicated decided that those times were just too distant to wait for. The former *Chuck-Walla* tyros finally shut down the *Times* in April 1908 and headed for Bishop to start a new magazine. The post office closed its doors in May. Arthur Kunze, old-timers say, walked away broke, giving his last possession, a $5,000 Pope Toledo, to his chauffeur when it got stuck in the sand on the way out. By June there was just one store and saloon left—the Furnace Mercantile company's, run by Ash Meadows rancher Ralph Fairbanks. When Fairbanks left the following year, he took the town with him, hauling away the last of Greenwater's buildings to the railroad siding of Shoshone on the Tonopah and Tidewater.[60]

The other Death Valley copper excitements stirred up by the Greenwater frenzy had also subsided by the end of 1908. Jack Salsberry had made one last push of his Ubehebe Copper Mines and Smelter Company stock with an expensive double-page spread in *Harper's Weekly* in the spring of 1908, before letting it quietly die. One of the Crackerjack mines had actually shipped several carloads of rock. The end of the boom there was signaled in March of 1908, when the *News* moved to Silver Lake to be born again as the *Miner*. When Tiger Lil left Greenwater, she too settled at Silver Lake for a while and ran the "hotel." The little copper flurry at Willow Creek, of course, had died in the summer of 1907, when gold was discovered at neighboring Gold Valley and miners found they could make as much as $50 a day working pockets of high-grade in arrastras. Several decamping Greenwater merchants moved to Gold Valley early in 1908, and Bill Brong even extended his Death Valley Chug Line to the camp. But it too died in the summer after the high-grade was worked out.[61]

Finally, on September 1, 1909, Greenwater's last hope vanished; its last illusion was swept away—the quest for the great sulphide bonanza was ended. The Copper Queen shaft had reached a depth of 1,404 feet without striking pay rock, and Charley Schwab decided to sink no farther. Patsy Clark had quit six months before at a depth of 800 feet. Schwab's superintendent, John McGee, discharged the last miners and contracted with Fairbanks to haul away the machinery. The following spring Clark and Schwab let their claims go for back taxes. Those wonderful claims they once touted as "the greatest copper belt the World has ever known," those marvelous claims they once sold on the New York Curb at a market value of over $15 million—all those claims were let go for taxes totaling exactly $21.36. George Graham Rice wasn't stretching it much when he called Greenwater "*the monumental mining-stock swindle of the century.*"[62]

Resurrection

Before it was over, the great Death Valley gold excitement even resurrected, if only fleetingly, the dead camps of yore—Lida, Palmetto and Sylvania, Gold Mountain, Tule Canyon and Tecopa—and finally came full circle to redeem that once-damned camp of Montgomery, where the boom had first begun. Only that poor old sinner Panamint was still beyond salvation. The millennium had come, a new day of judgment and reassessment, promising a bright future for those fallen camps. After all, there was proven metal in their old veins, not just the indications of some new, raw prospect. It mattered not that the mines had been closed, even abandoned, when the rich pockets of the past had been exhausted. Surely the technological wonders of the new century would triumph over the primitive methods of the past and by some new alchemy make profits from loss. There was faith in the ultimate perfectability not only of man but of machine. It was a faith held by many and exploited by a few. It all seemed sensible enough; it just didn't work that fast.

There had been only a few previous attempts at resurrecting the old camps, all failures. In the fall of 1885 the old State Line mine was reopened by a Carson City lawyer and champion of lost causes, Colonel A. C. Ellis, a former Confederate officer and a twice-defeated congressional candidate. He got the property at public auction after the litigation was settled and confidently sent his son Pearis with a couple of dozen miners to resurrect the mine and mill, vowing to work it "for all it's worth." By the spring of 1886 the old State Line had at last become a bullion producer, with monthly bullion shipments of a few thousand dollars each. By then the Colonel had also discovered that the bullion was costing more than it was worth, so he shut down the mine again. In 1890 he disposed of the property, passing it to a Silver Peak mining man, L. J. Hanchett, who finally tore down the old mill and hauled it away. That was the end of the State Line mine. But a handful of miners at what had come to be known as the Old Camp of Gold Mountain still made wages working pockets of high-grade there. They worked their ore on a steam-powered arrastra built in 1883 by a former State Line miner, Guy Thorpe. There weren't enough men there to support a store, but they did manage to keep a little post office called Oriental open from 1887 to 1900.[1]

In 1886 Robert Catherwood, then in his late sixties, retired from his Brooklyn construction business and turned his attention again to the old

Palmetto mine, which he and his brother still held. He tried for the next several years to interest British capital in the mine. To dress it up he even put up a new ten-stamp mill in the summer of 1888 and briefly had as many as thirty men at work reopening the old Champion. But declining silver prices had made the mine even less profitable than before, and even the British wouldn't buy it. But Catherwood had faith that the mine would pay someday, so he hired a watchman to see that no one made off with the mill this time, and he waited. He was still waiting when death overtook him in 1903 at the age of eighty-four. His faithful watchman, Ike McConnell, continued the vigil for another decade, until he and his dog died, too.[2]

In the spring of 1890 Sylvania pioneer William Kincaid had bonded his old Liberal mine to an enthusiastic promoter named Andrew Fife, who was looking forward to a new boom with the resumption of government silver purchases. With ore that ran 60 percent lead and 60 ounces of silver to a ton exposed in the old shaft, Fife even persuaded Owens Valley farmers to put their money into reopening the mine and building a new smelting furnace. He stirred up so much excitement, in fact, that two women and over a hundred men were lured to the camp, which briefly boasted two saloons and a string band. The notorious Jack Longstreet ran one of the dispensaries. Then the farmers backed out, and on the first of July the mine shut down and most of the hopefuls left. Within a month, however, Fife raised a little more money from a group of San Franciscans, headed by real estate broker James F. Turner. They formally organized as the Sylvania Mining Company and resumed work on a much more limited basis, delaying the furnace until more ore could be opened. But further exploration failed to reveal more ore, so all work was finally stopped in December. Most of the miners and merchants had been paid only in promises for several months. When the San Franciscans refused to settle accounts, one creditor attached the property, leaving the others to administer what they called "Indian justice" to the company's local manager, Robert Starrett. On a bitter cold night early in January 1891 Longstreet and a few other angry Sylvanians took Starrett from his cabin, stripped him naked in the snow, and warmed his hide with saplings.[3]

Thus the old camps lay dead or dying until the coming of the new millennium in the great gold excitement. The first stirrings of the reawakening began on the heels of the Tonopah rush. But it was not until the Bullfrog rush that the resurrection really got going, and the old camps began to rise again in the fall of 1904. For a time the whole north end of Death Valley was one big revival meeting of born-again mines and miners.

Lida led the way. Many were rushing to Bullfrog that fall of 1904 by way of the well-watered trail around the north end of Death Valley, and to any who would listen, Lida's lone storekeeper, Jerome Vidovich, told of the wonderful riches of the old camp and of his own venerable Florida mine in particular. The Florida, he said, had once produced $200,000 in silver and much more was still there, just waiting. Years before, he confided, a fortune in high-grade, running thousands of dollars a ton, had been exposed at the bottom of the shaft, when suddenly water was struck, the mine flooded, and all work stopped. All that was needed now was capital to pump out the water. It sounded like a sure thing to two rising young southern Californians, State Senator Howard Broughton and his brother Amos, so they bought the mine. With a few friends they hastily formed the Lida-Goldfield Mining Company, ordered pumps, a mill, and tons of other machinery, and put a crew to work cleaning out the old works.[4]

With that, the new rush to Lida began. By the end of the year hundreds of prospectors and promoters were on the ground. Foremost among them was "Judge" Francis L. Burton. A disarmingly smooth-talking lawyer recently arrived from Colorado with an invalid wife and a large amount of cash, Burton was one of the principal organizers of the new Goldfield Bank and Trust Company. Nevadans were yet to learn of his background, but his devoted attention to his paralytic wife inspired the admiration and confidence of those who met him. In a blitz of activity Burton virtually monopolized the camp of Lida. He swiftly secured bonds on many of the old mines and organized an array of mining companies, including two obvious imitations of the Broughtons's highly publicized Lida-Goldfield Mining Co., which he dubbed the Lida Gold Mining Co. and the Goldfield-Lida Gold Mining Co. In addition, he organized in rapid succession the Lida Townsite Co., Lida Water Co., Lida Bank and Trust Co., Goldfield-Lida Investment Co., Goldfield-Lida Auto Co., and the Big Pine, Lida and Tule Canyon Telephone and Transportation Co. Burton of course sold stock in them all. To help sales he also induced two Utah newspapermen, Newman H. Mix and Charles F. Spilman, to start a paper, the *Lida Enterprise,* which began on April 14, 1905.[5]

By May 1905 the camp of Lida had been born again, far livelier than before, with six hundred citizens, a dozen saloons, a weekly newspaper, and daily auto service. It had even been rechristened in blood when a luckless miner, Claude Logan, was found dead in a crib in the "squaw camp" with two bullet holes in the back of his head. The mines too were full of promise, although none was yet producing. The pumps were in place, ready to drain the Florida; its concentrating mill was nearly completed; and a score of other mines were being reopened, including an old favorite called the Buster. There was even a giant smelter in the offing. Lida's past glories were also growing daily. One promoter claimed the mines had first been worked almost a hundred years before by Spaniards,

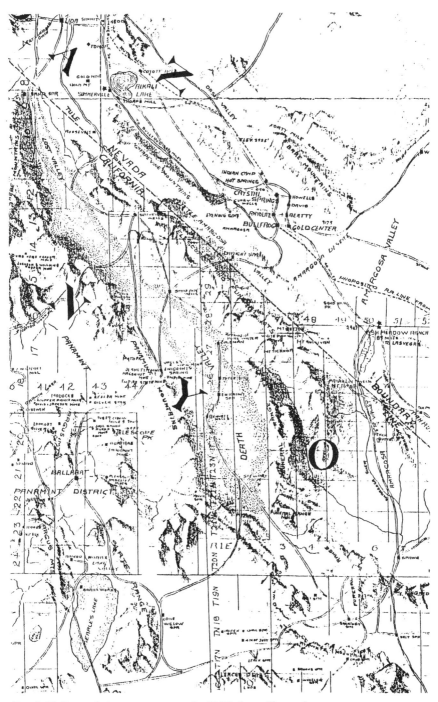

Death Valley and Amargosa camps in 1905, from Shearer's map.

while another simply swore that the camp was "so old that no living man knows when it was discovered." Every old mine that was reopened was said to have produced a quarter of a million dollars or more. On the old Brown's Hope, one booster insisted, $750,000 had been taken out of a dozen gopher holes. With every telling the production of these ancient mines was stretched a little further, to total $2.2, then $3.6, and finally $5.5 million! And there was much more just waiting to be recovered.[6]

Then suddenly the reborn Lida stumbled and fell; for Burton the archangel's past caught up with him. Burton had been a little too successful in his promotions, and succeeded in attracting the attention of a crusading Colorado Springs editor, Claude Sachs. He knew all about Burton's past, but hadn't known his present whereabouts. Sachs knew the Judge as a perfect prince of con men who had even swindled a Massachusetts prison superintendent and his assistant out of $20,000 on a Colorado mining scheme while doing time in their prison in 1903. The Judge was then serving eighteen months for defrauding the New York Central Railroad of $2,500 as an accident settlement for injuries he had actually received in a brawl in a Denver brothel. Sachs dutifully warned Nevadans of all this and more in the May 22 issue of his weekly magazine, the *Mining Investor*.[7]

Burton, it seems, learned of the impending exposé just a few days before, for he and an accomplice, J. B. Young, titular head of the banks, hastily cleaned out over $50,000 in cash and stock from the vaults and fled to San Francisco. So the same day Sachs's revelations appeared, Nevada depositors found the Goldfield and Lida banks closed. Subsequent investigations showed their total remaining assets amounted to just $16.05, in nickels and dimes left in a vault, plus a $5 gold piece that had rolled under a counter.[8]

Burton and Young were soon apprehended, but they escaped justice because Nevada had no laws governing banks. Burton disappeared for a few years after that, apparently living off his ill-gotten gains. But Nevadans didn't forget him, and when he resurfaced in December 1907 at the new boom camp of Rawhide, the local editor, J. Holman Buck, rallied a citizens' committee to put him on the next stage out of town. Burton, infuriated, threatened to kill Buck on sight. But the editor, armed with a sawed off shotgun, called his bluff and was quicker on the draw, ending the Judge's "evil career" with a double-barreled blast that nearly tore his head from his shoulders.[9]

Lida was paralyzed for months after Burton's hasty departure in May 1905. Not only did all of Burton's companies fold, including the new townsite, but miners and merchants lost all their working capital, deposited in his bank, and many other mines lay tied up for as much as a year until his options on them expired. The bulk of Lida's population moved on that summer to livelier camps, leaving only true believers, like Newman Mix of the *Enterprise*, who still had faith in Lida's resurrection. In the months that followed, even that faith was finally broken. First the promising Florida was pumped out and the new mill started up with fanfare on the Fourth of July, only to have it shut down after just one shipment of concentrates. Then all operations ceased in October when the Broughtons went bankrupt. "Bad management" was to blame, Mix claimed, but the fact was that the magnificent ore body waiting at the bottom of the flooded shaft simply vanished when the water was pumped out.[10]

There was also the matter of the promised smelter. Ground was broken in July for the 250-ton plant that the Nevada Ore Purchasing, Smelting and Refining Company said it would build just 4 miles west of Lida, where the company laid out a new town called Heinze. Mix was certain that "Copper Prince" F. Augustus himself was the "directing spirit" of this ten-million-dollar venture, and predicted that the furnace would be fired up by November. But once Gus Eisen and the other promoters had sold all the shares and lots they could, all pretense of work on the great smelter quietly ended.[11]

Lida's last hope lay in the old Buster, which was being reopened in solid style by the Lida Queen Mining Company. The Buster, a gold ledge 5 miles west of the camp, was first called the Fortunatus by its discoverer, Isaiah Rice, in the mid-1870s. Rice had bonded it to Easterners, who opened it to a depth of 180 feet, exposing several small ore pockets before they backed out, concluding that it wouldn't pay enough for full-scale development. Local miners, putting up two steam arrastras at nearby Pigeon Spring in the fall of 1884, successfully worked the high-grade pockets on and off for over a decade. Pigeon Spring rancher Charles Murphy even got Ike McConnell to start up the new Palmetto mill for a run on Buster ore in 1890. Others hauled in a four-stamp mill in the spring of 1898, and a cyanide plant was brought in the following year to work the tailings and lesser-grade ore. Then with the new revival, Henry Jagles relocated the ground. Claiming that the old mine had produced $200,000 in bullion and still had $600,000 worth of ore in sight, Jagles sold it for $50,000 in July 1905 to a Tonopah druggist, Robert Prouty, and his friends. They formed the Lida Queen Mining Company and began systematic exploration of the ledge to determine whether the property warranted the erection of a mill. Such work took time, of course, but the indications were promising enough to sustain the last of Lida's true believers for one more season.[12]

The great revival meanwhile was bringing about a reawakening in all the neighboring camps. At old Sylvania, John Buser, who had worked on a pocket mine next to Kincaid's with his father for twenty years, sold the old ground in the fall of 1904 to Goldfield broker George Patrick for a price advertised as $200,000 cash. Patrick floated a new $1 million Sylvania Mining Company on Pittsburgh capital and reopened the mines under the enthusiastic stewardship of W. D. Clair. By the fall of 1905 Clair had several thousand tons of ore on the dump and was making his first shipment. Several nearby claims were also being reopened, and the camp was lively once again.[13]

At Palmetto, a gold strike near the old mill in February 1905 brought in the first pilgrims of the new revival. They reorganized the district that fall, electing a young woman, Pauline Rodenkirk, as district recorder. The excitement prompted stockholders of the old company to talk about reviving the Champion, but the newcomers found even more attractive ground to reopen. The best was a mine, just 2 miles west of the old mill, which old Henry Jagles had worked on and off over the years. Harry Stimler, one of the discoverers of Goldfield, went in with Jagles, forming the Death Valley and Palmetto Gold Mining Company and putting men to work reopening the mine in January 1906. Before the end of the month they had struck bonanza rock running $20,000 a ton. The old camp came back to life in a wild rush. Within just three weeks there were six hundred faithful on the ground. Two hundred tents and frames lined the road for a mile, sprawling through three townsites—Palmetto, laid out by Stimler; a hastily added addition on the west; and a rival, Goldhorn, even farther west. Forty-foot lots were selling for as much as $500, as buildings and businesses were eagerly moved over from Lida and Goldfield. There was a post office, daily stage service, and a weekly newspaper, for even Lida's staunchest supporter, Newman Mix of the *Enterprise,* hedged his bets by starting a separate paper, the *Palmetto Herald,* on February 23. The camp was reborn far grander than before.[14]

Down in Tule Canyon, the revivalists were also busy, even though the placers there had never given up the ghost. They had been worked continuously for over thirty years, producing over a million dollars. Several gold ledges had also been opened in the adjacent hills. The most profitable of these was the Good Hope, discovered in September 1895 by Tom Jaggers a few miles west of the canyon. He had a pocket of ore running over $100 a ton, which he worked himself with a little five-stamp mill. He took out about $30,000 before he sold the mine in 1904.[15]

Since the placer miners all lived on their claims, scattered along the canyon for 6 miles or more, the only spot that could be called a "camp" was the general store that H. H. "Bob" Robinson put up in the fall of 1891. It also housed the post office, which opened that December and was named for its postmaster, an old German miner, Christian Senner. Robinson's store was also the scene of the only reported homicide in the canyon, which occurred when Jim Boone fatally stabbed Antone Bacoch in a squabble over $11 in November 1895. Boone fled across the Amargosa with Jack Longstreet in pursuit and was finally captured at Peach Springs, Arizona. Soon after that, Robinson sold the store to Bing Kee and Ah Chung and moved his family to Owens Valley.[16]

Then the revivalists came, taking options on thousands of acres of placer ground and talking of monster gold dredges "on the way." By the winter of 1904–05, more than a hundred men were at work on the placers, and three townsites had been laid out. The most promising was Roosevelt, near the lower end of the canyon, named for the progressive Teddy, while its streets were named for his predecessors. At the upper end of the canyon was the rival Fairbanks, named for his vice president, and in between was Summerville, named simply for its promoter, Thomas Summers—although one wag suggested that it would be more fitting if it were named for the Speaker of the House! All three lost out the following summer, however, to a new promotion, Tule City, which had water piped to every lot, a fire hydrant on every corner and, most important, the new post office.[17]

Over on Gold Mountain, the first revivalists had come in the wake of the Tonopah rush. In September 1902 Robert H. Stewart and William Douglas staked claim to a great white quartz ledge they called the Tokop—Shoshone for "snow"—located at the head of Oriental Wash about half a dozen miles northeast of the Old Camp. It was only a low-grade gold deposit, averaging barely $14 a ton, but they found a buyer the following summer in Tonopah promoter Lucien L. Patrick. He bonded the claims for $6,000 cash with a promise of $100,000 to $150,000 in stock, formed the Tokop Mining Company, and started a crew to work prospecting the ledge, sinking a well, and putting up an office, bunkhouse, and blacksmith shop. Other claims were staked nearby, and the fledgling camp of Tokop came into being. It only grew to eight tents and two frames before the discovery of bonanza ores at Goldfield in January 1904 drew almost everyone away, Patrick included. It was not until March 1905 that a strike of $2,600-a-ton ore sparked interest in Tokop again, and Stewart and Douglas found a new buyer, Christian B. Zabriskie, a protegé of Borax Smith. Zabriskie formed the Tokop Consolidated Gold Mining Company and put on a new crew to open the ledge at depth.[18]

By the spring of 1905, many of the old mines at Gold Mountain were being resurrected, or at least rejuvenated. The most promising of these—and also the most flamboyantly touted—was the old Rattlesnake, rechristened the Bonnie Clare, which had already quietly become Gold Mountain's biggest producer. Guy Thorpe had worked rich stringers in the mine intermittently from the early eighties until his death in 1893.

At first he treated the gold ore at his steam arrastra at Old Camp, 4 miles to the west, but later he built a little makeshift mill at Stinking Springs, renamed Thorpe's Well, 8 miles to the east, where there was more water. Thorpe willed a third interest in the mine to an energetic young Slav, Louis E. Chiatovich, who had helped him through illness in his last years. Chiatovich bought out the others and reopened the mine in 1896, putting up a new five-stamp mill and a cyanide plant. By the end of 1904 he had recovered $142,000 in bullion from ore pockets yielding $50 a ton or better, and had exposed a large body of ore he said would average over $25 a ton. It was clearly a proven and promising property—the perfect answer to a promoter's prayers.[19]

The prayers that the Rattlesnake answered were those of two none-too-saintly operators from Los Angeles, Fred Vahrenkamp and Willis George Emerson. Vahrenkamp, a graduate of the Colorado School of Mines, had learned the basic lessons of sharp promotion at Ballarat and had gotten a few advanced lessons in Los Angeles from a self-appointed geology "professor," Lawn H. Mitchell, just before Mitchell was arrested for mail fraud. Emerson was a former Kansas lawyer and banker, a tireless Republican campaigner, and a novelist of modest craft, who in his early forties had turned to mining speculation in a scandalous copper promotion at Grand Encampment, Wyoming, before setting himself up in the real estate business in Los Angeles. Their combined talents made the old Rattlesnake the flashiest and most skillful promotion of the whole revival at the north end of Death Valley.[20]

Emerson and Vahrenkamp bought a half interest in the Rattlesnake and adjacent claims in the spring of 1905, paying Chiatovich a reported $100,000 to $200,000. They immediately incorporated the property into a two-million-dollar stock venture, the Bonnie Clare Bullfrog Mining and Milling Company—named for Emerson's future wife, Bonnie O'Neal—and launched a promotional blitz. For his part, Emerson wrote romantic news stories with titles like "From Poverty to Plenty," which told how the plucky Chiatovich, a "famished boy of Death Valley twenty years ago . . . found fortune through kindness" when he "rode a bronco 300 miles across Death Valley" to help an ailing miner in his last days and was repaid with the bequest of a mine, which the boy, grown to manhood, single-handedly made into "one of the greatest mines in Nevada, without the assistance of any man or a single outside dollar of capital." These were such inspiring stories that they were printed and reprinted in paper after paper—a bonanza of free advertising. Mining engineer Vahrenkamp meanwhile reported "over four million dollars worth of ore . . . blocked out and in sight . . . ready for immediate conversion into the yellow metal," and that made news too.[21]

Emerson and Vahrenkamp also bought full-page ads in the Sunday papers, where they even predicted that "the possibilities of this great mine run into as high figures as the old Comstock from which $555,000,000.00 were actually taken out and paid to the stockholders in dividends"—or so they said! Here was a chance, they preached, for an "investment free from hazard, one that is underwritten by the forces of nature." Out of Christian charity, for a short time only, they offered a limited amount of this wonderful stock at a "rock bottom" price of only 60¢ a share, and predicted that the lucky buyers would earn dividends of 60 percent a year from the proceeds of the mine and make speculative profits of 400 percent a year from the rise in stock prices. Lest anyone hesitate, they were admonished, in the words of the Bard, that "There is a tide in the affairs of men, which, taken at the flood, leads on to fortune." These were indeed high-toned ads![22]

But Emerson and Vahrenkamp did more than just talk. With money from the first sale of treasury stock, they put over three dozen men to work reopening the old mine and ordered tons of machinery for a magnificent new mill. By the fall of 1906 they had 10,000 feet of underground works, exposing new ore pockets and opening up what one enthusiast proclaimed "a veritable catacomb of wealth." Sixteen carloads of machinery for a twenty-stamp mill, a 250-ton cyanide plant, a 100-ton concentrator, and a 50-ton smelter were being hauled in to the new mill site a mile west of Thorpe's Well. The town of Bonnie Clare had arisen on the flat just to the south. Construction trains of the Bullfrog Goldfield Railroad were running to within a mile of the mill, a connecting spur was being laid, and there were plans to extend it 6 miles farther west to where an aerial tram from the mine could deliver the ore. Although progress was slower than predicted and stock prices hadn't yet leaped to the hoped-for highs, Bonnie Clare was looking better and better with each passing day, and big profits seemed certain once the first stamps dropped in the new mill.[23]

By the fall of 1906, however, Bonnie Clare was the only living hope of the north-end revivalists, for all the other born-again camps had lapsed once more. Zabriskie had lost faith in Tokop, and the Tule Canyon gold dredging schemes had died aborning. The revelation had come to Sylvania's new investors that remote lead mines still wouldn't pay, although their zealous superintendent W. D. Clair refused to believe it and kept trying until the 1920s. Harry Stimler's miraculous Palmetto bonanza had pinched out precipitously, and the camp disbanded as quickly as it had formed. Mix blamed "injudicious boosting" when he folded up the *Palmetto Herald* in July. Just three months later he closed down the *Lida Enterprise* too, when his last hope, the Lida Queen, went under. A little group of San Luis Obispo businessmen, who had purchased most of the Lida Queen stock, had grown impatient for returns on their money as the company reported opening larger and larger ore reserves without attempting to work them. At the annual meeting in the spring of 1906, they took over the management of the company and emptied the treasury, rushing a ten-stamp mill to completion that fall. But when they dug into the ore reserves, they found the rock just wasn't rich enough to pay, so they shut down and went to court. That was the final blow to Lida's resurrection.[24]

Emerson didn't stay around to finish the Bonnie Clare story. He sold out his interest early in 1906 and returned to the real estate business, $175,000 richer. While the Bonnie Clare moved toward its inevitable conclusion, Emerson worked on a new story, *The Smoky God,* a fantastic tale of an electric civilization lost in the bowels of the earth, which moved one critic to rank him with Jules Verne. Vahrenkamp remained as general manager and worked out his fantasies right there at Bonnie Clare. He must have begun to believe all the liturgy of boundless wealth that he was preaching, for he raised the resurrection of the old Rattlesnake to new heights. With the financial indulgence of the new majority stockholders— Henry Timken, a septuagenarian roller-bearing magnate, and E. A. Forrester, another Los Angeles real estate man—Vahrenkamp managed to spend over a quarter of a million dollars on the old mine before he was through. He spared no expense, even on the boardinghouse fare, which included such desert luxuries as Lake Tahoe trout and fresh strawberries.[25]

Vahrenkamp at last started the first ten stamps of his expensive new mill in July 1907, and increased the crew to eighty-five men to run it around the clock. By then he had opened up nearly 3 miles of tunnels and drifts in ore he said would average $30 a ton. With the mill crushing 40 tons a day of ore, the mine could pay a handsome profit even with a monthly payroll of $10,000. But after a five-month run that yielded only about $60,000, the Bonnie Clare was $43,000 in debt and went into receivership in December. The ore had averaged only $15 a ton, and the costly mill had recovered just two-thirds of that, for a return that didn't even come close to meeting expenses. But the Bonnie Clare wasn't quite dead yet. The aged Timken still had faith. He paid off all the debts, took control of the stock, dumped Vahrenkamp, and elected himself president and manager of the company in the spring of 1908. He was certain he could make the mine pay by adding a slime plant to improve the returns, using traction engines to haul the ore, and opening up some richer ore pockets struck at depth.[26]

In the meantime, a fresh rush had suddenly revitalized all of Gold Mountain in one final, frantic gasp. A rich strike of hornsilver, running $1,600 a ton, had triggered the biggest stampede Gold Mountain had ever seen, as a thousand men dashed over in the spring of 1908. Three years previously, the Russell and Kavanaugh brothers—Jim and Howard, and Bill and Tom—had located a group of claims they called the Nettie L. near a little ridge known as Lime Point, about 4 miles north of the old State Line mine. They formed a partnership, grandly styled the Great Western Gold Mining and Milling Company, but they worked on the claims only sporadically until they struck shipping ore that averaged $155 a ton in silver in June 1907. Then they took in two more partners for operating capital and went to work in earnest. The mine was soon paying its own way. By March 1908 they had fifteen men at work and had shipped $14,000 worth of ore; then they struck the bonanza ore that started the stampede.[27]

The Russell brothers laid out a townsite, called Hornsilver, in a field of wildflowers on April 10. Within a week a hundred hopefuls had tramped down the flowers and raised in their place scores of tents, half a dozen saloons, several restaurants, lodging houses, and general stores, a barbershop and a livery stable. In less than a month at least five hundred men were on the ground; over a hundred tents and frames were up; lots were selling for as much as $2,500; and three townsite additions had been marked off. There was a daily auto service direct from Goldfield and a daily stage from Cuprite station on the railroad. Telephone lines were in, and water and power lines were planned. The stampede even spurred *Rhyolite Herald* publisher Earle Clemens to start a separate *Hornsilver Herald* on May 9. He stationed his assistant editor, A. B. Gibson, at the new camp to wire the news to Rhyolite, 80 miles away, where the paper was actually printed. By the end of May there was a post office, a miners' union—Local No. 221 of the Western Federation, a chamber of commerce and a volunteer fire department. The population swelled to eight hundred before most lost faith that summer; then it fell back to a hundred or so. The miners' union agreed to a wage cut in July, and Clemens buried the *Herald* that fall.[28]

While the spirit moved, however, countless old mines were resurrected and new ones christened all over Gold Mountain, and a host of new stock companies stepped forward to take their tithe. The Great Western partners refused to sell shares in their mine. But they did lease ground to miners for a 15 percent royalty on ore extracted, and obliged eager investors by forming a new stock venture, the Silver King Mining Company, on neighboring ground, offering 100,000 shares that were snapped up within a week at 15¢ apiece. Other paper promoters resorted to the usual ploys to sell their stock. Several made token ore shipments so that they could call their properties "shippers" like the Great Western and hopefully get a little more for their shares. That ploy was most dramatically exploited by Dr. Frances E. Williams. She was a versatile woman who claimed to have made a fortune in the shellac business, and to have lost it in Florida land, before she came to Nevada in 1903 as an "electro-therapist" at the age of sixty. She soon turned to stock promotion with such self-beatifying ventures as the St. Frances Williams Gold Mining Company. In May 1908 she draped a wagon with banners and paraded the streets of Goldfield to publicize the first shipment from her new Frances Lime Point company's ground. That summer, when a little slab of "picture rock" was accidentally discovered on another claim she held, called the Royal Flush, she announced assay returns of $329,000 a ton and brought in a young history professor from the University of Nevada to have it declared the one and only Lost Breyfogle! Then she formed a new promotion around it, called it the Frances Gold Mountain Mining Company, and laid out a Frances townsite nearby. There were only a few pounds of the jewelry rock, however, and it took three years to scrape together enough additional ore to make a shipment.[29]

An equally enterprising young sharp was W. H. Sills of Goldfield, who formed a $1.5 million promotion, the Nevada Empress Gold Mines and Milling Company, around a worked-out pocket near Old Camp. Sills put up a huge building that dwarfed the pathetic little gyratory mill he housed in it, but it looked very impressive from the outside and created the image of a producer in his promotional photos. For good measure and the chance to sell town lots to distant speculators, he also platted a new town of Gold Mountain.[30]

One of the most promising old mines was the Oriental, which had once held boulders of picture rock. It was relocated in 1908 as the Monarch by a prospector named Mike Drumm, who found new pockets of shipping ore and started a new camp called Drummville. Then previous relocators brought suit, charging Drumm with claim jumping and tying up everything in litigation until long after the excitement had passed.[31]

The Great Western was the only significant producer, however, shipping a total of $119,000 worth of ore before the Russells and Kavanaughs suspended operations in May 1909 and sold the mine to S. H. Brady, a Tonopah promoter. By then nearly all of the shipping ore had been picked out, and a mill was needed for any chance of further profits. Brady talked of a mill for nearly a decade before he finally succeeded in getting one up, and then it didn't pay.[32]

Henry Timken, meanwhile, had died before he could complete his new vision of the Bonnie Clare. But the task was quickly taken up by a close friend, Willard W. Whitney, a retired Ohio piano manufacturer and music publisher, also in his seventies, who pursued an even grander design than his predecessor. Whitney formed the New Bonnie Clare Company in April 1909 and hired an inspired manager named Andrew J. Trumbo. They not only finished remodeling the mill but doubled its size to twenty stamps in September 1910. Rather than use traction engines, they formed the Bonnie Clare and Gold Mountain Railroad Company and bought rails, locomotives, and other equipment from a smelting company at Needles. They planned to haul ore not only from the old Rattlesnake but from all of Gold Mountain as well. What they failed to do was find enough paying ore to keep the mill running. Trumbo even tried leasing the Great Western, but that wouldn't pay either. His faith shaken, he finally gave up in April 1911. To salvage what he could, Whitney leased the mill the following year to two Goldfield companies, the Jumbo Extension and the Florence. For the next two years they shipped from 50 to 100 tons of ore a day by rail 36 miles down to Bonnie Clare. By the time they quit in June 1914, the Bonnie Clare mill had produced altogether about a million dollars worth of bullion—but it hadn't come from Gold Mountain, for the north-end revival was over.[33]

The revival at the other end of Death Valley wasn't nearly as spectacular, but it was far more productive. The old Montgomery district, born again as the Johnnie, was only a renewed disappointment to most, although it produced nearly a third of a million dollars—more than all of the north-end revivals combined. The resurrected Tecopa mine also attracted very little attention, but in its own quiet way it produced over three million dollars, becoming the largest metal producer in the whole Death Valley and Amargosa country.

The Montgomery district revival began in the winter of 1903–04 with the purchase of the old Johnnie mine by two Angelenos, Carl F. Schader and T. A. Johnson, who had already reopened another old mine, the Keystone, at the other end of the Spring Mountains. Schader, the prime mover of the partnership, was a thirty-three-year-old neophyte from Arkansas who had dabbled in surveying, general merchandising, and banking before he converted to mining in 1896. With the financial and spiritual backing of other Angelenos, he and Johnson formed the Johnnie Consolidated Gold Mining Company, a 3 million share venture, in April 1904, and put a crew to work full time reopening the old workings. At the same time Harry Ramsey came back in partnership with Tonopah discoverer Jim Butler and others, relocated the old Chispa as the Congress in January 1904, and formed the Congress Mining Company to resurrect it, too. The following winter they officially rechristened the whole area the Johnnie Mining District.[34]

Johnnie's resurrectors expected great things. They had gotten a headstart on Bullfrog and confidently expected to stay at least one jump ahead of the upstart. But the revival of Johnnie was sadly retarded and never came close to matching the excitement of the north-end revivals, let alone that stirred up by the lively new Bullfrog. Perhaps most mining men considered the old district just too far from the new bonanzas at Tonopah, Goldfield, and Bullfrog to hold much promise. After all, even those dedicated mine makers, the Montgomery brothers, had given up on it. Worse yet, perhaps, Johnnie lacked the murky history and mystery of much older rivals. No one found an ancient arrastra around which to imagine Spaniards once working in the dim and distant past. No one even suggested it was the long-sought, long-lost Breyfogle any more. And certainly no one could claim that it had once produced millions; its meager showing was still too fresh in mind. Johnnie was, in fact, just too fresh a failure to excite any but the most zealous revivalists.

Thus, although the Johnnie and Congress mines were working fifty men by the summer of 1905, their efforts had attracted barely twice that number of outsiders to the district. Even when Schader struck a wonderfully rich pocket of picture rock assaying $180,000 a ton, no crowd rushed in. The old camp was resurveyed with wide new streets and rebaptized Johnnie, and the townsite company, boasting that lots were "selling like hot cakes," ran big ads promising that "$100 will earn you $500 while you sleep, if you buy a lot in Johnnie," but few actually bought. Even though they shouted in banner headlines, "WATCH JOHNNIE GROW!" poor little Johnnie just didn't grow anything like they had hoped.[35]

Not until Johnnie was a year old did the little camp of a few dozen tents even acquire the minimum essentials—a saloon, restaurant, store, post office, hotel, and feed yard. It took still another year—and the passage of the Las Vegas and Tonopah Railroad within a dozen miles in the spring of 1906—before Johnnie also got a telephone line and a daily auto service. That August, Johnnie finally had its first and only homicide when the gallant saloon keeper Dave Poste, late of the Lee district, shot the camp's faro dealer, Frank Gomez, in the stomach for threatening to kill his mistress. That and the brief specter of a claim-jumping war the following month were the extent of Johnnie's high jinks.[36]

The pace was just too slow for Harry Ramsey and his friends, who gave up on the Congress in the summer of 1906 to join the Greenwater rush. Schader was also growing weary of Johnnie. He had placed the stock on the San Francisco and Los Angeles exchanges, but he couldn't get any action. He even tried exhibiting a sack of picture rock in a Los Angeles jewelry-store window to stir up some excitement, but to little avail. Yet by the spring of 1907 he and his partners had opened over 6,000 feet of underground workings and blocked out, they said, some 80,000 tons of ore running $10 or better—a total of roughly $1 million ready for milling. But they still didn't have a mill, and at the rate Johnnie was moving it would be a few more years before they could hope to see any money from that ore, so they decided to sell out and get what they could. They found

WATCH
JOHNNIE
GROW!

THE NEW TOWN IN

JOHNNIE MINING DISTRICT

Fifty miles southeast of Beatty and Bullfrog. A natural location for a big TOWN.

A trip to Johnnie will convince you that Nevada will soon add another great gold camp to the list. The town has been laid out on land that has been patented, making title PERFECT.

The company has five miles of 2 inch pipe line, flowing sparkling artesian water from the mountains to town, a great sight on the DESERT.

For Particulars Call On or Address

FRED W. THOMAS or L. E. JOHNSON
BEATTY.   JOHNNIE.

(*Beatty Bullfrog Miner,* May 20, 1905)

a buyer in May, a sharp San Francisco broker, D. G. Doubleday, who bought nearly all the Johnnie stock at close to the market price of 10¢, for a total of almost $300,000, it was said. Schader and his friends must have gotten about two-thirds of that for their stock; $87,000 went to the company for treasury stock. Schader was through with mining for a while, and put his money into the real estate business in Santa Monica.[37]

Doubleday had no intention of waiting on all that ore to take his profit, either. He too was anxious for quick returns, but he knew how to get them. He promptly elected himself vice president and general manager of the Johnnie Con and went to work with the $87,000 he had paid into the company treasury. Ordering carloads of lumber and machinery and doubling the work force, he broke ground for the mill in September. In a whirlwind of activity that broke "all records . . . for rapid construction," Doubleday finished the mill and other improvements on Christmas Eve 1907. He had put up a modern sixteen-stamp mill and cyanide plant, a new hoisting works, drill compressor, and electric lights throughout the mine, all powered by three gasoline engines that drew on a 27,000-gallon fuel tank and delivered a total of 220 horsepower. With a milling capacity of 150 tons a day, Doubleday talked confidently of a bullion output of $30,000 a month. It was indeed an impressive accomplishment, and one that ultimately generated, at least briefly, the feverish excitement that Schader had only longed for. As if all that wasn't enough, Doubleday opened the new year with the announcement of a phenomenal strike on the adjoining Crown Point Globe ground, which he also held. It was "beyond question the richest ore ever found in a quartz ledge," he said, and who dared deny the claim? The ore ran $500,000 a ton, he said— almost as much as pure gold![38]

In just four months, Doubleday had made Johnnie the darling of the Los Angeles Stock Exchange, and he was just as quick to cash in on it. Johnnie Con stock had nearly doubled in value to 18¢ a share by December 1907, when Doubleday began to unload. He played out the stock for the next four months, selling the last, it is said, as the price on the bloated market fell to 9¢ in April. With that he closed his office and disappeared. Doubleday had dumped nearly 2.5 million shares, taking a profit, some said, of $100,000. Others swore, however, that he left a loser; but that may have been wishful thinking. The real losers, of course, were those who bought the stock at any price, for two months later it crashed to a penny a share![39]

As a parting gesture Doubleday had shipped the first gold bar from the Johnnie Con mill in late March, predicting that production would soon reach $50,000 a month. But when the stockholders met in May, they found that their fine new mill was turning out only $4,000 a month in bullion and generating debts of almost $2,000 a month, on top of unpaid construction bills totaling $12,000. That was the news that shattered stock prices.[40]

Then came the savior, Al Myers. Still blushing from having been suckered into Death Valley by Scotty, Myers seemed anxious to restore his reputation by showing just what a real mining man could do, even with a discredited mine like the Johnnie. He felt the mill hadn't paid simply because the ore wasn't properly sorted and too much worthless rock had been worked. So in October 1908 he reorganized the property as the Johnnie Mining and Milling Company, and after a quick renovation he started up the mill in December to show that he could make it pay. By May 1909 he had done just that, working 5,000 tons of ore and producing $39,000 worth of bullion for a net profit of over 40 percent. Myers went on to make the Johnnie a steady producer for the next two years, taking out over 50,000 tons and yielding $260,000. But as the work went deeper, mining costs rose and ore values fell, until by the end of 1911 there was hardly any paying rock left. After further exploration down to 1,000 feet revealed nothing but a few more pockets, Myers at last closed down, satisfied that he had proven his point.[41]

The scorned little Johnnie had produced roughly $300,000 in gold—far more than any other resurrected mine in Death Valley, save one. Johnnie's faithful stockholders could rejoice in that. But spiritual rewards were all they got—they never saw a dividend. Like a good mining man, Al Myers had sunk all the profits back into exploration for more ore, and he came up empty-handed. The Johnnie was sold by the sheriff in the spring of 1915 for debts amounting to $10,000.[42]

The one mine that surpassed not only the Johnnie but every other metal mine in the Death Valley and Amargosa country was of course Jonas Osborne's old Tecopa. The resurrection of the Tecopa was the realization of Osborne's dreams and the confirmation of his faith. With the help of a partner, San Bernardino banker Harry L. Drew, Osborne had faithfully ministered to the old mine for over a quarter of a century, trying now and then to revive it, but to no avail. He and Drew held a potential fortune in lead ore there, but it wasn't worth a thing unless it could be shipped cheaply to a smelter. Osborne had tried hauling the ore all the way to the Santa Fe Railroad at Daggett with his "self propelling steam wagon," and later to the California Eastern railhead at Manvel, but both times it cost more to haul than it was worth. Drew died still hoping. But Osborne held on and was at last rewarded when Borax Smith's Tonpah and Tidewater Railroad came within just half a dozen miles of the old mine.[43]

In June 1906, when the Tonopah and Tidewater construction crews first reached Amargosa Canyon a dozen miles from the Tecopa, Osborne and Drew's heirs bonded a half interest in the property to Rhyolite mining superintendent James H. Lester and several associates for two years. Lester, a "gritty little fellow," wasted no time reopening the old workings. He hired fifty men that summer to put up new buildings, grade a new road to the line of the railroad, and break down ore in anticipation of the trains. By the end of the year he and his partners were so impressed with the prospects of the mine that they rushed ahead with the purchase, even though the railroad construction was still stalled by slides in Amargosa Canyon. They formed the Tecopa Consolidated Mining Company with a nominal capital of $3 million and Lester as general manager. Early in January 1907 they paid Osborne and the Drew estate a total of $350,000, over half apparently secured by mortgages on the two principal mines, the Gunsight and the Noonday. After all those years of waiting, Osborne was rich at last. He was in his mid-seventies by then, and he didn't have many years left to spend it, but he did his best.[44]

Lester and his associates had no trouble raising working capital with their first stock offering of 100,000 shares of treasury stock, which was sold out at $1 par in less than forty-eight hours. But that brief flurry was about the only real excitement that the Tecopa revival ever generated. With gold fever in the air it was hard to work up much excitement over something as dull as lead. Moreover, the Tecopa company had started with twenty-one claims covering all the good ground and much more, and it went on to grab up four times that, blanketing the country for nearly 3 square miles. There was little room for others to get a foothold in the district, even if they'd wanted to. So the new camp of Tecopa that grew up at the mines never became more than a company town. Despite its swift and promising start, the Tecopa revival was headed for some hard and disappointing years before the old mine was fully resuscitated.[45]

By the time the Tonopah and Tidewater got out of Amargosa Canyon in May 1907 and reached the road from the mine, Lester had 600 tons of ore waiting there for shipment—enough to make up a "solid train of ore." Moreover, that first shipment paid nearly $29 a ton, returning an impressive profit of $19 a ton after costs of mining and shipping. By then too, Lester had 3½ miles of underground tunnels and drifts opened in ore just as rich, he said. That summer he doubled the crew to nearly a hundred men, and with more than a dozen wagons and over a hundred mules he was shipping about 75 tons of ore a day. By November he had shipped 7,500 tons to the Salt Lake smelters at a profit of $90,000. But then the smelters shut down under a court injunction arising from a suit brought by Salt Lake valley farmers for damages from smelter fumes. The Tecopa company, which had contracted with the smelter trust, had no other market for their ores and was forced to close in December.[46]

In September, before the shutdown, John W. Brock of the Tonopah Mining Company had bought a large, if not controlling interest in Tecopa

Con with an eye toward building a $1.5 million smelter at Beatty and using the Tecopa lead ore as a flux to treat the lower-grade, silicous ores from Tonopah and Goldfield. But he soon abandoned that idea in the tight money market that followed the failure of the Knickerbocker Trust, and sold his Tecopa shares the next summer to a fellow Philadelphian, Nelson Z. Graves. A shrewd but erudite man in his mid-fifties, Graves had begun as a language professor at Ellicott College in Maryland before going into the paint business, to make his fortune as one of the largest white-lead paint manufacturers in the country. Like Brock, Graves was interested not in the profits to be made from the mine but in the lead itself, in order to set up a vertical monopoly in his paint business, which consumed as much as 75 tons of lead a day.[47]

Work at Tecopa resumed in June 1908, as soon as Graves took over. Lester again had a crew of fifty or more men blocking out ore, and by the end of the year he had extended the underground workings to a total of 6 miles, exposing some 300,000 tons of ore worth an estimated $6 million. In the meantime, Graves was negotiating with Borax Smith for the construction of a railroad spur up to the mines. Both men wanted to build and operate the line, however, so they were stalemated until Graves finally threatened to build a smelter right at Tecopa and deprive Smith of all the ore-hauling revenues. Smith conceded, and construction of the little Tecopa Railroad began in July 1909. It was an 11-mile long, Y-shaped, standard gauge line, running from the Gunsight and Noonday mines at the upper ends to the Tonopah and Tidewater siding at the lower. It cost roughly $150,000, financed by a loan from Graves. Nearly a hundred men and over a hundred mules graded the roadbed and laid the ties and track under the supervision of C. H. Ellison, a construction engineer loaned from the Southern Pacific. Lester had overall charge of the work, however, and he and Ellison quarreled continuously. With the railroad barely half done, Ellison quit in disgust at the end of November. Lester, drunk and in a "murderous mood," tried to stop him from leaving, threatening him with a pocket derringer that discharged, hitting the engineer in the neck. Ellison was taken to Los Angeles, where he eventually recovered, and no charges were filed against Lester. But as soon as Lester completed the railroad in February 1910, Graves fired him.[48]

In the meantime, Graves had signed a new contract with the American Smelting and Refining Company guaranteeing to ship at least 300 tons of ore a day from Tecopa, apparently in exchange for a guaranteed delivery of 75 tons of lead a day at a favorable price to his paint plant in the East. Graves's new manager, J. P. Sullivan, fresh from Philadelphia, increased the payroll to 150 men and started shipping ore as fast as he could that June. There was talk of dividends in two months, and Tecopa Con stock, which had fallen well below par, jumped up to $1.60 a share. But two months later, instead of dividends, the entire crew was discharged and the mine was closed down without explanation. Stock prices tumbled to 30¢, held there briefly, then fell to 5¢. Disgruntled investors in the West saw the whole episode as a simple stock manipulation. But whether Graves, who then held between two-thirds and three-quarters of the stock, had indeed planned to pick up a little quick cash by letting the stock out at a high figure and buying it back low, remains quite literally a matter of speculation. What does seem certain is that the Tecopa mine, for all its real worth, was simply not able to fulfill the contract Graves had made with the smelter trust. The most that Sullivan was able to ship was 200 tons a day, and to do that he had to include so much low-grade rock that the shipments averaged only $16 a ton.[49]

The Tecopa mine remained closed for roughly two years, and Graves seems to have had second thoughts about the mining business. He even tried to interest Brock's Tonopah Mining Company into taking it back. But in 1912 he got a new, workable contract with the smelters and, even more important, he got a new, experienced general manager, Dr. Lincoln D. Godshall. A chemist and metallurgist then in his late forties, and a former intercollegiate pole-vaulting champion, Godshall had received his doctorate from Lafayette College in Pennsylvania in 1890, and had gone West to become superintendent and eventually a part-owner in a number of mining and smelting ventures. He came to Tecopa after he and his partners sold their Needles smelter to the United States Smelting, Refining, and Mining Company; with some of the proceeds, he may eventually have bought a sizable block of Tecopa stock, for he also became vice president of the company. The stock could have been had at bargain prices for several years, since it continued to slide under the weight of outstanding debts until it reached a penny a share, despite the resumption of production.[50]

Godshall reopened the Tecopa mine in November 1912 and began regular ore shipments in January 1913. For the next sixteen years the shipments came almost like clockwork, as he patiently and systematically worked the great ore reserves. He kept between fifty and seventy men at work taking out ore, and in 1916 he added a 75-ton concentrator so they could take out even lower-grade rock and enrich it for shipping. Although shipments never exceeded about 2,000 tons a month, the Tecopa was the largest silver-lead producer in California from 1917 through 1920. The continuity of production was interrupted only a few times: once by a tragic accident in the summer of 1913, when an overeager but inexperienced engineer lost control of the ore train on the downgrade and died in the derailing; then for most of the year 1921, when lead prices dropped to unprofitable values; and again the following summer, when excessive heat made the work unbearable.[51]

By the time declining lead prices and ore values finally forced the Tecopa to shut down in 1928, Godshall had shipped 148,000 tons of ore, averaging nearly $24 a ton—two-thirds of that in lead, the rest in silver with a trace of gold. By then the old Tecopa mine's production had reached nearly $4 million, making it without question the biggest metal producer in the Death Valley and Amargosa country. The old Tecopa also revealed that despite all the prospectors' lore and promoters' whoopla, the valley's most precious metal was not gold, silver, even copper, but just plain lead![52]

Yet despite Tecopa's wonderful production, even this venture proved to be a losing proposition to all but a select few of its stockholders. In all those years they saw only two dividends, totaling just 2½¢ a share and amounting to $75,000—barely 2 percent of the gross production. That was a good return after sixteen years only if you bought the stock at 1¢ a share. Important details of the company finances were not made public, but much of the early profits certainly went toward paying off the original mortgages and Graves's loan, which together were said to have amounted to $338,000. Those debts were undoubtedly paid off by 1918, when the first dividend was paid. Thus it seems likely that most of the potential profits of the following decade were simply lost to the mining company through reciprocal contracts for the purchase and sale of lead to Graves's paint company. After all, Graves only bought the mine for the lead in the first place and, as president and majority stockholder of both companies, he made the contracts.[53]

Facts, Fantasies, and Flivvers

Even during the great boom, it wasn't the lore of riches alone that lured men into Death Valley and the Amargosa. Some came simply to find the facts about the land of fantasy. They were a new crew of scientists who picked up where Wheeler's party had left off. They collected and catalogued many new species, measured and mapped much new ground, found new facts and tried to dispel old fantasies. But it was a handful of adventure seekers, also drawn by the lore of mystery and horror, who brought about the biggest changes. They were the daring young men in their newfangled autos. They pushed their machines to the limit, challenging the deadly valley, and they won. In a triumph of technology over terror, they conquered the valley in their flivvers and threw it open for all to follow. Death Valley and the Amargosa would never be the same again.

But by the time they came, the valley was shrouded in illusion. Once that awful name had been fixed upon it, Death Valley had become a place in the mind, far beyond geography and history. It had become a mirage not only of limitless wealth but of countless horrors, which had started in whispers around the campfires and in the saloons and which had spread through the Sunday supplements and penny dreadfuls to more reputable works. By the time the great rush began, a pervasive and pernicious lore had already turned the valley into a poisonous, unearthly inferno, a "dismal and dreary . . . fearful, uncanny place."[1]

The illusory valley wasn't just seasonally hot, one enthusiast swore, it was seized by "a straight forward, businesslike, independent, sizzling heat which keeps the thermometer in the region of 130 in the shade *all the time,* and . . . it knows no shade." It was a merciless place, where "no friendly clouds ever intercept the scorching rays of the sun. No moisture ever falls to cool the burning sand." It was a scarred and scoured land where "hot suffocating winds sweep down the chasm, laden with blinding sand." It was a waterless waste, where only "deadly poison, having the appearance of water, oozes from the salt and lava beds," and "poisonous gasses issue from fissures in the rocks." It was a hellish place, infested by creatures "conjured up by Satan . . . armed with weapons artfully contrived to aid their master in this terrible Kingdom of Death." It was a place where even the lowly gnat "swarms so thickly that it could probably sting a regiment of soldiers to death before the bugler had time to sound the signal for retreat," a place where even the most harmless mouse "plays a part in the diabolical scheme for the destruction of life in this den of the destroyer."[2]

Death Valley was a "death pit" from which "there is no escape—hemmed in on all sides by titanic rocks and majestic mountains, full of treacherous pitfalls, false surfaces and quivering quicksands." It was the "hopeless tomb" of a whole wagon train of emigrants and countless other lost souls, all lured by its mirages. It was a ghastly land "thickly strewn with dead," where corpses "will not decay, but will simply be shrivelled up to a mummy and lie there in the Valley of Death to all eternity, imperishable, staring up at the burning sky."[3]

"There is on all the globe no other spot so forbidding, so desolate, so deadly," raved one admirer. "It is a concentration of the hideousness of that whole hideous area . . . the Great American Desert." Thus it would always be, swore another,

> the one foul spot upon the fair face of our land. Population may press forward. Civilization may claim our country bit by bit. . . . Yet they can never enter here. This is the dominion of death. It is forever destined to stay in its state of primitive desolation and barrenness. By some mysterious decree of nature this pestilential place must remain the resort of venomous reptiles and vermin. It will ever be avoided alike by man and beast. It is the last and lasting remnant of the world as it probably was in that pleiocene period ere man was made to dominate and fructify the earth.[4]

And so it went, though not all the tales were so deadly somber. Indeed, by 1890 one lively scribbler had turned the horror into comic absurdity, twisting the devil's tail with a report of the farcical exploits of one Colonel John Jewks, who made Death Valley safe at last for all mankind. The dauntless Colonel ventured into the valley on stilts to keep his head above the deadly "sea of gas." Armed with only a "gasometer" and a pocket full of gophers, which he dropped one by one as he progressed, to test the fatal fumes, he mapped the extent and depth of the poisonous vapors, calculating their volume to be "6,000,000,000,000,000 meters—gas meters," that is. Moreover, in the very midst of the valley he found all of the hundreds of lost wagons and thousands of lost emigrants who had been drowned and petrified in the sea of gas. And spilled on the ground all around them, just out of reach of the stilted explorer, was a treasure of silver and gold. He pondered for days on how to get the treasure, before he finally lit upon the answer, climbed to the highest point above the valley, built a bonfire and pushed it into that "terrestrial hell." The gas ignited in a blinding flash that turned the Colonel's hair white as snow and shot flames a mile into the sky, barbecuing the great black cloud of buzzards that had hovered over the valley. But when the eager

Colonel rushed back into the valley to gather up the treasure, he found that the fierce heat of the flash had not only burned all of the gas but had vaporized every trace of the emigrants and their treasure. So he returned to Los Angeles penniless, but content that he had rid "Death's Valley" of its horrors at last.[5]

Even so enlightened a journal as the *Scientific American* succumbed to the deadly illusion, branding the valley the "Puit d'enfer"—the pit of hell into which "very few persons have ever gone . . . who returned to tell the tale." And its editor sadly lamented that the valley's awful "climatic violence" would never be known because "no man could survive there long enough to secure continuous observations of any extent." Such outrageous talk of hellish conditions and satanic creatures, of the unknown and the unknowable, was certain to arouse the interest of more scientific Americans, who couldn't resist coming to see it for themselves.[6]

First among them was the Death Valley Expedition of the Department of Agriculture. It was one of the first in a series of biological surveys of the West made by naturalist Clinton Hart Merriam, who studied the geographical distribution of plants and animals in order to define life zones that could be used to assess the suitability of land for farming and ranching Merriam was particularly interested in the Death Valley country, not for its dubious agricultural potential or for "deadly peculiarities," but for the possibility of finding strange new species of life and for the unique opportunity to study seven separate life zones in the short span from the valley floor to the peaks of the Panamints. For the expedition Merriam recruited government zoologists Vernon Bailey, Basil H. Dutcher, and Edward W. Nelson; ornithologists Albert K. Fisher and Theodore S. Palmer; entomologist Albert Koebele; botanists Frederick V. Coville and Frederick Funston; and an amateur naturalist, Frank Stephens, who later founded the San Diego Natural History Museum.[7]

The Washington press releases heralded the members of the expedition as "ten celebrated scientists," but most were fledglings in their early twenties, fresh from college. Even Palmer, who headed the expedition for the first three months before Merriam could join them, was only twenty-two. But their energy and enthusiasm more than made up for their lack of experience, and most eventually did become quite prominent. Funston, in fact, became a national hero, although not as a botanist. He took a canoe down the Yukon on another botanical survey after Death Valley, but he craved even more excitement, so he quit to join the rebel forces in Cuba in 1896. Two years later, he led a regiment of Kansas Volunteers to fight against Philippine rebels after the Spanish-American War. He showed such "reckless daring" there that President McKinley commissioned him a brigadier-general at thirty-five—the youngest general in the army. Funston died of a heart attack in 1917 while helping Pershing chase Pancho Villa on the border.[8]

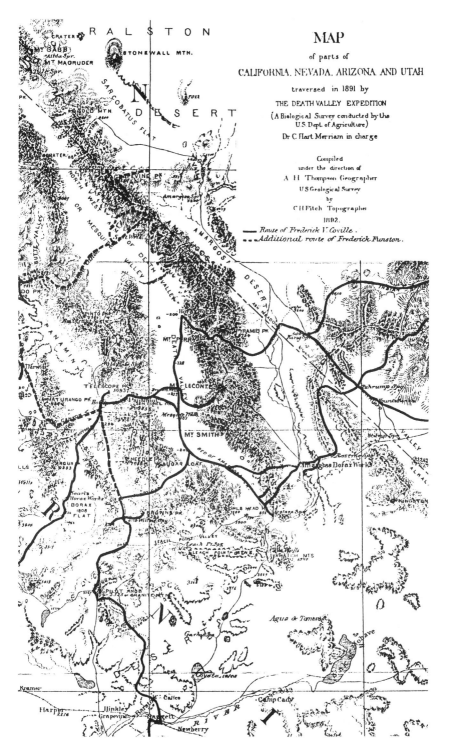

MAP

of parts of

CALIFORNIA, NEVADA, ARIZONA AND UTAH

traversed in 1891 by

THE DEATH VALLEY EXPEDITION

(A Biological Survey conducted by the
U.S. Dept. of Agriculture)

Dr C Hart Merriam in charge

Compiled
under the direction of
A. H. Thompson Geographer
U.S. Geological Survey
by
C H Fitch Topographer
1892.

—— Route of Frederick V. Coville .
▪▪ Additional route of Frederick Funston .

The expedition entered Death Valley through Wingate Pass in mid-January 1891 and spent the next six months crisscrossing the country from Panamint to Pahrump and Saratoga Springs to Sylvania, collecting every type of plant and animal they could find. They found the deadly valley full of life, though much of it was nocturnal. They sighted hundreds of birds, from hummingbirds to vultures, roadrunners to gnat-catchers. They shot sidewinders, coyotes, and mountain goats; trapped chuckwallas, horned toads, and kangaroo rats; caught pupfish, frogs and toads, and a myriad of beetles, moths, and gnats; and clipped or dug up hundreds of varieties of plants. They eventually published two fat books on the wildlife of Death Valley, and they would have published a third if they had had enough money to print it. They discovered more than 150 new species and two dozen new genera of plants and animals, mostly insects, but including new species of pupfish, poppy, and snail named for Merriam; a toad and a mountain goat for Nelson; a frog for Fisher; a lizard for Palmer; and a greasewood for Bailey, *Sarcobatus baileyi,* a name they gave in turn to Sarcobatus Flat east of the Grapevines.[9]

The Death Valley Expedition was a grand success, and, except for Funston's dog, which was "parboiled by the sun" in Saline Valley, they all got out alive, unlike Wheeler's expedition. There were, however, a couple of close calls. Bailey was left afoot about 6 miles from camp when his horse spooked and ran off after he stopped to shoot a rattlesnake but he made it back without incident. Palmer and a teamster, heading for Daggett to meet Merriam late in March, weren't quite as fortunate when their horses wandered off while they were camped for the night. They had to continue on foot for 40 miles with only what water they could carry. They just made it after three grueling days, with Palmer so close to death that he had to be hospitalized for three weeks.[10]

That summer, at Merriam's request, the Department of Agriculture's newly formed Weather Bureau also set up a temporary station in Death Valley to record that "climatic violence" that *Scientific American* was certain could never be measured. A fearless young weatherman, John H. Clery from Kansas City, packed in a full array of instruments to the old Harmony borax works, and for five months, from May through September, he dutifully recorded not only the fearsome temperatures but also the humidity, pressure, winds, and even occasional traces of rain. It was lonely duty, and he suffered more from boredom than from heat. But he whiled away his idle hours making up news items for the columns of an imaginary paper, the *Death Valley Mourner.* Although an assistant who was sent out to keep Clery company immediately got sick from the heat and left, the valley was not exceptionally hot that summer. The maximum temperature was only 122°, so the Salton Sink, with its record 130° set in 1885, remained the hottest known spot. The chief of the Weather

Bureau was nonetheless impressed enough by the severity of the climate to publish a lengthy report on the *Climate and Meteorology of Death Valley* as the bureau's first bulletin. Twenty years later, a permanent weather station was finally established at Furnace Creek Ranch. During the awful heat wave in the summer of 1913 the Salton Sink record was at last broken, when the thermometer topped out at 134° on July 10, and Death Valley officially became the hottest spot in America.[11]

Next came the surveyors to more accurately define the California-Nevada boundary after von Schmidt's survey was called into question. Cephas H. Sinclair of the U.S. Coast and Geodetic Survey was given the task this time. Starting at Lake Tahoe in 1893, he ran a new line across the north end of Death Valley and on through the Amargosa in the heat of the summer of 1895 and finally ended at the Colorado River in 1899. He successfully straightened out the boundary, moving it west by as much as a mile in the vicinity of Death Valley. But Sinclair inadvertently added much more to the fantasies of the valley than to the facts, for he was also the man who first brought to Death Valley its champion fantasizer of all time, the incomparable Walter Scott.[12]

Then came the geologists. First there was young Josiah E. Spurr of the Geological Survey, fresh from the Klondike. He brought his bride of a few months on an extended honeymoon through southern Nevada and across Death Valley in the summer and fall of 1899. Seeking to unravel the geological history of the region, he traced out most of the geological formations, but missed the rich mineralogical indications. It was left to a rancher, Jim Butler, to make the phenomenal strike the following spring which started the great rush to Tonopah. Spurr, perhaps chagrined, returned a few years later and reported unfavorably on the prospects of the district. Not until 1906, after the mines had produced nearly $10 million, did he change his mind, quit the survey, and become vice president of the Tonopah Mining Company, which eventually produced roughly $50 million.[13]

The rich strikes at Bullfrog and neighboring Death Valley districts attracted Frederick L. Ransome and several other government geologists in the summer and fall of 1905. They studied the various ore bodies and the surrounding geology to try to understand the relation between them. Then they picked out several areas where they expected ore should also be found, but these all proved barren. Their subsequent reports were of little value to potential investors, because promoters usually wouldn't let government men into the mines, not even proven bonanzas like the Montgomery Shoshone and the Keane Wonder. Thus the government had to rely on the promoters' estimates of the size and richness of the ore deposits, and what independent appraisals they did make were published too late.[14]

Death Valley's borax and other salt deposits also attracted the attention of geologists. In the spring of 1900 Marius R. Campbell of the Geological Survey made a hasty reconnaissance of the borate deposits, and the following winter Gilbert E. Bailey of the California State Mining Bureau began a much more extensive survey of all saline deposits. They mapped out different deposits and speculated on their origin and economic potential. But Bailey got carried away, publishing such an exaggerated description of some low-grade nitrate deposits in Death Valley that he started a stampede in the fall of 1902 which Campbell branded as "little short of insanity."[15]

Finally, the topographers came. From 1905 to 1907 Robert H. Chapman and half a dozen other surveyors from the Geological Survey mapped most of Death Valley and the Amargosa—over 10,000 square miles. They produced the first reliable maps of the region—the preliminary Amargosa sheet issued in the summer of 1906 and the Ballarat, Furnace Creek, and Lida quadrangles in the spring of 1908. The following year Walter C. Mendenhall, drawing mainly on the notes of Bailey and Chapman, issued a guide to the water holes of the entire desert country of eastern California and southern Nevada. The maps and guidebook were invaluable to later travelers and may have saved many lives. There was, in fact, an abrupt drop in the valley's annual death toll after their publication, but much of that was undoubtedly due to the sharp decline in activity following the great boom.[16]

As a part of these surveys, L. F. Biggs ran the first spirit level line into Death Valley early in 1907 and reported the lowest spot to be 274 feet below sea level. By then, even though the Salton Sink may have been deeper, the runaway waters of the Colorado River, which flooded the sink in 1905, had made Death Valley undeniably the lowest spot in America. A few wild-eyed reclamationists, however, still hoped to change that by flooding Death Valley, too. Every so often, to the amusement of the press, one of these dreamers would revive Stretch's old scheme of turning the Colorado River into Death Valley. Worse yet, one desert Noah feared that mother nature herself would flood the valley with seawater leaking in from the Gulf of California, so he built a fully rigged brig on the valley floor, just to be safe—or so it was reported by the mythmakers who still tried to keep at least one jump ahead of the fact finders.[17]

A few other truth seekers also came to the valley, and wrote some of its best works. Journalist John Randolph Spears came in the winter of 1891 to gather facts for the first book on the valley, his classic *Illustrated Sketches of Death Valley*. He brought out a bonanza of entertaining fact, but he perpetuated some tenacious old fantasies too—telling of how "more than a score of lives were lost in a day when the valley was christened"—

and he started some new yarns, like that of "Bellerin' Teck." A few years later that aged argonaut William Lewis Manly came forth to put the lie to the myths of the forty-niner tragedy with a "plain, unvarnished tale of truth" in his heroic *Death Valley in '49*. But so much truth only rankled some of his former companions, like the Briers, and so confused at least one popular writer that he concluded there must have been two Death Valley tragedies.[18]

Others came only in their mind's eye, seeking some deeper truths. There was a young moralist, Frank Norris, who brought the tormented dentist of his 1899 novel *McTeague* to a tragic end in the vengeful heart of Death Valley, handcuffed to the corpse of a man he murdered. There was a Lone Pine schoolteacher, Mary Austin, who eloquently portrayed the simple truths of that "land of lost rivers, with little in it to love," that valley of "endless sun and silence," in her first book, *The Land of Little Rain*, in 1903. And there was a fledgling Robinson Jeffers, fresh from college in 1907, who mused in his all-but-forgotten poem, "Death Valley":

> There is a Fate that sways this deadly land—
> A silent Fate that smiles and is accurst,
> Bearing strange gifts for men in each hand's hold.
> Loose on the open palm of the right hand
> Are death and madness and a hell of thirst—
> But in the tight-clenched left is yellow gold.[19]

Despite such heavy doses of truth, however, the contagious lore of the valley only spread faster. Even the poisonous gases held on tenaciously, despite the valiant Jewks, and mingled with them the boom brought ghostly lights and phantom voices, boiling rains and a "fountain spouting scalding blood!" One amateur theologian even swore that Death Valley was literally the roof of the Biblical Hell and that he could hear the "wails of the damned" crying out from the "Devil's domain" below. The "Poet-Prospector" Clarence Eddy, in contrast, fancied it was actually the fallen Eden, that long lost "pristine paradise . . . blasted, blackened, torn and accursed . . . after the shameful conduct there." Amateur archaeologists imagined in its rock formations the ruins of a lost civilization—a gigantic, ancient masonry dam, 200 feet high, complete with copper tools—at either the north or the south end of the valley; they couldn't agree on which. Rhyolite raconteur Mike Lane topped that with the discovery deep in the valley of an entire lost tribe of emigrants, the descendants of an errant band of argonauts who couldn't find their way out. With cockamamy tales like these abroad, the absurd fantasies of such calculating con men as Death Valley Scotty and B. X. Dawson seemed almost plausible by comparison.[20]

Go Automobiling
In Death Valley
With Alkali Bill

The Death Valley Chug Line

Runs cars daily from The Front on Borax Smith's railroad (The Tonopah Tidewater) and from Amargosa on the Las Vegas & Tonopah to Greenwater. Alkali Bill himself meets every train and whizzes you over the desert 45 miles by way of Death Valley and the famous Amargosa Canyon, to Greenwater in less than three hours.

Better write ahead or wire your reservations if you have time.

Alkali Bill's Death Valley Chug Line

Greenwater, Inyo County, California

(*Death Valley Chuck-Walla,* April 1, 1907, *courtesy of Bancroft Library*)

The adventure seekers were drawn more by all the lore than by the facts. Foremost among them were those daring young men in their flivvers who came to challenge the ultimate desert, pitting themselves and their machines against all the terrors, both real and imagined, that the deadly place possessed. Geologist Gilbert Bailey had first talked of outfitting a special automobile for a run into Death Valley in 1904, though nothing came of it. But with the Bullfrog rush early the following year, "Alkali Bill" Brong and other desert mahouts began regular auto runs to Rhyolite and camps bordering the valley. Then in the fall, Malcolm Macdonald cautiously took the first flivver on a brief run into the edge of the valley.[21]

In June 1906 George Graham Rice mounted the ultimate challenge, sending his front man, "Shanghai Larry" Sullivan, on a wild auto dash across the heart of Death Valley. It was a race to beat Charley Schwab's man to a new prospect at Emigrant Spring, Rice said. Yet it was the unbeatable, derring-do publicity for his Sullivan Trust Company that was foremost in Rice's mind, and he made it an incomparable tale of desert motoring. Shortly before midnight of June 15, Sullivan, Jack Campbell, and a driver, James Hopper, raced out of Goldfield in the company's 80-horsepower Pope Toledo. Sullivan and Campbell "leaned forward on the tonneau, their teeth crunching upon their cigars," Rice told, and

> urged the chauffeur on. The latter, a long, thin fellow all humped up, as if eternally cutting his way through a recalcitrant atmosphere, drove like a demon. The machine buzzed; at times, the iron flaps covering the engine raised with the friction of the air and she seemed to fly on extended wings. Above, the stars blazed—the Great Dipper overhead, Orion stalking with flaming scabbard across the horizon in front. On each side, distorted cacti lurked in the shadow like huge tarantulas.[22]

They flew into Rhyolite at three in the morning and stopped just long enough to grab breakfast, get gas and extra water, and pick up the Emigrant Spring claim-owner, Ed Chafey. Then they were off again, reaching Daylight Pass, Rice wrote,

> with the green sky of dawn behind them, and whirred down a dry wash. . . . The enfevered breath of the still invisible valley struck their faces, as if she were hissing warning to them. After a while, the canyon walls opened, and Death Valley was below them—a huge bowl, its bottom leprous with some loathsome-hued sediment. They whirred on, down a wash of black flint rock; with each plunge of the machine they entered a layer of air hotter than the preceding, till they panted as at the finish of a mile run. They rolled on, and the mountains rose on all sides, veiled, painted, mysterious mountains. Finally they were at the bottom, one hundred feet below sea level,

and stopped at Stove Pipe Springs, a hole in the sand from which a little black water oozed.

The mule wagon which Chafey had sent on ahead was there, driven by G. N. McCullough, a desert prospector of years' experience. They loaded up with the water from the spring for the machine, hoarding the better water for drinking, and then they went on across the valley of Death.

A half mile on, they reached the sand-dunes, and the big machine stuck, its wheels whirring impotently through the elusive stuff without catching.

"We can't make it," said the chauffeur.

"We've GOT to make it," answered Sullivan and Campbell in one breath. Before them, blue with the distance, rose the Panamints with its mine, the MINE that they were after.

The three men got out. With a shovel they cleared the sand heaped up before the wheels; they placed gunny sacks beneath the tires; then, putting their shoulders against the tonneau, they pushed and strained while the chauffeur applied full power. The wheels whizzed, caught the sacking, the men strained and toiled. The machine gave a jump—one foot, two feet, three! It stuck again. More shoveling, more placing of sacks under the wheels, more pushing and straining. The machine jumped six feet and then struck again. For two hundred yards, foot by foot, they went thus across the dunes. Then the sand grew deeper and their best efforts unavailing.

"Can't make it," said the chauffeur.

"Got to," said Sullivan and Campbell.

Before them, far, mysterious as a veiled woman, the Panamint Range rose with its promise of golden splendor.

They sat down upon the baking sand to consider the matter.

"The mules!" exclaimed Campbell at length.

"You've got it," said Sullivan.

With ropes they tied the wagon to the front axle of the auto. McCullough took the reins. "Yip! Yip! Yip!" he yelled, urging the animals with voice and gesture, while the chauffeur put on full power and the men pushed from behind. The machine vibrated, it jumped up and down in its tracks. There was a crash, and the mules started forward at a gallop, dragging McCullough with them, while the auto remained in place, immovable as a rock. The whiffle-tree had broken.

With the handle of a pick, Campbell and Sullivan improvised a new one. Then they hitched the mules directly to the auto. There was a sharp struggle. The mules tugged, the men pushed, the wheels whirred through the yielding sand. The auto began to move, an inch, a foot. The men panted. The wheels began to take hold, the machine gave a jump, and rolled forward.

For a hundred yards it went. Then the mules stopped, exhausted, and the men rolled over, half dead. The perpendicular sun fell upon them like drops of molten lead. The shimmering sand caught the heat and threw it back to the sun, which promptly poured it down again, till earth, sky, and air pulsated with a blinding glow. But ahead, far, mysterious, the Panamints rose with their purple promise of riches.

"Let's go on," said Sullivan.

They went on. For seven miles, by hundred-yard stretches, they heaved the machine over the sand. And finally they struck hard ground.

They left McCullough there with the wagon and the mules and a supply of water. They got into the auto and buzzed on across the shimmering alkali, a hundred feet below sea level, through an atmosphere that scorched. And ever before them the Panamints rose, veiled and inscrutable.

The machine struck a down grade and whizzed along. At the bottom of the grade, a faint, green mustiness was visible. The machine approached it with vertiginous speed. Suddenly, with an exclamation, the chauffeur leaned forward and put on both brakes. There was a thump, a screech of tortured steel, the machine skidded and jumped, then came to a full stop, like a cow pony that throws itself on its haunches. The front wheels were buried in the treacherous soil.

With infinite labor, they pulled her back out of it. They examined the ground and found that the road led through an alkali swamp. Over the oozy depths, a crust that seemed hard, but broke to weight, stretched like a shimmering white lie.

Chafey went up on a little knoll to reconnoitre. The heat waves, rolling like gigantic breakers, caused strange illusions. On the top of the knoll, Chafey seemed to be limping as if his left leg were cut off at the knee. Then he began running in an extraordinary fashion around in a circle. The rest of the party called him back, afraid. He assured them that he had been walking peaceably along the ridge. They were in the land of delusions, and everything was false.

They held a conference, and then decided upon taking a wild chance.

With only the chauffeur in it, the auto was backed far up the grade it had come down. The rest of the men spread along the path through the marsh, ready for any emergency. Sullivan dropped his handkerchief for a signal, and the machine started down the hill.

Right away, the chauffeur put on full speed. The steel flaps in front opened like wings. Silently at first, like a shadow, she whizzed down; then, as she caught the full impetus of power and grade, she began to buzz in a crescendo that rose till she roared like a bomb-shell. Down she came aroar, like a meteor from the skies. An involuntary cry came from the men in the marsh as she bore down upon them. She cleared the first hundred feet as if with one spring. She slowed, hesitated, yawed from side to side, then, the wheels catching a bit of harder ground, jumped forward again, through an oozy place, the wheels bespattering the skies. The men watched her, breathless. She struck a succession of hard spots between mud holes. Each time the wheels, catching the hard spot, jumped her over the next soft one, and thus, by a series of mad leaps, she went almost across, the chauffeur rising and falling upon his seat like the rider of a dromedary. On the further edge, a few feet from safety, she seemed to mire for good. She stopped, the wheels whirring madly through the slime. But the men alongside, frenzied, threw their coats, their hats, their shirts beneath the wheels, and slowly, inch by inch, she at length rose upon the hard ground.

Everything afterward was easy in comparison, though enough to daunt wills forged of baser metals than those of Sullivan, Campbell, and Chafey. An examination of the machine showed the frame that supported the engine to be cracked. It was braced with a drill and a shovel handle. Five miles from Emigrant Springs the party ran out of water, and the machine refused to go without it. Leaving Sullivan and the chauffeur with the small canteen that remained, Campbell and Chafey hiked on afoot with the empty water-bags. With the desert sun pumping the water out of their bones, it was a desperate race, their tongues were swollen almost out of their mouths before they reached the little pool of stagnant water. They filled all the bags and returned to the machine. Again in working order, the auto pumped slowly up the remainder of the grade, and at midnight rolled into the little camp at Emigrant Springs.

Even then it was not time to rest. Afoot the party climbed over the hills, and just at sun-up, they were standing upon a monstrous outcropping of gold-bearing quartz, the MINE so desperately won. Taking samples here and there, they returned to camp, "panned" them, and there and then, Sullivan, Chafey, and the prospectors closed the deal. Hardly had this been done when the puff-puff of an auto drew them outside of the tent. Slowly, painfully, a crippled automobile was rolling in from the other side of the mountains. Campbell recognized the man in the auto, a confidential agent of Charles M. Schwab, the great steel magnate. The race had been won, and just won.[23]

The "mine" was soon forgotten, but the auto had come to stay, revolutionizing travel throughout the Death Valley and Amargosa country. Other auto enthusiasts followed, after James Clark graded a good road across the valley to Skidoo and opened a roadhouse at Stovepipe Wells that winter. Over the new road too in February 1907 came J. H. Carson on the first motorcycle to cross the valley. Then in the spring of 1908 the little road became a leg of the great around-the-world auto race from New York to Paris.[24]

The "Great Race," really a 20,000-mile endurance run across America, Asia, and Europe, was the first and, as it turned out, the last auto race ever run around the globe. It was promoted by the Paris daily, *Le Matin*, and by the *New York Times,* with a dazzling World Tour Cup as the grand prize to stimulate interest in motoring and sales for the papers themselves. A crowd of 200,000 packed the streets of New York as the six contenders started from Times Square on February 12, 1908—an American Thomas Flyer, a German Protos, an Italian Brixia-Zust, and three French cars, a De Dion-Bouton, a Moto-Bloc, and a Sizaire-Naudin. Only three reached Death Valley; the last two French contenders dropped out early, and the German car broke down in Wyoming and was shipped on by rail.[25]

The first into Rhyolite was the Flyer, driven by the Thomas Motor Company's men, Harold Brinker and George Schuster. It arrived on Saturday afternoon, March 21—39 days and 3,120 miles out of New York. Most of the town turned out to see the daring racers as they stopped for gas and water and their navigator, Arctic explorer Hans Hansen, tore up an American flag to hand out as souvenirs. Then they were off for Death Valley, accompanied partway by Rhyolite's founder, Pete Busch, in his own new Thomas. Reaching Stovepipe Wells at 8 P.M., they crossed the dreaded valley over Clark's road by moonlight with little trouble. It was slow going nonetheless, and it took four hours to cover 8 miles through the sandiest stretch, where they had to let air out of the tires for better traction and frequently got out to push. At 3 A.M. Sunday morning they reached Ballarat, and got just three hours sleep before taking off again. At that point Brinker decided to take a shortcut over the old borax road to Mojave instead of going to Daggett as planned, unaware that his boss Edwin Thomas had come out to Daggett with the press to accompany the car to Los Angeles. The embarrassed auto manufacturer waited all day in the dusty little town amid growing fears that something awful had happened in Death Valley. At sundown word finally came from Mojave that the Flyer had passed through safely, headed for San Francisco. The disappointed newsmen from Los Angeles pleaded in vain for them to come back! Thomas promptly replaced Brinker with another man when they reached San Francisco.[26]

A week later the Zust arrived in Rhyolite, driven by Emilio Sirtori and Henri Haaga, and carrying a young London newspaper correspondent, Antonio Scarfoglio. They too drew a curious crowd and were treated to an elegant spread by an Italian saloon keeper. They headed for Death Valley early Sunday afternoon March 29, but took a wrong turn and ended up that evening at the virtual ghost camp of Greenwater, where only seven souls remained. Continuing through Zabriskie the following day, they crossed the south end of Death Valley to Cave Spring in the Avawatz. It was a fine spring day with wildflowers blooming by the road, and they encountered only a few bad stretches of sand, where they laid down canvas strips for traction. To fulfill the expectations of his readers, the obliging Scarfoglio later conjured up "a veritable inferno" with sun-bleached skeletons beside the road. "It seems as if the whole plain were flaming," he wrote, "burning like an immense pyre. We breathe in fire and a vestment of fire hangs on our limbs; our foreheads are bound by a circle of fire." Sapped of strength, he said, they collapsed in the meager shade of their car until the tormenting sun finally set and freed them from the "infernal valley." In fact they reached Daggett barely an hour after sundown, had a good night's rest, and went on to Los Angeles, where they were thronged by the eager reporters the Flyer had passed by.[27]

Last came the De Dion, driven by Alph Autran and G. Bourcier Saint Chaffray, correspondent for both the *Times* and *Le Matin*. They rolled into Rhyolite on April Fools Day and stayed just long enough for Saint Chaffray to telegraph his story to New York. Then they plunged into Death Valley at midday in the midst of a sandstorm, lost the road leaving Stovepipe Wells, and got stuck in the dunes. They tried digging their way out but were choked and blinded by the sand and quit until the wind died at sundown. Then they tried laying down their shirts and handkerchiefs under the tires for traction, making half a mile before the cloth was torn to shreds. Finally they hiked back to the roadhouse at Stovepipe Wells and telephoned to Rhyolite for help. A samaritan, John Murphy, set out that night with a wagon and team to rescue them, but the next morning the team returned without him. He was later reportedly found dead by the road with a broken neck, having fallen from the wagon. Meanwhile, Autran and Saint Chaffray returned to their stranded auto with canvas from an old tent. They laid this beneath the wheels and made some progress before it too was shredded. Finally the wind shifted and miraculously blew the sand out of their path. By the afternoon of April 2 they were almost out of the dunes when a second rescue team arrived and pulled them through. Free at last, after a day and a half in the Vallée du Mort, they raced out through Wildrose and Ballarat to Mojave to tell their tale.[28]

The Flyer, far in the lead, had sailed to Valdez, only to find that the next leg of the route across Alaska was impassable. The Flyer claimed victory for having gone the farthest, but the organizers withdrew the cup and instead offered a $1,200 prize to the first car to finish the race over a shortened route resuming at Vladivostok. The De Dion dropped out at that point, but the Protos was allowed to stay in the race with a handicap of 30 days for skipping the last thousand miles across the United States.

The Protos made the best time across Siberia and reached Paris on July 26. But the Flyer, with Schuster at the wheel, came in just four days later to win the race, having come 13,341 miles in 169 days. The Zust brought up the rear seven weeks later, and the world's longest auto race was finally over. The first American car to win an international competition, the Flyer returned victorious to Times Square, and Teddy Roosevelt personally congratulated the drivers. Thomas doubled Schuster's salary to $50 a week and gave him a $1,000 bonus. But the official prizes were slow in coming. After two years' prodding, the Thomas Company at last got a trophy, and sixty years after the race, the *Times* finally gave Schuster a $1,000 prize promised by a long-defunct auto club.[29]

The Thomas Motor Company, of course, had won publicity for their car that money couldn't buy. They followed up with a promotional booklet on *The Story of the New York to Paris Race,* making outrageous claims that the car had never been repaired, not even a spark plug replaced, during the entire race. Orders for cars soared, but the little Buffalo company couldn't keep up with the demand and turned out lemons trying. Sales soon collapsed, and the company went into receivership in 1912, a victim of its own success.[30]

Other auto makers got publicity for their cars with much less grueling tests—a trip across the country or just a run through the dreaded Death Valley. The Packard Motor Car Company proudly published *A Family Tour from Ocean to Ocean,* publicizing the "first amateur motor car journey" across the country. It was made by Jacob Murdock, who drove his family from Pasadena to New York across the south end of Death Valley in their Packard touring car in the spring of 1908. Four years later Studebaker got good press from the exploits of another Pasadenan, Lou Beck, the "Good Samaritan of Death Valley," who took his little Flanders all over the valley on roads "where no car has ever been before," to put up signs to guide thirsty travelers to the water holes.[31]

But when a Los Angeles Dodge dealer arranged to have one of his company's cars run through Death Valley at the peak of the summer heat in 1913, there were tragic results. For when Pete Busch and the dealer's driver, Roy Shaw, started across the valley for Rhyolite on the morning of July 8, they found themselves in the midst of the worst heat wave ever recorded there. They got stuck repeatedly on the sandy road, and finally, mired hub deep, "something broke" and the car would go no farther. They tried to walk out. Only Shaw made it; Busch died by the side of the road the next morning. Even the daring young men in their flivvers still had something to fear from Death Valley.[32]

Two years later, with much cooler weather and a more cautious driver, O. K. Parker, the Dodge Brothers at last got one of their cars across the valley. They too proudly brought out a booklet, *Through Death Valley in a Dodge Brothers Motor Car,* telling not only of the triumph of Parker's Dodge but also of the awful fate of poor Pete Busch. They made no mention, however, of the fact that Pete too had been driving a Dodge![33]

Although the real dangers of Death Valley still couldn't be ignored, those daring young men in their flivvers had transformed it, and it would never be the same again. The coming of the auto had robbed Death Valley of its remoteness, radically compressing space and time. A day's journey by horse and wagon had become less than an hour's drive, and millions would now come to see it for themselves.

Into Death Valley with Scotty in 1905 by A. Y. Pearl. (*Courtesy of California State Library*)

DEATH VALLEY VICTIMS. The coyote-ravaged corpse of an unknown
prospector who died of the desiccating summer heat about 1907, and the grave
of Furnace Creek Ranch caretaker Jim Dayton, covered with the bones of the
mules that perished with him in July of 1899. (*Courtesy of National Park Service*)

DEATH VALLEY FORTY-NINERS. William Lewis Manly, one of the heroes and namers of Death Valley, wrote the classic account of the forty-niners' ordeal, illustrated with this stark scene of their "Leaving Death Valley." (*Portrait courtesy of George Koenig*)

THE FIRST VIEWS OF DEATH VALLEY, published in an 1870 mining
prospectus, show the wagon road over the old Walker's cutoff—sought by the
forty-niners—looking west across the south end of the valley (BELOW) past Salt
Spring toward Walker Pass, and the luxuriance of Saratoga Springs (ABOVE),
the best camp on the road. (*Courtesy of Bancroft Library*)

PANAMINT, scene of Death Valley's first big mining bubble in 1874–75, looking up Main Street toward the Surprise Valley Company's great mill—the closest thing to a church Panamint ever had. (*Courtesy of U.S. Borax & Chemical Corp.*)

DEATH VALLEY'S FIRST HOMESTEADER, Andy Laswell, a hotheaded Kentuck known to legend as "Bellerin' Teck," started a hay ranch at Bennetts Well in 1874 and another at the mouth of Furnace Creek where the Greenland Ranch (BELOW) was later built by borax company superintendent Rudolph Neuschwander. (*Courtesy of Mojave River Valley Museum, Gertrude Alf Collection,* ABOVE, *and Henry E. Huntington Library & Art Gallery,* BELOW)

HARMONY BORAX WORKS. Chinese miners scraped up the borate salts from the floor of Death Valley from 1883 to 1888 while the famous twenty-mule teams hauled the refined borax to the railroad. (*Courtesy of U.S. Borax & Chemical Corp.*)

DEATH VALLEY PROSPECTORS. Shorty Harris, a "single blanket jackass prospector" (ABOVE) and a partner Ed Cross triggered the Bullfrog rush with their discovery of gold in 1904, while Death Valley Scotty (BELOW) in a blitz of publicity stunts, fired the imagination of the nation with his tales of the valley's hidden riches. (*Courtesy of Arizona Historical Foundation,* ABOVE, *and Nevada Historical Society,* BELOW)

THE MONTGOMERY BROTHERS. George (RIGHT) started Death Valley and Amargosa's great gold boom with rich strikes in the 1890s and Bob (LEFT) sustained the boom with the opening of Bullfrog's biggest bonanza, the Montgomery Shoshone mine (BELOW) which produced nearly $1,500,000 in gold from 1905 to 1911. (*Courtesy of Virginia Rhode,* ABOVE, *and Nevada Historical Society,* BELOW)

RHYOLITE, the "Queen City" of the Death Valley country was a model metropolis with 4,000 citizens, three railroads, three-story skyscrapers, and all the modern conveniences: running water, electricity and telephones, daily and weekly newspapers, and a monthly magazine—even a stock exchange and a rock-drilling contest every Fourth of July. (*Courtesy of Special Collections, University of Nevada Library,* ABOVE, *and Nevada Historical Society* BELOW)

THE BIGGEST BULLION PRODUCERS in Death Valley proper were Homer Wilson's Keane Wonder mill (BELOW) and Bob Montgomery's Skidoo mill (ABOVE)—each turned out about a million dollars worth of gold from 1906 to 1917. (*Courtesy of National Park Service,* ABOVE, *and U.S. Borax & Chemical Corp.,* BELOW)

SKIDOO. Joe "Hootch" Simpson, "boss bad man" of Skidoo (BELOW), was hung from a telephone pole by irate Skidoovians after he murdered a man on Easter Sunday 1908, and the town's doctor hung Hootch up again for this souvenir photo (LEFT), then cut off his head a few nights later for another memento. (*Courtesy of National Park Service,* LEFT, *and* BELOW)

GREENWATER. Patsy Clark's manipulation of the stock of this raw prospect (BELOW) to a market value of over $6,000,000 on the New York Curb in 1906 triggered the Greenwater copper frenzy that cost investors tens of millions of dollars. (*Courtesy of Eastern Washington State Historical Society,* ABOVE, *and Nevada Historical Society,* BELOW)

PATSY CLARK MINE, FURNACE CREEK & DEATH VALLEY CAL.

RESURRECTION. The old camps at the north end of Death Valley were resurrected in the great gold boom that brought new life to the main street of Palmetto in 1905 (ABOVE) and a gang of promoters to Lida and Tule Canyon, including the ill-fated Pete Busch (BELOW, FAR RIGHT). (*Courtesy of Nevada Historical Society*)

DEATH VALLEY'S
BIGGEST BONANZA.
"Borax King" Frances
Marion Smith opened the
first of the great colemanite
deposits, the Lila C.
(BELOW), in 1904 and
built a branch line from his
Tonopah & Tidewater
Railroad to the mine two
years later, after an abortive
attempt to haul out the ore
with a traction engine, Old
Dinah (UPPER RIGHT).
The Lila C. together with
other deposits opened in
1914 at New Ryan above
Furnace Creek (LOWER
RIGHT) eventually
produced over $30,000,000
worth of borax. (*Courtesy of
U.S. Borax & Chemical
Corp., and Henry E.
Huntington Library & Art
Gallery, Dinah*)

FLIVVERS. The automobile conquered Death Valley at the turn of the century, reducing a long day's trek to less than an hour's ride and robbing the valley of its isolation and much of its terror—unless there were problems. (*Courtesy of Hugh Tolford,* ABOVE, *and Nevada Historical Society,* BELOW)

MOVIES AND A MONORAIL. Death Valley gained new publicity in the 1920s when Eric von Stroheim shot the final scenes of his classic film *Greed* in the heart of the valley and a quixotic Los Angeles florist Thomas Wright built an ill-fated monorail to tap a laxative bonanza. (*Courtesy of Museum of Modern Art, Film Stills Archive,* ABOVE, and National Park Service, BELOW)

THE LAST HURRAH.
In a final flash of
flimflammery Charles
Courtney Julian hired a
whole train and a fleet of
cars to haul a thousand
faithful followers out to
Death Valley in March of
1926 to ogle at his
Leadfield "Jazz Baby."
(*Courtesy of UCLA
Library, Special Collections,*
RIGHT, *and National Park
Service,* BELOW)

SCOTTY'S
CASTLE. Death
Valley Scotty
captured national
attention again in
the 1920s when his
backer Albert M.
Johnson and wife
Bessie (BELOW)
began building the
mansion that soon
came to be known
as Scotty's Castle.
(Courtesy of
UCLA Library,
Special Collections)

TOURISTS. Bob Eichbaum opened Death Valley for tourists in 1926, building a toll road into his new Stove Pipe Wells resort. (*Courtesy of Tom G. Murray,* ABOVE, *and Pomona Public Library, Frasher Collection,* BELOW)

Early the following year the borax men, led by Frank Jenifer, opened the luxurious Furnace Creek Inn. (*Courtesy of U.S. Borax & Chemical Corp.*)

NATIONAL MONUMENT. Death Valley was saved for posterity in 1933 when National Park Service director Horace Albright (LEFT) got President Herbert Hoover to declare the valley a National Monument—just two weeks before he left office. (*Courtesy of National Park Service,* RIGHT, *and U.S. Borax & Chemical Corp.,* BELOW)

SALT AND SCENERY

Despite all the lore and lure of gold and silver, the real wealth of Death Valley and the Amargosa was simply in its salt and its scenery. And after decades of rainbow-chasers, that wealth still lay practically untouched at the end of the nineteenth century. Coleman's men had hardly scratched the surface of the enormous borate deposits before they quit, and old Jake Staininger had died still waiting for his Grapevine Ranch to become a popular spa. But with the new century, salt and scenery would at last become the Death Valley country's biggest businesses. Meanwhile, of course, the last of the mining sharps also conjured up more mental scenery to sell their stock, and those who bought it had to take their losses with a grain of salt.

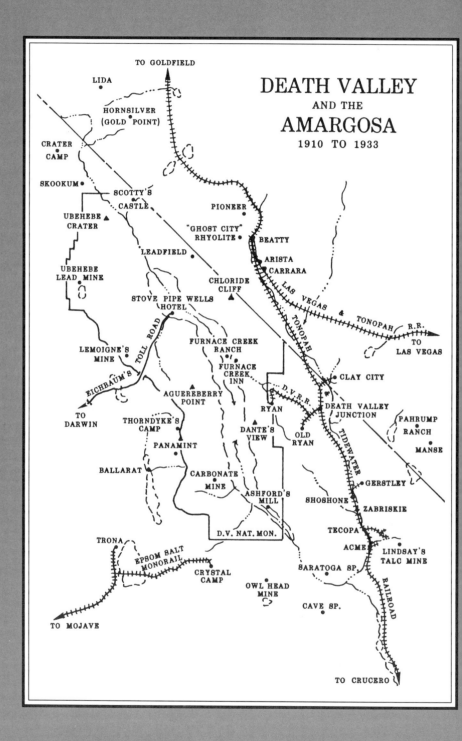

The Salt of the Earth

While thousands of hopefuls were rushing into Death Valley in the quest of its elusive gold, Borax Smith was heading back to open its real treasure—those vast but long-neglected deposits of colemanite. Borax mining out on the salt flats of Death Valley had ended with Coleman's failure in the spring of 1888, and when Smith took over Coleman's holdings two years later, he concentrated on the colemanite deposits at Calico, down on the Mojave close to the railroad. For the next sixteen years Calico was practically the sole producer of borax in America. But during these years Death Valley was not forgotten, as the rich lore of the valley and its twenty-mule teams became the star attractions in an advertising campaign to put a box of borax in every home. The campaign was so successful that by the turn of the century the ever-increasing demand for borax was rapidly depleting the Calico deposit. Only the great colemanite beds of Death Valley and the Amargosa seemed capable of supplying the long-term demand—and so they would, even after the "Borax King" had fallen.[1]

Frances Marion Smith liked to think of himself as a self-made man, and he was, to a large extent. He was hardworking and strong-willed, with a stubborn determination that saw him through adversity. His was certainly a rise from rags to riches. He had been a poor woodchopper living in a clapboard shack when he discovered borax at Teel's Marsh in 1872, at the age of twenty-six. Ten years later, with the help of his brother Julius and loans from Coleman, Smith had become the largest single borax producer in the country. Soon after Coleman's failure he formed a virtual monopoly of both the production and distribution of borax in America. By the time he set out to reopen the Death Valley deposits, he controlled the borax business worldwide, and was unquestionably the "Borax King." He had also amassed a personal fortune estimated at around $20 million. He had two palatial estates, the 25-acre "Arbor Villa" in Oakland and the 260-acre "Presdeleau" at the east end of Long Island; a private railroad car, the "Havoli"; a 211-foot steam yacht, the *Havoli II;* and a 93-foot sloop, the *Effort,* which took several racing cups. By then, too, Smith was speculating heavily in Oakland real estate and streetcar lines. Admirers have called him a visionary entrepreneur. But Smith had a great blind spot that kept him from recognizing the often crucial help of his closest associates, and cost him their loyalty. Moreover, he had a shortsighted view of finance that eventually proved catastrophic.[2]

The idea of drawing on the lore and mystique of Death Valley to promote borax sales was the brainchild of a bright young man named Stephen Tyng Mather, who was to become the founding director of the National Park Service. Mather's father, Joseph, a former Connecticut schoolteacher and California commission broker, played a key role in the formation of Smith's Pacific Coast Borax Company, obtaining the loans that made possible Smith's purchase of the Coleman property in 1890, and setting up a New York office to make a market for the product. It was the latter effort that attracted young Mather. Born in San Francisco on the Fourth of July, 1867, and graduated from the University of California twenty years later, Stephen had gone to work as a cub reporter on the *New York Sun,* but he was a "born salesman." He saw that the romance of Death Valley was the perfect vehicle to help make borax a household word, so he persuaded one of the *Sun's* feature writers, John Randolph Spears, just returned from Greenland, to go to Death Valley and write the story, if Borax Smith would agree to pay his salary and expenses. The harder task, it seems, was convincing Smith of the value of the venture. But Mather senior finally succeeded, and early in November 1891 Spears headed west. The result was the first popular book on the valley, *Illustrated Sketches of Death Valley and Other Borax Deserts of the Pacific Coast,* a classic that's still delightful reading today. Spears wrote the book in just three months, but it took six to find a publisher—at least two turned it down because of the promotional matter in it. Rand McNally finally brought it out as a 25¢ paperback in September 1892 to spread the borax story across the country. Mather senior also distributed it freely in the Congress when he went to lobby for a protective tariff on the versatile salt.[3]

Smith was so favorably impressed with the result that he hired young Mather in January 1893 to push an all-out campaign to make a home market for borax. But Smith wasn't willing to put out much money to buy newspaper ads, so the resourceful Mather had to do the best he could with planted press releases and letters to the editor. To propagate the latter he offered a dollar to anyone who sent in a *published* testimonial letter extolling the use of borax. This produced a bumper crop of epistles, which he harvested—along with his own plantings—and turned into a fat booklet entitled *Borax: From the Desert, Through the Press, Into the Home: 200 Best Borax Recipes from More than 800 Issues of 250 Different Publications in 33 States of the Union.* Mather also persuaded Smith to adopt the now famous "20 Mule Team" brand name. Smith had resisted the idea at first, because he wanted to use his own name. But he finally recognized that it was the logical choice. After all, his borax packages had been decorated for years with a distinctive little cartoon of a mule team and wagons, placed there by his brother, Julius, who had marketed the borax from Teel's Marsh before they had a falling out.[4]

To promote the brand, Smith resurrected two of the old Death Valley wagons, trained a new team, and sent them to the St. Louis Exposition in 1904. The great twenty-mule team created such a sensation that a motion picture company even made a short film of it, generating more free advertising for the product. At the same time, Smith put out another little booklet on *The 20-Mule Team and a Sketch of its Famous Driver: Borax Bill*. Its zealous writer, not wanting to spoil the romance, still had the teams hauling borax out of Death Valley in 1904—sixteen years after the fact. The "famous driver Borax Bill" was mostly an ad man's creation, too. Dubbed "Borax Bill" just for the occasion, William Parkinson had never driven the Death Valley teams, but he had worked for the Searles brothers west of the valley, and was kept on as a watchman when Smith bought their property in 1897. Parkinson played his new role well. A short, stout, feisty man with a walrus moustache, much like Borax Smith himself, he put the big team through its paces with a black snake whip and a string of curses that made the crowds gasp. The St. Louis appearance was so successful that Smith sent the team on an extended tour all over the East to hand out free samples of borax. Even Parkinson's sudden death the following summer didn't slow the promotion; Smith just recruited a new "Borax Bill," and the tours continued.[5]

To keep pace with the growing demand, Smith had thoroughly modernized his borax operations in 1898. He built a narrow gauge railroad, the Borate and Daggett, to haul the colemanite 8 miles from the Calico mine to the Santa Fe siding, replacing the last twenty-mule teams with two Heisler locomotives named Francis and Marion. He also built a roaster near Daggett to concentrate the lower-grade ores for shipment, making use of the fact that colemanite, when heated, decrepitates or shatters into a fine powder that can be easily separated from coarser impurities. Finally, he built a new, $1.25 million refinery at Bayonne, New Jersey to supply the Eastern market and take the load off Coleman's old remodeled soap works at Alameda. With all of this, Smith was able to triple borax production, which of course only hastened the depletion of the Calico deposits.[6]

These improvements as well as Smith's extensive personal speculations, were financed by a series of deals that secured not only much needed cash but virtual control of the borax industry worldwide as well. In the summer of 1896, Smith moved in on the European market through a merger with a British borax refinery, forming the Pacific Borax and Redwood's Chemical Works, Ltd. Through this company he soon bought up a number of other competitors, both at home and abroad, and in January 1899 he combined them into one of the first multinational corporations, Borax Consolidated, Ltd. This $12 million venture, with holdings scattered

Vol. I. No. 175.

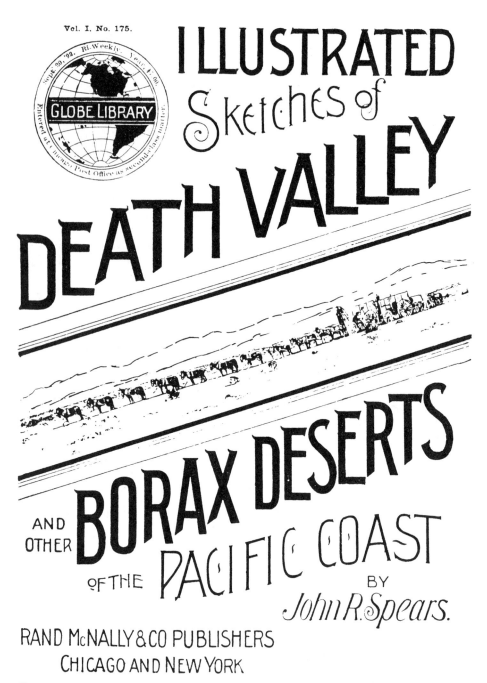

ILLUSTRATED Sketches of

DEATH VALLEY

AND OTHER BORAX DESERTS OF THE PACIFIC COAST

BY

John R. Spears.

RAND McNALLY & CO PUBLISHERS
CHICAGO AND NEW YORK

Borax Smith hired *New York Sun* correspondent John Spears to write this book to help sell the laundry miracle.

from Turkey to Chile, practically controlled the global production of borax. Smith, however, held control of the company without having to hold much more than $1.5 million worth of stock, since voting rights were limited to the ordinary shares, which made up only a quarter of those issued. Sale of his other shares thus brought in ready cash for his personal ventures, without causing him to lose control of the borax business. But even that money proved insufficient for Smith's ever-spiraling speculations, and he eventually mortgaged even his ordinary shares for more quick cash.[7]

Conservative old Joseph Mather, feeling used and abused, had quit in disgust after the first British deal over what he termed Smith's "devious" style of business. His son Stephen, his loyalties torn, stayed with Smith for several more years, but secretly began financing his friend Thomas Thorkildsen, another disgruntled former Smith employee, in a rival borax mining venture in Ventura County. The emotional strain eventually brought young Mather to a nervous breakdown in 1903, so he quit Smith and went into open competition. Mather and Thorkildsen were so successful that Smith finally bought them out in 1912. In the meantime, Smith's American marketing operations were taken up by an ambitious but officious young protégé from the Nevada borax fields, Christian B. Zabriskie, whom young Mather had trained. Smith had already found a more-than-able replacement for the elder Mather in his new associate, Richard C. Baker, who had been the senior partner of the British chemical company with which Smith had merged and who had become Borax Consolidated's managing director in Europe. Although Smith held voting control of the company, he relied on Baker to take care not only of foreign operations and global acquisitions but of all the financial affairs of the company as well. Smith worried only about the American operations, devoting an ever-increasing amount of his time and energy to his personal speculations.[8]

The depletion of the Calico deposits, however, was one problem that had the Borax King's full attention. The solution was simple enough— building a railroad to open the Death Valley deposits—but it became unduly complicated as Smith began to see in it yet another chance for personal profits. Smith had started thinking about opening the Death Valley deposits early in 1899, and after inspecting all of the colemanite claims, he decided to work the Lila C. first. This wasn't the richest or the largest deposit, but it was the most accessible, located just a few miles west of the Amargosa, and the easiest to reach by rail. In April 1900 Smith first wrote to Baker suggesting that they build a railroad to the Lila C. from the railhead of the old California Eastern at Manvel, a distance of 100 miles. Baker, who would have to raise the money for the venture, was cool to the idea. He wanted a cheaper way to get the ore out, one that would require less capital investment. The following year, Smith proposed a traction road along the same route. He had not given up the idea of a railroad, however—far from it. But he now saw the line as a highly profitable personal venture, for the Tonopah rush had begun, and Smith envisioned big money to be made with a railroad to the new camp. All he needed to cash in on it was a little help from the company.[9]

Smith had few illusions that a traction road could prove practical. He had already tried a Best steam tractor in 1894 on the short haul from the Calico mine, before he built the railroad there, and had found that the tractor couldn't even compete with mules. But Baker and his British associates were willing to finance a traction road, and Smith was quite willing to go along with the idea. Even though it wouldn't work, he would have a roadbed already graded for his railroad. Smith dutifully contracted with a Harlem firm to build three fancy tractor trains with seven cars each, capable of hauling a total of 300 tons of ore. The tractors were to be powered by a new, untested "electro-gasoline engine," which was to consist of two three-cycle, 75-horsepower gasoline engines turning a 100-kilowatt dynamo that ran electric motors geared to the rear wheels of each car.[10]

Work on the road began in June 1903, with a crew of seventy or more under the supervision of John Ryan, a hard-driving man who had worked for Smith since the Nevada marsh days. Ryan worked the men steadily for the next ten months, grading and cutting the 10-foot-wide road north across Ivanpah Valley, over State Line Pass, through Mesquite and Pahrump valleys, around the north end of the Resting Spring range, and across Ash Meadows to the Lila C.—104 miles in all, at a cost of $153,000. But when the road was completed in April 1904, the marvelous new "electro-gasoline" tractor was still on the drawing board. The designers just couldn't make it work, and Smith canceled the contract. In case his British associates still thought tractors might work, Smith hauled "Old Dinah," the Best tractor, and her two wagons out to the railhead at Ivanpah for a test run. To no one's surprise, the old tractor failed again; she just couldn't make the grade up State Line Pass. Her engine stuck, and she was dragged back to the railhead in humiliation by a team of mules.[11]

That was the end of the tractor business, and Smith promptly notified his partners that a railroad would have to be built after all. But he would take care of it himself; all the British company would have to do was to guarantee the bonds for construction costs in exchange for a very favorable hauling rate for their ore. Moreover, the cost should not be too great now, because he would use the traction road. Smith didn't mention, however, that the railroad wouldn't end at the Lila C. The British learned that in July, when Smith formed the Tonopah and Tidewater Railroad Company, with himself as president, Zabriskie as secretary-treasurer, and Ryan as general manager. Nonetheless, when the railroad issued $2.5 million in fifty-five-year debentures for construction, Borax Consolidated guaranteed them, and Baker dutifully placed them on the London market.[12]

The Goldfield boom and the new rush to Bullfrog that fall made the railroad's potential profits all the greater and its completion all the more urgent. But things didn't go as Smith planned. A reexamination of the traction road revealed that the grades and curves in State Line Pass were just too steep and sharp for a railroad, and there was no practical way to improve them. Much to his chagrin, Smith had to give up the traction road as a total loss, and Ryan set out to find another route. By the end of the year Ryan had one, starting at Soda Lake on Senator William Clark's nearly completed San Pedro, Los Angeles and Salt Lake Railroad. The route was a much gentler grade and a mile shorter than the traction road. It ran almost straight north, paralleling the old Spanish Trail from Silver Lake to Tecopa, and then crossed Ash Meadows to the Lila C. Bullfrog was an easy 50 miles on up the Amargosa valley, and Goldfield and Tonopah were just beyond.[13]

Before he could proceed, however, Smith would have to reach an agreement with Clark, who was also thinking about building a new line to Tonopah and the other boom camps from his Salt Lake road at Las Vegas. Clark's men finished a survey of that route in February 1905, with a 30-mile "Borax Branch" to the Lila C. Borax Consolidated could build the branch itself at only a small cost, but that didn't fit Borax Smith's plans, so he wouldn't hear of it—and was careful not to let Baker hear of it, either. What followed was a cat and mouse game between Clark and Smith that lasted for months, as each tried to outmaneuver the other. In April, one of Clark's close associates announced that Clark had decided to build a railroad from Las Vegas to Tonopah without delay; at the same time, Clark's brother announced that a deal was being worked out with Smith allowing him to connect his "borax line" with the Salt Lake Railroad at Soda Lake. But shortly after that Smith and Clark met face to face, and according to Smith, reached a verbal agreement that Smith would build the railroad from Las Vegas to Tonopah with a branch to the Lila C.[14]

Smith announced his new plans early in May. By the end of the month Ryan had assembled a grading crew of some forty men and fifty horses at Las Vegas, and started work without fanfare. By the end of June they had graded about 12 miles of roadbed and were ready to make a connection with the Salt Lake tracks when Clark's attorney ordered them off the right-of-way. Smith was furious and wired Clark, only to find that he was vacationing in Europe. Work came to a standstill while Ryan went East to confront Clark on his return in August. It was to no avail, however, for Clark simply told Ryan that he was going to build the railroad from Las Vegas, and publicly revealed that he had offered to let Smith build a branch to the Lila C., but that it hadn't suited Smith to do so. Moreover, he warned that there was "no room" for two railroads beyond the Lila C. The following month Clark formed the Las Vegas and Tonopah Railroad Company, gave Smith $30,000 for the 12 miles of grading already done, and put his own men to work.[15]

Smith was now more determined than ever to build his own railroad and beat Clark to Tonopah. He quickly worked out an arrangement with the Santa Fe to connect his Tonopah and Tidewater with their track at a station called Ludlow, just 26 miles south of Soda Lake. Late in August Ryan moved all of his men, teams, and equipment down from Las Vegas. The grading began at Ludlow, right on the heels of the surveyors, as they set out to tie in with the earlier survey line at Soda Lake. Smith, hoping to complete the road as far as Bullfrog in just six months, ordered Ryan to hire every man he could get. They started laying rails late in November at a rate of 1 mile a day. But they couldn't keep up the pace, and spring found the grading and track-laying crews barely 60 miles out of Ludlow, in the middle of that dreaded stretch of the old Spanish Trail once known as the jornada del muerto. As summer set in, Ryan had more than 200 men down in the south tip of Death Valley, working in as much as 140° heat for just $2.50 a day. Few men stayed long under those conditions, and Wash Cahill, Ryan's assistant, recalled that they often had three crews in the field at the same time—one on the way home, having just quit; one just starting work; and one on the way out, to replace the second crew when they quit. When the heat was at its worst, only half the men actually worked on the road; the other half were kept busy spraying them with water. By the end of July, Ryan couldn't keep enough men on the ground to continue, so work stopped until the fall.[16]

Seventy-five miles of track had been laid, but they were barely halfway to the Lila C., and the worst was yet to come, in Amargosa Canyon. When construction resumed that fall, Ryan had as many as nine hundred men and eight hundred animals laboring on the cuts and fills and trestles in that 11-mile stretch of canyon. Despite all that effort, they averaged fewer than 2 miles per month, at a cost of $55,000 a mile.[17]

When the railhead finally climbed out of Amargosa Canyon in May 1907, a small mountain of ore was sacked and waiting on the dump at the Lila C. Work on the mine had begun early in 1904, and a handful of men had been blocking out and knocking down ore ever since, opening 3,000 feet of underground workings. As soon as the trains could run up through the canyon, Smith commenced shipping. In a nostalgic gesture, the two old Death Valley borax wagons, left at Daggett, were hooked up to a twenty-mule team again by Seymour Alf, and on June 6, 1907 the old wagons were loaded with colemanite at the Lila C. to haul the first ore shipment 28 miles to the Tonopah and Tidewater railhead at Zabriskie. These sentimental journeys lasted only a couple of months, however, until the rails of the 7-mile branch from the main line reached the mine and the first trainload of ore rolled out of the Lila C. on August 21. The Calico mines closed down completely two months later, and the roasting plant and everything that could be moved was shipped to the new camp of Ryan at the Lila C.[18]

Smith, meanwhile, was pushing the Tonopah and Tidewater on across the Amargosa Desert to the Bullfrog district. But he was too late. He had lost the race to Clark back in Amargosa Canyon a year before. Clark's Las Vegas and Tonopah had passed through Rhyolite in the fall of 1906 and was now in Goldfield. Smith hadn't even come in second, for Brock's Bullfrog Goldfield had reached its destination in June. It wasn't until October 30, 1907, a week after the crash of the Knickerbocker Trust, that the last spike of the Tonopah and Tidewater was driven at Gold Center, by then a virtual ghost town. That was the end of the track—over two years, $3 million, and 167 miles from Ludlow. Half a dozen members of the Beatty Booster Club came down to celebrate the event with a bottle of Mum's, but there was little cause for cheer; the boom days were over. The big profits Smith had dreamed of had gone aglimmering. Even though Smith later leased the Brock line to run his trains on into Goldfield, the Tonopah and Tidewater would never make a profit. Nonetheless, the ill-starred railroad fulfilled its primary purpose very well, serving faithfully as the borax company's vital link between its mines and market.[19]

With the opening of the Lila C., the Death Valley and Amargosa country became the center of American borax mining, and the modest little mine itself quickly became the region's biggest producer. Day after day, month after month, year after year the Lila C. shipped around 100 tons of ore, selected and concentrated to nearly $30 a ton. Her shipments totaled over $1 million a year, and that rate was limited only by market demand. By the time she was finally shut down in 1915, the Lila C. had shipped a third of a million tons of colemanite, worth roughly $8 million— far more than all the other Death Valley mines combined.[20]

Despite this prodigious production, the camp of Ryan remained a quiet, dusty little company town. There was no wild rush of miners there, no townsite boom or highboot speculators, no miners' union or preacher, no gamblers or whiskey peddlers, not even a murder. Ryan never had a population of more than about 150, and for the three hottest months of each year, June through August, it was a virtual ghost town, with only a watchman in residence. It never had more than a couple of dozen

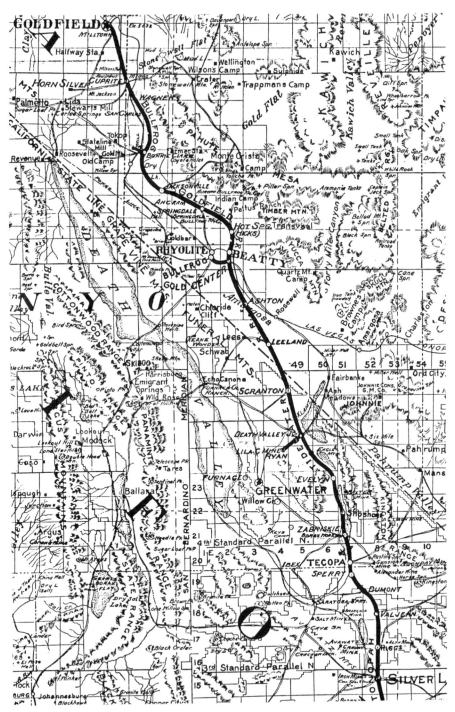

Death Valley and the Amargosa about 1909, from the Tonopah & Tidewater Railroad map.

buildings, either, and nearly all of them were secondhand, moved up from the Calico mines on the Tonopah and Tidewater. There was just the big roaster or concentrator, the company office, the blacksmith shop, a few sheds, the company store, the boardinghouse, a reading room, a bunkhouse, and a few dozen one-room cabins for the men, plus a couple of cottages for the mine and mill superintendents, Billy Smitheram and Fred Corkill, and their families. Aside from the reading room, the nearest entertainment was at the combination saloon, store, and brothel run by Bob Tubb and his wife 7 miles to the northeast at Death Valley Junction, where the branch line from the mine joined the main line of the Tonopah and Tidewater. But the men had little time on their hands, since they worked nine-hour shifts, seven days a week—at least until 1910, when California passed an eight-hour law. Miners' wages were $2.75 a day plus board, and muckers' were $1.75; these were cut by 25¢ when they went to eight-hour shifts. Jobs were scarce enough after the crash of 1907 that Smitheram and Corkill had little trouble keeping a crew of anywhere from 50 to 150—whatever size the borax market demanded.[21]

Although Borax Consolidated was prospering, paying steady dividends of more than a million dollars a year to its stockholders, the Borax King's personal ventures were on the verge of collapse. The Tonopah and Tidewater was the least of Smith's financial disappointments. His extensive land and streetcar speculations in Oakland had failed to generate the big profits he expected. As a result, his pyramiding of short-term loans was out of control; he had two brokers working constantly to place new loans, just to pay off old ones as they came due. In a desperate attempt to get more quick cash and create additional loan "security," Smith tried to water his stock just one more time, forming a gargantuan $200 million holding company, the United Properties Company of California, in December 1910, to take over all of his ventures. But the promotion fell through when he couldn't even free his stock from his creditors long enough to turn it over to the new company. With the collapse of this deal, nervous bankers started calling in his loans, totaling nearly $9 million, and the whole house of cards came down.[22]

On May 5, 1913 Smith signed his assets over to the bankers for liquidation. Since an auditor had estimated his net worth at around $25 million, he expected that the sale of his Oakland properties alone would more than satisfy his indebtedness, without the loss of the borax holdings. The bankers, however, failed to recover more than a fraction of Smith's debt from his other assets, so in the spring of 1914 they took his Borax Consolidated shares to London for disposal. Smith followed, trying to stop the sale, but to no avail. Dumping so large a block of stock on the market could have severely depressed the price, so Baker formed a syndicate to take all 400,000 shares for about $4 million. Through this, of course, Baker also gained absolute control of the business, and when Smith formally resigned from the company in November, Baker made himself managing director of the entire operation, a position he held until his death in 1937. Smith, bitter over the loss, never forgave Baker for his part in the deal.[23]

Francis Marion Smith was the Borax King no more. The title he had so proudly held for a quarter of a century had been suddenly stripped from him. But he was far from destitute. Shortly before the fall he had deeded to his wife both his mansions and considerable stock, including a controlling interest in the West End Consolidated Mining Company, which owned a profitable mine in Tonopah. The Smiths could still live well and at the age of 68, many another man would have been content to accept the loss and retire in luxury. But Smith was determined to get back into the borax business, and to the embarrassment of his former associates, he even ran a little ad in a mining journal, "To Prospectors. Borax Mine Wanted." That ad didn't bring any results, but several years later he did succeed in beating Borax Consolidated to a newly discovered colemanite deposit near Las Vegas. Diverting the profits of the West End mine into the new venture, he built up a modest borax operation there and at Searles Lake. Despite his success in breaking back into the business, Smith never came close to regaining his lost title, although he tried almost until he died on August 27, 1931, at the age of eighty-five.[24]

By the time the Lila C. was nearing exhaustion in 1914, plans were well underway to open new colemanite deposits to replace her. The next most accessible deposit of any significance was the Biddy McCarthy, on the west side of the Greenwater Range overlooking Furnace Creek Wash, a dozen miles northwest of Ryan. Nearby were several other promising claims—the Played Out, Grand View, Lizzie V. Oakey, and Widow—all of which had been patented by Coleman in 1886. John Ryan surveyed a new rail line from the Biddy to the Lila C. branch 4 miles out from Death Valley Junction, and was ready to begin construction in the fall of 1913. But the California Railroad Commission refused to allow Smith's debt-ridden Tonopah and Tidewater to issue new bonds to finance the work, so on January 26, 1914, a separate Death Valley Railroad Company was founded to do the job. Frank M. Jenifer, freight agent for the Tonopah and Tidewater, was named president, and its bonds were guaranteed by Borax Consolidated. Construction began in mid-February, with a crew of 325 men and 150 mules, in hopes of completing the road by the end of June. But the searing heat, a couple of high trestles, and heavy rock work to cut a ledge for the roadbed into a cliff on the final approach to the mine once again slowed the pace and raised the cost. It was not until

December 1 that the 17-mile railroad was a last completed, at a cost of $370,000.[25]

In the interim, Billy Smitheram had put most of his men to work opening the Biddy, and they began shipping ore as soon as the rails reached the dump. The Lila C. was shut down, and all of the old buildings in Ryan, except for the roaster, were loaded onto railroad cars once again and hauled to their new resting place on the slope adjacent to the Biddy. The company officially named the ensemble Devar, for the Death Valley Railroad, but sentiment and the post office restored it to Ryan before the old man retired in 1916. One train a day ran from Death Valley Junction to the new Ryan and back, bringing water in the morning and hauling out the ore in the afternoon. The company also fitted up a 1912 Cadillac touring car with flanged wheels and ran it on the rails, carrying mail and passengers.[26]

Fred Corkill had dismantled the roaster at old Ryan and hauled it to Death Valley Junction to make that spot the mill town. There the machinery was incorporated into a new half-million-dollar roasting plant that started up on Biddy ore early in January 1915. The company also built a modern new bungalow with indoor plumbing for the Corkills, quarters for the mill hands, and a company store that put Tubb out of the general mercantile business. Soon after that Tubb was forced to close his saloon, when Inyo County went dry in 1916, so he moved across the state line to Ash Meadows and turned to ranching.[27]

The other claims near the Biddy were put into production within a year or two. The Played Out, which lay right on the line of the railroad a couple of miles northeast of the Biddy, was opened first. Work then started on the Grand View and Lizzie V. Oakey, a mile or so south of Ryan, and a winding little 2-foot-gauge rail line, dubbed the Baby Gauge, was laid from Ryan to those mines in 1915 and 1916. Farther to the southeast was the Widow, which didn't look too promising at first, so the ore from there was packed to the railroad by mule. But after rich ore was struck at depth, the Baby Gauge was extended down to the Widow in 1919. By then the Baby Gauge was 7 miles long and had its own little gasoline engine and 3-ton cars. The company worked all of the mines at new Ryan year-round, with a crew of about a hundred. Their combined production ran over 200 tons a day—about double that of the Lila C.—and the new mill at Death Valley Junction ran twenty-four hours a day.[28]

Life at the new Ryan wasn't quite as tranquil as life at the old Ryan had been. The trouble started in 1916, after Baker sent over a young British engineer, Herbert W. Faulkner, to act as mining superintendent and replace the popular Billy Smitheram, who was dying of silicosis. Faulkner was a tall, thin, humorless chap, ill-suited to the raucous life in a Western camp. The miners dubbed him "Highpockets," and made him the butt of every joke imaginable. A few, led by Smitheram's son and a disgruntled former employee, James P. Hughes, who had either been fired by Faulkner or quit, stirred up even more trouble, jumping a number of the company's best claims on the Monte Blanco.[29]

These claims had been patented by Coleman as placers in the 1880s, along with the playa deposits, but around 1899 legal questions arose as to whether the colemanite deposits should be located as lodes instead. Just to be safe, Smith had the ground staked out again as lode claims and formed a separate company, United States Borax, to hold all of the undeveloped claims and do the annual assessment work, which was required to hold title, until the legal question was resolved or they could be patented. This was no small job, since the company was holding down some 37,000 acres—roughly 60 square miles—over half of it unpatented. It cost over $25,000 a year, for every fall the company sent out a crew of twenty or so to make the rounds of all the unpatented claims and do the necessary $100 worth of work on each.[30]

Suddenly, in the spring of 1916, Hughes, young Smitheram, and their confederates relocated a dozen or more of the richest claims, arguing that the company hadn't done the full $100 worth of work on each the previous fall. To add insult to injury, they named their new claims in such a way that they spelled out unrepeatable epithets directed at Faulkner, and finished with a pair that taunted, "Don't Get Peeved, Highpockets." In a huff, Faulkner went out with a deputy to order them off the ground. He found them securely barricaded on one of the claims up in Corkscrew Canyon, and quietly retreated after the deputy read the order amid the hoots and jeers of the jumpers. Faulkner then put his own men to work running a token two-by-four post and telephone-wire fence around the other contested claims, while the company lawyers worked on building a legal case.[31]

The case finally came to trial in the U.S. District Court in Los Angeles in December 1918. Hughes tried unsuccessfully to show that the work done by the company on each of the claims was worth only $77.50, not the required $100. In support, Hughes brought in one of the assessment crew members, who claimed he had loafed on the job and not done a full day's work, but under cross-examination he admitted to taking a full day's pay from the company. Faulkner and a crowd of company witnesses had little trouble convincing the judge that the required work had indeed been done, and the court ruled against Hughes, ordering him off the ground. Hughes, who had in the meantime secured some financial backing from unnamed parties interested in a chance to grab the ground, doggedly appealed the ruling all the way up to the Supreme Court, before he finally gave up in 1923.[32]

Although Hughes ultimately lost, the excitement of the claim-jumping case sparked the interest of a veteran borax miner, W. Scott Russell, in the spring of 1919. Russell, a shrewd but friendly fellow with an easy laugh and a twinkle in his eye, had discovered several borate deposits over the years, including a big claim down on the Mojave in the Kramer district which he had just sold to the borax company for $65,000. Poking around Furnace Creek Wash, he found some indications of colemanite on ground adjoining several of the company's claims, and staked neighboring claims of his own. But when he went to record these claims at the county courthouse in Independence, he discovered something much better—that a patent had not in fact been granted on one of the company's claims. This claim, the Clara, was one of many that United States Borax had applied for patents on in 1905. But the patent was not issued on the Clara because it happened to lie in a section of land that had been automatically transferred to the State of California as school land half a century earlier, when Henry Washington first surveyed it. The law allowed that if minerals were found on such land it could be transferred back to the federal government upon request, so that a patent could be granted. But the company's attorney had failed to make such a request and had let the application lapse in 1907. The forfeiture was not noted, however, in the company's land records, where it was mistakenly entered as a patented claim on which the company paid taxes but had to do no further assessment work.[33]

When Russell learned of the status of the Clara in June 1919, he hurried back to Furnace Creek and quietly staked claim to the ground himself, thoughtfully naming it the Boraxo, for one of the company's more popular products. He then quickly sank a shaft to demonstrate the value of the ground and formally requested that it be transferred back to the federal government so that he could patent it. Although Russell's camp was down in the wash just 2 miles west of Ryan, it was hidden from sight by a low ridge. Thus the borax company didn't learn of Russell's activities until he started shipping ore samples to San Francisco in February 1920. That brought an urgent telegram to Faulkner, who dispatched his assistant Harry Gower to investigate. Spotting fresh tracks, Gower finally found Russell's camp. Faulkner followed, ordering Russell and his men off the claim as trespassers, but Russell happily informed the superintendent that the company had no claim to the ground and that he now held clear title. And just as soon as the land was transferred, Russell applied for a patent.[34]

The company's attorneys opposed Russell's application and tried to have the original Clara application reinstated. When that failed, they decided to bring suit. In order to do so, the company had to be forcibly evicted from the ground. At the lawyers' insistence, in September 1921, just before Russell resumed work after a summer break, Gower took two big, burly miners from Ryan down to the claim to set up a tent. Russell and eight men arrived on September 18. After only a few words they obligingly tore down the tent and sent the company's men packing, with a couple of black eyes as evidence of forcible eviction. The lawyers then happily went to court to try to regain title. Great volumes of testimony were taken, but the judge finally ruled for Russell in April 1924. The lawyers appealed all the way to the Supreme Court, but it refused to hear the case.[35]

Russell meanwhile had organized the Death Valley Borax Company and talked of building his own refinery in Los Angeles. But his real aim was simply to sell the property to Borax Consolidated, and soon after his first court victory he offered it to them for $112,500. They turned him down, however, still hoping to win the appeal, and by the time the last appeal was lost in 1928 they were in no mood to buy him out. Russell eventually sold the claims for $75,000 to a speculator named Walter J. Thompson, who had to put up a Rube Goldberg mill and actually started producing borax before the company finally bought him out in 1934 for $138,000. That still wasn't the end of the matter, though, for the company lost the claim again as a result of an antitrust settlement. Tenneco eventually acquired the property and began open-pit operations in 1970.[36]

Long before the Hughes and Russell cases had been settled, the harried Faulkner had pleaded with Baker for a transfer. In the spring of 1920 his request was granted, but he soon discovered he had gotten out of the frying pan and into the fire, for Baker sent him to Turkey to reopen a mine there just as a war broke out with Greece. Most of his crew were slaughtered, and he barely escaped with his life.[37]

Faulkner's replacement in Death Valley in April 1920 was Major Julian Boyd, a former Australian army officer, veteran of Gallipoli, and graduate of the Royal School of Mines. He was a genial but energetic fellow who quickly won the admiration of the men at Ryan. The old cabins and bunkhouse, which dated from the Calico days, had become so bug-infested and dilapidated that many of the men had resorted to dugouts in the hillside. Faulkner had complained to Baker about the conditions without effect. But Boyd knew how to get things done: when he saw the ramshackle cabins, he simply dropped a lighted match and walked away. Four of the shacks were gone in a flash, and by autumn the company had built modern, new, fireproof dormitories and a dozen new cottages for the staff. Boyd also hauled the original Catholic church down from Rhyolite, stained glass windows and all, and set it up at Ryan as a recreation hall and movie theater.[38]

Over at Death Valley Junction, the company soon made even more elaborate improvements, after the popular Western writer, Zane Grey, penned an embarrassingly dismal description of the place in a travel story for *Harper's Magazine* and repeated it in one of his books. In response the company hired an architect, A. H. McCulloh, to design a thoroughly modern "Civic Center" to house the whole camp. The architect drew up a grand Spanish-style, U-shaped adobe with a colonade across the front. It measured 420 by 198 feet on a side and enclosed a 2-acre plaza. In the long west wing were sleeping quarters, showers, a gymnasium, and a swimming pool for the entire crew of two hundred; in the south wing were the kitchen, dining hall, clubroom, billiard parlor, branch library, barbershop, butcher shop, bakery, ice cream parlor, general store, post office, and company offices; and the north wing housed the staff apartments, hospital, and movie theater, then called Corkill Hall and now dubbed the Death Valley Opera House. The Civic Center was, in fact, a complete "town under one roof." It was painted corn yellow on the outside and an icy blue inside, and was cooled throughout by air "sucked through water sprays." The construction, begun in 1923, was completed in the fall of 1924 at a cost of $300,000, and the unique new company town was formally opened with a grand ball.[39]

In the meantime, Boyd had modernized the mining operations at Ryan, too. He replaced the last of the mules in the mines with gasoline engines, which not only cut costs but eliminated the flies that had plagued the camp. He also reopened the Lila C. in the fall of 1920, after a crew he had sent in to tear out the old timbers discovered a new ore body when part of the old works caved in. A narrow gauge track was laid back to the mine again, and a little Milwaukee gasoline engine hauled out ore for seven more years.[40]

Another rich new colemanite deposit was discovered quite accidentally in January 1922 by Johnny Sheridan, a frugal old eccentric who was said to share a cave with hydrophobic skunks and chuckwallas back of Shoshone. He happened upon the colemanite while out prospecting for clay in a gulch on Red Mountain, just 2 miles from the railroad northeast of Shoshone. Clarence M. Rasor, the borax company's field engineer, promptly bought the claim for $50,000, but Sheridan didn't get to enjoy his good fortune for long. A fast-footed gambler named Smoky Dixon quickly took half of the money on a grubstake claim, then plied poor old Sheridan with bad whiskey until he died. Dixon then got the rest of the money through probate.[41]

Rasor, meanwhile, opened the mine—which he named the Gerstley for one of the company's directors, James I. Gerstley—and made a deal with the company to buy the ore. He began shipping ore in 1924 after a new 3-mile "baby gauge" with its own gasoline engine and cars was laid from the Tonopah and Tidewater to the mine. With a crew of about forty men, Rasor shipped several carloads of ore per day, and a lively little camp flourished at the mine until all work stopped in the fall of 1927.[42]

By 1927, after two decades in Death Valley, Borax Consolidated had taken out over $30 million worth of borates from its mines at old and new Ryan, making it by far the biggest and most profitable mining venture in the Death Valley and Amargosa country. Although the company had barely tapped the vast borate reserves of the region, competition from new producers—especially the American Potash and Chemical Corporation at Searles Lake, which produced borax as a by-product and could afford to undercut its price—was beginning to cut heavily into the market. Thus the company needed a cheaper source than the Death Valley country could provide. It found it down on the Mojave, just a few miles from the Santa Fe Railroad, in the Kramer district, where Clarence Rasor discovered an enormous deposit of rich sodium borate in August 1926. Scattered borate deposits had first been found at Kramer in 1913 by a Los Angeles physician, John K. Suckow, while drilling a well for a desert homestead, and in the intervening years Borax Consolidated had spent several hundred thousand dollars buying up over 7 square miles of claims there. But exploratory drilling had failed to reveal anything spectacular until Rasor discovered bonanza ore.[43]

Within a year, the new mine, known as the Baker, was in operation, and the Death Valley mines were doomed. In October 1927 the company closed down the mines at Ryan and shifted all work to the new town of Boron. Since that time, the mine at Boron has been the principal borax producer in America. This marked the end of borate mining in Death Valley for many years, but it wasn't the end of Borax Consolidated operations there. The versatile company simply turned from salt to scenery and branched out into the tourist business.[44]

Mostly Mud and Rock

The two decades that followed the great gold boom were the most stable and productive years yet for mining in Death Valley and the Amargosa. Trainloads of borates and lead ores rolled out steadily on the Tonopah and Tidewater Railroad, and the oil and building booms in southern California spurred the opening of vast clay and talc deposits that further swelled the output. Although many found little enthusiasm for such minerals, there were a few truly dedicated promoters and dreamers who could even work up a flurry of excitement over salt, mud, and rock. The fast talkers hustled miracle mud and started niter and potash stampedes, while the dreamers hoped to quarry a whole mountain of marble and ran a quixotic little monorail to tap a hill full of laxative. In the course of it all, they added a flush of needed color to an otherwise dusty business.

The opening of the Death Valley colemanite deposits by Borax Smith had inspired various hopefuls to try their luck with other salts, both real and imagined. Certainly the most imaginative of these was a Greenwaterite C. W. Patrick, who in May 1907 announced the discovery of a wonderful new mineral—the answer to every desert denizen's dreams—a rock that was miraculously transformed into water by simply chewing or heating it! Patrick discovered a whole ledge of this "dry, white lime-like substance" just 7 miles west of Greenwater, he said, when his burro started happily nibbling on it. One piece exhibited in a local saloon was reported to have produced several quarts of water, and there was talk of forming a company to irrigate all of Death Valley by just heating up the rock as it lay.[1]

Not far behind came a self-styled chemistry professor, George L. Bossemeyer, who envisioned a whole pharmacopoeia in a little patch of "medical mud" around the hot springs at the mouth of Grapevine Canyon. He claimed that the venerable Panamint Tom, 107 years old and blind, had told him of the miraculous curative powers of the stuff. So Bossemeyer went out in the heat of July 1907 and staked claim to 160 acres all around the springs. He then made secret tests which showed, he said, that the marvelous mud would "cure all manner of diseases arising from fever"—everything from sprains and erysipelas to pneumonia and inflamed bowels! Moreover, he proclaimed that the ground was so "saturated with so many cure-alls and unpatented nostrums" that it was certain to "become a veritable Mecca for the old, the blind and the lame, rejuvenating them and restoring all of their lost faculties." Never mind that it didn't help poor old Tom.[2]

A miracle sanitarium could wait, however; it was the patented medicine market that Bossemeyer wanted first. The following spring he joined with that wily old ex-Senator William Stewart to form the Death Valley Chemical Company and market the stuff under the brand name of "ANTI-FEBRENE." They shipped a load of it to Chicago and placed sample packages in the drugstores. They also experimented with over a dozen other wonder products made from the mud, including a medicated complexion powder, cold cream, eye salve, foot powder, tooth powder, shampoo, and metal polish. At the same time they put out a fancy prospectus for the company's stock, and Bossemeyer told a romantic story of how the Shoshone and Washoe had once fought a long and bitter war for possession of the ground, and how the company now had hundreds of millions of tons of the miraculous mud just lying there waiting to be packaged and sold at a profit of 20¢ a pound—an incredible bonanza worth over $100 billion! But the public simply refused to buy much of the mud or the stock, and the whole deal dried up.[3]

Meanwhile, down at the south end of Death Valley, an asthmatic prospector, W. A. "Whispering" Kelly, had found a big deposit of rock salt near Saratoga Springs in the summer of 1905. Old Jonas Osborne joined him to form the Death Valley Salt Company in January 1906, with plans to start shipping as soon as Borax Smith's railroad came within reach. But nothing came of that. Then in 1909 the United States Smelting Company optioned the property and set up a lively little tent camp with some twenty men at Saratoga Springs, while they sank a number of exploratory shafts that fall and winter. Nothing more came of that, either. It was not until 1912 that Kelly finally found a buyer, William G. Kerckhoff, a millionaire California utility baron. Kerckhoff also bought up several square miles of gypsum deposits across the valley to the south and organized the Avawatz Salt and Gypsum Company. He had grand plans to build an 18-mile railroad out to the deposits from the Tonopah and Tidewater line and make it a million dollar a year business, shipping 150 tons of salt a day, worth up to $50 a ton. But he too soon realized what others before him had already learned; it just wouldn't pay. He hung onto the deposits, however, until the day he died in 1929, still hoping that they would pay someday.[4]

Elsewhere in the valley, others found traces of niter and potash which wishful thinking and a world war blew out of all proportion. Low-grade niter had been known on the Amargosa since the early 1890s. An overly enthusiastic geologist from the California State Mining Bureau, Gilbert E. Bailey, had stirred up the first fleeting excitement in 1902, with claims that niter beds in the south end of Death Valley could rival the famous deposits of Chile. Nine hundred niter hunters were said to have been in the valley or on their way to it that fall, before a U.S. Geological Survey official denounced the rush as "little short of insanity." But the notion, once planted, was slow to die, and one hopeful group of speculators after another held onto the ground. In 1910 a San Francisco grain merchant, Albert W. Scott, Jr., and some friends began acquiring the deposits. By the spring of 1914 they had over 13 square miles of "niter ground" and had formed the California Nitrate Development Company. When World War I broke out a few months later they issued a slick, illustrated prospectus, disarmingly entitled *A Story About Nitrate of Soda in Death Valley.* Stressing its use not only for explosives but for fertilizers, they pushed $200,000 worth of stock on the public at $10 a share, talking of profits in excess of $800,000 a year and holdings so immense that they were "almost beyond the power of computation." They built a couple of new cabins at Saratoga Springs, but they never shipped any marketable niter. The notion of a niter bonanza was finally laid to rest at the end of the war with a new government survey, which clearly showed that the deposits were too poor to pay.[5]

The potash excitement was precipitated in the spring of 1912 when Congress, reacting to a threatened German cut in potash exports, passed a law withdrawing all American potash land from entry after May 1 of that year. Prospectors and speculators descended on salt flats all over the West to stake "potash claims" before the deadline, whether or not they found a trace of it on the ground. Practically the entire sink of Death Valley was staked and quickly sold to Borax Smith or a couple of other syndicates, gambling on a chance of finding something. Test wells sunk on various claims during the next two years failed to turn up any significant potash, but that didn't detour one group of promoters, who got hold of 67 square miles of "potash land" and formed the Death Valley Potash Development Company to peddle $1 million in stock at $50 a share just weeks after the start of World War I.[6]

By far the most widely publicized of all the ill-fated salt ventures in Death Valley was an epsom salt mine. What attracted all the attention was not the mine itself, but the curious little monorail that was built to Death Valley to haul the salt out. The deposit was situated in the low, lavender Crystal Hills just south of the old borax road in Wingate Wash and not far from the scene of Death Valley Scotty's infamous "battles." The salts were discovered in the fall of 1917 by Jasper Stanley and two other amateur prospectors from Los Angeles, who found alum—potassium aluminum sulfate—and staked nine placer claims that they called the Aluminum group. It was not until the summer of 1919, however, that an acquaintance of Stanley's, Thomas H. Wright, found that the deposit was actually richer in magnesium sulfate, or epsom salt, commonly used as a bath salt and a laxative. Wright had run a little flower shop in Los Angeles for twenty years with his wife, Emeline. But he was a dreamer who had always hoped for grander things, and he suddenly saw in the epsom salts his chance of a lifetime. He eagerly bought a controlling interest in the claims, organized the grand-sounding American Magnesium Company, and began selling shares to his friends, neighbors, and customers to finance his vision.[7]

Situated so close to a road, most would simply have set to work scraping up the salts and trucking them out. But nothing so ordinary would do for the quixotic Wright. His mind was bursting with revolutionary new ideas. Even before he dreamed up the monorail, he fancied a far grander, holistic scheme to flush the salt out. It was a masterpiece of economy and efficiency—at least on paper—relying solely on the sun's heat and the earth's gravity for power. He would pipe water from mountain springs to the deposits by gravity, run it through a solar heater of copper pipe and glass, and blast the hot water out of fire hoses to hydraulically mine and dissolve the epsom salt out of the deposits. Then he would collect the warm brine in a pond and flush it down a drainpipe 28 miles long to the Trona Railroad at Searles Lake, running it into tanks there to let the sun evaporate the water and crystallize out the purified salts. With epsom salt selling for $50 a ton, Wright dreamed of grandiose profits by flushing out 100 tons of crude salt a day at a cost he estimated at only $5 a ton. But the first difficulty with the scheme was finding enough water and Wright scurried about for a couple of years, sinking dry wells at the deposit and surveying pipelines from the surrounding springs before he finally realized in the summer of 1922 that he just couldn't get enough water to do the job.[8]

By then, Wright had already conceived a new brainchild—his soon-to-be-famous Death Valley monorail—to replace the pipeline for bringing out the salt. This time nothing seemed to stand in the way of the dream. In the fall of 1922, he began construction of the monorail at Magnesium siding on the Trona Railroad, 6 miles south of the town. From there the rail ran due east across the south end of Searles Lake, up tortuous Layton Canyon and over the Slate Range, northeast across the tip of Panamint Valley, through Wingate Pass, and down the wash to the salt deposit at his Crystal Camp. It was 28 miles long in all, following the route he had planned for the pipeline. The monorail itself was a single steel rail spiked to a 6 by 8 inch riding beam supported on an A-frame trestle about 3 feet high. The specially designed locomotives and cars ran on two wheels, like motorcycles, with steel outriggers hanging down both sides to form another A-frame. They rode like pack saddles astride the track with carefully balanced cargo strapped low on both sides. Rollers mounted under the outriggers ran on wooden guide rails tacked to the sides of the trestle to help stabilize the swaying cars as they skimmed just inches above the ground.[9]

Construction took almost two years and cost roughly $200,000. That, together with the costs of half a dozen buildings at Crystal Camp and a refinery at Wilmington, exhausted the company treasury before they could even begin scraping up salt. So in May 1924 Wright tripled the stock issue to raise more money. The novelty of it all—a monorail into the dreaded Death Valley—was his biggest selling point, and attracted nation-wide publicity with illustrated feature articles in *Popular Mechanics, Scientific American,* and other magazines. These attracted more investors, newly captivated by the dream. But the novelty of the venture was also its greatest fault. For all of Wright's wonderful new ideas were, of course, untested, although he eagerly patented them all and ended up sinking nearly every new dollar of the company's money into trying to make things work. The wonderful monorail, which seemed so cheap and simple in concept, was in practice so plagued with problems that it proved to be nothing but a costly and unworkable failure.[10]

The locomotives were the most persistent source of trouble and expense. Wright had started with battery-powered motors, which worked well enough on the early construction across the flats of Searles Lake. But as the rail moved up Layton Canyon on a 10 percent rise, they were unable to make the grade, so Wright built two new locomotives with Fordson tractor engines. These were at least powerful enough to get up over the hills, but they weren't able to pull more than a single car with a total load of only 8 tons. Next he built a locomotive with a heavier Buda engine, which managed to carry 4 tons itself and tow two cars, for a total haul of 14 tons. But none of these machines seemed capable of making a trip without some kind of breakdown, overheating, twisting a driving rod, or what have you, and even the Buda's load still wasn't big enough to be profitable. Finally Wright contracted with a Los Angeles automotive engineer, A. W. Harrison, to build a much bigger gasoline-electric engine that could carry 20 tons by itself and pull a train of eight cars for a total of 60 tons. That engine, finished in the fall of 1925, essentially broke the back of the whole venture. The engine alone made a couple of successful trips with its 20 tons. But when several cars were added to make up a full train, the aging trestle, now cracked and warped in the furnace of a couple summers, collapsed under the weight.[11]

That smashed the dreams of most stockholders and all work stopped. But Wright wasn't quite ready to give up his dream, and early in 1927 he scraped up a little more money for one last try. He overhauled the whole line, built three new lightweight locomotives, bulldozed a big reservoir at Crystal Camp, enlarged the Wilmington refinery, and even bought perfume and bottles to finally start turning out bath salts. That

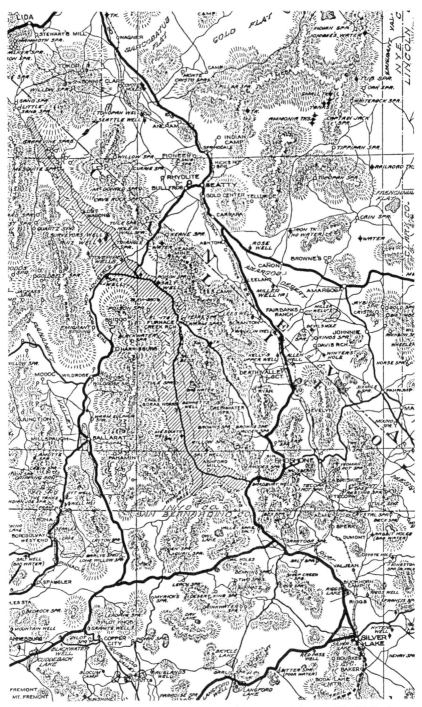

Death Valley and Amargosa roads in 1919. (*Courtesy of Automobile Club of Southern California*)

fall, despite one problem after another, Wright succeeded in hauling out and refining close to 1,000 tons of crude salt at a cost of around $20 a ton. But to get all that salt, the miners had to scrape the beds a little deeper, so the salt they shipped didn't carry enough epsom salts to pay even half the cost. That was the final blow, and everything shut down permanently that winter. The following spring the property was offered for sale, but there were no takers. Wright turned fleetingly to oil speculation, but gave that up after he was charged with stock fraud by the sheriff's bunko squad. Sobered at last from his binge of midlife crazies, he settled down again, ending his days at the one thing he knew how to do well— selling flowers.[12]

Other hopefuls sought their fortunes in a rich variety of minerals, from precious gems and marble to lowly talc and clay. A few even sniffed for oil. The success of their quests varied inversely with the amount of excitement they generated: precious stones were as scarce as hens' teeth and the marble was an extravagant disappointment, while common clay and talc became the region's most valuable products, aside from borates.

In the frenzied search for precious metals it was only natural that some would also look for precious stones in Death Valley, and it was only human nature that a few would claim to find them. The stage was set in the fall of 1908, when an excited prospector reported finding the "throat" of an extinct volcano with blue clays like those of the South African diamond fields, and predicted that diamonds would soon be found in the valley. Within a few weeks, one C. M. Hooten announced the discovery of emeralds instead, showing something the size of a quail's egg. Soon after that, an old desert rat named Tom McFarlane claimed he had found the diamonds high in the mountains that fringe Death Valley. He displayed a rough stone the size of his thumb, but no one else ever found any. Yet one persistent gem hunter, F. M. "Shady" Myrick, did manage to keep himself in grub for many years working little deposits of semi-precious gems that he found at the south end of Death Valley. He made his first strike in fire opals in the summer of 1911, and then he found topaz and a new gem—a blood-red chalcedony—which was named Myrickite in his honor.[13]

There were three fleeting oil excitements in Death Valley and the Amargosa, but all they ever produced were a few good stories and some stock. The first commotion was staged in April 1907, when a Goldfield lawyer, William Schnitzer, and self-styled oil expert John Frank announced that they had found strong "indications" of oil in a 500-foot-wide "channel" coming out of the hills just south of Gold Center. They staked 600 acres and dashed off to Los Angeles for a drilling rig. Little more was heard of them until a quarter of a century later, when the full story was finally told. The two schemers, it seems, had a wealthy old Angeleno who was so "eager to bite at anything smelling of oil" that they couldn't resist salting some ground for him. They secretly lugged a dozen barrels of crude up Bare Mountain and emptied it all into a "natural fissure." When the oil reappeared several hundred feet below, looking just "like a real oil seepage," they hurried to Los Angeles to get the old man. But before they could get back with him, some greenhorn set a match to the oil to see whether it was real, and the whole scheme went up in smoke.[14]

A couple of innocents at the Johnnie mine stirred up the next excitement in January 1918, when they discovered "oil float" in the wash below the mine. Men rushed in from all around, only to find that the "float" was just sludge dumped out a decade before, from an oil-burning generator there. The final excitement began in the fall of 1920, after new "indications" were reported at the south end of Death Valley. Fully 100,000 acres—150 square miles—of oil claims were filed, and the Death Valley Oil Company was floated. But all it ever produced was 30,000 shares at $10 par.[15]

Unlike diamonds, emeralds, or oil, there was no question about the existence of the great banded marble beds on Bare Mountain just south and east of Beatty. Nels Linn, a former stonecutter, discovered the marble in December 1905, at the peak of the Bullfrog excitement. He swore that it was as good as the famous Italian marble from Carrara. Others claimed it was even better—"the finest in the world." Best yet, it was all quite accessible, for Clark's railroad soon came within a few miles of it. There seemed to be an immense fortune just waiting there for the taking, but for those who tried to get it, that fortune proved just as elusive as the diamonds. It took a lot of time and money—over ten years and a million dollars—and seemingly endless frustrations, however, to find that out. That task fell to Park V. Perkins and his backers.[16]

Perkins was a stockbroker with no experience in mining, but he did appreciate the value of marble, for he was born and raised in Vermont among the finest marble quarries in the country. When Perkins saw the Bare Mountain deposit, he immediately saw a chance for big things. By the spring of 1908 he had acquired most of the marble claims and was trying to raise money to develop them. But most mining investors wanted to put their money into something more glamorous than stone. Thus it was not until the spring of 1911 that Perkins finally found backers in Ohio and succeeded in floating a company, American Carrara Marble. As vice president and general manager, Perkins then began the slow, systematic work of diamond-drill exploration to try to estimate the size of the deposit. By the beginning of 1913 he was convinced that he had tapped an incredible bonanza—10 billion cubic feet of commercial marble worth roughly $30 billion! By then he had laid 8 miles of pipe to bring in water from Gold Center, had strung 11 miles of wire to bring in electric power from Rhyolite, and had surveyed a 3-mile railroad to carry the quarried stone down to the Las Vegas and Tonopah siding. Perkins was at last ready to start cutting marble. With a crew of forty, he opened two quarries, one in black and white laminated marble and the other in almost pure white stone.[17]

At the same time, Perkins laid out the new town of Carrara alongside the railroad tracks. He launched it on May 8, 1913, bringing in a trainload of excursionists for a free picnic, an exhibition baseball game between Goldfield and Tonopah, and a dance to the music of the Goldfield Hippodrome Orchestra in the Hot Potato, a makeshift town hall. That same day his brother, A. B. Perkins, launched a weekly paper, dubbed the *Carrara Obelisk,* which he had printed in Salt Lake City. He filled it with quarry news and such inspired bits of booster doggerel as

For quality, variety, for quantity and showing
American Carrara Marble sure has got them going.

The embryo town, of course, couldn't really support a paper, nor were there enough subscribers in the whole Bullfrog district to do so, but there were enough stockholders in the marble company to make it worthwhile, so most of the papers were mailed to Ohio. The prize attraction of the town was its highly publicized fountain, touted as the "only one in Nevada." It shot a graceful spray 30 feet into the air, its boosters said; less partisan observers were a bit disappointed to see that this marvel was just a homely little upright pipe that didn't seem to squirt more than 6 feet. It was nonetheless a welcome spray on a summer day, and the surrounding pool came in handy as an impromptu swimming hole. Despite such attractions, however, the town of Carrara never succeeded in attracting more than a few businesses and a few dozen cabins and cottages, all derelicts hauled in from Rhyolite.[18]

Up at the quarry, the marble was being systematically cut out with channeling machines, one "floor" at a time, in massive blocks measuring about 6 feet on a side and weighing around 15 tons. Each block had to be hoisted out of the pit with a 60-foot power crane. It was a slow process, removing only about four floors a year. The slowness was particularly frustrating to Perkins and his backers because nearly all of the marble on the first five floors was so badly weathered that it was of no commercial value and could only be piled on the dump. Only one carload of carefully selected pieces was salvaged and shipped out in April 1914 to boost stockholder morale. That summer the quality of the marble began to improve, but just as it did, a fire destroyed the transformers and forced

Perkins to stop work for six months until new equipment could be installed. Even the *Obelisk* was temporarily suspended until work resumed in January 1915. By the time summer came, the marble had improved enough that Perkins decided it was time to build a cable railroad and a finishing plant to get it ready for market. Late in the spring of 1916 the first blocks of marble started rolling down from the quarry on his newly completed gravity cable road, affectionately nicknamed the Carrara-Pacific. That fall the finishing plant was completed and the big diamond-toothed gang saws began slicing the blocks of marble into finished slabs.[19]

By then the quarry was down almost 100 feet, to the fifteenth floor, and a small mountain of unweathered marble was ready to be finished. It seemed that the company could at last begin shipping marble, but before many blocks were finished, Perkins was faced with a frustrating new dilemma: the Nevada-California Power Company turned off the power south of Goldfield and started taking down the lines in December 1916. The quarry was forced to close down again, and that was the end of the *Obelisk*. But Perkins and his backers, stopped just on the brink of success, it seemed, mortgaged the property for $150,000 and built a diesel electric-generating plant in 1917 to produce their own power. No sooner was it finished, however, than it was destroyed by a fire. Not yet beaten, they floated a second mortgage for another $150,000 and rebuilt the generating plant. This only allowed them to come to their final defeat, however, for when they began cutting into the unweathered blocks again they found that, though the color and texture were as fine as could be, the marble was too highly fractured to be cut into profitable commercial sizes. That was finally the end of Carrara. Perkins and his backers had sunk a total of $1.1 million into the venture, and all they had to show for it were a few odd lots of marble good only for gravestones![20]

A pantheon of other minerals, including a whole mountain of a curious flexible slate, itacolumite, reported on the Amargosa, attracted fleeting followers. But gypsum and sulphur were actually mined, and clay and talc were the big bonanzas. The Gypsy Queen, a gypsum deposit near China Ranch, just a mile from the Tonopah and Tidewater in Amargosa Canyon, was opened in 1915 by the Acme Cement and Plaster Company. The railroad company laid a track up to the mine, where F. A. Brown and a dozen or more miners shipped out around 1,000 tons a month to the Acme plaster plant in Los Angeles. That steep little spur proved to be one of the most dangerous miles of track on the line when a runaway train coming down with a load derailed, killing the fireman and badly burning the engineer. The Gypsy Queen produced about $100,000 worth of gypsum before work stopped in 1918 after the works caved in, killing two men.[21]

The Crater sulphur deposit at the other end of Death Valley, high up in Hanging Rock Canyon in the Last Chance Range, was located by Frank Hicks and his brother Dan early in 1924. They opened up an estimated 150,000 tons of 99 percent pure brimstone and sold the property in the spring of 1928 to Woolworth dimestore millionaire Fred M. Kirby. He formed the Pacific Sulphur Company in June, bulldozed a 23-mile road in from Fish Lake Valley, set up a neat little camp called Crater with half a dozen buildings and a couple dozen men, and began blocking out ore. Kirby talked of building a railroad in from Owens Valley and hoped to challenge the great Texas sulphur monopoly. But the Crater deposit didn't turn out to be big enough for that, so he suspended operations in December 1930. There was nonetheless a lot of paying ore there, and in the fall of 1932 W. H. Sanger and Morris Albertoli of Big Pine leased the mine and started trucking out 10 tons of sulphur a day. They made $50 a day, which was good money in hard times, so work continued through the Depression.[22]

Next to borax, Death Valley's biggest bonanzas have been in plain white talc, which first found a ready market during the southern California building booms, when it was widely used in wall tile, paint, and sewer pipe. There is a vast talc belt exposed throughout the south end of the valley, stretching for over 60 miles from the Panamint Range on the west to the Alexander and Silurian Hills on the east. It has become one of the major sources of talc in the West and dozens of mines have been opened. The first big talc bonanza was a mine now known as the Western, opened in 1912 by Lycurgus Lindsay, Death Valley's would-be Talc King.[23]

Lycurgus Lindsay—who usually went just by his initial—was a staid-looking, silver-haired bank director and principal owner of two well-established pottery businesses, the Western Art Tile Works and the Independent Sewer Pipe Company, in the Los Angeles suburb of Tropico, near Glendale. Lindsay had made his money from speculation, however, in the opening of the great Mexican copper deposits at Cananea at the turn of the century, and he was still on the lookout for a new mining proposition—particularly new sources of clay and talc for his business. In June 1909 he bought a group of claims known simply as the Talc Mine. China Ranch owner Dave Morrison and two partners had located them the year before in the Alexander Hills just east of the ranch and about 7 miles from the Tonopah and Tidewater Railroad. Lindsay incorporated the claims and his tile works into a new $1 million venture, the Pacific Tile and Terra Cotta Company, and put a crew to work opening the deposit. By 1912 he was hauling about a wagonload of talc a day to the railroad for his pottery works. Shipments that year amounted to less than 1,000 tons worth roughly $10 a ton, but they grew steadily, reaching

5,000 tons in 1918 at $15 a ton. By then the talc mine had become a profitable venture in its own right, and Lindsay was beginning to see even greater possibilities. With visions of becoming the Talc King, he reorganized the company under the more expansive name of Pacific Minerals and Chemical, and threw himself into exploiting the mine. He found new buyers and steadily stepped up shipments to over 12,000 tons in 1920. By the end of that year he had taken out roughly half a million dollars worth of talc. That was just the beginning for the mine, but it was the end for the Talc King.[24]

Despite the soaring production of his talc mine, Lindsay was in deep financial difficulties. He had overextended his credit and overreached his capabilities in plunging headlong into the talc venture. Early in 1921 Lindsay and the Pacific Minerals and Chemical Company went under, although shipments from the talc mine continued almost without interruption. The mine was worked for a time under lease to a former employee, George W. Morton. It was then purchased by Gustave Martin, who carried on the work until 1928, when he signed over the mine on a ten-year lease to the Western Talc Company, organized by Fred H. Savell. The mine eventually produced over 300,000 tons of talc worth several million dollars. It was truly a talc bonanza.[25]

Others, meanwhile, had followed Lindsay's lead and opened talc deposits elsewhere in the valley. The Eclipse mine in the Ibex Hills, 8 miles southwest of Zabriskie, was worked intermittently by the Pacific Mineral Products Company and by its successor, the California Mineral Corporation, from 1912 through 1918. During that time it produced only a couple of thousand tons of talc, but it was reopened after World War II to produce some 45,000 tons. The Tremolite mine was discovered by Frank Riggs in 1911 in the Silurian Hills, 7 miles southeast of Riggs siding on the Tonopah and Tidewater. It was worked by the Western White Talc Company, starting in 1918, and later by the Pacific Coast Talc Company, eventually shipping over 160,000 tons. The Death Valley mine in Galena Canyon at the foot of the Panamints was discovered by Ash Meadows rancher "Dad" Fairbanks around 1911, but only sporadic attempts were made to develop it by the Death Valley Talc Refining and Manufacturing Company and the American-Italian Talc Company from 1920 through the early 1930s. It was not until the 1950s that it finally produced over 50,000 tons. The Warm Spring mine in the next canyon to the south has been the largest recent producer, rivaling the production of Lindsay's bonanza. It was truly a latecomer, discovered by Louise Grantham and Ernest Huhn in April 1932, just before the creation of Death Valley National Monument.[26]

The other big bonanza was in the worthless-looking filter clay deposits along the Amargosa. In a brief flurry in the late 1920s and early 1930s, these deposits produced several million dollars. The southern California oil boom generated the market for the clays—mostly hydrous magnesium silicates—which were used in the refineries to clean or clarify heavier oils. Dad Fairbanks was the first to recognize their commercial value, and it proved to be the biggest discovery of his life. As he fondly recalled,

> In 1916 I made the strike that I'd been jack-assing for thirty-five years trying to locate. Strange as it may seem, it wasn't gold I found, nor did I have to go very far to find it. I was browsing around out back of Shoshone one day and went into a Shoshone Indian camp. There I found an Indian woman, Panamint Tom's squaw, washing her hair. She was doing it in an old gold pan full of something that looked like a mixture of mud and water and about the thickness of buttermilk. I watched her and when she'd finished the job her hair was soft and clean and glossy. I asked her where she got the stuff and she pointed out a certain hill. I immediately went to the hill, and found a veritable mountain of valuable filtering clay, and staked out my claim on it. When I first began prospecting, this claim wouldn't have been worth a thin dime. But the change from oats to gasoline had made a big difference. . . . I held this claim until 1920, because not being poverty-stricken, as the majority of prospectors usually are, I didn't have to sell at the first figure offered. So, I hung onto it and shopped around for a buyer until the Associated Oil Company wanted it bad enough to take if off my hands for cash. . . . I don't want to state the figure I got for this claim. But I can say that it was a tidy fortune—a comfortable stake for Dad Fairbanks and Mother for the rest of their days.[27]

Although Fairbanks didn't sell his clay strike for several years, word of his discovery got out immediately and started others searching for clay up and down the Amargosa. S. Frank Brock, a mining engineer, hit the jackpot the following year in Ash Meadows, just across the Nevada line, about 8 miles north of Death Valley Junction. There he found an immense clay bed and staked claim to over 6 square miles of ground before he told anyone else about it. But after he did reveal his discovery, finding a buyer for the ground wasn't just a matter of holding out for the highest bid, as Fairbanks implied. The oil companies had to be convinced that the new "Death Valley clay," as it came to be known—or Brockonite, as Brock liked to call it—was better and more economical than the Fuller's Earth they were using. It took Brock a number of years to persuade them. He started by shipping several hundred tons to Standard Oil for testing in 1918, and shipped out that much or more to other companies over the next several years. It was a long, slow struggle, but it finally paid off handsomely. By 1925 Brock had convinced at least five companies—Associated, Union, Pan-American, Pacific, and Standard's subsidiary, General Petroleum—of the value of the clay, and each bought up a quarter section or more for a grand total of $350,000. With that, Brock was soon ready to retire.[28]

Following these sales, things moved rapidly. General Petroleum began work early in 1925 through a subsidiary, General Clay, with a crew of twenty shipping 400 tons a month. Pan-American and others started soon after, and by summer there were fifty men at work digging out 1,200 tons a month. At first the clay was simply dried in the open at the pits on a makeshift platform of old railroad ties and then trucked 3 or 4 miles across the state line to Bradford siding on the Tonopah and Tidewater for shipping. But in 1927 the operations were thoroughly mechanized, after most of the work was consolidated by leases to one company, United Death Valley Clay, under the management of an enterprising Kansas-born, Yale-educated engineer, G. Ray Boggs. Boggs brought in gasoline shovels to dig the clay, laid miles of baby gauge rails to each of the pits, and put a Plymouth locomotive with a couple of dozen gondolas to work hauling the clay to a drying, grinding, and screening plant that he built at the siding, powered by an old diesel submarine engine. Early the following year, he expanded even further, after Borax Consolidated closed down its operations at Ryan. He convinced the borax company to remodel its Death Valley Junction plant to handle the clay, and lay a third rail on the Tonopah and Tidewater to Bradford siding so that the Death Valley Railroad equipment could haul it. By then, working two shifts in the pits and three at the plant, Boggs was turning out as much as 5,000 tons of clay a month. It was worth about $16 a ton at the pits and as much as $40 a ton when refined and delivered to the oil refineries.[29]

Alongside the pits, the camp of Clay City sprang up. It was no quiet company town like the one the borax company had maintained at its mines. Clay City was a "rip-roaring" camp of close to a hundred roughnecks and camp followers, who boasted that it and its surroundings were the "toughest thousand acres left of the old West." It was a hodgepodge of boardinghouses, tin shacks, and tents clustered around a grocery store, several roadhouses offering gambling and bootleg whiskey, and a row of cribs—all bent on relieving the men of their $5.50 a day as fast as they made it. Its isolation attracted several bootleggers, who set up their stills in the surrounding brush and ran their surplus to Las Vegas at night.[30]

Clay City prided itself in having no police, jail, preacher, or graveyard. But it did make two concessions to civilization: a $2,500 schoolhouse, donated by Pan-American oil president Edward L. Doheny, and an air-port—or at least an airfield—built by United Death Valley Clay's chief backer, Fred E. Keeler, who was also president of Lockheed Aircraft and liked to drop in on one of the company's planes. For all its vaunted toughness, however, the closest Clay City ever came to real violence was the suicide of a despondent prospector who hung himself in the fall of 1927, and the tragic death of a Mexican laborer the following spring. The laborer was squashed under a 70-ton clay tank one morning, scraped into a hastily made box, carried out 2 miles into the brush that afternoon, and callously dropped into a hole without benefit of ceremony.[31]

The boom years for the clay pits were 1927 through 1929, when the annual clay shipments ran over 30,000 tons, worth over a million dollars a year at the refineries. Boggs finally left the clay business in 1929 to plunge into a bizarre gold venture at Carrara, and Keeler sold his interest in United Death Valley Clay to George W. Coen, who renamed it the Coen Companies. Production declined rapidly in the early 1930s, owing both to the stock market crash and the development of new techniques for clarifying oil. By 1933, output had been cut to less than 4,000 tons a year; two years later, it was only 600 tons and Clay City was dead. Even the bootleggers had cleared out when prohibition ended in 1933. That was the end of Clay City, but it was not the end of the clay beds, where much more money has been made in later revivals.[32]

The Hangers-on

Even though the big money was being made in borates, clay, and talc, most of Death Valley's lingering miners and diehard promoters were still intoxicated by metal mining. The lure of gold clouded their brains, but some went on a binge in lesser metals, when prices surged to record highs in World War I and again in the 1920s. Many had come in the heady days of the great gold boom and just couldn't believe the party was over. They were drunken hangers-on who didn't know when to go home, or had none to go to. They stayed on for twenty, thirty, even forty years, working out the last little pockets, looking for that one big bonanza, and waiting. Most were lucky if they just made wages. A few finally found their fortunes when skyrocketing metal prices made even that old antimony mine at Wildrose into a paying proposition, at least briefly. All the while, of course, the old Tecopa just kept on shipping trainloads of ore for Graves's paint plant year after year, becoming the largest metal mine in all of Death Valley and the Amargosa.

The mines of the Bullfrog district, where the great boom had started, were a favorite of the hopeful lingerers looking for that overlooked bonanza. None inspired more hope than the Original Bullfrog with its famous high-grade which, legend said, had once graced the windows of Tiffany's. Over the years the imagined product of that little mine jumped to fully $2 million. Moreover, it was whispered that the mine had closed only because the rich vein had been faulted and lost. Somewhere along the fault scarp, the rest of the treasure still lay untapped. The old Bullfrog finally leapt back into the headlines in 1924 when two leasers, sinking a shallow shaft, struck high-grade running $2,600 a ton. They shipped several thousand dollars worth of jewelry rock, certain they had found the long-lost "faulted vein." Over the next half dozen years a succession of companies were formed and reformed to work this fabled bonanza. They hauled in new machinery, built a little mill at Beatty, and one superintendent even refurbished the grand old Rhyolite station as his office and residence. It was claimed that over $10 million worth of ore was blocked out, but nothing more came of it.[1]

Over at Pioneer, Bill Tobin stayed on for a quarter of a century, patiently probing for a new bonanza for his Reorganized Pioneer and Consolidated Mayflower companies. Tobin steadily collected money on assessments from stockholders and faithfully put it into the ground, but never found any ore that would pay. In the hope that history would repeat itself, he finally sold the Pioneer in 1926 to Ruben Bryan, the lucky leaser who had found the original bonanza. With the backing of Hollywood friends Bryan searched for another decade, making test shipments and test runs on the old mill, but he couldn't repeat the feat.[2]

Others carried on the search with equal dedication in the neighboring districts. The Ashford brothers were particularly persistent but no more successful. They had a little mine they hopefully called the Golden Treasure, on the Death Valley side of the Black Mountains just south of Scotty's Canyon. It showed promising pockets of high-grade running over $1,000 a ton, but turned out to be an empty promise. As Carl Glasscock later observed, all the Ashfords got out of it was "just enough gold to keep them in groceries and lawsuits for more than a third of a century." The first lawsuit started right after Harold Ashford filed claim to the ground in January 1907. The ground was part of the sprawling holdings of the Key Gold Mining Company, but Ashford relocated it, claiming that the company hadn't done the annual assessment work. When the company refused to recognize his claim, he brought suit and finally won title three years later. Then he and his brothers, Henry and Louis, succeeded in opening enough ore to option it for $60,000 to a self-styled "Hungarian nobleman" and speculator known as Count Kramer. He in turn optioned it for $105,000 to a Los Angeles oil man, Benjamin W. McCausland and his son, Ross, in November of 1914.[3]

The McCauslands, with Ross as superintendent, developed the mine in good style, putting up a fancy 40-ton roller mill down in the valley and cutting a road up to the mine to truck out the ore. The mill started up in February 1915 and ran straight through the summer, with over fifty men working night and day in both mine and mill. Then suddenly in September all work stopped and the McCauslands defaulted on the purchase. They had spent $125,000 on labor and machinery, and had gotten back almost as much by cleaning out the high-grade. But they found that there wasn't enough left in the mine to pay back the bulk of the purchase money still owed, so they quit. The Ashfords, who had gotten only a small down payment, again went to court and eventually won title to both the property and the machinery. But it was a hollow victory, for even though they now had a mill, their mine had been gutted. Nevertheless, they held on for another quarter century, finding a few more little pockets of high-grade, nearly selling the mine a few more times, and resorting to the courts again and again. The ruins of the mill, right beside the road, have become Death Valley's most "conspicuous monument to disappointment."[4]

The most dedicated of all the hangers-on was Pete Aguereberry, who stuck with his Eureka mine at Harrisburg on and off for forty years, until the day he died on November 21, 1945. That could only be called a labor of love. For though he found a few small stringers and pockets of pay rock from time to time, it was only money from odd jobs and occasional grubstakes that kept beans in the pot.[5]

There was also that dedicated little band of "single blanket jackass prospectors," like Shorty Harris. They were without any real mine to call their own and lived mostly off the kindness of strangers, running out their lives trekking up and down Death Valley in that never-ending quest for a new strike in a picked-over land. For all their searching, their rewards were purely spiritual.[6]

A few lingerers, however, did find real gold at the end of the rainbow. W. D. Clair, after giving up his lonely search at Sylvania, at last found his reward in the tailings of the old Ratcliff mine above Ballarat. He started reworking the rock, which still held over $4 a ton, in 1930, and cleaned up over $60,000 in a couple years—in between skirmishes with two gun-toting sisters, Orpha Hart and Mary Ann Thompson, who held nearly all the other claims in Pleasant Canyon and tried to run him out.[7]

The biggest gold bonanza of those latter years was that found in the Orleans mine at Hornsilver. A former South African venture, Le Champ D'Or French Gold Mining Company, Ltd., looking for new fields bought the mine in 1912 and the following year their superintendent, J. William Dunfee, struck pay rock. In the next three years he reportedly took out $280,000 worth of ore, then got a lease on the mine, formed his own Orleans Mining and Milling Company, and recovered $260,000 more by 1921. Unfortunately much of that wonderful showing may have been hot air, since those production figures come from stock promoter A. I. D'Arcy, who took over Dunfee's lease in 1921. For state tax purposes, Dunfee had reported a total output of only $52,704. D'Arcy's promotion produced barely $35,000 in bullion before work was stopped by litigation over the lease. But there really was bonanza ore there. A new company, the Ohio Mines Corporation, resuming work in 1930 under Dunfee's direction, turned out a taxable $294,336 in gold over the next decade. That was reason enough to change the name of the camp from Hornsilver to Gold Point.[8]

That was the best that Death Valley's gold mines had to offer by then. But well before that, skyrocketing metal prices of World War I had made a much bigger bonanza out of that ancient antimony mine at Wildrose that had frustrated both miners and stockholders for over half a century. The old Christmas Gift had been relocated and abandoned several times since Dr. George's Combination Company had finally given up. Then in 1896 it was relocated as the Combination by a more tenacious prospector, Frank C. Kennedy, who got Ballarat's man of the hour, George Montgomery, to reopen it. A few sample shipments showed that it still wouldn't pay, and Montgomery too gave up. But Kennedy patented the claim, and patiently held onto it.[9]

Kennedy was finally rewarded in August 1914 when the war broke out, sending antimony prices to undreamed of highs and sending Kennedy an instant buyer, a Los Angeles mining engineer named Leslie C. Mott. Antimony, having sold for years at around 6¢ a pound, shot up to 12¢ within the first month of the war and ultimately reached 45¢. That turned the Combination into a high-grade bonanza with its antimony sulfide ores, averaging 40 percent metal, running to $360 a ton. Mott formed the Western Metals Company and set a crew to work taking out ore and building a smelting furnace to concentrate it for shipment. By spring the steadily rising metal prices had increased ore values so much that he didn't have to bother with the smelter and could ship the ore directly at a handsome profit.[10]

The antimony bonanza had been thoroughly exposed by the old Combination Company in its search for silver and gold, so all Mott's men had to do was break down the ore. Hauling it out of Wildrose was the only work. Located at the head of a steep side-canyon, the mine was inaccessible by truck, so old Frank Montgomery, the poor brother of the clan, was hired to pack the ore by burro to a chute, which dropped it to the upper end of the road. From there a fleet of half a dozen specially built wormdrive Moreland trucks hauled the rock 50 miles down Panamint Valley and over the Slate Range to the railroad at Trona. The old mine turned out about $3,000 worth of ore a day until all work stopped in the spring of 1916, when a surge of imported metal broke the price. By then, Mott had shipped roughly 4,000 tons of ore—about half of the total American production in the war years. The old Christmas Gift had finally proven its worth as a $1 million bonanza.[11]

Other "war baby" metals—manganese and tungsten—also created fleeting excitement, but fell far short of the Christmas Gift's showing. A large low-grade manganese deposit, a mile north of Owl Hole Springs, had been discovered by Alex Yeoman in February 1910, but the rock wouldn't pay to ship until metal prices took off after the start of the war. Then Yeoman opened both the lode and a new road across the south end of Death Valley to Riggs station on the Tonopah and Tidewater, and started hauling out ore in the spring of 1915 with two caterpillar tractors. Even at boom prices, however, the ore ran only $35 a ton, so it was a marginal operation. The following year, Yeoman optioned the mine for $40,000 to an Ohio steel man, Samuel Mollet, but the deal soon ended in litigation that closed the mine until the spring of 1918. Yeoman resumed work only briefly before declining metal prices forced him to quit. In all, the Owls Head mine had shipped less than 500 tons of ore. It was not until World War II that the mine finally became an important producer.[12]

The tungsten excitement was just a flash in the pan. Shorty Harris found some rich tungsten ore near Goldbelt Spring in the fall of 1915 and packed out $500 worth of rock. The following spring others made a strike at Cucomungo Spring, 40 miles to the north, causing a brief rush that attracted actress Marie Dressler's husband. A year later, both strikes were all but forgotten.[13]

Lowly lead, not gold or silver or some "war baby," was the Death Valley and Amargosa country's bonanza metal. Lincoln Godshall demonstrated that day after day, month after month, year after year from 1912 to 1928, as he shipped out nearly four million dollars worth of lead from the old Tecopa mines. Others recognized the value of the base metal too, but their prospects always lacked that one essential advantage that Godshall had—a railroad right to the mine dump. Cheap transportation still made the critical difference between success and failure. W. D. Clair searched faithfully at Sylvania for twenty years before he gave up trying to find lead ore rich enough to pay the freight 50 miles to the nearest railroad.[14]

The tripling of lead prices in World War I, however, temporarily made the difference for one mine right in the heart of Death Valley. That mine was the Carbonate, located at the foot of the Panamints, a mile south of Galena Canyon. In 1907, the Poet-Prospector Clarence Eddy had discovered the big galena cropping that gave the canyon its name. Others wandered in, and the following year a young, itinerant Nevadan, Chester A. Pray, found the Carbonate. When the mine later became a paying proposition the poet-prospector happily took credit for the discovery himself. Poor Pray wasn't around to contest the point by then. When others had moved on after the first excitement, however, Pray had stayed, certain that he had finally found his big bonanza. He worked for several years opening the deposit with financial help only from his fiancée. By the spring of 1913 he had blocked out enough ore to attract former Ubehebe booster Jack Salsberry and a partner to buy an interest in the mine. The three formed a closed corporation, Carbonate Lead Mines, with a modest nominal capital of $100,000. With promising ore ready to ship, Pray next set to work grading a 40-mile road down the valley and over the lower end of the Black Mountains to the Tonopah and Tidewater at Zabriskie. The future seemed bright, when suddenly one day in June, Pray wandered off from the road camp and shot himself in the head. A hastily convened coroner's jury called it a case of "mental derangement," resulting from a sunstroke he had suffered several years before.[15]

Salsberry took over the work and completed the road, over what is now known as Salsberry Pass, that fall. But after all that work, the ore, hauled by mule teams up to the pass, then by a traction engine down to the railroad, proved too poor to pay with lead at only 3½¢ a pound. The Carbonate was virtually closed down, and that might have been the end of it had it not been for the outbreak of the war. When lead prices doubled to 7¢ in 1915, the ore suddenly turned profitable and Salsberry rushed back to work the mine for all it was worth. By the summer of 1915 he

JACK SALSBURRY
STOCK BROKER

STOCK
BONDS

JACK OPENED UP
THE FIRST BROKERAGE
OFFICE IN TONOPAH — ·1901

HIS FAMOUS
ROCK-DRILLING
CONTEST
IN THE EARLY
DAYS OF TONOPAH

OPENED UP
THE CARBONATE
LEAD MINES CO.
IN DEATH VALLEY

Jack Salsberry, one of Death Valley's most persistent mining promoters, worked every angle for twenty years from Greenwater to Leadfield. (*Courtesy of Nevada Historical Society*)

had as many as sixteen trucks and sixty men hauling out ore that averaged over $50 a ton. Midway between the mine and Zabriskie, he had to set up a "hotel" to feed, bed, and rotate the truckers. Since shipping costs were still the biggest expense, running almost $15 a ton, Salsberry kept experimenting to find a cheaper way to haul the ore. Old borax man Harry

Gower claimed that Salsberry even tried a crazy contraption that had two big ore-filled tanks for wheels! Later in 1915 Salsberry switched from trucks to caterpillar tractors, but the continued rise of lead prices, which reached a high of 12¢ in 1917, made further cost-cutting seem less important. Moreover, mining costs were particularly low because Pray had blocked out so much ore that just three or four men could break down more rock than all the trucks and tractors could haul away each day. The miners made their "hotel" right in the mine, not only working underground but cooking, eating, and sleeping there to beat the heat.[16]

Salsberry kept up steady shipments of around 40 tons a week until metal prices broke at the end of the war. He shipped a total of about 6,500 tons of carbonate ore, worth roughly a third of a million dollars, and doubtless turned a good profit on his investment. After the war he also worked a quick stock job on the mine. In 1923 he leased it to a foundering Tonopah company called New Sutherland Divide, in which he had an interest. He then succeeded in getting a contract with the giant U.S. Smelting, Refining and Mining Company to sublease the mine, and he and his partners hastily worked up the stock from 5¢ to 50¢ a share within a few months while they tried to unload before the smelting company backed out. A few years later they subleased the mine to another corporate shell, the Reorganized Victory Divide Mining Company, run by A. I. D'Arcy, who made a show of reopening the Carbonate and the adjoining Queen of Sheba. Claiming they were "destined to be one of the biggest silver-lead producers in the United States," D'Arcy worked the Victory stock up from 3¢ to 13¢ while he unloaded his own holdings, then let it crash in the summer of 1926.[17]

The old mine became an honest producer again after the stock market crash in 1929, when labor costs fell further than metal prices. Salsberry's New Sutherland Company reopened the mine in 1930 and over the next several years, they shipped more than 4,000 tons of ore worth another $100,000 before they finally quit. By then the Carbonate had become the second most productive lead mine in the Death Valley and Amargosa country, although it took a world war and the Great Depression to do it.[18]

While Salsberry was working the Carbonate, two Bishop businessmen, W. W. Waterson and Archibald Farrington, tried to work a lead mine in his old Ubehebe district. They had held the Ubehebe lead claims for nearly a decade. In the fall of 1915, after lead prices shot up, they started hauling ore with a Yuba tractor over Salsberry's old road across Death Valley and up Grapevine Canyon to the railroad at Bonnie Clare. But even at boom prices the Ubehebe ore paid only $20 a ton, and finding that it was a losing proposition, they quit in April 1916, after shipping only about 250 tons. Leasers later struck a couple of pockets of high-grade running around $100 a ton and shipped some 1,500 tons in 1921 and 1928 all the way to Beatty at a good profit. But that was all there was of that kind of ore.[19]

Then there was the lead mine of poor Jean Lemoigne, who attracted far more attention in death than he ever did in life. "Old John," as most called him, was a quiet man, a dreamer and a recluse. Born in France in 1842, he had drifted into the Death Valley country by 1880, and there he remained for the rest of his days. He worked high-grade pockets in the Hemlock and other old Panamint mines on lease for a while. But about 1895 he found a mine of his own—one that he dreamed would make him rich. It was a big, low-grade lead deposit high up in the Cottonwood Mountains on the west side of Death Valley, just 5 miles north of Towne Pass at the head of what is now Lemoigne Canyon.[20]

Lemoigne wasn't alone in his dream. One overly enthusiastic visitor called it "the largest body of lead ore ever uncovered on the coast." Others declared it was nothing less than the legendary Lost Gunsight. None overvalued it more, however, than Lemoigne himself. He once turned down an offer of $75,000 during the heady days of the gold boom—not, as some would have it, because he didn't trust checks, but because he wanted a whole lot more—"a quarter of a million dollars, cash," he said. Lemoigne was confident that he could get his price, if he was patient. But he waited a quarter of a century—to the day he died—and all he ever got was the warm feeling that he had found his fortune, even if he couldn't spend it. For Old John, however, that seemed to be enough, even though he had to take odd jobs to get enough cash for grub.[21]

But it was Lemoigne's death in the summer of 1919, at the age of seventy-seven, alone with his burros under a mesquite bush near Salt Well out in the middle of Death Valley, that finally stirred up interest in him and his mine. Scotty happened upon his coyote-mauled remains that fall and sent word to Harry Gower at Ryan. Gower went out with Tom Wilson, buried Lemoigne, and collected $40 from the coroner for his trouble. It all seemed simple enough, but maybe $40 meant a whole lot more then, for over thirty years later Scotty publicly complained that he had actually buried Old John and Gower hadn't shared a cent with him. Then along came Frank Crampton with a little pamphlet called the *Legend of John Lemoigne*, claiming that it was really he and Shorty Harris who had found and buried Old John and deserved the money.[22]

Bill Corcoran, a hanger-on from Rhyolite, was also down at Furnace Creek Ranch that fall, and years later offhandedly included himself in the burial party, too. But Corcoran didn't want any part of the coroner's fee. Instead, he and Bev Hunter had quietly headed up Lemoigne Canyon and relocated Old John's mine. Corcoran, however, soon began to think that the mine was "jinxed." First they optioned it to a Bostonian named

Brandon, who was killed in an auto accident in June 1920, just before he could complete the purchase. Then they got Harry Stimler interested in it, but he and Corcoran nearly died just trying to get out to the mine that August, and that deal fell through, too. A few years later they finally optioned it to a former Goldfield mining man, John J. Reilly, who bought it in 1924 and died the following spring. That was the end of the fatalities for a while.[23]

By 1925 Reilly's partner, William R. McCrea, had opened the lode on leases and built a road 8 miles up the canyon. With lead back up to nearly 11¢ a pound, pockets of high-grade, which ran just over 50 percent lead with traces of silver and gold, could pay over $100 a ton. McCrea was hauling out two truckloads a day across Death Valley, 50 miles to the railroad at Beatty at a good profit. But despite Old John's dreams and a few inflated experts' estimates, there just wasn't much paying ore in the mine. McCrea and his leasers shipped just over 200 tons before closing down in 1927.[24]

Bill Corcoran, still worried about the "jinx," died suddenly at the age of forty-seven at Emigrant Spring in December 1930. Harry Stimler was shot to death by a deranged storekeeper at Tecopa the following August. Bill McCrea didn't believe in jinxes, however, and held onto the mine for another decade or more. It never made him rich, but it didn't do him any harm, either.[25]

The Last Hurrah

The heady days of mining in Death Valley and the Amargosa were almost a thing of the past by the mid-1920s. But they were to end, not with a whimper but with a bang, in a final burst of flamboyant flimflammery over fancied bonanzas of silver and lead high up in the Panamints and Grapevines, where two notorious pied pipers—E. G. Lewis and C. C. Julian—each took their faithful followers for all they were worth. This was Death Valley's last hurrah.

Those two good sheperds, in fact, brought a whole new twist to mining promotion. They were peculiarly charismatic con men, who had each in his own way assembled an attentive and faithful flock of investors who would follow them into any scheme. That was the key to their remarkable successes, not only in fleecing the public but in evading the toils of the law much longer than most in their calling. They were, indeed, such good shepherds, gaining the confidence of their flocks so fully, that their lambs came back to be sheared again and again, and almost never cried wolf. How they did it was a marvel in itself.

Edward Gardner Lewis led off in the spring of 1925, taking his tired flock on a new chase that he said would return them tens of millions of dollars in silver from the old Panamint mines. Born in 1869, the son of a Connecticut minister, Lewis was a frail, intense man with pale blue eyes and such a confidence-inspiring manner that he would have made an ideal preacher himself. But he was too ambitious and erratic for that. He dropped out of college in 1890 to pursue a far less pious calling, which would eventually land him in a federal penitentiary. Lewis maintained an aura of zealous idealism, however, and cloaked his schemes in grand and noble purposes. He was a crusading con man who would rid the world of the loathsome cockroach with a wintergreen-impregnated "Bug Chalk" they dared not cross, and who would banish poverty by an endless-chain lottery scheme in his *Winner* magazine. He would bring education to all at his "People's University" in Saint Louis and "uplift American woman-kind" through the columns of his *Woman's Magazine,* for which he once claimed the largest circulation of any publication in the world![1]

Through these and other high-minded schemes, Lewis gathered, over the course of twenty years, a dedicated following of nine thousand or more souls who gave him not only their hard-earned savings but their unfaltering faith as well. They gave him over twenty million dollars, and although

421

they lost every cent, Lewis magically kept their faith alive and strung them along from one failing scheme to another, getting them to put up just a little more on each new venture in the hopes of finally recouping all their losses and gaining much much more.

Even when the postal authorities issued a fraud order against Lewis and his creditors forced him into bankruptcy, the faithful stood by him. He flourished in his newfound martyrdom, hinting darkly at persecution and comparing himself with Martin Luther, Oliver Cromwell, and Patrick Henry. The faithful scrimped to give him more money for a new start, and he came to California in 1913 to found a "dream community" at Atascadero. It would be the "ideal city" populated only by the true believer, that "ideal Atascaderan . . . who sees no evil, hears no evil and does no evil." All his followers could live there in "peace, harmony and contentment" at the modest cost of just a few hundred dollars an acre. A dozen years and $10.8 million later the Atascadero dream had been transformed into a new string of failing ventures in real estate, oil, and mines, and in December 1924 Lewis was again forced into bankruptcy. Again hinting at an evil conspiracy to do him in, he rallied his flock to "contribute" to his Atascadero Reconstruction Fund in a new scheme to rebuild their dreams and regain their losses. At the heart of the Reconstruction Fund was Panamint.[2]

Panamint was the last great hope for Lewis's tired flock, and he didn't bother dressing it up in any altruistic garb, but sold it simply as a rescue mission for the faithful. In April 1925 he announced that he had bought a half interest in the "famous Panamint silver mines" from Al Myers for $300,000, with $25,000 down and the balance to be paid from returns of the mines. Myers had acquired title to most of the old mines at Panamint over a decade before, but he hadn't gotten around to reopening them until 1924, when he teamed up with a mining engineer William L. Seeley. After just six months of exploration, they found that leasers had pretty well picked out the last of the high-grade, and that the rest of the exposed ore still wouldn't pay. The only remaining chance of striking pay ore was to run a tunnel to cut the veins at depth in the hope that there was some hidden bonanza below. But that was a more expensive gamble than Myers wanted to take, so he found Lewis and sold him on the idea. Lewis was just opening his Reconstruction Fund to drill some wildcat wells in Maricopa and he snapped up the Panamint proposition, making it his last best hope instead.[3]

The Lewis Tunnel was started at the foot of the south wall of Surprise Canyon in June 1925, to tap the Wyoming vein at a distance of 1,500 feet or more and a depth of roughly 1,000 feet below its once-rich surface croppings, which had produced most of Panamint's ore. Seeley kept as many as forty men working around the clock, pushing the tunnel face forward with power drills and hauling out the rock with a little electric locomotive. They advanced steadily, averaging just over 5 feet a day.[4]

It was the ideal deal, with all the ingredients of a perfect con. There was the tantalizing history of "proven" production, which Lewis helpfully stretched a mere tenfold, to $5 million—half of it stolen by high-graders, he said. There was the promise of instant riches when the tunnel cut the vein, revealing as much as "fifty million dollars overnight," Lewis predicted. There was an atmosphere of romance and adventure in all the wonderful tales of the wild and woolly old camp, its stage robbers and enormous silver "balls." Lewis had the pastor of Atascadero's Federated Church serialize the history of the camp for his followers, and he spiced it with a yarn from a pulp magazine that the "balls," weighing 3,000 pounds each, had simply been let loose to roll down the canyon, squashing a stray mule and everything else in their path, and thus giving the place a new name—Kill Ball Canyon! Best of all, of course, there was the Lewis Tunnel itself, which provided not only the reason for raising money but the perfect stall, since the work could be stretched at will. Although by then California had a Blue Sky Law, specifically designed to protect innocent investors from being sold stock in such pieces of the firmament, Lewis got around that because he wasn't selling stock; he was only soliciting "contributions" to his Reconstruction Fund. The "contributions" were, in fact, paid directly into his personal bank account. All the contributors got in return was Lewis's promise that when the Panamint mines paid off, the faithful would be repaid many times over for all their contributions and past losses. There was the awful threat, too, that as soon as the vein was cut Lewis would refuse to take any more contributions, so that those wavering souls who hadn't "contributed" any tangible measure of their faith would be left out in the cold. There was indeed a heaven and a hell.[5]

Of course, there was at least a chance, however slim, that the mine might really pay off. But Lewis the compulsive embellisher couldn't just leave it at that. He had to make it seem like a certainty, so he steadily increased the value of the ore already in the old workings "ABSOLUTELY BLOCKED OUT AND PROVEN UP" to over $12 million by Christmas of 1925, in order to squeeze out those last reluctant dollars from his flock.[6]

By the spring of 1926 the Lewis Tunnel was in over 1,500 feet. But Lewis had revised his estimate of when the wonderful Wyoming vein would be cut to 1,680 feet, and when that mark was passed, he pushed the estimate even further. Day by day the anxiety mounted, as the treasure trove was more certain to be found with each new dawn and the last reluctant followers hurried to contribute their tithes before the hour of redemption arrived. All through April and May they waited and worried, clinging to ever more promising "indications," until finally the day arrived when, at 2,052 feet, Lewis proclaimed that the great vein was cut in a bonanza of $75 ore. Surely this was Panamint's "second coming." But Lewis was already farther into the future, talking of a $25 million stock flotation and a 1,000-ton mill, $5 million a year production and airplanes to fly out the bullion, and maybe even tunneling several miles farther, all the way to Ballarat, to tap the old gold veins too![7]

Then suddenly on June 1 all work stopped, as the law finally began closing in on Lewis. In a rare muckraking mood, *Sunset Magazine* had launched a lengthy exposé of the dedicated deceiver which ran from September 1925 to February 1926. The martyred Lewis decried this new conspiracy through his own *Lewis Journal,* but *Sunset's* revelations took their toll on his flock. Worse yet, they reawakened the postal authorities to his doings, and early in May investigators seized a whole truckload of his records in Atascadero. Two months later he was hauled before a federal grand jury in Los Angeles and indicted on multiple counts of mail fraud. Although many of his flock stood bravely by him, others finally turned against him. Lewis was tried and convicted on a total of two dozen charges, reaching back several years, and was sentenced to two concurrent prison terms totaling eleven years. He was paroled in 1934 after serving five years at McNeil Island penitentiary. By then his flock had dispersed and his career was ended. He died nearly broke in Atascadero in 1950.[8]

Lewis was never tried for his Panamint promotion; there were too many other bigger things to get him on. He had only received about $700,000 from his flock on his Panamint promises, and had probably put almost half of that into the mines and tunnel, and some into his dry holes in Maricopa as well. But the post office did issue a fraud order banning his Reconstruction Fund appeals from the mails, after the U.S. Geological Survey found in August 1926 that the wonderful $75 a ton bonanza at the end of Lewis's tunnel assayed only 65¢ a ton. All of those blocked-out "millions" in the old workings were equally worthless. Once again, Panamint was a crushing disappointment.[9]

Unlike Lewis, there was nothing spiritual or idealistic about Charles Courtney Julian. He was a flamboyant hayseed huckster with a pungent but disarmingly folksy style—a sly fox, thin, wiry, and shrewd, with a "long vulpine nose and close set eyes." He was slow in getting into the con games of high finance, but he finished fast and hooked his followers with a few real winners. Born on a farm on the plains of Manitoba in 1885, Julian grew up hustling papers on the streets of Winnipeg after his father died. He later worked at a variety of jobs, from driving a milk wagon to selling real estate in Saskatchewan, before he drifted to the southern California oil fields. There he worked his way up from roustabout to driller. Then in 1920 he went into business for himself, raising money through a string of frank, folksy ads to sink wildcat wells. The first few were dry, but early in 1922 he got a lease on 4 acres in the newly opened oil field at Santa Fe Springs and brought in five gushers. That won him wide publicity and an instant following who flocked to him, eager to share in his good fortune.[10]

Julian was quick to capitalize on their desires, forming several more drilling syndicates and finally a giant Julian Petroleum Company, popularly known as "Julian Pete," offering 400,000 shares at $50 a throw. Although he failed to bring in any more gushers, he found that his talent for bringing in cash was unbeatable. He flooded Los Angeles with more folksy ads for Julian Pete, calling, "Come On In Folks, The Water's Just Fine . . . You'll Never Make a Thin Dime Just Lookin' On . . . I've Got a Sure-Fire Winner This Time . . . We're All Out Here In California Where The Gushers Are And We Just Ought To Clean Up . . . We'll Make That Standard Oil Crowd Turn Flipflops . . . I'm Not Kiddin', Folks, You're Looking Opportunity In The Eye." Forty thousand eager folks agreed and put up close to $10 million within a few months. It was an unprecedented success, and Julian took $2 million off the top for his sales commission alone. Suddenly he was a celebrity and a millionaire. He bought a nineteen-room mansion, scattered money right and left, and caroused with movie stars. He even picked a fistfight with Charlie Chaplin.[11]

Julian Pete was a flop, however. Despite all the money poured into it, there wasn't enough to get it going. It had pipelines and tank farms but virtually no oil, service stations but no refinery, assets but no income. Millions more were needed to make it a real oil company; the California corporation commissioner was pressing an investigation of its affairs; Julian's followers were starting to jump ship; and the shares had crashed to $9. In a last-ditch effort, Julian held a mass meeting of his stockholders in the Hollywood Bowl. Claiming that the big oil companies, the banks, the press, and the corporation commissioner were conspiring against him, he tried to convince his followers to keep their stock off the market for two years, while he sold more treasury stock to buy a refinery and some producing wells. He failed. In December 1924, he resigned as president of Julian Pete and turned over his stock to a Texas lawyer-promotor, S. C. Lewis, who proposed to salvage it. Instead, he savaged it. Over the next couple years, through a fraudulent overissue of $150 million in Julian Pete stock, Lewis produced the biggest financial fiasco in southern California history—"The Great Los Angeles Bubble." But well before the bubble burst in May 1927, Julian had led many of his followers out of oil and into a hot new deal, way up in the Grapevines on the brink of Death Valley.[12]

His public heard little from Julian from the time he stepped out of

Pete until the first of February, 1926. Then he burst back into the papers with an outrageous new string of cornpone ads, shouting "Death Valley and Her Hidden Treasure—That's My Baby Now." This "JAZZ BABY," he revealed, was a chippy called the Western Lead Mines Company:

> I picked this baby with plenty of care and I can just feel it in my blood that she's going to be wicked . . . this is one "BABY" that "struts her stuff" . . . she is the biggest thing out doors today . . . A HUNDRED MILLION DOLLAR SILVER-LEAD MINE and might be twice or three times that big.
>
> There is one sure thing about "WESTERN LEAD," and that is, if she is the hundred million dollar property that I believe she is, you can be sure you'll get all of yours, because if "CALVIN COOLIDGE" himself was running this deal he couldn't run it squarer or cleaner than I will. . . .
>
> I really believe that I've stumbled onto the biggest "SILVER-LEAD MINE" that's been picked up in the United States during the last fifty years, and if I'm right—holy smoke!—what will each share eventually be worth?
>
> It makes me dizzy to even try to figure that out, and I'm not so slow with a pencil, either. . . .
>
> It's not at all unlikely that every dollar invested will bring a return of 30 or 40 for one if it's anything like what the dozen engineers that have examined it, predict it to be, and I'm frank to say to you, I'll be tetotally "COW-KIPPED" if I can figure how anyone with any gambling blood in them, can stay off "WESTERN LEAD."
>
> Possibly its's too close to your back door for you to realize that such an immense treasure could exist, but let me tell you that I'm not the biggest "DUMB-BELL" roaming at large, and I honestly believe I've got my arms around a "HUNDRED MILLION DOLLAR SILVER-LEAD MINE" and I'm advising every mother's son and daughter to pick yourself off some "WESTERN LEAD" SHARES while the picking's good, because I'm going to open this "BABY" up about as fast as anything you ever saw happen. . . .
>
> What's wrong with the average mining deal is that they go so dawg-gone slow, one gets grey headed waiting for returns, but not so with "WESTERN LEAD" and that's a promise now. . . .
>
> Our whole body of ore is above the grass roots, no shaft or expensive mining on this baby, in fact, I might say we Miners (get that "we" Miners stuff) feel that our layout is almost a steam shovel proposition and inside of 120 days from now, I'll show you plenty of ore on its way to the smelter at Salt Lake City, and plenty of fat checks in return. . . .
>
> The action I'm going to give you on "WESTERN LEAD" operations will make the whole world sit up and take notice. . . .

I'm hitting on all "EIGHT" now with "ACTION AS MY
SLOGAN," so just watch me go . . . and give you all that action that
every "up and going" American loves. . . .
Let's go, folks, on "WESTERN LEAD," because it's time to twist
her tail, and every day you postpone placing your "BUY" order is
costing you money.
This "BABY" is due for a rapid ride and she craves altitude. . . .
She's a "High Stepping Baby" and I don't mean maybe. . . .
Shut your eyes, say here goes nothing, and . . . mail your checks
direct to me . . . C. C. Julian.[13]

With a line like that, Julian hardly needed anything else. But there was
much more to his "JAZZ BABY" than just a flashy carnival pitch; he had
spent months getting her gussied up to turn this trick. It all started on a
blustery spring day in 1924, when a couple of Rhyolite hangers-on, Ben
Chambers and Frank Metts, grubstaked by a Tonopah laundryman, Larry
Christianson, found the big, low-grade lead deposit they called the March
Storm at the head of Titus Canyon. Julian boasted she was absolutely
virgin ground that nothing had "ever walked, crawled or crept over, but
a lizard, a rabbit or a mountain goat" until Chambers laid a pick into her.
But she had, in fact, been picked up and discarded almost twenty years
before by another hopeful, W. H. Seaman, during the Bullfrog excitement.
He had formed a company, Death Valley Consolidated, sold shares at two
for a nickel to raise a couple of thousand dollars, and worked at her for
about six months before he gave her up as worthless. Chambers and Metts
didn't do much for her either, until they showed her to Jack Salsberry,
who saw the possibilities and showed her to Ed Staunton and Jake
Berger. Then Berger showed her to his old friend and business associate
C. C. Julian. She was just what Julian was looking for.[14]

Salsberry, Staunton, and Berger bought the claims, fourteen in all, for
what Julian swore was "more real money than old Ben will ever know
how to spend," and formed the Western Lead Mines Company in August
1925, with a modest capitalization of 1.5 million shares at a dime each.
Two months later another half million shares were added and Julian
formally took over, getting a quarter of the 900,000 shares of promoters'
stock as a "gift," he said, taking nearly all of the remaining treasury stock
in exchange for putting up the development money, and naturally becoming president of the company. From then on she was practically his
exclusive property. He alone would profit from her, too, because he got
his partners to lock up 90 percent of all their promoters' stock in a bank
vault for two years while he sold his treasury stock to recoup his development costs—and, as it turned out, much more.[15]

Before Julian could sell his "baby," he had to dress her up. For starters,
he bought a bunch of glowing reports from carefully selected "experts"

whom he praised as "the foremost Engineers and Geologists of America." They obligingly found no ore specimens assaying less than $30 a ton, and the most compliant, Bruce L. Clark, a professor of paleontology at the University of California, blithely calculated that there was "nearly a million tons of milling ore," although he later admitted that he knew nothing about mineral deposits. That was close enough, however, for Julian to call her his "hundred million dollar baby." Then Julian unleashed a whirlwind of activity. On the first of December he started a crew grading a road up Titus Canyon to the mine. It was completed in six days, and more men, supplies, and equipment were sent in. They started two tunnels to open the deposit at depth, put up a boardinghouse and offices, laid out a townsite called Leadfield, and started a new, much longer road on up the canyon and over the Grapevines to Beatty.[16]

By the end of January, Julian's baby was ready to "strut her stuff." His tunnels were in over 100 feet in "wonderful milling ore," and his new road was almost finished. A pipeline was laid from a nearby spring and telephone and telegraph lines were being run from Beatty. Julian had a hundred men at work and another hundred curious and hopeful souls had trekked in. Most just staked out some of the surrounding ground, but a few actually bought lots in Leadfield, opening a general store, a restaurant, and a combination barbershop and bathhouse. Other mining companies were also being formed, but most of these were the creation of Julian and his partners. They had picked up about thirty additional claims and organized at least half a dozen new companies, among them the Leadfield New Road Mining Company, with a high-grade pocket discovered while blasting for the road. But Western Lead was Julian's real "baby," and she was finally ready to go public.[17]

On January 30, Western Lead opened on the Los Angeles Stock Exchange. She was "hot stuff" from the start, and Julian boosted her daily. He started her shares at $1.50, a classy price for a 10¢-par hooker, but he had a ready clientele among his followers. He raised her 7¢ the first day, and doubled her price in six weeks. Even Julian couldn't say enough about her in his daily ads, so he sent a former Alaska newspaperman, Bernie Stone, out to Leadfield to drum up some news items for the papers as well. Stone did a bang-up job. He not only let loose a barrage of news on Western Lead's whirlwind operations but also fired off some colorful copy that was certain to make a hit in the tabloids. Even the echoes made news in his hands, with the report that each evening at 9 P.M., just before he went to bed, the company's cook would shout, "It's 6 o'clock, Get up," and right on time the next morning the echo would return with a bang and wake the camp! In fact, to hear Stone tell it, Titus Canyon was just "second to the Grand Canyon in scenic beauty and splendor" and Wrigley, the "chewing gum king," would build a big hotel and fly in tourists from

Los Angeles. Stone did such a good job that on March 13 Julian set him up as editor of his own paper, the *Leadfield Chronicle,* which Stone had printed in Tonopah whenever he got enough copy together. Nevada's governor, James Scrugham, got so excited over the boom that he called for a new boundary survey to see whether Nevada could claim the camp. But a hasty reconnaissance made at night by searchlight from Daylight Spring confirmed that Leadfield was in California after all.[18]

All the ballyhoo finally reached a crescendo on Sunday, March 14, when Julian brought a whole trainload of investors to Leadfield for a free lunch and a firsthand chance to give his baby "the once over." He'd advertised for weeks a $30,000 extravaganza, a free excursion to quiet the last doubters. All the press and even the corporation commissioner were invited. "COME UP or SHUT UP," he taunted, when "THAT CHOO CHOO LEAVES FOR WESTERN LEAD ... You don't have to know anything about a mine to appreciate this 'Baby' ... I'm here to tell you she'll knock the eye out of anyone that takes a peek at her." Out of 1,500 eager souls begging to be taken, 340 got the nod, and by 4:30 Saturday afternoon they were all aboard when the "Julian Special" rolled out of Los Angeles with eleven Pullman sleepers, two diners, and an observation car. Arriving in Beatty Sunday morning, they piled into 90 private autos, hired by Julian, and joined more than 800 other enthusiasts who had driven down from Tonopah and Goldfield. In a grand caravan they set out on the 22-mile trek to Leadfield over Julian's new road, opened just a few weeks before at a cost of $40,000 to $60,000. Getting there was an adventure in itself, for Julian's road was, and still is, a "thriller" with a "hair raising series of corkscrew curves ... cut out of the sheer sides of mountains"— "one of the grandest and most rugged drives on the American Continent," one enthusiast proclaimed.[19]

With a chorus of squealing brakes and a staccato of dynamite blasts from the surrounding hills, the caravan wound its way into Leadfield. For a few hours the little camp actually looked like the lively boomtown the excursionists expected, as twelve hundred people and a few hundred cars jammed the main street. Julian's admirers hoisted him on their shoulders, the crowd cheered, and a motion-picture camera rolled to preserve it all for posterity. Then the hungry throng queued up at Ole's Inn for their free lunch of barbecued turkey, pork, beer, salad, and "all the trimmings," including some hot jazz from a six-piece band. After lunch they were treated to a few inspirational words from the lieutenant governor of Nevada, from Julian's prize expert, Letson Balliet, and from the great Julian himself. Then they were herded into the tunnels by Jack Salsberry to ogle the jazz baby in all her glory. It was a rousing success. The next day her stock jumped to a new high of $3.30 in record trading on the Los Angeles Stock Exchange.[20]

But it all came crashing down just two days later, when Corporation Commissioner Edwin Dougherty announced an investigation into Western Lead. The shares broke to $1.55, as thousands of panicked stockholders stormed the brokers' offices and blocked traffic on Spring Street in front of the exchange, where the police hastily erected barricades to keep them from swarming onto the trading floor. Julian had thought he was safe from California's Blue Sky Law, because only companies selling stock were required to get a permit, while individual sales weren't regulated, and he was, after all, only selling his personal shares in Western Lead. But after the *Engineering and Mining Journal* decried the outrageous fraudulence of Julian's ads and the embarrassed paleontologist publicly repudiated Julian's use of his report, the commissioner decided to hold public hearings into whether the sale of Western Lead was "unjust, unfair or inequitable" to investors. Julian denounced the inquiry as "unwarranted, unfair and un-American" and vowed to fight. He sought a restraining order to block the hearings and brought a $350,000 damage suit against the commissioner and the *Los Angeles Times,* which had stopped running his ads. When the last of those cases was thrown out of court as "unintelligible," he finally brought out his own paper, *The Truth,* to assure his followers that his baby was still all right and that the inquiry was just part of a conspiracy to keep him from gaining political power and naming the next governor![21]

The hearings were held nonetheless, and they were every bit as damning as Julian could have feared. His jazz baby was exposed as a tramp. His experts either recanted, like the paleontologist, or were discredited, like Letson Balliet, who was a convicted felon for mail fraud. Even Julian's own mining superintendent conceded that his baby was only a prospect, not a mine. Moreover, the commission's experts found that, despite all the wonderful reports, there were only 200 tons of ore in sight, and that it ran less than 6 percent lead—less than $10 a ton! They concluded that the annual dividends of 20 percent, which Julian had promised were simply "impossible" and that the venture was "doomed to certain failure." Brokers further revealed that Julian had gotten his baby listed on the exchange by offering blocks of her stock at cut-rate prices to members of the listing committee, and that he had subsequently rigged her extraordinary price rise by matching buy and sell orders. Thus the commissioner concluded that the sale of Western Lead was indeed "unjust, unfair and inequitable" and ordered the stock—which by then had fallen to 70¢— stricken from the exchange on May 27.[22]

That was too late for Julian's followers. He had already stuck them with at least three-quarters of a million shares for roughly $1.5 million, and he didn't have much left to sell them. It was only his partners who were still waiting to sell their stock, which was locked up in that bank vault. Julian's only real concern was trying to regain the confidence of his flock so that he could hit them again the next time around. In view of the revelations at the hearings, that might have seemed an insurmountable task, but he came through:[23]

> Folks, the whole drama surrounding WESTERN LEAD, whether you know it or not, has been nothing more or less than a game of checkers, and it is obvious that it is now my move and I know the eyes of this Community are on me.
>
> I'm frank to tell you that this next move has been a difficult one to figure out.
>
> The most important thing of all to me is to retain the steadfast confidence of the people, regardless of everything else.
>
> Clothed with the authority and dignity of the State of California, the Corporation Commissioner comes out and tells the world that WESTERN LEAD is worthless . . . and to those of you that don't know me and my methods of doing business, makes me look like an unscrupulous thief. . . .
>
> I am hog-tied until the development at the Mine proves who is right and who is wrong; consequently . . . I have concluded that on June 12th I will just lock my offices up and will not reopen the doors until Sept. 1st.
>
> I will proceed to the Mine and will hurry development work in every way possible, and . . . I feel that by Sept. 1st I will be able to show you at least a million tons or ten million dollars worth of commercial ore blocked out and ready for the mill, and don't forget I'm staking my reputation on my belief that WESTERN LEAD will develop into one of the greatest lead-silver mines in the world.
>
> This is a show-down between the Corporation Commissioner and C. C. Julian, and . . . the Corporation Commissioner says the stock is unjust and inequitable. I say, cart all you can get in to me . . . folks, if it was good enough for me to recommend to you, it's good enough for me to buy back from you. . . .
>
> FOR 7 DAYS ONLY, I will buy every share of WESTERN LEAD in circulation and will allow you $2 a share and in payment I will hand you my personal note payable 24 months from date, to bear interest at the rate of 10% per annum, payable twice yearly. . . .
>
> I want you to believe in my integrity. I want you to believe in my honesty. I want you to believe that I believe every word I have ever told you about WESTERN LEAD.[24]

It was a masterful move. His shareholders believed him and held their stock. One admirer, however, later blamed the entire collapse of Leadfield on this grand gesture, claiming that Julian "spent almost three million dollars buying up stock," so "there was no money left for Leadfield." It made a good story, but in fact at the end of those seven days Julian proudly reported that he had given out notes for only $187,504 worth of stock. That was less than an eighth of what he had unloaded. Many of the notes were soon turned back again for new stock, and it's doubtful that Julian ever bothered to pay off the rest, in view of all the suits that were later brought against him.[25]

Julian did keep one promise, however; he returned in September with another string of preposterous ads. But he wasn't pushing his old baby anymore. "It was a tough jolt," he said, but he finally "realized that all the King's horses and all the King's men could not bring WESTERN LEAD back again":

> Even though the mine developed into one of the biggest in the country, there would always remain a certain amount of doubt in people's minds.
> It was another case of giving a dog a bad name and hanging it. . . .
> The burning question with me was, what should I do, and while meditating on the situation I recalled of reading, many times during the past year, of all the great mergers of the different big industries of the United States . . . in fact, mergers of nearly every worthwhile big business, but never a MERGER OF BIG MINES did I see; so says I to myself, says I, "C. C. you're the bird to pull a Mine Merger."[26]

"The next move was to acquire a few real mines," Julian concluded, so he scoured the West from Mexico to Canada looking at over a hundred mines before settling on four to combine with Western Lead in his big new quintet, Julian Merger Mines Incorporated. The prize of the lot was the Monte Cristo, a seventeen-year-old Arizona silver mine that had never paid a dime, but for which, Julian said, he paid $1 million in cash, because it had "already in sight and blocked out in the neighborhood of TWELVE MILLION dollars worth of high-class commercial ore." The combined "assets" of his mines he calculated at $20 to $25 million so he capitalized his merger at a modest $15 million at $1 par, and invited all his old Western Lead holders to trade in their old stock, share for share, for the new, and buy a little more at a bargain, too. "Go sink the ship on this baby," he urged, "with all the dough you can beg, borrow or steal . . . because I consider her a sure shot, big winner . . . STRONGER THAN HORSERADISH . . . wild and woolly and a sure, big money maker anyway you play it, if you will only do it now."[27]

Julian made his merger sound so good, in fact, that he felt obliged to explain in his own touching way,

> Why let the public in on such a plum? I'm going to tell you why, but even while I'm telling you the whole truth, I don't expect a reader to believe me, because even I, as I write this, must admit it sounds

fishy, but be that as it may, I'm going to tell you, anyway. . . .

As I sat on the dump at the mine, I was perfectly satisfied that all I had to do to get all the money I ever needed, was to just go ahead and grind it out, and don't think I wasn't tempted to do it because I was.

Then I started to think of the people of Southern California, and the loyal way you have stood behind me. . . .

I thought of the many times you had shot your money down the line on any project I sponsored.

I thought of the times you had won on me, and I thought of the times you had lost on me, and I tried to make it balance, but I couldn't, I couldn't satisfy my conscience to pass you by, after all your kindness to me, on what I know better than anyone, is the only real legitimate opportunity to make something worthwhile that I have offered you in these six years. Was I going to let you in on all the gambles and when a cinch came along, hog it all to myself? I couldn't do it, folks, and that's the story, whether you believe it or not.[28]

It was quintessential Julian, and the faithful loved it. They turned in their Western Lead shares and pinned their hopes on Monte Cristo. Western Lead was all but dead. The exodus from Leadfield had begun in May, with the banning of stock sales. The camp had come and gone so fast that the Post Office Department didn't get an office opened until the summer, when nearly everyone had left, then took six months to realize the mistake and close it. Starting a new razzle-dazzle at the Monte Cristo, Julian had left only a small crew at Western Lead to push the tunnels a little farther on the off-chance he might still find some real ore. By the fall of 1926 there were barely two dozen men in the camp; by spring there were half a dozen; and by summer there was only one, a watchman who stayed until the last of the machinery was hauled away. Only the road was left—a spectacular drive that still excites and delights new travelers each year.[29]

Julian had put about $300,000 into his Death Valley baby, but he had gotten away with much more—$1.2 million, he later admitted. Through it all, he managed to hold onto most of his flock, too. He fleeced them again with his grand mine merger until it too was banned by the corporation commission that fall. Then he reorganized as the New Monte Cristo to take them in again. But suddenly in the spring of 1927 all hell broke loose, with the horrendous revelations of fraud in Julian Pete. The shocking exposes, scandals, and trials that ensued raised new suspicions about Julian himself, even though he was never implicated in the enormous stock overissue that was the cause of the final disaster. Some of his flock finally began to have doubts, and he was soon besieged with suits charging him with fraudulent sales of Western Lead and "gross and fraudulent

Julian sheared his lambs once again with this new variation on his Death Valley lead scheme.

mismanagement" of Monte Cristo. He fought hard, but he lost the suits, and that was the end of his mining schemes.[30]

The unsinkable Julian, however, moved on to Oklahoma and got back into oil. Once things had quieted down, he started all over again in 1930. Reassuring his former followers that he had only "SEEMED TO BE-TRAY THEM," he offered them yet another chance to "rear upon the dead ashes of our blasted hopes—A FINANCIAL STRUCTURE THAT SHOULD ULTIMATELY WITHSTAND THE ASSAULTS OF TIME"—namely, his grand new C. C. Julian Oil and Royalties Company. He might have gotten away with it, too, and carried on for decades just like E. G. Lewis, if it hadn't been for Jack Salsberry.[31]

Julian just shouldn't have tried to fleece Salsberry, too. Although Salsberry may have seemed like a happy, simple fellow, he had been around. He had been in on Greenwater and Ubehebe when Julian was still selling real estate in Saskatchewan. He had been the first to recognize the real possibilities in Western Lead, and he had played his part like a veteran. All he wanted was a share in the take. When Julian dropped Western Lead to push his merger and refused to settle with Salsberry for his 205,000 shares, which were still locked up in that bank vault, Salsberry got mad and filed suit. Julian ignored the suit at first and lost by default, then appealed and got the judgment thrown out. But Salsberry brought suit again and won a new judgment totaling $193,119. Julian refused to pay, but Salsberry wouldn't give up, and although he never got any money, he finally got revenge. He followed Julian to Oklahoma and stirred up so much trouble there that Julian was forced out of his new company and into bankruptcy, and was at last indicted for mail fraud.[32]

Not one to miss a chance to pick up a few more bucks, Julian made a final pitch to his followers to contribute to his "victory fund" to fight the new conspiracy. But just before he was to go to trial in February 1933, Julian jumped bail and fled to Shanghai. There he started writing his memoirs, "What Price Fugitive," talked of opening up China's oil reserves, and offered to help China raise money to build an air force. But nothing panned out, and on the evening of March 24, 1934, nearly penniless and in fear of being extradited, Julian had a last supper with his former stenographer, then took a lethal dose of amytal. He was buried in a pauper's grave.[33]

Julian's jazz-baby jive was a fitting finale for all the flimflammery in Death Valley and the Amargosa—a last hurrah that should have been the end of it all. But there were still a few echoes to be heard. The first reverberated down in Death Valley at a fleeting camp called Skookum in 1927, and the others were heard way over on the Amargosa at old Carrara two years later.

Skookum, a fad word for "mighty good" borrowed from the Chinook, was the last gold excitement in Death Valley proper. It was in the north end of the valley, up on Chuckawalla Hill, a spur of the Last Chance Range about 10 miles south of Sand Springs. Sol Camp, a one-time Goldfield stockbroker, had discovered gold in a big quartz ledge there in 1924 but lost interest in it. Then during the Leadfield excitement, some of his friends found surface rock running up to $276 a ton, relocated the ground, and cut him in when they formed the Death Valley Mines, Inc. That winter they built a road in, set up tents, and started exploratory work. When they started shipping out small lots of high-grade early in 1927, a rush for the surrounding hills began. Soon there were twenty tents and dozens of cars at Skookum, and a service station and store at Sand Spring.[34]

In the meantime, Camp and his partners had started work on a tunnel to tap the lode at depth and determine its worth. But like Al Myers at Panamint, they soon decided that that was a more expensive gamble than they wanted to take, so they got a beefy, balding Texas oil promoter, Chester R. Bunker, interested in the idea and sold him a controlling interest in the mine for a reported $100,000. Bunker was publisher of the Fort Worth *Western World,* an oleaginous weekly that had slipped through three states and four names in five years. But Bunker had finally collected a loyal following in 1925, after shares in a wildcat oil well that he had offered as a subscription bonus paid a million dollars. The following year he branched out into mining with an eclectic, $2 million venture he called the World Exploration Company, taking a fling with Texas quicksilver, New Mexico lead, and Arizona zinc—and now with Death Valley gold, his biggest and best yet.[35]

Though not on a par with Lewis or Julian, Bunker awed his followers with tales of "sensational new strikes" and "spectacular developments" all through the summer, as he pushed hard both the tunnel and the stock. "SKOOKUM!" he shouted from full-page ads, was nothing less than "The Hope of the West for the Mine of the Century":

SKOOKUM IS SO BIG IN SIZE AND IN PROMISE . . . THAT
SINGLE-HANDED IT CAN SWEEP WORLD EXPLORATION
COMPANY TO MAGNIFICENT SUCCESS—CAN RETURN TO EACH
AND EVERY STOCKHOLDER A FORTUNE IN CASH DIVIDENDS . . .
SKOOKUM CAN WIN—WIN SO STUPENDOUSLY—WIN SO
QUICKLY—THAT IT OVERSHADOWS EVERYTHING ELSE.

He played the tunnel for all it was worth, too, and even started a second one for good measure. Then with each new strike he taunted,

SKOOKUM is warning YOU—TELLING YOU TO GET IN RIGHT
NOW . . . SKOOKUM is saying: ACT NOW! . . . ACT QUICKLY!

QUICKLY!! QUICKLY!!! . . . Buy before the TWO tunnels, driving in
at SKOOKUM day and night, PROVE its magnificent promise of
GOLDEN WEALTH, and PUT WORLD EX STOCK BEYOND YOUR
REACH FOREVER . . . you must ACT—or prepare to regret as long
as you live that the WINNING OF A LIFE-TIME PASSED YOU BY.[36]

And so it went, week by week and foot by foot until mid-September,
when the main tunnel reached 550 feet and Bunker at last proclaimed
"SKOOKUM HAS IT! The Lower Tunnel Has Broken Into the 'Big'
Quartz . . . Finding Good Gold Values Right In Its Edge! . . . The BIG
STRIKE has come!" He promptly boosted the stock price from $1 to $1.50
and ordered in heavier machinery to drive crosscuts, drifts, and raises
through the "BIG QUARTZ in all directions, searching out . . . its riches."
In the weeks that followed he reported still more "spectacular sensations"
in his "wonder mine" and pushed the stock even harder, for the future
was now "virtually assured." But then Bunker suddenly brought out a
new "WINNER"—a silver mine over in Nevada—and poor Skookum began
to slip into oblivion. The last report from the "BIG QUARTZ" came in
December, with word that all the tunnels, crosscuts, drifts, and raises had
finally revealed a magnificent mass of "at least two hundred thousand tons
of quartz"—but not a mention of ore! The "Big Quartz" was just that,
and nothing more. By then no one was supposed to care: Nevada silver
was his new big thing. Skookum was just a misnomer. The machinery
was hauled away the following spring, and a year later Bunker too was
hauled off to jail for mail fraud.[37]

Over on the Amargosa, the clay company manager, G. Ray Boggs, had
watched Julian's show with only casual interest, but just a few years later
he found himself staging its last encore. It started simply enough, but one
thing led to another until matters suddenly got out of hand and the quiet,
middle-aged mining engineer was temporarily transformed into a wild-
eyed promoter-entrepreneur.

In May 1928 Boggs had optioned an old, low-grade gold mine, known
as the Bull Moose, just 2 miles north of the abandoned marble camp of
Carrara. Over a dozen years before, Jack Salsberry had tried and failed
to make the Bull Moose pay. But Boggs was convinced that there was
more than a million dollars worth of $10-a-ton ore in the old workings
that could be worked at a profit. He formed a little company, Gold Ace
Mining; with the backing of his boss, Fred Keeler, he leased the marble
company's old diesel-electric plant; and within six months he had brought
in water and power and put up a 100-ton ball mill. Boggs even put in an
airfield and personally flew out his first bullion bar to Los Angeles in
December.[38]

The costs were much higher and the gold recovery much lower than Boggs had expected, however; try as he might, he couldn't make it pay. By March 1929 he was ready to quit. But as a last resort he agreed to dig at a spot his wife Leila May had picked out some months earlier, in a sort of a seance between the stars and a batch of photos of the claim, hoping to divine the source of a stray piece of rich float. Within just a few feet of the surface they did in fact strike a pocket of jewelry rock, assaying as much as $23,692 a ton. That changed everything.[39]

Word of the sensational strike triggered a rush of veteran prospectors and weekend tourists, all eager to get a piece of ground nearby, or at least a piece of the fabulous rock. As many as six hundred people drove in one weekend to this roadside excitement, just off the highway from Las Vegas, and the exuberant Boggs gave them all glittering pieces of rock. Visitors were reported to have carried off between $10,000 and $15,000 worth of ore, and hopefuls across the country wrote in for samples. Many others wanted a share in the mine and were willing to pay for it.[40]

Boggs promptly quit the clay pits to become a budding entrepreneur. Just a few weeks after the big strike he got Gold Ace on the new Los Angeles Curb Exchange. He started the shares at $1.27, five times par, and they rose to $1.45 in the next two weeks as buyers clamored to get in. Brokers touted it as a "speculation of unusual merit," and even the Corporation Commission could find no fault with it. Boggs didn't try to mimic Julian's advertising jazz, but he did get the talented Bernie Stone to cook up some copy and put out a little booster paper, the *Carrara Miner,* distributing 10,000 copies to Gold Ace enthusiasts in Los Angeles. Then, with reports of a phenomenal new strike just to the north, Boggs launched a second venture, the Arista Mining Company, named for one of his wife's lucky stars. With Harry Stimler he laid out a new town of Arista just a mile up the road from Carrara, outfitting it with ornamental Marbellite streetlights and a railroad carload of "redi-cut" houses. Boggs also staged a big "Barbecue Day" at Arista on Saturday, June 22. He brought in a planeload of friends and a Pullman car full of Los Angeles brokers, while a couple of hundred carloads of other Angelenos and Nevadans brought themselves. All were treated to a tour of the mines, more free ore samples, a copy of the *Carrara Miner,* and a barbecued beef dinner, washed down with their choice of buttermilk or near beer, to the sounds of a six-piece dance band from Las Vegas.[41]

Harry Stimler had picked up some neighboring claims to float a Gold Ace Extension, and others tried to get a piece of the action with a Gold Ace Annex and the like. Sol Camp, late of Skookum, and some new friends even resuscitated the old Diamond Queen on the other side of the mountain, renaming it the Golden Ace. They shipped one carload of ore and pushed the stock out of a Los Angeles storefront with a free mining exhibit, movie, and gold raffle until the Corporation Commission cracked down on them. By the summer of 1929, there were more than a hundred men at work on the Gold Ace and surrounding claims, and the Tonopah and Tidewater hurriedly built a mile-long spur to Carrara. Boggs meanwhile took off in a new direction, launching on the Fourth of July the Nevada Airlines—the "world's fastest"—with daily flights from Los Angeles to Reno, Tonopah, and Las Vegas, and occasionally Carrara.[42]

The bubble burst that fall. The bonanza pocket pinched out at a depth of 16 feet, and after all of the picture rock had been picked out, Boggs shut down the mine in September. The Wall Street crash did the rest. Gold Ace was thrown off the Curb Exchange after it fell below 2¢. Then Boggs was sued by the owner of the mine for failing to make the payments due under the option and for fraudulently taking out $100,000 worth of ore. Nevada Airlines crashed too, and Boggs, almost $200,000 in debt, was forced into bankruptcy.[43]

The other Gold Ace imitations died soon after their namesake. But Harry Stimler kept the name alive, at least in spirit, in his next venture, the Western Ace Gold Mining Company, at a short-lived camp called Black Hills, 6 miles southeast of Tecopa—until a bullet cut him down in August 1931.[44]

The Gold Ace itself still held a curious attraction for some. In 1931 a visionary Hollywood inventor, Fred Kuenzel, tried to revive it with a scheme to make millions out of all the low-grade ore by working it at a cost of only 23¢ a ton with his revolutionary new Kuenzel Smelter. As a backup scheme he also put up some tourist cabins at Arista, which he renamed Hollywood, in the hopes of making it "a social mining center for the sportive butterflies of the film center." He never got around to building his smelter, however, and the closest his Hollywood ever came to attracting celebrities was in September, when a corpse, suspected to be that of a murdered movieland "mobster chieftan," turned up in the abandoned Tonopah and Tidewater freight shed. The mine itself may have attracted one notable, however, for in 1934 it was reported that men were once again at work reopening it, this time for a syndicate headed by former President Herbert Hoover.[45]

But even the last echoes finally died away. The wild mining rushes to Death Valley and the Amargosa were a thing of the past. It was time to move on, for the big rush of tourists had already begun.

A Nice Place to Visit

In the fall of 1925 a one-time Death Valley gold seeker, Bob Eichbaum, started work on a road over Towne Pass to a resort hotel he planned to build right in the heart of Death Valley, and a new era began. The dreaded purgatory was on its way to becoming a paradise for tourists. Death Valley's biggest bonanzas—its boundless beauty and inexhaustible lore—were at last to be opened. Despite all the horrors told about it before, a new whirlwind of publicity would now tell the world that Death Valley was, after all, a nice place to visit.

As early as the 1890s, old Jacob Staininger had dreamed of the day when the place would become a "famous pleasure resort." In the crazy days of the great gold boom, that dream went wild along with everything else. Boosters confidently predicted that the "awful abyss" would become "a winter resort that cannot be rivaled on the face of the universe," the perfect spot "to banish the languor of the idle rich seeking fresh pleasures to overcome the ennui of existence." Old desert denizens shuddered at the thought of "chappies with their dress suit cases and golf sticks . . . and conventions of short-haired women and long-haired men" all flocking there.[1]

Other enthusiasts proclaimed it a mecca for health seekers and victims of the great white plague, where

> the heretofore hopeless sufferer from tuberculosis may feel his lungs heal as if by miracle, see his chest expand with all the power of health, even watch the flesh come upon his emaciated body. . . . All the pulsations of life are renewed down in this hole of the earth which is a crucible for the segregation of the pure with its furnace for the destruction of the impure ever burning around it.[2]

Even the tyros of the *Chuck-Walla* took a poke at the dream in an April Fool ad:

> Would You Enjoy a Trip to Hell? . . . You Might Enjoy a Trip to Death Valley, Now! It has the advantages of hell without the inconveniences. It is a wonderful country with all the weird mysticism of Dante's Inferno, marvelous scenery, strange romanticism, fabulous wealth and absolute novelty. If you would enjoy a change from ordinary city life and fashionable summer resort outings you would find it here.[3]

441

At the same time, Skidoo road builder James Clark and his partners talked of turning their Stovepipe Roadhouse into a winter resort with comfortable bungalows, outdoor games, and "houses of entertainment." And for several years "Borax King" Francis Smith toyed with the idea of building a "grand hotel" at Furnace Creek Ranch to tempt "the jaded appetites of globe trotters." But nothing came of all the talk; the valley's wiles were still left to be appreciated only by the most adventuresome souls.[4]

Although dreams of a tourist paradise temporarily faded after the boom, the valley's repelling horror and alluring lore were pushed increasingly into the public eye by a small army of writers, moviemakers, and advertisers—especially the advertisers. In the fall of 1916 the Pacific Coast Borax Company resurrected the old twenty-mule team wagons again and recruited a colorful new "Borax Bill," Frank Wilson, to drive them from the Pasadena Rose Parade through the eastern states for another five or six years, stirring up once more the romance of the valley and sales of the laundry miracle. The lore of the valley had become so captivating that even New Englander Robert Ramsay of the Pneumatic Scale Corporation, which made the machines that boxed the borax for market, couldn't resist putting out a little book on *The Romance of the Desert*, which repeated the tales of the borax teams and told of his role in ensuring full measure in every box, so that old "Borax Bill . . . did not work in vain."[5]

The auto dealers were also busy cashing in on the valley's legendary terrors. In 1916 the Dodge Brothers Corporation had brought out their pioneering booklet, *Through Death Valley in a Dodge Brothers Motor Car,* which chronicled the thrilling triumph of their "Death Valley Dodge" in "the most strenuous trip ever recorded in the annals of motoring" through the most dreaded spot in America in 144° heat. Other publicity-minded dealers followed eagerly in their tracks to prove the prowess of such rivals as the Essex, the Pierce-Arrow, and the Franklin Camel. Each tried to outdo the other until a Nash dealer pulled off an unbeatable coup, sending veteran driver Rupert Larson into the Death Valley dunes in a touring car on the Fourth of July to pose for photos with a big thermometer registering 151°—"the highest temperature ever encountered by a motor car in any part of the world!" Standard Oil also got into the act with what they heralded as "the most grueling test of lubricating oil on record" in their booklet, *Across Death Valley in a Ford Car,* revealing "How a new oil for Model T Fords conquered the Hottest Place in the world." It all made such good copy that the dealers weren't even daunted by sharp criticism from the Southern California Auto Club that they had made Death Valley the "most maligned natural attraction in America," trying "to make the public think their cars are wonders because they penetrate the awful mysteries of the valley of death."[6]

Would You Enjoy a Trip to Hell?

Probably you would not. At least we will suppose so. Even if you would enjoy it there is no hurry about starting. If you are going you will do so sometime without having to plan ahead of time.

You Might Enjoy a Trip to Death Valley, Now!

It has all the advantages of hell without the inconveniences. It is a wonderful country with all the weird mysticism of Dante's Inferno, marvelous scenery, strange romanticism, fabulous wealth and absolute novelty. If you would enjoy a change from ordinary city life and fashionable summer resort outings you would find it here. You would see and learn of things of which you have never dreamed. *An automobile trip through hell* would certainly be a novelty. Such an excursion through Death Valley would be no less wonderful and much more comfortable. You may have this. If you are interested write to

The Mining Advertising Agency, Greenwater, Cal.

(*Death Valley Chuck-Walla,* April 1, 1907, *courtesy of Bancroft Library*)

In a more artful vein, poets and novelists also mined the lore of the valley in the early twenties. Some were familiar names, like the "Poet-Prospector" Clarence Eddy, who assembled two volumes of his Death Valley verse, *Ballads of Heaven and Hell* and *The Burro's Bray*, and former Rhyolite editor Paul DeLaney, who tried his hand at the great American novel with a reminiscent *Toll of the Sands*, "A Story of Love and Adventure in the Great Gold Rush into the Death Valley Country." Others were lured from afar, like the popular British poet Alfred Noyes of "Highwayman" fame, who spun a lyrical tale *Beyond the Desert* about a Wobbly who reforms after a mystical encounter with the forty-niners in Death Valley. And the valley naturally attracted writers of romantic Westerns, particularly Dane Coolidge and Zane Grey. Coolidge, a naturalist and collector of western lore, worked the valley and some of its characters into several of his novels—*Shadow Mountain, Wunpost, Lost Wagons, Horse Ketchum, Snake Bit Jones,* and *Trail of Gold*—with a clean, unvarnished style. But the baroque Grey, a onetime New York dentist who had become the most popular Western writer of the day, cloaked the valley in grotesque garb in his *Wanderer of the Wasteland*—"ghastly gray through the leaden haze, an abyss of ashes, iron walled and sun blasted, hateful and horrible as the portal of hell." He even conjured up that "poison air" again and unleashed a new horror, the deadly "midnight furnace winds." He had actually visited the valley for a week or two in March 1919 while writing the *Wanderer,* and he recounted his personal adventures as part of a travel series for *Harper's Magazine,* reprinted as *Tales of Lonely Trails.* One trip was enough to convince Grey that Death Valley would "never be popular with men," and was "fatal to women." It was the haunt only of a special breed, his "wanderers of the wastelands—men who go forth to seek and to find and to face their souls."[7]

Other adventure writers were also drawn to Death Valley. One imaginative free-lancer, John Edwin Hogg, challenged the length of the "blistering inferno" on a motorcycle in December 1919. He then wrote it up as a hair-raising, midsummer "Race for Life in Death Valley," complete with near-fatal mechanical breakdown, rattlesnakes and heat stroke, and final salvation in the gunpoint robbery of a passing motorist for water! A year later he planned to return in an airplane to penetrate those "scorched regions" where even the most daring desert rats had not "dared to leave their footprints." But that adventure fell through because Hogg couldn't get enough gasoline packed into the valley for refueling, so he turned to hunting wild burros in the Panamints on his motorcycle. In the meantime an adventuresome Cleveland matron, Edna Brush Perkins, and her friend Charlotte Jordan, seeking a "wild and lonely place and a different kind of freedom," had braved the old Walker cutoff across the south end of the valley in a car and then made a lengthy pilgrimage through the heart of it by wagon. She told of their "adventure with the outdoors" in an appealing book, *The White Heart of Mojave,* which deflated the tales of her macho rivals. Then she went on to conquer the Sahara.[8]

The moviemakers too had begun to tap Death Valley for its scenery and romance. The valley's first movie was a commercial made by Pacific Coast Borax in 1909, the two-reel *Trip to Death Valley,* filmed along the Tonopah and Tidewater tracks to old Ryan and shown from coast to coast by a dozen traveling sales teams to an audience of three million. Three years later Kalem studios shot their ill-timed *Death Valley Scotty's Mine,* just as the Mystery himself was forced to admit that he was a fake, but then the Death Valley scenes were also faked! It wasn't until November 1915 that the first movie was actually shot in the heart of the valley, when a somewhat reluctant New York director, Barry O'Neill, came out with a cast and crew to film the final scenes of Frank Norris's *McTeague,* later released as *Life's Whirlpool.* The Death Valley filming had been forced upon him by Norris's heirs as a condition for obtaining permission, and when it was all over O'Neill sighed, "I wouldn't take a million dollars for the experience. But I wouldn't go through it again for ten times the amount."[9]

In the years that followed, many more movies were shot in the valley. Foremost among them was Erich von Stroheim's great film classic, *Greed,* a savagely realistic remake of *McTeague.* A pioneer in cinema verité, *Greed* was the first feature film ever shot entirely on location, without a single studio set. Von Stroheim sought to draw real emotion from his actors as well, descending into the very heart of Death Valley in the white heat of August 1923 to film the closing scenes of his classic. Goldwyn studio executives tried to dissuade him, and their insurance company warned against such perils as arsenic-poisoned water holes, treacherous quicksands, and the ever-persistent "death-dealing gas and poison fumes." But von Stroheim scoffed at such nonsense, though he did make one concession to the studio, taking a shortwave radio so they could stay in constant contact with civilization. In a caravan of seven cars and trucks, von Stroheim descended into the valley in mid-August with his two stars, Gibson Gowland, playing McTeague, and Jean Hersholt, his pursuer; three cinematographers, William Daniels, Ben Reynolds, and Ernest Schoedsack; a violinist who provided mood music until his instrument cracked from the heat; some three dozen technicians; and one woman, script girl Eve Bessette.[10]

They suffered for six weeks in the valley, camped on army cots in the open outside the fence at Furnace Creek Ranch, while they filmed in the dunes and the salt flats. The heat set no special records that summer, but it reached 132° in the shade of the cameraman's umbrella out on the salt flats. Von Stroheim recalled temperatures of 142° and Hersholt, crawling over the glaring salt, was certain it got to 161°. It was hot enough that fourteen men fell ill from the heat and had to be taken out, while Hersholt lost 27 pounds, became delirious with sunburn, and had to be hospitalized for several weeks after the ordeal. It was "the most terrible experience any of us has ever gone through," Hersholt recalled, and before the filming was finished there was "murder . . . in our hearts." Toward the end, von Stroheim carried a pistol night and day, and wouldn't let anyone else near a loaded gun. By the time they got to the final scene—a fight to the death between Gowland and Hersholt—both actors were burned, blistered, and bleeding. Yet as they struggled, almost in a stupor, the uncompromising von Stroheim still pushed for more realism, taunting "Fight, Fight! Try to hate each other as you both hate me!"[11]

For von Stroheim, the real ordeal began when the filming ended and he started editing the 200 thousand-foot reels they had shot over nine months at a cost of $470,000. In January 1924 he emerged from the cutting room with his first version, a 42-reel, 9-hour film, which he planned to show in two parts with a dinner intermission. But before it was released Goldwyn studios merged with Metro and von Stroheim's nemesis, Louis B. Mayer, took over, demanding a much shorter film. Von Stroheim returned to the cutting room and finally came out with a 24-reeler. Mayer demanded still further cutting. Von Stroheim turned it over to a friend, Rex Ingram, who trimmed it to what he considered a bare minimum of 18 reels—a tight 3½-hour film. Even this was much too long for Mayer, and when von Stroheim refused to cut it further, Mayer gave it to a "hack cutter" who slashed it to 10 reels. In "black despair" von Stroheim refused to attend the premiere in December 1924. Years later, he still lamented, "I have made only one real picture in my life and nobody ever saw that. The poor, mangled, mutilated remains were shown as *Greed.*" Even shorn of much of its artistry, it was not a popular film. Indeed, *Variety* damned it as "morbid and senseless . . . a decisive and distinct flop." But decades later in Brussels it was named "one of the 12 best films of all time," and one enthusiast, Kenneth Rexroth, called it the "greatest of all movies."[12]

It was the less distinguished movies, however, that brought Death Valley its widest audience. Zane Grey's Death Valley epic *Wanderer of the Wasteland* was filmed by Irvin Willat of Paramount Pictures in the winter of 1923–24. It was Hollywood's first all-color movie and gave the world its first technicolor glimpses of the deadly valley. Willat then came back the next winter, restored the old Bottle House, and shot Rhyolite as "Ghost City" in a thoroughly modern Western called *The Air Mail,* complete with sky bandits. In the fall of 1926 Paul Powell came out to do a boy-and-his-dog movie under the title of *Death Valley*. With a quick eye for publicity, Powell even tried to get that old reprobate Johnny Cyty into it, after Cyty made the news by shooting Beatty's hotel keeper in the leg, but Cyty went to jail instead. Such were the movies that kept the valley on the screen.[13]

As if this wasn't publicity enough for the valley, its once great mystery man himself, the irrepressible Scotty, suddenly made a comeback with a brand new stunt—a million dollar castle right in the midst of Death Valley. After his humiliating public confession in 1912, Walter Scott had quietly retired to Twentynine Palms with Bill Key for a few years. But by 1915, his former grubstaker Albert Johnson had found that he missed his Death Valley vacations and Scotty's comraderie much more than he resented the con man's duplicity. Indeed, one of Johnson's closest associates was convinced that Johnson secretly admired Scotty for having outwitted him. Moreover, his association with Scotty had in its own peculiar way made Johnson something of a celebrity, too. Thus Johnson resumed his seasonal outings with Scotty to Death Valley and became one of the valley's earliest and most dedicated tourists. Soon after, he bought the old Staininger Ranch in Grapevine Canyon to serve as a base camp and a place for Scotty to stay between trips. When he went to buy the ranch, however, he found that there were several different claimants, each of whom had jumped the land after Staininger's death. Johnson couldn't figure out whose title, if any, was good, so he simply offered to pay $1,000 for the place, got them all to sign quit claims, and left them to fight over how the money was to be divided. Knowing that Scotty couldn't be trusted to keep up the ranch, Johnson also hired an old English remittance man, "Lord" Ely, to tend the 10 acres of orchard, vineyard, garden, and alfalfa.[14]

Scotty, with a renewed if modest allowance from Johnson, started trying to wrap himself once more in mystery. He threw a few big bills around, talked of fabulous gold and platinum mines, and promised that he would "soon startle the world again." It was all cheap amusement for Johnson who later confided, "I gave him the money because I got a kick out of watching him spend it. Scotty paid me back in laughs for every cent I gave him."[15]

But the real mystery that attracted the most attention was not in Scotty's time-worn antics, but quite inadvertently in what was starting to happen at the Grapevine Ranch. Johnson had begun to improve the accommodations there so that he could bring his wife, Bessie, and feel free to stay longer. At first he just put up a few wood-sided tents on a low shelf of ground not far from the dilapidated old ranch house. But in January 1922

Johnson hired builder F. W. Kropf and four carpenters to start work on a big, boxy two-story stucco house. And then the speculation started. Was it just a "millionaire's plaything," or did Scotty really have a mine after all, to which the building was somehow connected?[16]

The would-be mystery and his partner eagerly encouraged such speculations. Scotty rather cryptically dubbed it his "Hall of Fame," and Johnson began planning something much grander. He even commissioned Frank Lloyd Wright to design a Death Valley mansion for him, but the result was too avant-garde for his taste. Johnson finally hired a construction engineer and former Stanford classmate of his wife's, Matt Roy Thompson, to oversee the building. Thompson undertook a massive remodeling and enlargement of the existing "box" along more romantic lines, with Spanish arches and tile in the style of his alma mater. He began on a grand scale early in 1925, shipping in carloads of lumber, cement, pipe, and other materials and increasing the crew to thirty or more men. Thompson set out to build not only a great mansion but an entire self-sustaining underground system with its own water supply, sewers, hydroelectric generator, cold storage and ice plant, air conditioning and solar heating, way out there in the middle of nowhere. Johnson also hired designer C. Alexander MacNeiledge to draw up overall plans for the house and grounds, do all the interior decorating, bring in European artisans and craftsmen for the interior work, and eventually go on an extended buying trip abroad for antiques and custom furnishings. Needless to say, the construction took years and was in fact never really finished.[17]

In the summer of 1925, as the speculation about what the place was to be reached its bursting point, Scotty at last announced, "I am building myself a castle, so I can sit back and laugh at the world." And thus it became ever after "Scotty's Castle," even though Johnson officially named it Death Valley Ranch. By 1926 the curious were driving hundreds of miles over barely passable roads all the way from Los Angeles to see it in the making. Shrewd Nevada mine owners and railroad men—even the governor—crossed over the line to see it. All were royally entertained by the genial Scotty, and treated to a little of his camp-style cooking. That spring *Sunset Magazine,* between exposés of E. G. Lewis and C. C. Julian, brought out a generously illustrated, feature spread on "The Mysterious Son of the Desert," puzzling over Scotty's "baffling moves," asking "What's He Up To Now? Why is he building a mansion and an ice plant on the blistering sands? Has he a hidden gold mine?" *Sunset* finally concluded only that he was "a master of mystery." With that, Death Valley Scotty's comeback was complete—the Death Valley Mystery was born again.[18]

It was in the midst of all this whoopla carnival—the books, the movies, the derring-do auto trips, and the building of Scotty's Castle—plus Lewis and Julian's last hurrahs—that Bob Eichbaum returned to Death Valley to open it for tourism. Herman William Eichbaum, known as Bob, had been a green young electrical engineer just out of college in West Virginia when he joined the rush to Rhyolite and helped build its first electric plant in 1907. Broke after the boom, he had drifted to southern California. There he chanced to make a new start with a goat-cart concession at the beach in Venice, and eventually built up a very profitable sightseeing business on Catalina Island, then being promoted by chewing-gum king William Wrigley. The more Eichbaum learned about the tourist trade, the more clearly he saw the potential of Death Valley "with its beauty, its mystery and history," and he began to dream of going back someday to open it to the world. Early in 1925 he finally decided that day had come and, selling his island tour business to Wrigley, headed for Death Valley to try to make his dream pay.[19]

Eichbaum had dreamed of a big resort at Hell's Gate, near the Death Valley Buttes overlooking the valley above Stovepipe Wells. He envisioned a truly grand hotel with sunken gardens and a sweeping view that would make it "one of the wonders of the country." He planned to run daily tour buses from Los Angeles to bring in the tourists, but quickly found that the biggest obstacle was a lack of good roads.[20]

At the urging of such tireless campaigners for safe desert roads as George W. Parsons of the Los Angeles Chamber of Commerce and the energetic officers of the Automobile Club of Southern California, county, state and federal governments had appropriated funds for road signs to the desert water holes. The auto club had also put up many more signs of its own in Death Valley and had prepared reliable road maps for travelers. But except for the Midland Trail, a national highway from coast to coast that crossed the north tip of the valley through Lida, there was virtually no government money to improve or even maintain the roads themselves. All of the roads in the Death Valley and Amargosa country, like so many elsewhere at that time, had been built and maintained solely by their users, and those in Death Valley had deteriorated rapidly after the boom.[21]

Thus in addition to building his dream hotel, Eichbaum also had to build a good road to it. But he quickly realized that if he built a toll road it could eventually pay for itself, and might even give him virtual control of the valley's tourist business. So in the spring of 1925 he started petitioning the Inyo County supervisors for a franchise to build a scenic toll road through the valley. At first he proposed a road the full length of the valley from the national highway at Lida on out the south end to Mojave or

This grand design for Scotty's Castle was never completed. (*Courtesy of Death Valley National Monument Library*)

Silver Lake. But since that would have let travelers bypass Owens Valley, the supervisors strongly opposed it. Next he came back with a plan for a road through the south half of the valley, entering over Towne Pass from the Owens Valley road to Darwin. This didn't threaten Owens Valley business, but it drew opposition from the Pacific Coast Borax Company and others on the east side of the valley, who preferred to make do with the old roads rather than pay a toll. Eichbaum finally worked out a compromise with Clarence Rasor of the borax company, agreeing to build the road only as far as his planned hotel. In October 1925 the supervisors granted him a franchise for a toll road from Darwin Falls to Stovepipe Wells, even though some now complained it was a "road to nowhere."[22]

Eichbaum began grading early in November with a caterpillar tractor and a crew of half a dozen shovel men. Although one enthusiast hailed the road as "one of the most remarkable feats of engineering of the present day," it was road building at its simplest. Eichbaum didn't bother blasting away boulders on rocky outcroppings, he just detoured around them. Shortly before Christmas the road crew reached Towne Pass, and a month later they had graded the first cut all the way to the dunes. Surfacing and widening took another three months and on May 4, 1926, even though the road still wasn't finished across the dunes, the 38-mile Death Valley Toll Road was officially opened. The wondrous valley, "one of the most unusual and grotesquely beautiful scenic wonders of the world," could now be seen for a price of $2 per car and 50¢ per person, collected at toll gates at either end. Animals were $1 a head, while trucks and wagons were charged by weight anywhere from about $4.50 to $6.50 a ton. But summer was coming fast, so Eichbaum didn't collect many tolls until the valley cooled down again that fall and the first big tourist season began.[23]

In the meantime, Eichbaum had begun work on his resort, though it didn't live up to his dreams. The road construction had cut into his capital, so he could only afford a cluster of bungalows instead of a grand hotel. Then when the trucks loaded with lumber and building materials got stuck on the sandy road west of the dunes, a dozen miles short of his Hell's Gate site, he resigned himself to building the bungalows right there instead. Eichbaum made the best of it, however. Appropriating the name of the historic wells 5 miles to the northeast, he opened his Stove Pipe Wells Hotel on November 1, 1926—Death Valley's first tourist resort. Nicknamed both Bungalette and Bungalow City, it opened with a cluster of twenty neat green-and-white, open-air bungalows with screened windows and striped canvas awnings—a total of fifty rooms. At one end of the cluster was a restaurant topped with a searchlight to guide lost travelers, and at the other were a general store and filling station. Out back were a diesel electric plant and a well. Eight more bungalows, a swimming pool, tennis court, makeshift golf course, and airfield were added in the next few years.[24]

Now the whirlwind of publicity began, and an old Catalina friend of Eichbaum's, Alma Overholt, an artist, nurse and shameless publicist, led the way. She let loose the first round of stories to tell the world "Nature's Inferno" had at last been tamed: "the Mystery Spot of America" had been unveiled, and in its midst was the Stove Pipe Wells Hotel, "the most amazing and entrancing resort in the world—the eighth wonder!" To bring in the tourists, Eichbaum started a daily Mt. Whitney–Death Valley stage line in November 1926, running Studebaker phaetons from Los Angeles to Bungalow City. The tours also stopped in Lone Pine so that his guests could see both the "Highest and Lowest Points in America"— never mind that Whitney wasn't the highest. For the more adventuresome, he offered pack trips around the valley guided by old Johnny Cyty, who was out of jail again, and a couple of other desert rats.[25]

For the more spiritually inclined, Eichbaum held the first of many Easter Sunrise Services out in the dunes near the hotel in April 1927. As dawn broke over the Funerals, a cross was raised to the "Unknown Dead of Death Valley"; a eulogy was read by a former judge Benjamin Bledsoe; wildflowers were scattered by schoolchildren; and "Onward Christian Soldiers" resounded over the dunes. A special stage brought a crowd of Angelenos, and the bungalows were full that weekend. Skookum promoter Chester Bunker proclaimed it "the most unique and significant Easter Service that America has ever known," and then called upon his followers to pledge themselves to help him open up the valley's vast riches, so that all those valiant dead will "not have died in vain . . . it is both a glorious opportunity and a solemn responsibility."[26]

But Eichbaum didn't hold a monopoly on the Death Valley tourist business for long, because his arrival had finally spurred the borax men into action. Just three months after Eichbaum opened his bungalows, they opened the rival Furnace Creek Inn, which was soon to become the luxury hotel that Eichbaum had only dreamed of. Borax Smith, of course, had first talked of building a tourist hotel in Death Valley in 1906 and Frank Jenifer, the crusty but enterprising manager of Borax Consolidated's Tonopah and Tidewater, had resurrected the idea from time to time as a way of increasing the railroad's sagging revenues. But nothing happened for almost twenty years, until Eichbaum finally won his toll road franchise in October 1925.[27]

Then within weeks Jenifer got Harry Gower to sketch out plans for a ten- to twelve-room hotel at Furnace Creek Ranch, complete with a flagpole floating a T.&T.R.R. banner. Other borax officials had doubts about the practicality of building a hotel in the valley itself, but these were

(*Courtesy of Death Valley National Monument Library*)

dispelled after Jenifer brought out the owner of the popular Palm Springs Desert Inn, Nellie Coffman, who assured them that the valley was an ideal place for a resort. Finally Jenifer got the Union Pacific Railroad, which had taken over Senator Clark's San Pedro, Los Angeles, and Salt Lake road, to join with the Tonopah and Tidewater in promoting and running combination rail and bus tours to the valley to bring in tourists. The borax men at last agreed to build a resort, and a new subsidiary, the Death Valley Hotel Company, was organized, with Jenifer as president.[28]

Late in March 1926, Borax Consolidated President Richard Baker came over from England to join Jenifer and Zabriskie in selecting the hotel site on the low ridge at the mouth of Furnace Creek Wash, just above the ranch and just above sea level. Soon afterward Jenifer hired architect Albert C. Martin to draw up new plans for the rambling, two-story, adobe, stucco, and red tile mission-style structure that was to be the Furnace Creek Inn. Little work could be done that summer, but by November a crew of Shoshone and Paiute had finished making all of the adobe at Furnace Creek Ranch, and the day after Thanksgiving, construction began on the ridge. A mile long water line was laid from Texas Spring and the first wing of a dozen rooms, the dining room, kitchen, lobby, and electric plant were rushed to completion in just over two months. Painters were still putting on the finishing touches when the Inn opened for the first Union Pacific tour on February 1, 1927. To transport the tourists the borax men also purchased a new gasoline-powered passenger railcar for their Death Valley rail line, and Union Pacific brought in the big tour buses they used at Zion National Park in the summer.[29]

Union Pacific had begun drumming up business with a big advertising campaign for their new "Weirdly Strange and Thrilling! Death Valley Tours." They invited tourists to "view the dire and dreadful Death Valley—with all danger removed and all thrills retained" for as little as $40 on a two-day, all-expense-paid tour. They touted the valley's "deep mystery, wild, rugged beauty and . . . thrilling history!" Some ads even promised tourists that they could "stand at the lowest point on the continent—310 feet below sea level—and look up the country's highest peak, lofty Mt. Whitney!"[30]

Trying not to be outdone by the borax men, Eichbaum soon made rail connections of his own with the Southern Pacific's line from Mojave to Owens Valley. Then in December 1929 he arranged with the Martin Brothers Air Service to launch the first airline to Death Valley, flying six-passenger trimotor "air sedans" from Mills Field near San Francisco to the Stove Pipe Wells Hotel, and circling Yosemite and Mt. Whitney as a bonus en route. The borax men countered two months later, inducing the Curtiss-Wright Flying Service to start regular weekly flights with a ten-passenger Ford trimotor from Glendale's Grand Central Air Terminal to Furnace Creek Ranch. But it was the automobile, not buses, trains, or planes, that would bring most of the tourists to Death Valley.[31]

Meanwhile, the great whirlwind of promotion grew steadily, fed not only by Eichbaum, the borax men, and the railroad but by booster groups and auto clubs as well. The main thrust of it all was the reeducation of the nation to a Jekyll-Hyde transformation of the valley "from gruesome, death-dealing desert to health-giving winter resort." Professional publicists were hired, and the words poured forth. "Once the most forbidding place in America . . . the Furnace of the World," it became "Diabolical Divine Death Valley . . . the Winter Playground," "Yesterday grim, tragic as Dante's Inferno, today the mecca of tourists," "Once a malevolent mantrap . . . now a winter resort deluxe." It was a "Hell-hole" turned "Paradise," "Nature's Inferno" now a "Nation's Showplace," "Beauty and the Beast," "the land of fascination, romance and beauty," "the most romantic desert in America," "the most weird, heroic spot on earth"—in brief, "one of the most alluring and fascinating spots in existence." On and on the words flowed in a seemingly inexhaustible stream: "strange, mysterious, fantastic, bizarre, grotesque, lovely, peaceful, brilliant . . . awe-inspiring, terrific, the masterpiece of the Creator."[32]

Each season, more and more tourists flocked to the valley. A few thousand had come that first season, twice that the next, and over ten thousand came in 1928–29. By then tourism had become a million-dollar-a-year business in Death Valley. To keep up with the ever-increasing demand, the borax men had enlarged the Furnace Creek Inn, adding the twenty-room Terrace Wing during 1927 and 1928, plus a swimming pool and tennis courts. In the fall of 1929, a nine-hole golf course and airfield were laid out and an annex was built for the hotel staff, who had been housed in tents and cabins in back of the hotel. The following season yet another twenty rooms were added with the North Wing. By then the total cost of the Inn was said to have been $500,000.[33]

After the suspension of borate mining in Death Valley in the fall of 1927, when all work was shifted to Boron, the borax men turned their mining and milling communities into hotels as well. The giant Civic Center complex at Death Valley Junction was remodeled to become the Amargosa Hotel, and the dormitories at Ryan were made into the Death Valley View Hotel. These offered more economical accommodations for about two hundred guests, competing directly with Eichbaum. But when the Union Pacific finally conceded victory to the automobile and ended its regular tours in 1930, the Death Valley Railroad, left without any business, ceased operations too. The Death Valley View Hotel was shut down at the same time, left literally high and dry, since all the water had been hauled in daily by tank cars from Death Valley Junction. New, cheaper accommodations were set up at Furnace Creek Ranch by moving the old staff tents and cabins from behind the inn, plus twenty more cabins and a big boardinghouse from the abandoned Gerstley mine.[34]

Tourism brought an end to the macho image of the valley that Zane Grey and others had tried to promote, for all of the Death Valley Hotel Company's operations were managed by women. During the first two seasons, Beulah Brown, who ran the Old Faithful Lodge at Yellowstone during the summers, had brought down part of her staff to run the Furnace Creek Inn in the winters. Then in 1929 the inn management was turned over to Kathryn Ronan, a former teacher, lawyer, and juvenile court judge, who ran it throughout the Depression. Harry Gower's wife, Pauline, managed the short-lived Death Valley View Hotel before taking over the Amargosa Hotel. And the Furnace Creek Ranch foreman's wife, Edna Boswell, and her sister-in-law looked after the cabins there. Moreover, after Eichbaum died suddenly of meningitis in February 1932, his wife Helene carried on as sole owner and manager of the Stove Pipe Wells Hotel.[35]

Others got into the Death Valley tourist business too, but on much smaller scales. Panamint miner John Thorndyke dreamed of building a hotel atop Telescope Peak, at just over 11,000 feet. But he and his wife finally settled for a few tourist cabins half a mile lower on Mahogany Flat at the head of Wildrose Canyon. Even then, the cabins were so high that they were too cold for tourists most of the winter season, and by the time they warmed up enough to be comfortable in the late spring, the surrounding country was getting too hot. Down at the south end of Death Valley at Cave Spring, health seeker Adrian Egbert offered the most unusual accommodations. Settling at the springs in 1925, he blasted out and enlarged a number of the caves there for a residence, store, garage, gas station, and a couple of guest rooms. Over at Shoshone, old Dad Fairbanks and his son-in-law Charlie Brown, one-time sheriff of Greenwater, started a four-room hotel, dubbed the "Old Timer's Inn," in the winter of 1925–26; it kept pace with the tourist business by the addition of abandoned cabins from the surrounding mines. Out at Pahrump, one hopeful even leased the old Bennett spread to turn it into a dude ranch, and the eccentric Kuenzel opened his Hollywood tourist cabins at Carrara in the hope of attracting movie stars. But Beatty hotel keeper George Dalton, who helped boost the old town as the "Gateway to Death Valley," did the biggest business aside from Eichbaum and the borax men.[36]

The advent of tourists also brought out the souvenir sellers. A few hangers-on at Rhyolite set up tables on weekends to sell rocks and purple bottles at 50¢ to a few dollars a piece. But they soon complained that too many sightseers only brought "with them a dollar and a clean shirt and change neither." One enterprising couple, Bill and Edna Price, squatted on the old Jayhawker camp at Salt Creek in the winter of 1932–33, dug up a bunch of forty-niner relics, opened a trading post beside the road, and cleaned up $800 from passersby before they drifted on.[37]

Although most of the lure of Death Valley was in its grand illusions of hellishness, mystery, and riches, there were very real attractions in its history and scenery. Eichbaum and the borax men tried hard to develop these to best advantage, too. Topping the list of needed attractions was an accessible view point that would provide not only a sweeping view of the valley but a glimpse of Mt. Whitney as well. Thus tourists could have the thrill of seeing both the lowest and highest spots in the United States—that's the way the more scrupulous defined them, semantically excluding all the higher peaks in what was then only the Territory of Alaska.

Beatty businessmen tried to promote old Chloride Cliff, which they renamed "The Rim of Hell," as the perfect view spot. And when the Union Pacific began talking about running tours, the Beatty men got Nevada Governor Scrugham to widen the road in from Beatty right on across the California line so that it could handle big tour buses. Moreover, when the borax and railroad men came out to look at Chloride Cliff in April 1926, Scrugham came along to help persuade them that it was indeed just the place they were looking for. And so it would have been, if they hadn't stopped at Shoshone on their way back to Los Angeles and asked Charlie Brown if he knew of a better spot. Brown shrugged, "I don't pay much attention to scenery. But I know one view that made me stop and look." When he took them to it, they immediately agreed—it was the most spectacular view of the valley they had seen. On the glistening salt flats a mile below lay Badwater and the lowest spot on the continent; just across the valley, towering 2 miles above the desert floor, stood Telescope Peak, the highest point of the Panamints; and far beyond was the icy crest of the Sierra just north of Mt. Whitney. They christened it Dante's View, and called a point just below it Beatrice's, although the latter was later dubbed Poison Point, since "one drop was enough." That winter, with matching funds from the borax company and the county, Charlie Brown graded a road up from Furnace Creek Wash. When the Union Pacific bus tours started in February it was their first stop, handsomely outfitted with a little six-sided, glassed-in observatory and a guest book. Eichbaum was taking his guests over to Hell's Gate for a panoramic view of the valley, but that wasn't nearly as impressive, and they couldn't see Mt. Whitney. So in the winter of 1929–30 he scraped a road across Harrisburg Flat to a new spot of his own, with a view of the valley one way and Whitney the other, so he said. He called it Grand View, but it has since come to be known as Aguereberry Point.[38]

New roads were constructed to several other natural attractions as well. The borax men graded a road down to Pluto's Salt Pools and Badwater, to the Devil's Golf Course and other devilish sights, such as the Devil's Speedway and the Devil's Throne—a name they tried to stick on old Mushroom Rock. In Furnace Creek Wash just east of the Inn, they ran a little side road up to Zabriskie Point, a pinnacle overlooking the "Bad Lands," and to the south they put a road up Golden Canyon into the amphitheater below "Dripping Blood Mountain," which had so impressed Zane Grey that he was positive "something terrible had happened there." The great dunes were Eichbaum's biggest attraction and he held rolling and skiing contests on them, in addition to Easter services. Back behind his bungalows he broke hiking trails up Mosaic and Grotto canyons, and eventually helped run a road up the north end of the valley to Ubehebe Crater and on to Racetrack Dry Lake, where wind-driven rocks leave curious tracks when it's wet. But they didn't have to build the most spectacular and most costly road of all—that through Titus Canyon—for C. C. Julian had thoughtfully done that for his own ends just as the tourist rush began.[39]

In addition to natural attractions, the borax men proudly promoted all the romantic relics of their business, taking tourists to see the old Harmony Borax Works, two of the famous 20-mule team wagons, and Borax Smith's ill-fated traction engine, Old Dinah, which Harry Gower spirited down to the Furnace Creek Ranch one night from its resting place in Daylight Pass, despite Eichbaum's vehement protests. They also treated tourists to a trek through the colemanite deposits in Gower Gulch and 20 Mule Team Canyon, and to a ride on the Baby Gauge Railway into the depths of the idle borate mines at Ryan.[40]

Eichbaum was a bit short on historical attractions, although he did occasionally take tourists to the crumbling mud walls of Clark's original Stovepipe Roadhouse and directed them on to the wonderful "Ghost City" of Rhyolite with its photogenic ruins, its famous Bottle House and, of course, its long-gone little electric plant, which he had helped build in his youth. But Eichbaum couldn't just leave it at that; he had to concoct a whole cockamamy sideshow of "lost" thises and thats. He started simply enough, hauling to the hotel the old borax company wagon that had been abandoned at the north end of the valley in 1890, and touting it as the "Old Lost Wagon of 1849"—one of seven that had carried the lost argonauts to their doom. About the same time he started touting Marble Canyon as the secret site of a Lost "Dreifogel" mine from which, he said, the old recluse had taken a small fortune in gold before he was killed by Indians at the mouth of the canyon in the early eighties.[41]

Then with the help of a colorful old desert rat, John Weyland, whom he hired as a guide in the winter and a watchman in the summer, Eichbaum staged a "lost whiskey" strike—more tempting than gold to many in prohibition days. While driving tourists around the dunes, they would suddenly stop; Weyland would leap out and start digging under a mesquite bush. Then Eichbaum would explain to the puzzled passengers that back in the seventies a teamster with a wagonload of whiskey was supposed to have been lost and buried in a terrific sandstorm, right there in the dunes. Not a trace of either the man or the whiskey had ever been found, but just the night before Weyland had stubbed his toe on something and he wanted to see it in the daylight. Just as Eichbaum finished the talk, Weyland let out a big yell and all rushed over to see him uncovering a small keg. But when he lifted it out of the sand, it proved to be empty and was discarded in disgust—for the next time.[42]

But that was nothing compared to Eichbaum's startling announcement of the discovery of a legendary "lost cave" in the valley, "filled with blue-eyed giants gathered around a council table." To keep them from being "molested," however, the mouth of the cave was blasted shut! After that came his discovery of an entire "Lost City" in the north end of the valley. There he pointed out to tourists the foundations of ancient temples and gigantic houses, all laid out with small stones on the sands, alongside of which were traced big question marks! Close by, in what he called "Silica Canyon," Eichbaum discovered the pièce de résistance—a great stone tablet that told the fate of the "Lost Continent of Mu." Balanced atop the tablet was a rock resembling "the squat figure of a man in a posture of grief," and all over the tablet were chiseled ancient writings in the "Mayan hieratic alphabet." Eichbaum deciphered only a few words that told how the "lost continent" vanished, but he speculated that some day when all the inscriptions were deciphered, Death Valley would be revealed as the "cradle of Creation." What more could anyone want to see on a two-day tour?[43]

The tourists themselves, however, generally found other attractions more impressive. For some it was just the simple "thrill of motoring hundreds of feet below the level of the sea." For others it was more in the mind's eye. One enthusiast even found that the "refuse heaps took on an undisguised beauty of their own . . . the discarded milk and meat tins by the roadside reflected the sun's rays in a wonderful manner, and broken glass bottles sparkled like diamonds." For others the attraction was more spiritual, as the "uncanny silence . . . beat upon our senses like the surf of a supernatural ocean." "It is awesome, yet inspiring," another found "and under its spell one feels his proper place—a mere bit of clay in a

(*Courtesy of U.S. Borax & Chemical Corp.*)

universe of inconceivable magnitude and mystery." But it was the awful lore of the valley that shaped most impressions. "It is so terrific, so awful, that you sob aloud," one tourist claimed, and just entering the valley, "panic seizes you. You will go back! But irresistibly the road plunges downward, and you plunge with it . . . into the cauldron . . . into inferno itself." "It is a weird grotesque desolation—the ultimate of strange, cruel beauty," another swore, "it fascinates, but gives you the creeps." Still, most agreed that "no one can describe the place; it has to be seen and felt."[44]

For many, the valley's biggest attraction—indeed, its very personification—was the great mystery himself, Death Valley Scotty. One zealot claimed that "all Death Valley is divided into three parts: Death Valley, itself; the Death Valley mountain ranges; and Death Valley Scotty. And the greatest of these is Death Valley Scotty." The magic castle had made Scotty into a national celebrity once again. He was getting as many as five hundred letters a day from all over the country, and even from abroad. Most came addressed simply to Death Valley. Though there was no such post office, they found their way to him anyway—even those sent to Valle de la Muerte and Valleto della Morti. They weren't just fan letters, however. One blasted him as a "damned miser . . . for not dividing up your gold with all the poor people in the world." But most had more personal charity in mind, like the Texas widow who wanted $2,000 "right away please" to pay off her mortgage. Some sent photos with marriage proposals, while one already married woman just wanted to run off with him. Scotty rarely answered the letters, and after a while he even stopped opening most of them, just tossing them into a heap next to the fireplace.[45]

Scotty was more generous with visitors, however, especially newsmen and feature writers. They could always count on him for a good story and, as one noted, "Every Scotty story is an exclusive one. He never tells the same one twice." They repaid him well, of course, spreading his name and his yarns across the country and hailing him as "America's No. 1 Mystery Man" and even as the "Greta Garbo of the Great Open Spaces." The editor of the *Los Angeles Record* gave him the front page for eighteen days running with an imaginative life story. Another writer-publicist, Bourke Lee, did two lively pieces on Scotty for the *Saturday Evening Post,* then expanded them into the opening chapter of a book entitled *Death Valley Men.* Dane Coolidge gave Scotty an outlandish final chapter in his *Fighting Men of the West,* and then spun a whole novel around him as *Snake Bit Jones.* But Scotty didn't care too much what they said about him as long as they said something: "Praise me or condemn me, but don't ignore me," was all he really asked.[46]

The old performer was back in the limelight, the star of his own show. "This is a one-man circus," he roared. "I'm th' ringmaster, th' actors, th' menagerie an' th' rest of th' show. Death Valley is th' areno an' th' world is th' audience. I keep 'em guessin' an' that's the mark of a real showman. I've out-Barnumed Barnum an' had a whale of a time doin' it. . . . I'm the greatest one-man show on earth." He'd try any new trick to get attention. He even talked of setting up "the greatest television radio station in the world" right there in Death Valley to "raise all hell" broadcasting evangelical sermons in the daytime and Wild West shows at night.[47]

Scotty's biggest trick was simply claiming he was broke. He had tried to grab headlines after the Wall Street crash by announcing that he was going to Paris for a big spree, and even took the train as far as Chicago, but unsympathetic editors gave him no more than a few lines on the back pages. Then he saw a show about a rich man who had lost his money and realized that that was the game to play. Catching the next train for home, he told a reporter in Kansas City that the Paris trip was off because he had just lost $6 million on the stock market and was broke. That was what the newspapers wanted. The story made front pages from Los Angeles to New York and sold more papers, Scotty claimed, than Lindbergh's flight across the Atlantic. He even made money on the deal: the dining-car waiters took up a collection of $27 for him; newsboys in Los Angeles gave him $8 in nickels and pennies; and letters of sympathy and aid poured in—over 20,000 in all, Scotty said, bringing in a total of $4,481, plus 250 Owl cigars. Then he told the world it was just a joke, and that made headlines too![48]

Nothing Scotty did could quite match the Castle as an attention-getter, however. The Castle was being called "one of the wonders of the west" and threatened to become an even bigger attraction than Scotty himself. It drew hundreds of sightseers a week—so many that they got in the way of the workmen and construction boss Thompson complained that people seemed to "think we were running a side show"—so Johnson put up a high barbed-wire fence, posted "NO TOURISTS ALLOWED" signs, and ran ads in the newspapers asking everyone to "keep away" until all the work was finished.[49]

But still the curious came, and in the winter of 1930–31 Johnson finally hired a guide to start taking them through in an orderly manner. For a dollar a head they were shown all the fancy fountains and fireplaces, all the handcarved beams, handwoven Minorcan rugs, and hand-tooled leather drapes, the magnificent $125,000 organ and the great campanile that chimed out tunes from the famous cathedrals of Europe. By then Johnson had reportedly spent about $2.5 million on the Castle, doing everything he could to make it unique. Yet the most unique things about it were its location and its nickname. In Pasadena or Santa Barbara, as

Johnson's mansion it would hardly have been noticed. Only in Death Valley, as Scotty's Castle, was it suddenly famous.[50]

The Castle became so famous that Scotty occasionally showed signs of jealousy. "This may be a great castle to a lot of folks," he would complain, "but to me its just a lot of hooey." "I'm the one-man circus. The castle is just the tail of my kite." Yet other times he would beam,

> Thirty years ago I drempt about this joint. An' here it is. . . . I've fought Death Valley. . . . I've taken th' gold from its heart. I've slain th' horror of the mountains, like that guy who fought th' dragons . . . and I drempt of the day when I could live as its king in a castle. An' here I am, boy, right in that castle, and th' king of th' works. . . . Look 'er over and then tell me if you think Scotty's a hoax.

Still, Scotty mocked the "rag hanger" who designed the place and all the "goofy" things in it, from the fountains shaped like "insects and rattlers, spitting colored water all over" to the foreign words and phrases carved on the beams. He swore no one could read them, not even the architect, but he was sure they all said simply "make the job last as long as you can."[51]

At best, Scotty had a love-hate relationship with the Castle. It just didn't fit his style, and there was little place for him in it. He refused to sleep in the fancy $40,000 bedroom MacNeilledge designed for him. Most of the time, especially when the Johnsons were around, he stayed at his "hideaway"—a little bungalow Johnson built for him down at Grapevine Springs, on the edge of the valley several miles away. Even when Scotty had the Castle to himself, he usually camped out in the kitchen, sleeping on a smelly cot in the corner, surrounded by piles of dirty dishes and pans, and living on canned beef, pickles, catsup, and crackers.[52]

Then too there was Scotty's wife, Jack, long-suffering but faithful, and their teenage son, Walter "junior," born in 1914 during those dark days of Scotty's eclipse. Scotty hid them away at Reno in another bungalow that Johnson provided, visiting them only rarely and almost never allowing them to come to the Castle. There was simply no place for them, either. Such was the life of the Death Valley Mystery. Yet it was only the illusion that seemed to matter to Scotty, and with the help of Johnson and the Castle he did project a grand illusion.[53]

And season after season the illusion grew, as Johnson, Thompson, MacNeilledge, and a crew of sixty to eighty carried on the seemingly endless building and rebuilding. The work even continued right on through the great stock market crash and into the early years of the Depression. But suddenly in August 1931 all work stopped; Johnson paid off the workmen; Scotty cooked them a last supper; and the campanile tolled a parting lament. They locked up the place and put up a big sign, "THE CASTLE IS CLOSED. POSITIVELY NO ADMITTANCE." The problem was not that Johnson had finally lost his fortune—that was yet to come. The problem was that a government survey had just revealed that Johnson didn't own the land the Castle was on: the land he had bought was a mile away, and the Castle land still belonged to the government. Worse yet, Johnson couldn't even stake claim to it, because the land had been withdrawn from entry by President Hoover as part of a new plan to make Death Valley a national park! Thus they had to get out, at least temporarily, and Scotty stormed into Los Angeles grumbling, "All the galoots who want it for a national park can have it for all I care, to hell with them." They want to "steal my publicity," he howled, and "use us for scenery."[54]

The idea of making Death Valley a national park had been brewing for some time. It seems to have begun in 1926, soon after Jenifer, Zabriskie, and the others decided to go into the tourist business; the creation of the park was to be their coup de grace. The commercial advantages were obvious. By making Death Valley one of the nation's official wonders, it would become a "must" for millions of additional tourists. Moreover, the government would then help advertise it and maintain all those costly roads. And finally, since all lands within the park would be withdrawn from further settlement, the tourist bonanza could be kept in the hands of those already on the ground; no more newcomers could crowd in.[55]

It all should have been quite easy because former borax man and pioneering Death Valley publicist Stephen Mather was the founder and head of the National Park Service. But there were complications. That fall the borax men invited Mather out to Death Valley to see their new Inn and discuss the idea. He came early in January 1927 with his field director, Horace M. Albright, a former Inyo county boy and an old friend of Zabriskie's. Both agreed that the valley's unique scenic and historic attractions made it worthy of inclusion in the national park system. But because of his former borax company ties, Mather refused to recommend the idea to Congress without widespread public support. Thus nothing happened for the next couple of years, until failing health forced Mather's retirement and Albright replaced him in January 1929.[56]

Although Albright was mindful that he "might be unfairly accused of trying to do something at the Nation's expense for my boyhood friends," he was willing to start work on the idea and requested studies by park service men. At the same time a big new push was made to drum up more national interest in the valley. Eichbaum also quickly saw the advantages. A friend of his, a talented writer-publicist and former Navy flyer, Thomas Burke Lee, spearheaded the campaign with a series of articles on Death

Valley in the *Saturday Evening Post* in the summer of 1929, under the pen name of Bourke Lee. Lee followed up in April 1930 with a big, handsome book entitled *Death Valley*—the first popular work on the valley since Spears's book nearly forty years before. Lee did such a good job that even the *New York Times* reviewer raved that he "made the worst and hottest desert in the United States so luridly attractive that . . . it is all a normal person can do to resist dropping everything . . . and going there." Close on Lee's heels came Willie Chalfant, editor of the *Inyo Register,* Albright's hometown paper. Chalfant wrote a much slimmer book called *Death Valley, The Facts.* Lee came back that fall with a new *Saturday Evening Post* series on Death Valley Scotty and another lively book *Death Valley Men,* about a year later.[57]

At the same time, the Pacific Coast Borax's advertising agency, McCann-Erickson, Inc., was starting to reach an even wider audience with a novel new radio show, "Death Valley Days," which first aired on NBC on September 30, 1930, bringing the history and lore of the valley to tens of millions of Americans. The company spent a quarter of a million dollars a year on this half-hour, weekly series, which was researched and written by Ruth Cornwall Woodman. "Death Valley Days" attracted a faithful following and went on to become one of the longest running shows on the air—fourteen years on radio plus eighteen more on television—the latter hosted for a time by Ronald Reagan.[58]

Armed with park service studies strongly endorsing the creation of a Death Valley National Park or at least a national monument, Albright had begun to draw up boundaries and draft tentative legislation. On July 25, 1930, he got President Hoover to sign an executive order that temporarily withdrew over 2 million acres of land for possible inclusion in the park or monument. The order covered all government land in and around Death Valley, from Ubehebe Crater south to Wingate Pass and from Panamint Valley east to the California state line and Ryan.[59]

The plan was now public, and strong protests were soon heard from mining men who opposed the ban on new mining locations. In view of the strength of the opposition and the fact that, despite all the publicity, public support would be very difficult to rally, veteran California Senator Hiram Johnson and local Congressmen Harry Englebright and Sam Arentz warned Albright that it was doubtful that a Death Valley National Park bill could get through the Congress. Albright finally decided to give up the idea of a park and try to make Death Valley a national monument instead, since that could be done without congressional approval, simply by presidential proclamation. But since Hoover was a former mining man himself, some concession would still have to be made to mining interests.[60]

Surveys of the proposed boundary had turned up another complication—an error in von Schmidt's 1873 state line survey that caused most of the townships in the north end of the valley to be off by about a mile. That survey had left Johnson without title to the Castle ground, and the withdrawal order had prevented him from reclaiming it. But while Scotty was still howling to the press about the proposed park, Johnson came quietly to Albright to ask that the Castle be excluded. Johnson described the place in such glowing terms, however, that Albright couldn't resist having a little fun. After listening to Johnson tell what a great place it was, Albright started talking about what a great park headquarters, it would make, and happily concluded that, since it was after all on government land, the government ought to keep it. Johnson was looking terribly depressed by the time Albright admitted that he was only joking and promised to exclude the Castle as soon as Johnson sent him a map of the property lines.[61]

Months passed, however, and nothing more was heard from Johnson. In the meantime, Albright had quieted most of the objections of the mining men by promising to exclude the whole western side of the Panamints and to seek with Arentz special federal legislation restoring mining rights within the monument. Albright had also won Hoover's full support of the plan, with a little help from another Inyoite, an old friend of his and the president's, Ralph Merritt. All that was needed was Johnson's map so that the final boundary could be drawn. By then it was the winter of 1932–33 and time was running out, since Hoover had lost the election and would soon be out of office.[62]

Albright wrote Johnson but got no reply, and finally sent an urgent telegram. At last he heard through Arentz that Johnson didn't want the Castle land excluded from the monument after all. Johnson had learned that if the land was reopened to filing, war veterans would have first claim to it. Thus he too now wanted special legislation, which Arentz agreed to add to the mining rights bill, allowing him to simply buy the land at $1.25 an acre. The last stumbling block removed, Albright drew up the final boundaries, which embraced some 1,601,800 acres. On Saturday afternoon, February 11, 1933, just three weeks before the end of his term, Hoover finally signed the proclamation creating Death Valley National Monument.[63]

Death Valley was at last a certified national wonder. The terror of the West was officially caged, safe for all to see, and millions would indeed come to see it.

The deed was done, the borax men rejoiced, and there was a happy ending for all. Five months after Roosevelt took office Albright quit the Park Service to go to work for Zabriskie as vice president and general manager of Borax Consolidated's new subsidiary, U.S. Potash. The bill restoring mining rights had passed, and the mining men were happy again. The bill to let Johnson buy the Castle land took longer, but finally became law in 1935, so Johnson too had something to be happy about, although the great Depression had finally taken its toll on him. His insurance company had gone into receivership in 1933, leaving him with less than a million dollars of the tens of millions he was once reported to have had, and the Castle was never finished. Johnson finally resorted to renting out rooms, to the delight of tourists. Even Scotty, although he still complained occasionally, couldn't help but enjoy having a ready audience of admirers whenever he chose to put on a show.[64]

Certainly, Jenifer, Zabriskie, and the others couldn't have hoped for more. That first winter of 1933, nearly four hundred men from the newly created Civilian Conservation Corps were sent into the valley to start rebuilding the roads, digging wells, and opening campsites. Many more would follow, until the valley had more miles of road than any other place in the park system. The state also bought Eichbaum's road in December 1934 for $25,000, abolishing all tolls. The rush of tourists had doubled that first season to over 20,000, and it doubled again and again until nearly half a million had visited the valley by the end of the decade. The Furnace Creek Inn and Ranch and the Stove Pipe Wells Hotel were enlarged repeatedly to keep up with the demand. The monument boundaries were also expanded. Half a century later, over half a million people were coming each season. Tourism had established itself as the valley's biggest and most enduring moneymaker.[65]

Beyond all the commercial advantage, the creation of the National Monument was truly a great benefit for Death Valley and all who enjoy it. The monument saved the valley—saved it in a raw, if not quite virgin, state for all to see; saved it from becoming an army base, a naval weapons center, an air force bombing range, or a nuclear test site, like so much of the surrounding desert; and saved it too from that ultimate indignity of being subdivided into town lots, like Palm Springs and Las Vegas. Best of all the National Monument helped save the valley's great illusions of elusive riches and unfathomable mysteries and lurking deadliness, feeding and guarding them but leaving them plenty of room to run wild, so that they too are still there to see—in the mind's eye.

This, after all, was the culmination of a century—a hundred years of seeking and finding and losing, of dreaming and scheming and myth-making, of sweating and thirsting and dying—a hundred years of horse traders and horse thieves, lost emigrants and lost mine hunters, soldiers and surveyors, prospectors and promoters, miners and merchants, renegades and rainbow-chasers, politicians and preachers, boomers and brokers, hookers and hustlers, yahoos and yarn spinners, ranchers and railroadmen, scientists and scoundrels, poets and publicists, magazine writers and moviemakers. They opened the way for tourists—for all the rest of us. And that's what the taming of the West was all about—that, and making a buck.

Death Valley National Monument—California

———————•———————

BY THE PRESIDENT OF THE UNITED STATES OF AMERICA

𝔄 𝔓roclamation

WHEREAS it appears that the public interest would be promoted by including certain lands known as Death Valley, in California, within a national monument for the preservation of the unusual features of scenic, scientific, and educational interest therein contained:

NOW, THEREFORE, I, HERBERT HOOVER, President of the United States of America, by virtue of the power in me vested by section 2 of the act of Congress entitled "AN ACT For the preservation of American antiquities," approved June 8, 1906 (34 Stat. 225), do proclaim and establish the Death Valley National Monument and that, subject to all valid existing rights, the area indicated on the diagram hereto annexed and forming a part hereof be, and the same is hereby, included within the said national monument.

Warning is hereby expressly given to all unauthorized persons not to appropriate, injure, destroy, or remove any feature of this monument and not to locate or settle upon any of the lands thereof.

The Director of the National Park Service, under the direction of the Secretary of the Interior, shall have the supervision, management, and control of this monument as provided in the act of Congress entitled "AN ACT To establish a National Park Service, and for other purposes," approved August 25, 1916 (39 Stat. 535–536), and acts additional thereto or amendatory thereof.

IN WITNESS WHEREOF, I have hereunto set my hand and caused the seal of the United States to be affixed.

DONE at the City of Washington this 11'' day of February, in the year of our
[SEAL]   Lord nineteen hundred and thirty-three, and of the Independence of the United States of America the one hundred and fifty-seventh.

HERBERT HOOVER

By the President:

Henry L Stimson
    Secretary of State.

[No. 2028]

U. S. GOVERNMENT PRINTING OFFICE 1933

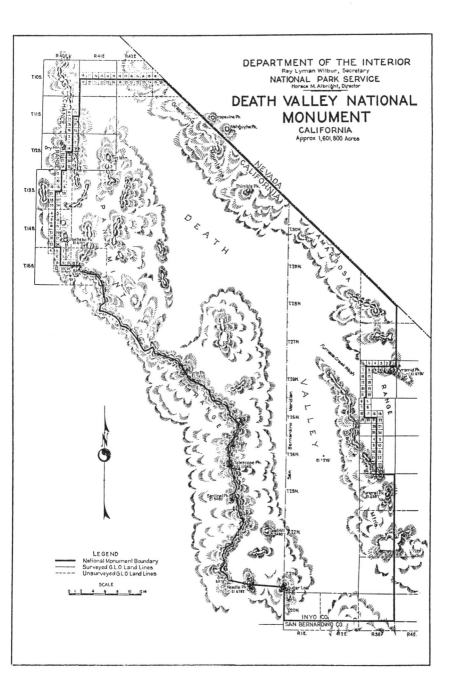

DEPARTMENT OF THE INTERIOR
Ray Lyman Wilbur, Secretary
NATIONAL PARK SERVICE
Horace M. Albright, Director

DEATH VALLEY NATIONAL MONUMENT
CALIFORNIA
Approx 1,601,800 Acres

LEGEND
National Monument Boundary
Surveyed G.L.O. Land Lines
Unsurveyed G.L.O. Land Lines

SCALE
0 1 2   4   6   8   10   12 M

NOTES

A Land of Extremes

1. Sacramento *Daily Union*, July 13, 1861; Visalia *Delta*, April 6, 1861; Los Angeles *Star*, April 7, 1860; M. T. Carr to J. H. Carleton June 10, 1860, B. F. Davis to J. H. Carleton June 21, 1860, National Archives, Record Group 393, Department of California Letters Received, quoted in Dennis G. Casebier, *Carleton's Pah-Ute Campaign* (Norco, Calif.: Dennis G. Casebier, 1972), 34–38 and 40–42, and G. H. Heap Statement April 5, 1855, National Archives, Microcropy 574, Roll 33, typescript courtesy of Dennis G. Casebier.
2. Sacramento *Daily Union*, July 13, 1861.
3. Josiah D. Whitney, *Geology, v. 1, Report of Progress and Synopsis of the Field-Work from 1860 to 1864* (Philadelphia: Caxton Press of Sherman and Co., 1865), 473–474; Josiah D. Whitney [On the Depression of Death Valley] *California Academy of Natural Sciences, 3* (1864), 129 and *3* (1868), 376; *Mining and Scientific Press*, November 23, 1867; Belmont *Silver Bend Reporter*, November 30, 1867.
4. U.S. Geographical Surveys West of the 100th Meridian, *Atlas Sheet No. 65(D)* (New York: Graphic Co. Photo-Lith., issued May 7, 1877); J. P. Widney, "The Colorado Desert," *Overland Monthly, 10* (1873), 44; Frederick V. Coville, *Botany of the Death Valley Expedition* (Washington, D.C.: Government Printing Office, 1893), map; Gilbert E. Bailey, *The Saline Deposits of California* (Sacramento: Supt. State Printing, 1902), 16; Marius R. Campbell, *Reconnaissance of the Borax Deposits of Death Valley and Mohave Desert* (Washington, D.C.: Government Printing Office, 1902), 90; Bishop *Inyo Register*, July 21, 1904.
5. Bishop *Inyo Register*, February 28, 1907; S. S. Gannett and D. H. Baldwin, *Results of Spirit Leveling in California 1896 to 1907, Inclusive* (U.S. Geological Survey, Bulletin 342, Washington, D.C.: Government Printing Office, 1908), 86, 90–91; California State Mineralogist, *Eleventh Annual Report . . . 1892* (Sacramento: State Printer, 1893), 384.
6. U.S. Geological Survey, *Bennetts Well* and *Furnace Creek, 15* Minute Series (1952).
7. Candelaria *True Fissure*, August 6, 1881; Mark W. Harrington, *Notes on the Climate and Meteorology of Death Valley, California* (U.S. Department of Agriculture, Weather Bureau, Bulletin No. 1), (Washington, D.C.: Weather Bureau, 1892), 21; John R. Spears, *Illustrated Sketches of Death Valley and Other Borax Deserts of the Pacific Coast* (Chicago: Rand, McNally and Co., 1892), 39; G. H. Willson, "The Hottest Region in the United States," *Monthly Weather Review, 43* (1915), 278–280, 341.

8. Willson, op. cit., n. 7; Arnold Court, "How Hot Is Death Valley?" *Geographical Review, 39* (1939), 217; Bessie Beatty, *Who's Who in Nevada* (Los Angeles: Home Printing Co., 1907), 200–202; Bishop *Inyo Register,* July 17, 1913; Goldfield *Tribune,* July 9, 10, 11, 1913; Margaret Long, *The Shadow of the Arrow* (Caldwell, Idaho: Caxton Printers, 1941), 69–71.

9. Court, op. cit., n. 8, 217.

10. Ibid., 218–220; Los Angeles *Times,* July 11, 1926; Charles B. Hunt, T. W. Robinson, Walter A. Bowles, and A. L. Washburn, *Hydrologic Basin, Death Valley, California* (Washington, D.C.: Government Printing Office, 1966), B9.

11. Spears, op. cit., n. 7, 36; Andrew H. Palmer, "Death Valley—The Hottest Known Region," *Monthly Weather Review, 50* (1922), 10–13.

12. Ernest E. Eklund, "Some Additional Facts About the Climate of Death Valley, Calif.," *Monthly Weather Review, 61* (1933), 34; Hunt et al., op. cit., n. 10, B5–B11; Spears, op. cit., n. 7, 36.

13. John C. Fremont, *Report of the Exploring Expedition to the Rocky Mountains in the Year 1842 and to Oregon and North California in the Years 1843–44* (Washington, D.C.: Gales and Seaton, 1845), 264; Greenwater *Death Valley Chuck-Walla,* March 15, 1907.

A Name on the Land

1. New York *World,* September 16, 1894.

2. Rhyolite *Daily Bulletin,* May 28, 1909.

3. See also E. I. Edwards, "The Mystery of Death Valley, How It Was Named," *Westerners, Los Angeles Posse Branding Iron No. 61* (June 1962), 4–8.

4. Independence *Inyo Independent,* July 27, 1889; Ruth Wood, *The Tourists' California* (New York: Dodd, Mead and Company, 1914), 230.

5. Margaret Long, *The Shadow of the Arrow* (Caldwell, Idaho: Caxton Printers, 1941), 235–237; Colton Scrapbook, op. cit., n. 1, v. 1, 12, 23, v. 2A, 135, 239; Charles F. Lummis, *Some Strange Corners of Our Country* (New York: Century Co., 1898), 39–40; Lorenzo Dow Stephens, *Life Sketches of a Jayhawker of '49* (San Jose: Nolta Bros., 1916), 22.

6. William Lewis Manly, *Death Valley in '49* (San Jose: Pacific Tree and Vine Co., 1894), 215–216.

7. San Jose *Pioneer,* April 28, 1877, May 15, June 15, 1895; L. Burr Belden, *Goodbye, Death Valley! The 1849 Jayhawker Escape* (Palm Desert: Desert Magazine Press, 1956), 54.

8. Los Angeles *Star,* March 18, 1861; San Francisco *Alta California,* April 26, December 1, 1860, April 12, 1861; Visalia *Delta,* April 13, 1861; Minard H. Farley, *Farley's Map of the Newly Discovered Tramontane Silver Mines in Southern California and Western New Mexico* (San Francisco: W. Holt, 1861); Panamint *News,* March 23, 1875.

9. W. L. Manly to J. B. Colton, February 17, 1890, Jayhawker Collection;

Manly, op. cit., n. 6, 212–213; Joseph Goldsborough Bruff, *Gold Rush; The Journals, Drawings, and Other Papers of J. Goldsborough Bruff* (New York: Columbia University Press, 1944), xlv–xlviii; Louis Nusbaumer, *Valley of Salt, Memories of Wine; A Journal of Death Valley, 1849,* edited by George Koenig, (Berkeley: Friends of the Bancroft Library, 1967), 55–59.

10. George Q. Cannon, "Twenty Years Ago: A Trip to California," *Juvenile Instructor,* 4 (1869), reprinted in LeRoy R. Hafen and Ann W. Hafen, *Journals of Forty-Niners, Salt Lake to Los Angeles* (Glendale: Arthur H. Clark Co., 1954), 254.

11. J. H. Beadle, *The Undeveloped West* (Philadelphia: National Publishing Co., 1873) 151–152; Independence *Inyo Independent,* October 4, 1873; Candelaria *True Fissure,* November 5, 1881; Colton Scrapbook, op. cit., n. 1, v. 2, 18, 121; Oliver Roberts, *The Great Understander, True Life Story of the Last of the Wells Fargo Shotgun Express Messengers* (Aurora, Ill.: William W. Walter, 1931), 211–212.

12. George Wharton James, *Heroes of California* (Boston: Little, Brown and Co., 1910), 86–93; Los Angeles *Times,* January 3, 1923; E. I. Edwards, "The Mystery of Death Valley's Lost Wagon Train," *Westerners, Los Angeles Posse Brand Book 11* (Los Angeles: Ward Ritchie Press, 1964), 181–240.

13. Julian H. Steward, *Basin-Plateau Aboriginal Sociopolitical Groups* (Washington, D.C.: Government Printing Office, 1938), 92, 273–281; Gordon L. Grosscup, "Note on Boundaries and Culture of the Panamint Shoshone and Owens Valley Paiute," *Contributions of the University of California Archaeological Research Facility, No. 35* (1977), 139–140; the Tomesha story appears in Sydney H. Ball, *A Geologic Reconnaissance in Southwestern Nevada and Eastern California (U.S. Geological Survey Bulletin No. 308)* (Washington, D.C.: Government Printing Office, 1907), 195; *Death Valley Magazine* (April 1908), 61; Bourke Lee, *Death Valley* (New York: Macmillan Co., 1930), 16; Willie A. Chalfant, *Death Valley, The Facts* (Stanford: Stanford University Press, 1930), v; Carl B. Glasscock, *Here's Death Valley* (Indianapolis: Bobbs-Merrill Co., 1940), 18; and George P. Putnam, *Death Valley and Its Country* (New York: Duell, Sloan & Pearce, 1946), 13.

Death in the Valley

1. Los Angeles *Times,* May 23, 1927; Los Angeles *Star,* July 27, October 5, 1861; Charles F. Lummis, *Some Strange Corners of Our Country* (New York: Century Co., 1898), 37–38.

2. For a partial list, see Daniel Cronkhite, *Death Valley's Victims, A Descriptive Chronology 1849–1980* (Morongo Valley, Calif.: Sagebrush Press, 1981).

3. Oscar Loew, "On the Physiological Effects of a Very Hot Climate," in George M. Wheeler, *Annual Report Upon the Geographical Surveys West of the One Hundredth Meridian* (Washington, D.C.: Government Printing

Office, 1876), 328–330; E. F. Adolph and Associates, *Physiology of Man in the Desert* (New York: Interscience Publishers, Inc., 1947), 132.

4. Adolph, op. cit., n. 3, 220–229.

5. See for example Cronkhite, op. cit., n. 2; Rhyolite *Herald,* June 16, July 21, August 4, 11, 18, 1905; Independence *Inyo Independent,* November 3, 1905; *Beatty Bullfrog Miner,* June 29, 1907.

6. Rhyolite *Herald,* July 21, August 11, September 1, 1905; Tonopah *Miner,* September 9, 1905; Rhyolite *Bullfrog Miner,* May 10, 1907.

7. Los Angeles *Times,* August 24, 1899; Bishop *Inyo Register,* August 31, 1899; Carl B. Glasscock, *Here's Death Valley* (Indianapolis: Bobbs-Merrill Co., 1940), 157.

8. Robert H. Chapman, "The Deserts of Nevada and the Death Valley," *National Geographic Magazine, 17* (1906), 495; Rhyolite *Herald,* August 18, 1905; Randsburg *Miner,* March 22, 1906; Independence *Inyo Independent,* November 14, 1931; Bishop *Inyo Register,* November 15, 1934; Los Angeles *Examiner,* January 8, 1954.

9. Virginia City *Territorial Enterprise,* July 2, August 30, 1874; London *Daily Telegraph,* August 3, 1874.

The People

1. Alice Hunt, *Archeology of the Death Valley Salt Pan, California* (Salt Lake City: University of Utah, 1960), 313 pp.; William J. and Edith Wallace, *Ancient Peoples: Cultures of Death Valley National Monument* (Ramona: Acoma Books, 1978) 34 pp.

2. Julian H. Steward, *Basin-Plateau Aboriginal Sociopolitical Groups* (Washington, D.C.: Government Printing Office, 1938), 57–100, 180–186; Gordon L. Grosscup, "Notes on Boundaries and Culture of the Panamint Shoshone and Owens Valley Paiute," *Contributions of the University of California Archaeological Research Facility, No. 35* (1977), 109–150; Inter-Tribal Council of Nevada, *Newe: A Western Shoshone History* (Salt Lake City: Univeristy of Utah Printing Service, 1976), 143 pp., and *Nuwuvi: A Southern Paiute History* (Salt Lake City: University of Utah Printing Service, 1976), 177 pp. Charles N. Irwin, ed., *The Shoshoni Indians of Inyo County, California: The Kerr Manuscript* (Socorro: Ballena Press, 1980), 92 pp.

3. Steward, op. cit., n. 2, 71, 92–93.

4. Frederick V. Coville, "The Panamint Indians of California," *American Anthropologist, 5* (1892), 352–355; Steward, op. cit., n. 2, 20, 27–28, 72–74.

5. R. Birnie, "Executive Report of Lieutenant R. Birnie, Jr.," in George M. Wheeler, *Annual Report Upon the Geographical Surveys West of the One Hundredth Meridian* (Washington, D.C.: Government Printing Office,

1876), 133; Coville, op. cit., n. 4, 352–356; B. H. Dutcher, "Piñon Gathering Among the Panamint Indians," *American Anthropologist, 6* (1893), 378–380; Steward, op. cit., n. 2, 19–34, 38–40, 82–83, 88.

6. Steward, op. cit., n. 2, 45.
7. E. W. Nelson, "The Panamint and Saline Valley Indians," *American Anthropologist, 4* (1891), 371–372; Dutcher, op. cit., n. 5, 377–378; Steward, op. cit., n. 2, 90–91, 237, 280; Julian H. Steward, "Cultural Element Distributions: XIII Nevada Shoshoni," *University of California Publications in Anthropological Records, 4* (1941), 232–234.
8. Steward, *Basin-Plateau* . . . op. cit., n. 2, 74–76, 90.
9. Ibid., 87, 90–91; Virginia City *Territorial Enterprise,* May 31, 1866.
10. Steward, *Basin-Plateau* . . . op. cit., n. 2, 86–91; Virginia City *Territorial Enterprise,* May 31, 1866; Birnie, op. cit., n. 5, 133.
11. Steward, *Basin-Plateau* . . . op. cit., n. 2, 69, 88–89; Steward, "Cultural . . ." op. cit., n. 7, 231.
12. Steward, *Basin-Plateau* . . . op. cit., n. 2, 84–85, 91–93; Maurice L. Zigmond, "Kawaiisu Territory," *American Anthropologist, n.s., 40* (1938), 634–638; Grosscup, op. cit., n. 2, 111–112, 138–139; Bishop *Inyo Register,* May 14, 1896.
13. Bishop *Inyo Register,* September 20, 1906.
14. Independence *Inyo Independent,* April 3, October 23, 1880, September 23, 1883, April 6, 1894, April 23, 1897; Bishop *Inyo Register,* April 15, 1897; Steward, *Basin-Plateau* . . . op. cit., n. 2, 85, 93; R. J. Fairbanks, "My 73 Years on Southwestern Deserts," *Touring Topics, 22* (June 1930), 22; J. C. Boyles, "He Witnessed the Death Valley Tragedy of '49," *Desert Magazine, 3* (February 1940), 6; Dane Coolidge, *Death Valley Prospectors* (New York: E. P. Dutton and Co., 1937), 39–43.
15. Bishop *Inyo Register,* May 14, 1896, August 12, 1897; Independence *Inyo Independent,* August 13, 1897; Nelson, op. cit., n. 7, 372; Steward, *Basin-Plateau* . . . op. cit., n. 2, 93; Grosscup, op. cit., n. 2, 139; Birnie, op. cit., n. 5, 132; Linda W. Greene, *Historic Resource Study: A History of Mining in Death Valley National Monument, Volume I* (Denver: National Park Service, 1981), 362–370.
16. Nelson, op. cit., n. 7, 372; Independence *Inyo Independent,* August 13, 1897; Boyles, op. cit., n. 14, 3–6; Bourke Lee, *Death Valley Men* (New York: Macmillan Co., 1932), 158.
17. Tonopah *Miner,* August 12, 1905; Bessie Beatty, *Who's Who in Nevada* (Los Angeles: Home Printing Co., 1907), 194–195; A. B. Christman, "Johnny Shoshone of Death Valley," *Desert Magazine, 16* (December 1953), 10–11; Harold O. Weight and Lucille Weight, *Rhyolite, The Ghost City of Golden Dreams* (Twentynine Palms: Calico Press, 3d ed., revised, 1959), 24; Jack Herron to author, October 30, 1981.
18. Steward, *Basin-Plateau* . . . op. cit., n. 2, 94–97.
19. Rhyolite *Bullfrog Miner,* September 7, 1906; Rhyolite *Death Valley Magazine,* January 1908, p. 12; Rhyolite *Herald,* July 24, September 18, October 16, 1909; Bishop *Owens Valley Herald,* July 9, 1909.

20. John W. Powell and G. W. Ingalls, "Report on the Condition of the Ute
     Indians of Utah; the Pai-Utes of Utah, Northern Arizona, Southern Nevada,
     and Southeastern California . . . ," in *Annual Report of Commissioner of
     Indian Affairs . . . 1873* (Washington, D.C.: Government Printing Office,
     1874), 51; Coville, op. cit., n. 4, 358; U.S. Department of the Interior,
     General Land Office, Survey Plat for T17S.R50E.MDM, 1882; Steward,
     Basin-Plateau . . . op. cit., n. 2, 181–182; Grosscup, op. cit., n. 2, 112–113;
     Rhyolite *Death Valley Prospector,* December 1907.
21. Powell and Ingalls, op. cit., n. 20, 50–51; Jose-Antonio Chavez, "Itineraire
     du Nord-Mexico a la Haute-Californie," *Bulletin de la Société de Geographie,
     Paris, 2d ser., 3* (1835), 322; Isabel T. Kelly, "Southern Paiute Bands,"
     American Anthropologist, n.s., 36 (1934), 559; Steward, *Basin-Plateau . . .*
     op. cit., n. 2, 182.
22. Steward, *Basin-Plateau . . .* op. cit., n. 2, 181–185.
23. Powell and Ingalls, op. cit., n. 20, 50–51; Kelly, op. cit., n. 21, 559;
     Steward, *Basin-Plateau . . .* op. cit., n. 2, 181–185; Beatty *Bullfrog Miner,*
     September 23, 1905; Orin S. Merrill, *"Mysterious Scott," The Monte Cristo
     of Death Valley and Tracks of a Tenderfoot* (Chicago: Orin S. Merrill, 1906),
     122–124.
24. Steward, *Basin-Plateau . . .* op. cit., n. 2, 51–70; U.S. Army, Camp Indepen-
     dence, Post Returns, August 31, 1870–July 20, 1877; Independence *Inyo
     Independent,* July 5, 1884.

Los Chaguanosos

1. The Spanish Trail has been studied extensively by: Joseph J. Hill, "The
    Old Spanish Trail," *Hispanic American Historical Review, 4* (August 1921),
    444–473; Eleanor F. Lawrence, "The Old Spanish Trail from Santa Fe to
    California" (Unpublished Master's thesis, University of California, Berkeley,
    1930), 148 pp., and her "Mexican Trade Between Santa Fe and Los Angeles
    1830–1848," *California Historical Society Quarterly, 10* (March 1931),
    27–39; LeRoy R. Hafen, "Armijo's Journal of 1829–30; The Beginning of
    Trade Between New Mexico and California," *Colorado Magazine, 27* (April
    1950), 120–131; LeRoy R. Hafen and Ann W. Hafen, *Old Spanish Trail,
    Santa Fe to Los Angeles* (Glendale: Arthur H. Clark Co., 1954), 377 pp.;
    and Elizabeth von Till Warren, "Armijo's Trace Revisited: A New Interpre-
    tation of the Impact of the Armijo Route of 1829–1830 on the Development
    of the Old Spanish Trail" (Unpublished Master's thesis, University of
    Nevada, Las Vegas, 1974), 195 pp.
2. Jose-Antonio Chavez, "Itineraire du Nord-Mexico a la Haute-Californie,"
    Bulletin de la Société de Geographie, Paris, 2d ser., 3 (1835), 316–323;
    Lawrence, "Old Spanish . . . , op. cit., n. 1, 8–9, 48–51; LeRoy R. Hafen,
    "Armijo's Journal," *Huntington Library Quarterly, 11* (November 1947),
    87–101; Hafen and Hafen, op. cit., n. 1, 150–170; Warren, op. cit., n. 1,

5–83. Biographical material on Armijo is in Alan P. Bowman, *Index to the 1850 Census of the State of California* (Baltimore: Genealogical Pub. Co., 1972), 446.

3. Departmental State Papers, XI, 131, in Bancroft Library; John C. Fremont, *Report of the Exploring Expedition to the Rocky Mountains in the Year 1842, and to Oregon and North California in the Years 1843–'44* (Washington: Gales and Seaton, 1845), 264; George W. Brewerton, "A Ride with Kit Carson Through the Great American Desert and the Rocky Mountains," *Harper's New Monthly Magazine, 7* (August 1853), 315–316; Lawrence, "Old Spanish . . ." op. cit., n. 1, 67–68.

4. Departmental State Papers, Angeles I, 109–113, and Benecia Military, LXXVI, 32–51; Lawrence, "Old Spanish . . ." op. cit., n. 1, 73–76; Hafen and Hafen, op. cit., n. 1, 230–232; LeRoy R. Hafen, "Elijah Barney Ward," *The Mountain Men and the Fur Trade of the Far West, 7,* LeRoy R. Hafen, ed. (Glendale: Arthur H. Clark Co., 1969), 347–348; Ardis M. Walker, "Joseph R. Walker," *The Mountain Men . . .* op. cit., n. 4, 5 (1968), 361–380.

5. Honolulu, *Sandwich Island Gazette and Journal of Commerce,* December 2, 1837; Antonio Maria Osio, "Historia de California," 321–347, Bancroft Library; Lawrence, "Old Spanish . . ." op. cit., n. 1, 82–84; Hafen and Hafen, op. cit., n. 1, 234–235; Janet Lecompte, "Jean-Baptiste Chalifoux," *The Mountain Men . . .* op. cit., n. 4, 7, 57–74.

6. Brewerton, op. cit., n. 3, 316; Horace Bell, *Reminiscences of a Ranger; or Early Times in Southern California* (Los Angeles: Yarnell, Caystile and Mathes, 1881), 281–283; Lawrence, "Old Spanish . . ." op. cit., n. 1, 84–87; Hafen and Hafen, op. cit., n. 1, 236; LeRoy R. Hafen, "Philip F. Thompson," *The Mountain Men . . .* op. cit., n. 4, 3 (1966), 339–347.

7. Departmental State Papers, Angeles, IV, 72, 88, 105, and San Jose, V, 71; Lawrence, "Old Spanish . . ." op. cit., n. 1, 87–88; Hafen and Hafen, op. cit., n. 1, 236–237; Lecompte, op. cit., n. 5, 68–69.

8. Departmental State Papers, Angeles, IV, 89–92, 96–98, and Benecia, VI, 70; Lawrence, "Old Spanish . . ." op. cit., n. 1, 88–91; George W. Beattie and Helen P. Beattie, *Heritage of the Valley: San Bernardino's First Century* (Pasadena: San Pasqual Press, 1939), 140–142; Hafen and Hafen, op. cit., n. 1, 238.

9. Departmental State Papers, Angeles, IV, 105; Lawrence, "Old Spanish . . ." op. cit., n. 1, 91; Beattie and Beattie, op. cit., n. 8, 142; Hafen and Hafen, op. cit., n. 1, 238–239.

10. Departmental State Papers, Angeles, IV, 99–100, 105–106; Brewerton, op. cit., n. 3, 313; Lawrence, "Old Spanish . . ." op. cit., n. 1, 91–92; Beattie and Beattie, op. cit., n. 8, 142–143; Hafen and Hafen, op. cit., n. 1, 239; Lecompte, op. cit., n. 5, 69–70; Harvey L. Carter, "Calvin Jones," *The Mountain Men . . .* op. cit., n. 4, 6 (1968), 207–208.

11. Departmental State Papers, Angeles, IV, 99–100, 105–106; Lawrence, "Old Spanish . . ." op. cit., n. 1, 91–92; Hafen and Hafen, op. cit., n. 1, 239.

12. Rufus B. Sage, *Scenes in the Rocky Mountains and in Oregon, California,*

New Mexico, Texas and the Grand Prairies (Philadelphia: Carey & Hart, 1846), 51; Brewerton. op. cit., n. 3, 316; Lawrence, "Old Spanish . . ." op. cit., n. 1, 92–93; Beattie and Beattie, op. cit., n. 8, 143; Hafen and Hafen, op. cit., n. 1, 241.

13.   Fremont, op. cit., n. 3, 261; Christopher H. Carson, *Kit Carson's Autobiography* (Chicago: Lakeside Press, 1935), 82–83.

14.   Fremont, op. cit., n. 3, 261–263; Carson, op. cit., n. 13, 83–84.

15.   Fremont, op. cit., n. 3, 262–263; Carson, op. cit., n. 13, 84; Charles Preuss, *Exploring with Fremont: The Private Diaries of Charles Preuss* (Norman: University of Oklahoma Press, 1958), 127–128.

16.   Fremont, op. cit., n. 3, 262–263; Preuss, op. cit., n. 15, 127–128.

17.   Fremont, op. cit., n. 3, 263–265; Carson, op. cit., n. 13, 85.

18.   Fremont, op. cit., n. 3, 265; Brewerton, op. cit., n. 3, 321–322; John C. Fremont, *Memoirs of My Life* (Chicago: Belford, Clark and Co., 1887), 409.

19.   Lawrence, "Old Spanish . . ." op. cit., n. 1, 43; Lawrence, "Mexican Trade . . ." op. cit., n. 1, 37–39.

20.   Lawrence, "Old Spanish . . ." op. cit., n. 1, 92–100; Hafen and Hafen, op. cit., n. 1, 241–246.

21.   San Francisco *Alta California,* April 6, 1855; Bell, op. cit., n. 6, 290; Lawrence, "Old Spanish . . ." op. cit., n. 1, 94–100; Beattie and Beattie, op. cit., n. 8, 65–66; Hafen and Hafen, op. cit., n. 1, 247–257; Julian H. Steward, *Basin-Plateau Aboriginal Sociopolitical Groups* (Washington, D.C.: Government Printing Office, 1938), 223–224, 229; Gustive O. Larson, "Walkara, Ute Chief," *The Mountain Men* . . . op. cit., n. 4, 2 (1965) 339–350; Paul D. Bailey, *Walkara Hawk of the Mountains* (Los Angeles: Westernlore Press, 1954), 185 pp.

The Trail to Gold

1.   For most of the known accounts and diaries of those who came down the Spanish Trail through Death Valley in the winter of 1849–50, see LeRoy R. Hafen and Ann W. Hafen, *Journals of Forty-Niners, Salt Lake to Los Angeles. With Diaries and Contemporary Records of Sheldon Young, James S. Brown, Jacob Y. Stover, Charles C. Rich, Addison Pratt, Howard Egan, Henry W. Bigler, and Others* (Glendale: Arthur H. Clark Co., 1954), 333 pp., and LeRoy R. Hafen and Ann W. Hafen, *Supplement to the Journals of Forty-Niners, Salt Lake to Los Angeles* (Glendale: Arthur H. Clark Co., 1961), 124 pp.

2.   Hafen and Hafen, *Journals* . . . op. cit., n. 1, 47–50; Hafen and Hafen, *Supplement* . . . op. cit., n. 1, 15–26.

3.   Hafen and Hafen, *Journals* . . . op. cit., n. 1, 51–53, 59–60; Hafen and Hafen, *Supplement* . . . op. cit., n. 1, 27–28; Thomas S. Wylly III, ed., "Westward Ho in '49, Memoirs of Captain Thomas S. Wylly, Part II," *Pacific Historian,* 22 (1978), 121–122.

4.   W. B. Lorton's letter dated Los Angeles, January 30, 1850, published in

Cleveland *Plain Dealer,* May 11, 1850, reprinted in John B. Goodman, III, *Over the Salt Lake Trail in the Fall of '49* (Los Angeles: privately printed, 1957), 18 pp., and in Hafen and Hafen, *Supplement . . .* op. cit., n. 1, 71–75; Addison Pratt's Diary, October 22 to November 3, 1849, published in Hafen and Hafen, *Journals . . .* op. cit., n. 1, 75–79; William Farrer's Diary, October 23, 1849, published in Hafen and Hafen, *Journals . . .* op. cit., n. 1, 197–198; George Q. Cannon's Narrative, published in Hafen and Hafen, *Journals . . .* op. cit., n. 1, 226–228; J. C. Fremont, *Map of Oregon and Upper California From the Surveys of John Charles Fremont . . .* (Baltimore: Litho. E. Weber & Co., 1848); LeRoy R. Hafen, "Elijah Barney Ward," *The Mountain Men and the Fur Trade of the Far West, 7* (Glendale: Arthur H. Clark Co., 1969), 343–351; Alan P. Bowman, *Index to the 1850 Census of the State of California* (Baltimore: Genealogical Pub. Co., 1972), 386: Clifford L. Stott, *Search for Sanctuary.* (Salt Lake City: University of Utah Press, 1984), 10–12.

5. Lorton, op. cit., n. 4; Pratt, op. cit., n. 4; and Farrar, op. cit., n. 4.

6. Addison Pratt's Diary, November 4, 1849, published in Hafen and Hafen, *Journals . . .* op. cit., n. 1, 79–81; J. B. Colton Scrapbook, v. 2, 136, 146, Jayhawker Collection in Henry E. Huntington Library and Art Gallery, San Marino, Calif.

7. Leonard Babcock's Recollections, published in Hafen and Hafen, *Supplement . . .* op. cit., n. 1, 65; William Lewis Manly, *Death Valley in '49* (San Jose: Pacific Tree and Vine Co., 1894), 111–114, 328–329.

8. Charles C. Rich's Diary, November 14 to 18, 1849, published in Hafen and Hafen, *Journals . . .* op. cit., n. 1, 188–189; Farrer's Diary, November 16 and 17, 1849, ibid, 211–212; George Q. Cannon, "Twenty Years Ago: A Trip to California," *Juvenile Instructor 4* (1869), reprinted in Hafen and Hafen, *Journals . . .* op. cit., n. 1, 250–251; Jacob Y. Stover, "History of the Sacramento Mining Company of 1849, written by one of its number," John W. Caughey, ed., *Pacific Historical Review, 6* (1937), 172–173, and also reprinted in Hafen and Hafen, *Journals . . .* op. cit., n. 1, 279–280; Lorton, op. cit., n. 4, 74–75; Pratt, op. cit., n. 4, 110–112. The suggestion by Hafen and Hafen, *Journals . . .* op. cit., n. 1, 280, and repeated by others, that the Stover party returned to the Spanish Trail at the Amargosa is refuted by Lorton and Pratt.

9. Lorton, op. cit., n. 4, 73–74; Stover, op. cit., n. 8, 173; Babcock, op. cit., n. 7, 65; Cannon, op. cit., n. 8, 250; Ransom G. Moody, "Biographical Sketch," *The Pioneer 1,* March 17, 1877, reprinted in Hafen and Hafen, *Supplement . . .* op. cit., n. 1, 109; Thomas Kealy's Letter dated William's Ranch, March 19, 1850, published in the *Michigan Expositor* and reprinted in Hafen and Hafen, *Supplement . . .* op. cit., n. 1, 104–105.

10. Henry W. Bigler, Journal Book B, November 25 and 27, 1849, published in Hafen and Hafen, *Journals . . .* op. cit., n. 1, 166–167; Peter Derr and J. D. Gruwell's accounts, ibid., 51–55; Pratt, op. cit., n. 4, 93–94.

11. Hafen and Hafen, *Journals . . .* op. cit., n. 1, 66–67, 112–113.

12. Pratt, December 1, 1849, op. cit., n. 4, 95–96; James S. Brown, *Life of a Pioneer, Being the Autobiography of James S. Brown* (Salt Lake City:

Geo. Q. Cannon & Sons Co., 1900), 139, and reprinted in Hafen and Hafen, *Journals* . . . op. cit., n. 1, 124.

13. Hafen and Hafen, *Journals* . . . op. cit., n. 1, 167, 190, 214, 315, and *Supplement* . . . op. cit., n. 1, 39, 62, 92.

"Into the Jaws of Hell"

1. Jacob Y. Stover, "History of the Sacramento Mining Company of 1849, Written by one of Its Number," John W. Caughey, ed., *Pacific Historical Review, 6* (1937), 172. For variants, see John B. Colton, Kansas City *Times,* February 5, 1890, clipping in J. B. Colton Scrapbook, v. 1, 21, Jayhawker Collection, Henry E. Huntington Library and Art Gallery, San Marino, Calif.; John W. Brier, "The Death Valley Party of 1849," *Out West, 18* (1903), 328; and Lorenzo Dow Stephens, *Life Sketches of a Jayhawker of '49* (San Jose: Nolta Bros., 1916), 19.

2. Stover, op. cit., n. 1, 173; W. B. Lorton's Letter dated Los Angeles, January 30, 1850, published in Cleveland *Plain Dealer,* May 11, 1850, reprinted in *Over the Salt Lake Trail in the Fall of '49,* John B. Goodman III, ed. (Los Angeles, 1957), and in LeRoy R. Hafen and Ann W. Hafen, *Supplement to the Journals of Forty-Niners, Salt Lake to Los Angeles* (Glendale: Arthur H. Clark Co., 1961), 74–75.

3. Stover, op. cit., n. 1, 180–181; see also St. Louis *Republican,* May 14, 1883, clipping in Colton Scrapbook, op. cit., n. 1, v. 1, 10–11.

4. Stover, op. cit., n. 1, 180–181; George Q. Cannon, "Twenty Years Ago: A Trip to California," *Juvenile Instructor, 4* (1869), reprinted in LeRoy R. Hafen and Ann W. Hafen, *Journals of Forty-Niners, Salt Lake to Los Angeles* (Glendale: Arthur H. Clark Co., 1954), 251–253; Leonard Babcock's Recollections in Hafen and Hafen, *Supplement* . . . op. cit., n. 2, 69–70; L. D. Stephens to C. B. Mecum and Brother Jayhawkers, January 21, 1880, and James W. Brier to Charles B. Mecum and others, January 21, 1880, in Colton Scrapbook, op. cit., n. 1, 5–6, 19; John W. Brier's letter dated Grass Valley, November 4, 1882, published in Independence *Inyo Independent,* July 26, 1884. The suggestion in Harold O. Weight, *Lost Mines of Death Valley* (Twentynine Palms: Calico Press, 1970), 14–15, and in George Koenig, *Beyond This Place There Be Dragons* (Glendale: Arthur H. Clark Co., 1984), 245–246 n., that Webster survived, comes from a badly abbreviated quote from a newspaper article in W. A. Chalfant, *Death Valley, The Facts* (Stanford: Stanford University Press, 1936), 113, and is clearly contradicted in the original article in the Independence *Inyo Independent,* March 22, 1873.

5. There are three known diaries of these Death Valley argonauts: (1) Sheldon Young, "Sheldon Young's Log 1849 Joliet Illinois to Rancho San Francisquito California," typescript Jayhawker Collection, op. cit., n. 1, published in Margaret Long, *The Shadow of the Arrow* (Caldwell, Idaho: Caxton Printers, 1941), 241–263, and exerpted in E. I. Edwards, *"Into an Alkali*

Valley," The First Written Account of Death Valley (Los Angeles: Edwards and Williams, 1948), 8 pp.; (2) Louis Nusbaumer, "Erlebnisse einer Reise nach den Goldregionen Californiens," March 20, 1849–March 10, 1850, 2 vol. manuscript in Bancroft Library, exerpts translated and published in Louis Nusbaumer, *Valley of Salt, Memories of Wine: A Journal of Death Valley, 1849,* George Koenig, ed. (Berkeley: Friends of the Bancroft Library, 1967), 67 pp., and in George Koenig, *The Lost Death Valley '49er Journal of Louis Nusbaumer* (Death Valley: Death Valley '49ers, Inc., 1974), 79 pp.; and (3) Asa Haynes Diary, photocopy in Jayhawker Collection, published in John G. Ellenbecker, *The Jayhawkers of Death Valley* (Marysville, Kans.: The Author, 1938), 124–128. There are also several important reminiscences. Foremost among these are (1) William Lewis Manly, *Death Valley in '49* (San Jose: Pacific Tree and Vine Co., 1894), 498 pp., his "From Vermont to California," published serially in the *Santa Clara Valley* 1887–1890, and a number of articles written for *The Pioneer* and collected as *The Jayhawkers' Oath and Other Sketches,* Arthur Woodward, ed. (Los Angeles: Warren F. Lewis, 1949), 170 pp; (2) John B. Colton's interviews in the Kansas City *Times* (1888), February 5, 1890, and February 5, 1893 clippings in Colton Scrapbook op. cit., n. 1, 14, 19, 21–24, 31–32; (3) James W. Brier's statement in Gwinn Harris Heap, *Central Route to the Pacific* (Philadelphia: Lippincott, Grambo and Company, 1854), 133–136, his letters to Charles B. Mecum, January 17, 1876, and to Dear Old Comrades, January 16, 1896, Jayhawker Collection, and his reminiscences published in the Los Angeles *Times* (c. 1887) clipping in Colton Scrapbook, op. cit., n. 1, v. 1, 12; (4) Juliet Brier's two accounts published in the San Francisco *Call,* December 25, 1898, and the Carson City *News,* June 8, 1913, both reprinted in L. Burr Belden, *Death Valley Heroine and Source Accounts of the 1849 Travelers* (San Bernardino: Inland Printing and Engraving Company, 1954), 19–35; (5) John Wells Brier, "The Death Valley Party of 1849," *Out West, 18* (1903), 326–335, 456–465, and his "The Argonauts of Death Valley, Being a Concise but Truthful Account of the Trials and Tribulations of that Pioneer Band Who Came to California by the Southern Route, as Told by One of the Survivors," *The Grizzly Bear, 9* (June 1911), 1–4, 7; (6) Lorenzo Dow Stephens, op. cit., n. 1; (7) John H. Roger's reminiscence in the Merced *Star,* April 26, 1894, reprinted in Belden, op. cit., n. 5, 63–68; and, for Shoshone views, (8) George Hansen's reminiscences in J. C. Boyles, "He Witnessed the Death Valley Tragedy of '49," *Desert Magazine, 3* (February 1940), 3–6, and (9) Tom Wilson's accounts in T. R. Goodwin, "White Man's History Through Red Man's Mouth," *Thor Shun* (August 24, 1936), 11–14, and in Dane Coolidge, *Death Valley Prospectors* (New York: E. P. Dutton & Co., 1937), 11–13, 18, which also contains two secondhand accounts attributed to Panamint Tom and Ash Meadows Charlie on pages 15–16 and 32–33, 37.

Lists of members of the various parties are given in: Carl I. Wheat, "The Forty-Niners in Death Valley: (A Tentative Census)," *Historical Society of Southern California Quarterly, 21* (1939), 102–117, and his "The Jayhawkers at the Missouri, A Remarkable Discovery," ibid., 22 (1940),

103–108; E. I. Edwards, *The Valley Whose Name Is Death* (Pasadena: San Pasqual Press, 1940), 122 pp.; Frank F. Latta, *Death Valley '49ers* (Santa Cruz: Bear State Books, 1979), 68–85; and George Koenig, *Beyond . . .* op. cit., n. 4, 240–243.

6. Young, op. cit., n. 5, November 11 through December 1, 1849: James W. Brier in Colton Scrapbook, op. cit., n. 1, v. 1, 12; John W. Brier, "The Argonauts . . ." op. cit., n. 5, 2; and Manly, op. cit., n. 5, 114–118, 330, 332; *Map of Oregon and Upper California From the Surveys of John Charles Fremont . . .* (Baltimore: Litho. E. Weber & Co., 1848); Thomas C. W. Sale to Hon. O. H. Irish, dated Meadow Valley, May 4, 1865 in *Report of the Secretary of the Interior (House Exec. Doc. No. 1, 1st Sess., 39th Cong. ser. 1248)* (Washington, D.C.: Government Printing Office, 1866), 324–325.

The tangled routes of the various parties remain only poorly defined, although they have been a persistent subject of speculation and controversy for over half a century, studied in varying degrees by Chalfant, op. cit., n. 4; John E. Wolff, *Route of the Manly Party of 1849–50 in Leaving Death Valley for the Coast* (Santa Barbara: Pacific Coast Pub., 1931), 29 pp.; T. R. Goodwin, "The Argonaut Trail," *Thor Shun* (December 9, 1935 through April 4, 1936), serially; John W. Caughey, "Southwest from Salt Lake in 1849," *Pacific Historical Review, 6* (1937), 143–164; Ellenbecker, op. cit., n. 5; John W. Beck, "Log of the Manly-Bennett-Jayhawker-Georgian Routes From Mt. Misery, Utah to the Floor of Death Valley," 12 pp. typescript, 1939, and his "A Tentative Correlation of the Logs of Asa Haynes, Sheldon Young and William H. Manly's Story," 11 pp. typescript, April 27, 1939, both in Henry E. Huntington Library and Art Gallery, San Marino, Calif.; Charles Kelly, "On Manly's Trail to Death Valley," *Desert Magazine, 2* (February 1939), 6–8, 41–43; Carl I. Wheat, "Trailing the Forty-Niners Through Death Valley," *Sierra Club Bulletin, 24* (June 1939), 74–108; Edwards, *The Valley . . .* op. cit., n. 5; Long, op. cit., n. 5; Dick Freeman, "On Manly's Trail in the Panamints," *Desert Magazine, 4* (March 1941), 4–8; Harry Coulter, "Escape from Death Valley," *Westways, 41* (September 1949), 2–3; L. Burr Belden, *Goodbye, Death Valley! The 1849 Jayhawker Escape* (Palm Desert: Desert Magazine Press, 1956), 61 pp., and his *The Wade Story "In and Out of Death Valley"* (San Bernardino: Inland Printing and Engraving Co., 1957), 15 pp.; John Southworth, *Death Valley in 1849; The Luck of the Gold Rush Emigrants* (Burbank: Pegleg Books, 1978), 132 pp.; Latta, op. cit., n. 5; and Koenig, *Lost . . .* op. cit., n. 5, and *Beyond . . .* op. cit., n. 4.

Here I have outlined their routes only in terms of what seem to be the most important and best defined landmarks, but even some of these are debatable.

7. Myron Angel, *History of Nevada* (Oakland: Thompson and West, 1881), 476; Colton, Kansas City *Times* (1888) op. cit., n. 5, John B. Colton's "Death Valley Mines," *The Pioneer, 10,* December 15, 1895; Rogers, op. cit., n. 5; William L. Manly's letters to A. C. Clay, November 25, 1894, and to J. B. Colton, July, 1894, in Jayhawker Collection; Brier, "Argonauts . . ." op. cit., n. 5, 2.

8. Young, op. cit., n. 5, December 7, 1849; Rogers, op. cit., n. 5; Manly, op. cit., n. 5, 125.

9. Young, op. cit., n. 5, December 7 through 20, 1849; Haynes, op. cit., n. 5; Colton, Kansas City *Times,* February 5, 1890 and February 5, 1893, op. cit., n. 5; Stephens, op. cit., n. 1, 19.

10. Julian H. Steward, *Basin-Plateau Aboriginal Sociopolitical Groups* (Washington, D.C.: Government Printing Office, 1938), 92; Boyles, op. cit., n. 5, 5; Wilson's accounts in Goodwin, "White . . ." op. cit., n. 5, 12 and Coolidge, op. cit., n. 5, 11–13; Juliet W. Brier, San Francisco *Call,* December 25, 1898, op. cit., n. 5; Rogers, op. cit., n. 5; and Manly, op. cit., n. 5, 139, 335.

11. Young, op. cit., n. 5, December 22 through 30, 1849; Stephens, op. cit., n. 1, 20; Manly, op. cit., n. 5, 140–141, 335–337.

12. Young, op. cit., n. 5, December 28, 1849; Juliet W. Brier, Carson City *News,* June 8, 1913, op. cit., n. 5; Manly, op. cit., n. 5, 337.

13. Nusbaumer, *Valley of Salt* . . . op. cit., n. 5, 38–41; Manly, op. cit., n. 5, 130–133, 137, 143; Steward, op. cit., n. 10, 95; Lewis Granger's letter to his father, dated Los Angeles, April 8, 1850, published in Hafen and Hafen, *Supplement* . . . op. cit., n. 2, 61–62; Coolidge, op. cit., n. 5, 32, 37.

14. Boyles, op. cit., n. 5, 5; see also Tom Wilson's and Panamint Tom's accounts in Coolidge, op. cit., n. 5, 16, 18.

15. Young, op. cit., n. 5, December 28–29, 1849; James W. Brier to Charles B. Mecum, January 17, 1876, op. cit., n. 5, and his reminiscences in the Los Angeles *Times,* op. cit., n. 5; Colton "Death Valley Mines" op. cit., n. 7, and his interview in the Kansas City *Times,* February 5, 1890, op. cit., n. 5; George Miller, "A Trip to Death Valley," *Historical Society of Southern California Annual Publication, 11* (1919), 56–57.

16. Colton, "Death Valley Mines" op. cit., n. 7, Miller, op. cit., n. 15, 56.

17. Colton, "Death Valley Mines" op. cit., n. 7, and his interview in Kansas City *Times,* February 5, 1890 op. cit., n. 5; Ed Mecum, "Jayhawks of '49," Perry, Iowa *Chief,* February 12, 1892, clipping in Colton Scrapbook, v. 1, 33, Jayhawker Collection; Miller, op. cit., n. 15, 57.

18. Henry G. Hanks, "An Undeveloped Region," San Francisco *Evening Bulletin,* February 10, 1869; Miller, op. cit., n. 15, 56; William Lewis Manly, "The Gunsight Lead," *The Pioneer, 9,* April 15, 1894 (gives Los Angeles as the place gunsight was made).

19. Colton interview in Kansas City *Times,* February 5, 1893, op. cit., n. 5, Stephens, op. cit., n. 1, 21; George B. Evans, *Mexican Gold Trail, The Journal of a Forty-Niner* (San Marino: The Huntington Library, 1945), 254–255, 259–263; Edward Coker's reminiscences in Manly, *Death Valley* . . . op. cit., n. 5, 373–376.

20. Wilson's accounts in Goodwin, "White . . ." op. cit., n. 5, 13–14, and in Coolidge, op. cit., n. 5, 18; Chalfant, op. cit., n. 4, 41. Carl I. Wheat also wrote of a purported interview with Hungry Bill entitled "Hungry Bill Talks," *Westways, 31* (May 1939), 18–19, but it is at least partially fictitious, since Wheat quotes the long-dead Bill as referring to the road over Towne Pass, which wasn't built until six years after Hungry Bill's death in 1919.

21. Young, op. cit., n. 5, January 6–7, 1850; James W. Brier's letters to Charles B. Mecum, January 17, 1876, to Dear Old Comrades, January 16, 1896, and to Deacon Richards, January 20, 1898, Jayhawker Collection; Juliet W. Brier, San Francisco *Call,* December 25, 1898, op. cit., n. 5; John W. Brier, "The Argonauts . . ." op. cit., n. 5, 4; Steward, op. cit., n. 10, 84; and Wheat, "Trailing the Forty-Niners . . ." op. cit., n. 6, 105.

22. Young, op. cit., n. 5, January 10–14, 1850; Nusbaumer, *Valley of Salt . . .* op. cit., n. 5, 45–46; James W. Brier's reminiscence in the Los Angeles *Times,* op. cit., n. 5, and his letters to Dear Old Comrades, January 16, 1896 and to Deacon Richards, January 20, 1898, op. cit., n. 21; Colton's interview in the Kansas City *Times,* February 5, 1890, op. cit., n. 5; Manly, *Death Valley . . .* op. cit., n. 5, 224; and Stephens, op. cit., n. 1, 22.

23. Young, op. cit., n. 5, January 15–February 5, 1850; James W. Brier's reminiscence in the Los Angeles *Times,* op. cit., n. 5; and Colton's interview in the Kansas City *Times* (1888) op. cit., n. 5; Manly, *Death Valley . . .* op. cit., n. 5, 162.

24. Young, op. cit., n. 5, January 28 and 30, 1850; James W. Brier's letter to Charles B. Mecum, January 17, 1876, op. cit., n. 5; Colton's interview in the Kansas City *Times* (1888) op. cit., n. 5; Manly, "The Gunsight . . ." op. cit., n. 18, his *Death Valley . . .* op. cit., n. 5, 365–366, and his "Charles Alvord" *The Pioneer, 10,* May 15, 1895. See also John E. Baur, "John Goller: Pioneer Angeleno Manufacturer," *Historical Society of Southern California Quarterly, 36* (1954), 14–27.

25. Nusbaumer, *Valley of Salt . . .* op. cit., n. 5, 10–11, 33, 47–53, 57; Manly, *Death Valley . . .* op. cit., n. 5, 113, 153; Manly, *Jayhawkers . . .* op. cit., n. 5, 28n; Rogers op. cit., n. 5; Stover, op. cit., n. 1, 166; Alan P. Bowman, *Index to the 1850 Census of the State of California* (Baltimore: Genealogical Pub. Co., 1972), 145, 498, 558; Louisa Burrel, "Across the Plains in 1849," *The Pioneer, 9,* December 15, 1894; Joseph Goldsborough Bruff, *Gold Rush: The Journals, Drawings and Other Papers of J. Goldsborough Bruff* (New York: Columbia University Press, 1944), xlv–xlviii. See also Wheat, "Forty-Niners . . ." op. cit., n. 5; Edwards, *Valley . . .* op. cit., n. 5; Southworth, op. cit., n. 6, 127–128; LeRoy and Jean Johnson, *Julia, Death Valley's Youngest Victim* (Roseville, Minn.: Author, 1981), 20 pp.

26. Manly, "From Vermont . . ." op. cit., n. 5 (March 1888), and his *Death Valley . . .* op. cit., n. 5, 144–147; Rogers, op. cit., n. 5.

27. Nusbaumer, *Valley of Salt . . .* op. cit., n. 5, 50–52; Manly, "From Vermont . . ." op. cit., n. 5, and his *Death Valley . . .* op. cit., n. 5, 148–150.

28. Manly, *Death Valley . . .* op. cit., n. 5, 150–153; Rogers, op. cit., n. 5; San Francisco *Alta California,* December 1, 1860; San Francisco *Chronicle,* January 25, 1891.

29. Manly, *Death Valley . . .* op. cit., n. 5, 201.

30. Manly, *Death Valley . . .* op. cit., n. 5, 202; Nusbaumer, *Valley of Salt . . .* op. cit., n. 5, 53–55, 61; Burrel, op. cit., n. 25; Belden, *Wade . . .* op. cit., n. 6, 11 mistakenly states that the Wades left Death Valley by way of Salt Spring.

31. Nusbaumer, *Valley of Salt* . . . op. cit., n. 5, 52–55; Manly, *Death Valley* . . . op. cit., n. 5, 202.

32. Manly, *Death Valley* . . . op. cit., n. 5, 198; L. D. Stephens to C. B. Mecum and Brother Jayhawkers, January 21, 1880, op. cit., n. 4; James W. Brier to Charles B. Mecum and others, January 21, 1880, op. cit., n. 4; Stover, op. cit., n. 1, 175; Wilson's account in Goodwin, "White . . ." op. cit., n. 5, 13–14; Southworth, op. cit., n. 6, 127–128.

33. Nusbaumer, *Valley of Salt* . . . op. cit., n. 5, 59–60.

34. Manly, *Death Valley* . . . op. cit., n. 5, 200–204.

35. Manly, "From Vermont . . .", op. cit., n. 5 (April–August 1888), and his *Death Valley* . . . op. cit., n. 5, 153–200.

36. Manly, "From Vermont . . ." op. cit., n. 5 (August 1888), and his *Death Valley* . . . op. cit., n. 5, 201–209.

37. Manly, "From Vermont . . ." op. cit., n. 5 (September 1888), and his *Death Valley* . . . op. cit., n. 5, 210–217; Wilson's account in Goodwin, "White . . ." op. cit., n. 5, 13.

38. Manly, "From Vermont . . ." op. cit., no. 5 (October–December 1888), and his *Death Valley* . . . op. cit., n. 5, 218–258.

39. Manly, *Death Valley* . . . op. cit., n. 5; Ellenbecker, op. cit., n. 5, 101–123; E. I. Edwards, "Death Valley's Neglected Hero," *Westerners, Los Angeles Posse, Brand Book, 12* (Los Angeles: 1966), 59–73.

A Hard Lesson

1. Addison Pratt, Diary, December 1, 1849, published in LeRoy Hafen and Ann Hafen, *Journals of Forty-Niners, Salt Lake to Los Angeles* (Glendale: Arthur H. Clark Co., 1954), 95–96; James S. Brown, *Life of a Pioneer* (Salt Lake: George Q. Cannon & Sons, 1900), 139; Mrs. Edward Burrel, "Across the Plains in 1849," *The Pioneer, 9,* December 15, 1894; Lindley Bynum, ed., "The Record Book of the Rancho Santa Ana del Chino," *Historical Society of Southern California, Annual Publications, 16* (1934), 36; Los Angeles *Star,* May 17, 1851. For biographical information on Benjamin D. Wilson, see John W. Caughey, "Don Benito Wilson: An Average Southern Californian," *Huntington Library Quarterly, 11* (April 1939), 289–300.

2. San Francisco *Alta California,* May 9, September 20, 1850; Los Angeles *Star,* May 17, 1851; Alan P. Bowman, *Index to the 1850 Census of the State of California* (Baltimore: Genealogical Pub. Co., 1972), 401.

3. Los Angeles *Star,* May 17, 1851.

4. Los Angeles *Star,* May 17, August 16, 1851; Doyce B. Nunis, Jr., *Andrew Sublette, Rocky Mountain Prince, 1808–1853* (Los Angeles: Dawson's Book Shop, 1960), 103–104.

5. Los Angeles *Star,* May 17, 1851.

6. Los Angeles *Star,* May 17, 1851; W. W. Robinson, *People versus Lugo* (Los Angeles: Dawson's Book Shop, 1962), 46 pp.

7. Los Angeles *Star,* May 17, 1851; Walter C. Mendenhall, *Some Desert Watering Places in Southeastern California and Southwestern Nevada* (U.S.G.S. Water Supply Paper 224; Washington, D.C.: Government Printing Office, 1909), 48–49.

8. Los Angeles *Star,* May 17, July 12, August 16, 1851.

9. Los Angeles *Star,* November 8, 1851, February 21, July 31, 1852.

10. Ibid.; Nunis, op. cit., n. 4, 107–108, 114–115.

11. George Beattie and Helen Beattie, *Heritage of the Valley: San Bernardino's First Century* (Pasadena: San Pasqual Press, 1939), 198; Sylvester Mowry, "Lt. Sylvester Mowry's Report on His March in 1855 from Salt Lake City to Fort Tejon," *Arizona and the West, 7* (1965), 340 (Lynn R. Bailey, ed.).

12. William B. Rice, "Early Freighting on the Salt Lake-San Bernardino Trail," *Pacific Historical Review, 11* (1942), 73–80; S. N. Carvalho, *Incidents of Travel and Adventure in the Far West* (New York: Derby & Jackson, 1857), 232–235.

13. Los Angeles *Star,* February 9, 1861; Los Angeles *News,* May 7, 1862, February 23, 1863.

14. San Bernardino County Recorder, Deeds Book E, 520; San Francisco *Alta California,* February 17, 1863; Los Angeles *News,* February 23, March 25, 1863.

15. Los Angeles *News,* February 23, March 2, 25, May 6, June 1, September 16, October 9, November 9, 1863, January 6, May 31, 1864; San Francisco *Alta California,* December 9, 1863, May 31, 1864; Independence *Inyo Independent,* April 11, 1874; Rossiter W. Raymond, *Statistics of Mines and Mining in the States and Territories West of the Rocky Mountains for the Year 1870* (Washington, D.C.: Government Printing Office, 1872), 14–15.

16. Henry G. Langley, *Langley's San Francisco Directory for the Year Commencing 1867 [through]* . . . *1875* (San Francisco: Valentine, 1862 through 1875); Richard E. Lingenfelter, *Steamboats on the Colorado River 1852–1916* (Tucson: University of Arizona Press, 1978), 43–51.

17. Los Angeles *News,* October 18, 29, 1864; *Mining and Scientific Press,* October 22, December 3, 1864; San Francisco *Alta California,* November 26, 28, 1864; Mrs. James A. Rousseau, "Rousseau Diary Across the Desert to California from Salt Lake City to San Bernardino in 1864," *San Bernardino County Museum Association Quarterly, 6* (Winter 1958), 11–12; San Francisco *Exchange,* January 31, 1882 Extra; *Gifford v. Carvill,* 29 Cal. 589 (1866).

18. Brown, op. cit., n. 1, 440–442.

Gunsight Silver and the Wonderful Bailey Ore

1. Henry G. Hanks, "An Undeveloped Region," San Francisco *Evening Bulletin,* February 10, 1869; James W. Brier to Deacon Richards, Lodi, January

20, 1898, J. B. Colton Scrapbook, Jayhawker Collection, in Henry E. Huntington Library and Art Gallery, San Marino, Calif.

2. William L. Manly, "The Gunsight Lead," *The Pioneer, 9,* April 15, 1894.

3. Hanks, op. cit., n. 1.

4. Beatty *Bullfrog Miner,* June 13, 1908; J. C. Boyles, "He Witnessed the Death Valley Tragedy of '49," *Desert Magazine, 3* (February 1940), 5; Henry G. Hanks, *Third Annual Report of the State Mineralogist* (Sacramento: James J. Ayers, Supt. State Printing, 1883), 31; John R. Spears, *Illustrated Sketches of Death Valley and Other Borax Deserts of the Pacific Coast* (Chicago: Rand, McNally & Co., 1892), 21.

5. Andrew Jensen, "History of the Las Vegas Mission," *Nevada State Historical Society Papers, 5* (1926), 217–218, 270–276; Independence *Inyo Independent,* March 22, 1873, February 12, 1904; Jacob Y. Stover, "History of the Sacramento Mining Company of 1849," *Pacific Historical Review, 6* (1937), 166.

6. Jensen, op. cit., n. 5, 218, 270–276; *Mining and Scientific Press,* June 9, 1862.

7. San Francisco *Alta California,* April 26, 1860, June 11, 1863; William L. Manly, "Men That I Knew," *The Pioneer, 10,* January 15, 1895; William L. Manly, *Death Valley in '49* (San Jose: Pacific Tree and Vine Co., 1894), 474–477.

8. San Francisco *Alta California,* April 26, June 2, 1860, June 11, 1863; San Francisco *Evening Bulletin,* June 9, 1860; William L. Manly, "How Furnace Creek Got Its Name," *The Pioneer, 8,* August 15, 1893, and his "Charles Alvord," *The Pioneer, 10,* May 15, 1895; Milo Page, "Unwritten History," Bishop *Inyo Register,* August 2, 1906 (found what may have been Bennett's first furnace near Anvil Spring).

9. Visalia *Delta,* April 7, 1860; Oroville *Butte Record,* July 21, 1860; San Francisco *Alta California,* July 25, 1860, June 11, 1863; Panamint *News,* March 9, 1875; Carl I. Wheat, "Death Valley After Forty-Niners," *California Historical Society Quarterly, 18* (1939), 200. See also Joseph E. Doctor, *Dr. E. Darwin French's Exploration of Death Valley* (Bishop: Chalfant Press, 1982), 16 pp.

10. Oroville, *Butte Record,* July 21, 1860; Visalia *Delta,* June 23, July 7, 1860, April 20, May 4, 1861; Los Angeles *Star,* January 5, March 9, July 27, October 5, 1861; San Francisco *Alta California,* July 25, 1860, March 10, 24, 1861; Minard H. Farley, *Farley's Map of the Newly Discovered Tramontane Silver Mines in Southern California and Western New Mexico, Comprising Those of Coso, Washington, Tiachipa, Russ, Potosi, Esmeralda, Holcomb and Bear Valley Districts* (San Francisco: W. Holt, 1861).

11. S. G. George, "Our Early History," Panamint *News,* March 9, 23, 1875; *Combination Gold and Silver Mining Co.* stock certificate, April 15, 1862, and assessment receipt, November 25, 1862, in the Wells Fargo History Room, San Francisco; San Francisco *Alta California,* July 28, 1861, February 10, 1869; Los Angeles *Star,* April 19, 1862; Bishop *Inyo Register,* January 22, 1891, March 17, 1904, September 20, 1906; Hanks, *Third Annual Report . . .* op. cit., n. 4, 36.

12. J. C. Boyles, "He Witnessed the Death Valley Tragedy of '49," *Desert Magazine, 3* (February 1940), 6; W. A. Chalfant, *The Story of Inyo* (Bishop: Chalfant, 1933), 147–229.

13. Oroville *Butte Record,* July 21, 1860; George, op. cit., n. 11.

14. Visalia *Delta,* January 19, June 6, 13, July 4, 1861; San Francisco *Alta California,* March 14, April 11, 1861; Farley, op. cit., n. 10.

15. San Francisco *Alta California,* April 11, 12, 13, 1861; Visalia *Delta,* June 6, July 11, 1861; Los Angeles *Star,* July 27, 1861; *Mining and Scientific Press,* July 6, 1861.

16. San Francisco *Alta California,* July 18, 1861; Los Angeles *Star,* July 27, 1861.

17. Los Angeles *Star,* July 27, August 10, September 21, November 23, 1861; Los Angeles *News,* July 26, 1861; *Mining and Scientific Press,* July 20, 27, August 3, 1861.

18. *Mining and Scientific Press,* August 10, 1861; *Proceedings of California Academy of Natural Science, 2* (1858–1862), 142.

19. *Mining and Scientific Press,* August 10, 1861; Los Angeles *Star,* September 28, 1861.

20. *Mining and Scientific Press,* July 27, 1861; J. Ross Browne, *Adventures in Apache Country* (New York: Harper & Brothers, 1869), 517–518; Bishop *Inyo Register,* February 4, 1904; Chalfant, op. cit., n. 12, 132.

21. *An Illustrated History of Southern California* (Chicago: Lewis Publishing Company, 1890), 199–201; San Francisco *Alta California,* July 18, 1861 (notes the sailing of the *Sûreté* on July 17).

Alvord and Breyfogle

1. Additional information on both Alvord and Breyfogle is given in Harold O. Weight, *Lost Mines of Death Valley* (Twentynine Palms: The Calico Press, 1961), 17–52).

2. William L. Manly, "Charles Alvord," *The Pioneer, 10,* May 15, June 15, 1895; San Francisco *Alta California,* April 26, June 2, 1860; San Francisco *Evening Bulletin,* June 9, 1860.

3. Manly, op. cit., n. 2; San Francisco *Alta California,* June 2, 1860; Los Angeles *Star,* October 6, 1860 (hotel arrivals); William L. Manly, *Death Valley in '49* (San Jose: Pacific Tree and Vine Co., 1894), 462, 475.

4. Manly, "Charles Alvord," op. cit., n. 2; Los Angeles *Star,* October 13, 1860; San Francisco *Alta California,* December 1, 1860.

5. Manly, "Charles Alvord," op. cit., n. 2; Bishop *Inyo Register,* October 29, 1903; Lieut. Charles E. Bendire, "Report of a Scouting Expedition Made in the Region East of Owens Valley, Cal.," May 26, 1867, Typescript, Collection of Dennis G. Casebier, Norco, Calif.

6. Manly, "Charles Alvord," op. cit., n. 2; Los Angeles *Star,* November 17, 24, 1860 (hotel arrivals).

7. Manly, "Charles Alvord," op. cit., n. 2.

8. Ibid.; S. G. George, "Our Early History," Panamint *News,* March 23, 1875.

9. Los Angeles *Star,* March 18, 1861; San Francsico *Alta California,* April 12, 1861; Minard H. Farley, *Farley's Map of the Newly Discovered Tramontane Silver Mines in Southern California and Western New Mexico* (San Francisco: W. Holt, 1861).

10. Manly, "Charles Alvord," op. cit., n. 2.

11. Ibid.; George, op. cit., n. 8; Sacramento *Daily Union,* September 17, 1861.

12. Los Angeles *Star,* July 26, 1862; *Mining and Scientific Press,* November 21, 28, 1891; Manly, "Charles Alvord," op. cit., n. 2.

13. Bishop *Inyo Register,* August 2, 1906; Los Angeles *Examiner,* June 15, 1919, quoted in Weight, op. cit., n. 1, 21–22; San Bernardino County, Superior Court, Cases No. 1065, *Loveland v. Osborne,* and No. 1491, *Stevens et al. v. Alvord Consolidated Quartz Mining Company et al.*

14. Bishop *Inyo Register,* August 24, 1899.

15. Standish Rood, "The Lost Ledge," *Whittaker's Milwaukee Monthly,* 4 (1872), 41; Lewis W. Breyfogle, "What I Know About the Breyfogle Family," typescript, Chanute, Kansas, 1963, Nevada Historical Society, Reno.

16. Breyfogle, op. cit., n. 15; "The Diary of Joshua D. Breyfogle, Sr. 1849," 34 pp., typescript, Nevada Historical Society, Reno; *History of Alameda County . . .* (Oakland: Myron H. Wood, 1883), 204, 220, 288–289; San Leandro *Alameda County Gazette,* August 27, 1859, March 24, April 14, 1860; Virginia City *Territorial Enterprise,* June 2, 1860; Austin *Reese River Reveille,* March 30, July 25, 29, September 9, 1863; Sacramento *Daily Union,* August 22, 1859.

17. Austin *Reese River Reveille,* October 19, 1866, November 6, 1869.

18. Austin *Reese River Reveille,* January 30, 1864, November 6, 1869. "Breyfogle's Trail" is shown on the Nevada map in Sterling M. Holdredge, *State, Territorial & Ocean Guide Book of the Pacific* (San Francisco: Grafton T. Brown, 1865).

19. Austin *Reese River Reveille,* March 17, 1864, October 19, 1866, November 18, 1871.

20. Austin *Reese River Reveille,* April 24, October 2, 1865, November 18, 1871; John Todd, *Map of the Reese River Mining Districts, Showing Explorations of D. E. Buel in 1864 and Joseph Todd in 1865* (New York: D. Van Nostrand, 1866).

21. Salt Lake *Telegraph,* June 9, 1865; Tonopah *Miner,* July 2, 1904; Beatty *Bullfrog Miner,* July 1, 1905; Rhyolite *Bullfrog Miner,* June 8, 1907; Dane Coolidge, *Death Valley Prospectors* (New York: E. P. Dutton & Co., 1937), 65–66.

22. Tonopah *Miner,* July 2, 1904; Salt Lake *Telegraph,* June 9, 1865.

23. Austin *Reese River Reveille,* October 30, November 1, December 16, 1865; Todd, op. cit., n. 20; Tom Wilson's account in Coolidge, op. cit., n. 21, 69–70.

24. Austin *Reese River Reveille,* November 18, 1871.

25. Mammoth City *Herald,* December 10, 1879.
26. Virginia City *Territorial Enterprise,* June 23–28, 1866; San Francisco *Bulletin,* June 15, 1866; Austin *Reese River Reveille,* November 18, 1871.
27. Austin *Reese River Reveille,* October 19, 1866; Virginia City *Territorial Enterprise,* October 17, 1866; Rood, op. cit., n. 15; 41–46, 89–94; Standish Rood, *Report of Standish Rood on the Pah-Ranagat Lake Silver Mines of Southeastern Nevada* (New York: William C. Bryant & Co., 1866), 23 pp.
28. Austin *Reese River Reveille,* February 1, 7, 1867; Rood, "Lost Ledge," op. cit., n. 15.
29. Myron Angel, *History of Nevada* (Oakland: Thompson and West, 1881), 436; Tonopah *Bonanza,* December 24, 1904; Searchlight *Searchlight,* May 26, 1905; Beatty *Bullfrog Miner,* June 10, 1905; William R. Breyfogle to Dane Coolidge, April 27, 1936, in Dane Coolidge Collection, Bancroft Library; Coolidge, op. cit., n. 21, 72–73; Weight, op. cit., n. 1, 36.
30. Virginia City *Territorial Enterprise,* November 22, 1871; Greenwater *Death Valley Chuck-Walla,* April 1, 1907; Tonopah *Bonanza,* December 24, 1904; W. A. Chalfant, *Death Valley, The Facts* (Stanford: Stanford University Press, 1936), 47; Tonopah *Miner,* July 2, 1904; Tonopah *Daily Sun,* December 27, 1905; K. R. Casper, "The Story of Breyfogle," *Sunset Magazine, 15* (1905), 591–593; Goldfield *Gossip,* January 1, 1907; Los Angeles *Times,* July 8, 1891; Albert Williams, "Lost Mines," *Chautauquan, 17* (1893), 693; Rood, "The Lost Ledge," op. cit., n. 15, 41.
31. *Mining and Scientific Press,* November 1, 1884; Tonopah *Miner,* July 2, 1904; Williams, op. cit., n. 30, 693; Goldfield *Gossip,* January 1, 1907; Searchlight *Searchlight,* May 26, 1905.

Camels, Frauds, and Lost Guides

1. San Francisco *Daily Herald,* August 25, September 21, 1853; Gwinn H. Heap, *Central Route to the Pacific: From The Valley of the Mississippi to California,* (Philadelphia: Lippincott, Grambo & Co., 1854), Appendix II, 133–136.
2. San Francisco *Daily Herald,* September 21, October 8, December 19, 20, 1853; George W. Cullum, *Biographical Register of the Officers and Graduates of the U.S. Military Academy* (Boston: Houghton, Mifflin and Co., 1891), v. 1, 333–334; Stewart Mitchell, "A Forgotten Exploration in Search of a Route Across the Sierra Nevada for the Pacific Railroad," *California Historical Society Quarterly, 34* (1955), 209–228.
3. San Francisco *Daily Herald,* December 20, 1853; George H. Goddard, *Britton and Rey's Map of the State of California* (San Francisco: Britton and Rey, 1857).
4. San Francisco *Daily Herald,* December 19, 20, 1853; Goddard, op. cit., n. 3.; Warren Holt, *Map of the State of Nevada* (San Francisco: W. Holt, 1866).

5. San Francisco *Daily Herald,* August 7, 1853; San Francisco *Alta California,* April 21, 1854; John C. Fremont, *Map of Oregon and Upper California From The Surveys of John Charles Fremont and other Authorities, Drawn by Charles Preuss* (Baltimore: 1848); John C. Fremont, *Central Railroad Route to the Pacific* (Washington: 1854), 7 pp.; Walt Wheelock, "Following Fremont's Fifth Expedition," *Westerners Brand Book, Los Angeles Posse, v. 12* (1966), 187–200.

6. *Annual Report of the Surveyor General of California:* (for 1855–56), 34th Cong., 3rd sess., Senate Ex. Doc. 5, 384–385; (for 1856–57), 35th Cong. 1st Sess., House Ex. Doc. 2., 221, 224; (for 1857–58), 35th Cong., 2nd Sess., House Ex. Doc. 2, 308, 324; *Map of Public Surveys in California to Accompany Report of Surveyor Genl., 1857;* Visalia *Delta,* April 6, 1861.

7. *Annual Report . . . (1857–58)* op. cit., n. 6, 803; Sacramento *Union,* July 31, 1861; San Francisco *Evening Bulletin,* June 13, 1860.

8. Los Angeles *Star,* January 28, March 31, April 7, 21, 1860; Dennis G. Casebier, *Carleton's Pah-Ute Campaign* (Norco, Calif.: Casebier, 1972), 4–10.

9. Casebier, op. cit., n. 8, 10–39.

10. Ibid., 40–42.

11. W. J. Tenney, *The Military and Naval History of the Rebellion in The United States, With Biographical Sketches of Deceased Officers . . .* (New York: D. Appleton and Co., 1867), 384, 759; Los Angeles *Star,* July 21, 1860.

12. San Francisco *Evening Bulletin,* April 30, June 13, October 25, 1860; San Francisco *Alta California,* October 25, November 27, 1860. See also Francois D. Uzes, *Chaining the Land: A History of Surveying in California* (Sacramento: Landmark Enterprises, 1977), 69–96.

13. San Francisco *Alta California,* October 25, December 20, 1860, March 4, 9, 1861; Visalia *Sun,* November 8, 1860.

14. San Francisco *Evening Bulletin,* September 13, 1860; San Francisco *Alta California,* December 20, 1860, March 9, 1861; J. R. N. Owen, Report to Hon. S. Mowry of a Reconnaissance along the Proposed Boundary Line of the State of California, April 15, 1861, California State Lands Commission, Sacramento, copy courtesy of Francois D. Uzes.

15. San Francisco *Alta California,* March 9, 10, 24, 1861; Arthur Woodward, *Camels and Surveyors in Death Valley* (Palm Desert: Desert Printers, Inc., 1961), 5–21; Harlan D. Fowler, *Camels to California* (Stanford: Stanford University Press, 1950), 71.

16. San Francisco *Alta California,* December 20, 1860, March 4, 1861; Los Angeles *Star,* March 9, 1861. Aaron Van Dorn's account of the expedition, entitled "Eastern Boundary Sketches," was published in the Sacramento *Daily Union,* June 25, 29, July 9, 11, 13, 31, August 7, 10, 1861, and reprinted in Woodward, op. cit., n. 15, 23–73. Although the articles were unsigned, Van Dorn's authorship is evident from the frequent professional references; from specific instances in which he is identified by Owen, op. cit., n. 14; and from the fact that, aside from one of the camel drivers, Van Dorn is the only member of the party not mentioned by name. In his

introduction to the reprint Woodward, op. cit., n. 15, repeats Carl Wheat's suggestion that James Hitchens was the author. Hitchens, however, wrote signed letters to the San Francisco *Alta California,* dated March 4, 10, 1861, that are clearly of different authorship from those in the Sacramento *Daily Union.*

17. Sacramento *Daily Union,* June 25, 29, July 9, 13, 1861; Owen, op. cit., n. 14.

18. Sacramento *Daily Union,* July 11, 13, 1861; Owen, op. cit., n. 14.

19. Sacramento *Daily Union,* July 13, 1861; Owen, op. cit., n. 14.

20. Sacramento *Daily Union,* July 13, 31, 1861.

21. Ibid.

22. *Report of the Secretary of the Interior, November 30, 1861* (37th Cong., 2nd Sess., Senate Ex. Doc. 1), 490–494; Visalia *Delta,* April 6, 13, 1861; San Jose *Tribune,* March 29, April 5, 1861; Myron Angel, *History of Nevada,* (Oakland: Thompson and West, 1881), 100.

23. Los Angeles *Star,* August 24, 1861, February 15, 1862; San Francisco *Alta California,* February 2, March 5, 1862.

24. Angel, op. cit., n. 22, 102; Sacramento *Daily Union,* June 15, 1865; C. H. Sinclair, "The Oblique Boundary Line Between California and Nevada," Appendix No. 3, *Report of the Superintendent of the Coast and Geodetic Survey, 1899–1900* (Washington, D.C.: Goverment Printing Office, 1901), 270.

25. Richard H. Stretch wrote a detailed account of Blasdel's expedition in a series of letters, "From the Exploring Expedition," published in the Virginia City *Territorial Enterprise* April 8, 13, 14, 15, 17, May 31, June 6, 10, 22, 23, 24, 26, 27, 28, 29, 1866, and an abbreviated "Journal of Explorations in Southern Nevada in the Spring of 1866 by His Excellency Governor Blasdel of Nevada," published as Appendix "E" of his *Annual Report of the State Mineralogist of the State of Nevada for 1866* (Carson City: Joseph E. Eckley, State Printer, 1867), 141–147; Gold Hill *News,* April 16, 1866.

26. Austin *Reese River Reveille,* March 31, 1864, October 2, 1865; Virginia City *Territorial Enterprise,* May 31, June 22, 24, 28, 1866; John Todd, *Map of the Reese River Mining Districts Showing Explorations of D. E. Buel in 1864 and Joseph Todd in 1865* (New York: D. Van Nostrand, 1866).

27. Virginia City *Territorial Enterprise,* June 6, 24, 26–28, 1866.

28. Ibid., June 29, 1866; Angel, op. cit., n. 22, 102; Austin *Reese River Reveille,* quoted in Gold Hill *News,* April 14, 1866.

29. Camp Independence, Post Returns, April 30, 1867, Record Group 393, U.S. National Archives; Camp Independence, Special Order No. 37, April 2, 1867; Lieut. Charles E. Bendire, "Report of a Scouting Expedition Made in the Region East of Owens Valley, Cal.," May 26, 1867, typescript, Collection of Dennis G. Casebier, Norco, Calif.

30. Bendire, op. cit., n. 29.

31. Ibid.; Francis B. Heitman, *Historical Register and Dictionary of the United States Army* (Washington, D.C.: Government Printing Office, 1903) v. 1, 209; *The Great Register of Inyo County for 1871* (Independence: *Inyo Inde-*

pendent, 1871), 4; Independence *Inyo Independent*, July 29, December 2, 1871.

32. Cullum, op. cit., n. 2, v. 2, 65–66; *Dictionary of American Biography* (New York: Scribner's Sons, 1936), v. 20, 47–48; George M. Wheeler, *Preliminary Report Concerning Explorations and Surveys Principally in Nevada and Arizona* (Washington: Government Printing Office, 1872), 96 pp., and Wheeler Scrapbook, 1871, in Bancroft Library. See also Richard A. Bartlett, *Great Surveys of the American West* (Norman: University of Oklahoma Press, 1962), 333–349; William H. Goetzmann, *Exploration and Empire, The Explorer and The Scientist in the Winning of the American West* (New York: Alfred A. Knopf, 1966), 467–488; and Dorothy C. Cragen, *The Boys in The Sky Blue Pants: The Men and Events at Camp Independence and Forts of Eastern California, Nevada and Utah, 1862–1877* (Fresno: Pioneer Pub. Co., 1976), 93–110.

33. Wheeler, op. cit., n. 32, 15; Independence *Inyo Independent*, July 29, 1871; San Diego *Union*, December 21, 1871; *Appleton's Cyclopaedia of American Biography* (New York: D. Appleton & Co., 1900), v. 4, 27.

34. Wheeler, op. cit., n. 32, 12–13; Cullum, op. cit., n. 2, v. 2, 66–67, 132; John Dickson, ed., *National Cyclopaedia of American Biography* (New York: J. T. White & Co., 1940), v. 28, 376.

35. Wheeler, op. cit., n. 32, 15–16; David A. Lyle, "Report of Second Lieutenant D. A. Lyle, Second United States Artillery," Appendix B of Wheeler, op. cit., n. 32, 77–80; Independence *Inyo Independent*, November 18, 1871.

36. Lyle, op. cit., n. 35, 80–81; Independence *Inyo Independent*, January 27, 1872.

37. Lyle, op. cit., n. 35, 81–82; Independence *Inyo Independent*, November 18, December 2, 1871, January 27, 1872.

38. Lyle, op. cit., n. 35, 82–83; Wheeler, op. cit., n. 32, 16.

39. Lyle, op. cit., n. 35, 83–84; Independence *Inyo Independent*, November 18, 1871, January 27, 1872.

40. Lyle, op. cit., n. 35, 84; Austin *Reese River Reveille*, October 13, 1871; Independence *Inyo Independent*, November 25, 1871, January 27, 1872.

41. Independence *Inyo Independent*, September 2, November 18, 25, December 2, 1871, January 27, 1872; Fred W. Loring, "Into the Valley of Death," *Appleton's Journal*, 6 (November 18, 1871), 574–575.

42. Independence *Inyo Independent*, November 25, 1871, January 27, 1872.

43. Ibid., November 18, 1871, May 10, 31, 1873, July 25, 1874.

44. Ibid., May 1, 1875.

45. *Reports of J. E. James and Richard H. Stretch, Civil Engineers &c. of the Practicability of Turning the Waters of the Gulf of California Into The Colorado Desert and The Death Valley (43rd Cong. 1st Sess., Sen. Misc. Doc. No. 84)* (Washington: Government Printing Office, 1874), 6–7; George M. Wheeler, *Annual Report upon the Geographical Surveys West of the One Hundredth Meridian (App. J J of the Ann. Rpt. of the Chief of Engineers for 1876)* (Washington, D.C.: Government Printing Office, 1876), 70–71, 109–111, 117.

Tom Shaw's Country

1. George M. Wheeler, *Preliminary Report Concerning Explorations and Surveys Principally in Nevada and Arizona* (Washington: Government Printing Office, 1872), 82–83; George M. Wheeler, *Geographical Explorations and Surveys West of the 100th Meridian, Atlas Sheet No. 65* (New York: The Graphic Co., [c. 1873]); A. Russell Crowell, *Miners Map of Death Valley, The Mojave, Amargosa and Nevada Deserts* (Las Vegas: A. Russell Crowell, 1905); U.S. Geological Survey, *Lida Quadrangle*, 60 Minutes Series (1908).

2. "Census of the Inhabitants of the State of Nevada, 1875," *Appendix to the Journal of the Senate and Assembly of the 8th Session of the Nevada State Legislature* (Carson City: State Printer, 1877), v. 2, 77; Virginia City *Territorial Enterprise*, August 3, 1866; Belmont *Silver Bend Reporter*, May 2, 1868; Belmont *Courier*, April 4, 1874.

3. Austin *Reese River Reveille*, November 27, 1865; Elko *Chronicle*, November 16, 1870; Independence *Inyo Independent*, September 24, October 7, 21, 1871.

4. Virginia City *Territorial Enterprise*, April 14, May 22, 1866; Francis B. Heitman, *Historical Register and Dictionary of the United States Army* (Washington: Government Printing Office, 1903), v. 2, 87; *Mining and Scientific Press*, November 4, 1865; *Annual Report of the State Mineralogist of the State of Nevada for 1866* (Carson City: Joseph E. Eckley, State Printer, 1867), 42; Independence *Inyo Independent*, September 2, 1871. See also Hugh A. Shamberger, *The Story of Silver Peak* (Carson City: Nevada Historical Press, 1976), 12–13.

5. Virginia City *Territorial Enterprise*, May 22, 1866; Austin *Reese River Reveille*, May 7, 1866.

6. Virginia City *Territorial Enterprise*, May 22, 1866; *Third Biennial Report of the State Mineralogist* [1869–1870] (Carson City: State Printer, 1871), 104–105; Belmont *Silver Bend Reporter*, June 22, September 28, November 23, December 7, 1867, February 8, May 30, June 24, 1868.

7. Wheeler, *Preliminary Report . . .* op. cit., n. 1, 47; Virginia City *Territorial Enterprise*, January 7, 1869; Austin *Reese River Reveille*, February 1, 1869; Independence *Inyo Independent*, January 16, 1875.

8. Austin *Reese River Reveille*, November 26, 1868, February 1, 1869; Independence *Inyo Independent*, June 17, 1871; Candelaria *True Fissure*, June 5, 1886.

9. Austin *Reese River Reveille*, June 19, 1869; Independence *Inyo Independent*, May 17, 1873, January 16, 1875; Candelaria *True Fissure*, January 29, 1881; New York *Times*, November 15, 1903.

10. Virginia City *Territorial Enterprise*, August 3, 1866; Ione *Nye County News*, August 11, 1866.

11. Belmont *Silver Bend Reporter*, May 2, 1868.

12. Ibid.; Wheeler, *Preliminary Report . . .* op. cit., n. 1, 47; Independence *Inyo Independent*, January 28, March 25, June 17, 1871; Camp Independence, Post Returns, November 30, 1870, February 28, March 31, 1871, April

30, 1872; U.S. National Archives, Micro copy 617, Roll 506.

13. Independence *Inyo Independent,* March 25, June 17, November 18, 1871; Wheeler, *Preliminary Report . . .* op. cit., n. 1, 47; *Biennial Report of the State Mineralogist of the State of Nevada for the Years 1871 and 1872,* (Carson City: State Printer, 1872), 43.

14. Austin *Reese River Reveille,* March 4, 1872; Independence *Inyo Independent,* February 17, March 9, June 1, 1872; *Biennial Report . . . 1871 and 1872,* op. cit., n. 13, 41–42; Rossiter W. Raymond, *Statistics of Mines and Mining in the States and Territories West of the Rocky Mountains; Being the Fourth Annual Report* (Washington: Government Printing Office, 1872), 183.

15. Myron Angel, *History of Nevada* (Oakland: Thompson and West, 1881), 420; Independence *Inyo Independent,* June 1, 8, July 13, September 28, November 20, 1872, April 26, May 3, 10, 17, July 19, November 8, 1873.

16. Independence *Inyo Independent,* May 10, 18 (Extra), 24, 31, June 2, November 8, 1873, March 7, 1874.

17. Ibid., November 21, 1870, January 7, 1871, February 17, 1872, August 16, 1873; *Mining and Scientific Press,* June 18, 1870; *The Great Register of Inyo County for 1871* (Independence: Inyo Independent, 1871), 5; Henry G. Langley, *The San Francisco Directory for the Year 1865 [through] 1873* (San Francisco: H. G. Langley, 1865 through 1873).

18. Independence *Inyo Independent,* October 31, November 21, 1870, January 7, February 4, 25, April 1, 15, 29, May 6, October 28, 1871, February 17, October 26, 1872; Austin *Reese River Reveille,* March 4, 1872; Wheeler, *Preliminary Report . . .* op. cit., n. 1, 49.

19. Independence *Inyo Independent,* February 17, March 9, 23, April 6, 27, May 11, 1872.

20. Ibid., July 9, 1870, April 13, June 1, October 26, November 23, 1872; *Biennial Report . . . 1871 and 1872,* op. cit., n. 13, 41–42.

21. Independence *Inyo Independent,* April 26, May 3, 10, 1873, January 10, 1874; *Biennial Report of the State Mineralogist of the State of Nevada for the Years 1873 and 1874* (Carson City: State Printer, 1874), 22.

22. Independence *Inyo Independent,* June 28, August 2, 16, October 4, 11, November 8, 1873, January 10, June 20, 1874.

23. Ibid., May 30, June 20, August 8, 1874; Henry G. Langley, *The San Francisco Directory for the Year Commencing March 1875* (San Francisco: H. G. Langley, 1875), 201.

24. Independence *Inyo Independent,* September 7, October 26, 1872, May 10, 1873, January 10, 1874; *Biennial Report . . . 1871 and 1872,* op. cit., n. 13, 43 and *. . . 1873 and 1874,* op. cit., n. 21, 23; Bishop *Inyo Register,* August 1, 1895.

25. Independence *Inyo Independent,* April 26, May 10, 1873.

26. Ibid., February 17, 24, 1872, May 10, 1873, November 12, 1881; Candelaria *True Fissure,* May 7, 1881.

27. Independence *Inyo Independent,* May 3, 10, 1873, January 10, 1874; *Biennial Report . . . 1873 and 1874,* op. cit., n. 21, 23; Angel, op. cit., n. 15, 468–469.

28. Independence *Inyo Independent,* October 4, June 20, July 4, August 8, 15,

September 26, October 24, November 14, 1874, December 4, 1875, November 12, 1881; Belmont *Courier*, August 22, 29, September 5, 1874; Candelaria *True Fissure*, July 3, 1880.

29. Independence *Inyo Independent*, September 26, 1874, April 3, 17, May 22, December 4, 1875; San Francisco *Alta California*, November 20, 1875; Langley, *San Francisco . . . 1875*, op. cit., n. 23, 579; California, Secretary of State, Division of Archives, Corporation Records, *Book 13*, 48, 62; Belmont *Courier*, May 22, 1875.

30. Independence *Inyo Independent*, June 28, October 4, 11, November 8, 1873, April 25, June 13, July 11, 18, 25, 1874, November 27, 1875, January 8, April 15, 22, May 13, June 10, 17, August 26, 1876; *Biennial Report . . . 1873 and 1874*, op. cit., n. 21, 21–22; John P. Mains, comp., *The Annual Statistician, 1878* (San Francisco: L. P. McCarty, 1878), 552; Aurora *Esmeralda Herald*, April 5, 1879.

31. Independence *Inyo Independent*, October 14, 1876, January 6, 1877, September 7, 1878; Columbus *Borax Miner*, April 3, 1875, January 1, 15, 1876; Virginia City *Territorial Enterprise*, July 12, 1878; Aurora *Esmeralda Herald*, March 11, 29, 1879.

32. Independence *Inyo Independent*, June 17, November 18, 1871, June 8, 1872, May 29, 1875; *Biennial Report . . . (1869–1870)*, op. cit., n. 17, 105, and *1873–1874*, op. cit., n. 21, 23; Aurora *Esmeralda Herald*, July 3, 1880; Candelaria *True Fissure*, February 12, 1881; Belmont *Courier*, August 25, 1883, August 30 1884; Bishop *Inyo Register*, December 25, 1890, June 18, 1891, June 9, August 25, 1892, April 6, December 14, 1893, November 8, 1894, August 1, 1895; Candelaria *Chloride Belt*, March 28, June 13, 1891, May 21, 1892; Tonopah *Bonanza*, June 28, 1902; Los Angeles *Examiner*, September 20, 1905; National Archives Record Group 29, Twelfth Census of the United States, 1900, Esmeralda County, Nevada, Tule Canyon Enumeration District No. 13.

33. "Census . . .," op. cit., n. 2, 77; Aurora *Esmeralda Herald*, November 22, 1879; Winnemucca *Silver State*, September 30, October 1, 1884.

Panamint—The Wonder of the World

1. A very entertaining but not always reliable account of the Panamint excitement can be found in Neill C. Wilson, *Silver Stampede: The Career of Death Valley's Hell-Camp, Old Panamint* (New York: The Macmillan Company, 1937), 319 pp.

2. Edward Doty letter to John B. Colton dated San Jose, November 14, 1871, Jayhawker Collection, in Henry E. Huntington Library and Art Gallery, San Marino, Calif.; George Miller, "A Trip to Death Valley," *Historical Society of Southern California, Annual Publication, 11* (1919), 56–64; Sacramento *Daily Union*, January 29, 1870; San Diego *Union*, February 17, 1870; Independence *Inyo Independent*, September 21, 1872, March 22,

April 19, 1873; James. W. Brier Letter to Charles B. Mecum, January 17, 1876, Jayhawker Collection.

3. Visalia *Delta,* July 28, 1860, May 28, 1863; Independence *Inyo Independent,* December 28, 1872, July 12, 1873, April 4, December 12, 1874; Havilah *Miner,* August 16, 1873; San Francisco *Mining and Scientific Press,* August 2, 1873; Milo Page, "Old Panamint History," in Bishop *Inyo Register,* July 19, 1906.

4. Page, op. cit., n. 3; William M. Stewart, *Reminiscences of Senator William M. Stewart of Nevada* (New York: Neale Publishing Company, 1908), 262.

5. Pioche *Record,* October 27, November 12 (letter list), December 22, 1872, August 29, 1902; San Francisco *Mining and Scientific Press,* August 2, 1873; Page, op. cit., n. 3; Stewart, op. cit., n. 4, 261–262; Harry M. Gorham, *My Memories of the Comstock* (Los Angeles: Suttonhouse Publishers, 1939), 108, 121; *Copy of the Great Register of Inyo County for 1875* (Independence: Inyo Independent, 1875), 2, 5, 16.

6. Independence *Inyo Independent,* May 10, 1873.

7. San Francisco *Mining and Scientific Press,* August 2, 1873; Havilah *Miner,* August 16, 1873; Salt Lake City *Utah Mining Gazette,* July 11, 1874; Panamint *News,* November 26, 1874; Independence *Inyo Independent,* August 16, 1873, December 4, 1874; Page, op. cit., n. 3; Inyo County, Recorder, Panamint Mining Register Book A, 27–29, 34–36, 41–43, 49–52, and Land, Water and Mining Claims, Book B, 49, 72.

8. Independence *Inyo Independent,* June 21, August 16, 1873, January 17, February 14, March 21, April 11, May 2, July 4, 25, August 1, 1874; San Francisco *Mining and Scientific Press,* September 13, November 29, 1873; Henry G. Langley, *San Francisco Directory for the Year Commencing March 1873* (San Francisco: H. G. Langley, 1873), 483, 547.

9. *Copy of the Great Register* . . . op. cit., n. 5, 14; Pioche *Record,* October 23, 1872; Salt Lake City *Utah Mining Gazette,* July 11, 1874; Independence *Inyo Independent,* November 22, December 20, 1873, November 4, 1876; William M. Stewart, "Panamint, Early History of Rich Mining Country," in Beatty *Bullfrog Miner,* July 7, 1906; Reno *Nevada Mining News,* August 20, 1908.

10. New York *Times,* April 11, 1874; Alonzo Phelps, *Contemporary Biography of California's Representative Men* (San Francisco: A. L. Bancroft & Co., 1881), 165–169, 223–230; Myron Angel, *History of Nevada* (Oakland: Thompson and West, 1881), 591–592; *The National Cyclopaedia of American Biography* (New York: James T. White & Co.), v. 1 (1892), 300, 325–326, and v. 13 (1906), 352–353; *Dictionary of American Biography* (New York: Charles Scribner's Sons, 1928–1935), v. 5, 188–189; v. 7, 208–209; v. 9, 13–15; Russell R. Elliot, *Servant of Power, A Political Biography of Senator William M. Stewart* (Reno: University of Nevada Press, 1983), 347 pp.

11. Gorham, op. cit., n. 5, 108–109; Independence *Inyo Independent* July 11, August 8, 15, October 31, November 14, December 5, 1874; Salt Lake

City *Utah Mining Gazette,* July 11, August 4, 1874; Virginia City *Territorial Enterprise,* July 15, 1874; Inyo County, Recorder, Panamint Mining Register Book A, 27–29, 34–36, 41–43, 49–54, 116, 176–181.

12. Pioche *Lincoln County Record,* August 29, 1902; Stewart, *Reminiscences* . . . op. cit., n. 4, 262; Stewart, "Panamint . . ." op. cit., n. 9; W. B. Daugherty reminiscences in Bishop *Inyo Register,* April 27, May 4, 1916; Willie A. Chalfant, *The Story of Inyo* (Bishop: Chalfant, 1933), 286.

13. San Bernardino *Guardian,* November 21, 1874; San Francisco *Mining and Scientific Press,* January 3, 1874; Independence *Inyo Independent,* January 10, November 21, 1874; New York *Engineering and Mining Journal,* October 17, 24, 1874.

14. San Francisco *Mining and Scientific Press,* September 5, 1874; Independence *Inyo Independent,* July 25, November 21, 1874; Eliot Lord, *Comstock Mining and Miners* (Washington: Government Printing Office, 1883), 244–249, 284; New York *Engineering and Mining Journal,* October 18, 25, 1890.

15. San Francisco *Mining and Scientific Press,* January 16, 1875; Belmont *Courier,* December 12, 1874; Austin *Reese River Reveille,* December 29, 1874; Phelps, op. cit., n. 10, 224; *Copy of the Great Register* . . . op. cit., n. 5, 11; Independence *Inyo Independent,* September 26, December 12, 1874.

16. Independence *Inyo Independent,* September 26, November 7, 1874, January 16, 23, 1875; Austin *Reese River Reveille,* October 23, November 23, 1874; San Francisco *Mining and Scientific Press,* November 21, 1874; San Francisco *Alta California,* February 1, 1875; Panamint *News,* March 2, 1875. For the Emma Mine promotion, see W. Turrentine Jackson, "The Infamous Emma Mine; A British Interest in the Little Cottonwood District, Utah Territory," *Utah Historical Quarterly, 23* (October 1955), 339–362, and Clark C. Spence, *British Investments and the American Mining Frontier 1860–1901* (Ithaca: Cornell University Press, 1958), Chap. VIII, 139–190.

17. J. Barr Robertson Letters to J. W. Walker, November 30, and December 7, 1874, Robertson Letterbook, Bancroft Library, quoted in Spence, op. cit., n. 16, 171; San Francisco *Evening Bulletin,* October 1, 1874; Belmont *Courier,* December 19, 1874; Independence *Inyo Independent,* October 10, 1874, January 30, 1875.

18. Lord, op. cit., n. 14, 281–286; Grant H. Smith, *The History of the Comstock Lode, 1850–1920* (Reno: University of Nevada, 1943), 128–130.

19. *The Wonder Consolidated Mining Company and the Wyoming Consolidated Mining Company* [Prospectus] (San Francisco: Stock Report, 1875); San Francisco *Mining and Scientific Press,* December 12, 1874; Independence *Inyo Independent,* January 16, 23, February 6, 1875; San Francisco *Alta California,* February 1, 1875.

20. San Francisco *Alta California,* January 30, February 1, 2, 1875; San Francisco *Chronicle,* January 30, 1875; Independence *Inyo Independent,* February 13, 1875.

21. Panamint *News,* March 6, 9, 1875; San Francisco *Mining and Scientific*

Press, April 24, May 1, 15, August 14, 1875; Independence, *Inyo Independent* May 22, 1875, June 24, 1882; New York *Graphic,* July 25, 1881.

22. Independence *Inyo Independent,* November 7, 21, December 19, 1874; Los Angeles *Herald,* November 10, December 16, 1874; Panamint *News,* November 26, 1874, March 6, 1875; San Francisco *Alta California,* February 1, 1875.

23. Independence *Inyo Independent,* November 10, 21, December 5, 1874, February 5, 1876; Panamint *News,* November 26, 1874, March 2, 6, 23, 27, April 24, 1875; Belmont *Courier,* January 23, 1875; San Francisco *Chronicle,* March 21, May 9, 1875; "Census of the Inhabitants of the State of Nevada, 1875," *Appendix to the Journal of the Senate and Assembly of the 8th Session of the Nevada State Legislature* (Carson City: State Printer, 1877), v. 2, 552.

24. Los Angeles *Express,* November 3, 20, 1874; San Bernardino *Guardian,* October 17, November 21, 1874; Independence *Inyo Independent,* October 31, November 7, December 12, 1874; Panamint *News,* November 26, 1874, February 27, March 6, 13, 18, 20, April 24, 1875; Richard E. Lingenfelter and Richard A. Dwyer, *The "Nonpareil" Press of T. S. Harris,* (Los Angeles: Glen Dawson, 1957), 11–26.

25. Austin *Reese River Reveille,* November 17, December 24, 1874; Independence *Inyo Independent,* July 25, December 19, 1874, February 6, March 6, April 24, 1875; Panamint *News,* February 25, March 23, 27, 1875.

26. Independence *Inyo Independent,* November 7, 1874; Panamint *News,* November 26, 1874.

27. Panamint *News,* March 9, May 18, 1875; San Francisco *Mining and Scientific Press,* January 2, May 8, 1875, March 18, 1876.

28. George M. Wheeler, *Annual Report Upon the Geographical Surveys West of the One Hundredth Meridian* (Washington, D.C.: Government Printing Office, 1876), 65–66; Independence *Inyo Independent,* December 5, 1874, January 2, 23, February 27, March 6, 1875, March 11, 1876; Panamint *News,* March 9, 1875; Harold O. Weight, "Emigrant Springs and the Lost Gunsight," *Desert Magazine, 41* (August 1978), 8–11, 39.

29. Independence *Inyo Independent,* February 19, 26, 1876; San Francisco *Mining and Scientific Press,* February 19, March 18, June 3, 1876; Darwin *Coso Mining News,* April 29, May 6, 1876; *Pacific Coast Annual Mining Review and Stock Ledger* (San Francisco: Francis and Valentine, October 1878), 31–32; Page, op. cit., n. 3.

30. Independence *Inyo Independent,* May 13, November 18, December 19, 1876, April 21, July 28, 1877; San Francisco *Mining and Scientific Press,* August 14, 1875, December 2, 1876, February 3, 17, April 7, June 23, September 8, October 27, December 22, 1877, March 30, May 25, June 8, 1878; Darwin *Coso Mining News,* May 12, 19, September 8, 1877; Bishop *Inyo Register* July 26, 1906; Phelps, op. cit., n. 10, 9–13; *Great Register of the County of Inyo, State of California, August 1st 1877* (Independence: Chalfant and Parker, 1877), 10, 11, 15; C. W. Ferguson, and R. A. Wright, "Tree-Ring Dates for Cutting Activity at the Charcoal Kilns,

Panamint Mountains, California," *Tree-Ring Bulletin, 24* (January 1962), 3–9; Robert J. Murphy, *Wildrose Charcoal Kilns* (Death Valley: Death Valley '49ers Inc., 1972), 23 pp.

31. Austin *Reese River Reveille,* July 30, August 13, 14, December 4, 5, 8, 1874, May 8, 1875; Eureka *Sentinel,* August 22, 1874, March 18, May 1, 7, 1875; Independence *Inyo Independent,* March 27, May 15, 1875, May 6, 1876. Wilson, op. cit., n. 1, 199–200, mistakenly assumes that Stewart arranged the Wells Fargo payoff for Small and McDonald, instead of the Gibbons gang, and invents an elaborate transaction.

32. Wheeler, op. cit., n. 28, 64; Independence *Inyo Independent,* July 17, December 11, 1875, April 28, 1877; Panamint *News,* February 25, March 2, 1875.

33. Independence *Inyo Independent,* November 21, December 12, 1874, February 27, 1875.

34. Panamint *News,* March 2, 1875; Independence *Inyo Independent,* December 26, 1874, May 22, September 4, October 9, 1875, March 4, 1876; San Francisco *Mining and Scientific Press,* August 22, 1874, June 5, August 7, September 25, October 9, 1875; San Francisco *Alta California,* February 1, 1875; San Diego *Union,* December 27, 1874, June 5, 1875; *Prospectus of the Panamint Mining and Concentration Works,* (San Francisco: Women's Print., 1875), 7 pp.

35. Panamint *News,* October 21, 1875; Independence *Inyo Independent,* July 10, September 11, 25, 1875; San Francisco *Mining and Scientific Press,* August 14, October 2, 1875.

36. Panamint *News,* October 21, 1875; Independence *Inyo Independent,* October 16, 1875, June 24, 1882; San Francisco *Mining and Scientific Press,* October 2, 1875; Los Angeles, *Mining Review,* November 11, 1905; Stewart, *Reminiscences . . .* op. cit., n. 4, 263–264; Stewart, "Panamint . . ." op. cit., n. 9.

37. *Emma Mine Investigation (49th Congress, 1st Session, House Report No. 579)* (Washington, D.C.: Government Printing Office, 1876), 141, 159, 184, 236, 459, 500, 553, 745, 802, 823, 868; *Congressional Record, 1st Session, 44th Congress* (May 25, 1876), 3337–3338; New York *Times,* March 3, 4, April 20, 22, May 3, 4, 26, 1876.

38. *Emma . . .* op. cit., n. 37, 868; San Bernardino *Times,* March 4, 18, 1876; Independence *Inyo Independent,* February 19, May 6, June 10, 1876; San Francisco *Mining and Scientific Press,* May 27, 1876; Los Angeles *Mining Review,* November 11, 1905.

39. Wilson, op. cit., n. 1, 294–296, fathered this fanciful catharsis, which has been repeated by many others, but contemporary records contradict it. Independence *Inyo Independent,* July 29, 1876, February 3, 1877; Darwin *Coso Mining News,* May 19, 1877.

40. Panamint *News,* October 21, 1875; Independence *Inyo Independent,* July 17, 1875, February 5, April 15, November 4, 1876; Henry G. Langley, *San Francisco Directory for the Year Commencing April 1874* (San Francisco: H. G. Langley, 1874), 548; Letters of Isaac Messic to his wife, April 21

and 23, 1876, in Death Valley National Monument Library; Darwin *Coso Mining News,* April 22, May 6, 1876; Bishop *Inyo Register,* March 30, 1933.

41. Independence *Inyo Independent,* June 10, 1876, June 30, December 8, 1877; San Francisco *Mining and Scientific Press,* May 27, 1876, January 20, December 22, 1877.

42. San Francisco *Alta California,* February 1, 1875; Independence *Inyo Independent,* January 23, 1874, July 10, 1875, November 1, 1879, June 24, 1882; San Diego *Union,* October 7, 1876, January 27, 1878; Page, op. cit., n. 3; Gorham, op. cit., n. 5, 109; Stewart, *Reminiscences . . .* op. cit., n. 4, 262–263; Panamint *News,* March 2, 1875; San Francisco *Mining and Scientific Press,* November 21, 1874, January 22, 1876; San Bernardino *Times,* March 4, 1876; Los Angeles *Mining Review,* November 11, 1905.

The Education of Jonas Osborne

1. San Francisco *Mining and Scientific Press,* February 15, 1868; Virginia City *Territorial Enterprise,* March, 3, 7, 1868.

2. Visalia *Delta,* June 23, October 6, 13, 1869, February 9, 16, May 11, 1870; *Biennial Report of the State Mineralogist of the State of Nevada for the Years 1871 and 1872* (Carson City: State Printer, 1872), 94–95; San Francisco *Alta California,* September 21, 1871; San Francisco *Mining and Scientific Press,* December 6, 1890. Erwin G. Gudde, *California Place Names* (Berkeley and Los Angeles: University of California Press, 3d ed., 1969), 66, erroneously attributes the name of Clark Mountain to a William Andrews Clark, who didn't come into the region until more than thirty years after the name came first into use.

3. San Bernardino *Guardian,* July 23, October 8, 1870, September 21, 1872, October 4, 1873; Los Angeles *Daily News,* May 23, 1872; Los Angeles *Herald,* January 24, 1874; Independence *Inyo Independent,* October 22, 1881.

4. San Bernardino *Guardian,* April 12, June 7, July 26, August 16, October 18, November 1, 1873; Bullfrog *Miner,* March 23, 1906; Beatty *Bullfrog Miner,* November 25, 1905.

5. Bodie *Free Press,* February 9, 1881; Aurora *Esmeralda Herald,* February 12, 1881; Candelaria *True Fissure,* May 21, 1881, July 31, 1886; Independence *Inyo Independent,* May 3, 1884; Belmont *Courier,* May 24, 1884; San Francisco *Mining and Scientific Press,* October 25, 1884; Beatty *Bullfrog Miner,* April 29, November 18, December 9, 1905, March 9, 1907.

6. San Bernardino *Times,* November 6, 1875, March 25, May 27, June 17, 1876; San Bernardino County Recorder, Deeds, Book O, 554, and Book R, 202; San Francisco *Mining and Scientific Press,* August 21, 1875; Theodore S. Palmer, *Places Names of the Death Valley Region in California and Nevada* (n.p.:1948), 13.

7. "Census of the Inhabitants of the State of Nevada, 1875," *Appendix to the*

Journal of the Senate and Assembly of the 8th Session of the Nevada State Legislature (Carson City: State Printer, 1877), v. 2, 287; Joseph S. Curtis, *Silver-Lead Deposits of Eureka, Nevada* (Washington, D.C.: Government Printing Office, 1884), 184; San Bernardino *Times,* February 26, March 25, October 7, December 17, 1876, February 3, 1877, March 16, April 20, 1878; Aurora *Esmeralda Herald,* January 5, 1878.

8.   San Bernardino *Times,* February 3, 1877, April 20, 1878; Independence *Inyo Independent,* June 23, 1877; San Bernardino County Recorder, Deeds Book R, 193, 200, and Book S, 274, 280; "Articles of Incorporation of the Los Angeles Mining and Smelting Company," May 22, 1877, California Secretary of State Archives, Sacramento.

9.   San Bernardino County Recorder, Deeds, Book R, 202; San Bernardino *Argus,* February 14, July 5, 1877, April 3, 1878; San Bernardino *Times,* February 2, May 25, August 24, 1878; Aurora *Esmeralda Herald,* January 5, 1878; Independence *Inyo Independent,* April 20, June 1, 1878.

10.   San Bernardino *Times,* March 9, April 24, May 25, 1878; Aurora *Esmeralda Herald,* April 13, 1878; Independence *Inyo Independent,* June 1, 1878, August 9, 1879; San Francisco *Mining and Scientific Press,* February 19, 1881.

11.   San Bernardino *Times,* May 25, 1878, January 11, February 22, 1879; San Francisco *Mining and Scientific Press,* September 14, 1878, March 1, 1879; Independence *Inyo Independent,* July 5, August 9, 1879; Henry G. Langley, *The San Francisco Directory for the Year Commencing February 1878* (San Francisco: Francis, Valentine and Co., 1878), 429.

12.   San Bernardino *Times,* January 11, 25, 1879; Independence *Inyo Independent,* August 9, 1879, June 19, 1880; Walter N. Frickstad, *A Century of California Post Offices 1848 to 1954* (Oakland: Philatelic Research Society, 1955), 53, 146–147.

13.   Independence *Inyo Independent,* July 5, August 9, 1879.

14.   San Bernardino *Times,* July 26, August 16, September 20, 1879; Independence *Inyo Independent,* July 5, November 8, 1879.

15.   San Bernardino *Times,* November 25, 1879; San Francisco *Mining and Scientific Press,* February 19, 1881; Independence *Inyo Independent,* July 30, 1881.

16.   Independence *Inyo Independent,* February 14, June 12, 19, August 7, 14, October 30, November 6, 1880; San Francisco *Mining and Scientific Press,* February 19, 1881; Bishop *Inyo Register,* December 7, 1893.

17.   San Bernardino *Times,* April 30, May 4, 1880.

18.   San Francisco *Mining and Scientific Press,* February 17, 1881; Independence *Inyo Independent,* May 21, July 19, 30, 1881; *Report of the Director of the Mint Upon the Production of the Precious Metals in the United States in the Calendar Year 1883* (Washington, D.C.: Government Printing Office, 1884), 166.

19.   San Bernardino County Recorder, Deeds, Book R, 354; U.S. Patent Office, *Official Gazette, 37* (1886), 631–632; Los Angeles *Mining Review,* March 25, 1899, January 12, 1901, July 7, 1906; San Francisco *Mining and*

Scientific Press, January 26, 1901; Rhyolite *Bullfrog Miner*, September 7, 1907; Bishop *Inyo Register*, Octrober 24, 1907; Beatty *Bullfrog Miner*, November 9, 1907; R. J. Sampson, "Mineral Resources of the Resting Springs Region, Inyo County," *California Division of Mines Report, 33* (1937), 264–270.

On The New York Exchange

1. Columbus *Borax Miner*, March 17, 24, 1877; Aurora *Esmeralda Herald*, November 3, 1877, January 18, 1879, September 4, 1880, February 18, 1882; Candelaria *True Fissure*, June 26, December 4, 1880, May 14, 1881; Francis B. Heitman, *Historical Register and Dictionary of the United States Army* (Washington, D.C.: Government Printing Office, 1903), v. 2, 101.

2. San Francisco *Mining and Scientific Press*, May 3, 1879; Independence *Inyo Independent*, May 3, 31, August 23, November 1, December 6, 1879, February 6, March 13, 1880, February 5, 1881; Denver *Tribune*, April 8, 1882; New York *Times*, April 2, 3, 1882.

3. San Bernardino *Times*, February 29, July 5, August 16, 1879; Independence *Inyo Independent*, November 22, December 6, 1879; Inyo County Recorder, Deeds, Book J, 541–543; Marshall Robinson, *Sketches in Prose and Rhyme* (Carson City: Daily Index Print, 1888), 10–11; Walter N. Frickstad, *A Century of California Post Offices, 1848–1954* (Oakland: Philatelic Research Society, 1955), 51; *Rand, McNally & Co.'s Indexed Atlas of the World* (Chicago: Rand, McNally & Co., 1882), 892; Bryan, Taylor & Co., *The People's Illustrative and Descriptive Family Atlas of the World* (New York: Bryan, Taylor and Co., 1891), 103.

4. Independence *Inyo Independent*, May 20, December 9, 1882, March 24, April 7, June 2, 1883, April 19, May 3, 1884, September 26, 1885, February 7, 1890; San Francisco *Mining and Scientific Press*, June 2, July 14, 1883, March 22, October 25, 1884; *Report of the Director of the Mint Upon the Production of the Precious Metals in the United States During the Calendar Year 1883* (Washington, D.C.: Government Printing Office, 1884), 166–167; California State Mining Bureau, *Ninth Annual Report of the State Mineralogist for the Year Ending December 1, 1889* (Sacramento: Supt. State Printing, 1890), 238–239, and *Tenth Annual Report . . . December 1, 1890* (Sacramento: Supt. State Printing, 1890), 213; Henry G. Langley, *The San Francisco Directory for the Year Commencing April 1882*, (San Francisco: Francis Valentine & Co., 1882), 780. See also John A. Latschar, *Historic Resource Study: A History of Mining in Death Valley National Monument, Volume II* (Denver: National Park Service, 1981), 693–699.

5. *Pacific Coast Annual Mining Review and Stock Ledger* (San Francisco: Francis and Valentine, October 1878), 48–49; San Francisco *Examiner*, December 25, 1901; New York *Engineering and Mining Journal*, January 4,

1902; Reno *Nevada Mining News,* June 18, 1908; San Francisco *Mining and Engineering Review,* June 15, December 15, 1900; William R. Balch, *The Mines, Miners and Mining Interests of the United States in 1882* (Philadelphia: Mining Industrial Pub. Bureau, 1882), 476–482; *The New York Mining Directory* (New York: Hollister & Goddard, 1880), 106, 110; Asbury Harpending, *The Great Diamond Hoax and Other Stirring Incidents in the Life of Asbury Harpending* (San Francisco: James H. Barry Co., 1913), 195–264; Bruce A. Woodard, *Diamonds in the Salt* (Boulder: Pruett Press, 1967). One has to read between the lines in the last two.

6. New York *Engineering and Mining Journal,* August 7, 1880; Richard E. Lingenfelter, *The Handrock Miners: A History of the Mining Labor Movement on the American West, 1863–1893* (Berkeley, Los Angeles, and London: University of California Press, 1974), 143–156.

7. Aurora *Esmeralda Herald,* September 4, 1880; Candelaria *True Fissure,* October 2, 1880; New York *Engineering and Mining Journal,* October 30, 1880; New York *Mining Review,* November 20, 1880, January 29, 1881; Independence *Inyo Independent,* January 15, November 12, 1881; Balch, op. cit., n. 5, 476; *Pacific Coast Annual . . .* op. cit., n. 5, 74–75.

8. New York *Bullion,* November 1, 1880; Independence *Inyo Independent,* November 13, 1880, January 15, May 28, 1881; Candelaria *True Fissure,* February 26, May 7, 1881; New York *Engineering and Mining Journal,* May 28, 1881; Clark C. Spence, *The Mining Engineers & the American West, The Lace-Boot Brigade, 1849–1933* (New Haven: Yale Univ. Press, 1970), 101, 133; Rodman W. Paul, *Mining Frontiers of the Far West, 1848–1880* (New York: Holt, Rinehart and Winston, 1963), 152–153; *Dictionary of American Biography* (New York: Scribner, 1933), v. 12, 163–164.

9. Aurora *Esmeralda Herald,* December 11, 1880, April 9, 16, 1881; Independence *Inyo Independent,* January 1, 15, 1881; Candelaria *True Fissure,* April 9, 16, May 7, 1881.

10. Aurora *Esmeralda Herald,* October 16, 1880, January 29, February 19, October 8, 1881; Independence *Inyo Independent,* February 5, 1881; Candelaria *True Fissure,* March 5, April 2, 30, 1881; New York *Daily Graphic,* May 28, 1881.

11. New York *Bullion,* November 1, 1880; Candelaria *True Fissure,* January 8, March 5, April 16, 30, May 14, 21, 28, 1881; Aurora *Esmeralda Herald,* February 19, March 26, May 7, 1881.

12. New York *Engineering and Mining Journal,* March 26, May 14, 21, 28, June 18, 1881; New York *Mining Record,* April 30, June 4, 1881; *State Line Gold Mining Company No. 1,* fifty share stock certificate #A996 (issued May 25, 1881), *No. 2* #A211 (May 10, 1881), *No. 4,* #A217 (May 17, 1881) and #A963 (May 26, 1881), *Oriental Gold Mining Company* #A524 (May 24, 1881), Collection of Ken Prag, Burlingame, Calif.

13. New York *Engineering and Mining Journal,* May 28, July 2, 1881; Independence *Inyo Independent,* June 11, July 23, 1881; *State Line . . .* op. cit., n. 12; Lingenfelter, op. cit., n. 6, 143–156.

14. New York *Daily Graphic,* May 28, 1881; New York *Tribune,* June 4, 13,

1881; New York *Engineering and Mining Journal,* June 18, July 2, August 6, 1881; Independence *Inyo Independent,* July 9, 1881; Candelaria, *True Fissure,* July 16, 1881.

15. New York *Engineering and Mining Journal,* June 18, July 16, August 6, 1881; Independence *Inyo Independent,* July 16, 1881; *State Line Gold Mining Company No. 1,* #A2993 (July 23, 1881), *No. 2,* #A3116 (July 26, 1881), *No. 4,* #A2706 (July 27, 1881), *Oriental Gold Mining Company,* #A3005 (August 10, 1881), Collection of Ken Prag, Burlingame, Calif.

16. New York *Engineering and Mining Journal,* August 6, 13, 20, 27, 1881; Rossiter Johnson, ed., *The Twentieth Century Biographical Dictionary of Notable Americans* (Boston: The Biographical Society, 1904), v. 1 (unpaged).

17. Independence *Inyo Independent,* September 17, October 22, November 12, 19, December 17, 1881, January 7, 1882; New York *Engineering and Mining Journal,* December 3, 10, 1881, February 18, 1882, February 10, 1883; New York *Mining Record,* November 19, 1881, January 7, 1882; Candelaria *True Fissure,* January 14, 1882; Aurora *Esmeralda Herald,* February 18, 1882.

18. Candelaria *True Fissure,* July 22, 1882, May 19, 1883, October 2, 1885; New York *Engineering and Mining Journal,* October 6, 1883, November 22, 1884.

19. New York *Engineering and Mining Journal,* July 2, 1881, February 4, 1882.

20. New York *Mining Record,* November 26, December 31, 1881; Reno *Nevada Mining News,* June 18, 1908; San Francisco *Examiner,* December 25, 1901; San Francisco *Chronicle,* December 25, 1901.

21. San Francisco *Alta California,* April 10, 1875; San Francisco *Chronicle,* July 29, August 21, 26, 1875; New York *Times,* August 26, October 2, 5, 1875, May 6, 8, 26, June 2, 10, September 15, 1877; New York *Tribune,* May 8, 10, 1877, February 14, 1879; John P. Young, *Journalism in California* (San Francisco: Chronicle Publishing Co., 1915), 84–89.

22. Independence *Inyo Independent,* September 25, 1875, May 15, 1880, April 23, 1881; New York *Graphic,* July 25, 1881; New York *Engineering and Mining Journal,* April 1, 1882; *The National Cyclopaedia of American Biography* (New York: James T. White & Co.), v. 3, (1893), 171–172.

23. New York *Graphic,* July 25, 1881; New York *Engineering and Mining Journal,* September 3, 17, October 15, 1881; Independence *Inyo Independent,* December 23, 1882.

24. Independence *Inyo Independent,* October 15, 29, November 12, 1881, January 7, June 24, 1882, May 12, 1883; New York *Engineering and Mining Journal,* May 5, 1883; Pioche *Record,* May 12, 1883.

25. Independence *Inyo Independent,* June 24, July 15, 1882; New York *Engineering and Mining Journal,* April 1, 1882; New York *Times,* November 16, 1882.

26. Independence *Inyo Independent,* June 24, July 22, September 16, November 4, December 23, 1882, January 6, 1883; New York *Engineering and Mining Journal,* April 8, October 21, 1882.

27. Independence *Inyo Independent,* December 23, 1882, January 6, March 3,

May 12, 1883; New York *Engineering and Mining Journal,* May 5, 1883.

28. New York *Engineering and Mining Journal,* May 5, 1883; Independence *Inyo Independent,* May 12, 1883; Bishop *Inyo Register,* August 20, 1885.

29. Independence *Inyo Independent,* September 5, November 14, 1885, August 21, November 27, December 11, 1886, December 10, 1887, March 24, 1888, May 25, 1889.

30. Ibid., May 13, 1876; New York Stock Exchange, Committee on Admissions, Hearing Transcripts, v. 12, June 3, 11, 17, 1880, and Copartnership Directory, v. 1, in NYSE Archives & Corporation Research Center, New York; San Bernardino County Recorder, Deeds Book 22, 446; New York *Graphic,* February 11, 1882; *The New York Stock Exchange* (New York: Historical Publishing Co., 1886), 73; New York *Times,* December 10, 11, 22, 1886, May 21, 28, June 5, 1889, April 8, 1896.

31. San Bernardino County Recorder, Deeds Book 26, 82–87, Book 27, 188–189; New York *Indicator,* November 10, 1881, quoted in San Bernardino *Times,* June 3, 1882; New York *Times,* January 15, 1882; New York *Engineering and Mining Journal,* November 5, 19, December 24, 31, 1881, January 21, April 22, 1882, February 10, 1883; *South Pacific Mining Co.,* 100 share certificates No. 1172 (November 10, 1881), 2302 (January 5, 1882), 3578 (January 11, 1882), and 4480 (May 20, 1882) Collection of Ken Prag, Burlingame, Calif.; San Francisco *Exchange,* January 31, 1882.

32. New York *Graphic,* January 14, 25, February 3, 10, 17, 1882; New York *Tribune,* January 14, 1882; New York *Times,* January 15, February 4, 1882.

33. New York *Tribune,* January 14, 1882; New York *Times,* January 15, 1882; San Bernardino *Times,* June 3, 1882.

34. New York *Engineering and Mining Journal,* November 5, 1881; San Francisco *Exchange,* November 23, 1881, January 28, 31, 1882; New York *Mining Record,* December 10, 1881; New York *Daily Stockholder,* quoted in New York *Graphic,* February 11, 1882.

35. New York *Engineering and Mining Journal,* May 6, 14, 20, 1882, June 9, 1883; San Bernardino *Times,* June 3, 1882; San Bernardino County, Superior Court, Case No. 410, Thomas E. Williams et al. v. South Pacific Mining Co.; August 4, 1883; New York *Times,* December 11, 1886; Copartnership Directory, v. 1, op. cit., n. 30; *The National Cyclopaedia of American Biography* (New York: James T. White & Co.), v. 11 (1901), 10–11.

"Starving to Death on a Government Claim"

1. Richard E. Lingenfelter, Richard A. Dwyer, and David Cohen, *Songs of the American West* (Berkeley and Los Angeles: University of California Press, 1968), 457–459; Panamint *News,* November 26, 1874, March 2, 1875; Candelaria *True Fissure,* January 8, 1881; Bishop *Inyo Register,* February 19, 1891; Orin S. Merrill, *"Mysterious Scott," The Monte Cristo of Death Valley and Tracks of a Tenderfoot* (Chicago: Merrill, 1906), 163.

2. Julian H. Steward, *Basin-Plateau Aboriginal Sociopolitical Groups* (Washington, D.C.: Government Printing Office, 1938), 94–97, 180–184; George M. Wheeler, *Preliminary Report Concerning Explanations and Surveys Principally in Nevada and Arizona* (Washington, D.C.: Government Printing Office, 1872), map; *Biennial Report of the State of Mineralogist of the State of Nevada for the Years 1871 and 1872* (Carson City: State Printer, 1872), 9, 96.

3. John R. Spears, *Illustrated Sketches of Death Valley and Other Borax Deserts of the Pacific Coast* (Chicago: Rand McNally & Co., 1892), 24–26.

4. W. A. Chalfant, *The Story of Inyo* (Bishop: Chalfant, 1922), 280; W. A. Chalfant, *Death Valley, The Facts* (Stanford: Stanford University Press, 1930), 46; Federal Writers' Project, *Death Valley, A Guide* (Boston: Houghton Mifflin Co., 1939), 30; Carl B. Glasscock, *Here's Death Valley* (Indianapolis: Bobbs-Merrill Co., 1940), 112; Edwin Corle, *Desert Country* (New York: Duell, Sloan & Pearce, 1941), 283–285; George Palmer Putnam, *Death Valley and Its Country* (New York: Duell, Sloan and Pearce, 1946), 48–49; William Caruthers, *Loafing Along Death Valley Trails* (Palm Desert: Desert Magazine Press, 1951), 22–23; W. Storrs Lee, *The Great California Deserts* (New York: G. P. Putnam's Sons, 1963), 127–129; Paul Bailey, *An Unnatural History of Death Valley* (Bishop: Chalfant Press, 1978), 41–49.

5. *Copy of the Great Register of Inyo County for 1875* (Independence: Inyo Independent, 1875), 9; Independence *Inyo Independent,* December 19, 1874, August 9, 1879; Pioche *Record,* December 15, 19, 1874; George M. Wheeler, *Geographical Explorations and Surveys West of the 100th Meridian, Atlas Sheet No. 65 (D)* (New York: Graphic Co., 1877).

6. Independence *Inyo Independent,* February 5, 1876; Pioche *Record,* August 12, October 3, December 3, 1875, November 26, 1876, October 16, 1880; San Bernardino *Times,* April 24, 27, July 3, 17, October 2, 1880; Colton *Semi-Tropic,* May 1, 1880; *Great Register of San Bernardino County for 1888,* (San Bernardino: 1888), #1701–1704.

7. *Copy of the Great Register* … op. cit., n. 5, 9; Wheeler, *Geographical Explorations … Atlas Sheet No. 65 (D)* … op. cit., n. 5; George M. Wheeler, *Annual Report Upon the Geographical Surveys West of the One-Hundredth Meridian* (Washington, D.C.: Government Printing Office, 1876), 132; Independence *Inyo Independent,* May 31, August 9, 1879; Bakersfield *Southern Californian and Kern County Weekly Courier,* April 18, 25, 1878, May 29, June 5, 1879; Bishop *Inyo Register,* May 14, 1896; William H. Boyd, *A California Middle Border: The Kern River Country, 1772–1880* (Richardson, Tex.: Havilah Press, 1972), 159.

8. Independence *Inyo Independent,* May 2, 1874, July 17, 1875, April 14, 1888, August 6, 1897, March 30, 1900; Capt. A. B. MacGowan, "Itinerary of Scouts made by Co. 'D' 12th U.S. Infantry during May, June, July and August 1875," San Francisco, August 21, 1875, in National Archives, Record Group 393; Aurora *Esmeralda Herald,* November 1, 1879; Bishop *Inyo Register,* May 8, June 19, December 25, 1890; San Francisco *Examiner,* January 11, 1891; Goldfield *Review,* November 9, 1905; Los

Angeles *Examiner,* November 23, 1938; Linda Greene, *Historic Resource Study, A History of Mining in Death Valley National Monument* (Denver: National Park Service, 1981), v. I, 765–768.

9.   Panamint *News,* March 9, 1875; Myron Angel and M. D. Fairchild, *History of Placer County* (Oakland: Thompson and West, 1882), 112; Wheeler, *Preliminary Report . . .* op. cit., n. 2, 84; Austin *Reese River Reveille,* October 13, 1871; Independence *Inyo Independent,* November 25, 1871; Pioche *Record,* March 4, 1873; Myron Angel, *History of Nevada* (Oakland: Thompson and West, 1881), 582.

10.   Pioche *Record,* March 4, 1873; Wheeler, *Geographical Explorations Atlas Sheet No. 66 . . .* op. cit., no. 5; Panamint *News,* November 26, 1874, March 27, 1875; Angel, op. cit., n. 9, 604.

11.   National Archives, Record Group 29, Tenth Census of the United States 1880, Lincoln County, Nevada, Ash Meadows, Enumeration District 59, 3; Pomona *Times-Courier,* April 10, 17, 1886 account of trip by T. W. Brooks, reprinted and edited by Anthony L. Lehman in *By Buckboard to Beatty, The California-Nevada Desert in 1886* (Los Angeles: Dawson's Book Shop, 1970), 8, 13, 38, 40; Independence *Inyo Independent,* October 12, 1894, June 26, 1903, June 30, 1904; Bishop *Inyo Register,* June 2, 1898 (tax list); Spears, op. cit., n. 3, 24, 62, 141; John R. Spears, "Through Death Valley," *California Illustrated Magazine, 3* (February 1893), 314–315; Walter C. Mendenhall, *Some Desert Watering Places in Southern California and Southwestern Nevada* (Washington, D.C.: Government Printing Office, 1909) (USGS Water-Supply Paper 224), 39–40; San Bernardino *Sun-Telegram,* November 15, 22, 1959.

12.   San Bernardino *Times,* May 27, 1876; Pioche *Record,* November 29, 1876; Candelaria *True Fissure,* May 12, 1881; Nye County Recorder, Deeds Book L, 104–105; Tenth Census . . . op. cit., n. 11; Independence *Inyo Independent,* August 9, 1879, May 19, 1883, June 30, 1904; Bureau of Land Management, Survey Plates of T17SR50E, T18SR50E, and T18SR51E, all filed February 18, 1882; Spears, *Illustrated Sketches . . .* op. cit., n. 3, 58–62; Lehman, op. cit., n. 11, xiii–xiv, 6, 8, 17–18, 30.

13.   Spears, *Illustrated Sketches . . .* op. cit., n. 3, 60, 84–86; Pioche *Record,* May 13, 1882; National Archives, Record Group 123, Indian Depredation Claim 3352, Joseph Yount v. the United States, July 17, 1891 (copy courtesy of Dennis G. Casebier); John Doherty, "The History of the Settling of the Manse Ranch and Territory," n.d., 6 pp. typescript, Nevada Historical Society, Reno; Belmont *Courier,* January 26, 1886, December 10, 1887, December 9, 1891; Beatty *Bullfrog Miner,* September 23, November 11, 1905, January 19, 1907; Bishop *Owens Valley Herald,* May 13, 1910; Lehman, op. cit., n. 11, 9–12; Mendenhall, op. cit., n. 11, 91–92.

14.   Belmont *Courier,* September 14, 1895, December 25, 1897; Inyo County Recorder, Deeds Book I, 645–646, Ah Foo to R. D. Morrison, April 16, 1900; Mendenhall, op. cit., n. 11, 40–41.

15.   San Jose *Pioneer,* January 15, 1895; Belmont *Courier,* September 12, 1896; Tonopah *Miner,* July 15, 1905; Rhyolite *Herald,* December 22, 1905, August 19, 1908; Independence *Inyo Independent,* February 9, 1906; Beatty

Bullfrog Miner, November 3, 1906; Rhyolite *Bullfrog Miner,* December 19, 1908; Rhyolite *Daily Bulletin,* October 7, December 15, 1908; Bishop *Owens Valley Herald,* December 25, 1908; *Great Register, County of Inyo . . . 1882* (Independence: Inyo Independent, 1882), 1 #65; Promissory Note, July 3, 1906 by Montillion Murray Beatty et al., manuscript and oral interview with M. M. Beatty, Jr., November 1, 1968, tape recording, both in Nevada Historical Society, Reno.

16. *Copy of the Great Register of Inyo County, California [1890],* (Independence: Inyo Independent, 1890), #546; Pioche *Record,* October 14, 1882, March 3, 1883, May 17, 1884, November 20, 27, December 4, 11, 27, 1886, September 28, 1888; Belmont *Courier,* November 30, 1889, December 17, 1892, October 5, 1895; Salt Lake City *Tribune,* September 10, 12, October 16, 1895; Bishop *Inyo Register,* February 27, 1896; Tonopah *Sun,* August 13, 1905; Tonopah *Nevada Mining Record,* July 28, 1928; Tonopah *Mining Record,* July 28, 1928; C. B. Glasscock, *Gold in Them Hills, The Story of the West's Last Wild Mining Days* (Indianapolis: Bobbs-Merrill Co., 1932), 212–216.

17. *Biennial Report . . .* op. cit., n. 2, 8–9; Panamint *News,* November 26, 1874, March 2, 1875 (market prices); Candelaria *True Fissure,* January 8, 1881; San Francisco *Mining and Scientific Press,* August 16, 1890; Belmont *Courier,* May 24, June 21, 1890; Beatty *Bullfrog Miner,* June 12, 1905.

18. *Biennial Report . . .* op. cit., n. 2, 9; Belmont *Courier,* January 2, December 4, 1886, December 19, 1891, December 17, 1892, December 15, 1894, December 25, 1897 (tax lists); Lehman, op. cit., n. 11, 12, 16.

19. San Bernardino *Times,* June 1, 1880; Pioche *Record,* May 13, 1882; Independence *Inyo Independent,* May 20, 1882; Belmont *Courier,* May 19, 1888; Bureau of Land Management, Survey Plat of T20SR53E filed May 14, 1882; Mendenhall, op. cit., n. 11, 91–92; Dougherty, op. cit., n. 13, 5.

20. Belmont *Courier,* December 19, 1891; Dougherty, op. cit., n. 13, 4–5; Spears, *Illustrated Sketches . . .* op. cit., n. 3, 56–57.

21. Spears, *Illustrated Sketches . . .* op. cit., n. 3, 56–57.

22. Belmont *Courier,* November 8, 1884.

23. Independence *Inyo Independent,* May 20, 1882, April 24, 1891, March 31, 1905, March 2, 1906; Spears *Illustrated Sketches . . .* op. cit., n. 3, 58–62; Belmont *Courier,* May 2, 1891; Dougherty, op. cit., n. 13, 6; Tonopah *Bonanza,* February 17, 1906; Greenwater *Death Valley Chuck-Walla,* June 1907; San Francisco *Call,* December 15, 1907; Rhyolite *Bullfrog Miner,* August 8, 1908; Dane Coolidge, *Death Valley Prospectors* (New York: E. P. Dutton & Co., 1937), 29–37.

24. Pioche *Record,* February 25, May 5, 26, June 2, 16, November 10, December 1, 1888, January 19, March 9, April 27, 1889, January 4, May 10, July 12, 1890, January 29, 1891, February 11, 25, 1892, March 2, 1893, June 21, 1894, September 12, 1895, December 29, 1898; Belmont *Courier,* May 19, December 8, 1888, November 30, 1889, May 24, June 20, December 6, 1890, December 19, 1891, December 17, 1892, December 23, 1893, December 15, 1894; Independence *Inyo Independent,* June 30, October 27, November 24, 1888, April 20, May 18, 25, June 1, 1889; San

Diego *Union,* August 14, 1888, May 21, 22, 1889; A. Russell Crowell, *Miners' Map of Death Valley, the Mojave, Amargosa and Nevada Deserts* (Manvel: 1903 Revised Las Vegas: 1905); David F. Myrick, *Railroads of Nevada and Eastern California* (Berkeley: Howell-North Books, 1963), 623–625.

25. "Census of the Inhabitants of the State of Nevada, 1875," *Appendix to the Journal of the Senate and Assembly of the 8th Session of the Nevada State Legislature,* (Carson City: State Printer, 1877), v. 2, 759; Virginia City *Territorial Enterprise,* January 22, 1867; Belmont *Silver Bend Reporter,* August 24, 1867; Belmont *Courier,* October 30, 1880; Angel, op. cit., n. 9, 347, 515–516; Reno *Nevada State Journal,* January 9, 1891; Bishop *Inyo Register,* March 31, 1892, May 14, 1896, August 12, 1897, July 15, 1909; C. H. Sinclair, "The Oblique Boundary Line Between California and Nevada," Appendix No. 3., *Report of the Superintendent of the Coast and Geodetic Survey 1899–1900* (Washington, D.C.: Government Printing Office, 1901), 304, 322; Mendenhall, op. cit., n. 11, 31; Hank Johnston, *Death Valley Scotty, "The Fastest Con in the West,"* (Corona del Mar: Trans-Anglo Books, 1974), 98; Greene, op. cit., n. 8, 771, 773.

Borax Bonanza

1. Further material on early borax mining in Death Valley and elsewhere in the West can be found in Harold O. Weight, *Twenty Mule Team Days in Death Valley* (Twentynine Palms, Calif.: Calico Press, 1955), 44 pp.; F. Ross Holland, Jr., and Robert V. Simmonds, *Eagle Borax Works, Harmony Borax Works, Death Valley National Monument, California* (San Francisco: National Park Service, Office of History and Historic Architecture, 1971), 53 pp.; Ruth C. Woodman and Ann Rosener, *Story of the Pacific Coast Borax Co.* (Los Angeles: Ward Ritchie, 1951), 58 pp.; Ruth C. Woodman, "History of Pacific Borax Company," 929 pp. manuscript in Ruth C. Woodman Papers, Special Collections Library, University of Oregon; W. E. Ver Planck, "History of Borax Production in the United States," *California Journal of Mines and Geology,* 52 (1956), 273–291; Linda W. Greene, *Historic Resource Study: A History of Mining in Death Valley National Monument, Volume I* (Denver: National Park Service, 1981), 976–989; George H. Hildebrand, *Borax Pioneer: Francis Marion Smith* (San Diego: Howell-North Books, 1982), 318 pp. and Norman J. Travis and E. J. Cocks, *The Tincal Trail, A History of Borax* (London: Harrap, 1984), 38–59. Annual production figures are summarized in *Mineral Resources of the United States . . . 1916,* pt. II, 387 and . . . *1927,* pt. I, A81. Death Valley reserves are discussed in Clarence Wendel, *Special Report on Borate Resources* (San Francisco: National Park Service, Mining and Minerals Division, 1978), 138 pp.

2. Independence *Inyo Independent,* April 19, May 10, 1873; San Francisco *Mining and Scientific Press,* November 22, 1873.

3. Independence *Inyo Independent,* February 3, 1877, November 26, 1881; *Great Register of the County of Inyo . . . August 1st, 1877* (Independence: Chalfant and Parker, 1877), 23; John R. Spears, *Illustrated Sketches of Death Valley and Other Borax Deserts of the Pacific Coast* (Chicago: Rand McNally & Co., 1892), 58–59.

4. Spears, op. cit., n. 3, 58–59.

5. Death Valley Borax and Salt Mining District [Record Book], Borax Museum, Death Valley National Monument; By-Laws of Death Valley Borax and Salt Mining District, in Inyo County Recorder, Land, Water and Mining Claims Book D, 345–349 and Claims Book C, 314–318; Independence *Inyo Independent,* February 4, April 15, 1882; Spears, op. cit., n. 3, 60; Greene, op. cit., n. 1, 1033–1036.

6. Eagle Mountain Borax and Salt Mining District, Vol. A, Borax Musuem, Death Valley National Monument; Independence *Inyo Independent,* April 15, 1882; Spears, op. cit., n. 3, 61.

7. Pioche *Record,* May 13, September 2, October 14, 1882, March 5, 1887; Belmont *Courier,* October 10, 1885, December 10, 1887; Spears, op. cit., n. 3, 61–62; Los Angeles *Mining Review,* October 21, 1899.

8. Organization and Laws of Monte Blanco Borax and Salt Mining District, copy courtesy of Linda Greene; Inyo County Recorder, Land, Water and Mining Claims Book D, 299–300, Notice of Location, Biddy McCarthy, February 2, 1883 and Book E, 145–146, Notice of Locaton, Lila C., February 9, 1884; Henry G. Hanks, *Report on the Borax Deposits of California and Nevada* (Sacramento: James J. Ayers, Supt. State Printing, 1883), 86–87; Spears, op. cit., n. 3, 62, 192–193; Wendel, op. cit., n. 1, 26; Woodman, op. cit., n. 1, Chap IV, 49–50; Greene, op. cit., n. 1, 1031.

9. Henry G. Langley, *San Francisco Directory for the Year . . . 1862 [through] 1884* (San Francisco: publisher varies, 1862–1884); Independence *Inyo Independent,* October 23, 1880; San Francisco *Alta California,* May 30, 1884; San Francisco *Chronicle,* May 30, 1884; Hanks, op. cit., n. 8, 33.

10. Independent *Inyo Independent,* June 24, September 2, 1882, May 5, 1883; San Francisco *Alta California,* May 30, 1884; Hanks, op. cit., n. 8, 36–37, 80; Inyo County Recorder, Land, Water and Mining Claims Book C, 487–488, Book D, 22–25, and Deeds Book M, 575–577.

11. Calico *Print,* October 21, 1882; Independence *Inyo Independent,* January 20, May 5, 1883; Hanks, op. cit., n. 8, 36–37; Holland and Simmonds, op. cit., n. 1, 47–48; Ed Stiles, "Saga of the Twenty-Mule Team," *Westways, 31* (December 1939), 8.

12. Articles of Incorporation of the Eagle Borax Mining Company, June 27, 1883, California Secretary of State, Archives, Sacramento; Independence *Inyo Independent,* May 5, July 14, 1883; Hanks, op. cit., n. 8, 37; Candelaria *True Fissure,* May 10, 1884; San Francisco *Stock Report,* May 29, 1884, clipping in William L. Locke's Scrapbook, 11–12, Locke Papers in Bancroft Library; San Francisco *Alta California,* May 30, 1884; Langley, op. cit. . . . 1882, n. 9, 420 and *1885,* 379, 499.

13. San Francisco *Stock Report,* May 29, 1884, clipping op. cit., n. 12; San Francisco *Alta California,* May 30, 1884.

14. Alonzo Phelps, *Contemporary Biography of California's Representative Men* (San Francisco: A. L. Bancroft & Co., 1881), 272–280; Hubert Howe Bancroft, *Chronicles of the Builders of the Commonwealth* (San Francisco: The History Co., 1891), v. 1, 301–391; A. S. Hallidie, "William T. Coleman," *Overland Monthly, 23* (1894), 71–75; *The National Cyclopaedia of American Biography* (New York: James T. White & Co., 1898), v. 8, 336; James A. B. Scherer, *"The Lion of the Vigilantes" William T. Coleman and the Life of Old San Francisco* (Indianapolis: Bobbs-Merrill Co., 1939), 335 pp.; New York *Engineering and Mining Journal,* February 5, 1876, December 22, 1877; Columbus *Borax Miner,* November 11, 1876; Aurora *Esmeralda Herald,* July 20, 1878; Candelaria *True Fissure,* December 4, 1880.

15. Articles of Incorporation of the Amargosa Borax Company, February 24, 1883; California Chemical Company, November 28, 1884; Greenland Borax Company, March 6, 1883; Harmony Borax Mining Company, May 15, 1884; Harmony Mining Company, March 30, 1883; Henry Clay Mining Company, March 30, 1883; Meridian Borax Company, November 10, 1884; and Meridian Mining Company, April 2, 1883, California Secretary of State, Archives, Sacramento; Langley, op. cit. . . . *1883,* n. 9; Independence *Inyo Independent,* June 23, July 7, 1883; Locke's Scrapbook, op. cit., n. 12, 10.

16. "Census of the Inhabitants of the State of Nevada, 1875," *Appendix to the Journal of the Senate and Assembly of the 8th Session of the Nevada State Legislature* (Carson City: State Printer, 1877), v. 2, 87; Columbus *Borax Miner,* August 21, 1875; Death Valley Borax and Salt Mining District, op. cit., n. 5; William T. Coleman's letter to D. W. Earl & Co., March 14, 1883, Mojave River Valley Museum, Barstow, quoted in Patricia Jernigan Keeling, ed., *Once Upon a Desert* (Barstow: Mojave River Valley Musuem Assoc., 1976), 101–102; Langley, op. cit. . . . *1881,* n. 9, 754.

17. Independence *Inyo Independent,* January 20, April 7, 1883, May 3, 1884, March 31, 1888; Bishop *Inyo Register,* March 29, 1888; Coleman to Earl op. cit., n. 16; R. Neuschwander's letter to D. W. Earl & Co., February 22, 1883, Mojave River Valley Musuem, quoted in Keeling, op. cit., n. 16, 106; Hanks, op. cit., n. 8, 32, 36–37; Spears, op. cit., n. 3, 27.

18. Independence *Inyo Independent,* May 3, October 18, 1884; Bishop *Inyo Register,* March 29, April 3, 1888; Candelaria *True Fissure,* July 29, 1882; San Francisco *Chronicle,* January 25, 1891; George A. Teague and Lynette O. Shenk, *Excavations at Harmony Borax Works* (Tucson: Western Archeological Center, 1977), 50, 71, 75, 179–181, 186–190.

19. Independence *Inyo Independent,* May 3, 1884, March 31, 1888; San Francisco *Mining and Scientific Press,* June 21, 1884; Coleman to Earl, op. cit., n. 16, Coleman Daybook [Store Ledger], Borax Museum, Death Valley National Monument; Journal Death Valley, Journal Amargosa, and Ledger in U.S. Borax Co. Account Books in Bancroft Library; Arthur J. Burdick, *The Mystic Mid-Region, the Deserts of the Southwest* (New York: G. P. Putnam's Sons, 1904), 150.

20. Journal Death Valley, op. cit., n. 19; Hanks, op. cit., n. 8, 37; Independence *Inyo Independent*, May 3, 1884; San Bernardino *Times*, November 11, 1886; San Francisco *Chronicle*, January 25, 1891; Spears, op. cit., n. 3, 86–87, 106. Most recent published maps of the borax routes perpetuate the errors of L. Burr Belden in the San Bernardino *Sun-Telegram*, December 7, 1952, showing a fictitious route from the Harmony Works to Saratoga Springs and failing to show that from the Amargosa Works to Mojave.

21. Spears, op. cit., n. 3, 86, 91–92; Weight, op. cit., n. 1, 15.

22. Independence *Inyo Independent*, March 31, 1888; Spears, op. cit., n. 3, 88–93, 99; Weight, op. cit., n. 1, 15.

23. Bishop *Inyo Register*, March 29, 1888; San Francisco *Chronicle*, January 25, 1891; Spears, op. cit., n. 3, 86, 98–99.

24. San Bernardino *Times*, November 4, 11, 1886, January 29, 1887; and a garbled account in Spears, op. cit., n. 3, 101–102.

25. Independence *Inyo Independent*, May 3, October 18, 1884, May 15, 1886, May 26, 1888; Pomona *Times Courier*, April 17, 1886; New York *Times*, March 25, May 9, 1888; Statement of J. W. Mather, in *Report [on Revision of the Tariff]* 50th Congress, 1st Session, Senate Report 2332 (Washington: Government Printing Office, 1888), pt. 2, 205–218; Gilbert E. Bailey, *The Saline Deposits of California* (Sacramento: Supt. State Printing, 1902), 41, (prices, but California product p. 39 is underestimated).

26. San Francisco *Alta California*, May 9, 1888; New York *Times*, May 9, 11, 1888; Independence *Inyo Independent*, May 26, 1888.

27. New York *Times*, May 10, 1888; Independence *Inyo Independent*, May 19, 1888, January 19, 1889; San Francisco *Mining and Scientific Press*, June 2, 1888; New York *Engineering and Mining Journal*, Septembr 14, 1889; Spears, op. cit., n. 3, 90; C. B. Zabriskie quoted in W. A. Chalfant, *Death Valley, The Facts* (Stanford: Stanford University Press, 1930), 9–10; Weight, op. cit., n. 1, 38.

28. New York *Times*, July 25, 1888; Hallidie, op. cit., n. 14, 75; Scherer, op. cit., n. 14, 310.

29. Inyo County Recorder, Deeds Book V, 324–431; Deeds, A. L. Tubbs, Assignee of Harmony Borax Mining Co., Meridian Borax Co., California Chemical Co., to F. M. Smith, dated March 12, 1890; New York *Engineering and Mining Journal*, May 3, 1890; San Francisco *Mining and Scientific Press*, November 29, 1890.

The Montgomery Brothers

1. *Supplemental Register of Inyo County . . . 1898* (Bishop: Inyo Register Print, 1898), 13; Bishop *Inyo Register*, February 25, April 7, 1892; Bessie Beatty, *Who's Who in Nevada* (Los Angeles: Home Printing Co., 1907), 192–196; *Out West*, 30 (April 1909), 384; *Press Reference Library* (Los Angeles: Los Angeles Examiner, 1912), 48; Los Angeles *Mining Review*, November 23,

1912; *Who's Who in the Pacific Southwest* (Los Angeles: Times-Mirror, 1913), 263; John S. McGroarty, *Los Angeles From the Mountains to the Sea* (Chicago: American Hist. Soc., 1921), v. 2, 211–212; Tonopah *Times-Bonanza*, August 27, 1934. Montgomery brothers genealogy, courtesy of Virginia Rhode, Victor, Idaho.

2. Independence *Inyo Independent*, April 3, 1891; Bishop *Inyo Register*, May 14, 1891; San Francisco *Mining and Scientific Press*, April 18, 1891; Needles *Eye*, September 1, 1894.

3. Independence *Inyo Independent*, April 3, 24, 1891; Bishop *Inyo Register*, April 9, May 14, 1891; Belmont *Courier*, May 2, June 6, September 26, 1891.

4. Independence *Inyo Independent*, April 24, 1891; Bishop *Inyo Register*, May 14, 28, 1891; Belmont *Courier*, May 2, 9, September 26, 1891; Candelaria *Chloride Belt*, May 16, June 6, 1891; William Caruthers, *Loafing Along Death Valley Trails; A Personal Narrative of People and Places* (Palm Desert: Desert Magazine Press, 1951), 88.

5. Bishop *Inyo Register*, May 7, July 2, 1891, February 4, 1892; Belmont *Courier*, June 6, September 26, October 31, 1891; Needles *Eye*, June 14, 1891; Candelaria *Chloride Belt*, June 27, July 16, 1891; San Francisco *Mining and Scientific Press*, July 25, 1891; Walter N. Frickstad and Edward W. Thrall, *A Century of Nevada Post Offices 1852–1957* (Oakland: Philatelic Research Society, 1958), 17, 19, 21. The little Kendall mill now rests at Furnace Creek Inn.

6. Bishop *Inyo Register*, February 25, April 7, 1892; Belmont *Courier*, August 29, September 19, 1891, February 13, 1892, January 6, May 5, August 18, 1894.

7. Articles of Incorporation of the Sterling Mining and Milling Company, July 3, 1894, Utah State Archives, Salt Lake City; Frank Esshom, *Pioneers and Prominent Men of Utah* (Salt Lake City: Pioneers Book Pub. Co., 1913), 793–794, 995, 1168, 1261; Panamint *News*, March 18, 1875; New York *Engineering and Mining Journal*, July 21, 1894, April 27, 1895; Belmont *Courier*, February 16, April 27, May 25, 1895; Independence *Inyo Independent*, April 5, 1895; Bishop *Inyo Register*, June 5, 1895; San Francisco *Mining and Scientific Press*, April 6, May 25, 1895; Salt Lake City *Tribune*, October 16, 1895.

8. Salt Lake City *Tribune*, September 10, October 16, 1895; Bishop *Inyo Register*, July 2, 1891.

9. Belmont *Courier*, September 14, 1895; Salt Lake City *Tribune*, September 10, 12, October 16, 1895.

10. Tonopah *Miner*, January 2, 1904; Greenwater *Death Valley Chuck-walla* May 1, 1907; Belmont *Courier*, September 14, October 5, 12, 26, 1895.

11. Bishop *Inyo Register*, January 2, 1896; Los Angeles *Times*, March 8, 1896; Caruthers, op. cit., n. 4, 88–89; Inyo County Recorder, Land, Water and Mining Claims Book H, 438, 441; Bishop *Inyo Register*, February 27, 1896, May 6, 1897; Independence *Inyo Independent*, February 26, 1897.

12. Bishop *Inyo Register*, November 28, 1895, January 2, February 27, May 7, 1896; San Francisco *Mining and Scientific Press*, May 16, 1891.

13. Bishop *Inyo Register,* February 27, May 7, 1896; Independence *Inyo Independent,* July 31, 1896; Salt Lake City *Tribune,* December 4, 1896; see also John A. Latschar, *Historic Resource Study: A History of Mining in Death Valley National Monument, Volume II* (Denver: National Park Service, 1981), 672–681.

14. Bishop *Inyo Register,* May 7, 1896; Salt Lake City *Tribune,* November 6, 1896; Los Angeles *Mining Review,* July 29, 1905.

15. Salt Lake City *Tribune,* October 28, 30, November 3, 6, December 4, 1896; Belmont *Courier,* November 7, 1896; Beatty *Bullfrog Miner,* April 15, 1905; Los Angeles *Times,* November 14, 1905; Independence *Inyo Independent,* December 7, 1906; Tonopah *Bonanza,* August 28, 30, 1910; Carl B. Glasscock, *Gold in Them Hills: The Story of the West's Last Wild Mining Days* (Indianapolis: Bobbs-Merrill Co., 1932), 214–215.

16. Independence *Inyo Independent,* October 14, 1898, July 12, 1901; Belmont *Courier,* December 3, 1898; Esshom, op. cit., n. 7, 793–794; Tonopah *Miner,* March 5, 1904; Rhyolite *Herald,* May 12, 1909.

17. Page's venture is described in the Independence *Inyo Independent,* April 21, 1883, May 4, 1889; Candelaria *True Fissure,* August 4, 1883; Calico *Print,* June 7, 1885; San Francisco *Scientific and Mining Press,* August 1, 1885; and Milo Page, "Searching for Lost Mines, The Goller Mine," *Sierra Magazine 2* (February 1909). Taylor's is described in the Independence *Inyo Independent,* June 15, September 14, 1889, December 29, 1899, and in Linda W. Greene, *Historic Resource Study: A History of Mining in Death Valley National Monument* (Denver: National Park Service, 1981), v. I, 90–95. McIntyre's appears in Bishop *Inyo Register,* May 17, August 23, 1894, January 24, 31, 1895, May 7, 1896; Independence *Inyo Independent,* April 19, 1895, June 1, 1899; Needles *Eye,* September 8, 1894; and *Great Register County of San Bernardino . . . 1892* (San Bernardino: John Flagg & Co., 1892), 120.

18. Bishop *Inyo Register,* August 23, 1894, May 7, 1896; Independence *Inyo Independent,* September 27, 1895, April 24, October 2, 1896; Inyo County Recorder, Land, Water and Mining Claims Book I, 390.

19. Bishop *Inyo Register,* January 21, March 25, April 8, May 20, 1897; Independence *Inyo Independent,* March 12, May 21, 1897.

20. Bishop, *Inyo Register,* March 25, April 8, May 20, October 7, November 4, December 9, 1897; Independence *Inyo Independent,* April 30, July 30, August 6, September 17, 24, October 22, 29, 1897. Additional information can be found in Paul B. Hubbard, Doris Bray, and George Pipkin, *Ballarat 1897–1917, Facts and Folklore* (Lancaster: Hubbard, 1965), 98 pp.

21. Independence *Inyo Independent,* February 25, March 11, 1898, April 21, 1899; Los Angeles *Mining Review,* April 29, May 27, 1899.

22. Bishop *Inyo Register,* March 9, May 25, 1899; Independence *Inyo Independent,* April 7, 21, 1899; Los Angeles *Mining Review,* April 29, November 4, 1899.

23. Independence *Inyo Independent,* April 21, June 9, July 21, December 8, 1899; Los Angeles *Mining Review,* April 29, June 10, 1899; Los Angeles City Directory Co., *Maxwell's Los Angeles City Directory for . . . 1897* (Los

Angeles: Los Angeles City Directory Co., 1897), 345; and . . . *1898*, 390; Bishop *Inyo Register,* June 1, 1899.

24. Independence *Inyo Independent,* September 16, 1898, January 13, 27, April 7, 21, May 26, 1899, August 6, 1900; Bishop *Inyo Register,* May 9, August 3, 1899; Los Angeles *Mining Review,* May 27, June 17, July 1, November 4, 1899, September 1, 22, 1900; San Francisco *Mining and Scientific Press,* January 20, 1900. Biographical notes on William W. and Albert J. Godsmark, Willard Library, Battle Creek, Michigan, courtesy of Jane Ratner.

25. Bishop *Inyo Register,* November 4, 1897, April 14, 1898, March 9, 30, 1899, August 30, 1900; Los Angeles *Mining Review,* May 27, December 23, 1899; September 1, 22, 1900.

26. Bishop *Inyo Register,* November 4, 1897, April 14, 1898, June 29, 1905; Independence *Inyo Independent,* February 25, June 24, August 26, 1898; Los Angeles *Mining Review,* April 29, 1899.

27. Inyo County Recorder, Mining Locations Book A, 224; Bishop *Inyo Register,* May 20, 1897, May 17, August 2, 30, December 13, 1900, November 9, 1905; Independence *Inyo Independent,* July 30, 1897, August 26, 1898, September 8, 1899, January 26, May 18, 1900; Los Angeles *Mining Review,* May 27, June 10, July 15, 1899, January 6, September 1, 22, 1900; Randsburg *Miner,* August 11, November 17, 1900.

28. Independence *Inyo Independent,* December 1, 29, 1899, January 26, February 6, April 27, May 18, 1900; San Francisco *Mining and Scientific Press,* November 24, 1900; Bishop *Inyo Register,* December 13, 1900, June 13, 1901.

29. Bishop *Inyo Register,* August 2, 30, December 13, 1900, Randsburg *Miner,* August 11, 1900; Los Angeles *Mining Review,* September 1, 22, 1900.

30. Los Angeles *Mining Review,* July 1, 1899, August 18, 1900; Independence *Inyo Independent,* February 16, May 17, 1900; Bishop *Inyo Register,* August 30, 1900, July 4, 1901; National Archives, Record Group 29, Twelfth Census of the United States, 1900, Inyo County, Ballarat and Panamint Precincts, Enumeration District no. 32.

31. Los Angeles *Mining Review,* July 15, August 12, 1899; Independence *Inyo Independent,* July 21, 1899, May 11, 1900; Bishop *Inyo Register,* November 2, 1905; Randsburg *Miner,* November 9, 1905; Tonopah *Nevada Mining Record-Reporter,* April 4, 1931.

32. Bishop *Inyo Register,* December 13, 1900, July 4, 1901, January 30, April 24, 1902. See also Russell R. Elliot, *Nevada's Twentieth-Century Mining Boom: Tonopah, Goldfield, Ely* (Reno: University of Nevada Press, 1966), 344 pp.

33. Bishop *Inyo Register,* August 22, 29, 1901, January 30, April 24, September 18, 1902, June 29, 1905.

34. Bishop *Inyo Register,* January 30, April 24, November 13, 1902, June 29, 1905; Los Angeles *Mining Review,* March 22, June 7, 1902; Independence *Inyo Independent,* September 16, 1904.

35. Independence *Inyo Independent,* June 6, October 10, 1902, February 5,

March 4, July 8, October 28, 1904, March 3, June 16, August 18, 1905; Bishop *Inyo Register,* October 23, 1902, January 22, 1903, May 19, 1904, June 8, 15, 29, August 10, October 26, 1905, January 18, 1906; *Los Angeles City Directory for . . . 1906* (Los Angeles: Los Angeles City Directory Co., 1906), 590; Articles of Incorporation of the Republican Mining Company, February 8, 1904, California Secretary of State, Archives, Sacramento.

36. Bishop *Inyo Register,* December 9, 1897, March 30, 1899, July 18, August 22, 1901, December 7, 1905; Los Angeles *Mining Review,* November 29, December 6, 13, 1902; San Francisco, *Mining and Scientific Press,* January 17, 24, March 4, July 25, November 21, 1903; Independence *Inyo Independent,* January 22, June 30, 1904, November 13, 1905; Wellington C. Wolfe, ed., *Men of California . . . 1900 to 1902* (San Francisco: Pacific Art Co., 1901), 416.

37. Inyo County Recorder, Deeds Book I, 38–39; Articles of Incorporation of the Gold Crown Mining Company, August 27, 1903, California Secretary of State, Archives, Sacramento; San Francisco *Mining and Scientific Press,* November 21, 1903; Independence *Inyo Independent,* March 4, April 1, 1904; Beatty *Bullfrog Miner,* July 8, 1905.

Bullfrog!

1. Additional material on the history of Bullfrog district can be found in Betsy Ritter [Mrs. Earle Clemens], *Life in the Ghost City of Rhyolite, Nevada* (Terra Bella, Calif.: Terra Bella News, 1939), 17 pp.; Harold and Lucile Weight, *Rhyolite, The Ghost City of Golden Dreams* (Twentynine Palms: Calico Press, 1970), 5th ed., revised and enlarged, 42 pp.; David F. Myrick, *Railroads of Nevada and Eastern California* (Berkeley: Howell-North Books, 1963), v. 2, 454–593; and John A. Latschar, *Historic Resource Study, A History of Mining in Death Valley National Monument* (Denver: National Park Service, U.S. Dept. of Interior, 1981), vol. II, 1–166. The history of the broader boom is told in Russell R. Elliott, *Nevada's Twentieth-Century Mining Boom* (Reno: University of Nevada Press, 1966), 344 pp.

2. Rhyolite *Bullfrog Miner,* March 29, 1907; Rhyolite *Herald* Pictorial Supplement, March 24, 1909; Frank Harris, "Half a Century Chasing Rainbows," (as told to Philip Johston), *Touring Topics,* 22 (October, 1930), 12–20, 55; *Inyo County, California, 1896, Great Register* (Bishop: Register Job Office, 1896), 19; *Index of the Great Register Inyo County, California, 1906,* (Bishop: Register Print, 1906), 9; Bishop *Inyo Register,* May 17, November 15, 1934; E. L. Cross letters to his wife, August 17, 20, 31, September 7, 1904, Tom G. Murray, ed., are published as "Letters from a Death Valley Prospector," *Desert Magazine, 26* (June 1963), 8–11; E. L. Cross's Reminiscences in Lucien M. Lewis, "He Was in on the Bullfrog Jackpot," *Desert Magazine, 10* (December 1946), 20–21.

3. Rhyolite *Herald,* August 18, 1905; Rhyolite *Herald* Pictorial Supplement, March 24, 1909; Harris, op. cit., n. 2; Cross's Reminiscences in Lewis, op. cit., n. 2.

4. Cross's letters, op. cit., n. 2; Tonopah *Miner,* September 3, 1904; Tonopah *Bonanza,* September 10, November 19, 1904; Rhyolite *Herald, Pictorial Supplement,* March 24, 1909; Harris, op. cit., n. 2; Cross's reminiscences in Lewis, op. cit., n. 2.

5. Tonopah *Miner,* September 3, 1904; Tonopah *Bonanza,* September 3, 1904, Harris, op. cit., n. 2.

6. Tonopah *Miner,* September 10, 1904; Beatty *Bullfrog Miner,* October 21, 1905; Rhyolite *Herald,* July 20, 1906; Rhyolite *Bullfrog Miner,* April 26, 1907.

7. Tonopah *Bonanza,* February 7, 1903; Bessie Beatty, *Who's Who in Nevada* (Los Angeles: Home Printing Co., 1907), 192–196; "Montgomery, Ernest Alexander," *Out West, 30* (April 1909), 384; Tonopah *Sun,* November 14, 15, 1905; Beatty *Bullfrog Miner,* January 6, 1906.

8. Tonopah *Sun,* November 15, 1905; Bessie Beatty, op. cit., n. 7, 194; Bob Montgomery's 1949 account of the Shoshone quoted in Harold and Lucile Weight, op. cit., n. 1, (1959), 3d ed., revised, 24; Jack Herron to author, October 30, 1981.

9. Tonopah *Sun,* October 25, November 15, 1905; Beatty *Bullfrog Miner,* January 6, 1906; Bessie Beatty, op. cit., n. 7, 194–195; New York *United States Mining Journal,* May 1905; Ralph D. Paine, *The Greater America* (New York: Outing Publishing Co., 1907), 296.

10. Tonopah *Miner,* February 25, March 4, 25, April 1, May 6, 1905; Tonopah *Bonanza,* April 8, 1905; Tonopah *Sun,* October 25, 1905; Rhyolite *Herald, Pictorial Supplement,* March 24, 1909.

11. Tonopah *Miner,* February 25, March 25, April 1, 15, 22, May 6, July 1, August 19, 1905; Tonopah *Bonanza,* April 29, 1905; New York *United States Mining Journal,* May 1905; Beatty *Bullfrog Miner,* May 20, October 28, 1905; Tonopah *Sun,* October 25, 1905; Rhyolite *Herald,* May 14, 1906.

12. George Graham Rice, *My Adventures With Your Money* (Boston: Richard G. Badger, 1913), 1–71; New York *Times,* November 11, 1894, April 20, 1895, September 30, 1910; New York *Engineering and Mining Journal,* November 6, 1909; Louis Guenther, "Pirates of Promotion, George Graham Rice," *World's Work, 36* (October 1918), 585–586.

13. Tonopah *Miner,* September 10, October 29, 1904, January 7, September 2, 1905; Tonopah *Bonanza,* September 10, October 1, 15, 1904, January 28, 1905; Rhyolite *Herald,* May 5, 1905; Beatty *Bullfrog Miner,* August 13, 1905; *Gold Center, The Future City of the Bullfrog Mining District, Nevada* (Goldfield: Lawton & Griffith, 1905) 2 pp; Rhyolite *Bullfrog Miner,* December 21, 1907.

14. Tonopah *Miner,* January 28, March 11, 18, 1905; Tonopah *Bonanza,* April 8, 15, May 6, 1905; Paine, op. cit., n. 9, 304–305; Rhyolite *Herald, Pictorial Supplement,* March 24, 1909.

15. Tonopah *Miner,* April 15, 1905; Beatty *Bullfrog Miner,* April 15, 1905;

Rhyolite *Herald,* May 5, June 2, 9, 1905; Tonopah *Bonanza,* July 15, 1905. For additional information on the Rhyolite *Herald* see Ritter op. cit., n. 1, and Alan Hensher, "Earle Clemens and the Rhyolite Herald: Twentieth Century Nevada Pioneers," *Southern California Quarterly, 49* (September 1967), 311–325.

16. Tonopah *Miner,* March 4, 1905; Tonopah *Bonanza,* March 18, 1905; Rhyolite *Herald,* May 5, 26, June 9, August 25, Sepember 8, December 1, 1905; Beatty *Bullfrog Miner,* June 17, 1905.

17. Tonopah *Miner,* March 25, May 13, September 30, 1905; Beatty *Bullfrog Miner,* April 8, 29, May 6, 13, 1905, October 13, November 3, 1906; Bullfrog *Miner,* March 23, 1906; Tonopah *Daily Sun,* May 24, 1905; Bessie Beatty, op. cit., n. 7, 220–221.

18. Rhyolite *Herald,* August 18, 1905; W. H. Shearer, *Atlas of the Goldfield Tonopah and Bullfrog Mining Districts of Nevada* (Chicago: Rand, McNally & Co., 1905), 35–83, Official Directory; *Handbook of Nevada Mines, Containing Such Information as Might be Valuable to Operations, Investors and Speculators in Nevada Mining Securities* (Goldfield: Goldfield News, 1906), 96 pp.; R. L. Polk & Co., *Nevada Sate Gazetteer and Business Directory, 1907–1908* (Salt Lake City, R. L. Polk & Co., 1907), 75–147, Corporations of Nevada; State of Nevada, *Biennial Report of the Secretary of State . . . 1911–12* (Carson City: State Printing Office, 1913), 193 pp.

19. Colorado Springs *Mining Investor,* October 16, 1905, February 18, 26, March 12, 19, April 16, 23, May 7, 1906; Forward Mining Development Company, *The First Year's Record of Bullfrog Nevada and Its Marvelous Mines* (Denver: App. Co., 1906), 4 pp. Promotional material from the Bullfrog-Colorado Mining Company, April 27, May 5, October 15, 1905; Bullfrog Charter Mining and Milling Co., April 29, 1905; Prospectus and flyers of the Bullfrog Keystone Gold Mining Company, 1906; Prospectus of Sunday-Nevada Gold Mining Company, 1906; all in the collection of Gil Schmidtmann.

20. Tonopah *Miner,* March 4, April 15, 1905; Salt Lake City *Tribune,* March 29, 1905; Tonopah *Bonanza,* April 29, 1905; Colorado Springs *Mining Investor,* March 26, 1906; Rhyolite postmistress Anna B. Moore quoted in Weight, op. cit., n. 1, 27.

21. Beatty *Bullfrog Miner,* April 8, May 6, 1905; Tonopah *Bonanza,* April 8, 29, 1905; Tonopah *Miner,* April 25, May 6, 13, 1905; Rhyolite *Herald,* May 5, 1905; New York *Times,* February 15, 1906; Rice, op. cit., n. 12, 66–71.

22. Beatty *Bullfrog Miner,* August 19, October 7, 1905; Tonopah *Miner,* September 2, 1905; Rhyolite *Herald,* October 6, 1905; Beatty, op. cit., n. 7, 88–89; Tonopah *Bonanza,* February 24, 1906; Searchlight *Bulletin,* January 11, 1907; "Montgomery . . . ," *Out West,* op. cit., n. 7.

23. Tonopah *Sun,* November 6–11, 13–18, 20, 1905; Beatty *Bullfrog Miner,* December 23, 1905, January 6, February 17, 1906; Rhyolite *Herald,* January 5, 1906; Tonopah *Miner,* January 6, 1906; New York *Times,* February 6, 1906.

24. Rhyolite *Herald,* February 9, 16, 1906; Beatty *Bullfrog Miner,* February 17, 1906; Colorado Springs *Mining Investor,* March 5, 1906; Rhyolite *Bullfrog Miner,* September 14, 1907; Bob Montgomery's Recollections in Tonopah *Mining Reporter,* December 15, 1928; Bob Montgomery's 1949 account . . . op. cit., n. 8.

25. Rhyolite *Herald,* May 4, 1906.

26. Tonopah *Bonanza,* October 21, 1905; Beatty *Bullfrog Miner,* November 10, 1906, April 29, 1908; Rhyolite *Bullfrog Miner,* September 14, 1907, December 5, 1908; Rhyolite *Herald,* September 2, 1908, February 19, 1909, August 6, 1910.

27. Searchlight *Searchlight,* July 21, 1905; Beatty *Bullfrog Miner,* September 23, 1905.

28. Arthur Goodrich, "The Head of the Great Steel Company," *World's Work, 1* (April 1901), 615–618; "The Career of Charles M. Schwab," *Outlook, 74* (August 15, 1903), 920–921; Alfred Henry Lewis, "Owners of America V. Charles M. Schwab," *Cosmopolitan Magazine, 45* (October 1908), 478–488; Bessie Beatty, op. cit., n. 7, 61–63; Eugene G. Grace, *Charles M. Schwab* (New York: E. G. Grace, 1947), 43 pp.; *Dictionary of American Biography, Supplement 2* (New York: Chas. Scribner's Sons, 1958), 601–603; Robert Hessen, *Steel Titan, The Life of Charles M. Schwab* (New York: Oxford University Press, 1975), 350 pp.

29. New York *Times,* January 14, 15, 23, February 8, 17, July 15, 1902; "The Career . . ." op. cit., n. 28; Lewis, op. cit., n. 28.

30. New York *Times,* July 2, August 5, October 23, November 2, 3, 1903; "The Career . . ." op. cit., n. 28; Henry Wysham Lanier, "One Trust and What Became of It," *World's Work, 7* (February 1904), 4445–4457; Arthur S. Dewing, *Corporate Promotions and Reorganizations* (Cambridge: Harvard University Press, 1914), Chaps. XVII–XVIII, The Promotion . . . and the Failure and Reorganization of the United States Shipbuilding Company, 464–509; Henry R. Seager and Charles A. Gulick, Jr., *Trust and Corporation Problems* (New York: Harper & Bros., 1929), Chap. XII, The United States Shipbuilding Company, 196–215.

31. New York *Times,* October 6–11, 15–17, 22, 23, December 23, 24, 1903, January 5, 8, 20, July 13, 17, 1904; Rhyolite *Herald,* October 6, 1905; Colorado Springs *Mining Investor,* October 16, 1905; Greenwater *Death Valley Chuck-Walla,* May 1, 1907; Rice, op. cit., n. 12, 66–69.

32. Rhyolite *Herald,* February 16, December 14, 1906, June 3, 1908, March 24, 1909 (Pictorial Supplement); Montgomery Shoshone Consolidated Mining Company, *Report on Properties* (New York: Miller Press, 1906), 16 pp.; Beatty *Bullfrog Miner,* March 30, 1907; Rhyolite *Bullfrog Miner,* March 31, 1907.

33. Rhyolite *Herald,* February 16, 1906; Beatty *Bullfrog Miner,* March 3, 1906, March 30, 1907; Reno *Nevada Mining News,* December 26, 1907.

34. Rhyolite *Herald,* December 14, 1906, March 20, April 12, November 1, 1907; Rhyolite *Bullfrog Miner,* July 13, 20, August 31, September 28, 1907; Rhyolite *Daily Bulletin,* October 24, 1907.

35. Rhyolite *Bullfrog Miner,* February 15, March 29, 1907; *Rhyolite: Metropolis of Southern Nevada* (Rhyolite: Richard E. Sinclair, 1907), 32 pp.

36. Rhyolite *Bullfrog Miner,* December 21, 1907; Rhyolite *Herald,* January 24, 1908; March 24, 1909 (Pictorial Supplement); Ritter, op. cit., n. 1, 15.

37. Rhyolite *Bullfrog Miner,* July 13, 1906, March 1, December 21, 1907; Rhyolite *Herald,* February 15, 1907, June 24, 1908, March 24, 1909, (Pictorial Supplement); Tonopah *Miner,* December 28, 1907; "Nevada's Bottle House is a Relic of Golden Days," *Sunset Magazine, 56* (February 1926), 47; Letter from Kay Kevil to Harold and Lucile Weight, July 9, 1951, courtesy of Harold Weight; Weight, op. cit., n. 1, 34.

38. Rhyolite *Herald,* January 18, 25, February 1, 8, March 29, April 5, 1907; Rhyolite *Bullfrog Miner,* January 25, February 15, 1907; *By-Laws of the Rhyolite Mining Stock Exchange, Adopted . . . January 1907* (Rhyolite: Bullfrog Miner Print, 1907), 29 pp.

39. Tonopah *Miner,* February 4, 25, March 4, July 22, 1905; Rhyolite *Herald,* August 18, 1905, June 1, 1906, April 19, October 11, 1907; Rhyolite *Bullfrog Miner,* June 8, August 3, 1906, July 6, 1907.

40. Rhyolite *Herald,* October 19, December 14, 21, 1906, March 4, 1908, March 12, 1910; Rhyolite *Bullfrog Miner,* June 22, November 30, 1907; Rhyolite *Daily Bulletin,* October 30, 1907, May 11, 1908; Myrick, op. cit., n. 1, v. 2, 454–536, 544–593.

41. Rhyolite *Bullfrog Miner,* March 30, 1906; Rhyolite *Daily Bulletin,* September 23, November 6, 1907, May 16, September 7, 1908; Rhyolite *Death Valley Prospector,* November, December 1907; Rhyolite *Death Valley Magazine,* January–October 1908.

42. Beatty *Bullfrog Miner,* May 13, 1905, May 19, 1906; Rhyolite *Herald,* May 19, August 18, 25, 1905; Rhyolite *Bullfrog Miner,* March 29, August 24, December 21, 1907; Boycott card in collection of Nevada Historical Society, Reno.

43. Rhyolite *Herald,* June 2, 1905, April 27, May 4, November 9, December 14, 1906, March 18, 1908, March 24, 1909 (Pictorial Supplement); Rhyolite *Bullfrog Miner,* March 8, 29, May 31, December 21, 28, 1907; Rhyolite *Daily Bulletin,* January 23, September 23, October 10, 1908.

44. Rhyolite *Herald,* March 8, April 5, 1907, January 17, April 29, 1908, June 25, August 13, 27, 1910; Rhyolite *Bullfrog Miner,* May 10, June 29, August 17, 1907, April 18, 1908; Rhyolite *Daily Bulletin,* November 20, 1908.

45. Rhyolite *Herald,* May 5, December 15, 1905, May 18, November 2, 1906, January 3, 10, 1908, November 6, 1909, February 19, 26, March 5, 12, 1910; Rhyolite *Bullfrog Miner,* December 7, 1906, May 3, 1907, January 4, 11, 1908; Rhyolite *Daily Bulletin,* March 26, 27, 28, 30, 1908; *State v. Skinner,* 104 Pac. 223.

46. Rhyolite *Bullfrog Miner,* August 3, 1906; Rhyolite *Herald,* November 10, 1905, August 3, 1906, January 8, 1908; Rhyolite *Daily Bulletin,* January 8, 1908.

47. Rhyolite *Herald,* August 4, 18, November 10, December 15, 22, 1905,

January 12, February 2, March 23, April 20, December 14, 1906, January 18, February 8, 15, 1907, January 13, 1909, February 26, September 10, 1910; Rhyolite *Bullfrog Miner,* March 23, April 20, 1906, January 4, February 8, July 13, August 3, 10, 1907; Rhyolite *Daily Bulletin,* January 29, March 4, 5, 9, 1909; Charles A. Kane, "An Act to Create and Establish the County of Bullfrog, Nevada," February 8, 1909, 20 pp., in Nevada Historical Society, Reno.

48. Rhyolite *Herald,* September 1, October 20, 1905, October 26, 1906, March 8, April 26, 1907, June 3, July 8, 29, 1908, May 7, 1910; Beatty *Bullfrog Miner,* September 23, 1905, March 3, October 5, 1906, April 27, May 18, 1907; Rhyolite *Bullfrog Miner,* March 8, May 24, July 13, 20, 27, August 10, 17, 1907, April 25, May 30, July 18, 1908; Tonopah *Miner,* June 1, 1907; Searchlight *Bulletin,* June 14, 1907.

49. Rhyolite *Bullfrog Miner,* March 23, 1906; Rhyolite *Herald,* May 4, October 12, December 14, 1906; Gold Center *News,* September 29, 1906.

50. Rhyolite *Herald,* March 30, April 6, 13, 20, May 4, 1906, November 22, 1907; Rhyolite *Bullfrog Miner,* March 30, 1906; Beatty *Bullfrog Miner,* March 31, April 7, 14, 1906; Transvaal *Miner,* April 14, 1906.

51. Rhyolite *Bullfrog Miner,* April 18, May 16, 1908; Rhyolite *Herald,* April 22, 29, May 13, 20, 1908; Beatty *Bullfrog Miner,* May 2, 16, 1908.

52. Rhyolite *Bullfrog Miner,* December 5, 1908; Rhyolite *Herald,* December 9, 16, 1908, March 24, 1909 (Pictorial Supplement).

53. Rhyolite *Herald,* December 16, 1908, January 27, 1909; Rhyolite *Daily Bulletin,* February 9, 12, 16, 26, 1909; Pioneer *Topics,* February 24, April 8, 1909; Rhyolite *Bullfrog Miner,* February 27, June 26, 1909.

54. Rhyolite *Daily Bulletin,* December 19, 1908, February 26, April 10, May 4, 1909; Rhyolite *Herald,* February 17, April 28, 1909; Pioneer *Topics,* February 24, May 27, 1909.

55. Rhyolite *Daily Bulletin,* March 20, 1909.

56. Rhyolite *Herald,* March 17, 31, April 28, December 25, 1909; Pioneer *Topics,* April 29, 1909.

57. Rhyolite *Daily Bulletin,* May 7, 8, 1909; Rhyolite *Bullfrog Miner,* May 8, 1909; Rhyolite *Herald,* May 12, July 7, 1909, September 10, 1910; Pioneer *Topics,* May 13, June 24, July 1, 8, 1909.

58. Rhyolite *Daily Bulletin,* May 4, 17, 1909; Pioneer *Topics,* May 13, 20, 27, June 3, 24, July 24, 1909; Rhyolite *Bullfrog Miner,* May 15, 29, 1909; Rhyolite *Herald,* June 2, 9, 1909, March 12, April 9, July 30, September 10, 1910; *Indiana Nevada Mining Co. v. Gold Hills Mining and Milling Co.,* 126 Pac. 965 (1912).

59. Rhyolite *Herald,* July 31, August 7, 14, 1909; *Indiana . . . op. cit.,* n. 58.

60. Rhyolite *Herald,* June 16, December 11, 18, 25, 1909, January 1, 8, 15, 22, February 12, 26, March 5, June 11, September 24, November 12, 19, 1910, February 25, March 18, April 22, June 17, November 4, 1911, February 3, 1912.

61. Rhyolite *Herald,* March 2, 1912; Los Angeles *Mining Review,* November 9, 1912; San Francisco *Mining and Scientific Press,* August 16, 1913;

Carrara *Obelisk,* March 8, 1914, May 1, 15, June 19, July 17, 1915.

62. Rhyolite *Herald,* January 4, 1907, March 24, 1909 (Pictorial Supplement); Rhyolite *Bullfrog Miner,* August 31, 1907; Harris, op. cit., n. 2; Latschar, op. cit., n. 1, vol. II, 23–37; Cross's Reminiscences, op. cit., n. 2.

63. Rhyolite *Herald,* March 16, 1906, October 16, 1909; Rhyolite *Bullfrog Miner,* December 21, 1907, March 27, 1909.

64. Rhyolite *Herald,* June 29, July 6, 1906, April 5, 1907, March 24, 1909 (Pictorial Supplement); Beatty *Bullfrog Miner,* August 31, 1907; Bessie Beatty, op. cit., n. 7, 98–103. For a detailed history of these two mines see Latschar, op. cit., n. 1, vol. II, 93–156.

65. Rhyolite *Bullfrog Miner,* February 22, 29, 2908; Rhyolite *Herald,* March 25, August 12, December 23, 30, 1908; Reno *Nevada Mining News,* May 7, 28, June 18, 1908; Bullfrog Gold Bar Mining Company, Presidents Statement, June 1, 1908, 2 pp., and letter from George D. Holt to manager Rhyolite *Herald,* August 25, 1908, in collection of Gil Schmidtmann; Latschar, op. cit., n. 1, vol. II, 105–122.

66. Rhyolite *Herald,* December 23, 1908; Carl B. Glasscock, *Gold in Them Hills, The Story of the West's Last Wild Mining Days* (Indianapolis: Bobb-Merrill Co., 1932), 204–241.

67. Rhyolite *Herald,* June 3, 24, July 29, August 26, 1908, January 20, March 24 (Pictorial Supplement), April 24, July 31, August 28, October 2, 9, 1909, July 2, 1910, March 25, November 11, 1911; Latschar, op. cit., n. 1, vol. II, 132–156.

68. Reno *Nevada Mining News,* October 23, 1907, April 30, 1908; Rhyolite *Herald,* October 25, 1907; Beatty *Bullfrog Miner,* October 26, November 2, 1907; Tonopah *Miner,* October 26, 1907.

69. Rhyolite *Herald,* December 27, 1907, February 26, 1908; Rhyolite *Bullfrog Miner,* December 28, 1907, February 22, 1908.

70. New York *Times,* April 30, May 1, 1908; Reno *Nevada Mining News,* April 30, 1908; Rhyolite *Daily Bulletin,* April 30, 1908.

71. Reno *Nevada Mining News,* April 30, May 7, 14, 1908; Rhyolite *Daily Bulletin,* April 30, May 6, 11, 1908; Beatty *Bullfrog Miner,* May 9, 1908; Rhyolite *Herald,* May 20, 1908; New York *Times,* May 1, 1908. Bernard M. Baruch's biography *Baruch, My Own Story* (New York: Henry Holt & Co., 1957), makes no mention of the Montgomery Shoshone.

72. Rhyolite *Herald,* December 9, 1908, February 10, June 3, 1909; Rhyolite *Bullfrog Miner,* February 20, 1909; *Report on the Montgomery Shoshone Consolidated Mining Company, February 10th 1909* (New York: 1909), 8 pp.

73. Reno *Nevada Mining News,* September 3, 1908; Rhyolite *Herald,* July 14, 1909, February 11, 1911.

74. Bishop *Inyo Register,* March 16, 1911; Rhyolite *Herald,* March 25, 1911, February 17, 1912; Rice, op. cit., n. 12, 67.

75. Rhyolite *Bullfrog Miner,* February 15, 1907; Rhyolite *Herald,* January 3, December 2, 1908, May 19, June 30, October 2, 1909, March 26, 1910; Rhyolite *Daily Bulletin,* June 8, 1909; Rhyolite *Death Valley Magazine,*

October 1908; Pioneer *Topics,* July 24, 1909; National Archives, Record Group 29, Thirteenth Census of the United States, 1910, Nye County, Nevada, Rhyolite Precint, Enumeration District 51.

76. Rhyolite *Herald,* December 31, 1910, April 8, 15, 1911, June 22, 1912; Bishop *Inyo Register,* April 13, 1911, November 13, 1913, July 30, 1914, December 7, 1916, April 19, 1917.

77. Harris, op. cit., n. 2; Cross's Reminiscences, op. cit., n. 2; Bob Montgomery's account of the Shoshone, op. cit., n. 8; Rice, op. cit., n. 12; New York *Times,* March 8, October 27, 1912; Grace, op. cit., n. 28; *Dictionary of American Biography, Supplement 2* (New York: Chas. Scribner's Sons, 1958), 601–603; Bishop *Inyo Register,* July 17, 1913.

Mysterious Scott

1. Much has been written about Death Valley Scotty, including Charles A. Taylor, *The Story of "Scotty" (Walter Scott) King of the Desert Mine* (New York: J. S. Ogilvie Pub. Co., 1906), 114 pp.; Orin S. Merrill, *"Mysterious Scott," The Monte Cristo of Death Valley and Tracks of a Tenderfoot* (Chicago: O. S. Merrill Pub., 1906), 210 pp.; Paul De Laney, "Life of 'Death Valley Scotty,'" serially in Rhyolite, *Death Valley Prospector,* December 1907, and *Death Valley Magazine,* January through October 1908; Sidney Norman, *Chasing Rainbows in Death Valley* (Los Angeles: L. A. Mining Review, 1909), 35 pp., reprinted from the Los Angeles *Times,* July 19, 1908; Bourke Lee, *Death Valley Men* (New York: Macmillan Co., 1932), Chap. I, 1–80, reprinted from the *Saturday Evening Post;* Dane Coolidge, *Fighting Men of the West* (New York: E. P. Dutton & Co., 1932), Chap. XII, 303–336, and his *Death Valley Prospectors* (New York: E. P. Dutton & Co., 1937), Chap. XI, 157–178; and Carl B. Glasscock, *Here's Death Valley* (Indianapolis: Bobbs-Merrill Co., 1940), Chaps. XII–XIV, 190–223. Much important material on Scotty can also be found in the testimony and correspondence presented in the 1940 case of *Julian M. Gerard v. Walter Scott, A. M. Johnson, et al.,* Civil Case No. 1134 BH in District Court of U.S., So. Dist. of California, Central Division (records in the Federal Record Center, Laguna Niguel, Calif.), and the Appeals Case No. 9979, Circuit Court of Appeals, Ninth Circuit (records in the Federal Record Center, San Bruno, Calif.). There is, however, only one comprehensive biography, the excellent work by Hank Johnston, *Death Valley Scotty, "The Fastest Con in the West"* (Corona Del Mar: Trans-Anglo Books, 1974), 160 pp.

2. Los Angeles *Examiner,* July 7, 10, 1905; New York *Tribune,* July 15, 1905; Rhyolite *Herald,* August 11, 1905; San Francisco *Chronicle,* August 27, 1905; Norman, op. cit., n. 1, 3, 7; A. M. Johnson in *Gerard v. Scott . . .* op. cit., n. 1, Testimony, vol. I, 165.

3. De Laney, op. cit., n. 1, February 1908.

4. National Archives, Record Group 29, Tenth Census of the United States

1880, Harrison County, Kentucky, Cynthiana, Enumeration District 100, p. 6; Los Angeles *Examiner,* July 2, 14, 1905, April 16, 1906; San Francisco *Chronicle,* August 27, 1905; Letter from Mrs. Ella Scott published in Rhyolite *Death Valley Magazine,* March 1908; Walter Scott in *Gerard v. Scott* . . . op. cit., n. 1, Testimony, vol. II, 267; and Johnston, op. cit., n. 1, 17–23.

5.   Scotty is mentioned in the Brooklyn *Sunday Advertiser,* May 20, 1894, in the clipping book for 1894, Buffalo Bill Historical Center, Cody, Wyoming, courtesy of Paul Fees, and in George H. Gooch, comp. *Route-Book Buffalo Bill's Wild West* (Buffalo: Matthews-Northrup, 1899), 7, 21–22; Needles *Eye,* December 9, 1893; Los Angeles *Examiner,* June 23, 1905; Ella Scott reminiscences quoted in Johnston, op. cit., n. 1, 21–23, see also 19–20.

Scotty repeatedly stated that he first saw Death Valley from the Grapevines while working for a government survey party headed by a man named "St. Clair"—see, e.g., San Francisco *Chronicle,* August 27, 1905; De Laney op. cit., n. 1; Los Angeles *Times,* July 19, 1908; Rhyolite *Bullfrog Miner,* November 7, 1908; Norman, op. cit., n. 1; Coolidge, *Fighting Men* . . . op. cit., 310; and *Gerard v. Scott* . . . op. cit., n. 1, Testimony, vol. II, 266. As is pointed out by Harold O. Weight in his *Lost Mines of Death Valley* (Twentynine Palms: The Calico Press, 1970), 80, this survey must have been that made in the summer of 1895 by the U.S. Coast and Geodetic Survey under C. H. Sinclair, a name easily confused with St. Clair. Contemporary newspaper accounts (e.g., Bishop *Inyo Register,* August 15, 1895) mention that there were twelve men in the party. Only three are named—and Scott is not one of them—in the official report by C. H. Sinclair, "The Oblique Boundary Line Between California and Nevada," Appendix No. 3, *Report of Supt. of Coast and Geodetic Survey* (Washington: Government Printing Office, 1901), and the survey records in the National Archives.

6.   Ella Scott Letter, op. cit., n. 4, and Reminiscences, op. cit., n. 5; Los Angeles *Times,* January 8, 1937.

7.   New York *Tribune,* April 20, 1902; Los Angeles *Examiner,* June 23, 1905; Ella Scott Reminiscences, op. cit., n. 5.

8.   Los Angeles *Examiner,* July 7, 1905; Los Angeles *Times,* July 12, 1905; *The '97 Class Book of the Sheffield Scientific School Yale University* (New Haven: Price, Lee and Adkins Co., 1897), 72–73; *Sexennial Record of the Class of 1897* . . . (New Haven: Dorman Litho. Co., 1903), 29; *History of the Class of 1897* . . . (New Haven: Tuttle, Morehouse and Taylor Co., 1907), 30–31; *Quarter Century Record of the Class of 1897* . . . (New Haven, 1922), 79; J. M. Gerard in *Gerard v. Scott* . . . op. cit., n. 1, Testimony, vol. II, 199, 209, 218–219; New York *Times,* February 27, 1944; *Obituary Record of Graduates of Yale University Deceased During the Year 1943–44* (New Haven: Yale Univ. Press, 1945), 233.

9.   *Gerard v. Scott* . . . op. cit., n. 1; Grubstake agreement between Scott and Gerard, April 23, 1902, Exhibit A, Gerard's Deposition, 4–8, 43, Gerard's Testimony vol. II, 199–201, 219–220, and Scott's Testimony, vol. I, 9.

10.   Ella Scott's reminiscences, op. cit., n. 5, 26.

11. Letters from Walter Scott to Julian Gerard, July 4, 1902, July 27, August 21, 1903, and August 17, 1904, in *Gerard v. Scott* . . . op. cit., n. 1, Gerard's Deposition, 18–21, 27–30, 35–37, 58–62, and Testimony, vol. I, 41–43, 58–61, 68–70.

12. Inyo County Recorder, Mining Locations, Book E, 422–423, Knickerbocker Quartz Mine Claim, located June 17, 1902 and recorded August 16, 1902, and Book G, 180–194, Knickerbocker Nos. 1–16, located September 4, 1904 and recorded October 7, 1904; letters from Walter Scott to Julian Gerard, July 4, 1902, June 13, August (?), October 14, 1903, January 10, February 23, 1904, in *Gerard v. Scott* . . . op. cit., n. 1, Gerard's Deposition, 18–24, 43–49, 64–67, 69–72, and Testimony, vol. I, 41–43, 56–57.

13. Letters from Walter Scott to Julian Gerard, May 27, July 4, 1902, June 13, July 27, 1903, February 23, March 14, August 17, 1904 in *Gerard v. Scott* . . . op. cit., n. 1, Gerard's Deposition, 13–21, 27–30, 58–62, 67–72, and Testimony, vol. I, 39–43, 58–61.

14. Letters from Walter Scott to Julian Gerard, July 4, 1902, July 27, August 16, 21, 25, October 14, 1903, January 10, 1904, in *Gerard v. Scott* . . . op. cit., n. 1, Gerard's Deposition, 18–21, 30–32, 34–37, 40–41, 44–49, 64–67, and Testimony, vol. I, 41–43, 61–62, 68–73; E. M. Wilkinson's report to Gerard, August 14, 1903 quoted in Johnston, op. cit., n. 1, 31; San Francisco *Call,* June 29, 1904; San Francisco *Chronicle,* June 29, 1904; Chicago *Record-Herald,* August 25, 1905; Los Angeles *Examiner,* July 6, 7, 1905, January 31, 1906; Los Angeles *Evening News,* March 9, 19, 1906.

15. Letters from Walter Scott to Julian Gerard, July 27, August 16, 21, 25, 1903 in *Gerard v. Scott* . . . op. cit., n. 1, Gerard's Deposition, 27–30, 34–37, 40–41, and Testimony, vol. I, 58–61, 68–73; and Gerard's trip West is described in his Deposition, 79–85, and Testimony, vol. I, 14–15, 77–79, and vol. II, 214–221.

16. Letters from Walter Scott to Julian Gerard, July 27, October 14, (?), 1903, March 14, 1904, in *Gerard v. Scott* . . . op. cit., n. 1, Gerard's Deposition, 27–30, 44–53, 69–72 and Testimony, vol. I, 58–61, 85.

17. Ella Scott's Reminiscences, op. cit., n. 5, 27; Letters from Walter Scott to Julian Gerard, October (?), 1903, February 23, 1904, in *Gerard v. Scott* . . . op. cit., n. 1, Gerard's Deposition, 50–53, 67–69, and additional material, 43, 83–85; Los Angeles *Examiner,* December 6, 7, 1904, June 23, 25, 1905; Los Angeles *Evening News,* March 20, 1906; "Charles Emmet Van Loan," *Who Was Who in America* (Chicago: Marquis Who's Who, 1943), vol. I, 1271.

18. Letter from Walter Scott to Julian Gerard, May 18, 1904, in *Gerard v. Scott* . . . op. cit., n. 1, 73–75; Los Angeles *Times,* July 6, 1905; Los Angeles *Examiner,* July 6, 1905; Los Angeles *Evening News,* March 19, 1906.

19. Rhyolite *Herald,* August 25, 1905; Los Angeles *Examiner,* August 29, December 23, 1905; Los Angeles *Evening News,* March 21, 30, 1906; Merrill, op. cit., n. 1, 124–127.

20. Albert Johnson's testimony in *Gerard v. Scott* . . . op. cit., n. 1, Testimony, vol. I, 125–129; Walter Scott's reminiscence and November 2, 1904

Grubstake Contract, both quoted in Johnston, op. cit., n. 1, 93–94; Los Angeles *Evening News,* March 19, 1906.

21. Independence *Inyo Independent,* July 8, 1904; Bishop *Inyo Register,* August 4, 1904; Los Angeles *Evening News,* March 19, 1906; *Los Angeles City Directory . . . 1906* (Los Angeles: Los Angeles City Directory Co., 1906), 639; San Bernardino *Daily Sun,* March 21, 1906; Los Angeles *Times,* July 19, 1908, June 19, 1912; Norman, op. cit., n. 1, 31. See also Glasscock, op. cit., n. 1, 194 and opp. p. 196; Johnston, op. cit., n. 1, 39; John A. Latschar, *Historic Resource Study, A History of Mining in Death Valley National Monument* (Denver: National Park Service, 1981), vol. II, 331–333.

22. Los Angeles *Examiner,* June 23, 1905.

23. Los Angeles *Examiner,* June 24, 25, 26, 27, 28, 29, July 1, 2, 3, 6, 7, 8, 1905.

24. Los Angeles *Examiner,* June 24, 26, July 2, 7, 1905.

25. New York *Times,* July 24, 1895, October 16, 1897, July 1, 1905; Rudyard Kipling, *"Captains Courageous" A Story of the Grand Banks* (New York: Century Co., 1897), chap. 9; Los Angeles *Examiner,* July 1, 6, 9, 1905; Los Angeles *Times,* July 1, 1905, June 19, 1912; San Bernardino *Daily Sun,* March 21, 1906; Scott's receipt for $5,500 from Santa Fe Railroad reproduced in Glasscock, op. cit., n. 1, opp. p. 196, from the original held by Gaylord's widow; Atchison, Topeka and Santa Fe Railway Co., *Record Breaking Run of the Scott Special* (n.p.; n.d.), 12.

26. Los Angeles *Examiner,* July 10, 1905; Los Angeles *Times,* July 10, 1905; Atchison, Topeka and Santa Fe Railway Co., op. cit., n. 25, 1–15.

27. Los Angeles *Examiner,* July 10, 12, 15, 1905; Los Angeles *Times,* July 10, 1905; Chicago *Record-Herald,* July 12, 1905; New York *Times,* July 15, 1905; New York *Tribune,* July 15, 1905.

28. Los Angeles *Examiner,* July 10, 11, 12, 1905; Chicago *Record-Herald,* July 11, 1905; New York *Tribune,* July 15, 1905; Atchison, Topeka and Santa Fe Railway Co., op. cit., n. 25, 1–6.

29. Los Angeles *Times,* July 12, 1905; Los Angeles *Examiner,* July 12, 1905; Chicago *Record-Herald,* July 12, 1905; New York *Times,* July 12, 1905; Atchison, Topeka and Santa Fe Railway Co., op. cit., n. 25, 8–9.

30. Los Angeles *Examiner,* July 12, 17, August 7, November 2, 1905, March 12, 1906; Chicago *Record-Herald,* July 12, 1905; San Francisco *Call,* March 26, 1906; Merrill, op. cit., n. 1; Taylor, op. cit., n. 1, Atchison, Topeka and Santa Fe Railway Co., op. cit., n. 25; "Earl Alonzo Brininstool," *Who Was Who in America* (Chicago: Marquis Who's Who, 1963), vol. III, 104; "Charles Alonzo Taylor," *Dictionary of American Biography, Supp. 3* (New York: Charles Scribner's Sons, 1973), 764–765.

31. Los Angeles *Times,* July 14, 1905; Los Angeles *Examiner,* August 18, September 3, 1905, February 7, March 19, 1906; Rhyolite *Herald,* September 15, 1905, October 11, 1907.

32. Los Angeles *Examiner,* July 13, 14, August 5, 1905; Los Angeles *Times,* July 13, 1905; New York *Times,* July 17, 1905.

33. Albert Mussey Johnson, clippings and papers in the deceased alumnus

folder, Dept. of Manuscripts and University Archives, Cornell University Libraries, Ithaca, New York; Albert and Bessie Johnson Papers 1900–1909, in Shadelands Ranch Historical Museum, Walnut Creek; Johnson Family Papers, 1899–1921, in Death Valley Ranch Archives, Death Valley National Monument; San Bernardino *Sun,* March 23, 1906; Los Angeles *Times,* January 8, 1948; New York *Times,* January 8, 1948; *Who Was Who in America* (Chicago: A. N. Marquis Co., 1950), vol. II, 282; Johnston, op. cit., n. 1, 91–94.

34. Letter of A. M. Johnson to R. D. Lay, c. February 1906, quoted in Johnston, op. cit., n. 1, 94.

35. Los Angeles *Examiner,* July 6, 7, 1905; Telegrams between Walter Scott and Julian Gerard, quoted in Johnston, op. cit., n. 1, 42–43.

36. Los Angeles *Examiner,* July 12, 13, 15, 17, 1905; Los Angeles *Times,* July 15, 1905; Chicago *Record-Herald,* July 15, 1905; New York *Tribune,* July 15, 1905; New York *Times,* July 15, 16, 17, 1905.

37. Los Angeles *Examiner,* July 18, 1905; New York *Times,* July 26, 1905; Agreement between Walter Scott and Julian Gerard, dated July 22, 1905, and Gerard's Reminiscences quoted in Johnston, op. cit., n. 1, 48, and A. M. Johnson's records cited on p. 95; Scott's testimony in *Gerard v. Scott . . .* op. cit., n. 1, Testimony, vol. I, 25–26.

38. Los Angeles *Examiner,* July 3, 6, 7, 8, 15, 1905; Chicago *Record-Herald,* July 12, 13, 1905; Los Angeles *Times,* July 13, 1905; New York *Times,* July 17, September 8, 1905; Tonopah *Daily Sun,* November 1, 1905.

39. New York *United States Mining Journal,* August 1905; Rhyolite *Herald,* December 15, 1905, January 19, 1906; Los Angeles *Examiner,* January 11, 1906; Latschar, op. cit., n. 21, 331–333, 385.

40. Los Angeles *Examiner,* August 4, 5, 23, 24, October 8, 10, 11, 12, 27, 1905.

41. Chicago *Record-Herald,* July 12, 1905; New York *Times,* July 12, 1905; New York *Tribune,* July 15, 1905; Los Angeles *Times,* July 15, 1905; Bishop *Inyo Register,* July 20, 1905; Wells *Nevada State Herald,* July 21, 1905; New York *United States Mining Journal,* August 1905; Los Angeles *Examiner,* December 23, 1905; Merrill, op. cit., n. 1, 83.

42. Rhyolite *Herald,* August 25, 1905; Los Angeles *Examiner,* August 27, 28, 1905; New York *Times,* August 29, September 8, 1905.

43. Los Angeles *Examiner,* August 8, 16, 18, September 5, 6, 7, October 8, 1905; Gerard's testimony in *Gerard v. Scott . . .* op. cit., n. 1, Gerard's Deposition, 88–89.

44. Los Angeles *Examiner,* August 16, 1905, March 21, 25, April 6, 7, 1906; New York *Times,* January 30, 1943; Rochester (New Hampshire) *Courier,* February 4, 1943.

45. Los Angeles *Examiner,* September 8, 14, 1905; San Bernardino *Sun,* April 11, 1906; Bill Keyes's Reminiscences in San Bernardino *Sun-Telegram,* January 19, 1958; Johnston, op. cit., n. 1, 61–62.

46. Los Angeles *Examiner,* September 30, October 3, 8, 9, 1905, March 20, 22, 1906; San Bernardino *Sun,* March 22, April 11, 1906.

47. Los Angeles *Examiner,* October 8, 10, 31, November 1, 7, 1905; New York *Times,* October 31, 1905.

48. Los Angeles *Examiner,* October 20, 21, November 2, 12, 1905; Los Angeles *Herald,* October 20, 1905; Taylor, op. cit., n. 1, 85–92; Marguerite Courtney, *Laurette* (New York: Rinehart & Co., 1955), 60–65.

49. Los Angeles *Express,* quoted in Goldfield *News,* October 20, 1905.

50. Los Angeles *Examiner,* December 13, 14, 15, 16, 20, 21, 1905; New York *Times,* December 21, 1905; Tonopah *Bonanza,* December 23, 1905.

51. Los Angeles *Examiner,* December 15, 20, 21, 22, 23, 24, 25, 26, 27, 1905; Tonopah *Bonanza,* December 23, 1905; Rhyolite *Herald,* January 5, 1906; Beatty *Bullfrog Miner,* January 6, 1906.

52. Los Angeles *Examiner,* January 3, 4, 1906; San Bernardino *Sun,* March 22, 1906.

53. Los Angeles *Examiner,* January 3, 4, 1906.

54. Los Angeles *Evening News,* March 19, 1906; Los Angeles *Examiner,* March 21, 1906; San Bernardino *Sun,* March 21, 1906; Keyes quoted in Johnston, op. cit., n. 1, 57.

55. Los Angeles *Examiner,* January 12, 16, 24, 1906.

56. New York *Commercial and Financial Chronicle,* June 6, 1903 (p. 1251); San Bernardino *Sun,* March 24, April 11, 1906; Los Angeles *Examiner,* April 16, 1906; "Thomas Coleman du Pont," *Dictionary of American Biography* (New York: Charles Scribner's Sons, 1944), Supp. 1, 271–272.

57. Antonio Apache letter to Julian M. Gerard, September 28, 1905, quoted in Johnston, op. cit., n. 1, 52–54; Los Angeles *Examiner,* January 3, 1906; Walter Scott letter to Julian M. Gerard, January 8, 1906, in *Gerard v. Scott* . . . op. cit., n. 1, Gerard's Deposition, 101–103.

58. Albert M. Johnson letter to Robert D. Lay, February 1906, quoted in Johnston, op. cit., n. 1, 94–95.

59. Los Angeles *Evening News,* March 19, 1906; Taylor, op. cit., n. 1, 103–114; Greenwater *Times,* October 23, 1906; Rhyolite *Herald,* January 24, 1908; Bill Keyes's Reminiscences in L. Burr Belden "The Battle of Wingate Pass," *Westways, 48* (November 1956), 8–9.

60. Los Angeles *Examiner,* March 3, 20, April 16, 1906; Los Angeles *Evening News,* March 19, 1906; San Bernardino *Sun,* March 21, 1906.

61. Los Angeles *Evening News,* March 19, 28, 1906; Los Angeles *Examiner,* March 20, 1906.

62. Los Angeles *Examiner,* March 2, 3, 19, 21, 1906; Los Angeles *Evening News,* March 19, 1906.

63. Los Angeles *Examiner,* March 2, 3, 19, 20, 21, 1906; Los Angeles *Evening News,* March 19, 1906; San Bernardino *Sun,* March 24, 1906; Keyes's Reminiscences . . . op. cit., n. 59, 8.

64. Los Angeles *Examiner,* March 2, 3, 21, 22, 1906; Los Angeles *Evening News,* March 21, 1906; San Bernardino *Sun,* March 24, 1906.

65. San Diego *Union,* March 1, 1906; Los Angeles *Examiner,* March 1, 2, 3, 4, 5, 6, 19, 1906; Los Angeles *Evening News,* March 3, 5, 1906; San Bernardino *Sun,* March 3, 1906.

66. Los Angeles *Examiner,* March 4, 7, 12, 26, 1906; Randsburg *Miner,* March 15, 1906; San Francisco *Call,* March 26, 1906; Taylor, op. cit., n. 1, 103–114.

67. Los Angeles *Examiner,* March 19, 20, 30, April 4, 1906; Los Angeles *Evening News,* March 12, 29, April 7, 11, 13, 1906; San Bernardino *Sun,* March 20, April 11, 12, 14, 1906; Rhyolite *Bullfrog Miner,* April 20, 1906.

68. Los Angeles *Evening News,* March 20, 23, April 7, 12, 1906; Los Angeles *Examiner,* March 23, 24, April 7, 8, 14, 1906; San Bernardino *Sun,* April 14, 1906.

69. Los Angeles *Evening News,* March 19, 20, 21, 22, 23, 26, April 7, 1906; Los Angeles *Examiner,* March 19, 20, 21, 22, 23, 24, 1906; Beatty *Bullfrog Miner,* April 7, 1906; San Bernardino *Sun,* April 8, 12, 1906; Randsburg *Miner,* April 12, 1906.

70. San Bernardino *Sun,* April 26, 27, 28, 1906; Los Angeles *Evening News,* April 26, 27, 1906; Bishop *Inyo Register,* May 3, 1906; Courtney, op. cit., n. 48, 65.

71. Los Angeles *Examiner,* April 16, 18, 1906; Articles of Incorporation of the Key Gold Mining Company filed August 21, 1906 in California, Secretary of State Archives, Sacramento; Greenwater *Times,* October 23, 1906; Rhyolite *Bullfrog Miner,* July 6, October 19, 1907; Rhyolite *Herald,* February 1, November 8, 1907, January 24, 1908, January 13, February 17, September 18, 1909, April 22, 1911; Independence *Inyo Independent,* February 14, March 6, 1908; Bishop *Inyo Register,* February 8, 1912, Keyes's reminiscences in San Bernardino *Sun-Telegram,* January 19, 1958; Latschar, op. cit., n. 21, 657–661.

72. Wells *Nevada State Herald,* June 1, 1906; Rhyolite *Bullfrog Miner,* July 20, 1906, June 15, 22, 29, 1907, January 25, 1908; Beatty *Bullfrog Miner,* August 4, 1906, Independence *Inyo Independent,* August 17, 1906; Randsburg *Miner,* October 18, 1906; Rhyolite *Herald,* April 5, 1907, January 24, 31, 1908; Rhyolite *Daily Bulletin,* January 21, 1908.

73. San Bernardino County Recorder, Mining Records, Book 52, 51–52; Bishop *Inyo Register,* January 17, 1907; Rhyolite *Bullfrog Miner,* July 27, August 16, 1907; Los Angeles *Times,* July 19, 1908; *Gerard v. Scott . . .* op. cit., n. 1, Agreement between W. Scott and J. M. Gerard dated August 9, 1907, in Gerard's Deposition, App. B., 1–4, and Scott's Testimony, vol. I, 92–98, and Johnson's Testimony, vol. I, 158–160, 164; Johnston, op. cit., 95–96.

74. Rhyolite *Herald,* February 14, March 11, July 15, 1908; Rhyolite *Bullfrog Miner,* February 15, 29, 1908; Johnston, op. cit., n. 1, 82–83.

75. Rhyolite *Daily Bulletin,* April 11, 1908; Rhyolite *Bullfrog Miner,* April 11, 1908; Rhyolite *Herald,* July 15, 1908.

76. Rhyolite *Bullfrog Miner,* June 12, July 31, 1909; Alfred MacArthur and Albert Johnson's exchange quoted in Johnston, op. cit., n. 1, 96.

77. Rhyolite *Daily Bulletin,* January 28, 1908; Rhyolite *Herald,* January 31, 1908; Rhyolite *Bullfrog Miner,* February 1, 1908.

78. Blair *Press,* June 20, 1908; Los Angeles *Times,* July 19, 1908; Norman, op. cit., n. 1; Glasscock, op. cit., n. 1, 209.

79. Los Angeles *Times,* July 19, 1908; Rhyolite *Herald,* August 5, 1908; Hornsilver *Herald,* August 8, 1908; Reno *Nevada Mining News,* August 20, 1908; Norman, op. cit., n. 1.

80. Rhyolite *Daily Bulletin,* December 4, 1908; Rhyolite *Herald,* September 18, 1909, July 30, August 20, September 10, 1910, February 25, July 1, 8, September 16, 23, 1911, April 13, 1912; Independence *Inyo Independent,* September 9, 1910; Los Angeles *Times,* June 20, 1912.

81. Los Angeles *Examiner,* May 30, June 16, 1912; Rhyolite *Herald,* June 1, 1912; Stock certificate of the Death Valley Scotty Gold Mining and Developing Company, reproduced in Johnston, op. cit., n. 1, 89.

82. Los Angeles *Times,* June 19, 1912; New York *Moving Picture World,* October 12, 19, November 9, 1912.

83. Los Angeles *Times,* June 11, 1912; Los Angeles *Examiner,* June 16, 1912.

84. Los Angeles *Times,* June 11, 16, 18, 19, 20, 21, 23, 1912; Los Angeles *Examiner,* June 16, 19, 1912.

85. San Francisco *Call,* June 24, 1912.

Heart of Gold

1. Inyo County Recorder, Mining Locations, Book F, 443–444; Independence *Inyo Independent,* July 29, 1904; Bishop *Inyo Register,* August 4, 1904; Rhyolite *Herald,* November 3, 1905; *Inyo County Great Register . . . for the Year 1898* (Bishop: Inyo Register Print, 1898), Supp. 12. A detailed history of the Keane Wonder Mine is given in John A. Latschar, *Historic Resource Study, A History of Mining in Death Valley National Monument* (Denver: National Park Service, 1981), v. II, 263–320.

2. Inyo County Recorder, Mining Locations, Book F, 568–570; Independence *Inyo Independent,* June 24, July 29, 1904; Bishop *Inyo Register,* June 2, 1904; Tonopah *Miner,* April 15, 1905; Rhyolite *Herald,* November 3, 1905; *Dictionary of American Biography* (New York: Scribner, 1931), v. 3, 210–211.

3. Inyo County Recorder, Mining Locations, Book F, 650–651; Independence *Inyo Independent,* June 24, July 8, 29, 1904, August 18, 1905; Bishop *Inyo Register,* August 4, 1904; Tonopah *Miner,* August 5, 1905.

4. Independence *Inyo Independent,* July 29, 1904, April 7, September 29, 1905; Tonopah *Miner,* February 25, April 15, September 30, October 28, 1905; Rhyolite *Herald,* November 3, 1905, January 26, March 2, April 6, June 8, 1906; Tonopah *Bonanza,* February 17, 1906; Beatty *Bullfrog Miner,* April 29, December 23, 1905, April 20, 1906; Los Angeles *Evening News,* March 19, 1906; Los Angeles *Times,* June 19, 1912; Latschar, op. cit., n. 1, 240–253.

5. Rhyolite *Herald,* March 2, June 8, August 10, 1906; Bishop *Inyo Register,* March 15, September 6, 1906; Beatty *Bullfrog Miner,* April 20, 1906; Rhyolite *Daily Bulletin,* March 31, 1908.

6. Bishop *Inyo Register,* March 15, 1906; Independence *Inyo Independent,* September 7, 14, 28, 1906; Rhyolite *Bullfrog Miner,* September 14, 1907; Bishop *Inyo Register,* March 19, 1931.

7. Rhyolite *Herald,* November 17, 1905, April 20, September 21, 1906; To-

nopah *Bonanza,* December 9, 1905; Rhyolite *Bullfrog Miner,* February 23, April 20, 1906; Bishop *Inyo Register,* May 24, 1906.

8. Inyo County Recorder, Mining Locations, Book G, 309; *Index to the Great Register, Inyo County . . . 1900* (Bishop: Inyo Register, 1900), 19; Independence *Inyo Independent,* December 16, 1904, March 31, 1905; Tonopah *Bonanza,* December 24, 1904; Rhyolite *Herald,* June 2, July 21, 1905, February 23, 1906, March 1, 1907; Beatty *Bullfrog Miner,* February 17, 1906; Rhyolite *Bullfrog Miner,* February 23, March 23, 1906, February 8, March 1, 1907. Latschar, op. cit., n. 1, 401–453 gives a detailed history of the Lee district.

9. Rhyolite *Herald,* June 2, 1905, January 5, June 8, 1906, February 22, 1907; Beatty *Bullfrog Miner,* September 16, 1905; Rhyolite *Bullfrog Miner,* February 8, March 1, 1907; Inyo County Recorder, Mining Locations, Book H, 273; Latschar, op. cit., n. 1, 463–475.

10. Rhyolite *Herald,* March 26, 1905, June 8, 1906, February 22, March 1, April 5, 12, 1907; Rhyolite *Bullfrog Miner,* March 29, April 5, May 3, 1907.

11. Rhyolite *Bullfrog Miner,* February 1, 22, March 8, April 19, May 3, June 29, August 17, October 12, 1907; Rhyolite *Herald,* March 1, October 18, 1907; Latschar, op. cit., n. 1, 422–441.

12. Rhyolite *Herald,* January 11, February 8, April 19, 26, 1907; Rhyolite *Bullfrog Miner,* March 1, April 19, May 3, 24, 1907.

13. Rhyolite *Herald,* December 28, 1906, March 22, April 5, 26, 1907; Rhyolite *Bullfrog Miner,* January 4, February 22, March 29, April 12, 1907; Greenwater *Death Valley Chuck-Walla,* June 1907; Latschar, op. cit., n. 1, 482–488, 492–493.

14. B. X. Dawson, *Death Valley Reclaimed, What Modern Science & Scientific Mining Engineering Has Accomplished* (Denver: Smith-Brooks Press, 1906), 4, 11, 14, and his *Death Valley of Superstition and Imagination, The Gold Valley of Today* (Denver: Smith-Brooks Press, 1906), 25, copies courtesy of Gil Schmidtmann; Colorado Springs *Mining Investor,* November 5, 1906.

15. Colorado Springs *Mining Investor,* December 4, 11, 18, 1905, February 5, 26, 1906; Dawson, *Death Valley Reclaimed . . .* op. cit., n. 14, 11–12; Dawson, *Death Valley of Superstition . . .* op. cit., n. 14, 5, 12–17.

16. Colorado Springs *Mining Investor,* December 4, 1905, February 26, 1906.

17. Dawson, *Death Valley Reclaimed . . .* op. cit., n. 14, 12.

18. Ibid., 2, 16; Colorado Springs *Mining Investor,* December 4, 11, 18, 1905. There is no mention of any of this business in the Rhyolite, Bullfrog, or Beatty papers of 1905–06.

19. Brooklyn *Daily Eagle* and Denver *Profit and Loss,* December 1905, quoted in Dawson, *Death Valley of Superstition . . .* op. cit., n. 14, 5, 12–17; Colorado Springs *Mining Investor,* December 4, 11, 1905, February 5, 26, 1906; Denver *Financial Bulletin,* February 20, 1906, quoted in Dawson, *Death Valley Reclaimed . . .* op. cit., n. 14, 7–10; Denver *Death Valley Dawsonian,* September 1, 1906, copy courtesy of Gil Schmidtmann; Dawson, *Death Valley of Superstition . . .* op. cit., n. 14, cover.

20. Colorado Springs *Mining Investor,* February 26, October 15, 1906, January 21, September 30, October 14, 1907; Dawson, *Death Valley Reclaimed . . .*

op. cit., n. 14, 3, 11; Denver *Death Valley Dawsonian,* September 1, 1906; Rhyolite *Bullfrog Miner,* April 12, June 22, 1907.

21. Independence *Inyo Independent,* December 30, 1904, January 20, March 25, 1905; Bishop *Inyo Register,* January 12, 1905; Linda W. Greene, *Historic Resource Study, A History of Mining in Death Valley National Monument* (Denver: National Park Service, 1981), v. I, 815–822.

22. Rhyolite *Herald,* July 7, September 1, 1905; Bishop *Inyo Register,* September 14, 1905; Independence *Inyo Independent,* September 15, 1905; Pete Aguereberry's Recollections of the discovery in Dane Coolidge, *Death Valley Prospectors* (New York: E. P. Dutton, 1937), 133–141 and in LeRoy and Margaret Bales, "He Belongs to the Panamints," *Desert Magazine,* 5 (November 1941), 17–21; Shorty Harris's Recollections of the discovery in his "Half a Century Chasing Rainbows," *Touring Topics,* 22 (October 1930), 20; Greene, op. cit., n. 21, 510–538. See also George C. Pipkin, *Pete Aguereberry, Death Valley Prospector and Gold Miner* (Trona, Calif.: Murchison Publications, 1982), 158 pp.

23. Inyo County Recorder, Mining Locations, Book J, 302–307, 569–571; Bishop *Inyo Register,* August 24, 1905; Rhyolite *Herald,* September 1, 1905; Independence *Inyo Independent,* September 15, 1905; Tonopah *Miner,* September 16, 1905; Randsburg *Miner,* September 28, November 9, 1905; Harris's Recollections . . . op. cit., n. 22.

24. Bishop *Inyo Register,* August 24, 1905; Rhyolite *Herald,* September 1, 15, 1905; Tonopah *Miner,* September 16, 1905; Tonopah *Bonanza,* September 23, 1905.

25. Independence *Inyo Independent,* September 15, November 3, 1905; Rhyolite *Herald,* September 29, 1906; Bishop *Inyo Register,* October 12, 1905; Tonopah *Miner,* November 4, 1905; Articles of Incorporation of the Cashier Gold Mining Company, September 12, 1905, and Midas Panamint Mining Company, January 24, 1906, in California Secretary of State, Archives, Sacramento; Inyo County Recorder, Deeds Book 7, 102.

26. Tonopah *Miner,* September 16, 1905; Independence *Inyo Independent,* November 3, 1905; Tonopah *Bonanza,* November 11, 1905.

27. Inyo County, Recorder Mining Locations, Book N, 21–35; Independence *Inyo Independent,* March 16, 1906; Rhyolite *Herald,* April 19, 1907; Rhyolite *Bullfrog Miner,* April 26, 1907; see also Greene, op. cit., n. 21, 608–680. C. B. Glasscock in his *Here's Death Valley* (Indianapolis: Bobbs-Merrill Co., 1940), 243 seems to be the originator of the fog story, but then he also thought Harry Ramsey was the discoverer.

28. Rhyolite *Herald,* June 8, December 14, 1906; Rhyolite *Bullfrog Miner,* April 25, May 10, 1907.

29. Beatty *Bullfrog Miner,* May 12, 1906; Los Angeles *Examiner,* February 7, 1906; New York *Mining Topics,* May 15, 1906; Rhyolite *Bullfrog Miner,* April 26, 1907; Bishop *Inyo Register,* April 23, 1908; Independence *Inyo Independent,* April 24, 1908.

30. Rhyolite *Herald,* May 4, 1906, March 1, 1907; Beatty *Bullfrog Miner,* June 23, 1906; Rhyolite *Bullfrog Miner,* April 26, 1907; Eric Partridge, *A Dictionary of Slang and Unconventional English* (New York: Macmillan Co.,

1970), 774. Glasscock, op. cit., n. 27, 243 is the source of the pipeline story, copied by almost every writer since.

31. Bishop *Inyo Register,* October 4, 1906; Rhyolite *Herald,* April 19, 1907; Rhyolite *Bullfrog Miner,* April 26, 1907; Beatty *Bullfrog Miner,* October 19, November 2, 1907; Bessie Beatty, *Who's Who in Nevada* (Los Angeles: Home Printing Co., 1907), 197–199.

32. Beatty *Bullfrog Miner,* June 23, 1906; Rhyolite *Herald,* July 20, September 28, 1906, December 13, 1907, January 3, 1908; Bishop *Inyo Register,* October 4, 1906, Rhyolite *Bullfrog Miner,* December 14, 1907; San Francisco *Mining and Scientific Press,* April 1, 1911.

33. Rhyolite *Bullfrog Miner,* July 13, August 24, 1906; Randsburg *Miner,* December 20, 1906; Rhyolite *Herald,* January 25, December 13, 20, 1907.

34. Beatty *Bullfrog Miner,* June 2, July 21, 1906; Rhyolite *Herald,* August 3, September 28, 1906, March 1, April 19, 1907; Bishop *Inyo Register,* September 6, 1906, January 17, 1907; Independence *Inyo Independent,* November 16, 1906; Inyo County Recorder, Plat of Town of Skidoo, November 22, 1906, reproduced in Greene, op. cit., n. 21, 627.

35. Rhyolite *Herald,* November 6, December 28, 1906, January 4, March 15, 1907; Skidoo *News,* December 28, 1906; Rhyolite *Bullfrog Miner,* April 26, May 17, 1907; Independence *Inyo Independent,* June 14, 1907; Randsburg *Miner,* July 23, 1907.

36. Rhyolite *Bullfrog Miner,* July 13, 1906, April 12, 26, 1907; Rhyolite *Herald,* August 3, 1906, March 15, April 19, October 18, 1907; Skidoo *News,* January 25, 1907, April 25, 1908; Randsburg *Miner,* April 4, 1907; Beatty *Bullfrog Miner,* May 10, 1907; Searchlight *Bulletin,* May 31, 1907; Rhyolite *Daily Bulletin,* October 2, 1907.

37. Rhyolite *Herald,* September 21, 1906, January 18, March 15, April 19, 1907; Skidoo *News,* January 25, 1907; Rhyolite *Bullfrog Miner,* February 22, 1907; Bishop *Inyo Register,* March 7, 1907; Randsburg *Miner,* April 25, 1907; Independence *Inyo Independent,* May 17, 1907; Greene, op. cit., n. 21, 888–897.

38. Rhyolite *Bullfrog Miner,* March 8, May 24, 1907; Rhyolite *Death Valley Magazine,* January 1908; Clarence E. Eddy, *The Pinnacle of Parnassus* (Salt Lake City: Tribune Printing Co., 1902), 104 pp.

39. Rhyolite *Bullfrog Miner,* March 8, May 24, 1907; Rhyolite *Herald,* April 19, 1907; see also Greene, op. cit., n. 21, 371–379.

40. Rhyolite *Bullfrog Miner,* May 31, June 8, 15, 22, July 13, August 3, 10, 17, September 21, November 23, 1907; Rhyolite *Herald,* July 26, November 22, 1907; Independence *Inyo Independent,* August 9, 1907.

41. Rhyolite *Death Valley Magazine,* February 1908.

42. Rhyolite *Herald,* November 22, December 27, 1907; Rhyolite *Bullfrog Miner,* November 23, 1907.

43. Randsburg *Miner,* August 22, 1907; Rhyolite *Bullfrog Miner,* October 19, November 2, 23, 30, 1907, January 25, February 15, 1908; Rhyolite *Herald,* December 27, 1907, January 24, 1908; Articles of Incorporation of the Death Valley Gold Placer Mining Company, August 20, 1907, California Secretary of State, Archives, Sacramento; Lincoln Steffens, "Taming of the West: Discovery of the Land Fraud System," *American Magazine, 64* (Sep-

tember 1907), 489–505; Francois D. Uzes, *Chaining the Land; A History of Surveying in California* (Sacramento: Landmark Enterprises, 1977), 173–193.

44. Rhyolite *Herald,* February 21, 28, 1908; Rhyolite *Bullfrog Miner,* February 22, 29, 1908; Rhyolite *Death Valley Magazine,* February 1908.

45. Bishop *Inyo Register,* March 7, 1912; Clarence E. Eddy, *Ballads of Heaven and Hell* (Salt Lake City: Western Printing Co., 1922), 14 pp., and *The Burro's Bray, A Book of Pomes* (Salt Lake City: 1923), 48 pp.

46. Rhyolite *Bullfrog Miner,* July 27, August 3, 10, October 12, 26, 1907; Rhyolite *Herald,* October 25, November 1, 15, 1907; Rhyolite *Daily Bulletin,* October 26, 1907.

47. Rhyolite *Herald,* May 13, June 3, September 23, 1908, January 13, 1909.

48. Rhyolite *Bullfrog Miner,* November 28, 1908; Bishop *Inyo Register,* March 18, 1909, January 21, 1915; Bishop *Owens Valley Herald,* April 2, 1909; Rhyolite *Herald,* July 7, 1909.

49. Rhyolite *Herald,* November 22, December 13, 1907, January 3, 1908; Rhyolite *Bullfrog Miner,* January 4, 1908.

50. Rhyolite *Herald,* December 20, 1907, May 13, June 3, 1908, April 21, 1909; Independence *Inyo Independent,* September 4, 1908; Bishop *Inyo Register,* January 21, March 25, 1909, January 21, 1915.

51. Independence *Inyo Independent,* May 31, July 19, 1907, April 24, May 1, 1908; Rhyolite *Daily Bulletin,* April 22, 23, 1908; Skidoo *News,* April 25, 1908; Bishop *Owens Valley Herald,* December 10, 1909; *Byrne v. Knight and Simpson,* 12 Cal. App. 56, 1909; Pipkin, op. cit., n. 22, 103.

52. Independence *Inyo Independent,* April 24, May 1, 1908; Skidoo *News,* April 25, 1908.

53. Skidoo *News,* April 25, 1908; Independence *Inyo Independent,* May 1, 1908.

54. Skidoo *News,* April 25, 1908; Rhyolite *Herald,* April 29, 1908; Independence *Inyo Independent,* May 1, 1908.

55. Rhyolite *Daily Bulletin,* April 23, 25, 1908; Skidoo *News,* April 25, 1908; Rhyolite *Bullfrog Miner,* April 25, 1908; Rhyolite *Herald,* April 29, 1908.

56. Skidoo *News,* April 25, 1908.

57. Los Angeles *Herald,* April 24, 1908; Los Angeles *Times,* April 24, 1908; Reginald Macdonald's account, quoted in Marcia Rittenhouse Wynn, *Desert Bonanza Story of Early Randsburg Mojave Desert Mining Camp* (Culver City: M. W. Samelson, 1949), 207. See also Daniel Cronkhite, *Death Valley's Victims, A Descriptive Chronology 1849–1980* (Morongo Valley: Sagebrush Press, 1981), 31–33, Plate 16. Glasscock, op, cit. n. 27, 249, appears to have originated the newspaper photographer story, repeated with embellishments by most later writers.

58. Rhyolite *Daily Bulletin,* April 25, 1908; George Cook's Reminiscences related in Myrtle Myles, "The Gruesome Encore," *Desert Magazine,* 27 (November 1964), 9; Pipkin, op. cit., n. 22, 105–106; Marcia Wynn Samelson, personal communication, October 17, 1981; George Pipkin, personal communication, October 17, 1981.

59. Cook, op. cit., n. 58; Pipkin, op. cit., n. 22, 105–107; George Pipkin, personal communication, October 17, 1981.

60. Rhyolite *Herald,* September 14, 1906, April 8, 1908; Independence *Inyo*

Independent, February 14, 1908; Shorty Harris's Recollections . . . op. cit., n. 22, Harris's and Aguereberry's Recollections in Coolidge, op. cit., n. 22, 133, 138; Thomas Edgar Crawford, *The West of the Texas Kid* (Norman: University of Oklahoma Press, 1962), 173–174. See also Pipkin, op. cit., n. 22, 81–86.

61. Bishop *Owens Valley Herald,* April 2, 1909; Rhyolite *Herald,* August 7, 1909; Rhyolite *Bullfrog Miner,* September 11, 1909; Crawford, op. cit., n. 60, 180–184.

62. Rhyolite *Bullfrog Miner,* March 13, 1909; Rhyolite *Herald,* August 7, 1909; Crawford, op. cit., n. 60, 184; Pipkin, op. cit., n. 22, 96–97; Greene, op. cit., n. 21, 531–532.

63. Rhyolite *Herald,* June 25, 1910, February 11, 1911; Crawford, op. cit., n. 60, 184; Pipkin, op. cit., n. 22, 94–96.

64. Rhyolite *Herald,* October 25, November 22, 29, December 13, 1907, March 18, April 15, August 18, 1908; Rhyolite *Daily Bulletin,* October 26, 1907; Rhyolite *Bullfrog Miner,* December 14, 1907.

65. Rhyolite *Herald,* December 27, 1907, January 28, February 7, 1908.

66. Rhyolite *Herald,* April 15, June 10, 1908, March 24 (Pictorial Supplement), 1909; Rhyolite *Bullfrog Miner,* June 13, 1908. See also Latschar, op. cit., n. 1, 439–441, 448–453.

67. Rhyolite *Herald,* February 19, May 14, August 13, September 10, October 15, December 17, 1910, April 27, 1912; Bishop *Inyo Register,* October 20, 1910.

68. Rhyolite *Bullfrog Miner,* October 26, 1907, February 8, 1908; Rhyolite *Herald,* February 21, 1908, November 27, 1909, April 15, 1911; see also Latschar, op. cit., n. 1, 276–320.

69. Rhyolite *Herald,* December 6, 1907, February 21, July 29, August 5, 1908, November 27, 1909, June 11, 1910; Rhyolite *Bullfrog Miner,* September 7, 1907, February 8, August 15, 1908, March 20, 1909; Independence *Inyo Independent,* March 20, 1908.

70. Independence *Inyo Independent,* May 10, 1907; Bishop *Inyo Register,* November 13, 1907; Rhyolite *Herald,* November 1, December 6, 1907, July 29, 1908, February 4, 1911; Rhyolite *Bullfrog Miner,* February 8, 1908.

71. Rhyolite *Herald,* April 12, December 6, 1907, July 31, October 23, 30, November 13, 1909; Rhyolite *Bullfrog Miner,* June 12, 26, July 31, 1909; Harry P. Gower, *50 Years in Death Valley—Memoirs of a Borax Man* (San Bernardino: Inland Printing, Inc., 1969), 26–27.

72. Tonopah *Daily Sun,* November 22, 1905; Reno *Nevada Mining News,* October 23, 1907; Rhyolite *Daily Bulletin,* November 9, 1907; Bishop *Inyo Register,* November 13, 1907, January 15, 1920; Rhyolite *Herald,* December 6, 1907; Bessie Beatty, op. cit., n. 31, 263–265; Blair *Press,* July 25, November 14, 1908.

73. Rhyolite *Herald,* October 14, November 18, 1908, April 14, 21, 1909; Rhyolite *Bullfrog Miner,* November 2, 1908; Blair *Press,* November 14, 1908; Bishop *Inyo Register,* November 25, 1915.

74. Rhyolite *Herald,* October 14, 1908, April 14, 21, 1909; Rhyolite *Daily*

Bulletin, April 13, 14, 1909; Rhyolite *Bullfrog Miner,* April 17, 1909.

75. Rhyolite *Daily Bulletin,* April 13, 14, 1909; Rhyolite *Herald,* April 14, 1909; Blair *Press,* April 16, 1909; Rhyolite *Bullfrog Miner,* April 17, 1909; Bishop *Owens Valley Herald,* April 23, 1909.

76. Rhyolite *Herald,* November 18, 1908, May 5, 26, 1909; Bishop *Inyo Register,* November 25, 1915.

77. Beatty *Bullfrog Miner,* April 13, 1907; Independence *Inyo Independent,* January 28, 1910; Rhyolite *Herald,* January 22, April 30, May 28, August 6, 1910, April 8, September 2, 1911, March 30, 1912; Latschar, op. cit., n. 1, 241–252.

78. Rhyolite *Herald,* December 15, 1905, August 7, 1909, May 7, June 25, August 27, September 10, October 15, 1910; Latschar, op. cit., n. 1, 385–388.

79. Rhyolite *Herald,* December 14, 1906, April 15, 1908; Rhyolite *Bullfrog Miner,* July 13, 1907, April 18, 1908; Rhyolite *Daily Bulletin,* April 13, 1908; Independence *Inyo Independent,* November 27, 1908; List of Stockholders of the Death Valley Big Bell Mining Co., as of October 1, 1907, Nevada State Museum, Carson City; Latschar, op. cit., n. 1, 331–350.

80. Rhyolite *Daily Bulletin,* November 23, 24, 25, 1908; Rhyolite *Herald,* November 25, December 5, 1908, April 7, November 20, 1909; Rhyolite *Bullfrog Miner,* November 28, 1908; Bishop *Owens Valley Herald,* November 28, December 4, 11, 1908, November 26, 1909, April 1, 1910; Independence *Inyo Independent,* December 4, 25, 1908, May 16, June 25, November 26, 1909, April 1, 1910; Bishop *Inyo Register,* April 8, November 25, 1909, May 31, 1910; *People v. Cyty* (November 12, 1909), 106 Pac 257.

81. Rhyolite *Herald,* February 4, March 11, April 1, October 14, November 25, 1911.

82. Bishop *Inyo Register,* May 25, July 6, 1911, July 23, August 22, 1912, January 1, 1914; Rhyolite *Herald,* August 5, 1911, January 27, February 3, March 9, 23, April 6, 13, 27, May 11, 18, June 22, 1912; Latschar, op. cit., n. 1, 312–318.

83. Rhyolite *Herald,* April 15, 1911; Bishop *Inyo Register,* August 22, 1912.

84. Bishop *Inyo Register,* August 22, 1912, June 5, 1913, January 29, February 19, 1914, November 25, 1915; San Francisco *Mining and Scientific Press,* November 15, 1913; Carrara *Obelisk,* December 4, 1915, July 29, 1916; Bishop *Owens Valley Herald,* July 14, 1916; Keane Wonder Mining Company stock certificate number 3293, issued February 20, 1919, signed by W. H. Wells, vice president, in the author's collection; Edna Brush Perkins, *The White Heart of Mojave, An Adventure with the Outdoors of the Desert* (New York: Boni and Liveright, 1922), 104–105.

85. Rhyolite *Daily Bulletin,* May 3, 1909; Bishop *Inyo Register,* January 23, June 12, September 18, 1913; San Francisco *Mining and Scientific Press,* February 1, April 19, 1913; *William B. Gray v. Skidoo Mines Company,* Case No. CC166ND in U.S. District Court for Southern District of California, Northern Division, in National Archive, Regional Branch, San Bruno, Calif., *Skidoo Fraction Mining and Milling Company v. Skidoo Mines Com-*

pany and E. A. Montgomery, Case No. 390 Civil, in U.S. District Court, Southern District of California, Southern Division, in National Archives, Regional Branch, Laguna Niguel, Calif.

86. Bishop *Inyo Register,* April 30, August 5, 1915.
87. New York *Engineering and Mining Journal,* September 22, October 6, 1917; Bishop *Inyo Register,* October 4, 1917; Greene, op. cit., n. 21, 696.
88. San Francisco *Mining and Scientific Press,* April 1, 1911; Bishop *Inyo Register,* January 21, 1915; J. H. Cooper, "The Skidoo Gold Mines, Data Supplemental to General Report," Archives, Death Valley National Monument.
89. Los Angeles *Mining Review,* July 27, November 23, 1912; San Francisco *Examiner,* August 17, 1917; *Press Reference Library* (Los Angeles: Los Angeles Examiner, 1912), 48; John S. McGroaty, *Los Angeles from the Mountains to the Sea* (Chicago: American Historical Society, 1921), v. 2, 211–212; Los Angeles *Times,* August 17, 1955; Clovis *News–Journal,* August 17, 1955.

A Copper Frenzy

1. Beatty *Bullfrog Miner,* January 12, 1907; Tonopah *Daily Sun,* October 17, 1907; Rhyolite *Herald,* November 8, 1907; George Graham Rice, *My Adventures With Your Money* (Boston: Richard G. Badger, 1913), 132–143. Additional material on the history of Greenwater can be found in Carl B. Glasscock, *Gold in Them Hills* (Indianapolis: Bobbs-Merrill Co., 1932), 264–286, and his *Here's Death Valley* (Indianapolis: Bobbs-Merrill Co., 1940), 224–238; Harold O. Weight, *Greenwater* (Twentynine Palms: Calico Press, 1969), 36 pp.; David F. Myrick, *Railroads of Nevada and Eastern California* (Berkeley: Howell-North Books, 1963), v. 2, 597–604; and John A. Latschar, *Historic Resource Study, A History of Mining in Death Valley National Monument* (Denver: National Park Service, 1981), v. II, 507–613.
2. Greenwater *Death Valley Chuck-Walla,* March 1, 1907.
3. Independence *Inyo Independent,* April 29, 1882; Beatty *Bullfrog Miner,* January 12, 1907; *Great Register of the County of Inyo . . . 1880* (Independence: Chalfant & Parker, 1880), 7, 9.
4. Inyo County Recorder, Mining Locations, Book B, 54 (March 3, 1898); *Supplemental Register of Inyo County, California 1898* (Bishop: Inyo Register Print, 1898), 13; Rhyolite *Bullfrog Miner,* October 12, 1907; Rhyolite *Herald,* November 1, 1907.
5. Frank Harris, "Half A Century Chasing Rainbows" (as told to Philip Johnston), *Touring Topics,* 22 (October 1930), 17.
6. Inyo County Recorder, Mining Locations, Book G, 4–11; Rhyolite *Bullfrog Miner,* November 2, 1906, October 12, 1907; Colorado Springs *Mining Investor,* December 17, 1906.
7. Independence *Inyo Independent,* December 7, 1906.

8. Inyo County Recorder, Mining Locations, Book H, 48–50; Rhyolite *Bullfrog Miner,* November 2, 1906; Independence *Inyo Independent,* December 7, 1906; Colorado Springs *Mining Investor,* December 17, 1906; Nelson W. Durham, *History of the City of Spokane* (Chicago: S. J. Clarke Publishing Co., 1912), v. 2, 295–296.

9. Independence *Inyo Independent,* May 5, 12, 1905; Rhyolite *Bullfrog Miner,* November 2, 1906.

10. Independence *Inyo Independent,* May 5, June 9, 1905, March 23, 1906; Rhyolite *Herald,* June 23, 1905; New York *Commercial and Financial Chronicle,* May 26, 1906; Rhyolite *Bullfrog Miner,* June 1, 1906; Colorado Springs *Mining Investor,* December 17, 1906.

11. Rhyolite *Bullfrog Miner,* March 9, June 1, 1906; Independence *Inyo Independent,* March 23, 1906; Los Angeles *Evening News,* April 2, 1906; New York *Commercial and Financial Chronicle,* June 30, 1906; Rhyolite *Herald,* July 27, 1906, November 8, 1907; Tonopah *Daily Sun,* October 3, 1906; Rice, op. cit., n. 1, 134; "The Modern Pirate," *World's Work,* 22 (October 1911), 14916–14918; "John Warne Gates," *Dictionary of American Biography* (New York: Charles Scribner's Sons, 1931), v. 7 188–190; Lloyd Wendt and Herman Kogan, *Bet A Million! The Story of John W. Gates* (Indianapolis: Bobbs-Merrill Co., 1948) 357 pp.; Robert Irving Warslow, *Bet-A-Million Gates: The Story of a Plunger* (New York: Greenberg, 1932), 187 pp.

12. Rhyolite *Bullfrog Miner,* June 1, 1906; Beatty *Bullfrog Miner,* September 1, 1906; Rice, op. cit., n. 1, 134.

13. Colorado Springs *Mining Investor,* December 17, 1906; Horace J. Stevens, *The Copper Handbook, vol. VII* (Houghton, Mich.: H. J. Stevens, 1907), 1196–1198, 1212–1213.

14. Independence *Inyo Independent,* December 15, 1905; Rhyolite *Bullfrog Miner,* July 13, 1906; New York *Mining Topics,* August 1, 1906; Bishop *Inyo Register,* August 9, 1906; Tonopah *Daily Sun,* August 18, 1906; Colorado Springs *Mining Investor,* December 17, 1906; Greenwater *Death Valley Chuck-Walla,* January 1, 1907; Albert H. Dutton, *Nevada Notables in Caricature* (n.p.:1915); Glasscock, *Here's Death Valley,* op. cit., n. 1, 228.

15. Bishop *Inyo Register,* August 9, 1906, January 31, 1907; Rhyolite *Herald,* August 10, 1906; Beatty *Bullfrog Miner,* September 1, 1906; New York *Mining Topics,* September 1, 1906.

16. Independence *Inyo Independent,* October 12, 1906, October 15, 1932; Greenwater *Times,* October 23, 1906; Rhyolite *Daily Bulletin,* May 5, June 5, 1909; Bishop *Inyo Register,* June 18, 1914; Glasscock, *Here's Death Valley,* op. cit., n. 1, 230.

17. Beatty *Bullfrog Miner,* July 21, August 11, 1906; Rhyolite *Bullfrog Miner,* August 10, 17, 1906; Rhyolite *Herald,* August 10, 17, September 7, 14, 28, 1906; Greenwater *Death Valley Chuck-Walla,* January 1, 1907.

18. Las Vegas *Times,* April 1, 1905, November 3, 1906; Rhyolite *Herald,* August 10, September 28, 1906; Beatty *Bullfrog Miner,* August 11, 1906; Independence *Inyo Independent,* September 21, 1906, January 4, 1907; Greenwater *Times,* October 23, 1906.

19. Rhyolite *Herald,* September 7, 1906; Tonopah *Daily Sun,* October 23,

November 12, 15, 1906; Greenwater *Death Valley Chuck-Walla,* January 1, 1907.

20. Tonopah *Daily Sun,* September 15, December 8, 1906; Beatty *Bullfrog Miner,* November 24, December 1, 1906; Rhyolite *Bullfrog Miner,* November 30, 1906; Rhyolite *Herald,* January 4, 1907; Reno *Nevada Mining Investor,* January 15, 1907.

21. Greenwater *Death Valley Chuck-Walla,* January 1, 1907.

22. Rhyolite *Herald,* July 27, 1906; Tonopah *Daily Sun,* September 7, 1906; Goldfield *News,* October 6, 1906; Colorado Springs *Mining Investor,* October 15, 1906; New York *Engineering and Mining Journal,* December 15, 1906; Bishop *Inyo Register,* December 20, 1906, June 18, 25, 1914; Independence *Inyo Independent,* January 4, 1907; Allan Patterson's Reminiscence is quoted in Weight, op. cit., n. 1, 13.

23. Greenwater *Times,* October 23, November 6, 1906; Tonopah *Daily Sun,* November 12, December 8, 31, 1906; April 24, 1907; Rhyolite *Bullfrog Miner,* November 30, 1906, January 4, March 29, April 26, 1907; Beatty *Bullfrog Miner,* December 1, 1906, February 2, May 24, 1907; Rhyolite *Herald,* December 14, 1906, January 4, 1907; Goldfield *News,* December 15, 1906; New York *Engineering and Mining Journal,* December 16, 1906, January 26, 1907; Colorado Springs *Mining Investor,* December 17, 1906; Greenwater *Death Valley Chuck-Walla,* January 1, February 15, 1907; Bishop *Inyo Register,* January 31, 1907.

24. Greenwater *Times,* October 23, 1906; Randsberg *Miner,* November 29, 1906; Tonopah *Daily Sun,* December 8, 1906, February 2, 1907; San Francisco *Mining and Scientific Press,* January 12, 1907; New York *Engineering and Mining Journal,* January 12, 1907; Greenwater *Death Valley Chuck-Walla,* January 15, February 15, 1907; Beatty *Bullfrog Miner,* March 9, 1907; Independence *Inyo Independent,* March 22, 1907; Rhyolite *Bullfrog Miner,* March 29, 1907; Goldfield *News,* March 30, 1907.

25. Greenwater *Times,* October 23, 1906; Bishop *Inyo Register,* June 25, 1914; Glasscock, *Here's Death Valley,* op. cit., n. 1, 233–235; Charles A. Brown's Reminiscences, published in Phil Townsend Hanna et al., eds., *Death Valley Tales* (Palm Desert: Desert Magazine Press, 1955), 45–46. Variants of the diamond tooth legend appear in Margaret Long, *The Shadow of the Arrow* (Caldwell: Caxton Printers, 1941), 54; William Caruthers, *Loafing Along Death Valley Trails* (Palm Desert: Desert Magazine Press, 1951), 60; and L. Burr Belden, *Mines of Death Valley* (Glendale: La Siesta Press, 1966), 35.

26. Tonopah *Daily Sun,* December 20, 24, 1906; Patterson's Reminiscence, op. cit., n. 22, 13; Brown's Reminiscences, op. cit., n. 25, 46.

27. Greenwater *Death Valley Chuck-Walla,* January 1, April 15, 1907.

28. Greenwater *Death Valley Chuck-Walla,* January 1 thru June 1907; Rhyolite *Bullfrog Miner,* January 25, 1907; Glasscock, *Here's Death Valley,* op. cit., n. 1, 231.

29. Greenwater *Death Valley Chuck-Walla,* January 1, March 1, 1907; Rhyolite *Bullfrog Miner,* January 25, 1907; Tonopah *Daily Sun,* January 31, 1907; Glasscock, *Here's Death Valley,* op. cit., n. 1, 167, 224, 231.

30. Articles of Incorporation of the Furnace Valley Copper Company filed October 13, 1906, Clark Copper Company, filed November 2, 1906, and Kempland Copper Company, filed November 5, 1906, in California, Secretary of State, Archives, Sacramento; Colorado Springs *Mining Investor,* December 17, 1906; Tonopah *Daily Sun,* December 18, 1906, January 7, 1907; Rhyolite *Herald,* December 28, 1906; Greenwater Copper Mines and Smelter Co., *Report . . . for the Year Ending December 31st, 1907* (New York: 1908), 2–3; Stevens, op. cit., n. 13, v. 8 (1908), 531, 701–703, 762.

31. Rhyolite *Herald,* July 27, September 7, November 9, December 28, 1906; Tonopah *Daily Sun,* August 11, October 3, 22, December 18, 1906, January 7, 1907; New York *Mining Topics,* September 1, 1906; Goldfield *News,* September 29, October 6, 1906; Colorado Springs *Mining Investor,* October 8, November 12, December 17, 1906; Reno *Nevada Mining Investor,* October 15, November 1, 1906; Independence *Inyo Independent,* October 19, December 21, 1906; Greenwater *Death Valley Chuck-Walla,* February 15, 1907.

32. Colorado Springs *Mining Investor,* October 1, 15, 29, November 5, 26, December 17, 1906; Independence *Inyo Independent,* October 12, 1906; Rhyolite *Bullfrog Miner,* April 26, 1907; Stevens, op. cit., n. 13, v. 8 (1908), 761–764; Rice, op. cit., n. 1, 143; Thomas W. Lawson, *Frenzied Finance— The Crime of Amalgamated* (New York: Ridgway-Thayer Co., 1905), 559 pp.; *Nation, 120* (February 25, 1925), 203.

33. Information on 111 Greenwater Mining Companies was obtained from Stevens, op. cit., n. 13, v. 8 (1908), 293, 303, 399, 437, 531, 556, 621, 647, 701–703, 719, 730, 746, 760–765, 768, 830, 839, 972, 1015, 1024–1025, 1100, 1126, 1256, and 1325; State of California, *Biennial Report of the Secretary of State . . . 1906–08* (Sacramento: Supt. State Printing, 1908), 68–69, 142–154; State of Nevada, *Biennial Report of the Secretary of State* (Carson City: State Printing Office, 1913), 17, 84–86, 120; together with various newspaper references summarized in Latschar, op. cit., n. 1, 585–588, 636. The known capital stock of 76 of these companies totals $167 million, or an average of about $2.2 million per company, which suggests a total capital stock for all of the companies of about $244 million.

34. Colorado Springs *Mining Investor,* October 15, December 10, 1906, February 18, 25, 1907; Greenwater *Death Valley Chuck-Walla,* February 15, March 15, 1907; Stevens, op. cit., n. 13, v. 8 (1908), 763–764, 768.

35. Colorado Springs *Mining Investor,* October 1, 8, 15, November 26, December 3, 1906, February 4, 18, 1907; Goldfield *News,* November 10, 1906; Tonopah *Daily Sun,* November 24, 1906.

36. Independence *Inyo Independent,* July 17, December 11, 1875, February 5, 19, 1897, July 21, October 27, 1899, September 16, 1904; Bishop *Inyo Register,* November 16, 1899, November 28, 1901, June 4, 1903. See also Linda Greene, *Historic Resource Study, A History of Mining in Death Valley National Monument* (Denver: National Park Service, 1981), v. I, 778–806.

37. Rhyolite *Bullfrog Miner,* October 5, 1906, May 3, 17, 24, June 15, 1907; Bishop *Inyo Register,* June 20, 1907.

38. Bishop *Inyo Register,* November 15, 1906, January 17, March 7, June 20, July 4, August 22, 1907; Rhyolite *Bullfrog Miner,* April 5, 19, 1907; Rhyolite *Herald,* April 12, 1907; Independence *Inyo Independent,* July 12, August 9, 23, 1907; Tonopah *Daily Sun,* September 27, 1907.

39. Rhyolite *Herald,* August 17, September 21, 28, November 16, 1906, September 16, 1908; Rhyolite *Bullfrog Miner,* December 28, 1906, May 17, 24, December 21, 1907; Bishop *Inyo Register,* June 25, 1914; see also Latschar, op. cit., n. 1, 625–643.

40. Rhyolite *Bullfrog Miner,* May 24, June 22, July 6, 20, December 21, 1907; Tonopah *Daily Sun,* July 2, 1907; Bishop *Inyo Register,* July 25, 1907.

41. Bishop *Inyo Register,* June 25, 1914; Charles Brown's Reminiscences in Weight, op. cit., n. 1, 26–27.

42. Bishop *Inyo Register,* September 5, 1907, July 29, 1915; Independence *Inyo Independent,* September 13, 1907; Rhyolite *Bullfrog Miner,* May 22, 1909; Rhyolite *Herald,* June 2, 1909, February 19, 1910; Latschar, op. cit., n. 1, 695–697.

43. San Francisco *Mining and Scientific Press,* May 8, June 12, 1886; Rhyolite *Herald,* December 8, 22, 1905; Randsburg *Miner,* December 14, 1905; Bishop *Inyo Register,* December 21, 1905; Latschar, op. cit., n. 1, 644–647.

44. New York *Engineering and Mining Journal,* September 20, 1902; Bishop *Inyo Register,* May 18, 1905; Rhyolite *Herald,* August 11, 1905, January 12, February 2, 1906, April 5, 1907, September 23, 1908, August 28, 1909; January 7, 1911; Tonopah *Bonanza,* August 26, 1905, January 27, 1906; Los Angeles *Examiner,* August 29, 1905; Randsburg *Miner,* August 31, 1905, July 26, September 20, 1906; Rhyolite *Bullfrog Miner,* January 12, November 16, 1906, April 5, May 10, 1907, March 7, 1908; Goldfield *News,* January 26, 1906; Greenwater *Death Valley Chuck-Walla,* May 1, 1907; Latschar, op. cit., n. 1, 697–698.

45. Rhyolite *Bullfrog Miner,* October 26, 1906, February 1, 8, 1907, March 28, 1908; New York *Engineering and Mining Journal,* November 10, 1906; Rhyolite *Herald,* February 8, 15, March 1, 1907, April 8, 1908; Beatty *Bullfrog Miner,* March 2, 9, April 6, May 4, 11, June 21, 1907; Searchlight *Bulletin,* May 3, 10, 24, 31, June 7, 1907; Walter N. Frickstad, *A Century of California Post Offices 1848 to 1954* (Oakland: Philatelic Research Society, 1955), 139.

46. Goldfield *Gossip,* December 1906; Rice, op. cit., n. 1, 132, 141.

47. New York *Times,* March 9, 26, 1901, July 13, 1937; New York *Tribune,* March 10, 11, 14, 16, 17, 19, 22, 23, 24, 31, April 16, 1901, December 1, 1906; Tonopah *Bonanza,* February 17, 1906; Rhyolite *Herald,* April 13, 1906; Goldfield *News,* December 8, 1906; Reno *Nevada Mining News,* January 16, 1908.

48. New York *Tribune,* December 1, 2, 5, 1906; Tonopah *Daily Sun,* December 3, 1906; Rhyolite *Herald,* December 7, 14, 1906, January 4, 11, 1907; New York *Ridgway's, A Militant Weekly for God and Country,* December 15, 22, 1906, January 12, 1907; Rice, op. cit., n. 1, 104–111.

49. Goldfield *News,* December 8, 15, 1906; New York *Ridgway's,* December 8, 1906; Colorado Springs *Mining Investor,* December 24, 1906; January

7, 1907; New York *Collier's,* January 26, 1907; Tonopah *Daily Sun,* January 28, 1906; Greenwater *Death Valley Chuck-Walla,* February 1, 1907.

50. Lindsay Denison, "The He-Siren of the Goldfields" and subsequent articles in *Ridgway's,* December 8, 1906 through January 12, 1907.

51. Colorado Springs *Mining Investor,* December 3, 1906, January 2, 1907; Beatty *Bullfrog Miner,* December 15, 1906; New York *Ridgway's,* December 22, 1906; Tonopah *Daily Sun,* January 9, 1907; Gold Center *News,* January 12, 1907; Rice, op. cit., n. 1, 119–122, 168–179.

52. Goldfield *Gossip,* December 1906.

53. Greenwater *Death Valley Chuck-Walla,* February 15, 1907; Goldfield *Gossip,* March 2, 9, April 13, 1907.

54. San Francisco *Mining and Scientific Press,* January 12, February 16, March 9, 1907; Greenwater *Death Valley Chuck-Walla,* June 1907; Reno *Nevada Mining News,* July 27, October 23, 1907; Sidney Norman's Reminiscences in Weight, op. cit., n. 1, 14, 16.

55. New York *Times,* January 6, 1907, January 5, 1908, and daily stock reports.

56. Greenwater *Death Valley Chuck-Walla,* March 1, 1907; Beatty *Bullfrog Miner,* September 7, 1907; San Francisco *Mining and Scientific Press,* September 14, 1907; Colorado Springs *Mining Investor,* October 14, 1907; Tonopah *Sun,* October 1, 17, 1907; Reno *Nevada Mining News,* October 23, 1907; Rhyolite *Herald,* November 8, December 6, 1907, February 26, 1908; Rhyolite *Bullfrog Miner,* June 6, 1908; Greenwater Copper Mines & Smelter Co., op. cit., n. 30, 2–6.

57. Rhyolite *Herald,* December 6, 1907, March 13, 1909; Bishop *Inyo Register,* March 11, 1909.

58. Rhyolite *Bullfrog Miner,* May 24, June 29, 1907; Beatty *Bullfrog Miner,* June 15, September 7, 1907; Tonopah *Sun,* June 25, November 4, 1907; Bishop *Inyo Register,* July 4, 1907; New York *Engineering and Mining Journal,* October 19, 1907.

59. Bishop *Inyo Register,* June 25, 1914; Glasscock, *Gold* . . . op. cit., n. 1, 274–275 and *Here's* . . . op. cit., n. 1, 234–237.

60. Rhyolite *Herald,* March 25, April 15, 1908; Rhyolite *Bullfrog Miner,* June 6, 1908; Bishop *Inyo Magazine,* July 1908; Bishop *Owens Valley Herald,* July 30, 1909; Bishop *Inyo Register,* November 4, 1909, June 25, 1914; O. J. Fisk, "Ghosts of Greenwater," *Westways,* 32 (November 1940), 9; Frickstad, op. cit., n. 45, 51.

61. Rhyolite *Bullfrog Miner,* July 13, November 2, 1907, March 28, 1908; Rhyolite *Daily Bulletin,* November 30, 1907, February 24, 1908; Independence *Inyo Independent,* February 14, 1908; Rhyolite *Herald,* April 8, 1908; New York *Harper's Weekly,* April 11, 1908; Stevens, op. cit., n. 1, v. 10 (1910), 1713; W. H. Brown Reminiscence quoted in San Bernardino *Sun-Telegram,* January 24, 1960.

62. Bishop *Inyo Register,* May 18, 1909, June 2, 1910; Rhyolite *Bullfrog Miner,* September 11, 1909; Rhyolite *Herald,* January 8, 15, 1910; New York *Copper, Curb and Mining Outlook,* February 15, 1911; Walter H. Weed, *The Mines Handbook, vol.* 15 (Tuckahoe, New York: Mines Handbook Co., 1922), 1218; Rice, op. cit., n. 1, 142–143.

Resurrection

1. Candelaria *True Fissure,* April 21, 1883, October 2, November 14, 1885; Independence *Inyo Independent,* May 26, 1883, December 19, 1885, April 10, 1886; Bishop *Inyo Register,* February 4, 1886; New York *Engineering and Mining Journal,* February 13, 1886; San Francisco *Mining and Scientific Press,* December 20, 1890; Candelaria *Chloride Belt,* October 17, 1891; Belmont *Courier,* April 27, 1895; Walter N. Frickstad and Edward W. Thrall, *A Century of Nevada Post Offices 1852–1957* (Oakland: Philatelic Research Society, 1958), 21.

2. Candelaria *True Fissure,* June 5, 12, August 28, September 11, 25, 1886; Bishop *Inyo Register,* May 12, 1887, March 22, 1888, May 8, June 19, 1890, December 7, 1893; Independence *Inyo Independent,* April 14, June 30, 1888; New York *Engineering and Mining Journal,* November 3, 1888, January 5, 1889; New York *Times,* November 15, 1903; Goldfield *Tribune,* May 29, 1913; Bishop *Owens Valley Herald,* December 29, 1916.

3. Bishop *Inyo Register,* March 27, April 24, May 8, June 19, 26, July 3, 10, September 18, October 2, 9, 16, 30, November 6, 20, 1890; Independence *Inyo Independent,* April 4, May 30, August 8, December 5, 1890, January 16, 1891; California Secretary of State, Archives, Articles of Incorporation of the Sylvania Mining Co., October 4, 1890; San Francisco *Examiner,* January 11, 1891.

4. Tonopah *Bonanza,* October 8, December 10, 1904; Bishop *Inyo Register,* December 1, 1904, January 5, 1905; Tonopah *Miner,* December 17, 1904; Los Angeles *Examiner,* January 14, 1906.

5. Tonopah *Bonanza,* April 15, 1905; Bishop *Inyo Register,* April 20, 27, June 1, 1905; Pioche *Record,* April 28, 1905; Beatty *Bullfrog Miner,* May 13, 1905; Los Angeles *Examiner,* May 23, 1905; Los Angeles *Times,* May 23, 1905; Tonopah *Miner,* May 27, 1905; Independence *Inyo Independent,* June 9, 1905; W. H. Shearer, *Atlas of the Goldfield, Tonopah and Bullfrog Mining Districts of Nevada* (San Francisco: W. H. Shearer Pub. Co., 1905), 56, 69.

6. Tonopah *Bonanza,* December 10, 1904, March 25, April 1, October 28, 1905; Bishop *Inyo Register,* March 30, May 11, 18, June 22, 1905; Rhyolite *Herald,* May 19, 1905; Tonopah *Miner,* June 3, 1905; New York *United States Mining Journal,* June 1905; Goldfield *Review,* November 2, 1905.

7. *Commonwealth v. Francis L. Burton* (June 5, 1903), 183 Mass 461; Colorado Springs *Mining Investor,* May 22, 1905, December 16, 1907.

8. Los Angeles *Examiner,* May 23, 24, 25, 1905; Los Angeles *Times,* May 23, 24, 1905; Los Angeles *Herald,* May 24, 1905; Tonopah *Miner,* May 27, 1905; Independence *Inyo Independent,* June 2, 1905.

9. Tonopah *Miner,* May 27, 1905; Goldfield *Review,* November 9, 1905, January 25, 1906, December 14, 1907; Goldfield *News,* November 10, 1905, December 14, 1907; Los Angeles *Examiner,* December 11, 1907; New York *Times,* December 11, 1907; Rhyolite *Herald,* December 13, 1907, July 3, 1908; *Sunset Magazine,* 56 (February 1926), 48.

10. Independence *Inyo Independent,* June 9, 23, 1905; Goldfield *Review,* June 29, October 19, 1905; Goldfield *News,* July 14, August 11, 1905; Bishop *Inyo Register,* July 27, August 17, October 26, 1905; Tonopah *Miner,* July 29, 1905; Tonopah *Bonanza,* August 26, 1905; Los Angeles *Examiner,* January 14, 1906.

11. Goldfield *Review,* July 13, September 7, 1905; Goldfield *News,* July 14, 21, 1905; Colorado Springs *Mining Investor,* July 24, 1905; Bishop *Inyo Register,* July 27, August 3, 17, 1905.

12. Columbus *Borax Miner,* January 1, 1876; Aurora *Esmeralda Herald,* February 7, March 6, 1880; Independence *Inyo Independent,* September 6, 1884, April 14, 1888; Bishop *Inyo Register,* May 8, June 19, December 25, 1890, June 23, 1898, March 30, June 8, 1899, September 21, 1905, February 8, 1906; Candelaria *Chloride Belt,* December 5, 1891, November 26, 1892; Tonopah *Miner,* September 9, 1905; Goldfield *Review,* November 9, 1905; Palmetto *Herald,* June 1, 1906.

13. Bishop *Inyo Register,* March 22, 1888, July 3, October 16, 1890; Tonopah *Miner,* September 24, November 4, December 17, 1904, January 14, 1905; Tonopah *Bonanza,* June 24, September 23, October 28, 1905.

14. Tonopah *Bonanza,* February 11, July 22, October 21, 1905, February 10, 17, 24, March 10, 1906; Goldfield *Review,* December 21, 1905; January 4, February 22, April 5, 1906; Goldfield *News,* February 2, 9, 23, 1906; Bishop *Inyo Register,* February 8, 22, March 1, 1906; Palmetto *Herald,* March 9, 16, 1906; Frickstad and Thrall, op. cit., n. 1, 21.

15. Bishop *Inyo Register,* September 26, 1895, December 15, 1904; Tonopah *Miner,* April 29, 1905; Los Angeles *Examiner,* September 20, 1905.

16. Candelaria *Chloride Belt,* June 13, October 17, 1891, February 6, 1892; Bishop *Inyo Register,* March 31, 1892, November 8, 1894, November 28, December 5, 12, 1895, January 2, 30, 1896; National Archives Record Group 29, Twelfth Census of the United States, 1900, Esmeralda County, Nevada, Tule Canyon, Enumeration District No. 13; Frickstad and Thrall, op. cit., n. 1, 26.

17. Tonopah *Miner,* November 12, December 10, 1904, March 11, August 26, 1905; Bishop *Inyo Register,* December 8, 15, 29, 1904, January 5, February 2, August 17, 1905; Frickstad and Thrall, op. cit., n. 1, 29.

18. Tonopah *Miner,* October 3, 1902, August 1, September 3, 26, 1903, August 20, 1904, April 1, 1905; Tonopah *Bonanza,* October 4, 18, 1902, July 11, August 22, October 10, 1903, March 12, August 20, 1904; Independence *Inyo Independent,* March 31, 1905; Helen S. Carlson, *Nevada Place Names, A Geographical Dictionary* (Reno: University of Nevada Press, 1974), 233.

19. Candelaria *True Fissure,* April 21, 1883, November 27, 1886; Independence *Inyo Independent,* May 22, 1896; Bishop *Inyo Register,* July 2, August 20, September 24, 1896, May 11, 1899; Belmont *Courier,* December 26, 1896; Tonopah *Bonanza,* June 4, 1904, May 27, September 30, 1905; Los Angeles *Times,* May 26, 1905; Beatty *Bullfrog Miner,* June 24, 1905.

20. Material on Vahrenkamp and Mitchell is from Los Angeles *Times,* May 26, 1905; Bessie Beatty, *Who's Who in Nevada* (Los Angeles: Home Printing Co., 1907), 174–175; Tonopah *Sun,* April 13, 1906, February 2, 1907;

and material on Emerson is from New York *Times,* May 17, 1902, June 16, July 28, 1906, August 1, 1915; Horace J. Stevens, *The Copper Handbook* (Houghton, Mich.: Horace J. Stevens), v. 4 (1904), 549–551, v. 6 (1906), 810, v. 10 (1911), 1394; Los Angeles *Times,* May 26, 1905; Rhyolite *Bullfrog Miner,* May 18, 1906; *Book Review Digest* (1906), 98 (1915), 147 (1919), 162; *Who Was Who in America, vol. 1, 1897–1942* (Chicago: Marquis, 1943), 371.

21. Los Angeles *Times,* May 26, 1905; Tonopah *Bonanza,* May 27, July 15, September 30, 1905; Tonopah *Miner,* June 10, 1905; Rhyolite *Herald,* June 30, September 22, 1905; Los Angeles *Examiner,* September 3, 1905; *Who Was Who* . . . op. cit., n. 20.

22. Los Angeles *Times,* September 3, 1905; Los Angeles *Examiner,* September 3, 1905.

23. Tonopah *Bonanza,* September 9, 1905; Rhyolite *Herald,* September 29, 1905, August 24, October 26, November 16, 1906; Beatty *Bullfrog Miner,* August 11, November 29, 1906.

24. Palmetto *Herald,* June 1, 1906; Bishop *Inyo Register,* July 26, 1906, June 17, 1909, January 26, February 16, 1911, December 18, 1919; Blair *Press* February 1, August 22, 1908.

25. Rhyolite *Bullfrog Miner,* May 18, 1906, May 31, 1907; Bessie Beatty, op. cit., n. 20, Goldfield *News* (2nd Annual Number), February 1907; Willis George Emerson, *The Smoky God; or, A Voyage to the Inner World* (Chicago: Forbes & Co., 1908), 186 pp.; Hornsilver *Herald,* September 12, 1908; San Diego *Union,* March 17, 1909; *Who Was Who* . . . op. cit., n. 20, v. 4, 944; *Dictionary of American Biography* (New York: Charles Scribner's Sons, 1936), v. 4, 555.

26. Rhyolite *Bullfrog Miner,* May 31, 1907; January 25, April 4, 1908; Goldfield *Review,* July 20, 1907; Beatty *Bullfrog Miner,* August 3, September 21, 1907; Rhyolite *Herald,* November 29, December 20, 1907, April 8, May 23, 1908.

27. Goldfield *Review,* November 9, 1905, June 22, 1907, May 30, 1908; Blair *Press,* January 25, February 22, April 18, 1908; Hornsilver *Herald,* May 9, 1908.

28. Goldfield *Review,* April 18, May 9, 1908; Rhyolite *Herald,* April 22, 29, 1908; Rhyolite *Bullfrog Miner,* April 25, May 9, 1908; Hornsilver *Herald,* May 9, 16, 23, 30, June 6, July 4, September 12, 1908.

29. Rhyolite *Herald,* April 29, 1908; Hornsilver *Herald,* May 9, June 13, 1908; Royal Flush Mine, Reports and Papers, 1908–1930, and Letter of Frances E. Williams to Jeanne E. Wier, November 7, 1908 in Nevada Historical Society, Reno; Frances Gold Mountain Mining Company, *Report of Officers for Corporate Year and Report of Director for Quarter Ending July 31, 1910* (Goldfield: 1910), 18 pp. Material on Frances E. Williams is from Tonopah *Bonanza,* October 31, 1903, August 27, September 3, 10, 1904; Tonopah *Miner,* January 2, 1904; Hornsilver *Herald,* May 16, July 11, 25, 1908; Rhyolite *Herald,* July 26, October 7, November 18, 1908, December 23, 1911; Goldfield *Review,* May 30, 1908; Rhyolite *Bulletin,* November 17, 1908; Goldfield *News,* March 27, 1909.

30. Rhyolite *Herald,* May 6, June 10, 17, 1908; Goldfield *Review,* September 19, 1908.

31. Rhyolite *Herald,* September 2, 1908; Bishop *Inyo Register,* November 12, 1908; Blair *Press,* November 14, December 3, 1908, February 19, April 23, 1909; Bishop *Owens Valley Herald,* December 11, 1908; Pioneer *Topics,* June 10, 1909.

32. Rhyolite *Bullfrog Miner,* December 19, 1908, June 19, 1909; Rhyolite *Herald,* June 16, 1909, September 24, 1910, May 4, 1912; Walter H. Weed, *The Mines Handbook, v. 12* (New York: Stevens Copper Handbook Co., 1916), 1061; *v. 14* (New York: Weed, 1920), 1105, 1107; Walter G. Neale, *The Mines Handbook, v. 17* (New York: Mines Handbook Co., 1926), 1260.

33. San Diego *Union,* March 17, 1909, January 2, 1923; Rhyolite *Herald,* April 7, June 30, July 31, September 18, 1909, February 12, April 2, 23, May 21, July 23, August 20, September 24, 1910, April 29, September 23, 1911; Bishop *Inyo Register,* August 25, 1910; San Francisco *Mining and Scientific Press,* November 23, December 28, 1912, January 25, April 26, June 7, September 20, October 18, November 22, 1913; Weed, *v. 14,* op. cit., n. 32, 499, 653. Biographical information on Willard W. Whitney is from San Diego *Union,* January 2, 3, 1923.

34. Tonopah *Miner,* March 5, 1904; Searchlight *Searchlight,* May 27, November 25, 1904, January 13, 1905; Tonopah *Bonanza,* March 4, July 22, 1905; Los Angeles *Mining Review,* April 1, July 29, 1905; Beatty *Bullfrog Miner,* April 22, 1905. Biographical information on Carl F. Schader is from George W. Burton, *Men of Achievement in the Great Southwest* (Los Angeles: Los Angeles Times, 1904), 116–117; Goldfield *News,* Second Annual Number, February 1907; *From Pueblo to City* (Los Angeles: Le Berthon Pub. Co., 1910), 49; John S. McGroarty, *History of Los Angeles County* (Chicago: American Historical Society, Inc., 1923), v. III, 334–336; Los Angeles *Times,* March 10, 1934.

35. Tonopah *Bonanza,* March 4, July 22, 1905; Beatty *Bullfrog Miner,* April 22, May 20, June 17, 1905, April 7, 1906; Los Angeles *Times,* June 20, 1905; Rhyolite *Herald,* July 7, 1905.

36. Beatty *Bullfrog Miner,* Arpil 22, 1905, June 9, 1906; Los Angeles *Mining Review,* July 29, 1905; Rhyolite *Bullfrog Miner,* August 31, 1906; Rhyolite *Herald,* August 31, September 21, October 26, 1906; Colorado Springs *Mining Investor,* October 15, 1906; Frickstad and Thrall, op. cit., n. 1, 15.

37. Tonopah *Bonanza,* March 24, 1906; Randsburg *Miner,* June 28, 1906; Goldfield *News,* December 1, 1906; Rhyolite *Herald,* February 1, December 27, 1907, January 17, October 21, 1908; Rhyolite *Bullfrog Miner,* July 13, 1907; Beatty *Bullfrog Miner,* November 16, 1907; Reno *Nevada Mining News,* June 18, 1908; Goldfield *News,* October 10, 1908; Joseph L. King, *History of the San Francisco Stock and Exchange Board* (San Francisco: Joseph L. King, 1910), 340; *From Pueblo . . .* op. cit., n. 34.

38. Rhyolite *Bullfrog Miner,* July 13, 1907; Beatty *Bullfrog Miner,* August 17, September 28, October 5, 1907; Rhyolite *Herald,* November 8, December 27, 1907, January 17, 1908, May 12, 1909; Reno *Nevada Mining News,*

June 18, 1908; Goldfield *News,* October 10, 1908.

39. Beatty *Bullfrog Miner,* October 5, 1907; Reno *Nevada Mining News,* December 19, 1907, April 2, 9, June 18, 1908.

40. Beatty *Bullfrog Miner,* March 21, 1908; Reno *Nevada Mining News,* June 18, 1908.

41. Beatty *Bullfrog Miner,* July 18, 1908; Rhyolite *Bullfrog Miner,* July 18, 1908; February 13, May 29, 1909; Los Angeles *Times,* July 19, 1908; Rhyolite *Herald,* October 21, December 30, 1908, January 13, April 3, May 12, 1909, July 23, 1910, July 8, 1911; Los Angeles *Mining Review,* November 2, 1912; Bertrand F. Couch and Jay A. Carpenter, *Nevada's Metal and Mineral Production (1859–1940 inclusive)* (Reno: Univ. of Nevada, 1943), 112–113.

42. New York *Engineering and Mining Journal,* March 20, 1915; Carrara, *Obelisk,* April 17, 1915; Couch and Carpenter, op. cit., n. 41.

43. U.S. Patent Office, *Official Gazette, 37* (1886), 631–632; Los Angeles *Mining Review,* March 25, 1899, January 12, 1901, July 7, 1906; San Francisco *Mining and Scientific Press,* January 26, 1901; Rhyolite *Bullfrog Miner,* September 7, 1907; Bishop *Inyo Register,* October 24, 1907; Beatty *Bullfrog Miner,* November 9, 1907; San Bernardino County, Superior Court Case No. 5409 *Osborne v. Osborne.*

44. Beatty *Bullfrog Miner,* June 23, July 28, October 27, 1906, February 2, 1907; Los Angeles *Mining Review,* July 7, 1906; Randsburg *Miner,* January 17, 1907; Rhyolite *Bullfrog Miner,* January 25, 1907; Bishop *Inyo Register,* January 20, 1910; Articles of Incorporation of the Tecopa Consolidated Mining Company, filed January 29, 1907, in California Secretary of State Archives, Sacramento; San Bernardino County, Superior Court, Probate No. 4141, Jonas B. Osborne, 1913.

45. Randsburg *Miner,* January 17, 1907; Beatty *Bullfrog Miner,* February 2, 1907; Rhyolite *Herald,* July 25, 1907, January 27, 1909.

46. Rhyolite *Herald,* March 22, October 25, November 29, 1907, January 31, 1908; Los Angeles *Mining Review,* April 20, June 8, 1907; Rhyolite *Bullfrog Miner,* May 10, July 6, August 24, 1907; Denver *Mining Reporter,* November 28, 1907; Rhyolite *Bulletin,* January 30, March 24, 1908; Charles H. Fulton, *Metallurgical Smoke* (Washington, D.C.: Government Printing Office, 1915), 82–83.

47. Rhyolite *Bullfrog Miner,* September 7, 1907; Rhyolite *Herald,* October 25, November 29, 1907, January 27, 1909; Beatty *Bullfrog Miner,* November 2, 1907; Rhyolite *Bulletin,* April 17, 1908; Bishop *Inyo Register,* November 12, 1908; Los Angeles *Mining Review,* December 5, 1908. Biographical information on Nelson Z. Graves is from New York *Times,* December 8, 1930; Philadelphia *Bulletin,* December 8, 1930; Philadelphia *Public Ledger,* December 8, 1930; *Who Was Who in America, vol. 4* (Chicago: A. N. Marquis Co., 1969), 374.

48. Rhyolite *Herald,* June 24, 1908, January 27, March 31, May 26, July 24, September 18, October 2, December 4, 1909, March 12, 1910, February 11, 1911; Bishop *Inyo Register,* November 12, 1908, January 20, 1910, June 1, 1916; Bishop *Owens Valley Herald,* October 22, November 26,

December 10, 1909; Independence *Inyo Independent,* December 10, 1909; San Francisco *Mining and Scientific Press,* February 11, 1911.

49. Los Angeles *Mining Review,* April 15, 1908; Rhyolite *Herald,* March 12, July 9, August 6, 1910, February 11, 18, 1911, April 20, 1912; San Francisco *Mining and Scientific Press,* February 11, 1911; Bishop *Inyo Register,* February 15, 1912.

50. Bishop *Inyo Register,* February 15, 1912, August 19, 26, 1915; Rhyolite *Herald,* April 20, 1912; San Francisco *Mining and Scientific Press,* November 23, 1912. Biographical information on Lincoln D. Godshall is from Rossiter Johnson, *The Twentieth Century Biographical Dictionary of Notable Americans* (Boston: Biographical Society, 1904), v. 4; Stevens, op. cit., n. 20, v. 10 (1911), 1258–1259; *Who's Who In California . . . 1928–29* (San Francisco: Who's Who Publishing Company, 1929), 209; *Who Was Who In America, vol. 5* (Chicago: Marquis Who's Who, 1973), 273.

51. San Francisco *Mining and Scientific Press,* November 23, 1912, March 7, 1914; Bishop *Inyo Register,* April 10, October 16, 1913, January 1, July 30, 1914, January 21, August 26, 1915, June 1, 1916, July 27, November 9, 1922; New York *Engineering and Mining Journal,* June 17, 1916, March 27, 1920, February 4, 1922, December 17, 1925; Independence *Inyo Independent,* February 19, 1921; California State Mineralogist, *Report of State Mineralogist, v. 15* (1915–16), 95–96, 103–104; *v. 22* (1927), 485, 491–492; *v. 34* (1938), 440–442, 448–450; Weed, op. cit., n. 20, *v. 14* (1920), 486; *v. 15* (1922), 536; *v. 16* (1924), 627; *v. 17* (1926), 546; *v. 18* (1931), 674; W. B. Tucker and R. J. Sampson, "Mineral Resources of the Resting Spring Region, Inyo County," *California Journal of Mines and Geology, v. 33* (1937), 264–269; David F. Myrick, *Railroads of Nevada and Eastern California* (Berkeley: Howell-North Books, 1963), v. 2, 596.

52. California State Mineralogist, op. cit., n. 51, v. 34 (1938).

53. Bishop *Inyo Register,* February 15, 1912; Weed, op. cit., n. 20, *v. 14* (1920), 486, *v. 17* (1926), 546.

Facts, Fantasies, and Flivvers

1. Titus Fey Cronise, *The Natural Wealth of California* (San Francisco: H. H. Bancroft and Co., 1868), 102; Mary Cone, *Two Years in California* (Chicago: S. C. Griggs and Co., 1876), 58.

2. Independence *Inyo Independent,* January 22, 1887; New York *World,* September 16, 1894.

3. San Francisco *Mining and Scientific Press,* December 20, 1890; unidentified newspaper clipping dated June 12, 1894 in John B. Colton's Scrapbook v. 2, 57, in Jayhawker Collection, Henry E. Huntington Library and Art Gallery, San Marino, Calif.; New York *World,* September 16, 1894.

4. Charles F. Lummis, *Some Strange Corners of Our Country* (New York: The Century Co., 1892), 37–38; New York *World,* September 16, 1894.

5. Los Angeles *Times,* January 19, 1890.

6. New York *Scientific American,* September 19, 1885.

7. San Francisco *Mining and Scientific Press,* December 20, 1890; San Francisco *Examiner,* February 28, 1891; New York *Times,* July 27, 1891; R. S. Dix, "Death Valley," *Chautauquan, 13* (August 1891), 629; A. K. Fisher et al., *The Death Valley Expedition, Part II* (Washington, D.C.: Government Printing Office, 1893), 3; Frederick V. Coville, *Botany of the Death Valley Expedition* (Washington Printing Office, 1893), 1; Vernon Bailey, "Into Death Valley 50 Years Ago," *Westways, 32* (December 1940), 8. Biographical material on Bailey can be found in *Who Was Who In America, v. 2* (Chicago: Marquis Who's Who, 1950), 37 and New York *Times,* April 22, 1942; on Coville in *National Cyclopaedia of American Biography, v. 27* (New York: J. T. White and Co., 1939), 239 and *Who Was . . .* op. cit., *v. 1,* 266; on Fisher in *National . . .* op. cit., *v. 37,* 473–474 and *Who . . .* op. cit., *v. 2,* p. 137; on Funston in *National . . .* op. cit., *v. 11,* 40–41, *Dictionary of American Biography, v. 4* (New York: Charles Scribners, 1932), 73–75 and *Who . . .* op. cit., *v. 1,* 433; on Merriam in *National . . .* op. cit., *v. 13,* 264, *Who . . .* op. cit., *v. 2,* 369, *Dictionary . . .* op. cit., *supp. v. 3,* 517–519, and New York *Times,* March 21, 1942; on Nelson in *National . . .* op. cit., *v. 26,* 434–435, *Who . . .* op. cit., *v. 1,* 890, and *Dictionary . . .* op. cit., *supp. v. 1,* 571–572; on Palmer in *National . . .* op. cit., *v. 44,* 312 and *Who . . .* op. cit., *v. 3,* 662–663; and Stephens in San Diego *Union,* October 6, 1937.

8. Independence *Inyo Independent,* November 14, 1890; San Francisco *Examiner,* February 28, 1891; and biographical material cited in note 7.

9. Theodore S. Palmer, Diary, December 1890–May 1891, in Henry E. Huntington Library and Art Gallery, San Marino, Calif.; San Francisco *Mining and Scientific Press,* January 10, 1891; San Francisco *Examiner,* January 28, February 28, May 31, June 7, 1891; New York *Times,* July 27, 1891; Fred W. Koch, "Through Death Valley, A Brief Account of a Trip from Daggett to Furnace Creek," *Sierra Club Bulletin, v. 1* (June 1893), 40–53; Fisher, op. cit., n. 7; Coville, op. cit., n. 7, 3–10; Bailey, op. cit., n. 7, 8–11. See also Albert K. Fisher, Papers 1827–1957, Clinton H. Merriam, Death Valley Expedition Journals I & II, March–July 1891 in his Papers and Journals 1873–1938; and Theodore S. Palmer, Papers 1887–1954, all in Manuscripts Division, Library of Congress.

10. Palmer, Diary . . . op. cit., n. 9; New York *Times,* May 7, 1891; Bishop *Inyo Register,* July 16, 1891; Colton's Scrapbook . . . op. cit., n. 3, v. 2, 16, 23; Bailey, op. cit., n. 7, 9–11.

11. Bishop *Inyo Register,* March 12, 1891; Candelaria *Chloride Belt,* August 8, 1891; San Francisco *Chronicle,* December 20, 1891; Colton's Scrapbook . . . op. cit., n. 3, v. 2, 4–5, 10; Mark V. Harrington, *Notes on the Climate and Meteorology of Death Valley, California (Weather Bureau Bulletin No. 1)* (Washington, D.C.: Weather Bureau, 1892), 1–50; G. H. Willson, "The Hottest Region in the United States," *Monthly Weather Review, 43* (July 1915), 278–280.

12. Belmont *Courier,* April 6, 1895, June 24, 1899; Bishop *Inyo Register,* August 15, 1895; C. H. Sinclair, "The Oblique Boundary Line Between

California and Nevada," Appendix No. 3, *Report of the Superintendent of the Coast and Geodetic Survey 1899–1900* (Washington, D.C.: Government Printing Office, 1901), 301–308; San Francisco *Chronicle,* August 27, 1905; Paul DeLaney, "Life of 'Death Valley Scotty,'" Rhyolite *Death Valley Magazine,* February 1908; Rhyolite *Bullfrog Miner,* November 7, 1908.

13.   Josiah E. Spurr, *Descriptive Geology of Nevada South of the Fortieth Parallel and Adjacent Portions of California (U.S. Geological Survey Bulletin No. 208)* (Washington, D.C.: Government Printing Office, 1903), 15–16, and his "Developments at Tonopah, Nevada, During 1904" in *Contributions to Economic Geology, 1904 (U.S. Geological Survey Bulletin No. 260)* (Washington, D.C.: Government Printing Office, 1905), 148–149; *Who . . .* op. cit., n. 7, *v. 3,* 810; *Dictionary . . .* op. cit., n. 7, *supp. v. 4,* 764–766.

14.   Sydney H. Ball, "Notes on Ore Deposits of Southwestern Nevada and Eastern California" in *Contributions to Economic Geology, 1905 (U.S. Geology Survey Bulletin No. 285)* (Washington, D.C.: Government Printing Office, 1906), 53–55, 61, and his *A Geologic Reconnaissance in Southwestern Nevada and Eastern California (U.S. Geological Survey, Bulletin No. 308)* (Washington, D.C.: Government Printing Office, 1907), 13–15, 113, 174–176; Frederick L. Ransome, *Preliminary Account of Goldfield, Bullfrog, and Other Mining Districts in Southern Nevada (U.S. Geological Survey Bulletin No. 303)* (Washington, D.C.: Government Printing Office, 1907), 7, 40, 52, 58; Frederick L. Ransome, W. H. Emmons, and G. H. Garrey, *Geology and Ore Deposits of the Bullfrog District, Nevada (U.S. Geological Survey Bulletin No. 407)* (Washington, D.C.: Government Printing Office, 1910), 10–11, 92.

15.   Marius R. Campbell, *Reconnaissance of the Borax Deposits of Death Valley and Mohave Desert (U.S. Geological Survey Bulletin No. 200)* (Washington, D.C.: Government Printing Office, 1902), 8, 13–19; Gilbert E. Bailey, *The Saline Deposits of California (California State Mining Bureau Bulletin No. 24)* (Sacramento: Supt. State Printing, 1902), 7, 154 ff.; San Francisco *Chronicle,* October 8, 9, 14, 1902; Bishop *Inyo Register,* October 9, November 27, 1902.

16.   Ball, *A Geologic . . .* op. cit., n. 14, 13–15; Robert H. Chapman, "The Deserts of Nevada and the Death Valley," *National Geographic Magazine, 17* (September 1906), 483–497; U.S. Geological Survey, Topographic Maps (1:250,000), *Amargosa Region* (July 1906), *Ballarat* and *Furnace Creek* (first eds. March 1908), and *Lida* (first ed. June 1908); Tonopah *Miner,* July 21, 1906, June 22, 1907; Walter C. Mendenhall, *Some Desert Watering Places in Southeastern California and Southwestern Nevada (U.S. Geological Survey Water-Supply Paper 224)* (Washington, D.C.: Government Printing Office, 1909), 7–8; Rhyolite *Herald,* May 26, 1909; S. G. Benedict, "Mapping Death Valley a Quarter Century Ago," *Touring Topics, 23* (November 1931), 12–15, 43.

17.   Saint Louis *Globe-Democrat,* June 16, 1894 clipping and an unidentified clipping dated June 12, 1894 in Colton's Scrapbook . . . op. cit., n. 3, v. 2, p. 57; Bishop *Inyo Register,* February 28, 1907; Rhyolite *Herald,* March 15, 1907; Beatty *Bullfrog Miner,* October 26, December 14, 1907; Tonopah

Miner, October 12, 1907; S. S. Gannett and D. H. Baldwin, *Results of Spirit Leveling in California, 1896 to 1907, Inclusive* (*U.S. Geological Survey Bulletin No. 342*) (Washington, D.C.: Government Printing Office, 1908), 86, 91.

18. John R. Spears, *Illustrated Sketches of Death Valley and Other Borax Deserts of the Pacific Coast* (Chicago: Rand, McNally & Co., 1892), 13, 24; William Lewis Manly, *Death Valley in '49* (San Jose: Pacific Tree and Vine Co., 1894), 498 pp.; George Wharton James, *Heroes of California* (Boston: Little, Brown and Co., 1910), 86–93.

19. Frank Norris, *McTeague* (New York: Doubleday & McClure Co., 1899), 442 pp.; Mary Austin, *The Land of Little Rain* (Boston: Houghton, Mifflin, and Co., 1903), 280 pp.; Robinson Jeffers, "Death Valley," *Out West, 26* (May 1907), 443; Mary Austin, *Earth Horizon, Autobiography* (Boston: Houghton, Mifflin, and Co., 1932), 233.

20. Independence *Inyo Independent,* January 22, 1897, June 3, 1904; Tonopah *Miner,* June 25, 1904; Rhyolite *Herald,* April 19, 1907; Rhyolite *Bullfrog Miner,* June 29, July 6, 1907, July 11, August 1, 8, 1908; Beatty *Bullfrog Miner,* July 20, 1907; Rhyolite *Death Valley Prospector,* December 1907; Rhyolite *Daily Bulletin,* December 11, 1908.

21. Bishop *Inyo Register,* October 13, 1904; Tonopah *Bonanza,* March 18, October 28, 1905; Rhyolite *Herald,* May 5, June 9, September 8, 1905, June 22, 29, 1906; Beatty *Bullfrog Miner,* June 23, 1906.

22. Beatty *Bullfrog Miner,* June 23, 1906; Rhyolite *Herald,* June 29, 1906.

23. Rhyolite *Herald,* June 29, 1906.

24. Rhyolite *Herald,* September 28, 1906, January 18, February 22, December 27, 1907; Independence *Inyo Independent,* December 21, 1906; Rhyolite *Bullfrog Miner,* February 22, 1907, April 4, 1908; Goldfield *Gossip,* May 11, 1907.

25. New York *Times,* November 25, 28, December 10, 1907, February 9, 12, 13, 1908; Rhyolite *Bullfrog Miner,* April 4, 1908. In addition to extensive newspaper coverage, there are four books by participants in the New York to Paris Race: E. R. Thomas Motor Company, *The Story of the New York to Paris Race* (Buffalo: [1908]), 75 pp; Hans Koeppen, *Im Auto um die Welt* (Berlin: Verlag von Ullstein, 1908), 355 pp.; Antonio Scarfoglio, *Round the World in a Motor-Car* (London: Grant Richards, 1909), 368 pp.; and George Schuster with Tom Mahoney, *The Longest Auto Race* (New York: John Day Company, 1966), 160 pp.

26. Rhyolite *Daily Bulletin,* March 21, 1908; New York *Times,* March 22, 23, 24, 25, 30, 1908; Rhyolite *Herald,* March 25, 1908; Rhyolite *Bullfrog Miner,* March 28, 1908; Schuster, op. cit., n. 25, 66–70.

27. Rhyolite *Daily Bulletin,* March 30, 1908; New York *Times,* March 30, 31, April 7, 1908; Scarfoglio, op. cit., n. 25, 138–145.

28. Rhyolite *Daily Bulletin,* April 1, 2, 1908; Rhyolite *Herald,* April 1, 8, 1908; New York *Times,* April 2, 3, 4, 1908; Rhyolite *Bullfrog Miner,* April 4, 1908.

29. New York *Times,* April 11, 12, 13, 17, July 27, 31, August 18, 21,

September 18, 1908, January 9, 1910, June 12, 19, 1968, July 5, 1972;
Schuster, op. cit., n. 25, 12, 132–141.

30.   Schuster, op. cit., n. 25, 143–144.

31.   Rhyolite *Herald,* April 22, 1908; Jacob M. Murdock, *A Family Tour From
Ocean to Ocean* (Detroit: Packard Motor Car Co., [1908]), 32 pp.; Los
Angeles *Times,* June 23, 30, 1912; Howard C. Kegley, "Lou Wescott
Beck," *American Magazine, 76* (September 1913), 30–32; Carey S. Bliss,
*Autos Across America, A Bibliography of Transcontinental Automobile Travel:
1903–1940* (Austin: Jenkins & Reese Companies, 1982), 10–11.

32.   Goldfield *Tribune,* July 9, 10, 11, 1913; Dodge Brothers Corporation,
*Through Death Valley in a Dodge Brothers Motor Car, A True Story of O. K.
Parker's Memorable Trip Through This Arid Desert Land* (Detroit: Dodge
Brothers, 1916), 16 pp.; Margaret Long, *The Shadow of the Arrow*
(Caldwell, Idaho: Caxton Printers, 1941), 69–71.

33.   Dodge Brothers, op. cit., n. 32.

The Salt of the Earth

1.   The colemanite operations in Death Valley have been described in detail in
Ruth C. Woodman's manuscript, "History of Pacific Coast Borax Company,"
chap. IX–X, XIII–XV, and XIX in the Ruth C. Woodman Papers, Special
Collections Library, University of Oregon; and many anecdotal incidents
are told in Harry P. Gower, *50 Years in Death Valley—Memoirs of a Borax
Man* (San Bernardino: Inland Printing, Inc., 1969), 145 pp. Additional
information is in the Borax Consolidated, Ltd. Records, 1899–1928, in the
Archives of the Companies Registration Office, Board of Trade, London,
microfilm in Bancroft Library; William E. Ver Planck, "History of Borax
Production in the United States," *California Journal of Mines and Geology,
52* (1956), 283–287; David F. Myrick, *Railroads of Nevada and Eastern
California* (Berkeley: Howell-North Books, 1963), 544–593, 608–621;
James M. Gerstley, *Borax Years, Some Recollections 1933–1961* (Los
Angeles: U.S. Borax & Chemical Corp., 1979), 8–9; George H. Hildebrand,
Borax Pioneer: Francis Marion Smith (San Diego: Howell-North Books,
1982), 68–92; Norman J. Travis and E. J. Cocks, *The Tincal Trail, A
History of Borax* (London: Harrap, 1984), 60–84, 114–145, 168–175.

2.   John R. Spears, *Illustrated Sketches of Death Valley and Other Borax Deserts
of the Pacific Coast* (Chicago and New York: Rand, McNally & Co., 1892),
178–186; "The Borax Industry and its Chief Promoter," *Overland Monthly,
42* (July 1903), 24–28; Beatty *Bullfrog Miner,* April 14, 1906; Henry A.
Lafler, "'Borax' A True Fairy Tale of the West," *Sunset, 26* (April 1911),
418–423; James K. Steel, "Frank M. Smith," in Evarts I. Blake, ed.,
Greater Oakland, 1911 (Oakland: Pacific Printing Co., 1912), 274–282;
The National Cyclopaedia of American Biography (New York: James T.
White Co., 1930), v. A, 171–172, v. 28, 81–82; *Dictionary of American*

Biography (New York: Charles Scribner's Sons, 1936), v. 9, 267; Woodman, op. cit., n. 1, chaps. I, III; Hildebrand, op. cit., n. 1, 17–22, 26, 42, 101–132, 152–189, 191–192, 239–241.

3. Letters of Joseph W. Mather to Francis M. Smith, November 6, 10, 1891, March 8, August—,1892, June 3, September 19, 1893 exerpted in Woodman notes and manuscript, op. cit., n. 1, chap. VI, 31–36, chap. VIII, 1–6; Spears, op. cit., n. 2; Robert Shankland, *Steve Mather of the National Parks* (New York: Alfred A. Knopf, 1951), 13–26. Additional biographical sketches of Mather and Spears can be found in *National Cyclopaedia . . .* op. cit., n. 2, v. 9 (1907), 162, v. 26 (1937), 210; *Dictionary . . .* op. cit., n. 2, v. 6 (1933), 398–399; *Who Was Who in America* (Chicago: Marquis Who's Who, 1943), v. 1, 788, 1160.

4. *Borax: From the Desert, Through the Press, Into the Home: 200 Best Borax Recipes from More than 800 Issues of 250 Different Publications in 33 States of the Union* (San Francisco, Chicago, New York: Pacific Coast Borax Co., 1895), 80 pp.; Woodman, op. cit., n. 1, chap. VIII, 7–8, 12–16; Shankland, op. cit., n. 3, 26–31.

5. "Twenty Mule Team, St. Louis Exposition," motion picture by American Mutoscope and Biograph Co., 1904 in National Archives; *The 20-Mule Team and a Sketch of Its Famous Driver: Borax Bill* (New York, Chicago, San Francisco: Pacific Coast Borax Co., 1904), 16 pp., reprinted by Sagebrush Press, Morongo Valley, 1980; Bishop *Inyo Register,* May 19, 1904; Randsburg *Miner,* July 6, 13, 1905; *Lecture on Death Valley, the Borax Industry and 20 Mule Team Borax Products, Arranged for the Moving Picture and Stereopticon Exhibits of the Pacific Coast Borax Company* (San Francisco: Pacific Coast Borax Co., 1909), 5–6.

6. Bishop *Inyo Register,* September 15, 1898; New York *Commercial and Financial Chronicle,* September 24, 1898; Woodman, op. cit., n. 1, chap. VII, 30–32, chap. VIII, 54–55; Ver Planck, op. cit., n. 1, 281; Myrick, op. cit., n. 1, 823–826; Hildebrand, op. cit., n. 1, 46–47.

7. Pacific Borax and Redwood's Chemical Works, Ltd. *Prospectus* (London: 1896) broadside; Borax Consolidated, Ltd. *Prospectus* (London: 1899) broadside, and *Memorandum and Articles of Association* (London: Doherty & Co., 1899), 40 pp.; *Lafayette Hoyt DeFreise Esq. and Mr. Henry Evan Thomas on Behalf of Borax Consolidated Limited, Agreement for Sale* (London: Doherty & Co., 1899), 17 pp; London *Times,* January 11, 1899; New York *Commercial and Financial Chronicle,* February 18, 1899, March 17, July 28, 1900; Woodman, op. cit. n. 1, chap. VIII, 63–66; Hildebrand, op. cit., n. 1, 44–53, 101.

8. Candelaria *True Fissure,* November 6, 1886; Rhyolite *Herald,* February 26, 1908; Shankland, op. cit., n. 3, 33–37; Woodman, op. cit., n. 1, chap. VIII, 36–40, 44–47; Gerstley, op. cit., n. 1, 4–7, 13–14; Hildebrand, op. cit., n. 1, 55–59, 152–189.

9. F. M. Smith letters to R. C. Baker, February 3, March, 1899, April 21, 1900, April 5, 1901, and May 5, 1902 exerpted in Hildebrand, op. cit., n. 1, 63–66, 72; Bishop *Inyo Register,* April 13, 1899.

10. Independence *Inyo Independent,* October 30, 1903; Searchlight *Searchlight,*

October 30, December 4, 1903; Tonopah *Bonanza,* April 9, 1904; W. W. Cahill, "Half a Century with the Pacific Coast Borax Company and Subsidiary Companies," 4, typescript in Ruth Woodman Papers; Woodman, op. cit., n. 1, chap. VII, 25; Hildebrand, op. cit., n. 1, 72–73.

11. Tonopah *Bonanza,* August 8, 1903; Independence *Inyo Independent,* October 30, 1903, February 26, 1904; Searchlight *Searchlight,* November 27, 1903, May 13, August 26, 1904, May 19, 1905; Beatty *Bullfrog Miner,* April 14, 1906; Cahill, op. cit., n. 10, 5; Woodman, op. cit., n. 1, chap. IX, 3; Hildebrand, op. cit., n. 1, 73.

12. F. M. Smith's annual report to Borax Consolidated, Ltd., 1904 exerpted in Woodman, op. cit., n. 1, chap. IX, 3; Letters of F. M. Smith to R. C. Baker, April 29, July 4, 1904, exerpted in Hildebrand, op. cit., n. 1, 73; Searchlight *Searchlight,* August 26, 1904; New York *Commerical and Financial Chronicle,* December 23, 1905, May 23, 1908; Myrick, op. cit., n. 1, 546.

13. Tonopah *Bonanza,* December 24, 1904; Searchlight *Searchlight,* December 30, 1904, February 3, 1905; Independence *Inyo Independent,* February 10, 1905; F. M. Smith's annual report to Borax Consolidated, Ltd., 1905, exerpted in Woodman, op. cit., n. 1, chap. IX, 4.

14. S.P.L.A. & S.L.R.R. Map of Reconnaisance Survey Las Vegas to Tonopah February 25, 1905, reproduced in Myrick, op. cit., n. 1, 457; Beatty *Bullfrog Miner,* April 22, 1905; Cahill, op. cit., n. 10, 5; Woodman, op. cit., n. 1, chap. IX, 4–6.

15. Independence *Inyo Independent,* May 12, 1905; Searchlight *Searchlight,* May 19, July 28, 1905; Las Vegas *Age,* May 20, 27, June 3, July 1, 8, 29, August 12, 19, September 30, 1905; Beatty *Bullfrog Miner,* September 30, 1905; Cahill, op. cit., n. 10, 5, and W. W. Cahill's answers on letter from R. C. Woodman January 25, 1949; Woodman, op. cit., n. 1, chap. IX, 7–10; Myrick, op. cit., n. 1, 546.

16. Los Angeles *Examiner,* August 30, September 3, 1905; Las Vegas *Age,* September 2, December 9, 1905; Beatty *Bullfrog Miner,* October 7, December 30, 1905, June 30, July 7, 28, 1906; Independence *Inyo Independent,* April 27, 1906; Cahill's answers, op. cit., n. 15; Woodman, op. cit., n. 1, chap. IX, 14–18; Myrick, op. cit., n. 1, 548–549.

17. Beatty *Bullfrog Miner,* October 27, 1906, January 25, 1908; Los Angeles *Mining Review,* December 29, 1906; Myrick, op. cit., n. 1, 548.

18. Independence *Inyo Independent,* February 26, 1904; Tonopah *Bonanza,* September 9, 1905, January 27, 1906; Los Angeles *Mining Review,* June 8, 1907; Rhyolite *Bullfrog Miner,* June 22, August 17, 1907; Beatty *Bullfrog Miner,* June 29, 1907; Bishop *Inyo Register,* September 5, 1907; F. M. Smith's report to Borax Consolidated, Ltd. for October 1, 1907 to September 20, 1908, in R. C. Woodman Papers; Hoyt C. Gale, "The Lila C. Borax Mine at Ryan, Cal.," *Mineral Resources of the United States . . . 1911* (Washington, D.C.: Government Printing Office, 1912), pt. 2, 861; Woodman, op. cit., n. 1, chap. IX, 23–24, 32–33; Myrick, op. cit., n. 1, 555.

19. Rhyolite *Herald,* October 19, 1906; Rhyolite *Bullfrog Miner,* June 22, November 30, 1907; Rhyolite *Bulletin,* October 30, 1907, May 11, 1908; Myrick, op. cit., n. 1, 475, 489, 518, 556–557.

20. Rhyolite *Herald,* November 15, 1907; Bishop *Inyo Register,* February 18, 1909, November 3, 1910; Charles G. Yale and Hoyt S. Gale, "Borax," *Mineral Resources of the United States . . . 1916* (Washington, D.C.: Government Printing Office, 1917), pt. 2, 387; Woodman, op. cit., n. 1, chap. X, 36.

21. Bishop *Inyo Register,* September 5, 1907, February 18, 1909, November 3, 1910, December 14, 1916; Rhyolite *Herald,* November 15, 1907, September 2, 1911; Bishop *Owens Valley Herald,* October 15, 1909; Gale, op. cit., n. 18, 864–865; Woodman, op. cit., n. 1, chap. X, 10–20, 33, chap. XV, 2, 9; Gower, op. cit., n. 1, 63.

22. New York *Commercial and Financial Chronicle,* July 25, 1914; Woodman, op. cit., n. 1, chap. XIII, 1–4; Hildebrand, op. cit., n. 1, 196–205, 216–220.

23. New York *Commercial and Financial Chronicle,* May 17, December 27, 1913, June 13, July 25, September 12, 26, 1914; Woodman, op. cit., n. 1, chap. XIII, 22–28; Hildebrand, op. cit., n. 1, 205–209, 219.

24. San Francisco *Mining and Scientific Press,* November 21, 1914; Bishop *Inyo Register,* September 3, 1931; Woodman, op. cit., n. 1, chap. XIII, 32–36; Hildebrand, op. cit., n. 1, 208, 224–226, 238, 246–260.

25. Independence *Inyo Independent,* November 20, 1886 (patent applications); Los Angeles *Times,* November 23, 1913, March 21, December 17, 1914; Bishop *Inyo Register,* November 27, 1913, April 2, July 23, 30, December 24, 1914; New York *Commercial and Financial Chronicle,* March 21, July 25, September 12, 1914; Carrara *Obelisk,* April 4, 1914; Woodman, op. cit., n. 1, chap. XIV, 1–10; Myrick, op. cit., n. 1, 608–611; Gower, op. cit., n. 1, 4–5, 17.

26. Los Angeles *Times,* December 17, 1914; *Scientific American,* October 1, 1921; Woodman, op. cit., n. 1, chap. XIV, 5, 10, 35; Myrick, op. cit., n. 1, 609, 615; Gower, op. cit., n. 1, 40.

27. Los Angeles *Times,* December 17, 1914; Bishop *Inyo Register,* January 21, 1915, December 14, 1916; Woodman, op. cit., n. 1, chap. XV, 2–10.

28. Woodman, op. cit., n. 1, chap. XIV, 54–55; Gower, op. cit., n. 1, 18, 31–32, 55.

29. C. R. Dudley Reminiscences of Hughes case, 11 pp., and W. W. Cahill Reminiscences, 3 pp., in Ruth C. Woodman Papers; Woodman, op. cit., n. 1, chap. XIV, 10–12; Gower, op. cit., n. 1, 33–35.

30. Independence *Inyo Independent,* May 3, June 14, 1884, November 20, 1886; F. M. Smith's annual report to Borax Consolidated, Ltd. for 1910 and United States Borax Company notes in Ruth C. Woodman Papers; *James P. Hughes v. United States Borax Co.,* Circuit Court of Appeals, Ninth Circuit, January 22, 1923 (286 Fed 24); Woodman, op. cit., n. 1, chap. X, 32–33, chap. XIV, 12–13.

31. Bishop *Inyo Register,* December 30, 1920; Independence *Inyo Independent,* March 12, 1921; Dudley Reminiscences, op. cit., n. 29; Cahill, op. cit., n. 29; Woodman, op. cit., n. 1, chap. XIV, 12–15; Gower, op. cit., n. 1, 36.

32. Bishop *Inyo Register,* December 30, 1920, April 7, 1921; Independence *Inyo Independent,* March 12, 1921; Los Angeles *Times,* March 5, 1922;

Hughes v. U.S. Borax Co., op. cit., no. 30; Dudley Reminiscences, op. cit., n. 29; Woodman op. cit., n. 1, chap. XIV, 18–34.

33. Independence *Inyo Independent,* September 22, 1905; Bishop *Owens Valley Herald,* December 21, 1921; *United States Borax Company v. Death Valley Borax Company, et al.,* Civil Case 5802, Second Appellate District, Division One, June 25, 1928 (92 Cal. App. 724); C. R. Dudley, "Clara Lode Claim," 15 pp., and H. P. Gower Reminiscences, 2 pp., in Ruth C. Woodman Papers; Woodman, op. cit., n. 1, chap. XIX, 12.

34. Independence *Inyo Independent,* May 31, 1924; Gower Reminiscences, op. cit., n. 33; Woodman, op. cit., n. 1, chap. XIX, 13–16.

35. Bishop *Owens Valley Herald,* May 30, 1923; Independence *Inyo Independent,* May 31, 1924; *United States Borax . . .* op. cit., n. 33; Gower Reminiscences, op. cit., n. 33; C. B. Glasscock, *Here's Death Valley* (Indianapolis: Bobbs-Merrill Co., 1940), 272–274; Woodman, op. cit., n. 1, chap. XIX, 1–19; Gower, op. cit., n. 1, 43–44.

36. California Secretary of State, Archives, Articles of Incorporation of the Death Valley Borax Co., August 9, 1920; Independence *Inyo Independent,* May 31, 1924; Harry P. Gower Letter to Ruth C. Woodman August 15, 1949, in Ruth C. Woodman Papers; J. W. Minette and G. Muehle, "Colemanite from the Thompson Mine, Death Valley," *Mineralogical Record, 5* (1974), 67–73.

37. Woodman, op. cit., n. 1, chap. XIV, 52–53; Gower, op. cit., n. 1, 40, 52–53.

38. Bishop *Inyo Register,* November 18, 1920; Julian Boyd Reminiscences in Ruth C. Woodman Papers; Woodman, op. cit., n. 1, chap. XIV, 53–55; Gower, op. cit., n. 1, 35, 40–41.

39. Zane Grey, "Death Valley," *Harper's Magazine, 140* (April 22, 1920), 758–759, and his *Tales of Lonely Trails* (New York and London: Harper & Brothers, 1922), 374–375; Bishop *Inyo Register,* November 27, 1924; Los Angeles *Times,* March 15, 1925; *Arrowhead Magazine* (December 1926/January 1927), 11–12; Woodman, op. cit., n. 1, chap. XV, 23–27.

40. Bishop *Inyo Register,* November 11, 1920; Boyd Reminscences, op. cit., n. 38; Woodman, op. cit., n. 1, chap. XIV, 55–56, chap. XXI, 48; Myrick, op. cit., n. 1, 587.

41. Tonopah *Mining Reporter,* January 21, August 12, 1922; Bishop *Owens Valley Herald,* February 8, 1922; Bishop *Inyo Register,* August 17, 1922; L. F. Noble, "Note on a Colemanite Deposit Near Shoshone, Calif.," *U.S. Geological Survey Bulletin 785-D* (Washington, D.C.: Government Printing Office, 1926), 71–72; Tonopah *Nevada Mining Record-Reporter,* January 9, 1932; H. P. Gower to R. C. Woodman, July 11, 1949; Woodman, op. cit., n. 1, chap. XIX, 1–4; Gower, op. cit., n. 1, 82–83.

42. Tonopah *Nevada Mining Record,* October 15, 1927; Noble, op. cit., n. 41; Woodman, op. cit., n. 1, chap. XIX, 5–8; Myrick op. cit., n. 1, 587; Gower, op. cit., n. 1, 83; Gerstley, op. cit., n. 1, 7, 10.

43. Tonopah *Nevada Mining Record,* October 15, 1927; Yale and Gale, op. cit., n. 20, and Frank J. Katz, *Mineral Resources of the United States 1927* (Washington, D.C.: Government Printing Office, 1930), pt. 1, A81 list a

total U.S. borax production from 1907 through 1927 of about $44 million, over two-thirds of which must have come from Death Valley and the Amargosa; *The American Potash and Chemical Corporation* (San Bernardino: Sun Printing and Publishing, 1940) 8–9; Woodman, op. cit., chap. XXI, 1–10; Ver Planck, op. cit., n. 1, 287–288; Gerstley, op. cit., n. 1, 23.

44.   Tonopah *Nevada Mining Record,* October 15, 1927; Woodman, op. cit., n. 1, chap. XXI, 47–48; Ver Planck, op. cit., n. 1.

Mostly Mud and Rock

1.   Rhyolite *Bullfrog Miner,* May 10, 24, 1907; Goldfield *News,* May 18, 1907; Goldfield *Review,* June 15, 1907; Beatty *Bullfrog Miner,* July 20, 1907.

2.   Rhyolite *Bullfrog Miner,* August 3, September 7, 1907; Rhyolite *Herald,* December 9, 1908; Bishop *Owens Valley Herald,* December 11, 1908.

3.   Rhyolite *Bullfrog Miner,* May 16, December 5, 1908; Rhyolite *Herald,* June 24, December 9, 1908.

4.   Beatty *Bullfrog Miner,* September 9, 1905, January 20, 1906; Rhyolite *Herald,* October 2, 1909; Independence *Inyo Independent,* February 25, 1910; Los Angeles *Mining Review,* September 21, 1912; Bishop *Inyo Register,* October 3, 1912, May 24, September 20, 1917; California *Report of State Mineralogist,* 27 (Sacramento: State Printer, 1931), 395–396.

5.   Needles *Eye,* November 4, 1893; Independence *Inyo Independent,* February 7, 14, 1896; Bishop *Inyo Register,* January 24, 1901, October 9, November 27, 1902, August 8, 1918, November 9, 1922; San Francisco *Chronicle,* October 8, 9, 14, 1902; Gilbert E. Bailey, *The Saline Deposits of California (California State Mining Bureau Bulletin 24)* (Sacramento: Supt. State Printing, 1902), 154 ff; Beatty *Bullfrog Miner,* March 9, 1907; Rhyolite *Bullfrog Miner,* June 15, 1907; Bishop *Owens Valley Herald,* September 24, 1909; Independence *Inyo Independent,* March 11, 1910; California Nitrate Development Company, *A Story About Nitrate of Soda in Death Valley California* (San Francisco:1914), 21 pp.; L. F. Noble, G. R. Mansfield, and others, *Nitrate Deposits in the Amargosa Region Southeastern California (U.S. Geological Survey Bulletin No. 724)* (Washington, D.C.: Government Printing Office, 1922), 97 pp.; John A. Latschar, *Historic Resource Study, A History of Mining in Death Valley National Monument, vol. II* (Denver: National Park Service, 1981), 721–726. Biographical information on Albert W. Scott, Jr., is in *Who Was Who in America, v. 5* (Chicago: Marquis Who's Who, 1973), 646.

6.   Rhyolite *Herald,* April 27, May 25, 1912; Bishop *Inyo Register,* October 10, 1912, April 17, 1913, March 21, 1914; Los Angeles *Mining Review,* April 19, 1913; Hoyt S. Gale, "Prospecting for Potash in Death Valley, California," in *Contributions to Economic Geology (U.S. Geological Survey Bulletin No. 540)* (Washington, D.C.: Government Printing Office, 1914), 407–415; *Moody's Manual of Railroads and Corporation Securities 1916, vol. II* (New York: Moody Manual Co., 1916), 2085.

7.   San Bernardino County Recorder, Mining Locations Book 131, 373–375, Book 133, 272–273, 311; Deeds, Book 662, 131, and Book 664, 70; Nevada Department of State, Articles of Incorporation of American Magnesium Company, September 18, 1919; Bishop *Owens Valley Herald,* January 2, 1924; David G. Thompson, *The Mohave Desert Region (U.S. Geological Survey, Water Supply Paper No. 578)* (Washington, D.C.: Government Printing Office, 1929), 591–592. Thomas H. Wright's flower shop is listed in the *Los Angeles City Directory* for 1903 through 1924.

8.   Bishop *Inyo Register,* June 10, 1920, June 15, 1922; Los Angeles *Times,* November 20, 1921; John Anson Ford, "Tap Wealth of Death Valley with Monorail," *Popular Mechanics, 40* (July 1923), 36–37.

9.   California State Mining Bureau, *Monthly Chapter of Report XVIII of the State Mineralogist* (October 1922), 742; Ford, op. cit., n. 8; Charles Hardy, "Monorail Transportation for Magnesium Ore in California," *Engineering and Mining Journal,* July 21, 1923; *Engineering News,* September 27, 1923. The monorail has also been described in Cora L. Keagle, "Tale of the Mono Rail," *Desert Magazine, 7* (May 1944), 9–12; Richard H. Jahns, "The Epsom Salts Line—Monorail to Nowhere," *Engineering and Science Monthly 14, 18–21* (April 1951); N. M. Thompson's Recollections in "Historic Photos of the High-Riding 'Magnesium Flyer,'" *Desert Magazine, 26* (January 1963), 12–15; David F. Myrick, *Railroads of Nevada and Eastern California* (Berkeley: Howell-North Books, 1963), v. 2, 808–814; Linda W. Greene, *Historic Resource Study, A History of Mining in Death Valley National Monument, vol. I* (Denver: National Park Service, 1981), 225–237.

10.   Hardy, op. cit., n. 9; *Engineering News,* September 27, 1923; Independence *Inyo Independent,* December 29, 1923; *Index of Patents Issued from the United States Patent Office, 1923* (Washington, D.C.: Government Printing Office, 1924), 602; "Conquering Excessive Grades and Curves with a Monorail Line," *Scientific American, 130* (April 1924), 249; Nevada Department of State, Amended Articles of Incorporation of American Magnesium Company, May 24, 1924; Bourke Lee, *Death Valley Men* (New York: Macmillan, 1932), 220.

11.   Ford, op. cit., n. 8; Independence *Inyo Independent,* December 29, 1923; *Scientific American, 130* (April 1924), 249; Phoenix *Arizona Mining Journal,* November 30, 1925; Thompson's Recollections, op. cit., n. 9, 14; A. W. Harrison's Reminiscences in San Bernardino *Sun-Telegram,* December 10, 1957; Keagle, op. cit., n. 9, 12.

12.   Los Angeles *Times,* February 28, March 28, April 25, July 4, 1927, December 27, 1928; Phoenix *Arizona Mining Journal,* March 15, April 15, May 15, 1927; Tonopah *Nevada Mining Record,* September 17, 1927; *Los Angeles City Directory,* 1929–1942; W. A. Chalfant, *Death Valley, The Facts* (Stanford: Stanford University Press, 1930), 118; Keagle, op. cit., n. 9, 12.

13.   Rhyolite *Bullfrog Miner,* October 3, 1908; Bishop *Inyo Register,* October 22, 1908, January 28, 1909, September 14, November 30, 1911, February 22, August 1, November 14, 1912, August 7, 1913, March 12, July 23, 1914; California State Mineralogist, *Fifteenth Report . . . 1915–16* (Sacra-

mento: State Printer, 1919), 863; Harold O. Weight, "Shady Myrick, Pioneer Gem Prospector of the Mojave," *Calico Print, 7* (September/October 1951), 4–6.

14. Rhyolite *Herald,* April 5, June 22, 1907; Rhyolite *Bullfrog Miner,* April 5, 1907; Beatty *Bullfrog Miner,* April 6, 1907; Tonopah *Nevada Mining Record-Reporter,* March 14, 1931.

15. Independence *Inyo Independent,* December 18, 1920; California Secretary of State, Archives, Sacramento, Articles of Incorporation of Death Valley Oil Company, August 2, 1922; Los Angeles *Times,* December 31, 1923; California State Mining Bureau, *Summary of Operations, California Oil Fields, 10* (July 1924), 119; Clinton C. Ball, "'Oil' on the Amargosa," *Desert Magazine, 17* (March 1954), 12.

16. Beatty *Bullfrog Miner,* December 30, 1905; Rhyolite *Herald,* April 1, 1911; Tonopah *Mining Reporter,* March 18, 1922.

17. Rhyolite *Bullfrog Miner,* June 20, 1908; Rhyolite *Herald,* July 14, 1909, April 1, May 6, September 2, December 23, 1911, April 27, May 11, 1912; Goldfield *Tribune,* February 24, May 1, 2, 7, 9, 14, 1913; Carrara *Obelisk,* May 8, 1914. See also Charles H. Labbe, *Rocky Trails of the Past* (Las Vegas: C. H. Labbe, 1960), 176–177; Myrick, op. cit., n. 9, 604–607.

18. Goldfield *Tribune,* May 2, 9, 14, 1913; Carrara *Obelisk,* May 2, 8, 1914, March 20, May 15, July 31, 1915; Myrick, op. cit., n. 9, 606.

19. Goldfield *Tribune,* May 1, 1913; Carrara *Obelisk,* April 11, May 8, June 27, 1914, January 2, February 6, April 17, May 1, 8, June 19, September 18, October 16, November 13, 27, December 11, 1915, July 8, 15, August 26, September 2, 9, 1916.

20. Bishop *Inyo Register,* December 7, 1916, January 25, 1917; Tonopah *Mining Reporter,* March 18, 1922, April 3, 1926; Tonopah *Nevada Mining Record,* January 22, 1927; Fort Worth *Western World,* April 7, 1928; Labbe, op. cit., n. 17, 177.

21. Bishop *Inyo Register,* February 21, 1889; California State Mineralogist, *Fifteenth Report . . .* op. cit., n. 13, 85–86, and *Seventeenth Report . . . 1920,* 282; Myrick, op. cit., n. 9, 568, 586, 589; Harry P. Gower, *50 Years in Death Valley—Memoirs of a Borax Man* (San Bernardino: Inland Printing, Inc., 1969), 48–50.

22. Tonopah *Mining Reporter,* July 11, 1925, February 12, 1927; Tonopah *Nevada Mining Record,* February 5, 1927, May 18, June 13, October 26, 1929; Bishop *Inyo Register,* October 24, 1929; *The Mines Handbook, v. 18* (Suffern, N.Y.: Mines Information Bureau, 1931), 641; Independence *Inyo Independent,* November 26, 1932; California State Mineralogist, *Thirty-fourth Report . . .* (Sacramento: State Printer, 1938), 489.

23. Lauren A. Wright, *Talc Deposits of the Southern Death Valley Kingston Range Region, California (California Division of Mines and Geology, Special Report 95)* (San Francisco: 1968), 79 pp.

24. San Bernardino County Recorder, Mining Records, Book 65, 117–118, and Deeds, Book 483, 40–47 and Book 675, 155–156; J. S. Diller, "Talc and Soapstone," in *Mineral Resources of the United States . . . 1913. Part II Non-Metallic* (Washington, D.C.: Government Printing Office, 1915), 157–

160; *Mineral Production of California in 1916 (California Division of Mines Bulletin 74)* (Sacramento: State Printer, 1917), 106; Bishop *Inyo Register,* August 8, 1918; California Secretary of State, Amended Articles of Incorporation of Pacific Minerals and Chemical Company, September 26, 1919; California State Mineralogist, *Seventeenth Report . . .* op. cit., n. 21, 367–368. Biographical information on Lycurgus Lindsay may be found in *Press Reference Library, Notables of the West, vol. I* (New York: International News Service, 1913), 192–193; William A. Spalding, *History of Los Angeles City and County* (Los Angeles: J. R. Finnell and Sons, 1931), v. 3, 54–56; Los Angeles *Times,* September 13, 1931; and C. L. Sonnichsen, *Colonel Greene and the Copper Skyrocket* (Tucson: University of Arizona, 1974), 44, 78–81, 213–214.

25. San Bernardino County Recorder, Deeds, Book 716, 6–8, and Official Records Book 603, 221–251; "Talc and Soapstone" in *Mineral Resources . . .* op. cit., n. 24, 1920 through 1927; Los Angeles *Times,* July 28, 1921, July 15, 1922; California State Mineralogist, *Seventeenth Report . . .* op. cit., n. 21, 367–368; Wright, op. cit., n. 23, 74–75.

26. Eclipse Mine: California State Mineralogist, *Fifteenth Report . . .* op. cit., n. 13, 126; Wright, op. cit., n. 23, 44. Tremolite Mine: San Bernardino County Recorder, Deeds, Book 618, 313, Book 650, 278–282, Book 727, 334–338; Bishop *Inyo Register,* August 8, 1918; California State Mineralogist, *Seventeenth Report . . .* op. cit., n. 21, 369–370, *Twenty Sixth Report . . . 1930,* 325, *Twenty Seventh Report . . . 1931,* 100–104; *California Journal of Mines and Geology,* v. 49 (1953), 208–209. Death Valley Mine: Independence *Inyo Independent,* June 26, July 8, 1920; Tonopah *Mining Reporter,* August 26, 1922; Tonopah *Nevada Mining Record,* September 28, 1929, March 28, 1931; Bishop *Inyo Register,* June 30, 1932; Wright, op. cit., n. 23, 40–42; Greene, op. cit., n. 9, 350–353. Warm Spring Mine: Wright, op. cit., n. 23, 48; Greene, op. cit., n. 9, 262–271.

27. Ralph J. Fairbanks, "My 73 Years on Southwestern Deserts," *Touring Topics,* 22 (June 1930), 24–25; California State Mineralogist, *Seventeenth Report . . .* op. cit., n. 21, 297–298; Victor E. Kral, *Mineral Resources of Nye County, Nevada* (Reno: University of Nevada, 1951), 14–15.

28. *Mineral Resources of the United States . . .* op. cit., n. 24, 1917 and 1918; Bishop *Inyo Register,* January 23, 1919; Tonopah *Mining Reporter,* April 25, 1925, April 2, 1927; Tonopah *Nevada Mining Record,* June 23, 1928; Tonopah *Nevada Mining Record-Reporter,* February 28, 1931; Kral, op. cit., n. 27, 13.

29. Tonopah *Mining Reporter,* April 25, July 11, 1925, January 8, 1927; Bishop *Inyo Register,* October 1, 1925, February 23, June 21, 28, 1928; Tonopah *Nevada Mining Record,* June 19, August 28, November 13, 1926, May 14, 1927, February 4, 25, June 23, October 13, December 1, 1928, February 9, 1929; New York *Engineering and Mining Journal-Press,* March 6, 1926; California Secretary of State, Archives, Articles of Incorporation of United Death Valley Clay Co., filed March 14, 1927; *Walker's Manual of Pacific Coast Securities, Twenty-First Annual Number* (San Francisco: Walker's Manual, Inc., 1929), 504–505; Myrick, op. cit., n. 9, 610. Bio-

graphical information on George Raymond Boggs is from *Who's Who in Los Angeles County, 1928–29* (Los Angeles: Charles J. Lang, 1928), 51, and Alumni Records Office, Yale University, New Haven, Conn.

30. Tonopah *Nevada Mining Record,* November 13, 1926; Independence *Inyo Independent,* March 30, October 12, 1929; Helen McInnis's Reminiscences, "Boom Days at Ash Meadows," *Frontier Times, 39* (June/July 1965), 12–14.

31. Tonopah *Mining Reporter,* January 8, November 19, 1927; Tonopah *Nevada Mining Record,* February 4, May 5, 1928.

32. Bishop *Inyo Register,* February 14, 1929, May 7, 1931; *Walker's Manual* op. cit., n. 29, 1929 and 1935, 513–514; Tonopah *Nevada Mining Record,* January 31, 1931; McInnis Reminiscences, op. cit., n. 30, 14. Production figures valued only at the pit price are given in Bertrand F. Couch and Jay A. Carpenter, *Nevada's Metal and Mineral Production (1859–1940, Inclusive)* (Reno: University of Nevada, 1943), 111–112, 117–118; and Kral, op. cit., n. 27, 14–15.

The Hangers-on

1. Tonopah *Mining Reporter,* July 5, 1924, January 8, August 6, 1927; Gilbert *Record,* November 14, 1925, April 24, 1926; Tonopah *Nevada Mining Record,* October 23, 1926, May 28, July 2, November 5, December 31, 1927, January 7, February 25, March 10, 1928; Tonopah *Nevada Mining Record-Reporter,* May 17, September 13, November 8, 1930, January 3, February 14, 28, November 7, 1931; *Mines Handbook, v. 18* (Suffern, N.Y.: Mines Information Bureau, 1931), 1348, 1543, 1553; John A. Latschar, *Historic Resource Study, A History of Mining in Death Valley National Monument, vol. II* (Denver: National Park Service, 1981), 35–37.

2. Alfred H. Dutton, *Notable Nevadans in Caricature* (n.p.: 1915); *Mines Handbook . . .* op. cit., n. 1, *v. 15* (1922), 1174, 1314, *v. 17* (1926), 1155, 1285, and *v. 19* (1937), n. 1, 250, 797; Tonopah *Nevada Mining Record,* November 27, December 18, 1926; Tonopah *Mining Reporter,* May 14, September 3, 1927, December 8, 1928; Tonopah *Nevada Mining Record-Reporter,* April 5, 1930, May 9, 1931.

3. Rhyolite *Herald,* February 26, 1908; Independence *Inyo Independent,* November 12, 1909, January 28, 1910; Bishop *Inyo Register,* January 27, 1910, January 27, 1910, January 14, 21, August 26, 1915; California State Mineralogist, *Fifteenth Report . . .* (Sacramento: State Printing Office, 1916), 78–79; *Los Angeles City Directory* (Los Angeles: L.A. City Directory Co., 1915), 1513; Carl B. Glasscock, *Here's Death Valley* (Indianapolis: Bobbs-Merrill Co., 1940), 252; Latschar, op. cit., n. 1, 663–665.

4. Bishop *Inyo Register,* January 14, 21, July 29, August 26, 1915, September 29, 1921, July 14, August 11, 1932; Carrara *Obelisk,* May 22, 1915; New York *Engineering and Mining Journal,* July 10, September 25, 1915; California State Mineralogist, *Fifteenth Report . . .* op. cit., n. 3, 78–79,

Twenty-second Report . . . *1926,* 469, and *Thirty-fourth Report* . . . *1938,* 383; Tonopah *Mining Reporter,* September 24, October 15, 1921; *Mines Handbook,* v. 18, op. cit., n. 1, 571; W. A. Chalfant, *Death Valley, The Facts* (Stanford: Stanford University Press, 1930) 117; Glasscock, op. cit., n. 3, 252–254; Latschar, op. cit., n. 1, 665–668.

5. LeRoy and Margaret Bales, "He Belongs to the Panamints," *Desert Magazine, v. 5* (November 1941), 17–21, and Obituary, *v. 9* (February 1946), 34; George C. Pipkin, *Pete Aguereberry, Death Valley Prospector and Gold Miner* (Trona: Muchison Publications, 1982), 158 pp.; Linda W. Greene, *Historic Resource Study, A History of Mining in Death Valley National Monument, vol. I* (Denver: National Park Service, 1981), 534–535.

6. Frank Harris, "Half a Century Chasing Rainbows," *Touring Topics, 22* (October 1930), 12–20, 55; Bishop *Inyo Register,* May 17, November 15, 1934; Dane Coolidge, *Death Valley Prospectors* (New York: E. P. Dutton & Co., 1937), chaps. VII through X, 85–156.

7. Bishop *Owens Valley Herald,* November 4, 1925; Independence *Inyo Independent,* August 3, 1929, November 29, 1930; Bishop *Inyo Register,* July 24, 31, 1930; Tonopah *Nevada Mining Record-Reporter,* August 2, 1930; California State Mineralogist, *Twenty-eight Report . . . 1928,* 373–376.

8. Walter R. Skinner, *Mining Manual for 1910* (London: Skinner, 1910), pp. 342–343; *Mines Handbook . . .* op. cit., n. 1, *v. 15* (1922), 1298, and *v. 18* (1931), 1404; Tonopah *Mining Reporter,* October 21, December 9, 1922; Tonopah *Nevada Mining Record,* February 5, 1927; Tonopah *Nevada Mining Record-Reporter,* December 28, 1929, February 8, March 22, April 19, 1930; Bernard F. Couch and Jay A. Carpenter, *Nevada's Metal and Mineral Production (1859–1940, Inclusive)* (Reno: Nevada State Bureau of Mines, 1943), 54.

9. Independence *Inyo Independent,* January 3, 24, 1890, April 18, 1902, June 26, 1903, September 13, 1907, May 21, 1909; Bishop *Inyo Register,* August 2, September 13, 1900; Greene, op. cit., n. 5, 452–458.

10. Bishop *Inyo Register,* September 24, November 26, 1914, January 21, April 8, September 17, 1915; *Mineral Resources of the United States, 1915* (Washington: Government Printing Office, 1917), pt. 1, 837–838 and *1918* (1920), pt. 1, Table I, 33–34; Greene, op. cit., n. 5, 458–459.

11. Bishop *Inyo Register,* April 8, 15, June 3, September 17, December 16, 1915, February 24, 1916; Bishop *Owens Valley Herald,* August 13, 1915; California State Mineralogist, *Fifteenth Report . . .* op. cit., n. 3, 60–62 and *Thirty-fourth Report . . .* op. cit., n. 4, 378; *Mines Handbook . . .* op. cit., n. 1, *v. 12* (1916), 752; Donald E. White, *Antimony Deposits of the Wildrose Canyon Area, Inyo County, California (U.S. Geological Survey Bulletin 922–K)* (Washington, D.C.: Government Printing Office, 1940), 307–308; Greene, op. cit., n. 5, 459–461.

12. San Bernardino County Recorder, Mining Records, Book 74, 307, Deeds, Book 594, 115–119; Carrara *Obelisk,* May 22, 1915; Los Angeles *Times,* August 29, 1915; Bishop *Inyo Register,* March 23, June 1, 1916; Walter W. Bradley et al., *Manganese and Chromium in California (California State Mining Bureau Bulletin 76)* (Sacramento: California State Printing

Office, 1918), 19, 62–64; Parker D. Trask, *Manganese in California* (*California Division of Mines Bulletin 125*) (Sacramento: State Printers, 1943), 203–205; *California Journal of Mines and Geology, 49,* 119–120.

13. Bishop *Inyo Register,* April 6, 20, 1916, November 1, 1917; Bishop *Owens Valley Herald,* May 19, 1916; Greene, op. cit., n. 5, 817–818.

14. Information on Sylvania is from Bishop *Inyo Register,* December 18, 1919; Tonopah *Mining Reporter,* May 1, 1926; *Mines Handbook* . . . op. cit., n. 1, *v. 16* (1924), 1246.

15. Goldfield *Tribune,* June 9, 11, 1913; Bishop *Inyo Register,* June 12, 19, 1913, February 26, 1914; Clarence Eddy, *The Burro's Bray, A Book of Pomes* (Salt Lake City: [author], 1923); Green, op. cit., n. 5, 320.

16. Bishop *Inyo Register,* September 4, 11, 18, October 16, November 6, 1913, February 26, 1914, January 21, July 22, 29, August 26, June 1, 1916; Carrara *Obelisk,* May 22, 1915; *Mines Handbook* . . . op. cit., n. 1, *v. 12* (1916), 321; California State Mineralogist, *Fifteenth Report* . . . op. cit., n. 3, 89–90; Harry P. Gower, *50 Years in Death Valley—Memoirs of a Borax Man* (San Bernardino: Inland Printing, Inc., 1969), 20; Greene, op. cit., n. 5, 320–325.

17. Tonopah *Mining Reporter,* April 28, 1923, January 30, March 6, April 24, July 3, 1926, February 12, 1927; New York *Engineering and Mining Journal,* December 1, 1923; *Mines Handbook* . . . op. cit., n. 1, *v. 16* (1924), 1439; Bishop *Owens Valley Herald,* March 3, 24, 31, April 14, 1926; Independence *Inyo Independent,* May 1, 1926; Greene, op. cit., n. 5, 326–331.

18. *Mines Handbook* . . . op. cit., n. 1, *v. 18* (1931), 521–522, 628, 1584; California State Mineralogist, *Thirty-fourth Report* . . . op. cit., n. 4, 430–431; Paul K. Morton, *Geology of the Queen of Sheba Lead Mine, Death Valley, California* (*California Division of Mines and Geology Special Report 88*) (San Francisco, 1965), 7; Greene, op. cit., n. 5, 331–334.

19. Bishop *Inyo Register,* January 30, 1908, October 21, 1915, January 13, March 23, 1916; Bishop *Owens Valley Herald,* October 15, 1915; California State Mineralogist, *Fifteenth Report* . . . op. cit., n. 3, 109; Independence *Inyo Independent,* October 16, 1920, January 8, 1921; Tonopah *Nevada Mining Record,* February 11, 1928; Tonopah *Mining Reporter,* September 8, 1928; James F. McAllister, *Geology of Mineral Deposits in the Ubehebe Peak Quadrangle, Inyo County, California* (*California Division of Mines, Special Report 42*) (San Francisco: 1955), 21–23; Greene, op. cit., n. 5, 824–830.

20. *The Great Register of the County of Inyo, State of California, A.D. 1884* (Independence: Independent Print, 1884), 5; Bishop *Inyo Register,* April 3, 1890; Independence *Inyo Independent,* April 5, 1895, February 7, 1896, August 6, 1897, December 29, 1899, April 15, 1904; Coolidge, op. cit., n. 6, 117; Greene, op. cit., n. 5, 733–738.

21. Independence *Inyo Independent,* April 15, 1904, August 14, 1920; Bourke Lee, *Death Valley Men* (New York: Macmillan Co., 1932), 172; Coolidge, op. cit., n. 6, 118–119.

22. Bishop *Inyo Register,* October 16, 1919; Eleanor J. Houston, *Death Valley Scotty Told Me* (Louisville: Franklin Press, 1954), 85; Frank A. Crampton, *Legend of John Lamoigne and Song of the Desert-Rats* (Denver: Sage Books, 1956), 26–27; Gower, op. cit., n. 16, 90–82; Green, op. cit., n. 5, 745–748.

23. Independence *Inyo Independent,* August 14, 28, September 11, October 2, 1920, December 1, 1923, June 28, 1924, April 4, 1925; Bishop *Inyo Register,* August 26, 1920; Tonopah *Mining Reporter,* January 31, 1925; Lee, op. cit., n. 21, 173–174.

24. Tonopah *Mining Reporter,* January 31, May 23, August 15, 1925; Bishop *Inyo Register,* March 12, July 30, 1925; Independence *Inyo Independent,* April 4, 1925, March 20, May 22, 1926; New York *Engineering and Mining Journal,* December 17, 1925; Tonopah *Nevada Mining Record,* July 10, 24, 1926; California State Mineralogist, *Twenty-second Report . . .* op. cit., n. 4, 488; *Mines Handbook . . .* op. cit., n. 1, *v. 18* (1931), 508; Wayne E. Hall and Hal G. Stephens, *Economic Geology of the Panamint Butte Quadrangle and Modoc District, Inyo County, California* (*California Division of Mines and Geology, Special Report 73*) (San Francisco: 1936), 36–37.

25. Independence *Inyo Independent,* December 13, 1930; Tonopah *Nevada Mining Record-Reporter,* August 22, 1931; Lee, op. cit., n. 21, 173–174, 187; Greene, op. cit., n. 5, 750–751.

The Last Hurrah

1. Edward Gardner Lewis, *Order Number Ten: Being Cursory Comments on Some of the Effects of the Great American Fraud Order* (University City: University City Pub. Co., 1911), 216 pp.; Sidney L. Morse, *The Siege of University City, the Dreyfus Case of America* (University City: University City Pub. Co., 1912), 772 pp.; Walter V. Woehlke, "The Champion Borrower of Them All," serially in *Sunset Magazine 55–56,* September 1925 through February 1926; *Who Was Who In America, v. 5* (Chicago: Marquis Who's Who, 1973), p. 429; Atascadero *News,* August 10, 1950.

2. New York *Times,* January 1, 1925; Atascadero *News,* April 10, 1925, April 23, 1926; Woehlke, op. cit., n. 1.

3. Los Angeles *Mining Review,* March 2, 1912; Independence *Inyo Independent,* September 24, 1915; Atascadero *News,* April 10, 17, May 22, 29, June 5, 1925; F. MacMurphy, "Geology and Ore Deposits of a Part of the Panamint Range, California," Unpublished M.S. thesis, California Institute of Technology, Pasadena, 1929, 87–88.

4. Atascadero *News,* May 29, June 5, December 18, 1925; Bishop *Inyo Register,* August 20, 1925; Atascadero *Lewis Journal,* November 1925; California State Mineralogist, *Twenty-second Report . . .* (Sacramento: State Printing Office, 1926), 495.

5. Atascadero *News,* June 26, September 4, 11, October 2, 30, December 18, 25, 1925; Atascadero *Lewis Journal,* November, 1925; Woehlke, op. cit., n. 1 (February 1926), 73.

6. Atascadero *News*, May 22, August 7, December 18, 25, 1925; Atascadero *Lewis Journal*, November 1925; MacMurphy, op. cit., n. 3, 98–103.

7. Atascadero *News*, August 21, December 18, 1925, January 1, 8, March 26, April 9, 16, 23, 30, May 7, 1926, April 15, 1927.

8. Atascadero *News*, September 4, October 30, 1925, May 7, 1926, August 10, 1950; Woehlke, op. cit., n. 1; California State Mineralogist, *Twenty-second Report . . .* op. cit., n. 4, 495; Los Angeles *Times*, July 18, 29, November 4, 1926, July 13, September 10, 14, 16, 1927, January 25, March 25, April 6, May 1, 1928, April 10, 1934, January 2, 1935.

9. Los Angeles *Times*, March 24, 1927; Atascadero *News*, March 25, April 15, May 20, 1927.

10. Tonopah *Mining Reporter*, March 20, 1926; Los Angeles *Times*, May 27, 1927, March 27, 1934; Walter V. Woehlke, "The Great Julian Pete Swindle," serially in *Sunset Magazine 59*, September through November 1927; Guy W. Finney, *The Great Los Angeles Bubble, A Present-Day Story of Colossal Financial Jugglery and of Penalties Paid* (Los Angeles: Milton Forbes Co., 1929), 203 pp.; Lorin L. Baker, *That Imperiled Freedom* (Los Angeles, 1932), 448 pp. Since Julian usually used only his initials, some confusion surrounds his full name. The most likely seems to be Charles Courtney Julian, the name listed in the coroner's inquest (Shanghai, *China Press*, March 30, 1934), although when pressed for a first name Julian listed himself as Courtney C. (e.g., *Los Angeles City Directories*, 1922–1925). Further confusion was created by Finney, op. cit., n. 10, 27, who erroneously called him Chanucey C.; that error was spread by a number of later writers, including Carey McWilliams, *Southern California Country* (New York: Duell, Sloan and Pearce, 1946), 242–246.

11. Woehlke, "The Great Julian . . . " op. cit., n. 10 (September 1927), 13–14; Finney, op. cit., n. 10, 27–31; Los Angeles *Times*, January 23, 24, 1924.

12. Woehlke, "The Great Julian . . . " op. cit., n. 10; Finney, op. cit., n. 10.

13. Los Angeles *Times*, February 1, 5, 8, 13, 14, March 3, 7, 1926.

14. Rhyolite *Herald*, December 8, 22, 1905, March 16, 23, May 18, 1906; Tonopah *Mining Reporter*, January 2, February 6, April 17, 1926, August 6, 1927; Los Angeles *Times*, February 1, 21, 1926; Bishop *Owens Valley Herald*, February 3, 1926; California State Mineralogist, *Twenty-second Report . . .* op. cit., n. 4, 504, 509. Additional information on Western Lead and Leadfield can be found in Harold O. Weight, "Leadfield Died of Complications," *Desert, 40* (November 1977), 34–39, 46, and John A. Latschar, *Historic Resource Study, A History of Mining in Death Valley National Monument, vol. II* (Denver: National Park Service, 1981), 187–210.

15. California Secretary of State, Archives, Sacramento, Articles of Incorporation of Western Lead Mines Company, August 19, 1925; Gilbert *Record*, November 28, December 19, 1925; Los Angeles *Times*, February 1, March 12, 18, 28, April 7, 1926, March 17, 1930; Los Angeles *Examiner*, April 7, 1926; *J. Salsberry v. C. C. Julian*, Civil Case No. 6216, District Court of Appeal, 2nd District, Division 1, California, May 28, 1929 (278 Pac 257).

16. Tonopah *Mining Reporter*, December 5, 19, 1925, January 2, 23, February 6, 1926; Bishop *Inyo Register*, January 7, February 18, 1926; Los Angeles

Times, February 1, 14, April 14, 1926; New York *Engineering and Mining Journal,* February 20, March 13, 1926.

17. Tonopah *Mining Reporter,* January 23, 30, February 6, 1926; Los Angeles *Times,* February 1, 1926; Bishop *Inyo Register,* February 18, 1926; California Secretary of State, Archives, Sacramento, Articles of Incorporation of Leadfield Bonanza Mining Company, Leadfield Burr-Welch Mines Company, Leadfield Carbonate Mines Company, Leadfield Consolidated Mines Company, Leadfield New Road Mining Company, and Leadfield Northern Mining Company, March 29, 1926; Los Angeles *Examiner,* March 30, 1926; Tonopah *Nevada Mining Record-Reporter,* March 30, 1929; *Mines Handbook, v. 18* (Suffern, N.Y.: Mines Information Bureau, 1931), 595–597.

18. Tonopah *Mining Reporter,* January 23, February 6, 13, 20, 27, March 6, 20, 27, April 3, 10, 1926; Los Angeles *Times,* January 31, February 1, March 15, 1926; Bishop *Owens Valley Herald,* February 3, 1926; Bishop *Inyo Register,* March 11, 18, 1926; Leadfield *Chronicle,* March 22, 1926.

19. Tonopah *Mining Reporter,* January 23, February 6, 27, March 20, 1926; Bishop *Owens Valley Herald,* February 3, March 17, 1926; Gilbert *Record,* February 6, 1926; Los Angeles *Times,* February 7, 8, 18, March 7, 10, May 28, 1926; Leadfield *Chronicle,* March 22, 1926; Tonopah *Nevada Record-Reporter,* July 4, 1931.

20. Los Angeles *Times,* March 16, 18, 1926; Tonopah *Mining Reporter,* March 20, 1926; Leadfield *Chronicle,* March 22, 1926.

21. New York *Engineering and Mining Journal,* February 20, March 13, 1926; Los Angeles *Times,* March 18–21, 26, 28, April 4, 7, 10, 24, 1926; Los Angeles *Examiner,* April 7, 8, 1926.

22. Los Angeles *Times,* April 6–9, 13–15, 21, 28, May 28, 1926.

23. Los Angeles *Times,* April 7, 1926; Los Angeles *Examiner,* April 7, June 2, 1926.

24. Los Angeles *Examiner,* June 2, 1926.

25. Los Angeles *Examiner,* June 11, 1926; Bourke Lee, *Death Valley* (New York: Macmillan Co., 1930), 156.

26. Los Angeles *Examiner,* September 19, 1926.

27. Los Angeles *Examiner,* September 19, 26, October 3, 8, 12, 1926.

28. Los Angeles *Examiner,* October 12, 1926.

29. Tonopah *Mining Reporter,* June 19, September 18, 1926, April 23, June 11, 1927, February 18, August 11, 1928; Bishop *Inyo Register,* April 21, June 16, 1927, August 16, 1928; Carl B. Glasscock, *Here's Death Valley* (Indianapolis: Bobbs-Merrill Co., 1940), 284; Walter N. Frickstad, *A Century of California Post Offices 1848 to 1954* (Oakland: Philatelic Research Society, 1955), 52.

30. Los Angeles *Times,* September 30, October 16, 1926, May 18, 28, June 9, December 30, 1927, May 25, July 5, 6, 13, September 17, October 6, December 29, 1928, January 22, 1929, January 15, March 21, 1930; Woehlke, "The Great Julian . . . " op. cit., n. 10 (September 1927), 81.

31. Los Angeles *Times,* January 15, February 6, 1930, July 14, 1931.

32. Alfred E. Dutton, *Notable Nevadans in Caricature* (n.p.: 1915); Tonopah

Mining Reporter, April 17, 1926; Los Angeles *Times,* September 30, 1926, March 14, 17, 26, December 9, 1930, April 10, May 5, 16, 21, 23, 29, June 11, 12, 13, July 14, September 26, 1931, June 17, 1932; *Salsberry v. Julian,* op. cit., n. 15; Bishop *Inyo Register,* April 3, 1930.

33.   Los Angeles *Times,* February 15, November 15, 1932, February 4, 5, April 25, 28, August 6, 1933, January 31, February 5, March 25, 26, 27, 28, May 11, 1934; New York *Times,* March 25, 30, 1934; Shanghai *China Press,* March 26, 27, 30, May 12, 1934.

34.   Independence *Inyo Independent,* November 20, 1926, February 5, May 7, 1927; Tonopah *Nevada Mining Record,* January 1, 29, February 19, March 5, April 16, 23, July 30, 1927; Tonopah *Mining Reporter,* February 5, 19, April 16, 1927; Bishop *Owens Valley Herald,* February 9, 23, 1927; Fort Worth *Western World,* February 12, 1927. See also Linda W. Greene, *Historic Resource Study, A History of Mining in Death Valley National Monument, vol. I* (Denver: National Park Service, 1981), 876–882.

35.   Fort Worth *Western World,* October 9, 1926, February 12, 26, April 2, May 21, 28, June 4, 1927; Tonopah *Mining Reporter,* April 16, May 7, 28, 1927, October 5, 1929; Tonopah *Nevada Mining Record,* April 23, May 28, June 11, 1927; Bishop *Owens Valley Herald,* June 8, 1927.

36.   Fort Worth *Western World,* June 4, 11, 18, 25, July 2, 9, 16, 23, 30, August 6, 13, 20, 27, 1927; Tonopah *Nevada Mining Record,* June 11, 25, July 2, 30, August 13, 20, September 3, 17, 1927; Tonopah *Mining Reporter,* July 2, 30, August 6, September 3, 10, 1927.

37.   Fort Worth *Western World,* September 10, 17, 24, October 1, 8, 15, 22, 29, November 5, 26, December 3, 17, 1927; Tonopah *Nevada Mining Record,* September 17, 1927, May 12, 1928, October 12, 1929; Tonopah *Mining Record,* September 17, 24, October 29, November 5, 1927, October 5, 1929; Fort Worth *Star-Telegram,* October 2, 1929; *Mines Handbook, v. 18,* op. cit., n. 17, 470.

38.   Carrara *Obelisk,* May 8, 1914, December 4, 1915, September 2, 1916; Tonopah *Mining Reporter,* June 16, July 14, 1928; Tonopah *Nevada Mining Record,* June 30, August 25, October 27, December 1, 1928, January 5, December 7, 1929; Los Angeles *Times,* July 9, September 24, 1928; Carrara *Miner,* July 11, 1929.

39.   Tonopah *Nevada Mining Record,* March 30, April 6, 13, 1929; Tonopah *Mining Reporter,* April 13, 20, 1929; Carrara *Miner,* July 11, 1929.

40.   Tonopah *Nevada Mining Record,* April 6, 13, 20, May 11, 1929; Los Angeles *Times,* April 8, 1929; Tonopah *Mining Reporter,* April 13, 20, 1929.

41.   Tonopah *Nevada Mining Record,* April 20, 27, May 4, June 1, 15, 1929; Los Angeles *Times,* April 20, 21, 25, 28, May 1, 1929; Los Angeles *Examiner,* April 21, 1929; Tonopah *Mining Reporter,* June 15, 29, 1929; Carrara *Miner,* July 11, August 10, 1929.

42.   Tonopah *Nevada Mining Record,* May 4, 11, June 29, July 13, 27, September 28, November 2, 1929; Tonopah *Mining Reporter,* May 25, July 13, 1929; Los Angeles *Times,* June 6, 1929; Carrara *Miner,* July 11,

August 10, 1929; *Arrowhead Magazine,* August 1929, 11; Los Angeles *Record,* February 20, 22, 24, 25, 1929.

43. Tonopah *Mining Reporter,* August 24, September 21, 28, 1929; Los Angeles *Times,* December 4, 1929, January 1, 1931; Tonopah *Nevada Mining Record,* December 7, 1929; Tonopah *Nevada Mining Record-Reporter,* April 19, August 23, 1930; *Mines Handbook, v. 18,* op. cit., n. 17, 1455.

44. Tonopah *Nevada Mining Record-Reporter,* February 28, June 6, August 22, 1931; Bishop *Inyo Register,* July 9, August 20, 27, 1931.

45. Tonopah *Nevada Mining Record-Reporter,* May 16, June 20, 27, September 12, October 10, 17, December 19, 26, 1931, May 14, 1932; Los Angeles *Times,* October 15, 1934.

A Nice Place to Visit

1. Bishop *Inyo Register,* March 31, 1892, March 22, 1906; Beatty *Bullfrog Miner,* March 3, 1906; Rhyolite *Bullfrog Miner,* February 15, 1908; Carrara *Obelisk,* April 18, 1914.

2. Independence *Inyo Independent,* February 9, 1906; Goldfield *Review,* August 17, 1907; Rhyolite *Bullfrog Miner,* December 5, 1908; Rhyolite *Herald,* December 9, 1908; Bishop *Owens Valley Herald,* December 11, 1908.

3. Greenwater *Death Valley Chuck-Walla,* April 1, 1907.

4. Randsburg *Miner,* July 26, 1906; Beatty *Bullfrog Miner,* July 28, 1906, February 23, 1907; Rhyolite *Herald,* April 19, 1907; Greenwater *Death Valley Chuck-Walla,* June 1907; Rhyolite *Bullfrog Miner,* February 15, 1908; Carrara *Obelisk,* April 18, 1914.

5. Bishop *Inyo Register,* November 16, 1916, January 25, 1917, September 17, 1918; San Francisco *Chronicle,* February 17, 1917, April 18, 1919; Wash Cahill, "20 Mule Team on Tour," March 1, 1947, 4 pp., and C. R. Dudley, "The 20 Mule Team (For Advertising)," 4 pp., and Notes, 5 pp. in Ruth C. Woodman Papers, Special Collections Library, University of Oregon; Robert E. Ramsey, *The Romance of the Desert* (Norfolk Downs, Mass.: Pneumatic Scale Corp., 1924), 36 pp.

6. Dodge Brothers Corporation, *Through Death Valley in a Dodge Brothers Motor Car, A True Story of O. K. Parker's Memorable Trip Through This Arid Desert Land* (Detroit: Dodge Brothers, 1916), 16 pp.; Los Angeles *Times,* February 29, 1920, March 27, December 18, 1921, December 31, 1922, April 12, 1925, February 7, July 11, October 16, 1926; *Standard Oil Bulletin,* September 1926, 3–9; Standard Oil Company of California, *Across Death Valley in a Ford Motor Car. How a new oil For Model T Fords conquered the Hottest Place in the world* [n.p.: Standard Oil Co., 1926], 16 pp.

7. Clarence E. Eddy, *Ballads of Heaven and Hell* (Salt Lake City: Western Printing Co., 1922), 14 pp., and *The Burro's Bray* (Salt Lake City: [author], 1923), 48 pp.; Paul DeLaney, *The Toll of the Sands* (Denver: Smith-Brooks Printing Co., 1920), 333 pp.; Alfred Noyes, *Beyond the Desert. A Tale of*

Death Valley (New York: Frederick A. Stokes Co., 1920), 85 pp.; Dane Coolidge, *Shadow Mountain* (New York: W. J. Watt & Co., 1919), 311 pp.; *Wunpost* (New York: E. P. Dutton & Co., 1920), 273 pp.; *Lost Wagons* (New York: E. P. Dutton & Co., 1923), 256 pp., *Horse-Ketchum* (New York: E. P. Dutton & Co., 1930), 236 pp.; *Snake Bit Jones* (New York: E. P. Dutton & Co., 1930), 280 pp., and *The Trail of Gold* (New York: E. P. Dutton & Co., 1937), 252 pp.; Zane Grey, *Tales of Lonely Trails* (New York: Harper & Brothers, 1922), 373–394, *Wanderer of the Wasteland* (New York: Harper & Brothers, 1923), 419 pp., especially 165, 173, 199, 205, 221, 233, 256, and 264; and "Death Valley," *Harper's Monthly Magazine, 140* (May 1920), 758–770. For Grey's trip to Death Valley, see also his diary, quoted in Frank Gruber, *Zane Grey, A Biography* (New York: World Publishing Co., 1970), 147–148, and Frank A. Crampton, *Deep Enough, A Working Stiff in the Western Mine Camps* (Denver: Sage Books, 1956), 242–243.

8. Bishop *Inyo Register,* January 8, 1920; Los Angeles *Times,* February 24, March 2, 1921, June 26, 1922; John Edwin Hogg, "A Race For Life in Death Valley," *Wide World Magazine 50* (October, 1922), 58–72; Edna Brush Perkins, *The White Heart of Mojave, An Adventure With the Outdoors of the Desert* (New York: Boni and Liveright, 1922), 229 pp.; *National Cyclopaedia of American Biography, v. 26* (New York: J. T. White & Co., 1937), 448–449.

9. Bishop *Owens Valley Herald,* May 7, 1909; Rhyolite *Herald,* June 16, 1909; *Lecture on Death Valley, The Borax Industry and 20 Mule Team Borax Products, Arranged for the Moving Picture and Stereopticon Exhibits of the Pacific Coast Borax Company* (San Francisco, 1909), 16 pp., copy courtesy of Joe Kern, U.S. Borax and Chemical Corporation; Pacific Coast Borax Co., *Annual Report for 1909* and "Movie History" notes in Woodman Papers, op. cit., n. 5; Los Angeles *Times,* June 19, 1912; New York *Moving Picture World,* October 12, 19, November 9, 1912, December 11, 1915, January 1, 15, 1916; Kevin Brownlow, *The War, The West and The Wilderness* (New York: Alfred A. Knopf, 1979), 244–245.

10. Los Angeles *Times,* December 10, 1922, February 1, May 20, August 12, 1923; New York *Times,* December 5, 1924; Ruth Woodman's Interview with Jean Hersholt c. 1949 in Woodman Papers, op. cit., n. 5; Erich Von Stroheim's Reminiscences in Peter Noble, *Hollywood Scapegoat: The Biography of Erich von Stroheim* (London: Fortune Press, 1950), 51–53; Jean Hersholt's Reminiscences in Noble, op. cit., n. 10, 48–50; William Daniels's Reminiscences in Charles Higham, *Hollywood Cameraman: Sources of Light* (London: Thames and Hudson, 1970), 63–67; Thomas Quinn Curtiss, *Von Stroheim* (New York: Farrar, Straus and Giroux, 1971), chap. 10, 158–181; Joel W. Finler, ed. *Greed, A Film by Erich von Stroheim* (New York: Simon and Schuster, 1972); Herman G. Weinberg, comp. and ed., *The Complete Greed of Erich von Stroheim* (New York: E. P. Dutton & Co., 1973), unpaged; Richard Koszarski, *The Man You Loved to Hate, Erich von Stroheim and Hollywood* (Oxford: Oxford University Press, 1983), 135–138.

11. Los Angeles *Times,* August 12, 1923; Woodman interview, op. cit., n. 10;

Heusholt's Reminiscences, op. cit., n. 10; Daniels's Reminiscences, op. cit., n. 10; von Stroheim's Reminiscences, op. cit., n. 10.

12. New York *Times,* December 5, 1924; New York *Variety Weekly,* December 10, 1925; von Stroheim's Reminiscences, op. cit., n. 10; Finler, op. cit., n. 10; Weinberg, op. cit., n. 10.

13. New York *Times,* July 8, 1924, March 17, 1925, November 22, 1927; "Nevada's Bottle House," *Sunset Magazine, 56* (February 1926), 47; Bishop *Owens Valley Herald,* March 10, 1926; Bishop *Inyo Register,* March 11, November 18, 25, December 9, 1926, June 21, 1928; Tonopah *Nevada Mining Record,* November 13, 1926; Fort Worth *Western World,* February 18, 1928.

14. Bishop *Owens Valley Herald,* October 15, 1915; Bishop *Inyo Register,* January 16, 1919, December 30, 1920, June 9, 1921; Tonopah *Mining Reporter,* October 22, 1921; Bourke Lee, *Death Valley Men* (New York: Macmillan Co., 1932), 54; Dane Coolidge, "Scotty's Castle," *Westways, 31* (March 1939), 8–10; *Gerard v. Scott et al.,* May 7, 1942 Case No. 9979, Circuit Court of Appeals Ninth Circuit, *128 Fed* 2d *120;* Albert Mussey Johnson, clippings and papers in the deceased alumni folder, Department of Manuscripts and University Archives, Cornell University Libraries, Ithaca, New York: Johnson Family Papers in Death Valley Ranch Archives, Death Valley National Monument; Hank Johnston, *Death Valley Scotty, "The Fastest Con in the West"* (Corona Del Mar: Trans-Anglo Books, 1974), 98–101.

15. Bishop *Inyo Register,* January 16, 1919, December 30, 1920, August 27, 1931; Johnson, op. cit., n. 14.

16. Tonopah *Mining Reporter,* December 27, 1923; Coolidge, "Scotty's Castle," op. cit., n. 14; Johnston, op. cit., n. 14, 98.

17. Los Angeles *Times,* January 27, 1924, April 12, 1925, Tonopah *Mining Reporter,* February 21, May 30, August 15, November 21, 1925; Edward A. Vandeventer, "Death Valley Scotty, Mysterious Son of the Desert," *Sunset Magazine, 56* (March 1926), 22–25, 72–73; Tonopah *Nevada Mining Record,* November 6, 1926; Randall Henderson, "He Built Scotty's Castle," *Desert Magazine, 15* (September 1952), 4–10; Johnston, op. cit., n. 14, 104–110.

18. Los Angeles *Times,* September 14, 1925; Vandeventer, op. cit., n. 17.

19. Rhyolite *Herald,* December 14, 1906, April 19, 1907; Tonopah *Nevada Mining Record,* November 13, 1926; Bishop *Owens Valley Herald,* November 24, 1926; Los Angeles *Times,* February 17, 1932, January 1, 1933; Independence *Inyo Independent,* February 20, 1932. See also Mary DeDecker, *The Eichbaum Toll Road* (San Bernardino: Inland Printing and Engraving Co., 1970), 20 pp., and Linda W. Greene, *Historic Resource Study: A History of Mining in Death Valley National Monument, vol. 1* (Denver: National Park Service, 1981), 897–900.

20. Bishop *Owens Valley Herald,* October 7, 1925; Tonopah *Mining Reporter,* October 13, 1925, November 27, 1926; Bishop *Inyo Register,* September 2, 1926.

21. Los Angeles *Times,* July 13, October 8, 1905, December 14, 1912, March

15, November 7, 1920, March 27, 1921; "The Need of Desert Signs," *Touring Topics, 1* (August 1909), 9–11; "Life Saving in Death Valley," *Touring Topics, 2* (August 1910), 5–7; Rhyolite *Herald,* October 8, 1910; Bishop *Inyo Register,* December 8, 1910, July 24, 1913, November 1, 1917, April 10, 1919, March 31, 1921, April 27, 1922; O. K. Parker, "Motor Exploration in Death Valley," *Touring Topics, 6* (January 1914), 8–14; *Streams, Springs, and Water Holes on Public Lands in the State of California (64th Cong. 1st Session House Report No. 9)* 1915, 3 pp. *(Senate Report No. 460),* 1916, 5 pp.; George W. Parsons, *A Thousand Mile Desert Trip and Story of the "Desert Sign Post"* (Los Angeles: Parsons, 1918), 16 pp.; "Mysterious Death Valley is Unmasked," *Touring Topics, 13* (April 1921), 14–15, Bishop *Owens Valley Herald,* May 25, 1921; David G. Thompson, *Routes to Desert Watering Places in the Mohave Desert Region, California (USGS Water Supply Paper 490-B)* (Washington, D.C.: Government Printing Office, 1921), 1–3.

22. Bishop *Inyo Register,* May 7, October 8, 1925; Bishop *Owens Valley Herald,* May 13, June 10, August 12, October 7, 1925; Alma Overholt, "Death Valley's Road to Nowhere," *World's Work, 59* (July 1930), 48–49; DeDecker, op. cit., n. 19, 6–7.

23. Bishop *Inyo Register,* October 22, 1925; Tonopah *Mining Reporter,* October 31, 1925, May 15, 1926; Gilbert *Record,* January 23, February 6, 1926; Bishop *Owens Valley Herald,* March 3, May 12, November 24, 1926; Los Angeles *Times,* May 23, 1926; Alma Overholt, "Death Valley The Mystery Spot of America," *Arrowhead Magazine* (August 1926), 12; DeDecker, op. cit., n. 19, 8, 13.

24. Tonopah *Mining Reporter,* May 15, July 3, 1926; Bishop *Inyo Register,* September 2, 1926; Tonopah *Nevada Mining Record,* October 30, November 13, 1926; Bishop *Owens Valley Herald,* November 24, 1926; Los Angeles *Times,* January 23, February 27, 1927; Alma Overholt, "Death Valley from the Air," *Sunset Magazine, 62* (January 1929), 35; Harry P. Gower, *50 Years in Death Valley—Memoirs of a Borax Man* (San Bernardino: Inland Printing, Inc., 1969), 112; Greene, op. cit., n. 19, 901–907.

25. Overholt, "Death Valley The Mystery . . . " op. cit., n. 23, 9–19; Tonopah *Nevada Mining Record,* September 11, 1926; Bishop *Owens Valley Herald,* November 24, 1926, February 23, 1927; Los Angeles *Times,* January 23, February 27, 1927; Mt. Whitney-Death Valley Transportation Co., *Death Valley,* [c. 1929] folder.

26. Bishop *Owens Valley Herald,* March 30, April 13, 1927; Los Angeles *Times,* March 20, 1927; Fort Worth *Western World,* April 23, 1927; Independence *Inyo Independent,* April 7, 14, 1928.

27. Randsburg *Miner,* July 26, 1906; Carrara *Obelisk,* April 18, 1914; John Edwin Hogg, "Farming in Death Valley," *Popular Mechanics, 33* (March 1920) 394; Los Angeles *Times,* December 16, 1923; Gilbert *Record,* November 21, 1925.

28. Harry Gower to Frank Jenifer, Letter dated November 6, 1925, quoted in *Death Valley National Monument, Hearings Before a Subcommittee of the*

Committee on Government Operations, House of Representatives, 88th Congress 2nd Session (Washington: Government Printing Office, 1965), 470–471; Gilbert *Record,* April 10, 1926; California Secretary of State, Archives, Sacramento, Articles of Incorporation of the Death Valley Hotel Company, December 31, 1926; Tonopah *Mining Reporter,* January 22, 1927; Harry P. Gower to Ruth Woodman, Letter dated August 24, 1949, in Ruth C. Woodman Papers; Gower, *50 Years . . .* op. cit., n. 24, 115–116. See also Greene, op. cit., n. 19, 918–928.

29. Gilbert *Record,* April 10, 1926; Tonopah *Nevada Mining Record,* October 30, 1926; Tonopah *Mining Reporter,* November 27, 1926; Roy B. Gray, "Now For Death Valley," *Arrowhead Magazine* (December 1926/January 1927), 8–9, 13, 22; Harvey S. Bliss to Albert C. Martin, reports dated January 22, 29, 1927, in *Death Valley National Monument . . .* op. cit., n. 28, 474–475; Gower to Woodman, op. cit., n. 28; David F. Myrick, *Railroads of Nevada and Eastern California* (Berkeley: Howell-North Books, 1963), v. 2, 614–615.

30. *Arrowhead Magazine* (Los Angeles: Union Pacific), (December 1926/January 1927), 7–22, (September 1927), 17, (November 1927), 9 (December 1927), 9, 17–29 (October 1928), 13–19 (November 1929), 13–15 (January 1930), 15–18; Union Pacific Systems, *Death Valley Winter Tours, Region of Mystery, Desolation and Grandeur by Rail and Motor* (Los Angeles: Bert Rosen Co., 1928), 10 pp., and their *California's Unique Winter Resort in Death Valley, Land of Mystery and Romance* (Omaha: Acorn Press, 1929), 24 pp.

31. Independence *Inyo Independent,* December 14, 1929; Los Angeles *Examiner,* February 9, 1930; Lee, op. cit., n. 14; 99–100; Stove Pipe Wells Hotel, *Death Valley* (Los Angeles: Hyatt, Jones & Patrick, 1930), 7; Death Valley Hotel Company, *Death Valley—Furnace Creek Inn, Death Valley Junction—Amargosa Hotel* (Los Angeles: 1930), 4.

32. *Sunset Magazine, 56* (March 1926), 73; Bishop *Owens Valley Herald,* February 2, 1927; Tonopah *Nevada Mining Record,* April 23, 1927; C. G. Milham, "The Paradise of Death Valley," *Country Life, 53* (January 1928), 64; Independence *Inyo Independent,* November 24, 1928; Phil Townsend Hanna, "Beauty and the Beast," *Touring Topics, 20* (December 1928), 38; *Arrowhead Magazine* (November 1929), 13 (January 1930), 15, 18 (October 1931), 11; Los Angeles *Examiner,* December 18, 1930, February 15, 1931; Los Angeles *Times,* February 22, 1932, February 26, June 4, 1933.

33. Tonopah *Mining Reporter,* April 16, 1927, September 25, 1929; Tonopah *Nevada Mining Record,* September 28, 1929; Tonopah *Nevada Mining Record-Reporter,* December 14, 1929; *Arrowhead Magazine* (December 1930), 21; Gower to Woodman, op. cit., n. 28, Gower, *50 Years . . .* op. cit., n. 24, 117.

34. *Arrowhead Magazine* (October 1928), 13; Death Valley Hotel Company, *Death Valley, Where Earth Is Still Fresh From the Casting* (Los Angeles: 1928), 8 pp.; Tonopah *Mining Reporter,* September 25, 1929; Tonopah

Nevada Mining Record, September 28, 1929; Los Angeles *Times,* December 11, 1929; Tonopah *Nevada Mining Record-Reporter,* March 1, 1930, January 31, 1931; Gower to Woodman, op. cit., n. 28; Gower, *50 Years . . .* op. cit., n. 24, 5, 121–123.

35. Los Angeles *Times,* February 16, 17, 1932; Alma Overholt, "The First Lady of Death Valley. The Story of Helene W. Eichbaum," *Los Angeles Times Sunday Magazine,* June 4, 1933, 3–4; C. B. Glasscock, *Here's Death Valley* (Indianapolis: Bobbs-Merrill Co., 1940), 294; Gower to Woodman, op. cit., n. 28; Gower, *50 Years . . .* op. cit., n. 24, 117, 122–123.

36. Gilbert *Record,* November 21, 1925, January 30, 1926; Gower to Jenifer op. cit., n. 28; Bishop *Inyo Register,* November 18, 1926, May 26, 1932; Bishop *Owens Valley Herald,* July 20, 1927; Tonopah *Nevada Mining Record,* October 8, 1927, October 12, November 9, 1929; Independence *Inyo Independent,* April 14, 1928, April 5, 1930; Glenn D. Willaman, "Impressions of Death Valley Trails," *California Real Estate Magazine, 9* (April 1929), 53; Walter Ford, "Samaritan of Cave Springs," *Desert Magazine, 3* (November 1939), 12–15; Greene, op. cit., n. 19, 424–431.

37. Alma Overholt, "Motoring Through Death Valley," *Travel, 55* (October 1930), 49; Edna C. Price, *Burro Bill and Me* (Idyllwild: Strawberry Valley Press, 1973), 44–58.

38. Bishop *Inyo Register,* July 1, September 2, 1920; Gilbert *Record,* January 30, March 20, April 10, 1926; Los Angeles *Times,* March 20, 1926, March 25, 1928, October 20, 1929; Vandeventer, op. cit., n. 17, 72; *Arrowhead Magazine* (August 1926), 11 (December 1926/January 1927), 12–13 (December 1927), 16 (January 1930), 18; Tonopah *Mining Reporter,* November 27, 1926; Tonopah *Nevada Mining Record,* December 25, 1926; H. P. Gower to F. M. Jenifer, January 20, 1927 in *Death Valley National Monument . . .* op. cit., n. 28, 475; R. B. Gray, "Death Valley De Luxe," *World Traveler, 19* (April 1927), 27; Independence *Inyo Independent,* January 18, 1930; Overholt, "Motoring . . . " op. cit., n. 37, 50; William Caruthers, *Loafing Along Death Valley Trails* (Palm Desert: Desert Magazine Press, 1951), 147–148.

39. Grey, *Tales . . .* op. cit., n. 7, 383; *Arrowhead Magazine* (December 1926/January 1927), 12–14 (October 1925), 17–19 (December 1930), 22–23; Los Angeles *Times,* December 31, 1927, October 20, 1929, March 9, 16, October 26, 1930, October 25, 1931; Bishop *Inyo Register,* January 2, March 6, 1930; Tonopah *Nevada Mining Record-Reporter,* January 11, 1930; Overholt, "Motoring . . ." op. cit., n. 37, 38; Jackson A. Graves, *California Memories* (Los Angeles: Times-Mirror Press, 1930), 313–314; "Seeing Death Valley in Five Days," *Touring Topics, 24* (March 1932), 30.

40. *Arrowhead Magazine* (August 1926), 11, 13 (December 1926/January 1927), 15–16, 19–21, (December 1927), 24–26 (October 1928), 17; Los Angeles *Times,* March 16, 1930; Gower, *50 Years . . .* op. cit., n. 24, 26–27.

41. Los Angeles *Times,* March 8, 1925, November 6, 1927, March 25, 1928, March 9, 16, 1930, October 25, 1931; "Nevada's Bottle House," op. cit., n. 13, 47; Overholt, "Death Valley The Mystery . . . op. cit., n. 23, 14–15; Overholt, "Motoring . . . " op. cit., n. 37, 49.

42. Bishop *Owens Valley Herald*, November 9, 1927; Los Angeles *Times,* March 15, 1931.

43. Bishop *Inyo Register,* September 26, 1929; Los Angeles *Examiner,* February 15, October 25, 1931; Los Angeles *Times,* March 15, October 25, 1931; and see also James Churchward, *The Lost Continent of Mu* (New York: Ives Washburn, 1931), 208–209.

44. Harold J. Shepstone, "Amazing Death Valley," *Contemporary Review, 134,* (November 1928), 633; Los Angeles *Times,* February 22, 1932, February 26, 1933; E. J. van Name, "Death Valley Trails," *Overland Monthly and Out West Magazine, 90* (August 1932), 182; Harry Carr, *The West is Still Wild* (Boston: Houghton Mifflin Co., 1932), 235; Basil Woon, *Incredible Land* (New York: Liveright Pub. Corp., 1933), 258.

45. Los Angeles *Record,* March 6, 1930; Tonopah *Nevada Mining Record-Reporter,* March 29, August 2, 1930; Bourke Lee, *Death Valley Men* (New York: Macmillan Co., 1932), 1, 43.

46. Los Angeles *Record,* February 17 through March 8, 1930; Bourke Lee, "Death Valley Scotty," *Saturday Evening Post, 204,* November 29, December 6, 1930; Lee, *Death Valley Men,* op. cit., n. 45, 1–80; Dane Coolidge, *Fighting Men of The West* (New York: E. P. Dutton & Co., 1932), 303–336, and *Snake Bit Jones,* op. cit., n. 7; Harry MacPherson, "Scotty Goes To Town," *Westways, 28* (January 1936), 16–17.

47. Tonopah *Nevada Mining Record,* November 9, 1929; Tonopah *Nevada Mining Record-Reporter,* February 1, 1930; New York *Times,* February 5, 1930; Los Angeles *Record,* February 20, 1930; Lee, *Death Valley Men,* op. cit., n. 45, 77.

48. Los Angeles *Times,* February 5, 1930; New York *Times,* February 5, 1930; Tonopah *Nevada Mining Record-Reporter,* June 14, November 8, 1930; Lee, *Death Valley Men,* op. cit., n. 45, 46–47, 74–78.

49. Tonopah *Nevada Mining Record,* December 1, 1928, November 9, 1929; Bishop *Inyo Register,* December 20, 1928; Los Angeles *Record,* February 21, 1930; Tonopah *Nevada Mining Record-Reporter,* August 16, 1930, April 11, 1931; Lee, *Death Valley Men,* op. cit., n. 45, 72.

50. Los Angeles *Times,* February 5, 1930; Los Angeles *Record,* February 19, 1930; Tonopah *Nevada Mining Record-Reporter,* April 11, August 22, 1931; Independence *Inyo Independent,* January 17, 1931; Los Angeles *Examiner,* February 15, 1931; Charlotte Arthur, "Castle in the Desert," *Country Life, 62* (June/July 1932), 35–38, 76–78; Henderson, op. cit., n. 17, 9; Johnston, op. cit., n. 14, 105–113.

51. Tonopah *Mining Reporter,* January 28, February 4, 1928; Los Angeles, *Record,* February 17, 19, 1930; Tonopah *Nevada Mining Record-Reporter,* July 26, 1930.

52. Tonopah *Nevada Mining Record,* August 3, 1929; Los Angeles *Record,* February 17, 21, 1930; Tonopah *Nevada Mining Record-Reporter,* November 8, 1930; Glasscock, op. cit., n. 35, 221.

53. Johnston, op. cit., n. 14, 97, 125–126.

54. Tonopah *Nevada Mining Record-Reporter,* November 30, 1929, June 14, August 16, October 18, 1930, March 7, 28, April 11, August 22, 1931;

Los Angeles *Examiner,* February 15, 1931; Johnston, op. cit., n. 14, 120.
55.   Horace M. Albright, "Creation of the Death Valley National Monument" in *The Story of Death Valley: Its Museum and Visitor Center* (San Bernardino: Inland Printing and Engraving, Co.:), 6, and his "Founding of Death Valley National Monument," 1, typescript of an interview on February 17, 1982 by Walt Wheelock (copy courtesy of the latter). See also Walt Wheelock, *The Founding of Death Valley National Monument, Honoring its Golden Anniversary 1933–1983* (Death Valley: Death Valley '49ers, 1983), 20 pp.
56.   Los Angeles *Times,* December 24, 1926, January 6, 1927; Albright, "Creation . . . " op. cit., n. 55, 6–8, and "Founding . . . " op. cit., n. 55, 3. Biographical information on Albright is given in his autobiographical sketch dated January 31, 1972 in the Horace M. Albright Papers, Special Collections Library, University of California, Los Angeles, and Donald C. Swain, *Wilderness Defender Horace M. Albright and Conservation* (Chicago: University of Chicago Press, 1970), 347 pp.
57.   Bishop *Inyo Register,* January 17, 1929; Independence *Inyo Independent,* February 16, 1929; Bourke Lee articles "Death Valley," "Lost in Death Valley," and "Death Valley Prospectors," *Saturday Evening Post,* 202 August 10, September 7, 14, 1929; Bourke Lee, *Death Valley* (New York: Macmillan Co., 1930), 210 pp.; W. A. Chalfant, *Death Valley, The Facts* (Stanford: Stanford University Press, 1930), 155 pp.; New York *Times Book Review,* June 1, 1930, 13; Lee, "Death Valley Scotty," op. cit., n. 46; Lee, *Death Valley Men,* op. cit., n. 45; Albright, "Creation . . . " op. cit., n. 55, 8–9. Biographical information on Thomas Burke (Bourke) Lee is given in his autobiographical sketch dated February 26, 1931 in California State Library, Sacramento, and *Register of The Commissioned and Warrant Officers of the U.S. Navy and Marine Corps* (Washington: Government Printing Office, 1927), 82 and (1929), 406. Unfortunately he wrote only one other book, *Blonde Interlude* (New York: Simon and Schuster, 1932), 314 pp., a novel about "the frenzy of the advertising world."
58.   Death Valley Days radio scripts, September 30, 1930 through July 13, 1944, in Ruth Cornwall Woodman Collection, Special Collections Library, University of Oregon, Eugene; "Twenty Mule Team Borax," *Fortune,* 6 (November 1933), 22; "Death Valley Days Gets New Look," *Pioneer,* 1 (October 1959), 23; Los Angeles *Herald-Examiner,* July 1, 1969.
59.   Herbert Hoover, *Executive Order 5408,* July 25, 1930 in *Proclamations and Executive Orders, Herbert Hoover March 4, 1929 to March 4, 1933, vol. 1,* (Washington, D.C.: Government Printing Office, 1974), 636–637.
60.   Los Angeles *Examiner,* August 2, 1930; Bishop *Inyo Register,* August 14, November 20, 1930; Tonopah *Nevada Mining Record-Reporter,* November 15, 1930; Albright, "Creation . . . " op. cit., n. 55, 8–9, and "Founding . . . " op. cit., n. 55, 4.
61.   Map of Upper and Lower Grapevine Ranches, 1927, reproduced in Greene, op. cit., n. 19, 773; Township plats T10 and 11S, R42E MDBM in Survey Records Office, Bureau of Land Management, Sacramento; Tonopah *Nevada Mining Record-Reporter,* December 6, 1930; Francois D. Uzes, *Chaining the Land: A History of Surveying in California* (Sacramento: Land-

mark Enterprises, 1977), 173–193; Albright, "Creation . . . " op. cit., n. 55, 10–11, and "Founding . . . " op. cit., n. 55, 4.

62. Herbert Hoover, *Proclamation No. 2028 Death Valley National Monument* February 11, 1933 in *U.S. Statutes at Large (1933),* v. 47, pt. 2, 2554 and map; Horace Albright, memo Re: Ralph P. Merritt, August 19, 1964 in Albright Papers, op. cit., n. 56; Albright, "Creation . . . " op. cit., n. 55, 10–12, and "Founding . . . " op. cit., n. 55, 5.

63. Hoover, *Proclamation . . .* op. cit., n. 59; Los Angeles *Times,* February 12, 26, 1933; Los Angeles *Examiner,* February 12, 1933; New York *Times,* February 13, 1933; Bishop *Inyo Register,* February 16, 1933; *Extend the Mining Laws of the United States to the Death Valley National Monument in California, and for Other Purposes (72nd Cong. 2nd Sess. House Report 2107)* February 24, 1933, 3 pp; Albright, "Creation . . . " op. cit., n. 55, 12, and "Founding . . . " op. cit., n. 55, 5.

64. An Act to extend the mining laws of the United States to the Death Valley National Monument in California (Public Law No. 49, June 13, 1933), *U.S. Statutes at Large (1933), v. 48, pt. 1, 139;* Bishop *Inyo Register,* June 22, July 6, 20, 1933; An Act to grant a patent to Albert M. Johnson and Walter Scott (Private Law No. 256, August 22, 1935), *U.S. Statutes at Large (1935), v. 49, pt. 2,* 2159; *Death Valley National Monument, Fifth Report by the Committee Government Operations (89th Cong. 1st Sess. House Rpt. 193)* (Washington, D.C.: Government Printing Office, 1965), 51; Albright, "Creation . . . " op. cit., n. 55, 12–13, and autobiographical sketch op. cit., n. 56; Johnston, op. cit., n. 14, 120, 140–141.

65. Bishop *Inyo Register,* October 26, November 16, 23, 1933, May 17, October 4, 18, December 27, 1934; Los Angeles *Examiner,* November 30, 1933; S. W. Lowden, "Famous Death Valley Toll Road Purchased, Making it a Free Highway," *California Highways and Public Works, 13* (January 1935), 4; Martin Sedgwick, "The History of the Civilian Conservation Corps in Death Valley," *Thor Shun, 2* (April 4, 1936), 6–7; Gower to Woodman, op. cit., n. 28; *Death Valley National Monument Hearings . . .* op. cit., n. 28, 488; Albright, "Founding . . . " op. cit., n. 55, 6.

BIBLIOGRAPHY

MANUSCRIPTS

Albright, Horace M. "Founding of Death Valley National Monument." 9 pp. transcript of interview, February 17, 1982, by Walt Wheelock.
————. Papers, Special Collections Library, University of California, Los Angeles.
Babcock, Leonard. Reminiscences, 1889. Bancroft Library, University of California, Berkeley.
Bancroft Scraps. California Counties, vol. 1, pp. 264–289, Inyo County. Bancroft Library, University of California, Berkeley.
Beatty, Montillion Murray, Jr. Transcript of interview, November 1, 1968. Nevada Historical Society, Reno.
Beatty Townsite Company. Papers, 1907. Nevada Historical Society, Reno.
Beck, John W. "Log of the Manly-Bennett-Jayhawker-'Georgian' Routes From 'Mt. Misery,' Utah to the Floor of Death Valley." 12 pp. typescript, 1939. Henry E. Huntington Library and Art Gallery, San Marino, Calif.
————. "A Tentative Correlation of The Logs of Asa Haynes, Sheldon Young and William Manly's Story." 11 pp. typescript, April 27, 1939. Henry E. Huntington Library and Art Gallery, San Marino, Calif.
Bendire, Lt. Charles E. "Report of a Scouting Expedition Made in the Region East of Owens Valley, Cal." May 26, 1867. 9 pp. typescript. Collection of Dennis G. Casebier, Norco, Calif.
Bigler, Henry William. Diaries and Papers. Henry E. Huntington Library and Art Gallery, San Marino, Calif.
————. Memoirs and Journals, 1815–1899. Bancroft Library, University of California, Berkeley.
Borax Consolidated, Ltd. Records, 1899–1951. Archives of the Companies Registration Office, Board of Trade, London. Microfilm copy in Bancroft Library, University of California, Berkeley.
Breyfogle, Joshua D., Sr. "The Diary of Joshua D. Breyfogle, Sr., 1849." 34 pp. typescript. Nevada Historical Society, Reno.
Breyfogle, Lewis W. "What I Know About the Breyfogle Family." 114 pp. typescript. Chanute, Kansas, 1963. Nevada Historical Society, Reno.
Bullfrog and Greenwater Mining Promotion Letters and Other Material, Collection of Gil Schmidtmann, Mentone, Calif.
Bullfrog Bank and Trust Company, Rhyolite. Records c. 1909–1913. Bancroft Library, University of California, Berkeley.
Cannon, George Quayle. Diary 1849–1852. Historical Department, Church of Jesus Christ of Latter-day Saints, Salt Lake City.
Casebier, Dennis G., comp. "Quotations From Original Sources Pertaining to California Desert Regions, Including the General Areas of Kingston Area

& Salt Lake Trail, Ivanpah, Greenwater, Old Woman Mountains, Dale Mining District, Chuckwalla-Orocopia." 989 pp. typescript, 1978. Bureau of Land Management, Riverside, Calif.

Chichering, Martha A. "The Saga of an Old-Time Prospector [William David McClellan)" 4 pp. typescript, 1964. Nevada Historical Society, Reno.

Coleman, William Tell. Biographical materials, 1870–1893. Bancroft Library, University of California, Berkeley.

Colton, John Burt. Jayhawker Collection, 1849–1938. Henry E. Huntington Library and Art Gallery, San Marino, Calif.

Cook, George E. "A True Story of My Life." 6 pp. typescript, 1961. Nevada Historical Society, Reno.

Cook, John S., and Company, Rhyolite. Ledgers, 1906–1908. Special Collections Library, University of Nevada, Reno.

Coolidge, Dane. Collection, 1889–1942. Bancroft Library, University of California, Berkeley.

Cooper, J. H. "The Skidoo Gold Mines, Data Supplement to General Report." 3 pp. typescript, c. 1915. Archives, Death Valley National Monument.

Death Valley Borax and Salt Mining District, [1881–1886] Manuscript ledger 226 pp. Borax Museum, Death Valley National Monument.

Derr, Peter. "Account of Experiences of Peter Derr . . . who came through on the First Train South from Salt Lake to California, 1849." Bancroft Library, University of California, Berkeley.

Doherty, John. "The History of the Settling of the Manse Ranch and Territory." 6 pp. typescript, n.d. Nevada Historical Society, Reno.

Eagle Mountain Borax and Salt Mining District, Vol. A [1882–1884]. Manuscript ledger. 357 pp. Borax Museum, Death Valley National Monument.

Egan, Howard. "Journal Kept by H. Egan on a Trip from Fort Utah to California, November 18, 1849 to February 23, 1850." Beinecke Rare Book and Manuscript Library, Yale University Library, New Haven, Conn.

Farrer, William. Diary, 1849–1854. Harold B. Lee Library, Brigham Young University, Provo, Utah.

Fisher, Albert Kenrick. Papers, 1827–1957. Manuscript Division, Library of Congress, Washington, D.C.

Goff, Francis W. "Death Valley Bibliography." 32 pp. typescript, June 1934. California State Library, Sacramento.

Granite Contact Mines Company. "Report," March 1, 1908. 16 pp. typescript. Nevada Historical Society, Reno.

Greenland Ranch Store. Day Book (1884–1887, 1902, 1906–1916) Manuscript ledger. Borax Museum, Death Valley National Monument.

Gregory, McClure. "Pidgeon Springs Mining Property." 2 pp. typescript, 1932. Nevada Historical Society, Reno.

Gruwell, J. D. Dictation, 1887. Bancroft Library, University of California, Berkeley.

Hamelin, Joseph P. Diary, 1849–50. Beinecke Rare Book and Manuscript Library, Yale University, New Haven, Conn.

Heyser, John A. "Death Valley Walter Scott." 11 pp. typescript, 1939. Nevada Historical Society, Reno.

Hoover, Herbert. Presidential Papers, 1929–1933. Herbert Hoover Presidential Library, West Branch, Iowa.

Johnson, Albert Mussey. Alumnus folder, Dept. of Manuscripts and University Archives, Cornell University Libraries, Ithaca, N.Y.

———. Family Papers, 1899–1921. Death Valley Ranch Archives, Death Valley National Monument.

Johnson, Albert and Bessie. Papers, 1900–1909. Shadelands Ranch Historical Museum, Walnut Creek, Calif.

Jones, John Percival. Papers, 1819–1936. Henry E. Huntington Library and Art Gallery, San Marino, Calif.

———. Family Papers, 1847–1946. Special Collections Library, University of California, Los Angeles.

Kane, Charles A. "An Act to Create and Establish the County of Bullfrog, Nevada." February 8, 1909. 20 pp. typescript. Nevada Historical Society, Reno.

Kensler, Charles D. "Survey of Historic Structures: Southern Nevada and Death Valley." Prepared for U.S. Department of Energy, Nevada Operations Office by URS/John A. Blume & Assoc. 671 pp. typescript, 1982. Nevada Historical Society, Reno.

Locke, William Lovering. Papers, c. 1883–1913. Bancroft Library, University of California, Berkeley.

Long, Margaret. Collection. Western History Collection, University of Colorado Library, Boulder.

Lorton, William B. Diary, September 1848–January 1850. 8 vol. Bancroft Library, University of California, Berkeley.

Lyman, Amasa Mason. Diaries, 1832–1877. Historical Department, Church of Jesus Christ of Latter-day Saints, Salt Lake City.

Mayflower Leasing Company. Correspondence and Papers, 1908–1916. Nevada Historical Society, Reno.

Merriam, Clinton Hart. Death Valley Expedition Journals I and II, March–July 1891, in his Papers and Journals, 1873–1938. Manuscript Division, Library of Congress, Washington, D.C.

Mining Stock Certificates, Collection of Ken Prag. Burlingame, Calif.

Moffat, Emma Louise. Papers and Correspondence, 1907–1909. Nevada Historical Society, Reno.

Myrick, Donald. "Death Valley in 1927." 6 pp. typescript, 1957. Nevada Historical Society, Reno.

Narratives of the Journey of Jefferson Hunt's Wagon Train from Utah to Southern California in 1849. 83 pp. typescript. Bancroft Library, University of California, Berkeley.

New York Stock Exchange. Copartnership Directory and Committee on Admissions Records. NYSE Archives and Corporation Research Collection, New York.

Nusbaumer, Louis. "Erlebnisse einer Reise nach den Goldregionen Californiens" [March 20, 1849–March 10, 1850] 2 vol. Bancroft Library, University of California, Berkeley.

Osio, Antonio Maria. "Historía de California," 506 pp. manuscript. Bancroft

Library, University of California, Berkeley.

Owen, J. R. N. "Report of J. R. N. Owen to Hon. S. Mowry of a Reconnaissance Along the Proposed Boundary Line of the State of California," April 15, 1861. California State Lands Commission, Sacramento. Copy courtesy of Francois D. Uzes. 11 pp. typescript, 1977.

Palmer, Theodore Sherman. Diary, December 1890–May 1891 and Papers. Henry E. Huntington Library and Art Gallery, San Marino, Calif.

———. Papers, 1887–1954. Manuscript Division, Library of Congress, Washington, D.C.

Pearson, Gustavus C. "Recollections of Gustavus C. Pearson a California '49er." 5 pp. manuscript, 1880. Bancroft Library, University of California, Berkeley.

Pratt, Addison. Diary, 1849–1850. Historical Department, Church of Jesus Christ of the Latter-day Saints, Salt Lake City.

Pratt, Orville C. Diary 1848. Beinecke Rare Book and Manuscript Library, Yale University, New Haven, Conn.

Pratt, Parley Parker. Journal 1851–1852. Harold B. Lee Library, Brigham Young University, Provo, Utah.

———. Journal 1852–1854. Historical Department, Church of Jesus Christ of Latter-day Saints, Salt Lake City.

Rich, Charles Coulson. Diaries, 1849–1851 and 1855. Historical Department, Church of Jesus Christ of the Latter-day Saints, Salt Lake City.

Robertson, J. Barr. Letterbook. Bancroft Library, University of California, Berkeley.

Robinson, Douglas. "Lida, Nevada." 12 pp. typescript, 1949. Nevada Historical Society, Reno.

Rollins, James Henry. Recollections, 1898. Utah State Historical Society, Salt Lake City.

Royal Flush Mine. Reports and Papers, 1908–1930. Nevada Historical Society, Reno.

Scott, A. W. "Niter Lands of California." Photo album c. 1910. Library, Death Valley National Monument.

Seeley, David. "Biographical Sketch," 1885. Bancroft Library, University of California, Berkeley.

Shannon, Thomas. "Journey of Peril with the Jayhawkers in Death Valley Fifty Three Years Ago." San Jose, 1903. Bancroft Library, University of California, Berkeley.

Shearer. Diary, 1849. Transcript. Bancroft Library, University of California, Berkeley.

State Line Mining Company, Gold Mountain. Ledger, 1881–1882. Nevada Historical Society, Reno.

Stewart, William Morris. Papers, 1887–1904. Nevada Historical Society, Reno.

Stover, Jacob Y. "History of the Sacramento Mining Company of 1849, written by one of its number." n.d. Henry E. Huntington Library and Art Gallery, San Marino, Calif.

Sublette Family. Papers. Missouri Historical Society, St. Louis.

Surprise Valley Mill and Water Company. Cash Book, 1874–1877. Library, Death Valley National Monument.

———. Store Ledger, November–December, 1874. Special Collections Library, University of California, Los Angeles.

U.S. Borax. Account Books, 3 vol.: Journal Death Valley, July 1882–March 1885, 176 pp.; Journal Amargosa, April 18, 1882–March 1885, 320 pp.; and Ledger, 1883–1904, 436 pp. Bancroft Library, University of California, Berkeley.

Von Schmidt, Allexey W. Field Notes of the Eastern Boundary of the State of California. National Archives, Record Group 49.

———. "Narrative Description of the Survey of the Southerly portion of the Eastern Boundary of the State of California," San Francisco, January 10, 1874. 10 pp. manuscript. National Archives, Record Group 49.

Wallace, William J. "An Enterprise That Failed: Death Valley's Eagle Borax Works." 25 pp. typescript, 1974. Collection of Western Archeological Center, National Park Service, Tucson, Ariz.

———. "Exploratory Excavations at the Harmony Borax Works, Death Valley National Monument." typescript, 1972. Collection of Western Archeological Center, National Park Service, Tucson, Ariz.

Warren, Elizabeth von Till, and Ralph J. Roske. "Cultural Resources of the California Desert, 1776–1880: Historic Trails and Wagon Roads." 172 pp. typescript, 1978. Bureau of Land Management, Riverside, Calif.

Weiss, Harry A. "Some Observations on Desert Trails," 11 pp. typescript, 1932. Bancroft Library, University of California, Berkeley.

Wheeler, George Montague. Papers. Beinecke Rare Book and Manuscript Library, Yale University, New Haven, Conn.

———. Scrapbook and Related Material, 1871–1886. Bancroft Library, University of California, Berkeley.

Wilson, Benjamin Davis. Papers. Henry E. Huntington Library and Art Gallery, San Marino.

Woodman, Ruth C. "History of Pacific Coast Borax Company." 929 pp. Manuscript, 1949. Special Collections Library, University of Oregon, Eugene.

———. Papers, 1914–1969. Special Collections Library, University of Oregon, Eugene.

Young, Sheldon. "Log, 1849, Joliet Illinois to Rancho San Francisquito, California." Transcript. Henry E. Huntington Library and Art Gallery, San Marino, Calif.

GOVERNMENT RECORDS

Arizona. Secretary of State, Archives. Articles of Incorporation.

California. Departmental State Papers, Archivo de California, Angeles, Benecia and San Jose. Records. Bancroft Library, University of California, Berkeley.

———. Inyo County. Recorder's Office. Deeds; Land, Water and Mining Claims;

Mining Locations; Panamint Mining District Records (1873–1874).

———. San Bernardino County, Recorder's Office. Deeds; Mining Claims.

———. Secretary of State. Division of Archives. Articles of Incorporation.

Nevada. Esmeralda County, Recorder's Office. Deeds; Mining Locations.

———. Lincoln County, Recorder's Office. Deeds; Book of Surveys.

———. Nye County, Recorder's Office. Deeds; Mining Locations.

———. Secretary of State. Division of Archives. Articles of Incorporation.

U.S. Army. Camp Independence, Post Returns, 1862–1877. National Archives.

———. Corps of Engineers, Wheeler Survey Records, 1869–1883, National Archives.

———. Corps of Engineers, Wheeler Survey, Field Notebooks, 1871, Special Collections Library, University of Nevada, Reno.

U.S. Bureau of the Census. Ninth (1870), Tenth (1880), Twelfth (1900) and Thirteenth (1910) Censuses of the United States. California: Inyo and San Bernardino counties; Nevada: Esmeralda, Lincoln and Nye counties. National Archives.

U.S. Bureau of Land Management. Sacramento Office. Township Survey Plats, 1857–1884.

Utah. Secretary of State, Articles of Incorporation.

THESES AND DISSERTATIONS

Ardolf, Genevieve Marie. "The Development of Death Valley with Special Reference to Transportation." Unpublished Master's thesis, University of Southern California, 1930, 84 pp.

Bard, Robert Charles. "Settlement Patterns of the Eastern Mojave Desert." Unpublished Ph.D. dissertation, University of California, Los Angeles, 1972, 291 pp.

Elliott, Russell R. "The Tonopah-Goldfield-Bullfrog Mining Districts, 1900–1916, History of a Twentieth Century Mining Boom." Unpublished Ph.D. dissertation. University of California, Berkeley, 1946, 296 pp.

Kirk, George. "A History of the San Pedro, Los Angeles, and Salt Lake Railroad." Unpublished Master's thesis, University of California, Berkeley, 1935, 71 pp.

Lawrence, Eleanor F. "The Old Spanish Trail from Santa Fe to California." Unpublished Master's thesis, University of California, Berkeley, 1930, 148 pp.

Mack, Effie Mona. "Life and Letters of William Morris Stewart, 1827–1909." Unpublished Ph.D. dissertation, University of California, Berkeley, 1930, 375 pp.

MacKellar, Christine P. "The History of Death Valley, 1849–1933." Unpublished Master's thesis, University of California, Berkeley, 1941, 89 pp.

MacMurphy, F. "Geology and Ore Deposits of a Part of the Panamint Range, California." Unpublished Master's thesis, California Institute of Technology, Pasadena, 1929, 177 pp.

Sawyer, Byrd F. "The Gold and Silver Rushes of Nevada, 1900–1910." Unpublished Master's thesis, University of California, Berkeley, 1931, 172 pp.

Warren, Elizabeth von Till. "Armijo's Trace Revisited: A New Interpretation of the Impact of the Antonio Armijo Route of 1829–1830 on the Development of the Old Spanish Trail." Unpublished Master's thesis, University of Nevada, Las Vegas, 1974, 195 pp.

MAPS

American Carrara Marble Company. *Geological Survey and Structure in the Immediate Vicinity of White Marble Quarry . . . Carrara, Nevada.* n.p.: 1920. Blueprint.

Automobile Club of Southern California. *Arrowhead Trail From Salt Lake City, Utah to Los Angeles, California.* Los Angeles: 1923.

———. *Desert Area.* Los Angeles: 1962.

———. *Guide to Death Valley.* Los Angeles: 1976.

———. *Map of a Portion of Southern California and Southwestern Nevada, Embracing the Arid Region of Mojave Desert, Colorado Basin and Death Valley.* Los Angeles: 1919.

———. *Map Showing Various Roads from Los Angeles to Points in Southwestern Nevada, Also Showing Region and Roads in Vicinity of Death Valley.* Los Angeles: 1913.

———. *Road Map of Inyo County, California.* Los Angeles: 1915.

Bailey, G. E. *Map of the Saline Deposits of the Southern Portion of California.* San Francisco: California State Mining Bureau, 1902.

———. *Official Prospectors' and Miners' Map of California and Nevada Deserts.* Los Angeles: *Times,* 1905.

Bradford, Strange, and Collier. *Map of Bullfrog Mining District, Nye County, Nevada.* n.p.: 1905, in W. H. Shearer, *Atlas of the Goldfield, Tonopah and Bullfrog Mining Districts of Nevada.* Chicago: Rand, McNally & Co., 1905.

Bullfrog-Goldfield Railroad. *Filing Map Sheet No. 2 [and] No. 3 Showing Present Adopted Location of the Bullfrog-Goldfield R.R. Esmeralda and Nye Counties, Nevada.* Tonopah: 1906.

California State Mining Bureau. *Map of Greenwater Mining District, Inyo County, California.* San Francisco: 1908.

———. *Map of Mining District in Immediate Vicinity of Greenwater, Inyo County, California.* San Francisco: 1908.

———. *Map of the Ubehebe Mining District, Inyo County, California.* San Francisco: 1908.

Cannon, R. M. *Rhyolite and Adjacent Mines, Bullfrog District, Nye County, Nev.* Rhyolite: Clemens & Keene, 1905. Reproduced in Rhyolite *Herald,* September 29, 1905.

Clason Map Company. *Clason's Map of Nevada.* Denver: 1916.

———. *Map of Nevada and the Southeastern Portion of California.* Denver: 1906, 12 pp., and 1907, 16 pp.

Crossman, James H. *Map of Inyo County California, Compiled from Authentic Sources.* n.p.: 1883.

Crowell, A. Russell. *Miners' Map of Death Valley, the Mojave, Amargosa and Nevada Deserts.* Manvel: 1903 Revised Las Vegas: 1905.

Deady, C. L. *Map of Pahrump Valley, Nye County, Nevada.* n.p.: August 15, 1914.

Death Valley Hotel Company. *A Picture Map of Points of Interest In and About Death Valley.* Los Angeles: 1928.

Dixon, W. G. *Territory and Resources Tributary to the Carson and Colorado Branch of the Southern Pacific R.R.* [San Francisco: c. 1900].

Doubleday, D. G. *Portion of Nye and Esmeralda Counties Showing the Road from Tonopah to Bullfrog.* San Francisco: 1905. Reproduced in Tonopah *Miner,* May 6, 1905.

Farley, Minard H. *Farley's Map of the Newly Discovered Tramontane Silver Mines in Southern California and Western New Mexico, Comprising those of Coso, Washington, Tiachipa, Russ, Potosi, Esmeralda, Holcomb & Bear Valley Districts.* San Francisco: W. Holt, 1861.

Fitch, C. H., comp. *Map of Parts of California, Nevada, Arizona and Utah Traversed in 1891 by the Death Valley Expedition.* Washington, D.C.: Norris Peters Co., 1892.

Forward Mining Development Company. *Map of the Bullfrog Mining District, Nye County, Nevada.* Denver: Williamson-Haffner Co., 1907.

Freese, Harry. *Map of Esmeralda County, Nevada.* Oakland: n.d.

———. *Map of Nye County, Nevada.* Oakland: n.d.

Fremont, John Charles. *Map of Oregon and Upper California From the Surveys of John Charles Fremont and Other Authorities, Drawn by Charles Preuss.* Baltimore: Litho. E. Weber & Co., 1848.

Gibbes, Charles Drayton. *Map of the States of California and Nevada, Carefully Compiled from the Latest Authentic Sources.* San Francisco: Warren Holt, 1878.

Giles, Edwin S. *Map of Esmeralda County, Nevada and Vicinity.* Goldfield: December 1927.

———. *Map of the Hornsilver Mining District, Esmeralda County, Nevada.* Goldfield: 1922.

Goddard, George H. *Britton & Rey's Map of the State of California.* San Francisco: Britton & Rey, 1857. [Lt. Moore's Route 1853 and East Camp shown.]

Graham, W. S. *Plat of the Claim of the Keane Wonder Mining Co. Sheets 1 [through] 5.* San Francisco: 1909.

Hamman & Armstrong. *Map of Nevada Showing Proposed County Subdivisions, Present Boundaries Shown by Full Lines, Changes Indicated by Dotted Lines.* n.p.: 1906. Reproduced in Rhyolite *Herald,* December 14, 1906. [Shows proposed Bullfrog County.]

Holdredge, Sterling M. *State, Territorial & Ocean Guide Book of the Pacific.* San Francisco: Grafton T. Brown, 1865. ["Breyfogle's Trail" shown on map of Nevada.]

Holt, Warren. *Holt's Map of the Owen's River Mining Country.* San Francisco: 1864.

———. *Map of the State of Nevada.* San Francisco: 1866.

James, George D. *Map of Death Valley and Panamint Districts, Inyo Co. California.* Reno: 1905. Reproduced in *Engineering and Mining Journal,* November 18, 1905.

Keeler, J. M. *Mining Map of Inyo County.* San Francisco: Daily Stock Report, 1883.

Kenyon Company. *Map of Inyo County California.* Des Moines: 1920.

Las Vegas & Tonopah Railroad. *Filing Map. No. 1A, No. 2 Amended, No. 3 [and] No. 5. Showing Definite Location of the Las Vegas & Tonopah Railroad, Nye and Lincoln County Nevada.* n.p.: 1905 [and] 1906.

———. *Station Map of Amargosa, Nye County, Nevada.* Los Angeles: June 1909.

Lawton & Griffin. *Map Showing Relative Position of Gold Center, Nye County, Nevada.* Goldfield: 1905.

Macdonald, Moran, and Pennington. *Map of the Greenwater Mining District Inyo Co., California.* Greenwater: 1906. Part reproduced in Colorado Springs, *Mining Investor,* December 17, 1906.

MacGowan, A. B. *Map of Country Adjacent to Camp Independence, Cal. with Line of Scouts by Co.'s B and D 12th U.S. Inf.* San Francisco: July 27, 1874. National Archives, Record Group 393. Reproduced in Levy.

———. *Itinerary of Scout made by Co. "D" 12th U.S. Infantry, Commenced April 30th and ending May 25th 1875.* San Francisco: June 25, 1875. National Archives, Record Group 393. Reproduced in Levy.

———. *Itinerary of Scouts made by Co. "D" 12th U.S. Infantry during May, June, July and August 1875.* San Francisco: August 21, 1875. National Archives, Record Group 393. Reproduced in Levy.

MacMurphy, F. *Claim Map of the Panamint District, Inyo County, Calif.* [Pasadena]: 1927.

Manhattan-Goldfield Brokerage Company. *Office Map of the Bullfrog Mining District, Nye County, Nevada.* Goldfield: 1905.

Manly, William L. *Map* in Jayhawker Collection and *Map* in T. S. Palmer Collection, Henry E. Huntington Library and Art Gallery, San Marino, Calif. Reproduced in Wheat (1939) and Koenig (1984) respectively.

———. *Map Oct. 7, 1894* in Death Valley National Monument Library. Reproduced in Walker, *The Manly Map . . .* (1954).

Map Showing the Mines of the Wonder Consolid. & Wyoming Consolid. Min. Co., Surprise Cañon, Panamint Mining District, Inyo Co., California. San Francisco: Britton, Rey & Co., 1875.

Mendenhall, Walter C. *General Map Showing Approximate Location of Better Known Springs and Wells in the Mohave and Adjacent Deserts, Southeastern California and Southwestern Nevada.* Washington, D.C.: U.S. Geological Survey, 1909.

Montgomery Shoshone Consolidated Mining Company. *Map Showing Claims of the Montgomery Shoshone Con. Mng. Co., Nye Co., Nev. Aug. 23, 1906.*

New York: 1906.

———. *Underground Workings, Montgomery Shoshone Con. Mng. Co., Nye County—Nevada. August 23–06.* New York: 1906.

Nicklin, T. G. *Map of Bullfrog Mining District.* Beatty: *Bullfrog Miner,* 1905.

O'Brien, Joseph D. *Pioneer Mng. Dist., Nye Co. Nevada.* Pioneer: 1911.

Pacific Coast Borax Co. *Death Valley—the bottom of the Western Desert Basin, showing the Railroads and Highways Leading thereto from East and West, [and] showing the location of Furnace Creek Inn, Amargosa Hotel, Death Valley View Hotel.* Los Angeles: 1930.

———. *Map of Death Valley Showing Principal Points of Interest and Furnace Creek Inn, Death Valley Hotel, Amargosa Hotel.* [Los Angeles: c. 1929].

Pheby, F. S. *Map showing the still unprospected area along the Nevada-California state line. Good roads and many springs.* Goldfield: F. S. Pheby & Co., 1905.

Ransome, Frederick L., et al. *Geologic Map and Sections of the Bullfrog District, Nevada.* Washington, D.C.: U.S. Geological Survey, 1910.

———. *Geologic Reconnaissance Map of Portions of Southwestern Nevada and Eastern California.* Washington, D.C.: U.S. Geological Survey, 1907.

Rasor, Clarence M. *Pacific Coast Borax Co. Death Valley Properties.* Los Angeles: 1941.

Rueger, Henry. *Rueger's Automobile and Mines' Road Map of Southern California.* Los Angeles: November 1903.

San Pedro, Los Angeles & Salt Lake Rail Road. *Map of Reconnaissance Survey, Las Vegas to Tonopah.* Las Vegas: February 25, 1905. Reproduced in Myrick (1963), p. 457.

Sanborn Map and Publishing Company. *Rhyolite, Nye Co., Nevada.* New York: July 1909 and September 1912.

Schader-Johnson Company. *Map of the Town of Johnnie and Johnnie Mining District, Nye County, Nevada.* Los Angeles: 1905. Reproduced in Los Angeles *Times,* July 11, 1905.

Shearer, W. H. *Map of Tonopah, Goldfield and Bullfrog Mining Districts and Region Adjacent Showing Railroads, Wagon Roads and Trails* in his *Atlas of the Goldfield, Tonopah and Bullfrog Mining Districts of Nevada.* Chicago: Rand, McNally & Co., 1905.

Sherer, George E., and W. B. Milliken. *New Official Map of the Bullfrog Mining District, Nye County, Nevada.* San Francisco: Britton & Rey Photo-Litho., 1905.

Spurr, Josiah E. *Geological Reconnaissance Map of Nevada South of the 40th Parallel and Adjacent California.* Washington, D.C.: U.S. Geological Survey, 1903.

Steele, C. H. *Route Marched by Co. "1", First Cavalry Commanded by Capt. C. C. C. Carr, First Cav. from June 8th to June 25th.* San Francisco: July 30, 1875. National Archives, Record Group 393. Reproduced in Levy, 1969.

Stirling, James. *Johnnie Mining District, Nye County, Nevada. 1906.* Reproduced in Butte *Mining World,* November 24, 1906.

Taylor, C. C. *Pahrump Valley, Nye Co., Nevada.* Carson City: August 1, 1925.

Thompson, David G. *Relief Map of Part of Mohave Desert Region, California.*

Washington, D.C.: U.S. Geological Survey, 1921. Sheets I through V.

Thurston, Albert G. *Desert Map.* Los Angeles: Western Map & Publishing Co., 1915.

———. *Thurston's Auto-Highway, Mountain and Desert Map.* Pasadena: 1919.

Todd, John. *Map of the Reese River Mining Districts, Showing Explorations of D. E. Buel in 1864, and Joseph Todd in 1865.* New York: D. Van Nostrand, 1866. [Shows explorations in Death Valley.]

Tonopah and Tidewater Company. *Tonopah & Tidewater Railroad, Bullfrog Goldfield Railroad and Tributary Country.* [n.p.: c. 1909].

Tonopah-Goldfield Trust Company. *Map Showing the Famous Bullfrog Mining District.* Gold Center: [c. 1906].

Treadwell, J. B. *Map of the County of Inyo, State of California.* n.p.: 1884.

Union Pacific System. *Map Showing the Death Valley Tour, Rail and Motor.* Omaha: 1929.

U.S. General Land Office. *Plat of the Townsite of Beatty, Nevada.* Washington, D.C.: Norris Peters Co. Photo Litho., 1908.

———. *Plat of the Townsite of Rhyolite, Nevada.* Washington, D.C.: Norris Peters Co. Photo Litho., 1908.

U.S. Geological Survey. *Death Valley National Monument and Vicinity.* (1974).

———. Topographic Maps, 1 Degree Series (1:250,000). *Amargosa Region* (1906), *Avawatz Mountains* (1933), *Ballarat* (1908), *Furnace Creek* (1908), *Lida* (1908), *Searles Lake* (1915).

———. Topographic Maps, 15 Minute Series (1:62,500). *Ash Meadows* (1952), *Avawatz Pass* (1948), *Bare Mountain* (1954), *Bennetts Well* (1952), *Big Dune* (1952), *Bullfrog* (1954), *Chloride Cliff* (1952), *Confidence Hills* (1950), *Darwin* (1950), *Dry Mountain* (1957), *Eagle Mountain* (1951), *Emigrant Canyon* (1952), *Funeral Peak* (1950), *Furnace Creek* (1952), *Grapevine Peak* (1957), *Horse Thief Springs* (1956), *Kingston Peak* (1955), *Last Chance Range* (1958), *Lathrop Wells* (1961), *Leach Lake* (1948), *Magruder Mountain* (1957), *Manly Peak* (1950), *Marble Canyon* (1951), *Maturango Peak* (1951), *Mount Stirling* (1957), *Pahrump* (1958), *Panamint Butte* (1951), *Quail Mountains* (1948), *Ryan* (1952), *Searles Lake* (1949), *Shoshone* (1951), *Silurian Hills* (1956), *Springdale* (1966), *Stewart Valley* (1958), *Stovepipe Wells* (1952), *Tecopa* (1950), *Telescope Peak* (1952), *Thirsty Canyon* (1966), *Tin Mountain* (1957), *Trona* (1949), *Ubehebe Crater* (1957), *Ubehebe Peak* (1950), *Wingate Pass* (1950), *Wingate Wash* (1950).

———. Topographic Maps, 7.5 Minute Series (1:31,250). *Amargosa Flat* (1968), *Bonnie Claire* (1968), *Bonnie Claire NW* (1968), *Bonnie Claire SE* (1967), *Bonnie Claire SW* (1968), *Gold Point* (1968), *Gold Point SW* (1968), *High Peak* (1968), *Lida* (1968), *Mount Jackson* (1982), *Mount Schader* (1968), *Mount Schader SE* (1968), *Scotty's Junction* (1968), *Scotty's Junction NE* (1968), *Scotty's Junction SW* (1982), *Stonewall Pass* (1968).

———. Topographic Maps, Special (1:24,000) *Bullfrog* (1906).

U.S. National Park Service. *Death Valley National Monument.* [Washington, D.C.: Government Printing Office, 1933].

U.S. Surveyor General. *Map of Public Surveys in California to Accompany Report of Surveyor Gen'l., 1857.* [Philadelphia: Wagner & McGuigan, 1858].

Vance, J. J. *Geographical Map of Skidoo, Wild Rose Mining District, Inyo Co., California.* Skidoo: Skidoo Publishing Co., 1907.

Von Schmidt, Allexey W. *Map of the Eastern Boundary of the State of California as Surveyed, 1872.* National Archives, Record Group 49.

Waring, C. A. *Geological Map of Inyo County California.* San Francisco: State Mining Bureau, 1917.

Weber, C. F. & Company. *Map of Inyo County, California.* San Francisco: 1914.

———. *Map of San Bernardino County, California.* San Francisco: 1914.

Wheat, Carl I. *Map Showing Probable Routes of Forty-Niner Parties Through Death Valley.* San Francisco: Sierra Club, 1939.

Wheeler, George M. *Explorations and Surveys South of Central Pacific R.R. War Department Preliminary Topographical Map . . . from Surveys . . . during the Summer and Fall of 1871.* [Washington, D.C.: 1872].

———. *Geographical Explorations and Surveys West of the 100th Meridian, Topographical Atlas, Parts of Eastern California and Southern Nevada, Atlas Sheets No. 57, 58, 65, 65D and 66.* [Washington, D.C.: 1874–1876].

Wilson, John Hoppes. *Official Map of the Mayflower Section in the North East Part of the Bullfrog District, Nye Co., Nevada.* Rhyolite: Hamman & Armstrong, 1907.

COURT CASES

Byrne v. Knight and Simpson, 12 Cal. App. 56 (1909).

Commonwealth v. Burton, 183 Mass. 461 (1903).

Ex Parte Rickey, 100 Pac. 134 (1909).

Gerard v. Scott, Johnson, et al., Civil Case No. 1134BH, U.S. District Court, Southern District of California, Central Division (1941). Records in Federal Records Center, Laguna Niguel, Calif.

Gerard v. Scott, Johnson, et al., 128 Fed. 2nd 120, Appeals Case No. 9979, Circuit Court of Appeals, Ninth Circuit (1942). Records in Federal Records Center, San Bruno, Calif.

Gifford v. Carvill, 29 Cal. 589 (1866).

Gray v. Skidoo Mines Co., Case No. CC166ND, U.S. District Court for Southern District of California, Northern Division (1912). Records in Federal Records Center, San Bruno, Calif.

Hughes v. United States Borax Co., 286 Fed. 24 (1923).

Indiana Nevada Mining Co. v. Gold Hills Mining & Milling Co., 126 Pac. 965 (1912).

Keane Wonder Mining Co. v. Cunningham, 222 Fed. 821 (1915).

People v. Cyty, 106 Pac. 257 (1909).

Salsberry v. Julian, 278 Pac. 257 (1929).

Skidoo Fraction Mining and Milling Co. v. Skidoo Mines Co. and Montgomery, Case No. 390 Civil, U.S. District Court, Southern District of California, Southern Division (1915). Records in Federal Records Centers, Laguna Niguel, Calif.

State v. Skinner, 104 Pac. 223 (1909).

United States v. Rhyolite Townsite and Mining Company, Supplemental Argument for Contestee, Before the General Land Office. Washington: J. D. Milans & Sons, 1909, 39 pp.

United States Borax Co. v. Death Valley Borax Co. et al., 92 Cal. App. 724 (1928).

Williams et al. v. South Pacific Mining Co., Superior Court, Case No. 410, San Bernardino County, California (1883). Records in San Bernardino County Clerk's Office.

Yount v. United States. Indian Depredation Claim 3352 (1891). Record Group 123, National Archives, Washington, D.C.

GOVERNMENT PUBLICATIONS

Aubury, Lewis E. *The Copper Resources of California (California State Mining Bureau, Bulletin 23).* Sacramento: Supt. State Printing, 1902, 282 pp.

———. *The Copper Resources of California (California State Mining Bureau, Bulletin 50).* Sacramento: W. W. Shannon, Supt. State Printing, 1908, 366 pp.

Bailey, Gilbert E. *The Saline Deposits of California (California State Mining Bureau, Bulletin 24).* Sacramento: Supt. State Printing, 1902, 216 pp.

Ball, Sydney H. *A Geologic Reconnaissance in Southwestern Nevada and Eastern California (U.S. Geological Survey Bulletin No. 308).* Washington, D.C.: Government Printing Office, 1907, 218 pp.

———. "Notes on Ore Deposits of Southwestern Nevada and Eastern California," in *Contributions to Economic Geology 1905 (U.S. Geological Survey Bulletin No. 285).* Washington, D.C.: Government Printing Office, 1906, 53–73.

Biographical Directory of the American Congress, 1774–1971. Washington, D.C.: Government Printing Office, 1971, 1,972 pp.

Bradley, Walter W., et al. *Manganese and Chromium in California (California State Mining Bureau Bulletin No. 76).* Sacramento: State Printing Office, 1918, 248 pp.

California Secretary of State. *Biennial Reports . . . 1900 [through] 1908.* Sacramento: Supt. of State Printing, 1900 through 1908.

California State Mineralogist. *Report . . . Third [through] Thirty Fourth.* Sacramento: State Printer, 1883 through 1938.

Campbell, Marius R. *Reconnaissance of the Borax Deposits of Death Valley and Mohave Desert. (U.S. Geological Survey, Bulletin 100).* Washington, D.C.: Government Printing Office, 1902, 23 pp.

"Census of the Inhabitants of the State of Nevada, 1875," *Appendix to the Journal of the Senate and Assembly of the 8th Session of the Nevada State Legislature.* Carson City: State Printer, 1877, 2 v.

Clark, William B. *Gold Districts of California (California Division of Mines and Geology, Bulletin 193).* San Francisco: State Printing Office, 1970, 186 pp.

Coville, Frederick V. *Botany of the Death Valley Expedition. (Contributions from the U.S. National Herbarium, v. 4, U.S. Department of Agriculture, Division of Botany).* Washington, D.C.: Government Printing Office, 1893, 363 pp.

Curtis, Joseph S. *Silver-Lead Deposits of Eureka Nevada.* Washington, D.C.: Government Printing Office, 1884, 200 pp.

Death Valley National Monument, Fifth Report by the Committee on Government Operations (89th Cong., 1st Sess., House Rpt. 193), Washington, D.C.: Government Printing Office, 1965, 108 pp.

Death Valley National Monument, Hearings Before a Subcommittee of the Committee on Government Operations, House of Rep. (88th Cong., 2nd Sess.) Washington, D.C.: Government Printing Office, 1965, 660 pp.

Deposits of Borax, Hearing Before the Committee on Mines and Mining, House of Representatives on S. 4008, An Act Defining the Manner in Which Deposits of Borax, Borate of Lime, Borate of Soda, and Borate Material May be Acquired. Washington, D.C.: Government Printing Office, 1913, 19 pp.

Emma Mine Investigation, Report on the (44th Cong., 1st Sess., House Rpt. 579). Washington, D.C.: Government Printing Office, 1876, 879 pp.

Evans, James R., Gary C. Taylor, and John S. Rapp. *Mines and Mineral Deposits in Death Valley National Monument, California (California Division of Mines and Geology, Special Report 125).* Sacramento: State Printing Office, 1976, 61 pp.

Extend the Mining Laws of the United States to the Death Valley National Monument in California, and for Other Purposes (72nd Cong. 2nd Sess. House Rpt. 2107). Washington, D.C.: Government Printing Office, 1933, 3 pp.

Fisher, A. K., et al. *The Death Valley Expedition: A Biological Survey of Parts of California, Nevada, Arizona and Utah. Part II. (North American Fauna No. 7).* Washington, D.C.: Government Printing Office, 1893, 393 pp. [Part I was never published.]

Fremont, John Charles. *Central Railroad Route to the Pacific (33rd Cong., 2nd Sess., House Misc. Doc. 8).* Washington, D.C.: Government Printing Office, 1854, 7 pp.

———. *Report of the Exploring Expedition to the Rocky Mountains in the Year 1842, and to Oregon and North California in the Years 1843–'44. (28th Cong., 2nd Sess., Senate Ex. Doc. 174).* Washington, D.C.: Gale and Seaton, 1845, 693 pp.

Gale, Hoyt S. "The Lila C. Borax Mine at Ryan, Cal.," in *Mineral Resources of the United States ... 1911.* Washington, D.C.: Government Printing Office, 1912, pt. 2, 861–865.

———. "Prospecting for Potash in Death Valley, California," in *Contributions to Economic Geology (U.S. Geological Survey Bulletin No. 540).* Washington, D.C.: Government Printing Office, 1914, 407–415.

Gannett, S. S., and D. H. Baldwin. *Results of Spirit Leveling in California, 1896 to 1907 Inclusive (U.S. Geological Survey Bulletin No. 342).* Washington, D.C.: Government Printing Office, 1908, 172 pp.

Greene, Linda W. *Historic Resource Study: A History of Mining in Death Valley National Monument, Volume I.* Denver: National Park Service, 1981. 1036 pp. [See John A. Latschar for Volume II.]

Hall, Wayne, E., and Hal G. Stephens. *Economic Geology of the Panamint Butte Quadrangle and Modoc District, Inyo County, California (California Divi-*

sion of Mines and Geology, Special Report No. 73). San Francisco: 1963, 39 pp.

Hanks, Henry G. *Report on the Borax Deposits of California and Nevada, Giving the Production, Consumption, Uses, History, Chemistry and Mineralogy of Boracic Acid and Its Compounds. (Part 2. Third Annual Report of the State Mineralogist*). Sacramento: James J. Ayers, Supt. State Printing, 1883, 111 pp.

Harrington, Mark W. *Notes on the Climate and Meteorology of Death Valley, California (U.S. Department of Agriculture. Weather Bureau. Bulletin No. 1*). Washington, D.C.: Weather Bureau, 1892, 50 pp.

Heitman, Francis B. *Historical Register and Dictionary of the United States Army.* Washington, D.C.: Government Printing Office, 1903, 2 v.

Hill, James M. *The Mining Districts of the Western United States (U.S. Geological Survey Bulletin No. 507*). Washington, D.C.: Government Printing Office, 1912, 309 pp.

Holland, F. Ross, Jr., and Robert V. Simmonds. *Eagle Borax Works, Harmony Borax Works, Death Valley National Monument, California.* San Francisco: National Park Service, Office of History and Historic Architecture, 1971, 53 pp.

Hoover, Herbert. *Proclamation No. 2028 Death Valley National Monument.* February 11, 1933 in *U.S. Statutes at Large, 47*, pt. 2, 2554.

————. *Proclamations and Executive Orders, March 24, 1929 to March 4, 1933.* Washington, D.C.: Government Printing Office, 1974, 2 v., 1566 pp.

Hunt, Charles B., and Don R. Mabey. *Stratigraphy and Structure, Death Valley, California (U.S. Geological Survey, Professional Paper 494-A*). Washington, D.C.: Government Printing Office, 1966, 162 pp.

Hunt, Charles B., T. W. Robinson, Walter A. Bowles, and A. L. Washburn. *Hydrologic Basin, Death Valley, California (U.S. Geological Survey, Professional Paper 494-B*). Washington, D.C.: Government Printing Office, 1966, 138 pp.

Inyo County, *Great Register of Inyo County for 1871 [through] 1908.* Independence: [publisher varies] 1871–1908.

James, J. E., and Richard H. Stretch. *Practicability of Turning the Waters of the Gulf of California into the Colorado Desert and the Death Valley (43rd Cong. 1st Sess., Senate Misc. Doc. No. 84*). Washington, D.C.: Government Printing Office, 1874, 7 pp.

King, Chester, and Dennis G. Casebier. *Background to Historic and Prehistoric Resources of the East Mojave Desert Region.* Riverside, Calif.: Bureau of Land Management, 1976, 363 pp.

Latschar, John A. *Historic Resource Study: A History of Mining in Death Valley National Monument, Volume II.* Denver, Colo.: National Park Service, 1981, 786 pp. [See Linda W. Greene for Volume I.]

Levy, Benjamin. *Death Valley National Monument: Historical Background Study.* Washington, D.C.: National Park Service, Division of History, 1969, 244 pp.

Loew, Oscar. "On the Physiological Effects of a Very Hot Climate," in

George M. Wheeler, *Annual Report Upon the Geographical Surveys West of the One Hundredth Meridian.* Washington, D.C.: Government Printing Office, 1876, 328–330.

Lord, Eliot, *Comstock Mining and Miners.* Washington, D.C.: Government Printing Office, 1883, 451 pp.

Mattes, Merrill J. *Charcoal Kilns, Wildrose Canyon, Death Valley National Monument.* San Francisco: National Park Service, 1970, 103 pp.

McAllister, James F. *Geology of Mineral Deposits in the Ubehebe Peak Quadrangle, Inyo County, California (California Division of Mines Special Report No. 42).* San Francisco: 1955, 63 pp.

Mendenhall, Walter C. *Some Desert Watering Places in Southeastern California and Southwestern Nevada (U.S. Geological Survey, Water Supply Paper, 224).* Washington, D.C.: Government Printing Office, 1909, 98 pp.

Mineral Resources of the United States . . . 1911 [through] 1927. Washington, D.C.: Government Printing Office, 1912–1928.

Morton, Paul K. *Geology of the Queen of Sheba Lead Mine, Death Valley, California (California Division of Mines and Geology, Special Report No. 88).* San Francisco: 1965, 18 pp.

Nevada Secretary of State. *Biennial Report . . . 1911–12.* Carson City: State Printing Office, 1913, 193 pp.

Nevada State License and Bullion Tax Agent. *Annual Reports (1910 through 1916).* Reno: State Printing Office, 1911 through 1917.

Nevada State Mineralogist. *Report of the State Mineralogist of the State of Nevada for 1866 [through] 1878.* Carson City: State Printer, 1867 through 1879.

Noble, Levi F. *Note on a Colemanite Deposit Near Shoshone, Calif. (U.S. Geological Survey Bulletin No. 785-D).* Washington, D.C.: Government Printing Office, 1926, 63–73.

Nobel, Levi F., et al. *Nitrate Deposits in the Amargosa Region Southeastern California (U.S. Geological Survey Bulletin No. 724).* Washington, D.C.: Government Printing Office, 1922, 97 pp.

Norman, L. A., Jr., and R. M. Stewart. "Mines and Mineral Resources of Inyo County," *California Journal of Mines and Geology,* 47 (January 1951), pp. 17–223.

Norwood, Richard N., Charles S. Bull, and Ronald Quinn. *A Cultural Resource Overview of the Eureka, Saline, Panamint and Darwin Region; East Central, California.* Riverside, Calif.: Bureau of Land Management, 1980, 219 + 26 pp.

Powell, John W., and G. W. Ingalls. "Report on the Condition of the Ute Indians of Utah; the Pai-Utes of Utah, Northern Arizona, Southern Nevada, and Southeastern California . . . ," in *Annual Report of Commissioner of Indian Affairs . . . 1873.* Washington, D.C.: Government Printing Office, 1874, 41–74.

Ransome, Frederick L. *Preliminary Account of Goldfield, Bullfrog, and Other Mining Districts in Southern Nevada (U.S. Geological Survey Bulletin No. 303).* Washington, D.C.: Government Printing Office, 1907, 98 pp.

Ransome, Frederick L., W. H. Emmons, and G. H. Garrey. *Geology and Ore*

Deposits of the Bullfrog District, Nevada (U.S. Geological Survey Bulletin No. 407). Washington, D.C.: Government Printing Office, 1910, 130 pp.

Raymond, Rossiter W. *Statistics of Mines and Mining in the States and Territories West of the Rocky Mountains.* Washington, D.C.: Government Printing Office, 1872 through 1877.

Register of Mines and Minerals, Inyo County, California. Sacramento: State Mining Bureau, 1902, 14 pp.

Register of Mines and Minerals, San Bernardino County, California. Sacramento: State Mining Bureau, 1902, 20 pp.

Sampson, R. J. "Mineral Resources of a Part of the Panamint Range," *Mining in California, 28* (July and October 1932), 357–376.

———. "Mineral Resources of the Resting Springs Region, Inyo County," *California Division of Mines Report, 33* (October 1937), 264–270.

San Bernardino County. *Great Register of San Bernardino County for 1872 [through] 1898.* San Bernardino: [publisher varies], 1872 through 1898.

Sinclair, Cephas H. "The Oblique Boundary Line Between California and Nevada." Appendix No. 3, *Report of the Superintendent of the Coast and Geodetic Survey, 1899–1900.* Washington, D.C.: Government Printing Office, 1901, 255–484.

Spurr, Josiah E. *Descriptive Geology of Nevada South of the Fortieth Parallel and Adjacent Portions of California (U.S. Geological Survey Bulletin No. 208).* Washington, D.C.: Government Printing Office, 1903, 229 pp.

Steward, Julian H. *Basin-Plateau Aboriginal Sociopolitical Groups (Smithsonian Institution, Bureau of American Ethnology, Bulletin 120).* Washington, D.C.: Government Printing Office, 1938, 346 pp.

———. "Culture Element Distributions: XIII Nevada Shoshoni," *University of California Publications in Anthropological Records, 4* (1941), 209–359.

Streams, Springs, and Water Holes on Public Lands in the State of California (64th Cong. 1st Sess. House Rpt. 9). Washington, D.C.: Government Printing Office, 1915, 3 pp. and (*Senate Report No. 460*) 1916, 5 pp.

Stretch, Richard H. "Journal of Explorations in Southern Nevada in the Spring of 1866 by His Excellency Governor Blasdel of Nevada," Appendix E, *Annual Report of the State Mineralogist of the State of Nevada for 1866.* Carson City: Joseph E. Eckley, State Printer, 1867, 141–147.

Teague, George A., and Lynette O. Shenk. *Excavations at Harmony Borax Works.* Tucson: Western Archeological Center Publications in Anthropology No. 6, 1977, 236 pp.

Thompson, David G. *The Mohave Desert Region (U.S. Geological Survey, Water Supply Paper No. 578).* Washington, D.C.: Government Printing Office, 1929, 759 pp.

———. *Routes to Some Desert Watering Places in the Mohave Desert Region, California (U.S. Geological Survey, Water Supply Paper No. 490-B).* Washington, D.C.: Government Printing Office, 1921, 269 pp.

Trask, Parker D. *Manganese in California (California Division of Mines Bulletin No. 125).* Sacramento: State Printing Office, 1943, pp. 51–215.

Tucker, W. B., and R. J. Sampson. "Mineral Resources of Inyo County," *Califor-*

nia Journal of Mines and Geology, 34 (October 1938), 368–500.

Tucker, W. B., and R. J. Sampson. "Mineral Resources of San Bernardino County," *California Journal of Mines and Geology, 39* (October 1943), 427–549.

U.S. National Park Service. *A Bibliography of National Parks and Monuments West of the Mississippi River.* Washington, D.C.: National Park Service, 1941, v. I, 3–26, Death Valley National Monument.

———. *Death Valley National Monument.* Washington, D.C.: Government Printing Office, 1933, 4 pp., and 1934, 20 pp.

———. *Death Valley National Monument, A Bibliography.* Death Valley: 1963, 116 pp.

———. *Guide for Motorists in Death Valley National Monument, California.* Washington, D.C.: Government Printing Office, 1934, 31 pp.

U.S. Surveyor General. *Annual Report . . . 1855–6 [through] 1857–8* in *Annual Report of the Secretary of the Interior.* Washington, D.C.: Government Printing Office, 1856 through 1858.

U.S. Treasury Department. *Report of the Director of the Mint Upon the Production of the Precious Metals in the United States During the Calendar Year 1880 [through] 1883.* Washington, D.C.: Government Printing Office, 1881 through 1884.

Ver Planck, W. E. "History of Borax Production in the United States," *California Journal of Mines and Geology, 52* (July 1956), 273–291.

Wallace, William J. *Death Valley National Monument's Prehistoric Past: An Archaeological Overview.* Tucson: National Park Service, 1977, 266 pp.

Waring, Gerald A. *Ground Water in Pahrump, Mesquite and Ivanpah Valleys, Nevada and California (U.S. Geological Survey, Water Supply Paper No. 450-C.* Washington, D.C.: Government Printing Office, 1920, 51–86.

Warren, Claude N., Martha Knack, and Elizabeth von Till Warren. *A Cultural Resource Overview for the Amargosa-Mojave Basin Planning Units.* Riverside, Calif.: Bureau of Land Management, 1980, 268 pp.

Wendel, Clarence. *Special Report on Borate Resources.* San Francisco: National Park Service, Mining and Minerals Division, 1978, 138 pp.

Wheeler, George M. *Annual Report Upon the Geographical Surveys West of the One Hundredth Meridian (App. JJ of the Ann. Rpt. of Chief of Engineers).* Washington, D.C.: Government Printing Office, 1876, 355 pp.

———. *Preliminary Report Concerning Explorations and Surveys Principally in Nevada and Arizona.* Washington, D.C.: Government Printing Office, 1872, 96 pp.

———. *Report Upon United States Geographical Survey West of the One Hundredth Meridian.* Washington, D.C.: Government Printing Office, 1889, v. 1.

White, Donald E. *Antimony Deposits of the Wildrose Canyon Area, Inyo County, California (U.S. Geological Survey Bulletin No. 922-K).* Washington, D.C.: Government Printing Office, 1940, 307–325.

Wright, Lauren A. *Talc Deposits of the Southern Death Valley-Kingston Range Region, California (California Division of Mines and Geology, Special Report No. 95).* San Francisco: 1968, 79 pp.

Wright, Lauren A., et al. "Mines and Mineral Deposits of San Bernardino County,

California," *California Journal of Mines and Geology, 49* (January–April 1953), 49–259 + 192 pp. table.

NEWSPAPERS AND PERIODICALS

Atascadero, Calif. *Lewis Journal,* 1925.
Atascadero, Calif. *News,* 1925–1926.
Aurora, Nev. *Esmeralda Herald,* 1877–1882.
Aurora, Nev. *Esmeralda Union,* 1867–1868.
Austin, Nev. *Reese River Reveille,* 1863–1871, 1874.
Bakersfield, Calif. *Southern Californian,* 1878–1879.
Beatty, Nev. *Beatty Bullfrog Miner,* 1905–1908.
Belmont, Nev. *Courier,* 1874–1899.
Belmont, Nev. *Silver Bend Reporter,* 1867–1868.
Bishop, Calif. *Bishop Creek Times,* 1881–1882.
Bishop, Calif. *Inyo Magazine,* 1908.
Bishop, Calif. *Inyo Register,* 1885–1934.
Bishop, Calif. *Owens Valley Herald,* 1908–1927.
Bishop, Calif. *Sierra Magazine,* 1909.
Blair, Nev. *Press,* 1908–1910.
Bullfrog, Nev. *Miner,* 1905–1906.
Butte, Mont. *Mining World,* 1906.
Calico, Calif. *Print,* 1882.
Candelaria, Nev. *Chloride Belt,* 1890–1892.
Candelaria, Nev. *True Fissure,* 1880–1886.
Carrara, Nev. *Miner,* 1929.
Carrara, Nev. *Obelisk,* 1914–1916.
Chicago *Record-Herald,* 1905.
Colorado Springs, Colo. *Mining Investor,* 1905–1907.
Columbus, Nev. *Borax Miner,* 1873–1877.
Daggett, Calif. *Calico Print,* 1885.
Darwin, Calif. *Coso Mining News,* 1875–1877.
Delamar, Nev. *Lode,* 1895–6.
Denver, Colo. *Death Valley Dawsonian,* 1906.
Denver, Colo. *Mining Investor,* 1907.
Denver, Colo. *Mining Record,* 1896–1913.
Denver, Colo. *Mining Reporter,* 1907.
Eureka, Nev. *Sentinel,* 1875.
Fort Worth, Tex. *Western World,* 1926–1928.
Gilbert, Nev. *Record,* 1925–1926.
Gold Center, Nev. *News,* 1906–1907.
Gold Hill, Nev. *News,* 1866.
Goldfield, Nev. *Gossip,* 1906–1907.
Goldfield, Nev. *Market Letter,* 1906–1907.
Goldfield, Nev. *Nevada Mining News,* 1906.
Goldfield, Nev. *News,* 1906–1907.

Goldfield, Nev. *Review,* 1905–1908.
Goldfield, Nev. *Tribune,* 1913.
Goodsprings, Nev. *Gazette,* 1916–1921.
Greenwater, Calif. *Death Valley Chuck-Walla,* 1907.
Greenwater, Calif. *Times,* 1906.
Havilah, Calif. *Miner,* 1872–1874.
Hornsilver, Nev. *Herald,* 1908.
Independence, Calif. *Inyo Independent,* 1870–1932.
Ione, Nev. *Nye County News,* 1864–1866.
Las Vegas, Nev. *Age,* 1905–1933 (Indexed).
Leadfield, Calif. *Chronicle,* 1926.
London *Times,* 1899 (Indexed).
Los Angeles *Arrowhead Magazine,* 1920–1934.
Los Angeles *Evening News,* 1906.
Los Angeles *Examiner,* 1904–1907, 1926–1935.
Los Angeles *Mining Review,* 1899–1913.
Los Angeles *News,* 1862–1866, 1872.
Los Angeles *Record,* 1930.
Los Angeles *Southern News,* 1860–1862.
Los Angeles *Star,* 1851–1863.
Los Angeles *Times,* 1881–1894, 1912–1935 (Indexed).
Mammoth City, Calif. *Herald,* 1879.
Needles, Calif. *Needles Eye,* 1891–1894.
New York *Bullion,* 1880.
New York *Commercial and Financial Chronicle,* 1898–1914 (Indexed).
New York *Copper, Curb and Mining Outlook,* 1911.
New York *Engineering and Mining Journal,* 1869–1933 (Indexed).
New York *Graphic,* 1881–1882.
New York *Mining Record,* 1880–1881.
New York *Mining Topics,* 1906.
New York *Moving Picture World,* 1912, 1915–1916.
New York *Times,* 1851–1933 (Indexed).
New York *Tribune,* 1875–1906 (Indexed).
New York *United States Mining Journal,* 1905–1906.
New York *World,* 1894.
Oroville, Calif. *Butte Democrat,* 1860–1861.
Palmetto, Nev. *Herald,* 1906.
Panamint, Calif. *News,* 1874–1875.
Phoenix, Ariz. *Mining Journal,* 1925–1927.
Pioche, Nev. *Record,* 1872–1906 (Indexed).
Pioneer, Nev. *Topics,* 1909.
Randsburg, Calif. *Miner,* 1900–1907.
Reno, Nev. *Nevada Mining Investor,* 1907.
Reno, Nev. *Nevada Mining News,* 1907–1909.
Rhyolite, Nev. *Bulletin,* 1907–1909.
Rhyolite, Nev. *Bullfrog Miner,* 1906–1909.
Rhyolite, Nev. *Death Valley Magazine,* 1908.

Rhyolite, Nev. *Death Valley Prospector,* 1907.
Rhyolite, Nev. *Herald,* 1905–1912.
Rhyolite, Nev. *Market Letter,* 1906–1907.
Sacramento, Calif. *Union,* 1860–1861, 1865.
Salt Lake City, *Tribune,* 1895–1896, 1905.
San Bernardino, Calif. *Guardian,* 1869–1871.
San Bernardino, Calif. *Sun,* 1906.
San Bernardino, Calif. *Times,* 1875–1882.
San Diego, Calif. *Union,* 1868–1902 (Indexed).
San Francisco *Alta California,* 1850–1854, 1859–1864, 1875, 1884, 1888.
San Francisco *Bulletin,* 1860, 1869.
San Francisco *Call,* 1904, 1912.
San Francisco *Chronicle,* 1875, 1884, 1902, 1904, 1917, 1919.
San Francisco *Examiner,* 1891, 1901.
San Francisco *Exchange,* 1881–1884.
San Francisco *Herald,* 1853.
San Francisco *Mining and Scientific Press,* 1860–1922 (Indexed).
San Jose, Calif. *Tribune,* 1861.
San Leandro, Calif. *Alameda County Gazette,* 1859–1861.
Searchlight, Nev. *Bulletin,* 1906–1911.
Searchlight, Nev. *Searchlight,* 1903–1906.
Shanghai *China Press,* 1934.
Silver Peak, Nev. *Post,* 1906.
Skidoo, Calif. *News,* 1907, 1908.
Tonopah, Nev. *Bonanza,* 1901–1906, 1910.
Tonopah, Nev. *Miner,* 1902–1907.
Tonopah, Nev. *Mining Reporter,* 1921–1929.
Tonopah, Nev. *Nevada Mining Record,* 1926–1929.
Tonopah, Nev. *Nevada Mining Record-Reporter,* 1929–1932.
Tonopah, Nev. *Sun,* 1905–1907.
Transvaal, Nev. *Miner,* 1906.
Virginia City, Nev. *Territorial Enterprise,* 1866–1879 (Indexed).
Visalia, Calif. *Delta,* 1859–1866.
Visalia, Calif. *Sun,* 1860.
Wells, Nev. *Nevada State Herald,* 1905–1906.

ARTICLES

"Across Death Valley," *Standard Oil Bulletin, 14* (September 1926), 3–9.
Albright, Horace, M. "Creation of the Death Valley National Monument," in *The Story of Death Valley Its Museum and Visitor Center*. San Bernardino: Inland Printing and Engraving Co., 1966, 5–14.
Allred, Jacob. "Driving A 20-Mule Team in Death Valley," *Travel, 61* (September 1933), 23–25, 38.
———. "Driving the Last Twenty Mule Team Across Death Valley," *Popular Mechanics, 45* (April 1926), 610–614.

———. "The Death Valley Teamsters," *Wide World Magazine, 58* (November 1926).

"Amazing Death Valley, America's Most Interesting Winter Tour," *Arrowhead Magazine* (January 1930), 15–18.

"Amazing Death Valley Winter Playground of Thrilling Interest and Romance," *Arrowhead Magazine* (November 1929), 13–15.

Anderson, B. "Railroad Taps Death Valley," *Technical World, 23* (July 1915), 498–499.

Anderson, Helen Ashley. "Gold for the Vaults of America," *Desert Magazine, 5* (May 1942), 5–7.

Arthur, Charlotte. "Castle in the Desert," *Country Life, 62* (June/July 1932), 35–38, 76–78.

Bailey, Philip. "Another Breyfogle," *Calico Print, 7* (December 1951), 2.

Bailey, Vernon. "Into Death Valley 50 Years Ago," *Westways, 32* (December 1940), 8–11.

Bales, LeRoy and Margaret. "He Belongs to the Panamints," *Desert Magazine, 5* (November 1941), 17–21.

———. "They Never Locked the Door of the Jail at Ballarat," *Desert Magazine, 4* (March 1941), 10–14.

Ball, Clinton C. "'Oil' on the Amargosa," *Desert Magazine, 17* (March 1954), 12.

Bauer, Harry J. "Death Valley Development," *Touring Topics, 24* (May 1932), 9.

Baur, John E. "John Goller: Pioneer Angeleno Manufacturer," *Historical Society of Southern California Quarterly, 36* (March 1954), 14–27.

Bechdolt, Frederick R. "How Death Valley Was Named," *Saturday Evening Post, 192* (July 19, 1919), 30, 32, 34, 66.

Belden, L. Burr. "The Battle of Wingate Pass," *Westways, 48* (November 1956), 8–9.

———. "Death Valley's New Survey," *Westways, 46* (November 1954), 2–3.

Benedict, S. G. "Mapping Death Valley a Quarter Century Ago," *Touring Topics, 23* (November 1931), 12–15, 43.

Benton, Arthur, R. "The Wrong Turn," *Desert Magazine, 241* (April 1961), 6–9.

Bigler, Henry W. "Extracts from the Journal of Henry W. Bigler," *Utah Historical Quarterly, 5* (April–October 1932), 35–64, 87–112, 134–160.

"The Borax Industry and Its Chief Promoter," *Overland Monthly, 42* (July 1903), 24–28.

Boyles, J. C. "He Witnessed the Death Valley Tragedy of '49," *Desert Magazine, 3* (February 1940), 3–6.

Brewerton, George D. "A Ride with Kit Carson through the Great American Desert and the Rocky Mountains," *Harper's New Monthly Magazine, 7* (August 1853), 306–334.

Brier, John Wells. "The Argonauts of Death Valley, Being a Concise But Truthful Account of the Trials and Tribulations of that Pioneer Band Who Came to California by the Southern Route, as Told by One of the Survivors," *The Grizzly Bear, 9* (June 1911), 1–4, 7.

———. "The Death Valley Party of 1849," *Out West, 18* (March and April 1903), 326–335, 456–465.

Britt, Henry. "Breyfogle," *Calico Print, 7* (April 1951), 8.

Brown, Charles. "The Law at Greenwater," *Calico Print, 9* (January 1953), 22–23.

Brown, W. H. "With a 20 Mule Team on the Borax Trail—in 1939," *Calico Print, 7* (December 1951), 5.

Burns, Colette Wagner. "Plan Now To Visit Death Valley," *Sunset Magazine, 65* (November 1930), 15–17.

Burrel, Louisa. "Across the Plains in 1849," *The Pioneer, 9* (December 15, 1894), 2.

Bynum, Lindley, ed. "The Record Book of the Rancho Santa Ana del Chino," *Historical Society of Southern California, Annual Publications, 16* (1934), 1–55.

Campbell, Marius R. "Basin-Range Structure in the Death Valley Region of Southeastern California," *American Geologist, 31* (May 1903), 311–312.

Cannon, George Q. "Twenty Years Ago: A Trip to California," *Juvenile Insructor, 4* (1869), Serially, 6–7, 13–14, 21–22, 28, 36–37, 44, 52–53, 60, 68, 78–79, 84, 92.

"The Career of Charles M. Schwab," *Outlook, 74* (August 15, 1903), 920–921.

Carter, Harvey L. "Calvin Jones," *The Mountain Men and the Fur Trade in the Far West, 6* (LeRoy R. Hafen, ed.). Glendale: Arthur H. Clark Co., 1968, 207–211.

———. "Kit Carson," *The Mountain Men and the Fur Trade in the Far West, 6* (LeRoy R. Hafen, ed.). Glendale: Arthur H. Clark Co., 1968, 105–131.

Carter, Oscar S. C. "Death Valley," *Journal Franklin Institute, 154* (September 1902), 193–199.

Caruthers, William. "Long Man," *Desert Magazine, 6* (May 1943), 11–14.

———. "Shorty and the Lost Chinaman," *Desert Magazine, 7* (November 1943), 25–26.

———. "Shorty Harris and Hungry Bill," *Calico Print, 7* (July 1951), 2.

Casper, K. R. "The Bullfrog Bonanza, How Recent Gold Discoveries Have Awakened Southern Nevada and Added New Towns to the Map," *Sunset Magazine, 15* (August 1905), 316–326.

———. "The Story of Breyfogle," *Sunset Magazine, 15* (October 1905), 591–593.

Caughey, John W., "Don Benito Wilson: An Average Southern Californian," *Huntington Library Quarterly, 11* (April 1939), 285–300.

———. "Southwest from Salt Lake in 1849," *Pacific Historical Review, 6* (June 1937), 143–164.

Chapman, Robert H. "The Deserts of Nevada and the Death Valley," *National Geographic Magazine, 17* (September 1906), 483–497.

Chavez, Jose-Antonio, "Itineraire du Nord-Mexico a la Haute-Californie," *Bulletin de la Société de Geographie, Paris, 2d. ser., 3* (1835), 316–323.

Cheesman, David W. "By Ox Team from Salt Lake to Los Angeles, 1850, A Memoir by David W. Cheesman," *Historical Society of Southern California, Annual Publications, 14* (1930), 271–337. (Mary E. Foy, ed.).

Christman, A. B. "Johnny Shoshone of Death Valley," *Desert Magazine, 16* (December 1953), 10–11.

Clawson, Elliott J. "The Sheriff of Greenwater. A Story of the Death Valley Slope," *Overland Monthly, 54* (November & December 1909), 481–489, 577–584.

Clyde, Norman. "High-Low, The Story of a Sunrise to Sunset Journey from the Summit of Mt. Whitney to Death Valley," *Touring Topics, 22* (November 1930), 30–31.

Colton, John B. "The Death Valley Mines," *The Pioneer, 10* (December 15, 1895), 4.

"Conquering Excessive Grades and Curves with a Monorail Line," *Scientific American, 130* (April 1924), 249.

Coolidge, Dane. "Scotty's Castle," *Westways, 31* (March 1939), 8–10.

Cooper, Lloyd. "Landmarks of Death Valley," *Touring Topics, 18* (June 1926), 32–33.

Coulter, Harry. "Escape from Death Valley," *Westways, 41* (September 1949), 2–3.

Court, Arnold. "How Hot is Death Valley?" *Geographical Review, 39* (April 1949), 214–220.

Coville, Frederick V. "Descriptions of New Plants from Southern California, Nevada, Utah and Arizona," *Proc. Biological Society of Washington, 7* (May 1892), 65–80.

———. "The Panamint Indians of California," *American Anthropologist, 5* (October 1892), 351–361.

———. "Sketch of the Flora of Death Valley, California," *Science, 20* (December 16, 1892), 342–343.

Cross, Ernest L. "Letters from a Death Valley Prospector," *Desert Magazine, 26* (June 1963), 8–11. (Tom G. Murray, ed.).

Davis, Alfred. "Death Valley," *Overland Monthly, 50* (July 1907), 81–83.

"Death Valley," *Forest and Stream, 38* (August 20, 1891), 83.

"Death Valley," *Scientific American, 53* (September 19, 1885), 177.

"Death Valley, A National Monument," *American Review of Reviews, 87* (May 1933), 43.

"Death Valley Beckons," *Standard Oil Bulletin, 21* (January 1934), 2–6, 13, 16.

"Death Valley Becomes a National Monument," *American Forests, 39* (April 1933), 178.

"Death Valley Days Gets a New Look," *Pioneer, 1* (October 1959), 23.

"Death Valley From Chloride, Cliff," *Arrowhead Magazine* (August 1926), 19.

"Death Valley in Winter, Nature's Amazing Beauty Spot May Now Be Visited in Comfort," *Arrowhead Magazine* (December 1930), 20–24.

"Death Valley Proposed As National Park," *Touring Topics, 24* (April 1932), 28.

"Death Valley Tours," *Arrowhead Magazine* (December 1926/January 1927), 22 and (October 1928), 18–19.

"Death Valley's Natural Bridge—A New Death Valley Attraction," *Standard Oil Bulletin, 22* (January 1935), 8–11, 16.

DeGroot, Henry. "Crossing the California Sahara," *Overland Monthly, 8* (July 1886), 52–57.

Delameter, John A. "My 40 Years Pulling Freight," *Touring Topics, 22* (August 1930), 24–29, 56. (As told to John E. Hogg).

DeLaney, Paul. "The Jayhawkers, of '49," *Death Valley Magazine, 1* (June through September 1908), 99–102, 115–117, 155–156.

———. "Life of 'Death Valley Scotty,'" serially in *Death Valley Prospector* (December 1907) and *Death Valley Magazine* (January through October 1908).

Denison, Lindsay. "The He-Siren of the Goldfields" and subsequent articles in *Ridgways, A Militant Weekly for God and Country* (December 8, 1906 through January 12, 1907).

"Depth of Death Valley," *Journal of Geography, 6* (September 1907), 75.

Dix, R. S. "Death Valley," *Chautauquan, 13* (August 1891), 629–633.

Dutcher, B. H. "Piñon Gathering Among the Panamint Indians," *American Anthropologist, 6* (October 1893), 377–380.

Edwards, E. I. "Death Valley's Neglected Hero," *Westerners, Los Angeles Posse, Brand Book 12.* Los Angeles: Westerners, 1966, 59–73.

———. "The Mystery of Death Valley, How It Was Named," *Westerners, Los Angeles Posse, Branding Iron No. 61* (June 1962), 4–8.

———. "The Mystery of Death Valley's Lost Wagon Train," *Westerners, Los Angeles Posse, Brand Book 11.* Los Angeles: Ward Ritchie Press, 1964, 181–240.

Eklund, Ernest E. "Some Additional Facts About the Climate of Death Valley, Calif.," *Monthly Weather Review, 61* (February 1933), 33–35.

Fairbanks, E. E. "Forty-Niners Starved in the Midst of Plenty," *Scientific American, 146* (June 1932), 348–349.

Fairbanks, H. W. "Mineral Deposits of Eastern California," *American Geologist, 17* (March 1896), 144–158.

Fairbanks, Ralph J. "My 73 Years on Southwestern Deserts," *Touring Topics, 22* (June 1930), 20–25, 53. (As told to John E. Hogg).

"Farming in Death Valley," *Literary Digest, 64* (March 20, 1920), 38–39.

Farnsworth, Harriett. "Dolph Nevares of Death Valley," *Desert Magazine, 21* (December 1958), 16–18.

Ferguson, C. W., and R. A. Wright. "Tree-Ring Dates for Cutting Activity at the Charcoal Kilns, Panamint Mountains, California," *Tree-Ring Bulletin, 24* (January 1962), 3–9.

Fisk, O. J. "Ghosts of Greenwater," *Westways, 32* (November 1940), 8–9. (As told to Philip Johnston).

Flint, Thomas. "Diary of Dr. Thomas Flint, California to Maine and Return, 1851–1855," *Historical Society of Southern California, Annual Publication, 11* (1923), 53–127. (Waldemar Westergaard, ed.).

Ford, John Anson, "Tap Wealth of Death Valley with Monorail," *Popular Mechanics, 40* (July 1923), 36–37.

Ford, Walter. "Samaritan of Cave Springs," *Desert Magazine, 3* (November 1939), 12–15.

Frasher, Burton. "Portfolio of Desert Area Photographs from 1920 to 1939," *Westerners, Los Angeles Posse, Brand Book 11.* Los Angeles: Ward Ritchie Press, 1964, 57–76.

Freeman, Dick. "On Manly's Trail in the Panamints," *Desert Magazine, 4* (March 1941), 4–8.

Gally, James W. "Ghosted," *Overland Monthly, 8* (August 1886), 120–125.

Gates, Charles Richard. "Gold Amid the Sagebrush," *Pacific Monthly, 17* (June 1907), 739–742.

Gilbert, Dick. "Lost Woman's Lost Mine?" *Calico Print, 9* (September 1953), 18–19.

———. "Old Joe Ward . . . Desert Man, Prospector and Poet," *Calico Print, 9* (November 1953), 8–9.

Glass, H. L. "Borax Ore Preparation in Death Valley," *Chemical and Metallurgical Engineering, 37* (May 1930), 296–298.

Goodrich, Arthur. "The Head of the Great Steel Company," *World's Work, 1* (April 1901), 615–618.

Goodwin, T. R. "The Argonaut Trail," *Thor Shun* (December 9, 25, 1935, January 3, February 6, 22, March 11, April 4, 1936). Serially.

———. "The Development of Death Valley," *American Forests, 41* (May 1935), 215–218, 253.

———. "The Invasion of Death Valley by the CCC," *Thor Shun* (February 1938), 7.

———. "White Man's History Through Red Man's Mouth," *Thor Shun* (August 24, 1936), 11–14.

Gower, Harry P. "The Night We Brought 'Old Dinah' Home to Furnace Creek," *Pioneer, 1* (January 1960), 14–15.

Gray, Fred. "Memories of Ballarat," *Westways, 32* (September 1940), 8–10. (As told to Philip Johnston).

Gray, Roy B. "Amazing Death Valley, Once Dreaded Place Now Lure For Tourists," *Arrowhead Magazine* (December 1927), 17–26.

———. "Death Valley De Luxe," *World Traveler, 19* (April 1927), 26–27, 46, 52.

———. "Now For Death Valley," *Arrowhead Magazine* (December 1926/January 1927), 7–21.

Greeves-Carpenter, C. F. "Road Construction in Death Valley," *Highway Magazine, 27* (February 1936), 28–31.

Grey, Zane. "Death Valley," *Harper's Monthly Magazine, 140* (May 1920), 758–770.

Grosscup, Gordon L. "Notes on Boundaries and Culture of the Panamint Shoshone and Owens Valley Paiute," *Contributions of the University of California Archaeological Research Facility, No. 35* (1977), 109–150.

Guenther, Louis. "Pirates of promotion: George Graham Rice," *World's Work, 36* (October 1918), 584–591.

Guthrie, J. A. "Rhodes Told Me of the Lost Gunsight," *Calico Print, 8* (August/September 1952), 26–27.

Hafen, LeRoy R. "Armijo's Journal," *Huntington Library Quarterly, 11* (November 1947), 87–101.

———. "Armijo's Journal of 1829–30; The Beginning of Trade Between New Mexico and California," *Colorado Magazine, 27* (April 1950), 120–131.

———. "Elijah Barney Ward," *The Mountain Men and the Fur Trade in the Far West, 7* (LeRoy R. Hafen, ed.). Glendale: Arthur H. Clark Co., 1969, 343–351.

———. "Philip F. Thompson," *The Mountain Men and the Fur Trade in the Far*

West, 3 (LeRoy R. Hafen, ed.). Glendale: Arthur H. Clark Co., 1966, 339–347.

Hallidie, A. S. "William T. Coleman," *Overland Monthly,* 23 (January 1894), 71–75.

Hanna, Phil Townsend. "Aboriginal Derelicts of Death Valley," *Touring Topics,* 21 (February 1929), 44–45, 55.

————. "Beauty and the Beast," *Touring Topics,* 20 (December 1928), 38–39, 49.

————. "Greenwater and Its Press," *Westways,* 32 (November 1940), 9.

————. "The Origin and Meaning of Some Place Names of the Death Valley Region," *Touring Topics,* 22 (February 1930), 42–43, 54.

————. "Something Different in Deserts," *Touring Topics,* 20 (March 1928), 25, 46.

————. "The Valley of Death and Delight," *Touring Topics,* 22 (December, 1930), Rotogravure Section.

————. "When Death Valley Took Its First Toll," *Touring Topics,* 19 (December 1927), 14–17, 40–42.

Harcourt, Carmen. "Death Valley and the Mojave Desert," *Overland Monthly, 31* (June 1898), 488–495.

Harris, Frank. "Half a Century Chasing Rainbows," *Touring Topics,* 22 (October 1930), 12–20, 55. (As told to Philip Johnston).

Hart, Edward. "Death Valley, California, and Its Borax Industry," *American Ceramic Society Transactions, 5* (1903), 64–73.

Helm, James P. "Did They Find the Lost Breyfogle Mine?" *Desert Magazine, 16* (September 1953), 17–19.

Henderson, R. C. "Building Roads in Death Valley," *Highway Magazine, 32* (July 1941), 159–161.

————. "Death Valley Has Come To Life," *Nations' Business, 18* (May 1930), 76, 79–80, 83.

————. "Opening Death Valley To Tourists," *Highway Magazine, 24* (September 1933), 199–201.

Henderson, Randall. "He Built Scotty's Castle," *Desert Magazine, 15* (September 1952), 4–10.

Hill, Joseph J. "The Old Spanish Trail," *Hispanic American Historical Review, 4* (August 1921), 444–473.

Hilton, John W. "Mystery of Jake Abram's Lost Wagon," *Desert Magazine, 9* (December 1945), 19–22.

Hensher, Alan. "Earle Clemens and the Rhyolite Herald: Twentieth-Century Nevada Pioneers," *Southern California Quarterly, 49* (September 1967), 311–325.

"History of Death Valley," *Arrowhead Magazine* (December 1927), 27–29.

Hogg, John Edwin. "Farming in Death Valley," *Popular Mechanics, 33* (March 1920), 339–344.

————. "A Race for Life in Death Valley," *Wide World Magazine, 50* (October 1922), 58–72.

"How a Motorist Flirted with Death in Death Valley," *Literary Digest, 97* (May 12, 1928), 51, 53–54, 56.

Hoyt, Franklin. "The Los Angeles and Independence Railroad," *Historical Society of Southern California, Quarterly, 32* (December 1950), 293–308.

Hubbard, George Davis. "Death Valley," *Journal of Geography, 13* (May 1915), 277–280.

Hutchinson, W. H. "The Law Comes to Panamint," *Westways, 42* (July 1950), 10–11.

Huntington, Ellsworth. "Death Valley and Our Future Climate," *Harpers Magazine, 132* (May 1916), 919–928.

"In Death Valley," *Pacific Rural Press, 49* (April 20, 1895), 241.

"Jack Stewart's Lost-Ace-In-The-Hole Ledge," *Desert Magazine, 11* (November 1947), 22–23.

Jackson, W. Turrentine. "The Infamous Emma Mine; A British Interest in the Little Cottonwood District, Utah Territory," *Utah Historical Quarterly, 23* (October 1955), 339–362.

Jaeger, Edmund C. "Marcus Jones . . . Flower Hunter Pedaled a Bicycle Over Death Valley Trails in 1897," *Calico Print, 8* (October/November 1952), 8–9, 25.

———. "River of the Bitter Waters," *Desert Magazine, 21* (July 1958), 24–27.

Jahns, Richard H. "The Epsom Salts Line—Monorail to Nowhere," *Engineering and Science Monthly 14* (April 1951), 18–21.

Jeffers, Robinson. "Death Valley," *Out West, 26* (May 1907), 443. Poem.

Jensen, Andrew. "History of the Las Vegas Mission," *Nevada State Historical Society Papers, 5* (1926), 117–284.

Johnston, Philip. "Along the Eastern Rim of Death Valley," *Westways, 29* (January 1937), 8–11.

———. "America's Great Natural Chemical Crucible," *Touring Topics, 19* (September 1927), 14–17, 33–35.

———. "Cities That Passed in the Night," *Touring Topics, 19* (April 1927), 26–28, 37–40.

———. "Days and Nights in Old Panamint," *Touring Topics, 20* (December 1928), 22–25, 50–51.

———. "Death Valley Canyons," *Westways, 26* (March 1934), 10.

———. "Gold is Where You Put It," *Westways, 32* (March 1940), 16–17.

———. "In Quest of the Lost Breyfogle," *Touring Topics, 21* (February 1929), 18–21, 56–57.

———. "River of Bitterness," *Westways, 31* (April 1939), 8–9.

———. "Skidoo Has 23'd," *Westways, 28* (February 1936), 8–10.

———. "To the Roof of the Panamints," *Touring Topics, 19* (October 1927), 20–23, 37–38, 40, 42, 44.

Jones, Idwal. "Journey With Funston," *Westways, 44* (October 1952), 14–15.

Keagle, Cora L. "Tale of the Mono Rail," *Desert Magazine, 7* (May 1944), 9–12.

Kegley, Howard C. "Lou Wescott Beck," *American Magazine, 76* (September 1913), 30–32.

Kelly, Charles. "On Manly's Trail to Death Valley," *Desert Magazine, 2* (February 1939), 6–8, 41–43.

Kelly, Isabel T. "Southern Paiute Bands," *American Anthropologist, n.s. 36* (October-December 1934), 548–560.

Kirk, Frances C. "Amazing Death Valley As Seen By An Artist," *Arrowhead*

Magazine (October 1928), 13–17.

Kirk, Ruth E. "Where Hungry Bill Once Lived," *Desert Magazine, 16* (March 1953), 15–18.

Koch, Fred W. "Through Death Valley," *Sierra Club Bulletin, 1* (June 1893), 40–53.

Koenig, George. "Zeroing In On the Gunsight," *Westerners, Los Angeles Posse, Branding Iron No. 69* (June 1964), 6–7.

Kramer, Irving. "Portrait of a Death Valley Man," *Westways, 29* (April 1937), 25 [Harold Ashford].

Lafler, Henry A. "'Borax,' A True Fairy Tale of the West," *Sunset, 26* (April 1911), 418–423.

Lanier, Henry W. "One Trust and What Became of It," *World's Work, 7* (February 1904), 4445–4457.

Larson, Gustive O. "Walkara, Ute Chief," *The Mountain Men and the Fur Trade in the Far West, 2* (LeRoy R. Hafen, ed.). Glendale: Arthur H. Clark Co., 1965, 339–350.

———. "Walkara's Half Century," *Western Humanities Review, 6* (Summer 1952), 235–259.

Lawrence, Eleanor. "Horse Thieves on the Spanish Trail," *Touring Topics, 23* (January 1931), 22–25, 55.

———. "Mexican Trade Between Santa Fe and Los Angeles 1830–1848," *California Historical Society Quarterly, 10* (March 1931), 27–39.

———. "On the Old Spanish Trail," *Touring Topics, 22* (November 1930), 36–39.

———. "Walkara, The Napoleon of the Desert," *Touring Topics, 24* (May 1932), 18–20, 37–39.

Layne, J. Gregg. "Route of the Manly Death Valley Party: 1849–1850," *Westways, 44* (May 1952), 18.

Leadabrand, Russ. "Boom and Bust at Leadfield," *Desert Magazine, 20* (January 1957), 11–12.

———. "Photographer of the Desert," *Westerners, Los Angeles Posse, Brand Book 11.* Los Angeles: Ward Ritchie Press, 1965, 47–56.

Lecompte, Janet. "Jean-Baptiste Chalifoux," *The Mountain Men and the Fur Trade in the Far West, 7* (LeRoy R. Hafen, ed.). Glendale: Arthur H. Clark Co., 1969, 57–74.

Lee, Bourke [Thomas Burke Lee]. "Death Valley," *Saturday Evening Post, 202* (August 10, 1929), 3–5, 98, 102.

———. "Lost in Death Valley," *Saturday Evening Post, 202* (September 7, 1929), 20–21, 140–141, 145–146, 149.

———. "Death Valley Prospectors," *Saturday Evening Post, 202* (September 14, 1929), 66, 89–90, 93, 97–98, 101.

———. "Death Valley Scotty," *Saturday Evening Post, 204* (November 29, 1930), 10–11, 106, 108–110 and (December 6, 1930), 32, 34, 60, 62, 64, 67.

Leuba, Edmond. "Bandits, Borax and Bears: A Trip to Searles Lake in 1874," *California Historical Society Quarterly, 17* (June 1938), 99–117. (Alan L. Chickering, transl.).

———. "A Frenchman in the Panamints," *California Historical Society Quarterly,*

17 (September 1938), 208–218. (Alan L. Chickering transl.).

Lewis, Alfred Henry. "Owners of America: V. Charles M. Schwab," *Cosmopolitan Magazine, 45* (October 1908), 478–488.

Lewis, Lucien M. "He Was In on the Bullfrog Jackpot," *Desert Magazine, 10* (December 1946), 20–21.

"Life Saving in Death Valley," *Touring Topics, 2* (August 1910), 5–7.

Lloyd, Audrey Walls. "Saga of Death Valley's Jimmy Dayton," *Desert Magazine, 21* (June 1958), 15–17.

Loring, Fred W. "Into the Valley of Death," *Appleton's Journal, 6* (November 18, 1871), 574–575.

Lowden, S. W. "Famous Death Valley Toll Road Purchased, Making It a Free Highway," *California Highways and Public Works, 13* (January 1935), 4, 22.

"Lowest Point in the United States," *National Geographic Magazine, 18* (December 1907), 824–825.

McAdie, Alexander, George. "Relative Humidity in Death Valley," *Monthly Weather Review, 41* (June 1913), 931.

McClure, James D. "Death Valley, 'A Region of Fancied Lore and Fascinating Realities,'" *National Motorist, 9* (February 1932), 5–6.

McGaffey, Ernest. "In the Beginning, God Created Desolation—Death Valley," *Touring Topics, 14* (June 1922), 16–20, 34–36, 38, 40, 42.

———. "The Valley of the Shadow," *Overland Monthly and Out West Magazine, 91* (October 1933), 139–140.

McGee, W. J. "Thirst in the Desert," *Atlantic Monthly, 81* (April 1898), 483–488.

McInnis, Helen. "Boom Days at Ash Meadows," *Frontier Times, 39* (June/July 1965), 12–14.

MacMurphy, F. "Geology of the Panamint Silver District, California," *Economic Geology, 25* (June 1930), 305–325.

MacPherson, Harry, "Scotty Goes to Town," *Westways, 28* (January 1936), 16–17.

Maguire, Don. "Death Valley," *Scientific American Supplement, 55* (April 25, 1903), 22838–22839.

Manly, William Lewis. "Charles Alvord," *The Pioneer, 10* (May 15, 1895), 8 and (June 15, 1895), 4.

———. "From Vermont to California," *Santa Clara Valley, 4–7* (June 1887–July 1890). Serially.

———. "A Faithful Pioneer," *The Pioneer, 8* (November 15, 1893), 8.

———. "The Gunsight Lead," *The Pioneer, 9* (April 15, 1894), 8.

———. "How Furnace Creek Got Its Name," *The Pioneer, 8* (August 15, 1893), 1.

———. "Is He a Jayhawker," *The Pioneer, 11* (April 15, 1896), 8.

———. "The 'Jayhawkers'' Oath," *The Pioneer, 9* (June 15, 1894), 4.

———. "Looking For a Lost Lead," *The Pioneer, 9* (July 15, 1894), 4.

———. "Men That I Knew," *The Pioneer, 10* (January 15, 1895), 5.

———. "Mines That Can't Be Found," *The Pioneer, 10* (June 15, 1895), 4.

———. "The Original Jayhawkers," *The Pioneer, 9* (March 15, 1894), 2.

———. "Pioneer Holidays," *The Pioneer, 8* (December 15, 1893), 1.

———. "Pioneer Reunions," *The Pioneer, 10* (April 15, 1895), 4.

———. "A Relic of '49," *The Pioneer, 8* (October 15, 1893), 5.

———. "Reunion of Pioneers," *The Pioneer, 10* (August 15, 1895), 5.

———. "Still Living," *The Pioneer, 11* (May 15, 1896), 4.

———. "Telescope Peak, in Death Valley," *The Pioneer, 11* (April 15, 1896), 8.

———. "Visit to a Pioneer," *The Pioneer, 10* (July 15, 1895), 2.

———. "W. L. Manly—How He Crossed the Plains—Description of an Adventurous Journey—Death Valley Experiences," *The Pioneer, 1* (April 21, 1877), 1 and (April 28, 1877), 1.

Mannix, Frank P. "Bullfrog and Its Suburbs," *Harper's Weekly, 52* (April 11, 1908), 20–21.

Martin, Al H. "The Land of Burning Silence, A Legend of Death Valley," *Out West, n. s. 2* (July 1911), 99–100.

Martineau, James H. "A Tragedy of the Desert," *Improvement Era, 31* (July 1928), 771–772.

Means, Thomas H. "Death Valley," *Sierra Club Bulletin, 17* (February 1932), 67–76, and *18* (February 1933), 110–111.

Merriam, C. Hart. "Charles E. Bendire," *Science, 5* (February 12, 1897), 261–262.

Milham, C. G. "The Paradise of Death Valley," *Country Life, 53* (January 1928), 64–65.

Miller, George. "A Trip to Death Valley," *Historical Society of Southern California Annual Publication, 11* (1919), 56–64.

Minette, James W., and Gerhard Muehle. "Colemanite from the Thompson Mine," *Mineralogical Record, 5* (March–April 1974), 67–73.

Minster, Joe. "The Lost Mines of the Great Southwest," *Adventure Magazine, 4* (September 1912), 97–105, and (October 1912), 42–48.

Mitchell, Stewart. "A Forgotten Exploration in Search of a Route Across the Sierra Nevada for the Pacific Railroad," *California Historical Society Quarterly, 34* (September 1955), 209–228.

"The Modern Pirate," *World's Work, 22* (October 1911), 14916–14918.

"Montgomery, Ernest Alexander." *Out West, 30* (April 1909), 384.

Moody, Ransom G. "Biographical Sketches, Ransom G. Moody, One of the Emigrants of '49–An Adventurous Trip Across the Plains," *The Pioneer, 1* (March 17, 1877), 1, 4.

Moreau, W. T. "Death Valley," *American Auto News, 1* (November 1929).

———. "Death Valley—Land of Strange Contrasts," *National Motorist, 10* (February 1933), 5–6.

Mowry, Sylvester. "Lt. Sylvester Mowry's Report on His March in 1855 from Salt Lake City to Fort Tejon," *Arizona and the West, 7* (Winter 1965), 329–346. (Lynn R. Bailey, ed.).

Murbarger, Nell. "Forgotten Ghost of Gold Mountain," *Desert Magazine, 14* (May 1951), 8–12.

———. "Ghost Town Dwellers," *Desert Magazine, 22* (February 1959), 4–8.

———. "The Ghost Towns of Inyo," *Westerners, Los Angeles Posse, Brand Book*

11. Los Angeles: Ward Ritchie Press, 1964, 1–18.

——. "Golden Treasure of Tule Canyon," *Desert Magazine, 14* (December 1951), 4–9.

——. "Pilgrimage into the Past," *Desert Magazine, 19* (May 1956), 11–15.

Myles, Myrtle. "The Gruesome Encore," *Desert Magazine, 27* (November 1964), 8–9.

"Mysterious Death Valley Is Unmasked," *Touring Topics, 13* (April 1921), 14–15.

"The Need of Desert Signs," *Touring Topics, 1* (August 1909), 9–11.

Nelson, E. W. "The Panamint and Saline Valley Indians," *American Anthropologist, 4* (October 1891), 371–372.

"Nevada's Bottle House is Relic of Golden Days," *Sunset Magazine, 56* (February 1926), 47.

Norman, Sidney. "Furnace Was My Town!" *Calico Print, 9* (September 1953), 8–11, 31–33.

Nunis, Doyce B. Jr. "Andrew Whitley Sublette," *The Mountain Men and the Fur Trade in the Far West, 8,* Glendale: Arthur H. Clark Co., 1969, 349–363. (LeRoy R. Hafen, ed.)

Nye, William. "A Winter Among the Piutes," *Overland Monthly, 7* (March 1886), 293–298.

Overholt, Alma. "A Famous Desert of the Cinema. Death Valley: Its Dreams, Mirages and Realities," *World Today, 58* (July 1931), 37–43.

——. "Death Valley from the Air," *Sunset Magazine, 62* (January 1929), 34–36.

——. "Death Valley: The Mystery Spot of America," *Arrowhead Magazine* (August 1926), 9–18.

——. "Death Valley's Road to Nowhere," *World's Work, 59* (July 1930), 48–51.

——. "The First Lady of Death Valley. The Story of Helene W. Eichbaum," *Los Angeles Times Sunday Magazine* (June 4, 1933), 3–4.

——. "Motoring Through Death Valley," *Travel, 55* (October 1930), 36–38, 49–50.

Pack, Arthur Newton. "Into the Valley of Death," *Nature Magazine, 12* (October 1928), 228–230, 267–268.

Page, Milo. "Searching for Lost Mines, The Goller Mine," *Sierra Magazine, 2* (February 1909), 3–11.

Palmer, Andrew H. "Death Valley–The Hottest Known Region," *Monthly Weather Review, 50* (January 1922), 10–13.

Parker, O. K. "Legends of Death Valley," *Arrowhead Magazine* (April 1920), 12–14.

——. "Motor Exploration in Death Valley," *Touring Topics, 6* (January 1914), 8–14.

Pascoe, Ruth Martin. "Dante's View," *Touring Topics, 22* (December 1930), Rotogravure Section, poem.

Patterson, Allan. "Life at Greenwater," *Calico Print, 9* (January 1953), 18–21.

Peirson, Erma. "Bottle House," *Desert Magazine, 6* (January 1943), 28.

Perry, Pearl. "When Mule Teams Came to Death Valley," *Westways, 47*

(November 1955), 4–5.

"Phantom Desert Terror," *Touring Topics, 15* (September 1923), 14.

Poste, Dave. "Breyfogle," *Calico Print, 7* (September/October 1951), 8.

Power, Ralph. "A Radio Adventure in Death Valley," *Radio Romances* (May 1925), 30–31, 80–81.

Pratt, Parley P. "A Mormon Mission to California in 1851—From the Diary of Parley Parker Pratt," *California Historical Society Quarterly, 14* (March and June 1935), 59–73, 175–182. (Reva H. Stanley and Charles L. Camp, eds.).

Price, Edna, "The 'Other People' Who Come to the Waterholes," *Desert Magazine, 17* (July 1954), 16–17.

"The Record-Breaking Climate of Death Valley," *American Review of Reviews, 65* (May 1922), 552–553.

Rice, William B. "Early Freighting on the Salt Lake-San Bernardino Trail," *Pacific Historical Review, 11* (March 1942), 73–80.

Rinehart, Robert E. "Death Valley Borax Beds," *Overland Monthly, 54* (October 1909), 356–362.

———. "Seizing the Desert's Last Stronghold," *World's Work, 15* (April 1908), 10143–10150.

Robertson, Dorothy. "Talzumbie Was Born in the Tragic Year," *Desert Magazine, 22* (November 1959), 25.

Rocha, Guy Louis. "Rhyolite: 'Don't Know the Date and Don't Give a Damn,'" *Nevada Historical Society Quarterly, 22* (Spring 1979), 41–47.

Rood, Standish. "The Lost Ledge," *Whittaker's Milwaukee Monthly, 4* (August and September 1872), 41–46, 89–94.

Rossiter, Kensett. "The Uncharted Valley," *Overland Monthly, 52* (July 1908), 30–35.

Rousseau, Mrs. James A. "Rousseau Diary Across the Desert to California from Salt Lake City to San Bernardino in 1864," *San Bernardino County Museum Association Quarterly, 6* (Winter 1958), 1–21.

Russell, A. M. "We Lost a Ledge of Gold," *Desert Magazine, 31* (November 1968), 14–17, 34–35.

Ryan, Clyde F. "Story of the 'Desert Sign Post,'" *American Quarterly,* (October 1, 1926), 73–86.

Saunders, Charles Francis. "The Lowest, Hottest, Dryest Spot in America," *Travel, 34* (December 1919), 25–28, 48.

"Scenes in Death Valley," *Pacific Rural Press, 73* (March 2, 1907), 129, 145.

Sedgwick, Martin. "The History of the Civilian Conservation Corps in Death Valley," *Thor Shun, 2* (April 4, 1936), 6–7.

"See Death Valley and (Don't) Die," *Literary Digest, 94* (September 3, 1927), 23.

"Seeing Death Valley in Five Days," *Touring Topics, 24* (March 1932), 28–30.

Serven, James E. "The Ill-Fated '49er Wagon Train," *Historical Society of Southern California Quarterly, 42* (March 1960), 29–40.

Shepstone, Harold J. "Amazing Death Valley," *Contemporary Review, 134* (November 1928), 633–639.

———, and John L. Von Blon. "The Conquest of Death Valley, The Romance of Its Borax Deposits," *World's Work, 40* (August 1922), 226–230.

Smith, George A. "New Tale of the Lost Breyfogle," *Calico Print, 8* (March 1952), 2.

Spears, John R. "A Desert Journey," *Goldthwaite's Geographical Magazine, 4* (July 1892), 507–513.

——. "Death Valley—The Arroyo del Muerte," *Goldthwaite's Geographical Magazine, 3* (April and May 1892), 292–299, 357–363.

——. "Ed Hadley, Desert Teamster," *Cosmopolitan, 17* (May 1894), 109–116.

——. "Miners' Homes in the Mojave Desert," *Chautauquan, 18* (March 1894), 713–717.

——. "Through Death Valley," *California Illustrated Magazine, 3* (February 1893), 312–321.

Standish, Hal. "Fred Fearnot's Cowboy Guide, or The Perils of Death Valley." *Work and Win, No. 997* (January 11, 1918), 1–18.

Stephens, Lorenzo D. "The Jayhawkers Meet," *The Pioneer, 9* (March 15, 1895), 1.

Steward, Julian H. "Linguistic Distributions and Political Groups of the Great Basin Shoshoneans," *American Anthropologist, n.s. 39* (October–December 1937), 625–634.

——. "Some Observations on Shoshonean Distributions," *American Anthropologist, n.s. 41* (April–June 1939), 261–265.

Stewart, Robert. "Making a Resort of Death Valley," *Mentor, 16* (August 1928), 42–47.

Stiles, Ed. "Saga of the Twenty-Mule Team," *Westways, 31* (December 1939), 8–9. (As told to Philip Johnston).

Stoddard, Carl. "This Is the Breyfogle Legend," *Calico Print, 7* (March 1951), 4.

Stout, Wesley. "Rainbow's End," *Saturday Evening Post, 203* (March 21, 1931), 20–21, 117–120.

Stover, Jacob Y. "History of the Sacramento Mining Company of 1849, written by one of its number," *Pacific Historical Review, 6* (Summer 1937), 165–181. (John W. Caughey, ed.).

Tallman, Clay M. "The Bullfrog District," *Proceedings of the American Mining Congress, 12* (1909), 428–437.

Talman, C. F. "A Valley of Death and Prosperity," *Mentor, 12* (July 1924), 55.

"Taming Death Valley," *Popular Mechanics, 71* (February 1939), 169–171, 154A, 156A, 159A.

Taylor, Frank J. "Death Valley: A New National Park in the Offing," *Motorland, 27* (November 1930), 9–11, 14.

Terrell, Clyde. "Lost Woman of the Mojave," *Calico Print, 9* (May 1953), 8–9.

Terrell, Starle W. "The Lost 'By Fogle' Mine," *Calico Print, 7* (May 1951), 2.

Thomas, Everett B. "Death Valley," *Touring Topics, 22* (October 1930), 54, poem.

Thompson, N. M. "Historic Photos of the High-Riding 'Magnesium Flyer,'" *Desert Magazine, 26* (January 1963), 12–15.

Toll, Roger W. "Death Valley," *American Civic Annual, 3* (1931), 35–40.

"Tours to Death Valley, Land of Fascination, Romance and Beauty," *Arrowhead*

Magazine (October 1931), 11–14.

"Twenty Mule Team Borax," *Fortune, 6* (November 1932), 40–43, 122.

"Ubehebe Copper Mines & Smelter Co.," *Harper's Weekly, 52* (April 11, 1908), 42–43.

Vaile, Fred. "Burro Prospector," *Westerners, Los Angeles Posse, Brand Book 10.* Los Angeles: Westerners, 1963, 201–208.

Vandeventer, Edward A. "Death Valley Scotty, Mysterious Son of the Desert," *Sunset Magazine, 56* (March 1926), 22–25, 72–73.

Van Dorn, Aaron. "Eastern Boundary Sketches," serially in *Sacramento Daily Union,* June 25, 29, July 9, 11, 13, 31, August 7, 10, 1861. [Reprinted in Woodward.]

Van Dyke, Dix. "Death Valley," *Desert, 1* (January 1930), 106–107.

Van Dyke, Walter. "Overland to Los Angeles, by the Salt Lake Route in 1849," *Historical Society of Southern California, Annual Publication, 3* (1894), 76–83.

Van Name, E. J. "Death Valley Trails," *Overland Monthly and Out West Magazine, 90* (April through August 1932), 71–73, 93, 145–146, 179–180, 182.

Vickrey, J. W. "Death Valley Roads Taken Into State System Provide 223 Mile Loop Tour," *California Highways and Public Works, 11* (September 1933), 4–5, 8.

Von Blon, John L. "A 'Garden of Allah' in Death Valley," *Scientific American, 134* (April 1926), 242–243.

———. "Dad of Death Valley," *Sunset Magazine, 55* (September 1925), 50–51. [R. J. Fairbanks.]

———. "Death Valley Transportation: How Borax is Transported from the Hottest Regions to the Nearest Rail Connection," *Scientific American, 125* (October 1921), 232.

———. "Lost Gold of Salt Spring," *Desert Magazine, 13* (February 1950), 23–27.

Von Engeln, O. D. "In the Desert," *Journal of Geography, 32* (February 1933), 81–84.

———. "The Ubehebe Craters and Explosion Breccias in Death Valley, California," *Journal of Geology, 40* (November/December 1932), 726–738.

Wackman, Howard, "The Argonauts of Death Valley," *Grizzly Bear, 27* (May 1920), 4, 9.

Wales, R. E. "Financial Power of Borax," *World Today, 21* (July 1911), 805–810.

Walker, Ardis M. "Joseph R. Walker," *The Mountain Men and the Fur Trade in the Far West, 5* (LeRoy R. Hafen, ed.). Glendale: Arthur H. Clark Co., 1968, 361–380.

Weight, Harold O. "Emigrant Springs and the Lost Gunsight," *Desert Magazine, 41* (August 1978), 8–11, 39.

———. "Greenwater, The Ghost that Went Away," *Calico Print, 9* (January 1953), 14–17.

———. "Leadfield Died of Complications," *Desert, 40* (November 1977), 34–39, 46.

———. "Mining Gold in Death Valley," *Desert Magazine, 37* (November 1974), 32–35, 46.

————. "On the Trail of Alvord's Lost Gold," *Desert Magazine, 13* (June 1950), 5–10.

————. "Shady Myrick, Pioneer Gem Prospector of the Mojave," *Calico Print, 7* (September/October 1951), 4–6.

————. "Was This the Lost Breyfogle?" *Calico Print, 7* (March 1951), 4–6.

Weight, Harold O., and Lucile Weight. "Rhyolite, Ghost City of Golden Dreams," *Calico Print, 6* (December 1950), 4–7.

Weight, Harold O., and Lucile Weight. "Wm. B. Rood," *Calico Print* (August/September 1952), 16–23.

Wheat, Carl I. "The Forty-Niners in Death Valley: (A Tentative Census)," *Historical Society of Southern California Quarterly, 21* (December 1939), 102–117.

————. "Hungry Bill Talks," *Westways, 31* (May 1939), 18–19.

————. "The Jayhawkers at the Missouri, A Remarkable Discovery," *Historical Society of Southern California Quarterly, 22* (September 1940), 103–108.

————. "Pioneer Visitors to Death Valley After the Forty-Niners," *California Historical Society Quarterly, 18* (September 1939), 195–216.

————. "Trailing the Forty-Niners Through Death Valley," *Sierra Club Bulletin, 24* (June 1939), 74–108.

Wheelock, Walt. "Following Fremont's Fifth Expedition," *Westerners, Los Angeles Posse, Brand Book 12.* Los Angeles: Westerners, 1966, 187–200.

Whitney, Josiah D. [On the Depression of Death Valley] *California Academy of Natural Sciences, 3* (1864), 129 and *3* (1868), 376.

Widney, J. P. "The Colorado Desert," *Overland Monthly, 10* (January 1873), 44–55.

Willaman, Glenn D. "Impressions of Death Valley Trails," *California Real Estate Magazine, 9* (February 1929), 48–49; (March 1929), 57–58, 76; and (April 1929), 52–53, 76.

Williams, Albert, Jr. "Lost Mines," *Chautauquan, 17* (September 1893), 692–696.

Williams, David. "Crossing the Desert By Gasoline Camel," *Illustrated World, 27* (June 1917), 574–575.

Willson, G. H. "The Hottest Region in the United States," *Monthly Weather Review, 43* (June and July 1915), 278–280, 341.

Wilson, Neill C. "How Not to Go A-Maying in Death Valley," *National Motorist, 4* (August 1927), 14–15.

————. "Telescope Peak from Death Valley," *Sierra Club Bulletin, 13* (February 1928), 36–39.

Woehlke, Walter V. "The Champion Borrower of Them All, The Story of E. G. Lewis," *Sunset Magazine, 55–56* (September 1925 through February 1926). Serially.

————. "The Great Julian Pete Swindle," *Sunset Magazine, 59* (September through November 1927). Serially.

Woodward, Arthur. "When Manly Returned to Death Valley," *Desert Magazine, 2* (May 1939), 24–27.

Wright, W. G. "A Naturalist in the Desert," *Overland Monthly, 4* (September 1884), 279–284.

Wylly, Thomas S. "Westward Ho in '49, Memoirs of Captain Thomas S. Wylly," *Pacific Historian, 22* (Spring through Winter 1978), 71–96, 120–144, 274–297, 327–352.

Zigmond, Maurice L. "Kawaiisu Territory," *American Anthropologist, n.s., 40* (October–December 1938), 634–638.

BOOKS AND PAMPHLETS

Ackerman, G. Frank. *A Walking Tour of Death Valley Ranch.* Bishop: Chalfant Press, 1981, 24 pp.

Adler, Pat, and Walt Wheelock. *Walker's R.R. Route-1853.* Glendale: La Siesta Press, 1965, 64 pp.

Adolph, E. F., and Associates. *Physiology of Man in the Desert.* New York: Interscience Publishers, Inc., 1947, 357 pp.

Albert, Herman W. *Odyssey of a Desert Prospector.* Norman: University of Oklahoma Press, 1967, 260 pp.

Alice Gold Mining Company. *Prospectus of the Alice Gold Mining Company Mines at the Tule Canon, Nevada.* Denver: 1905, 12 pp.

The American Potash & Chemical Corporation. San Bernardino: Sun Printing and Publishing House, 1940, 41 pp.

Angel, Myron. *History of Nevada with Illustrations and Biographical Sketches of its Prominent Men and Pioneers.* Oakland: Thompson & West, 1881, 680 pp.

Appleton's Cyclopaedia of American Biography. New York: D. Appleton & Co., 1894–1900, 7 v.

Arnold, Emmett L. *Gold-Camp Drifter, 1906–1910.* Reno: University of Nevada Press, 1973, 186 pp.

Ashbaugh, Don. *Nevada's Turbulent Yesterday: A Study in Ghost Towns.* Los Angeles: Westernlore Press, 1963, 346 pp.

Atchison, Topeka, and Santa Fe Railway Co. *Record Breaking Run of the Scott Special.* (n.p.:n.d.), 15 pp.

Austin, Mary. *The Land of Little Rain.* New York: Houghton, Mifflin, & Co., 1903, 281 pp.

———. *Lost Borders.* New York: Harper & Brothers, 1909, 208 pp.

Averett, Walter R. *Directory of Southern Nevada Place Names.* Las Vegas: Averett, 1962 rev. ed., 114 pp.

Bailey, Paul D. *An Unnatural History of Death Valley.* Bishop: Chalfant Press, 1978, 84 pp.

———. *Walkara Hawk of the Mountains.* Los Angeles: Westernlore Press, 1954, 185 pp.

Baker, Laura N. *Ground Afire: The Story of Death Valley National Monument.* New York: Atheneum, 1971, 166 pp.

Balch, William R. *The Mines, Miners and Mining Interests of the United States in 1882.* Philadelphia: Mining Industrial Pub. Bureau, 1882, 1191 pp.

Balliet, Letson. *Pioneers of the Wasteland, A Story of the Conquest of the Great American Desert.* Tonopah: c. 1925, 12 pp.

Bancroft, Hubert Howe. *Chronicles of the Builders of the Commonwealth.* San Francisco: The History Co., 1891–1892, 7 v.

Bartlett, Richard A. *Great Surveys of the American West.* Norman: University of Oklahoma Press, 1962, 408 pp.

Bartlett, W. P. *Happenings.* Los Angeles: Times Mirror Pub. Co., 1927, 267 pp.

———. *More Happenings.* Los Angeles: Christopher Pub. House, 1928, 193 pp.

Baruch, Bernard M. *Baruch, My Own Story.* New York: Henry Holt & Co., 1957, 337 pp.

Beadle, John H. *The Undeveloped West; or Five Years in the Territories.* Philadelphia: National Publishing Co., 1873, 823 pp.

Beattie, George W., and Helen P. Beattie. *Heritage of the Valley: San Bernardino's First Century.* Pasadena: San Pasqual Press, 1939, 459 pp.

Beatty, Bessie. *Who's Who in Nevada.* Los Angeles: Home Printing Co., 1907, 276 pp.

Bechdolt, Frederick R. *When the West Was Young.* New York: Century Co., 1922, 309 pp.

Belden, L. Burr. *Death Valley Heroine and Source Accounts of the 1849 Travelers.* San Bernardino: Inland Printing and Engraving Co., 1954, 78 pp.

———. *Goodbye, Death Valley! The 1849 Jayhawker Escape.* Palm Desert: Desert Magazine Press, 1956, 61 pp.

———. *Mines of Death Valley.* Glendale: La Siesta Press, 1966, 71 pp.

———. *The Mississippians and the Georgians of the Death Valley 1849 Party.* Pasadena: Castle Press, 1975, 13 pp.

———. *Old Stovepipe Wells.* San Bernardino: Inland Printing and Engraving Co., 1968, 12 pp.

———. *The Wade Story "In and Out of Death Valley."* San Bernardino: Inland Printing & Engraving Co., 1957, 15 pp.

Bell, Horace. *On the Old West Coast.* New York: William Morrow & Co., 1930, 336 pp.

———. *Reminiscences of a Ranger; or Early Times in Southern California.* Los Angeles: Yarnell, Caystile and Mathes, printers, 1881, 457 pp.

Bigler, Henry W. *Bigler's Chronicle of the West . . . Henry William Bigler's Diaries.* Berkeley and Los Angeles: University of California Press, 1962, 145 pp. (Erwin G. Gudde, ed.).

Bitton, Davis. *Guide to Mormon Diaries and Autobiographies.* Provo: Brigham Young University Press, 1977, 417 pp.

Bliss, Carey S. *Autos Across America, A Bibliography of Transcontinental Automobile Travel: 1903–1940.* Austin: Jenkins and Reese Co., 1982, 83 pp.

Bonsal, Stephen. *Edward Fitzgerald Beale, A Pioneer in the Path of Empire, 1822–1903.* New York: G. P. Putnam's Sons, 1912, 312 pp.

Borax Consolidated, Ltd. *Directors' Report and Statement of Accounts . . . 1908* [*through*] *1929.* London: Crowther and Goodman, 1909 [through] 1930. Annual.

———. *Lafayette Hoyt DeFriese Esq. and Mr. Henry Evan Thomas on behalf of Borax Consolidated Limited. Agreement for Sale.* London: Doherty & Co., 1899, 17 pp.

———. *Memorandum and Articles of Association*. London: Doherty & Co., 1899, 40 pp.

———. *[Prospectus.]* London: 1899, 1 p.

———. *Prospectus . . . Issue of 30,000 Six Percent Preferred Ordinary Shares of £5 each*. London: 1909, 3 pp.

———. *Prospectus . . . Issue of 250,000 Deferred Ordinary Shares of £1 each*. London: 1919, 3 pp.

Borax Producers of the Pacific Coast. *Facts and Figures Regarding Borax, And An Appeal in Behalf of This Desert Industry*. [n.p.: 1893], 23 pp.

Bowman, Alan P. *Index to the 1850 Census of the State of California*. Baltimore: Genealogical Pub. Co., 1972, 605 pp.

Boyd, William Harland. *A California Middle Border: The Kern River Country, 1772–1880*. Richardson, Tex.: Havilah Press, 1972, 226 pp.

Brewerton, George D. *Overland with Kit Carson, A Narrative of the Old Spanish Trail in '48*. New York: Coward-McCann, Inc., 1930, 301 pp.

Brooks, Thomas W. *By Buckboard to Beatty. The California-Nevada Desert in 1886*. Los Angeles: Dawson's Book Shop, 1970, 42 pp. (Anthony L. Lehman, ed.).

Brown, James S. *Life of a Pioneer, Being the Autobiography of James S. Brown*. Salt Lake City: Geo. Q. Cannon & Sons Co., 1900, 520 pp.

Browne, J. Ross. *Adventures in the Apache Country. A Tour Through Arizona and Sonora with Notes on the Silver Regions of Nevada*. New York: Harper & Brothers, 1869, 535 pp.

Brownlow, Kevin. *The War, the West and the Wilderness*. New York: Alfred A. Knopf, 1979, 602 pp.

Bruff, Joseph Goldsborough. *Gold Rush: The Journals, Drawings, and Other Papers of J. Goldsborough Bruff*. New York: Columbia University Press, 1944, 2 v., 1404 pp.

Buel, Arthur V. *Notable Nevadans, Snap-Shots of Sagebrushers, Who Are Doing Things*. Reno: 1910, 188 pp.

Bullfrog District Chamber of Commerce. *Bullfrog Mining District*. Rhyolite: Rhyolite Herald, 1909, 16 pp.

Bullfrog Gold Bar Mining Company. *Asset and Liability Statement, April 1st, 1908*. Goldfield: 1908. Broadside.

———. *President's Statement*. [Goldfield]: June 1908. Broadside.

Bullfrog Golden Sceptre Mining Company. *Official Statement, November First, Nineteen-o-six*. Philadelphia: 1906, 14 pp.

Bullfrog Keystone Gold Mining Company. *Prospectus*. [New York: 1906]. Folder.

Burdick, Arthur J. *The Mystic Mid-Region, The Deserts of the Southwest*. New York: G. P. Putnam's Sons, 1904, 237 pp.

Burton, George W. *Men of Achievement in the Great Southwest*. Los Angeles: Los Angeles Times, 1904, 149 pp.

Butte and Greenwater Mining Company. *Preliminary Prospectus*. Rhyolite: Taylor & Griffiths [1907], 4 pp.

Cain, Joseph, and Arieh C. Brower. *Mormon Way-Bill to the Gold Mines*. Great Salt Lake City: W. Richards Printer, 1851, 32 pp.

California Nitrate Development Company of San Francisco. *A Story About Nitrate of Soda in Death Valley, California.* [San Francisco: 1912], 21 pp.

Cannon, George Q. *A Trip to California.* [n.p.: 19—], 40 pp.

Carlson, Helen S. *Nevada Place Names: A Geographical Dictionary.* Reno: University of Nevada Press, 1974, 282 pp.

Carr, Harry. *The West is Still Wild.* Boston: Houghton Mifflin Co., 1932, 257 pp.

Carson, Christopher H. *Kit Carson's Autobiography.* Chicago: Lakeside Press, 1935, 192 pp. (Milo M. Quaife, ed.).

Cartter, George R. *Twilight of the Jackass Prospector: Death Valley Area Portraits of the 1930s.* Morongo Valley, Calif.: Sagebrush Press, 1982, 61 pp.

Caruthers, William. *Loafing Along Death Valley Trails, A Personal Narrative of People and Places.* Palm Desert: Desert Magazine Press, 1951, 186 pp.

Carvalho, Solomon N. *Incidents of Travel and Adventure in the Far West with Col. Fremont's Last Expedition.* New York: Derby & Jackson, 1857, 380 pp.

Casebier, Dennis G. *Carleton's Pah-Ute Campaign.* Norco, Calif.: Casebier, 1972, 58 pp.

Chalfant, Willie Arthur. *Death Valley, The Facts.* Stanford: Stanford University Press, 1930, 155 pp.; 1936 ed., 160 pp.

———. *The Story of Inyo.* Bishop: Chalfant, 1922, 358 pp.; rev. ed., 1933, 430 pp.

Chapman, Robert H. *The Deserts of Nevada and the Death Valley.* Washington: Judd and Detweiler, Inc., 1906, 15 pp. Reprint of *National Geographic* article.

Clements, Lydia. *Indians of Death Valley.* Hollywood: Hollycrofters, 1953, 23 pp.

Cone, Mary. *Two Years in California.* Chicago: S. C. Griggs & Co., 1876, 238 pp.

Coolidge, Dane. *Death Valley Prospectors.* New York: E. P. Dutton and Co., 1937, 178 pp.

———. *Fighting Men of the West.* New York: E. P. Dutton & Co., 1932, 343 pp. Chap. XII, Death Valley Scotty, pp. 303–336.

———. *Horse-Ketchum.* New York: E. P. Dutton & Co., 1930, 236 pp.

———. *Lost Wagons.* New York: E. P. Dutton & Co., 1923, 256 pp.

———. *Shadow Mountain.* New York: W. J. Watt & Co., 1919, 311 pp.

———. *Snake Bit Jones.* New York: E. P. Dutton & Co., 1936, 280 pp.

———. *The Trail of Gold.* New York: E. P. Dutton & Co. Inc., 1937, 252 pp.

———. *Wunpost.* New York: E. P. Dutton & Co., 1920, 273 pp.

Corle, Edwin. *Coarse Gold.* New York: Duell, Sloan & Pearce, 1942, 251 pp.

———. *Death Valley and the Creek Called Furnace.* Los Angeles: Ward Ritchie Press, 1962, 60 pp.

———. *Desert Country.* New York: Duell, Sloan & Pearce, 1941, 357 pp.

Couch, Bertrand F., and Jay A. Carpenter. *Nevada's Metal and Mineral Production (1859–1940 Inclusive).* Reno: University of Nevada, 1943, 159 pp.

Coulter, Charles C. *The "Little Mining Bradstreet" Containing a List of 200 of the Best Mining Properties in the State of Nevada.* Goldfield: Coulter, 1907, 41 pp.

Cragen, Dorothy C. *The Boys in the Sky-Blue Pants: The Men and Events at Camp Independence and Forts of Eastern California, Nevada and Utah, 1862–1877.* Fresno: Pioneer Publishing Co., 1976, 211 pp.

Crampton, Frank A. *Deep Enough, A Working Stiff in the Western Mine Camps*. Denver: Sage Books, 1956, 275 pp.

———. *Legend of John Lamoigne and Song of the Desert-Rats*. Denver: Sage Books, 1956, 32 pp.

Crawford, Thomas Edgar. *The West of the Texas Kid 1881–1910*. Norman: University of Oklahoma Press, 1962, 202 pp.

Cronise, Titus Fey. *The Natural Wealth of California*. San Francisco: H. H. Bancroft and Co., 1868, 696 pp.

Cronkhite, Daniel L. *Death Valley's Victims. A Descriptive Chronology 1849– 1980*. Morongo Valley, Calif.: Sagebrush Press, 1981, 3d ed. rev. and enlarged, 77 pp.

Cullum, George W. *Biographical Register of the Officers and Graduates of the U.S. Military Academy . . . 1802 to 1890*. Boston: Houghton, Mifflin Co., 1891, 3 v.

Curtiss, Thomas Quinn. *Von Stroheim*. New York: Farrar, Straus and Giroux, 1971, 357 pp.

Dawson, B. X. *Death Valley of Superstition and Imagination, The Gold Valley of To-day*. Denver: Smith-Brooks Press, 1906, 32 pp.

———. *Death Valley Reclaimed, What Modern Science & Scientific Mining Engineering Has Accomplished*. Denver: Smith-Brooks Press, 1906, 16 pp.

Death Valley Airways. Los Angeles: [c. 1930s], 4 pp.

Death Valley Copper Glance Mining Company. [New York: 1907], 4 pp.

Death Valley Hotel Company. *Death Valley, Where Earth Is Fresh From the Casting*. Los Angeles: 1928, 8 pp.

———. *Death Valley—Furnace Creek Inn, Death Valley Jc't.—Amargosa Hotel*. Los Angeles: 1930, 9 pp.

———. *Death Valley*. Los Angeles: 1931, 16 pp.

———. *Death Valley*. Los Angeles: 1932, 12 pp.

———. *Death Valley—Season 1935–36*. Los Angeles: 1935, 16 pp.

Death Valley Scotty's Castle. Goldfield: Castle Publishing Co., 1941, 74 pp.

DeDecker, Mary. *The Eichbaum Toll Road*. San Bernardino: Inland Printing and Engraving Co., 1970, 20 pp.

DeLaney, Paul. *The Toll of the Sands*. Denver: Smith-Brooks Printing Co., 1920, 333 pp.

DeNogales, Rafael. *Memoirs of a Soldier of Fortune*. New York: Harrison Smith Inc., 1932, 380 pp.

Dewing, Arthur S. *Corporate Promotions and Reorganizations*. Cambridge: Harvard Univ. Press, 1914, 615 pp. Chaps. XVII–XVIII [Schwab], pp. 464– 509.

Dickson, John, ed. *National Cyclopaedia of American Biography*. New York: J. T. White & Co., 1892–1971, 53 v.

Dictionary of American Biography. New York: Scribner's Sons, 1928–1937, 20 v.

Dobie, J. Frank. *Coronado's Children. Tales of the Lost Mines and Buried Treasures of the Southwest*. Dallas: Southwest Press, 1930, 367 pp.

Doctor, Joseph E. *Dr. E. Darwin French's Exploration of Death Valley*. Bishop: Chalfant Press, 1982, 16 pp.

Dodge Brothers Corp. *Through Death Valley in a Dodge Brothers Motor Car, A True Story of O. K. Parker's Memorable Trip Through This Arid Desert Land*. Detroit: Dodge Brothers, 1916, 16 pp.

Driskill, Earl C. *Death Valley Scotty Rides Again. Tales told by Death Valley Scotty, Winter 1952–1953 at Scotty's Castle*. Death Valley: Stovepipe Wells, 1955, 60 pp.

Dutton, Alfred H. *Cartoons and Caricatures of Men Who Made Good in Nevada*. Salt Lake City: A. H. Dutton and A. L. Lovey, 1907, 88 pp.

———. *Notable Nevadans in Caricature*. n.p.: 1915, 94 pp.

The Echo-Lee Gold Mining Co. Rhyolite: Bullfrog Miner Print., 1907, 4 pp.

Eddy, Clarence E. *Ballads of Heaven and Hell*. Salt Lake City: Western Printing Co., 1922, 14 pp.

———. *The Burro's Bray. A Book of Pomes*. Salt Lake City: 1923, 48 pp.

Edwards, Benjamin F., and C. Grace Sperry. *Eighteen Days in Nevada*. Oakland: [authors], 1907, 66 pp.

Edwards, Elza Ivan. *Desert Treasure—A Bibliography*. Los Angeles: Edwards and Williams, 1948, 42 pp.

———. *Desert Voices, A Descriptive Bibliography*. Los Angeles: Westernlore Press, 1958, 215 pp.

———. *The Enduring Desert, A Descriptive Bibliography*. Los Angeles: Ward Ritchie Press, 1969, 306 pp.

———. *"Into An Alkali Valley." The First Written Account of Death Valley*. Los Angeles: Edwards and Williams, 1948, 8 pp.

———. *The Valley Whose Name Is Death*. Pasadena: San Pasqual Press, 1940, 122 pp.

Egan, Howard R. *Pioneering the West: 1846 to 1878, Major Howard Egan's Diary*. Richmond, Utah: Howard R. Egan Estate, 1917, 302 pp.

Ellenbecker, John G. *The Jayhawkers of Death Valley*. Marysville, Kans.: The Author, 1938, 130 pp.

———. *Supplement To The Jayhawkers of Death Valley*. n.p.: 1942, 5 pp.

Elliott, Russell R. *Nevada's Twentieth-Century Mining Boom: Tonopah, Goldfield, Ely*. Reno: University of Nevada Press, 1966, 344 pp.

———. *Servant of Power, A Political Biography of Senator William M. Stewart*. Reno: University of Nevada Press, 1983, 347 pp.

Emerson, George. *The Smoky God; or, A Voyage to the Inner World*. Chicago: Forbes & Co., 1908, 186 pp.

Esshom, Frank E. *Pioneers and Prominent Men of Utah*. Salt Lake City: Pioneers Book Pub. Co., 1913, 1319 pp.

Evans, George W. B. *Mexican Gold Trail, The Journal of a Forty-Niner*. San Marino: The Huntington Library, 1945, 340 pp.

Evans, John Henry. *Charles Coulson Rich—Pioneer Builder of the West*. New York: Macmillan Co., 1936, 400 pp.

Farnham, Thomas Jefferson. *Travels in the Californias and Scenes in the Pacific Ocean*. New York: Saxton & Miles, 1844, 416 pp.

Federal Writers' Project. *Death Valley, A Guide*. Boston: Houghton, Mifflin Co., 1939, 75 pp.

Finler, Joel W., ed. *Greed. A Film by Erich von Stroheim.* New York: Simon and Schuster, 1972, unpaged.

Finney, Guy W. *The Great Los Angeles Bubble, A Present-Day Story of Colossal Financial Jugglery and of Penalties Paid.* Los Angeles: Milton Forbes Co., 1929, 203 pp.

Fisher [*Robert D.*] *Manual of Valuable and Worthless Securities.* New York: Fisher & Co., 1933–1951, 9 v.

Fleming, Andrew M. *The Gun Sight Mine.* Boston: Meador Pub. Co., 1929, 210 pp.

Forward Mining Development Company. *The First Year's Record of Bullfrog Nevada and Its Marvelous Mines.* Denver: App Co., 1905, 4 pp.

———. *Prospectus of the Forward Mining Development Co., Goldfield and Bullfrog, Nevada.* Denver: App Co., 1905, 12 pp.

Fowler, Harlan D. *Camels to California: A Chapter in Western Transportation.* Stanford: Stanford University Press, 1950, 93 pp.

Frances Gold Mountain Mining Company. *Reports of Officers for Corporate Year and Report of Board of Directors for Quarter Ending July 31, 1910.* Goldfield: 1910, 18 pp.

Fremont, John Charles. *Memoirs of My Life.* Chicago and New York: Belford, Clarke and Co., 1887, 655 pp.

Frickstad, Walter N. *A Century of California Post Offices 1848 to 1954.* Oakland: Philatelic Research Society, 1955, 395 pp.

Frickstad, Walter N., and Edward W. Thrall. *A Century of Nevada Post Offices 1852–1957.* Oakland: Philatelic Research Society, 1958, 40 pp.

Frothingham, Robert. *Trails Through the Golden West.* New York: Robert M. McBride & Co., 1932, 272 pp.

Gerstley, James M. *Borax Years, Some Recollections 1933–1961.* Los Angeles: U.S. Borax and Chemical Corp., 1979, 93 pp.

Gilbert, Edward M. *Panamint Legend.* Los Angeles: Hesperus Press, 1957, 16 pp.

Glasscock, Carl B. *Gold in Them Hills, The Story of the West's Last Wild Mining Days.* Indianapolis: Bobbs-Merrill Co., 1932, 330 pp.

———. *Here's Death Valley.* Indianapolis: Bobbs-Merrill Co., 1940, 329 pp.

Goetzmann, William H. *Exploration and Empire, The Explorer and the Scientist in the Winning of the American West.* New York: Alfred A. Knopf, 1966, 656 pp.

Gold Center: The Future City of the Bullfrog Mining District, Nevada. Goldfield: Lawton and Griffin, 1905, 2 pp.

Goldfield News, Annual Number 1905–1906. Goldfield: 1906, 50 pp.

Goldfield News, Second Annual Edition 1906–1907. Goldfield: 1907, 142 pp.

Gorham, Harry M. *My Memories of the Comstock.* Los Angeles: Suttonhouse Publishers, 1939, 222 pp.

Gower, Harry P. *50 Years in Death Valley—Memoirs of a Borax Man.* San Bernardino: Inland Printing Inc., 1969, 145 pp.

Grace, Eugene G. *Charles M. Schwab.* New York: E. G. Grace, 1947, 43 pp.

Grand Central Mining Corporation. *The Road to Gold.* Tonopah: [193?] 4 pp.

Granger, Lewis. *Letters of Lewis Granger.* Los Angeles: Glen Dawson, 1959, 50 pp. (Introduction by LeRoy Hafen).

Graves, Jackson A. *California Memories*. Los Angeles: Times-Mirror Press, 1930, 330 pp.

Greenwater Copper Mines and Smelter Company. *Report . . . for the Year Ending December 31st 1907*. New York: 1908, 8 pp., and . . . *1908*. New York: 1909, 8 pp.

———. *Notice . . . October 29, 1909*. [New York]. Broadside.

Greenwater Copper Mining Syndicate. Carson City: Nevada Press Co., [1906], 8 pp.

Greenwater Red Boy Copper Company. *A Copper Fortune in Gold For You*. Goldfield: D. Mackenzie & Co., [1906], 4 pp.

Grey, Zane. *Tales of Lonely Trails*. New York: Harper & Brothers, 1928, 394 pp.

———. *Tappan's Burro, and Other Stories*. New York: Harper & Brothers, 1923, 253 pp.

———. *Wanderer of the Wasteland*. New York: Harper & Brothers, 1923, 419 pp.

Gruber, Frank. *Zane Grey; A Biography*. New York: World Publishing Co., 1970, 284 pp.

Gudde, Erwin G. *California Gold Camps: A Geographical and Historical Dictionary of Camps and Localities Where Gold Was Found and Mined*. Berkeley: University of California Press, 1975, 467 pp.

———. *California Place Names: The Origin and Etymology of Current Geographical Names*. Berkeley and Los Angeles: University of California Press, 1969, 3d ed., 416 pp.

Gun Sight Mining Company. New York: 1880, 3 pp.

Hafen, LeRoy R., ed. *The Mountain Men and the Fur Trade of the Far West*. Glendale: Arthur H. Clark Co., 1965–1972, 10 v.

Hafen, LeRoy R., and Ann W. Hafen. *Journals of Forty-Niners, Salt Lake to Los Angeles. With Diaries and Contemporary Records of Sheldon Young, James S. Brown, Jacob Y. Stover, Charles C. Rich, Addison Pratt, Howard Egan, Henry W. Bigler, and Others*. Glendale: Arthur H. Clark Co., 1954, 333 pp.

Hafen, LeRoy R., and Ann W. Hafen. *Old Spanish Trail, Santa Fe to Los Angeles*. Glendale: Arthur H. Clark Co., 1954, 377 pp.

Hafen, LeRoy R., and Ann W. Hafen. *Supplement to the Journals of Forty-Niners, Salt Lake to Los Angeles*. Glendale: Arthur H. Clark Co., 1961, 124 pp.

Handbook for Mining Investors. Denver: General Publishing Syndicate, 1909, 219 pp.

Handbook of Nevada Mines, Containing Such Information as Might be Valuable to Operators, Investors and Speculators in Nevada Mining Securities. Goldfield: Goldfield News, 1906, 96 pp.

Hanna, Phil Townsend, et al. *Death Valley Tales*. Palm Desert: Desert Magazine Press, 1955, 59 pp.

Harpending, Asbury. *The Great Diamond Hoax and Other Stirring Incidents in the Life of Asbury Harpending*. San Francisco: James H. Barry Co., 1913, 283 pp.

Harper, Olive [Helen D'Apery/Mrs. Ellen Gibson]. *Through Death Valley. A Moving Story of Mormon Life*. New York: J. S. Ogilvie Pub. Co., 1907, 124 pp.

Heap, Gwinn Harris. *Central Route to the Pacific; From the Valley of the Mississippi to California.* Philadelphia: Lippincott, Grambo and Co., 1854, 136 pp.

Herbert, Miranda C., and Barbara McNeil. *Biography and Genealogy Master Index.* Detroit: Gale Research Co., 1980, 8 v. and 1982, 3 v. supplement.

Hermann, Ruth. *Gold and Silver Colossus. William Morris Stewart and His Southern Bride.* Sparks: Dave's Printing & Publishing, 1975, 429 pp.

Hessen, Robert. *Steel Titan, The Life of Charles M. Schwab.* New York: Oxford Univ. Press, 1975, 350 pp.

Higham, Charles. *Hollywood Cameraman: Sources of Light.* London: Thames and Hudson, 1970, 176 pp.

Hildebrand, George H. *Borax Pioneer: Francis Marion Smith.* San Diego: Howell-North Books, 1982, 318 pp.

Hill, David W. *Mojave Desert, High Sierra Topographical Quadrangle Map Index.* Bishop: Chalfant Press, 1968, 116 pp.

History of Alameda County . . . and Biographical Sketches of Early and Prominent Citizens. Oakland: Myron H. Wood, 1883, 1001 pp.

Hobbs, James. *Wild Life in the Far West—Personal Adventures of a Border Mountain Man.* Hartford: Wiley, Waterman & Eaton, 1872, 488 pp.

Horan, James D. *Timothy O'Sullivan, America's Frontier Photographer.* Garden City: Doubleday & Co., 1966, 334 pp.

Houston, Eleanor J. *Death Valley Scotty Told Me.* Louisville: Franklin Press, 1954, 106 pp.

Hubbard, Paul B., Doris Bray, and George Pipkin. *Ballarat 1897–1917. Facts and Folklore.* Lancaster: Hubbard, 1965, 98 pp.

Hufford, David Andrew. *Death Valley; Swamper Ike's Traditional Lore: Why, When, How?* Los Angeles: Hufford & Co., 1902, 43 pp.

Hunt, Alice. *Archeology of the Death Valley Salt Pan, California (University of Utah. Anthropological Papers No. 47).* Salt Lake City: University of Utah, 1960, 313 pp.

Hunt, Charles B. *Death Valley: Geology, Ecology, Archaeology.* Berkeley, Los Angeles, London: University of California Press, 1975, 234 pp.

An Illustrated History of Southern California, Embracing the Counties of San Diego, San Bernardino, Los Angeles and Orange. Chicago: Lewis Publishing Co., 1890, 898 pp.

Ingersoll, Luther A. *Ingersoll's Century Annals of San Bernardino County, 1769 to 1904.* Los Angeles: Ingersoll, 1904, 887 pp.

Ingraham, Prentiss. *Buffalo Bill's Mascot: or, The Death Valley Victim No. 13. Beadle's Dime Library No. 761.* New York: Beadle & Adams, 1893.

Inter-Tribal Council of Nevada. *Newe: A Western Shoshone History.* Salt Lake City: Univ. of Utah Printing Service, 1976, 143 pp.

————. *Nuwuvi: A Southern Paiute History.* Salt Lake City: Univ. of Utah Printing Service, 1976, 177 pp.

Irwin, Charles N., ed. *The Shoshone Indians of Inyo County, California: The Kerr Manuscript.* Socorro: Ballena Press, 1980, 92 pp.

Jaeger, Edmund C. *A Naturalist's Death Valley.* Palm Desert: Desert Magazine Press, 1957, 68 pp.

James, George Wharton. *Heroes of California.* Boston: Little, Brown and Co.,

1910, 515 pp.

Johnson, LeRoy, and Jean Johnson. *Julia, Death Valley's Youngest Victim.* Roseville, Minn.: Author, 1981, 20 pp.

Johnson, Russ, and Anne Johnson, comps. *Death Valley 1933 Scrapbook.* Bishop: Chalfant Press, 1983, 48 pp.

Johnston, Rossiter, ed. *The Twentieth Century Biographical Dictionary of Notable Americans.* Boston: The Biographical Society, 1904, 10 v.

Johnston, Hank. *Death Valley Scotty "The Fastest Con in the West."* Corona del Mar: Trans-Anglo Books, 1974, 160 pp.

———. *Death Valley Scotty, The Man and the Myth.* Yosemite: Flying Spur Press, 1972, 48 pp.

Keeling, Patricia Jernigan, ed. *Once Upon A Desert.* Barstow: Mojave River Valley Museum Assoc., 1976, 260 pp.

King, Joseph L. *History of the San Francisco Stock and Exchange Board.* San Francisco: Jos. L. King, 1910, 373 pp.

Kinkenbinder, C. E. *Mojave Desert Trails, Mojave Desert, Death Valley, Boulder Dam.* Los Angeles: Author, 1940, 72 pp.

Kirk, Ruth. *Exploring Death Valley: A Guide For Tourists.* Stanford: Stanford University Press, 1956, 82 pp.

Kockler, Nicholas. *Old Harmony Borax Works.* San Bernardino: Inland Printing and Engraving Co., 1962, 15 pp.

Koenig, George. *Beyond This Place There Be Dragons. The Routes of the Tragic Trek of the Death Valley 1849ers Through Nevada, Death Valley and on to Southern California.* Glendale: Arthur H. Clark Co., 1984, 263 pp.

———. *The Lost Death Valley '49er Journal of Louis Nusbaumer.* Death Valley: Death Valley '49ers, Inc., 1974, 79 pp.

———. *"23" Skidoo and Panamint, Too!* San Bernardino: Inland Printing and Engraving Co., 1971, 17 pp.

Koszarski, Richard. *The Man You Loved to Hate, Erich von Stroheim and Hollywood.* Oxford: Oxford University Press, 1983, 343 pp.

Kral, Victor E. *Mineral Resources of Nye County, Nevada.* Reno: Univ. of Nevada, 1951, 223 pp.

Kyne, Peter B. *The Parson of Panamint and Other Stories.* New York: Grosset and Dunlap, 1929, 387 pp.

Labbe, Charles H. *Rocky Trails of the Past.* Las Vegas: C. H. Labbe, 1960, 222 pp.

LaMontagne, P. *Nevada, The New Gold State: An Up-to-Date Description of the Mining Interests of Tonopah, Goldfield, Bullfrog, Diamondfield, Goldreed, etc.* San Francisco: D. G. Doubleday, 1905, 56 pp.

Langley, Henry G. *Langley's San Francisco Directory for the Year . . . 1861 [through] 1895.* San Francisco: [publisher varies], 1861 through 1895.

Latta, Frank F. *Death Valley '49ers.* Santa Cruz: Bear State Books, 1979, 365 pp.

Lawson, Thomas W. *Frenzied Finance—The Crime of Amalgamated.* New York: Ridgway-Thayer Co., 1905, 559 pp.

Leadabrand, Russ. *A Guidebook to the Mojave Desert of California, Including Death Valley, Joshua Tree National Monument and the Antelope Valley.* Los Angeles: Ward Ritchie Press, 1966, 180 pp.

Lee, Bourke [Thomas Burke Lee]. *Death Valley*. New York: Macmillan Co., 1930, 210 pp.

————. *Death Valley Men*. New York: Macmillan Co., 1932, 319 pp.

Lee, W. Storrs. *The Great California Deserts*. New York: G. P. Putnam's Sons, 1963, 306 pp.

Lewis, Edward Gardner. *Order Number Ten; Being Cursory Comments on Some of the Effects of the Great American Fraud Order*. University City: University City Pub. Co., 1911, 215 pp.

Lillard, Richard G. *Desert Challenge, an Interpretation of Nevada*. New York: Alfred A. Knopf, 1942, 388 pp.

Lincoln, Francis C. *Mining Districts and Mineral Resources of Nevada*. Reno: Nevada Newsletter Publishing Co., 1923, 295 pp.

Lingenfelter, Richard E. *The Hardrock Miners: A History of the Mining Labor Movement in the American West, 1863–1893*. Berkeley, Los Angeles, London: University of California Press, 1974, 278 pp.

————. *Steamboats on the Colorado River 1852–1916*. Tucson: University of Arizona Press, 1978, 195 pp.

Lingenfelter, Richard E., and Richard A. Dwyer. *The "Nonpareil" Press of T. S. Harris*. Los Angeles: Glen Dawson, 1957, 59 pp.

Lingenfelter, Richard E., Richard A. Dwyer, and David Cohen. *Songs of the American West*. Berkeley and Los Angeles: University of California Press, 1968, 595 pp.

Lingenfelter, Richard E., and Karen Rix Gash. *The Newspapers of Nevada, A History and Bibliography, 1854–1979*. Reno: University of Nevada Press, 1984, 337 pp.

Long, Margaret. *The Shadow of the Arrow*. Caldwell, Idaho: Caxton Printers, 1941, 310 pp., and enlarged ed. 1950, 354 pp.

Lorton, William B. *Over the Salt Lake Trail in the Fall of '49*. Los Angeles: privately printed, 1957, 18 pp. (Introduction by John B. Goodman III).

Los Angeles City Directory . . . 1890 [through] 1933. Los Angeles: Los Angeles Directory Co., 1890 through 1933.

Lummis, Charles F. *Mesa, Canyon and Pueblo*. New York: Century Co., 1925, 517 pp.

————. *Some Strange Corners of Our Country*. New York: Century Co., 1898, 270 pp.

McCoy, William M. *The Valley of the Sun*. New York: H. K. Fly Co., 1921, 308 pp.

McGroarty, John S. *Los Angeles From the Mountains to the Sea*. Chicago: American Historical Society, 1921, 3 v.

McWilliams, Carey. *Southern California Country, An Island on the Land*. New York: Duell, Sloan & Pearce, 1946, 387 pp.

Mains, John P., comp. *The Annual Statistician, 1878*. San Francisco: L. P. McCarty, 1878.

Majors, Alexander. *Seventy Years on the Frontier*. Chicago: Rand, McNally & Co., 1893, 325 pp.

Manly, William Lewis. *Death Valley in '49*. San Jose: Pacific Tree and Vine Co.,

1894, 498 pp. Several later editions.

———. *The Jayhawkers' Oath and Other Sketches.* Los Angeles: Warren F. Lewis, 1949, 170 pp. (Arthur Woodward, ed.).

Manning, Jacolyn. *The Law in Death Valley, A Drama of the Desert.* Pasadena, 1931, 61 pp.

Marcy, E. L. *The Resurrection of Death Valley.* Maywood: W. P. Beaumont Pub., 1966, 48 pp.

Marcy, Randolph B. *The Prairie Traveler, A Handbook for Overland Expeditions, with Maps, Illustrations and Itineraries of the Principal Route Between the Mississippi and the Pacific.* New York: Harper and Brothers, 1859, 340 pp.

Merrill, Orin S., *"Mysterious Scott" The Monte Cristo of Death Valley and Tracks of a Tenderfoot.* Chicago: Orin S. Merrill, 1906, 210 pp. Facsimile reprint, Bishop: Chalfant Press, 1972.

Miller, Ron. *Fifty Years Ago at Furnace Creek Inn.* Pasadena: Castle Press, 1977, 16 pp.

Milligan, Clarence P. *Death Valley and Scotty.* Los Angeles: Ward Ritchie Press, 1942, 194 pp.

Mitchell, John D. *Lost Mines & Buried Treasures Along the Old Frontier.* Palm Desert: Desert Magazine Press, 1953, 240 pp.

Moffat, James R. *Memoirs of an Old-Timer, A Personal Glimpse of Rhyolite, Nevada, 1906–07.* Verdi: Sagebrush Press, 1963, 9 pp.

Mohawk-Johnnie Mining Company. *Announcement of the Treasury Stock Issue.* Los Angeles: 1907. 4 pp.

Montgomery Shoshone Consolidated Mining Company. *Report on Properties, Dated September 17, 1906.* New York: Miller Press, 1906, 16 pp.

———. *Report on the Montgomery Shoshone Consolidated Mining Company, February 10th, 1909.* New York: 1909, 8 pp.

Moody's Manual of Railroads and Corporate Securities. New York: Moody Manual Co., 1906–1933. Annual.

Morris, Henry Curtis. *Desert Gold and Total Prospecting.* Washington, D.C.: Author, 1955, 60 pp.

Mt. Whitney-Death Valley Transportation Company. *Death Valley.* Los Angeles: c. 1929. Folder.

Murdock, Jacob M. *A Family Tour From Ocean to Ocean.* Detroit: Packard Motor Car Co., 1908, 32 pp.

Murbarger, Nell. *Ghosts of the Glory Trails.* Palm Desert: Desert Magazine Press, 1956, 291 pp.

Murphy, Robert J. *Wildrose Charcoal Kilns.* Death Valley: Death Valley '49ers Inc., 1972, 23 pp.

Murray, Tom G. *Death Valley Scotty.* [n.p.: 1961], 36 pp.

Myrick, David F. *Railroads of Nevada and Eastern California.* Berkeley: Howell-North Books, 1963, 2 v., 933 pp.

Nevada Syndicate. *Special Report on the Butler Gold Mining Company.* Reno: 1933, 4 pp. [Goldpoint District.]

The New York Mining Directory. New York: Hollister & Goddard, 1880, 111 pp.

The New York Stock Exchange. New York: Historical Publishing Co., 1886, 224 pp.

Newhall, Nancy, et al. *Death Valley*. San Francisco: 5 Associates, 1954, 56 pp.

Noble, Peter. *Hollywood Scapegoat: The Biography of Erich von Stroheim*. London: Fortune Press, 1950, 246 pp.

Norman, Sidney. *Chasing Rainbows In Death Valley*. Los Angeles: L. A. Mining Review, 1909, 35 pp.

Norris, Frank. *McTeague: A Story of San Francisco*. New York: Doubleday & McClure Co., 1899, 442 pp.

Noyes, Alfred. *Beyond the Desert. A Tale of Death Valley*. New York: Frederick A. Stokes Co., 1920, 85 pp.

Nunis, Doyce B., Jr. *Andrew Sublette, Rocky Mountain Prince, 1808–1853*. Los Angeles: Dawson's Book Shop, 1960, 123 pp.

Nusbaumer, Louis. *Valley of Salt, Memories of Wine: A Journal of Death Valley, 1849*. Berkeley: Friends of the Bancroft Library, 1967, 68 pp. (George Koenig, ed.).

O'Conley, Mary Ann. *Upper Mojave Desert: A Living Legacy*. Detroit: Harlo Press, 1969, 112 pp.

Pacific Borax and Redwood's Chemical Works. *[Prospectus]*. London: 1896, 1 p.

Pacific Coast Annual Mining Review and Stock Ledger. San Francisco: Francis and Valentine, October 1878, 264 pp.

Pacific Coast Borax Company. *Borax: From the Desert, Through the Press, Into the Home: 200 Best Borax Recipes from More than 800 Issues of 250 Different Publications in 33 States of the Union*. San Francisco, Chicago, New York: Pacific Coast Borax Co., 1895, 80 pp.

———. *High Spots of "Death Valley Days."* Los Angeles, 1939, 65 pp.

———. *Lecture on Death Valley, the Borax Industry and 20 Mule Team Products, Arranged for the Moving Picture and Stereopticon Exhibits of the Pacific Coast Borax Company*. San Francisco: Pacific Coast Borax Co., 1909, 16 pp.

———. *The 20-Mule Team and a Sketch of Its Famous Driver Borax Bill*. New York, Chicago, San Francisco: Pacific Coast Borax Co., 1904, 16 pp. Facsimile reprint, Morongo Valley, Calif.: Sagebrush Press, 1980.

Paher, Stanley W. *Captain Gibson, the Last of the Death Valley Teamsters*. Las Vegas: Nevada Publications, 1972, 6 pp.

———. *Death Valley Ghost Towns*. Las Vegas: Nevada Publications, 1973, 48 pp.

———. *Nevada Ghost Towns and Mining Camps*. Berkeley: Howell-North Books, 1970, 492 pp.

Paine, Ralph D. *The Greater America*. New York: Outing Publishing Co., 1907, 327 pp.

Palmer, Theodore S. *Chronology of the Death Valley Region in California, 1849–1949. An Index of the Events, Persons and Publications Connected With Its History*. Washington: Byron S. Adams, Printer, 1952, 25 pp.

———. *Place Names of the Death Valley Region in California and Nevada*. n.p.: 1948, 80 pp. Facsimile reprint, Morongo Valley, Calif.: Sagebrush Press, 1980.

Panamint Mining and Concentration Works. *Prospectus*. San Francisco: Women's Print., 1875, 7 pp.

Parsons, George W. *A Thousand Mile Desert Trip and Story of the "Desert Sign*

Post." Los Angeles: Parsons, 1918, 16 pp.

Paul, Rodman W. *Mining Frontiers of the Far West 1848–1880.* New York: Holt, Rinehart and Winston, 1963, 236 pp.

Pearson, Gustavus C. *Overland in 1849 From Missouri to California by the Platt River and the Salt Lake Trail.* Los Angeles: Privately Printed, 1961, 55 pp. (Introduction by John B. Goodman III).

Peck-Judah Company. *Death Valley, All-Expense Tours.* Los Angeles: 1931, 8 pp.

————. *Death Valley-Bolder Dam Rail Motor Tours.* Los Angeles: n.d., 8 pp.

Perkins, Edna Brush. *The White Heart of Mojave, An Adventure With the Outdoors of the Desert.* New York: Poni and Liveright, 1922, 229 pp.

Perkins, George E. *Pioneers of the Western Desert: Romance and Tragedy Along the Old Spanish or Mormon Trail and Historical Events of the Great West.* Los Angeles: Wetzel Publishing Co., Inc., 1947, 103 pp.

Peters, Dewitt C. *The Life and Adventures of Kit Carson . . . From Facts Narrated by Himself.* New York: W. R. C. Clark & Co., 1858, 534 pp.

Pettit, Edwin. *Biography of Edwin Pettit.* Salt Lake City: Arrow Press, n.d., 22 pp.

Phelps, Alonzo. *Contemporary Biography of California's Representative Men.* San Francisco: A. L. Bancroft & Co., 1881, 2 v.

Pipkin, George C. *Pete Aguereberry, Death Valley Prospector and Gold Miner.* Trona: Murchison Publications, 1982, 158 pp.

Piute Company of California and Nevada. San Francisco: Edward Bosqui & Co., 1870, 23 pp.

Polk, R. L. & Co. *Nevada State Gazetteer & Business Directory, 1907–1908* through *1914–1915.* Salt Lake City: R. L. Polk & Co., 1907 through 1914.

Poor's Manual of Railroads. New York: Poor's Railroad Manual Co., 1906–1933, Annual.

Powers, Prof. *"Death Valley," Land of Mystery. Millions in Sight! $$$$$$$ Suggestions to Prospectors.* Los Angeles: Efficiency Printing and Publishing Co., January 1919, 11 pp.

Pratt, Parley P. *Autobiography of Parley Parker Pratt.* New York: Russell Brothers, 1874, 502 pp.

Prescott, Paul J. [Leslie Artley Irons]. *The Cannibal Chief; or, The Mountain Guide. Frank Starr's American Novels, No. 51.* New York: Frank Starr & Co., 1870, 83 pp.

Press Reference Library, Notables of the West. New York: International News Service, 1913–1915, 2 v.

Preuss, Charles. *Exploring with Fremont: The Private Diaries of Charles Preuss, Cartographer.* Norman: University of Oklahoma Press, 1958, 162 pp. (Erwin G. and Elisabeth K. Gudde, transl. and eds.).

Price, Edna Calkins. *Burro Bill and Me.* Idyllwild: Strawberry Valley Press, 1973, 275 pp.

Probert, Thomas. *Lost Mines and Buried Treasures of the West, Bibliography and Place Names—From Kansas West to California, Oregon, Washington, and Mexico.* Berkeley, Los Angeles, London: University of California Press, 1977, 593 pp.

Putnam, George Palmer. *Death Valley and Its Country.* New York: Duell, Sloan & Pearce, 1946, 231 pp.
———. *Death Valley Handbook.* New York: Duell, Sloan & Pearce, 1947, 84 pp.
Ramsey, Robert E. *The Romance of the Desert.* Norfolk Downs, Mass: Pneumatic Scale Corp., 1924, 36 pp.
Red Fox Bullfrog Mining Company. *Prospectus.* Denver: App Co., 1905, 4 pp.
Remy, Jules and Julius Brenchley. *A Journey to Great-Salt-Lake City.* London: W. Jeffs, 1861, 2 v., 1113 pp.
Ressler, Theo C. *Trails Divided, A Dissertation on the Overland Journey of Iowa "Forty-Niners" of the Sacramento Mining Company.* Williamsburg, Iowa, 1964, 290 pp.
Rhyolite Herald, Pictorial Supplement. Rhyolite: 1909, 56 pp.
Rhyolite: Metropolis of Southern Nevada. Rhyolite: Richard E. Sinclair, 1907, 32 pp.
Rhyolite Mining Stock Exchange. *By-Laws of the Rhyolite Mining Stock Exchange Adopted by Governing Board January, 1907.* Rhyolite: Bullfrog Miner Print, 1907, 29 pp.
Rice, George Graham [Jacob Simon Herzig]. *My Adventures With Your Money.* Boston: Richard G. Badger, 1913, 363 pp.
Ritter, Betsy [Mrs. Earle Clemens]. *Life in the Ghost City of Rhyolite, Nevada.* Terra Bella, Calif.: Terra Bella News, 1939, 17 pp. Reprinted by Morongo Valley, Calif.: Sagebrush Press, 1982.
Roberts, Oliver. *The Great Understander, True Life Story of the Last of the Wells Fargo Shotgun Express Messengers.* Aurora, Ill.: William W. Walter, 1931, 315 pp. (William W. Walter, comp.).
Robinson, Marshall. *Sketches in Prose and Rhyme.* Carson City: Daily Index Print, 1888, 80 + 32 pp.
Robinson, W. W. *People versus Lugo.* Los Angeles: Dawson's Book Shop, 1962, 46 pp.
Rolt-Wheeler, Francis. *The Boy with the U.S. Survey.* Lathrop, Lee and Shepherd Co., 1909, 381 pp.
Rood, Standish. *Report of Standish Rood on the Pah-Ranagat Lake Silver Mines of Southeastern Nevada.* New York: William C. Bryant and Co., 1866, 23 pp.
Sage, Rufus B. *Scenes in the Rocky Mountains and in Oregon, California, New Mexico, Texas, and the Grand Prairies.* Philadelphia: Carey & Hart, 1846, 303 pp.
Scarfoglio, Antonio. *Round the World in a Motor-Car.* London: Grant Richards, 1909, 368 pp.
Scherer, James A. B. *"The Lion of the Vigilantes" William T. Coleman and the Life of Old San Francisco.* Indianapolis: Bobbs-Merrill Co., 1939, 335 pp.
Schuster, George, with Tom Mahoney. *The Longest Auto Race.* New York: John Day Co., 1966, 160 pp.
Scudder, Marvyn. *Manual of Extinct or Obsolete Companies.* New York: Marvyn Scudder Manual, Inc., 1926–1930, 3 v.
Seager, Henry R., and Charles A Gulick, Jr. *Trust and Corporation Problems.* New York: Harper & Bros., 1929, 719 pp. Chap. XII [Schwab], 196–215.

Shally, Dorothy, and William Bolton. *Scotty's Castle*. Yosemite: Flying Spur Press, 1973, 40 pp.

Shamberger, Hugh A. *The Story of Silver Peak*. Carson City: Nevada Historical Press, 1976, 111 pp.

Shankland, Robert. *Steve Mather of the National Parks*. New York: Alfred A. Knopf, 1951, 326 pp.

Shearer, W. H. *Atlas of the Goldfield, Tonopah and Bullfrog Mining Districts of Nevada*. Chicago: Rand, McNally and Co., 1905, 93 pp.

Shuck, Oscar T. *The California Scrap-Book,* San Francisco: H. H. Bancroft & Co., 1869, 704 pp.

Shumate, Albert. *Historical Mining Certificates: The Skidoo Mines Company*. Los Angeles: Ward Ritchie Press, 1971, 4 pp.

Smith, Grant H. *The History of the Comstock Lode, 1850–1920*. Reno: University of Nevada, 1943, 297 pp.

Smythe, Roland M. *Obsolete American Securities and Corporations*. New York: Smythe, 1904 and 1911, 2 v.

Snell, George. *And If Man Triumph*. Caldwell, Ida.: Caxton Printers, 1938, 215 pp.

Sonne, Conway B. *World of Wakara*. San Antonio: Naylor Co., 1962, 235 pp.

Southworth, John. *Death Valley in 1849: The Luck of the Gold Rush Emigrants*. Burbank: Pegleg Books, 1978, 132 pp.

Spears, John Randolph. *Illustrated Sketches of Death Valley and Other Borax Deserts of the Pacific Coast*. Chicago: Rand, McNally and Co., 1892, 226 pp. Facsimile reprint, Morongo Valley: Sagebrush Press, 1977.

Spence, Clark C. *British Investments and the American Mining Frontier 1860–1901*. Ithaca: Cornell University Press, 1958, 288 pp.

―――. *The Mining Engineers & the American West. The Lace-Boot Brigade, 1849–1933*. New Haven: Yale University Press, 1970, 407 pp.

Standard Oil Company of California. *Across Death Valley in a Ford Car. How a new oil for Model T Fords conquered the Hottest Place in the world*. [n.p.: Standard Oil Co., 1926], 16 pp.

Stephens, Lorenzo Dow. *Life Sketches of a Jayhawker of '49*. San Jose: Nolta Bros., 1916, 68 pp.

Stevens, Horace, J., ed. *The Copper Handbook, v. 4 [through] 11*. Houghton, Mich.: H. J. Stevens, 1904 through 1913. [11th vol. edited by Walter Weed.]

Stewart, William M. *Reminiscences of Senator William M. Stewart of Nevada*. New York: Neale Publishing Co., 1908, 358 pp. (George R. Brown, ed.).

The Story of Death Valley, Its Museum and Visitor Center. San Bernardino: Inland Printing and Engraving Co., 1966, 30 pp.

Stott, Clifford L. *Search for Sanctuary: Brigham Young and the White Mountain Expedition*. Salt Lake City: University of Utah Press, 1984. 297 pp.

Stove Pipe Wells Hotel. *Death Valley*. Los Angeles: Hyatt, Jones & Patrick, 1930, 8 pp.

―――. *Death Valley, Land of Mystery—Gold and Romance*. Los Angeles: c. 1937, 8 pp.

Sunday-Nevada Gold Mining Company. *Prospectus.* New York: John J. Bunte Co., 1906, 8 pp.

Swain, Donald C. *Wilderness Defender Horace M. Albright and Conservation.* Chicago: University of Chicago Press, 1970, 347 pp.

Sylvania Mining Company. *Prospectus.* [Tonopah: 1904], 12 pp.

Taylor, Charles A. *The Story of "Scotty," (Walter Scott) King of the Desert Mine.* New York: J. S. Ogilvie Pub. Co., 1906, 114 pp.

Tenney, W. J. *The Military and Naval History of the Rebellion in the United States, With Biographical Sketches of Deceased Officers.* New York: D. Appleton and Co., 1867, 843 pp.

Thomas (E. R.) Motor Company. *The Story of the New York to Paris Race.* Buffalo: E. R. Thomas Motor Co., 1908, 75 pp.

Tolford, Hugh C. *The Ties That Bind, A Biographical Sketch of Horace M. Albright.* Los Angeles: Death Valley '49ers, 1973, 24 pp.

———. *Zabriskie Point and Christian Brevoort Zabriskie, The Man.* Pasadena: Castle Press, 1976, 14 pp.

Tonopah Promotion Association. *Nye County, Nevada, and the Mineral Resources of Her Fifty Mining Camps.* Tonopah: 1909, 8 pp.

Travis, Norman J., and E. J. Cocks. *The Tincal Trail, A History of Borax.* London: Harrap, 1984, 311 pp.

Travis, Norman J., and Carl L. Randolph. *United States Borax and Chemical Corporation. The First One Hundred Years.* New York: Newcomen Society, 1973, 24 pp.

Tyler, Daniel. *A Concise History of the Mormon Battalion in the Mexican War, 1846–1847.* Salt Lake City, 1881, 376 pp.

Union Pacific Systems. *California's Unique Winter Resort in Death Valley, Land of Mystery and Romance.* Omaha: Acorn Press, 1929, 24 pp.

———. *Death Valley Winter Tours, Region of Mystery, Desolation and Grandeur, by Rail and Motor.* Los Angeles: Bert Rose Co., 1928, 10 pp.

United States Borax & Chemical Corporation. *100 Years of U.S. Borax 1872–1972.* Los Angeles: 1972, 47 pp.

———. *The Story of Borax.* Los Angeles: 1965. 40 pp. and revised edition 1979, 56 pp.

Uzes, Francois D. *Chaining the Land: A History of Surveying in California.* Sacramento: Landmark Enterprises, 1977, 315 pp.

Vredenburgh, Larry M., Gary L. Shumway, and Russell D. Hartill. *Desert Fever, An Overview of Mining in the California Desert.* Canoga Park: Living West Press, 1981, 323 pp.

Walker, Ardis Manly. *Death Valley & Manly. Symbols of Destiny.* San Bernardino: Inland Printing and Engraving Co., 1962, 43 pp.

———. *Freeman Junction . . . The Escape Route of the Mississippians and Georgians from Death Valley in 1849.* San Bernardino: Inland Printing and Engraving Co., 1961, 16 pp.

———. *The Manly Map and the Manly Story.* Palm Desert: Desert Mag. Press, 1954, 24 pp.

Walker's Manual of Pacific Coast Securities. San Francisco: Walker's Manual, Inc.,

1909–1933. Annual.

Wallace, William J. *Desert Foragers and Hunters, Indians of the Death Valley Region*. Ramona: Acoma Books, 1979, 44 pp.

Wallace, William J., and Edith Wallace. *Ancient Peoples and Cultures of Death Valley National Monument*. Ramona: Acoma Books, 1978, 34 pp.

Warns, Melvin Owen. *The Nevada "Sixteen" National Banks and Their Mining Camps*. Washington, D.C.: Society of Paper Money Collectors, 1974, 390 pp.

Warshow, Robert Irving. *Bet-A-Million Gates: The Story of a Plunger*. New York: Greenberg, 1932, 187 pp.

Weed, Walter H., ed. *The Mines Handbook, v. 12 [through] 18*. New York: Mines Handbook Co., 1916 through 1931.

Weeks, Ernst A. *Death Valley: A Brief History of Early Passage to the Goldfields and a Story of Personal Adventure in Search of a Copper Mine*. Morrill, Neb.: J. W. Snyder, 1941, 68 pp.

Weeks, George F. *California Copy*. Washington, D.C.: Washington College Press, 1928, 346 pp.

Weight, Harold O. *Greenwater*. Twentynine Palms: Calico Press, 1969, 34 pp.

———. *Lost Mines of Death Valley*. Twentynine Palms: The Calico Press, 1953, 72 pp., 2d ed. 1961, 80 pp., 3d ed. 1970, 86 pp.

———*Twenty Mule Team Days in Death Valley*. Twentynine Palms: Calico Press, 1955, 44 pp.

Weight, Harold O., and Lucile Weight. *Rhyolite, The Ghost City of Golden Dreams*. Twentynine Palms: Calico Press, 3rd ed. rev., 1959, 32 pp.; 5th ed. rev. and enlarged, 1970, 42 pp.

Weight, Harold O., and Lucile Weight. *William B. Rood, Death Valley '49er*. Twentynine Palms: Calico Print, 1952, 32 pp.

Weinberg, Herman G., comp. and ed. *The Complete Greed of Erich von Stroheim*. New York: E. P. Dutton and Co., 1973, unpaged.

Wendt, Lloyd, and Herman Kogan. *Bet A Million! The Story of John W. Gates*. Indianapolis: Bobbs-Merrill Co., 1948, 357 pp.

Wentworth, May. *Fairy Tales from Gold Lands*. New York: A. Roman and Co., 1867, 234 pp. Chap. 10 Death's Valley; or, The Golden Boulder, pp. 204–234.

Wheat, Carl I. *Trailing the Forty-Niners Through Death Valley*. San Francisco: Taylor and Taylor, 1939, 37 pp. Reprint of his *Sierra Club Bulletin* article.

Wheelock, Walt. *The Founding of Death Valley National Monument, Honoring its Golden Anniversary 1933–1983*. Death Valley: Death Valley '49ers, 1983, 20 pp.

Whitney, Josiah D. *Geology, v. 1, Report of Progress and Synopsis of the Field-Work From 1860 to 1864*. Philadelphia: Caxton Press of Sherman and Co., 1865, 498 pp.

Who Was Who In America. Chicago: Marquis Who's Who, 1943–1973, 5 v.

Who's Who in Los Angeles County 1928–29. Los Angeles: Charles J. Lang, 1928, 338 pp.

Wilson, Neill C. *Silver Stampede: The Career of Death Valley's Hell-Camp, Old Panamint*. New York: The Macmillan Co., 1937, 319 pp.

Wilson, Warren. *History of San Bernardino and San Diego Counties, California.* San Francisco: Wallace W. Elliott & Co., 1883, 204 pp. Facsimile reprint, Riverside: Riverside Museum Press, 1965.

Wolff, John E. *Route of the Manly Party of 1849–50 in Leaving Death Valley for the Coast.* Santa Barbara: Pacific Coast Pub., 1931, 29 pp.

The Wonder Consolidated Mining Company and The Wyoming Consolidated Mining Company. San Francisco: Stock Report, 1875, 7 pp.

Wood, Ruth. *The Tourist's California.* New York: Dodd, Mead and Co., 1914, 395 pp.

Woodard, Bruce A. *Diamonds in the Salt.* Boulder: Pruett Press, 1967, 200 pp.

Woodman, Ruth C., and Ann Rosener. *Story of the Pacific Coast Borax Co. Division of Borax Consolidated, Limited.* Los Angeles: Ward Ritchie Press, 1951, 59 pp.

Woods, S. D. *Lights and Shadows of Life on the Pacific Coast.* Funk and Wagnalls Co., 1910, 474 pp.

Woodward, Arthur. *Camels and Surveyors in Death Valley, The Nevada-California Border Survey of 1861.* Palm Desert: Desert Printers, Inc., 1961, 73 pp.

Woon, Basil. *Incredible Land.* New York: Liveright Pub. Corp., 1933, 374 pp.

Worth, Pauline Wilson. *Death Valley Slim and Others Stories.* Los Angeles: Segnogram Press, 1906, 48 pp.

Wynn, Marcia Rittenhouse. *Desert Bonanza, Story of Early Randsburg Mojave Desert Mining Camp.* Culver City: M. W. Samelson, 1949, 263 pp.

Young, John P. *Journalism in California.* San Francisco: Chronicle Publishing Co., 1915, 360 pp.

Zimmerman, Joseph. *Mines Register, v. 19.* New York: Mines Publications Inc., 1937, 1340 pp. Follows *Mines Handbook.*

INDEX

Bullfrog Gold Bar Mining Company, 236–237

Bullfrog Goldfield Railroad, 224, 229, 231, 322, 347, 387; stock certificate, 223

Bullfrog mine, Original, 203–204, 233–234, 412

Bullfrog Miner, 210–211, 224, 229, 239, 240, 327

Bullfrog mining district: gold discovery, 203–204; maps, 206, 213; naming, 203; newspapers, 210–211, 224, 229–233, 239–241; principal mines, 207–209, 212–219, 230–239; promotions, 208–209, 211–212, 214; railroads, 222–224, 229; rush, 204–207; towns, 209–211, 219, 222, 224–231, 239–241

Bullfrog Mountain, 203

Bullfrog Pioneer Gold Mines Company, 230–232

Bullfrog Pioneer Leasing & Milling Company, 230–232

Bullfrog Townsite Company, 211

Bull Moose mine, 438–440

Bungalow City, 451, 452

Bunker, Chester R., 437–438, 452

Buried treasure, 43–45, 171

Burton, Francis L., 340, 342

Burton brothers, 72

Busch, Frank, 209, 330

Busch, Peter A., 5, 209, 241, 330, 373, 375

Buser, John, 343

Buster mine, 340, 343

Butler, Jim, 200, 212, 351, 365

Butte Valley, 19, 194

Byrne, John J., 253

C. C. Julian Oil & Royalties Company, 436

Cahill, William W. "Wash," 386

Cajon Pass, 25, 27, 30, 55

Calico (town), 184, 302

Calico mine, 185–186, 379, 381, 383, 384, 387, 389

California Academy of Natural Science, 67

California Chemical Company, 180

California Corporation Commission, 431, 434, 439, 440

California Eastern Railroad, 248, 355, 383

California Mineral Corporation, 408

California-Nevada boundary: dispute, 4, 86, 89; surveys, 3, 86–89, 243, 365, 430, 465

California Nitrate Development Company, 399

California Railroad Commission, 390

California State Mineralogist, 4

California State Mining Bureau, 366, 398

Calloway, John, 200

Camels, 3, 87–89

Camp, Martha, 124, 125, 132

Camp, Sol, 437, 439

Campbell, John D., 333, 369–372

Campbell, John F., 276

Campbell, Marius R., 366

Camp Cady, 85

Camp Dawson, 281–282

Camp Hold Out, 249, 259, 260, 267

Camp Independence, 90, 92, 93

Camp Sagebrush, 105

Candelaria, 190

Cane Spring, 42

Cannibalism, 39

Cannin, William M., 115, 124

Cannon, George Q., 10, 191

Cannon, Hugh J., 191–195

Carbonate mine, 416–418

Carleton, James H., 85

Carnegie, Andrew, 216–217, 280

Carpenters' & Joiners' Union, 225

Carr, Richard, 224

Carrara, 404–406, 438–440, 456

Carrara Miner, 439

Carrara Obelisk, 405–406

Carrara-Pacific railroad, 406

Carrillo, Jose Antonio, 27–28

Carson, Christopher "Kit," 29–30

Carson, J. H., 372

Carson & Colorado Railroad, 150, 173

Cashier Gold Mining Company, 285, 293–294, 299–300

Catherwood, Edwin C., 102

Catherwood, Robert B., 102–103, 338–339

Cave Spring, 182, 263, 373, 456

Cave Springs (town), 331

Cecil R. Gold Mining Company, 201

Cemetery mine, 7

Center, James, 175

Cerro Gordo, 91

Cerro Gordo Freighting Company, 124, 126, 140

Chafey, Ed, 369–372

Chaguanosos, 25–28, 30–31

Chalfant, Willie, 465

Chalifoux, Jean Baptiste, 26

Challenge claim, 116–117

Chambers, Ben, 428

Champion mine, 102–103, 339, 344

Chapman, Robert H., 366

Charcoal kilns, 126, 129

Chemehuevi Indians, 58

Designer: Linda M. Robertson
Compositor: Prestige Typography
Printer: Vail-Ballou Press
Binder: Vail-Ballou Press
Text: 10/12 Monticello
Display: Bauer Bodoni